WITHDRAWN

W9-CPE-435

JAN 20 2000

ART PAST THIRD EDITION
ART PRESENT

ART PAST
ART PRESENT

THIRD EDITION

DAVID G. WILKINS
BERNARD SCHULTZ
KATHERYN M. LINDUFF

HARRY N. ABRAMS, INC.,
PUBLISHERS

FOR OUR STUDENTS

Project Director: Julia Moore
Editor: Jean Smith
Art Director: Lydia Gershey
Design and Production: Lydia Gershey with Yonah Schurink of Communigraph
Photo Editors: Lauren Boucher and Catherine Ruello

Wilkins, David G.
     Art past, art present / David G. Wilkins, Bernard Schultz,
Katheryn M. Linduff.—3rd ed.
              p.   cm.
     Includes bibliographical references and index.
     ISBN 0-8109-1981-8
     1. Art—History.   I. Schultz, Bernard,   1948–   II. Linduff,
Katheryn M.   III. Title.
N5300.W64   1997
709—DC21   96-49510

Text copyright © 1990, 1994, 1997 Prentice Hall, Inc.
Illustrations copyright © 1990, 1994, 1997 Harry N. Abrams, Inc.
Published in 1997 by Harry N. Abrams, Incorporated, New York

All rights reserved. No part of the contents of this book may be reproduced in any form
or by any means without the written permission of the publisher.

Printed and bound in Japan

Harry N. Abrams, Inc.
100 Fifth Avenue
New York, NY 10011
www.abramsbooks.com

front cover: Jenny Holzer. *Untitled (Selections from Truisms, Inflammatory Essays, The Living Series, The Survival Series, Under a Rock, Laments, and Mother and Child Text).* 1989. Temporary installation with extended helical tricolor LED electronic display signboard. Installed at the Solomon R. Guggenheim Museum, New York, which commissioned the work. Detail of figure 10-140. Partial gift of the artist, 1989

back cover: Temple of Borobudur, Java, Indonesia. Sailendra dynasty, 835–60. Figure 4–48

pages 14–15:   Nam June Paik. *Electronic Superhighway.* 1995. Installation with video monitors, laser disks, and neon, 32 x 54'. Temporary installation at Holly Solomon Gallery, New York. Detail of figure 1-1

pages 36–37:   Stonehenge, Salisbury Plain, Wiltshire, England. c. 2750–1300 BCE. Detail of figure 2-9

pages 48–49:   Exekias. *Achilles and Ajax Playing Droughts,* detail of black-figure decoration on an amphora. c. 560 BCE. Vatican Museums, Rome. Detail of figure 3-54

pages 144–45: Interior, Mosque, Córdoba. Spain. Begun 786. Detail figure 4-41

pages 240–41: The Limbourg Brothers. *February,* calendar page from the *Trés Riches Heures du Duc de Berry.* Before 1416. Musée Condé, Chantilly, France. Detail of figure 5-11

pages 292–93: Michelangelo Buonarroti. *The Last Judgment.* 1534–41. Sistine Chapel, Vatican, Rome. Detail of figure 6-49

pages 346–47: Jacob van Ruisdael. *Dutch Landscapes from the Dunes at Overveen.* c. 1760. Mauritshuis, The Hague, The Netherlands. Detail of figure 7-49

pages 392–93: Angelica Kauffmann, *Cornelia, Mother of the Gracchi.* 1785. Virginia Museum of Fine Arts. Richmond. Detail of figure 8-23

pages 412–13: Paul Cézanne. *Mont Ste.-Victoire.* 1904–6. Private collection. Detail of figure 9-75

pages 484–85: Robert Colescott. *Les Demoiselles d'Alabama: Vestidas.* 1985. New York, Collection of Hanford Yang. Detail of figure 10-127

CONTENTS

PART 4
ART FROM 200 TO 1400 144

PART 5
FIFTEENTH-CENTURY ART 240

PART 6
SIXTEENTH-CENTURY ART 292

PART 7
SEVENTEENTH-CENTURY ART 346

PART 10
TWENTIETH-CENTURY ART 484

PREFACE AND ACKNOWLEDGMENTS TO THE THIRD EDITION

In writing *Art Past/Art Present,* we have held these as underlying assumptions: that art is a result of the human experience of life and that art is itself fundamentally expressive. Quite simply, visual culture is something we live with and to which artists respond.

We have written *Art Past/Art Present* especially for the person with a general interest in learning about art and art history, and for the one-semester introductory course in art history or art appreciation. Our goal has been to present a clear, concise treatment of a limited number of artistic monuments from around the globe. In fact, *Art Past/Art Present* is the only introduction to art that integrates world cultures in a meaningful and thoughtful way. Further, the book discusses how the visual arts functioned and were viewed at the time of their creation, and its unique chronological presentation enhances this emphasis on the historical and cultural context.

The organization of *Art Past/Art Present* is chronological, from prehistory through the twentieth century. In thumbing through the book, you will note that highlighted dates in the upper corner of right-hand pages follow a strict chronological sequence, reflecting the exposition of the developments of art as they happened around the globe.

The presentation of *Art Past/Art Present* is contextual. Each part is introduced by an overview that lays out the broadest developments in history and in art for that period. Sections within the introduction also discuss the status and role of the artist and the patron in each culture or period. Following

the introduction are units that present major styles and periods (for example, Early Buddhist art in India, Roman imperial, Gothic), followed by sequenced double-page units discussing works of that style or period (such as the pyramids, the Pantheon, Japanese cinema). These approximately 150 double-page or four-page units form the basis of *Art Past/Art Present;* each focuses on a key work or works and is complete in itself.

The structure of *Art Past/Art Present* is flexible. The introductions to each part form a narrative of the history of art that gives the background necessary for understanding the works that follow. In condensing the history of art into a limited space, we have had to selectively represent some significant movements by a single work or a single artist. Nevertheless, the individual works are given a more complete treatment than is found in many survey books, and because each discussion is self-contained, this book can be customized by the reader or the teacher. *Art Past/ Art Present* is brief enough that all the material can be covered, for example, in a single semester, providing a truly global perspective on art. Or one can choose a smaller number of units, still with a world view, or can focus entirely on Western art.

Other features from earlier editions that have proved especially popular have been retained: The **techniques and processes** (such as post-and-lintel construction and etching) crucial for understanding works of art are explained in boxes within the chronological sequence at the point when their development had an impact on the evolution of art.

Contemporary documents have been quoted extensively within the narrative, giving the words of those who lived when the art was created a particular force and authority. **Extended captions** for illustrations often include significant historical and factual information and are best read in tandem with the main text; when known, **the patron for a work is indicated in the caption.** The Glossary defines terms and gives references to illustrations or passages in the text where the term, bold-faced, is further explained and/ or illustrated in a diagram or work of art. Seeing terms in their historical narratives and in relation to illustrations clarifies their meaning.

New coverage of art in the third edition includes more than **100 new images,** most of them in color; a **thorough revision and updating of twentieth-century art** and many other sections; and **new spreads** on the Indus Valley, the Shang dynasty, the temple at Borobudur, and Japanese prints and series.

New features in the third edition have been **added in response to past readers:** In addition to the **world map** on pages 6 and 7, we have added **twenty-two detail maps in color** throughout the book, within context, where they will be most useful. Within Part 1–9, we have added **Timescopes, schematic diagrams that include the major works of art and historical events during that period,** organized by year and geographical area; Timescopes graphically show the interrelationships among art and history and organize material in a way that makes it easy to master. **Chronologies in each section focus on the world events in the** narrow time period when that work was created.

A text of this breadth requires the generous efforts and insights of many people, especially colleagues at the University of Pittsburgh and West Virginia University who willingly shared their expertise: Robert Anderson, Kahren Arbitman, William Arnett, Vange Beldecos, Laura Crary, Roger Crum, Urban Couch, Robert H. Getscher, Ann Sutherland Harris, Fil Hearn, Marcia Meniham, Kristina Olson, Margaret Rajam, Patricia Rice, Matthew Roper, John Super, Thomas Tavella C.S.P., Frank Toker, H. Anne Weis, John Whitty, and John Williams all lent their authoritative understanding to different parts of the text.

Among those professionals who offered guidance for this edition, we acknowledge Madhu Wangu, Ed De Carlso, and Hsu Miao-lin. The expanded, up-to-date bibliography is the work of Rebecca L. Wilkins.

At Prentice Hall, Norwell "Bud" Therien, Jr., brought integrity to this project, and at Harry N. Abrams we were supported by the most professional of teams. We are especially grateful to Julia Moore, Jean Smith, Monica Mehta, Lauren Boucher, John McKenna, Lydia Gershey and Yonah Schurink for their erudite perceptions, indefatigable support, and unmatched dedication to quality.

David G. Wilkins
Bernard Schultz
Katheryn M. Linduff
1997

1-1. Nam June Paik. *Electronic Superhighway.* 1995. Installation with video monitors, laser disks, neon, 32 x 54'. Temporary installation at Holly Solomon Gallery, New York City

INTRODUCTION TO EXPERIENCING ART

Imagine—You are walking in New York City. As you pass the large windows of an art gallery, you notice, out of the corner of your eye, a familiar image, a huge map of the continental United States. When you pause to look more closely, you can see that it fills an entire wall, and that the borders of the states are defined in brilliant neon (fig. 1-1). You see flickering colored lights, barely discernible at this distance, but you can't really make out what they are. The familiarity of the map image puts you at ease while the unusual materials and format simultaneously provoke your interest. Is this map a work of art? You know that a museum's mission is to display and preserve works of art—but a commercial art gallery is here to sell art, so you hesitate to go inside for a closer look at this intriguing map. But it is so compelling that you overcome your hesitation and open the door. The gallery staff acknowledge your visit with a welcome.

As you approach the dazzling wall, you discover that the entire "map" is backed by video monitors of various sizes—this explains the flickering lights you noticed.

Clusters of monitors can be seen within each state's borders, and the images on their screens differ from state to state. Viewed as a whole, the work seems overwhelming; the steady glare of the neon contrasts with the patterns of color and movement that, state by state, dance across the video screens. You search the wall to find a place where you can focus your attention on a single sequence of images. This, you believe, just might be a way to open a path of understanding to the complexities of this unexpected work.

As you stare at the monitors within one state's neon borders, you begin to recognize some of the images. In Alabama, you see the Reverend Martin Luther King, Jr., and the early struggles of the civil rights movement, while to your left, scenes from the 1943 Rodgers and Hammerstein musical *Oklahoma!* identify that state; harsh realities and human triumphs are thus juxtaposed to an imaginative Broadway musical. As you look from state to state, you find more conflicting images. American historical traditions are recounted with images of Abraham Lincoln in Illinois and the Alamo in Texas—but the Texas videos also include television footage of the 1993 fire that consumed the Branch Davidian compound near Waco. Gradually, you begin to sort out the visual information on the monitors; you can, more and more, identify images with states. But just as you are becoming more comfortable with the visual and ideological complexity, you are surprised again. When you look at New York, you see *yourself* on the video monitor, viewing this very work at this very moment. Unlike the monitors from other states, whose images primarily depict historical sequences or scenic views, the monitors within the borders of New York State are linked to closed-circuit video cameras pointed at onlookers in the gallery. The immediacy of the present moment is thus inserted into the work; the image of you and your interaction with the "map" instantly becomes an element of the work itself: as you are viewing it, you become part of it.

Your latest discovery about this work is captivating; you have seen works of art before, but they remained still objects before you, allowing time for quiet contemplation. This work challenges the traditional interaction between you and art at the same time as the work is bombarding you with many simultaneous layers of information; the work in its present form could not exist without your participation. The rapid, compressed delivery is familiar to you from watching TV, but the immensity of it—and the insertion of *you* as an active participant—leads you to question some of your assumptions about art.

Now is the moment to find out more about this work. You read in the label nearby on the wall that the artist is Korean-born Nam June Paik (b. 1932) and that the work, which is composed of neon, video monitors, and laser disks, is called a video **installation**.♦ This installation was especially created by Paik for this specific gallery location, the Holly Solomon Gallery. The title, *Electronic Superhighway*, is now a familiar term in our culture. It evokes the promise of new modes of communication, but Paik's video installation also reveals that communication is not merely a matter of crossing distances, but of traversing time as well.

The panorama of diversity and rapidly changing images in *Electronic Superhighway* is, in many ways, a meditation on the meaning of the United States—its past and its present, and even how they may merge to form the future. Before you, perception collides with history, dreams with reality. And *you*, by your presence in New York City at this time, are a participant in this colossal structure of images and meanings.

Nam June Paik's *Electronic Superhighway* is a work of our time, founded on the recognition that electronic communications media are cultural forces in contemporary society. It disturbs our preconceptions about art and introduces real time as an element in our dialogue with

the work at the same time that it questions the construction of history. In the broader view, it could be argued that Paik's demonstration of how communication crosses time, from past to present, touches the heart of our experience of art no matter when it was created.

When you encounter an unfamiliar work of art in a gallery or museum—or even when you're walking down the street—one way to open your communication with it is to ask some general questions that can help you to understand that work as a visual expression and as a historical experience. Some questions you might ask are:

➤ Does the work of art communicate specific emotions and feelings? That is, what is its **expressive content**?
➤ Does it belong to a clearly recognizable artistic tradition? Is it related to a particular **historical style**?
➤ Who was the artist (or artists), and did the artist's personality play a role in the creation of the work?
➤ Does the work demonstrate **individual style**?
➤ What can a visual examination and analysis of the work tell us? How can a **formal analysis** be useful?
➤ How are the various visual elements of the work arranged? What is its **composition**?
➤ What materials is it made of? What is the **medium**?
➤ How have the artist or artists used these materials? What **techniques** were employed to make the work?
➤ Did someone commission the artist or artists to create the work and did they also pay for it? Who were the **patrons**?
➤ Why was it made? What purpose did it fulfill? What was its **function** when it was first created?
➤ Was it created for a specific location, and did the artist adjust the composition for that location? Has the artist used **collocation**?
➤ What is its subject matter and what does it represent? What are its **iconography** and **iconology**?
➤ What can it tell us about the ideas, beliefs, or attitudes current in the period when it was created? What is its **historical significance** and its **historical context**? Who was its audience?
➤ As a member of the audience, you can also ask what it is that you bring to this work, and how your personal history and experiences might give you a very particular response to the work. What is your personal response?

These questions are not a comprehensive list, nor do all these questions apply to every work. The key concept in each question is restated with highlighted terms (**bold-faced** in the question above and the discussion below) that are part of a specialized vocabulary for sharing ideas and information about works of art.

♦ Terms that are bold-faced in the text are defined in the Glossary at the back of the book, beginning on page 604.

VIEWING ART

1-2. *Menkaure and His Wife, Queen Khamerernebty II,* found at Menkaure's temple complex, next to his pyramid at Giza, Egypt. Dynasty 4, c. 2515 BCE. Greywacke, height 54^1/2". Museum Expedition, Courtesy, Museum of Fine Arts, Boston. Commissioned by King Menkaure

What is there about a statue of rulers who lived thousands of years ago that attracts our interest? How can even mythological figures, so far removed from our experiences, engage our attention? Art's power to communicate to us rests on an analysis of a work's visual qualities and an understanding of the work's **expressive content** and its relationship to its historical period.

One central goal of art history, then, is to increase our understanding of sometimes puzzling works from past cultures, and even from our own. This book attempts to provide a global perspective, but we need to recognize from the very beginning that most of us have a greater familiarity with the traditions of relatively recent Western (European and American) art than with those of other cultures and historical periods. This means that we must often make an additional effort to understand works from cultures outside of the Western tradition.

To construct a framework for analyzing art created in the past, as well as in the present, modern art historians use classifications that rely on the concept of **style**. The word *style* (from the Latin *stylus*) originally referred to a writing instrument, but over time the meaning changed to include the manner—or art—of handwriting. Each of us writes differently, and our handwriting has a personal quality related to whether we are left-handed or right-handed, how we learned to write, and even the period in which we live. Documents from past centuries easily demonstrate how handwriting styles have changed over time. In art history, **historical style** is the term used to describe how the appearance of a work of art is tied to the period during which it was created. Works of art from the same historical period and culture often share similar visual characteristics. In art history, specific periods and cultures tend to be examined within a chronology, or time sequence, and the history of art is often presented as a succession of period styles.

The term *style*, however, can also have a more intimate meaning, referring to the particular manner of visual expression used by an individual artist, which is known as **individual style**. This style can change as the artist develops and matures. Relationships may also be detected between the individual style of an artist and the historical style of the time in which he or she lived. To study style, art history uses a technique called **formal analysis**, which is an examination of the visual aspects of a work and how its integral parts unite to produce a distinctive historical and individual style.

The vocabulary of formal analysis, introduced in some of the questions at the end of the previous section, enables us to describe the visual structure of works of art.

To begin to understand the many ways in which works of art can be approached, we shall consider in some detail three examples from different historical and cultural periods.

The sculpture *Menkaure and His Wife, Queen Khamerernebty* (fig. 1-2), carved in ancient Egypt about 4,500 years ago, proclaims stability; the poses of the Egyptian king and his queen are confined within a rectangular **composition**, and there is no suggestion of movement. There is a slight hint of portraiture in their faces, but their bodies are **idealized**, abstracted to conform to a standard of perfection dictated by Egyptian cultural preferences. The value of stability is also proclaimed in the work of the eleventh-century Chinese artist Guo Xi (c. 1020–90), titled *Early Spring* (fig. 1-3). This scroll painting represents a mountainous landscape with parts of the scene "lost" in dense atmosphere. Waterfalls cascade down the lower portion of the mountain to the right. As with the Egyptian sculpted figures, a rectangular format encloses the composition. The monumentality of the mountain is reinforced by its central and dominant position; it occupies almost the entire painted surface of the scroll. The craggy rocks and skeletal trees suggest that we are also viewing the understructure, the essence of nature.

The perception of *Menkaure and His Wife, Queen Khamerernebty* as both stable and rigid results from several visual elements: The **axis**, an imaginary center line passing through each figure, conforms to a vertical line. Vertical or horizontal components appear to be balanced

1-3. Guo Xi. *Early Spring.* Northern Song dynasty, 1072. Hanging scroll, ink and slight color on silk, length 5'. National Palace Museum, Taipei, Taiwan, Republic of China

and in equilibrium. The vertical axes combine with the rectangular composition to communicate a contained, balanced stability. The vertical axes also contribute to the stiff posture of the figures, producing a rigidity reinforced by the compact outlines of the sculpture, which is a monolithic, rectangular solid.

The enormous mountain in Guo Xi's painting peaks in the center of

the composition; this work too has an **axial composition**. Although curvilinear elements (those bounded by curved lines) and diagonal elements can be seen in the painting—for example, in the bending branches, the flow of water over the tiered falls, and the outcropping of rock at the bottom—the soaring verticality of the central mountain dominates the scene. Set within a rectangular format, the visual authority of this axial mountain establishes stability within the composition.

Although both works communicate a sense of stability and permanence, each makes a distinct impact on us. The individual expression of each work is related to the **media** (materials) and **technique** that the artist employed. *Menkaure and His Wife, Queen Khamerernebty,* carved by an anonymous artist or workshop of artists, is made of schist, a dense, hard, and brittle stone found in Egypt. In contrast, the subtle atmospheric, spatial, and structural effects in *Early Spring* are achieved by Guo Xi's adept handling of brush and ink.

The subject matter of the two works is also distinctive. The art-historical examination of subject matter is expressed on two levels: What is the subject matter? What is its meaning within the work's historical context? **Iconography** (from the Greek *eikon*, "image," and *graphein*, "to describe" or "to write") is the art-historical study of the specific subject matter of the work, while **iconology** (from the Greek for "image discourse") interprets the *meaning* of the subject matter as it can be understood within the historical culture that produced it.

Menkaure and his queen ruled in ancient Egypt, and the iconography of the sculpture is their representation as royal personages. The subject of Guo Xi's painting is the landscape, a visual investigation of the appearance and structure of nature in China. Inquiry into the iconology of these works, however, leads to the realm of **historical significance** and **historical context**, for religious, political, social, economic, scientific, philosophic, and

1-4. Gianlorenzo Bernini. *Apollo and Daphne.* 1622–25. Marble, height 8'. Galleria Borghese, Rome. Commissioned by Cardinal Scipione Borghese

other values can all come to bear on the interpretation of a work's meaning and function.

The portrait of Menkaure and his wife is one of several similar sculptures intended to provide a home for the enduring aspect of the individual personality, called the *ka*, that the Egyptians believed continued after death; this was its **function** when it was created. Its original location was within a funerary precinct, close to the king's pyramidal tomb. The stable, rigid form of the sculpture conveys its expressive content, a majestic and enduring presence. More importantly, this form also protects it from breakage, thus safeguarding the home of the *ka* in the afterlife. This enduring

strength is reinforced by the use of schist as a medium.

Within the Chinese tradition, landscape paintings were not simply depictions of nature; rather, they were intended to express the continuing essence of the living, natural world. Artists such as Guo Xi were highly educated, and the paintings they created were intended to enrich the human spirit by allowing the individual viewer, through contemplation, to become aware of a universal order that governs natural and human affairs. In the Western tradition, values of stability, permanence, and constancy were often associated with the human figure in art, but in China these qualities were expressed in landscape painting.

Possibly, too, the underlying stability of both works bears some relationship to the powerful centralized governments that controlled both Egypt and China during the periods when the works were created.

Apollo and Daphne (fig. 1-4), created in Italy by Gianlorenzo Bernini (1598–1680), communicates an expressive content that is markedly different from *Menkaure and His Wife, Queen Khamerernebty* and *Early Spring*. This sculpture, with its emphasis on dramatic movement, is from the Baroque period in Western art; its stylistic qualities of visual, dynamic flux are shared with painting and architecture from that period. The figures, representing the mythological story of Apollo and Daphne, express a transient moment forever caught in time. This Baroque sculpture is also **naturalistic**, for the figures, drapery, landscape, and tree segments all reproduce the appearance of these forms in nature. (The term **realism**, which is sometimes confused with *naturalism*, refers to subject matter drawn from everyday life.)

Unlike the formal qualities of the two earlier works, which emphasized axial stability and stasis, Bernini's sculpture is composed primarily on a diagonal axis. Diagonal components, which break the equilibrium of the vertical and horizontal, communicate movement. If *Menkaure and His Wife, Queen Khamerernebty* appears closed and self-contained in space, *Apollo and Daphne* seems open and expansive. This openness is due to the extension of the figures' limbs and drapery out into the immediate space; here the surrounding space is energized by the sculptural form.

The medium, it is important to note, is Italian marble, which is soft and more easily carved than schist.

The iconography of Bernini's sculpture is drawn from a specific literary source from ancient Rome, Ovid's *Metamorphoses* (I, 545–59), written in the late first century BCE or the early first century CE♦:

> So ran the god and [Daphne],
>   one swift in hope,
> The other in terror, but he ran
>   more swiftly,
> Borne on the wings of love, gave
>   her no rest,
> Shadowed her shoulder,
>   breathed on her streaming
>   hair.
> Her strength was gone, worn
>   out by the long effort
> Of the long flight; she was
>   deathly pale, and seeing
> The river of her father, cried,
>   "O help me,
> If there is any power in the
>   rivers,
> Change and destroy the body
>   which has given
> Too much delight!" And hardly
>   had she finished,
> When her limbs grew numb
>   and heavy, her soft breasts
> Were closed with delicate
>   bark, her hair was leaves,
> Her arms were branches, and
>   her speedy feet
> Rooted and held, and her head
>   became a tree top,
> Everything gone except her
>   grace, her shining.

♦This book uses the abbreviations BCE ("before the common era") and CE ("common era") rather than BC ("before Christ") and AD ("Anno Domini," "year of our Lord").

Although the figures of Apollo and Daphne are represented naturalistically, they are legendary figures from Greek mythology. As described in the passage from Ovid, the god Apollo desires the lovely Daphne, daughter of a river god. She prays to her father to be delivered from Apollo's unwanted advances, and when he finally catches her, her father transforms her into a laurel tree. In Bernini's sculpture, Daphne's left side is metamorphosing into a trunk, while her fingers and hair become branches and leaves. The expression Bernini puts on Apollo's face is a complex mixture of joy, at the attainment of his goal, and wonder, as his hand embraces Daphne only to touch not flesh but bark.

The iconology of Bernini's sculpture communicates both general and particular aspects of Italian Baroque culture. It demonstrates the popularity in seventeenth-century Italy of literature and art from ancient Greece and Rome—Ovid's writings were popular sources for learning Latin, so all educated people would have known this tale. Besides delighting visitors, *Apollo and Daphne* also showed off the intellectual and artistic taste of its **patron**, Cardinal Scipione Borghese, an important member of the Roman aristocracy and an official of the Catholic Church.

Discerning style, formal analysis, iconography, iconology, function, and historical context are beginning steps to understanding the meaning of a work of art. Works of art themselves are far from being mute—but to hear them speak, we must be open to the expression and content of their language.

ANALYZING ART

1-5. Pond and garden of Katsura Imperial Villa, near Kyoto, Japan. 1620–63. Commissioned by Prince Hachijo Toshihito and his son Toshitada. This view looks toward the pond from a narrow veranda and through two rooms of a wing of the villa. The white-based veranda on the left is a corner of the first-built section of the rambling villa (compare figures 7-46 and 7-47).

Your personal approach to works of art may begin with queries about the historical or cultural significance, with an interest in individual style and the biography of the artist, or with an examination of subject matter. But the most fundamental approach is to look carefully at the work as a visual object and to begin to analyze how it communicates to us. This section sets out to help you understand how to do a formal analysis.

One element that is common to almost all forms of visual expression is the manipulation of space. We have an immediate relationship with space—we exist and move in it, and during much of our daily lives, we are sheltered by structures that enclose space.

Three-dimensional space is real space. Artists and architects who work with real space often use space as a positive element in the composition or design. This perception of space, and the merging of interior with exterior space, is, for example, a key feature in understanding the architecture of the

Katsura villa near Kyoto, Japan (fig. 1-5). The design of these rooms, inspired by some of the tenets of Zen Buddhism, creates a subtle integration of the building with its environment. The architectural features are restrained and simple; wooden supports reveal their natural beauty, and the translucent paper of the sliding screen walls produces a soft interior light. As the sliding walls are moved, different vistas of the garden appear and the spatial definitions of the rooms change. The emphasis on delicate horizontals and verticals makes the irregularity of nature even more evident; the distinction between the artificial and the natural is emphasized. The design of this Japanese royal retreat reminds us that the boundaries between architectural and real space are not always immutable—an understanding that also guides our experience of Fallingwater, designed by Frank Lloyd Wright (1867–1959).

Both the twentieth-century Fallingwater (fig. 1-6) and the sixteenth-century Villa Rotonda (fig. 1-7) by

Palladio (1508–80) were designed as country homes for private patrons: Fallingwater for the Kaufmann family of Pittsburgh, who used the home as a summer retreat, and the Villa Rotonda for a retired official of the Catholic Church, who used the villa for receptions and entertaining. Like the Katsura villa, each structure communicates a particular architectural effect, and each relates to its setting in a different manner.

The most striking feature of Fallingwater is the way the structure cooperates with the site, a characteristic of many of Wright's designs. The architect once commented: "A good building is one that makes the landscape more beautiful than it was before." In creating Fallingwater, he integrated the design with the natural environment, while at the same time establishing in the landscape a forceful abstract arrangement of rectangular forms. The large terraces allowed the Kaufmanns and their guests to enjoy the sun and views into the surrounding forest.

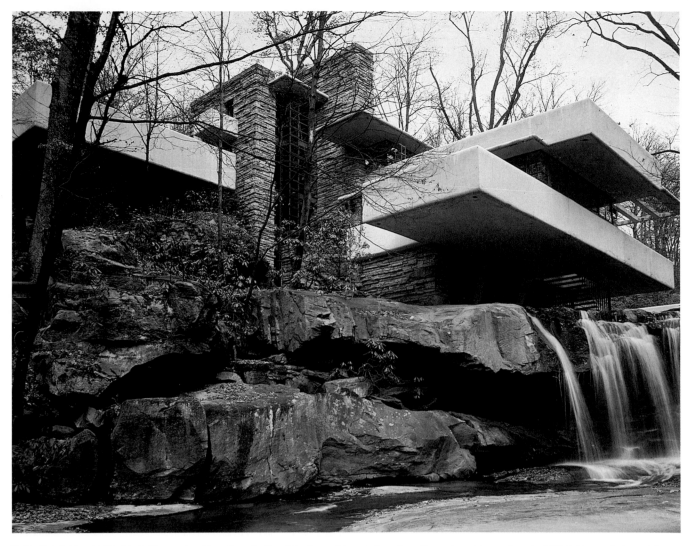

1-6. Frank Lloyd Wright. Fallingwater, Bear Run, in the Allegheny Mountains of southwestern Pennsylvania. 1936. Commissioned by Pittsburgh business executive Edgar Kaufmann

1-7. Palladio. Villa Rotonda (also known as the Villa Almerico and the Villa Capra), Vicenza, Italy. c. 1567–70. Commissioned by Paolo Almerico, Apostolic Referendary of popes Pius IV and Pius V

1-8. Palladio. Plan of Villa Rotonda

1-9. Frank Lloyd Wright. Plan of Fallingwater

The ledges of rock that form the falls at the site create a horizontal pattern. This is echoed in the thrusting, horizontal terraces above, which project out from a massive vertical core faced with local stone quarried near the site. Nature's design has been reinterpreted and reinforced by the abstract architectural forms integrated within it.

Situated very differently—on the crest of a hill and backed by a wooded area—the Villa Rotonda is an impressive and commanding structure. Its four porches, set at right angles to each other and extending from a central domed core, dominate the site. These porches serve a practical as well as an aesthetic function, for they afford the guests varied views of the surrounding countryside and, since each is partially enclosed on the sides, they offer the possibility of always being able to find a shady

spot away from the hot Italian summer sun.

The exterior design of the Villa Rotonda expresses a stable harmony. Symmetry governs the arrangement of the architectural forms, and vertical and horizontal elements are carefully balanced. The visual equilibrium revealed on the exterior also governs the interior design. The plan (fig. 1-8) is composed of proportional geometric shapes: a central, circular space is circumscribed by a square plan. From the central space, halls radiate to each porch. The cross axes of the halls are aligned with the cardinal points—north, south, east, and west. This desire to orient a building in relation to a perceived order in nature was an aspect of the Renaissance aesthetic that formed the basis of Palladio's architecture.

In contrast, the exterior design of Fallingwater is asymmetrical. A

unified composition is achieved, nevertheless, by balancing the horizontal thrust of the terraces against the vertical massing of the central core. Another unifying feature is the adherence to rectangular forms throughout. The asymmetrical balance of Wright's exterior concept also characterizes the plan and interior (figs. 1-9, 1-10). Rooms and hallways repeat the rectangular forms of the exterior. Like the Villa Rotonda, the rooms also correspond to the cardinal points, but Wright's asymmetrical design allows for the largest room, the living room, to have a southwest exposure, which maximized the Kaufmanns' enjoyment of the afternoon sun. Following a concept similar to that expressed in the Japanese pavilion (see fig. 1-5), Wright extends the rooms of the house into the space of the environment, while in Palladio's design the distinction

1-10. Frank Lloyd Wright. Interior, Fallingwater

between the building and its environment is firmly stated.

The Villa Rotonda was built to accommodate many guests, and its plan provided easy access into and out of the building; the symmetry of the halls and rooms around the central space allowed for clearly understood patterns of circulation. Fallingwater, by contrast, was designed for a family of three, and although the living room and terraces are large, the bedrooms are small, the halls narrow. As a private home for a small family, Fallingwater had no need for expansive patterns of circulation.

The principles of construction used to build the Villa Rotonda have a long tradition in architectural history. They include the use of **walls**, the **post-and-lintel** system (see page 68), and the **arch** (see pages 132–33). The design confers a stable dignity on the building that recalls the tradition of ancient Greece and ancient Rome.

In contrast, the manner in which Fallingwater's terraces are thrust out over the waterfall creates a dramatic effect. This adventurous architectural achievement was accomplished by the use of modern construction materials that have a high **tensile strength**—that is, they strongly resist the strain of the architectural load and the pull of gravity. In Fallingwater, the terraces are made of concrete reinforced with steel rods. The availability of these materials gave Wright the possibility of using the **cantilever**, a horizontal projection into space (see page 513).

Architecture serves both utilitarian and aesthetic purposes. Buildings are expressions of their time. As we encounter different forms of architecture, we would do well to recall the understanding of John Ruskin, the influential nineteenth-century English art critic, who wrote, "All architecture proposes an effect on the human mind, not merely a service to the human frame."

Like architecture, sculpture is an art of real space, and space is an integral element in analyzing sculpture.

1-11. Daniel Chester French. *Minuteman.* 1874–75. Bronze with granite base, height 7'. Old North Bridge, Concord, Massachusetts. The American writer Ralph Waldo Emerson proposed French for this commission. Commissioned by the Town of Concord

Depending upon the composition of the sculpture, the surrounding space can play a role in the effect and communication of the work. *Minuteman* (fig. 1-11), by Daniel Chester French (1850–1931), and *Cubi XIX* (fig. 1-12), by David Smith (1906–65), though very different in appearance, nevertheless share a similar spatial involvement.

The bronze statue of the Minuteman at Concord was commissioned to celebrate the centennial of the famous Revolutionary War battle fought there. The heroically scaled statue depicts the citizen-soldier of the American Revolution poised with a plow in one hand and a musket in the other. The figure stands alert and determined. The sculpture is **representational**, and although the medium is bronze, the artist has finished the surface to create the illusion of different textures: the flesh suggests the anatomical structure beneath, the folds of the clothing respond to the body, and these textures contrast with the cold metallic handle of the plow. Such representational qualities help us recognize the forms and realize the sculpture's commemorative, historical purpose.

David Smith's *Cubi XIX* is a **nonrepresentational** work of art, for it does not imitate actual figures or objects. In Smith's sculpture, the medium is stainless steel. Smith has wire-brushed the surface of the steel, giving a textural unity. The brushed steel surfaces reflect, in a diffused way, the atmospheric light around them. The appearance of the sculpture, then, changes in response to atmospheric conditions; it might appear dull gray-blue on an overcast day or reflect a slight golden glow on a sunny day.

Both *Minuteman* and *Cubi XIX* are examples of **sculpture in the round**, that is, sculpture finished on all sides, to be viewed from many different vantage points. And, as noted above, these sculptures share a similar relationship with space. Both have forms that develop from a vertical axis—the arms and right leg of *Minuteman* and the rectangular and rounded steel forms of *Cubi XIX*. Both sculptures are set on bases. The large granite base of *Minuteman* contributes to our recognition of the statue as a commemorative work; *Cubi XIX*'s base primarily offers support, but its design is in keeping with the nonrepresentative composition. The composition of each work is also animated by a suggested movement. With *Minuteman*, this sense is created by the contrast of the vertical axis of the figure with the diagonals of the right leg and musket. *Cubi XIX* offers an interplay of vertical, horizontal, and diagonal forms.

The compositions of French's *Minuteman* and Smith's *Cubi XIX* urge us to consider the sculptures from different viewpoints. The diagonal of the Minuteman's musket, which is reinforced by the implied movement of the right leg, creates an oblique motion that invites us to walk around the sculpture. In a similar way, diagonal elements break the planarity, or two-dimensional, view of Smith's work, drawing us around the sculpture to consider how the composition changes from varying points of view. Both sculptures make use of the three-dimensional space in which they, like ourselves, exist.

Minuteman and *Cubi XIX* are alike in yet another way; as a sculptural object, each remains stationary. Although movement is implied in each sculpture, movement actually occurs only when the viewer walks around each work. This situation is radically different when we consider the *Bird of the Night (But-*

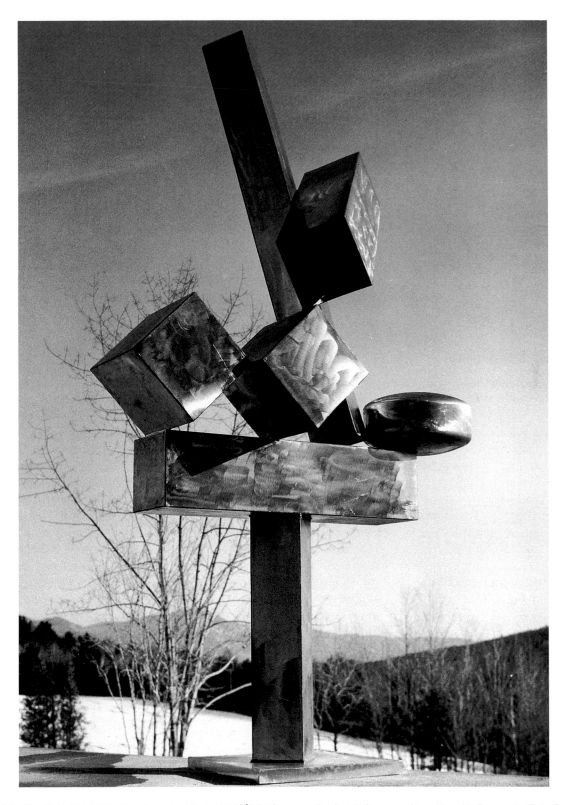

1-12. David Smith. *Cubi XIX*. 1964. Stainless steel, height 9'5¹/8". Photographed at Bolton Landing, New York; now in Tate Gallery, London. The abstract title of this sculpture reinforces its nonobjective content. It is number 19 in a series of twenty-eight sculptures by Smith that present variations on compositions of rectangular and cylindrical stainless-steel forms.

© 1997 Estate of David Smith/VAGA, New York, N.Y.

1-13. Bwa culture, Africa. Ritual dancer wearing painted wooden *Bird of the Night* (*Butterfly*) mask and raffia body suit. 20th century. Wood, paint, and raffia. Burkina Faso, Upper Volta River region

terfly) mask from the Bwa ethnic group in Africa (fig. 1-13). Although we are used to seeing African masks displayed in cases in museums and galleries, such static presentations deny their original function, which can only be understood within the context of village rituals.

In these rituals, the *Bird of the Night* figure appears after the first rains of the season. The mask adorns a dancer whose other garments cover the entire body. The fluttering movements of a butterfly are imitated by the dancer. In these rituals, the mask, created by a carver, is united with the ephemeral garment, with musicians, and with the movements of the dancer—a combination intended to express the essence, not an exact visual representation, of the butterfly. The purpose of the mask is thus only fulfilled in the context of the ritual as a whole. To try to understand this Bwa mask as a sculptural form, we must consider it within this dynamic context and within the spiritual context of the village and the participation in the ritual of the onlookers.

Although the villagers may remain static, the mask, garment, and dancer constantly energize the space of the village through actual movement. On a more profound level, the ritual is meant not merely to transform the space of the village but also to affect the quality of life.

Sculpture that incorporates the concept of movement is encountered in many works, especially during the twentieth century. As we have seen, our understanding of Paik's *Electronic Superhighway* (see fig. 1-1) was in part based in observing motion on the video screens.

Some aspects of twentieth-century art share another quality with the Bwa mask, garment, and ritual: they are ephemeral, lasting for only a short time. The materials in the African mask will wear out after a period of continued use—unless it is preserved out of its original context, perhaps within a museum. The creation of the mask, its use, and its eventual disintegration are part of a cyclical continuation of daily life and ritual within many African societies. The concept

of permanence, which underlies much Western art, is not a characteristic of this work. In fact, the emphasis on permanence in Western art has been challenged in the twentieth century as such ephemeral art forms as conceptual, performance, and earth art (see Part 10) have gained popularity.

Installation art, too, denies the tradition of the work of art as a singular static object by fashioning an environment, often temporary, within a museum, gallery, or other public space. Although there are almost as many types of installation art as there are examples, many of these works set out to charge and transform the space within which the viewer is moving.

One American installation artist, Judy Pfaff (b. 1946), responded to a literally enormous challenge when she accepted a commission for a work for the Pennsylvania Convention Center in Philadelphia. *cirque, Cirque* (fig. 1-14), developed over a period of several years, took seven months to execute; the installation itself, when many fragile forms had to be hung from the ceiling of the huge space, was especially difficult. The result, however, is a sequence of colorful forms that flow and surge through what was once just empty space above visitors' heads. But what happens when that "space" does not really exist, as is the case with the two-dimensional medium of painting?

An understanding of space is crucial for understanding the traditional medium of painting. Artists who have worked with two-dimensional surfaces usually have attempted either to create the illusion of three-dimensional space or to accept and emphasize the flatness of that surface. The distinction is apparent in the two paintings illustrated here.

In *Christ Giving the Keys to Saint Peter* (fig. 1-15), Pietro Perugino (1450–1523) painted recognizable figures, landscape, and architecture

1-14. Judy Pfaff. *cirque, Cirque*. 1995. Installation with 9 miles of steel and aluminum tubing and with glass orbs that extends across 70,000 square feet of space. Installed at the Pennsylvania Convention Center, Philadelphia. Commissioned by the City of Philadelphia and the State of Pennsylvania, together with the Pennsylvania Convention Center's One Percent for Art Program

from the visual world. Perugino's painting is **illusionistic**, for the objects represented seem to be tangible and weighty and appear to exist within actual space. In contrast, the painting by Piet Mondrian (1872–1944) does not have forms that resemble those in the visual world (fig. 1-16). The work is **nonobjective**, or nonrepresentational.

Traditionally, a **painting** can be defined as a two-dimensional surface to which liquid colors or inks have been applied. Flatness, the most distinctive attribute of paintings, is a starting point in their analysis. The flat surface is known as the **picture plane**, and in Mondrian's painting the two-dimensional colors and shapes reinforce the flatness of this plane. In illusionistic paintings, such as Perugino's, the picture plane seems transparent, like a large window.

Both paintings are made up of shapes. Mondrian's are black lines and squares or rectangles of a single color. Perugino's shapes are naturalistic objects: figures, trees, mountains, a public square, and a building. In both paintings, forms are organized into a composition. Perugino's composition is arranged to emphasize the figures of Christ and Saint Peter in the middle. A row of Christ's disciples on each side frames them, and the Renaissance-style structure in the background helps draw attention to them. The receding lines of the square's pavement converge at a central point. Perugino's composition is balanced, symmetrical, and centralized.

The composition of Mondrian's painting is neither centralized nor symmetrical, but it is balanced. Although Mondrian's square format is placed diagonally, his black lines are

horizontal and vertical, and they meet the edges of the painting at 45-degree angles. We are drawn to the edges of the composition by these angles and by the red, yellow, and blue found there. These colors are placed so that they balance each other, with no single color dominating. One subtlety of Mondrian's painting is that the only complete square, the area of color in the center of the composition, is a slightly more pure white than the other, surrounding areas of white. Mondrian's composition, however, might be described as decentralized, for it leads us to the periphery without concentrating our attention on any single area or element. His painting seems simple, but he has developed such a perfect balance that any change in color or composition would destroy the work's equilibrium.

Mondrian's composition is easier

1-15. Pietro Perugino. *Christ Giving the Keys to Saint Peter*, fresco in the Sistine Chapel, Vatican, Rome. 1482. 11'5¹/₂" x 18'8¹/₂". Commissioned by Pope Sixtus IV

1-16. Piet Mondrian. *Diamond Painting in Red, Yellow, and Blue.* 1921–25. Oil on canvas on fiberboard, 56¹/₄ x 56". National Gallery of Art, Washington, D.C.

Gift of Herbert and Nannette Rothschild, 1971. Courtesy of the Mondrian Estate/Holzman Trust

to analyze than Perugino's, for it exists completely in two dimensions. Perugino's composition must be analyzed both in terms of the patterns on the two-dimensional surface and as an illusion of three-dimensional reality. Note, for example, that when we analyze the painting as a two-dimensional object, the lines of the pavement converge toward a central point, but in actual space, these lines would be parallel to each other. This controlled spatial effect is a system of creating depth (**perspective**) known as **scientific perspective**. Other devices used by Perugino to help create his illusion are **atmospheric perspective** (the sky shades from blue toward white at the horizon, and the forms near the horizon are blurry and softened in color), **diminution** (forms in the distance are smaller), and **overlapping** (forms are placed in front of other forms).

Perugino's medium was the technique of painting directly on a wet plaster wall, known as **fresco**, or buon fresco; Mondrian's was painted in **oil paint** on canvas. Both artists used a technique of smooth, regular brushstrokes. Because most of the forms in both paintings are sharply defined, with precisely delineated edges, they can be termed **linear** (the opposite effect, in which broad, free brushstrokes are used to define form, is termed **painterly**; for an example see figure 6-44).

Perugino's colors are naturalistic, that is, taken from nature, which enhances his illusionism. Mondrian's selection of **hue** (the property that gives a color its name) is restricted to the **primary colors**: red, blue, and yellow. Perugino changed the **value** (relative darkness or lightness of the color) and **intensity** (the level of richness or saturation of the color) of his colors

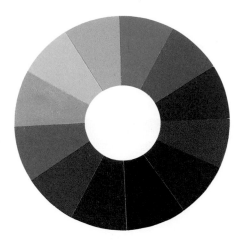

1-17. Color wheel. In the technical terminology used to discuss light and color, black and white are not considered to be colors. When color is understood in terms of light, black is understood as the absence of all color and white as the mixture of all colors. On the color wheel red, yellow, and blue are known as the primary colors because all other colors are made of a combination of these three hues; the secondary colors are orange, green, and purple. Complimentary colors, often juxtaposed by artists to achieve vivid coloristic contrasts, are the colors directly opposite each other on the color wheel, such as blue and orange or red and green.

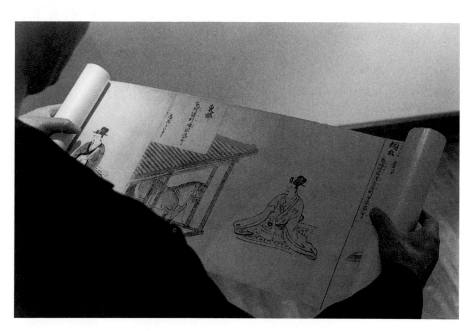

1-18. A scholar studying a Chinese hand scroll

to suggest the changes in value and intensity that result when light hits a form and creates highlights and shading; these changes are called **modeling**. Mondrian used pure colors, which are colors at their maximum or full intensity (fig. 1-17).

Perugino's painting was created during the Renaissance in Italy; it is one of a series of paintings of the lives of Moses and Christ that decorate the side walls of the Sistine Chapel in Rome. *Christ Giving the Keys to Saint Peter* reveals the abilities of a Renaissance artist to reproduce natural effects within a harmonious and clear composition. Mondrian's painting, on the other hand, is related to his personal philosophy and to the principles of the de Stijl movement (see page 533). While searching for a truly "universal means of expression," Mondrian wrote that beauty and harmony could only be expressed

by "abstraction of form and color, that is to say, in the straight line and the clearly defined primary color." His search for pictorial balance must be related to the search for political balance—peace in the years following World War I. Despite their pronounced differences, these two paintings share a surprisingly similar expressive content: they are orderly, serene, and, ultimately, calming. Both artists achieve visual harmony and balance. The formal analysis we have undertaken for each painting has a clear relationship to the historical and cultural background important for each work.

In addition, these works also conform to the common expectations that paintings adorn walls or ceilings. In some cultural traditions, however, two-dimensional works can only be seen in more intimate circumstances. A horizontal Chinese hand scroll (fig. 1-18) is meant to be viewed by one person or, at most, a limited group of people, in a quiet, contemplative atmosphere. And unlike the paintings by Perugino and Mondrian, a scroll painting is not seen in its entirety at one time. Usually only one or two feet of a longer scroll can be seen at a time,

as you unroll it from right to left. This format is intensely personal, with you controlling the pace of the journey; time thus becomes an important element in the experience of the work. The movement of simultaneously turning the two ends of the scroll to advance it cannot be rushed, which encourages contemplation. Perugino's large-scale illusionism is typical of much of Western art, but the more abstracted vision of nature seen in the typical Chinese hand scroll is consistent with the small-scale intimacy of the scroll format and the emphasis on the surface of the painting that is apparent when you unroll it. When the viewing is complete, you roll and tie the hand scroll and place it in a box out of sight for safekeeping.

Whether we are considering a work of art as public as an installation in a civic building or as intimate as a hand scroll, the artist's ability to transform our experience—and even our environment—is an important factor in the constantly evolving art at the end of the twentieth century. But the artist's role and impact throughout history have not always been so clearly recognized.

ART AND ARTISTS IN HISTORY

1-19. Käthe Kollwitz. Self-Portrait. 1934. Lithograph, 8 1/16 x 7 3/16". Philadelphia Museum of Art. This German artist was the first woman to be elected to the Prussian Academy of Arts.

Given by Dr. and Mrs. William Wolgin. © 1996 Artists Rights Society (ARS), New York/VG Bild-Kunst, Bonn

1-20. Ancient Greek, "Leningrad Painter." *Greek Potters at Work*, detail of Greek vase. c. 450 BCE. Private Collection, Milan

The impact of *Self-Portrait* (fig. 1-19) by Käthe Kollwitz (1867–1945) is direct and penetrating. Her face occupies the entire surface and demands that we confront her somber expression. Kollwitz published several series of prints depicting the social and political struggles of the poorer classes in Germany in the late nineteenth and early twentieth centuries. These struggles, with which she identified, have left their mark on *Self-Portrait*. As we can see in this image, one of the powers of art and the artist is the representation of the world, revealing its spirit.

Virtually all cultures, whether ancient or modern, have nurtured specialists who design and/or embellish everyday items or materials used in ritual. Whether Polynesian, Hopi, African, Mesoamerican, European, or Asian, these men and women were highly skilled workers. Sometimes those considered best at such expression were recognized as

"artists" and were elevated in their society to a high level of regard; in some cultures they were encouraged to sign their works. Although not all of these creators are recognized as artists, the visual arts—grand or modest, public or private, religious or secular—are a regular feature of human culture and those who create these works are fundamental to most societies in the world. Some were invested with special abilities, inspiration, and/or obligations to create artifacts that were beyond the ordinary.

Sometimes cultures such as fifth-century China and fifteenth-century Italy, among others, began to write down their aesthetic aspirations and deeply held values as expressed in the visual arts.

Throughout most of Western history, definitions of art were different from our modern view. The word *art* is derived from the Latin *ars*, meaning either "manual skill" or

"professional activity." The term has historically been used broadly, encompassing what we now think of as the sciences, as well as many practical handicrafts and occupations. An artist, for example, might practice the art of painting, while a physician practices the art of medicine.

As far back as the classical world of ancient Greece and Rome, the making of art was generally viewed as a manual profession taught in workshops, and it was not related to the more esteemed liberal arts—mathematics, grammar, philosophy, and logic—which were distinguished by intellectual, speculative thinking. This workshop tradition is illustrated in *Greek Potters at Work* (fig. 1-20), a vase painting by a Greek artist known as the Leningrad Painter, who worked in the fifth century BCE. Apprentice vase painters, some of them female, are working side by side with the head of the shop. Although we know that wom-

1-21. Johann Zoffany. *The Life Drawing Class at the Royal Academy.* 1772. Oil on canvas, 40 x 58". Collection Her Majesty the Queen, Windsor Castle, Windsor, Berkshire, England. Zoffany's painting shows all the members of the Royal Academy except for Angelica Kauffmann and Mary Moser, women who, within this restrictive academic climate, were not permitted to attend the life drawing class because of the nude male models. Zoffany ingeniously included them by showing their portraits hanging on the back wall. The sculpted figure with a raised right arm, just below the lamp, is an *écorché*, a sculpture of a flayed anatomical figure used to study surface muscles.

en were sometimes involved in the workshops, they must have been given lesser positions, for no Greek vase signed by a woman is known.

During the Middle Ages in the West, from about 500 to 1500 CE, art continued to be identified as a manual profession. Artists formed **guilds**—legal organizations rather like trade unions. While guilds assured professional standards, they also reinforced the distinction that was then drawn between manual arts—including the production of works of art—and the so-called liberal arts.

The traditional classification of the Western visual arts as manual, or mechanical, arts was transformed in the fourteenth and fifteenth centuries, during the Renaissance.

Both artists and writers began to emphasize the scientific and intellectual aspects of art, often incorporating the liberal arts into the education of artists. It was argued that arithmetic, for example, was necessary for the study of proportion, and that geometry figured in the proper calculation of perspective. The artist was beginning to be seen as an educated professional versed in both the practice and the theory of art. This new attitude that the artist had to be a skilled and educated individual was accompanied by a new social status: artists became the companions of intellectuals, princes, popes, and emperors.

This evolution affected the classification of the visual arts in Europe.

By the sixteenth century, painting, sculpture, and architecture were grouped together as the arts of *disegno* (an Italian word that refers both to the making of drawings and to the concept of design) and were elevated to a status higher than other utilitarian arts. Discussion of art theory became commonplace among intellectuals, and treatises were written that defined art and discussed its developing history. By the later sixteenth century, art academies began to replace the workshop tradition; artists were now educated in both the practical and the theoretical aspects of art, as can be seen in the late-eighteenth-century painting (fig. 1-21) depicting the male members of London's

1-22. Unknown Chinese painter. *Portrait of Ni Zan.* Ming dynasty, c. 1340. Scroll, ink on paper, 11 1/8 x 24". National Palace Museum, Taipei, Taiwan, Republic of China. Chinese literati painters worked alone, seated at desks in their studios. Paintings were executed on the flat surface of the table with natural-bristle brushes in watercolor and ink on silk or paper. All necessary brushes, paints, and inks were close at hand. For a painting by Ni Zan, see figure 4-4.

Royal Academy attending a class with live models. Plaster casts of the great works of classical sculpture, which were thought to exemplify the highest ideals of art, line the walls. The members of the academy are involved in rational discourse on the subject of life drawing.

This association of the arts of *disegno* with the intellectualism of the liberal arts was one of the mainstays of the new academic education given to artists. By the eighteenth century, art academies had proliferated throughout Europe. From this academic wellspring, a definition of the fine arts (*les beaux arts*) developed that included painting, sculpture, poetry, music, and dance on the basis that these are the arts that delight us. Arts that primarily serve a utilitarian purpose continued to be termed mechanical arts, while architecture, which was considered to combine usefulness with beauty, occupied a third, independent category.

Although our understanding of art's role within the fine arts is relatively recent, developments in the West since the nineteenth century have already begun to challenge those academic definitions of art. Early in the nineteenth century, when dramatically changing economic and social conditions were transforming Western cultural values, the concept of the artist as a member of the **avant-garde** (French for "vanguard") was born; in the 1980s and 1990s Chinese artists began to follow the same principles. Attacking the conservatism of academic training and public taste, many artists assumed roles as prophets, leading society toward a modern, often utopian, vision of life. In our time, the parameters within which visual artists work have changed. **Happenings** and performance art have blurred the distinctions between the traditional media of the visual arts and other art forms, including speech, music, dance, film, and video.

Among cultures outside the Western tradition, China nurtured the oldest continuous painting tradition in the world. Its historical isolation, imperial patronage, art academies (begun as early as the eighth century CE), and a bureaucratic elite of Confucian scholar-officials contributed to a unique tradition in the visual arts. Most Chinese artists were not only painters but also poets, calligraphers, government officials, antiquarians, scholars, collectors, connoisseurs, and mystics. Painters such as Ni Zan (fig. 1-22) were part of the cultured elite, the *wen-jen*, or literati, who were the main participants in the Chinese classical tradition. Among the Chinese aristocracy, painting and **calligraphy** were revered media for examination and for the preservation of social, political, and aesthetic values.

In other cultures, the position of artists varies. In Africa, for example, the early artist was traditionally a prominent member of the community, not only as the creator of pictures on rock surfaces but also as the one who decorated implements for hunting and other daily activities. In Africa today, artists hold a respected position within their respective ethnic groups, although the social status is not the same everywhere.

There often continues to be a sharp dividing line between the arts practiced by men and women. In some regions, men are still responsible for house building, tool making, and carving, while women are known for their dyeing, spinning, weaving, and pottery making.

In Africa, professional techniques are usually learned and handed down from father to son or mother to daughter, and certain crafts are family enterprises. In some cases, there is also apprenticeship—for instance, if a young male shows talent for **carving**, he might apprentice with a well-known sculptor and his family would be obligated to provide the teacher with gifts. If his skill comes to the attention of the chief, the artist is ordered to help create the elaborate attributes of chiefdom: thrones, crowns, scepters, drums, portraits, and articles of personal adornment. Village artists live solely on the patronage of their particular chief, and their talents and ideas usually conform to his wishes. The artists' role nevertheless often has great significance to the village as a whole through their creation of ritual objects.

In northeast Nigeria, Wodaabe women carve gourds into objects called calabashes that are important in both daily and ceremonial life (fig. 1-23). Only a few of these calabashes are used as utensils to hold porridge and milk; a greater number are treasured as ceremonial possessions (newborn babies are traditionally bathed in calabashes) and are a woman's riches and source of prestige. Calabashes are covered with elaborate designs that the artist cuts into the surface after the gourd is dried in the sun until hard. Most of the patterns are geometric motifs: triangles, half moons, suns, and sinuous lines. The designs are passed down from generation to generation and vary only slightly according

1-23. Wodaabe woman decorating a calabash, northeast Nigeria. c. 1981. The woman is probably decorating the calabash for her personal use.

to individual imagination. The patterns are thought to protect both the receptacle and its contents. Likewise, part of the daily obligation of village women in India is to maintain the exterior walls or plaza ofs of their homes with painted designs or rice-powder patterns (see fig. 10-18). These "painted prayers" are thought to protect their families and locate tremendous spiritual power in the artistic activity of women.

In India, as elsewhere, religion is a major force that stimulates art and architecture. Most systems of Indian thought consider the phenomenal world to be illusory, perceived and interpreted by the senses. These perceptions yield information of a personal rather than a universal nature. The challenge for the Indian artist is, therefore, to express concepts beyond the limits of the phenomenal world. The artist creates symbolic devices, or *murtis* (images, icons, or sculpture), that refer to the ultimate Truth and render the abstract, transcendent realm more approachable and comprehensible. Communication of uni-

versal religious ideals, not egoistic expression, is the goal of the Indian sculptor. As a result, variations on traditional artistic "rules" are limited, and few names of ancient artists are known. However, the task of the artist, whether the creator of Hindu temple sculpture or painter of house designs, is an extremely important one, for a devotee can gain access to spiritual power by viewing an image or by being in the presence of a great person. Such a belief, therefore, gives the visual artist an especially important role in Indian culture.

What we call art has assumed many different forms and functions in world history, and the role of the creative individuals we call artists has constantly been reformulated.

Imagine—You are walking in New York City. As you pass an art gallery, you notice a familiar image, a map of the continental United States. You are curious about what the artist is communicating, so you go inside to look more closely. You enter into the world of art.

2-1. *Cattle, Horses, Bison, and Deer*, axial gallery, Lascaux cave, Dordogne, France. Paleolithic in Europe, c. 15,000–13,000 BCE. Cave painting, animals lifesize

2-2. Plan of the Lascaux cave. Like most cave paintings, those at Lascaux are not all near the entrance and many are rather difficult to reach, supporting the theory that they are ritualistic rather than decorative.

INTRODUCTION TO PREHISTORIC ART

In a cave at Lascaux, France, painted animals—cattle, horses, bison, and deer—roam across walls and ceilings (fig. 2-1; see also fig. 2-3). The **naturalism** of these Paleolithic images is striking, for the animals are represented by means of a lively application of line and color that reveals careful observation and a profound understanding of the animals' anatomy and movement. In some areas, the natural undulation of the cave's surface matches the painted forms to give the animals a subtle three-dimensionality, and their apparent animation would have been enhanced by the quivering flames of the lamps or torches used for illumination when they were painted. These images, created in the period known as prehistory—the time before the development of writing—present many mysteries; their function and meaning are still uncertain.

THE PALEOLITHIC PERIOD

The origins of image making go back at least as early as the Paleolithic (c. 35,000–8000 BCE), a period characterized by the use of worked stone tools (the term *Paleolithic*, "Old Stone Age," is derived from the Greek words *palaios*, "old," and *lithos*, "stone"). Most Paleolithic people were migratory hunter-gatherers who journeyed in bands with twenty to thirty or even more

2-3. *Bulls*, rotunda, Lascaux cave

members. Their contact with other groups may explain similarities in Paleolithic art over vast geographic areas. As they followed the migrations of animal herds, men hunted while women, in addition to bearing and caring for children, gathered mainstay dietary staples—plants, fruits, nuts, and fish.

The Paleolithic period overlapped the last Ice Age, and glacial ice extended to areas in southern Europe. During the warmer months, when temperatures reached 60° Fahrenheit, people probably lived in tents covered with animal skins. As cold weather approached, however, many sought protection in rock shelters, in mammoth-bone shelters, or in mouths of caves. But some caves were sought out for other purposes, which we still do not fully understand; it is in these caves that we find their remarkable paintings.

THE DISCOVERY OF PALEOLITHIC PAINTING

During the summer of 1879, a Spanish archaeologist was digging near the entrance of a cave near Altamira, in northern Spain. He was hoping to find artifacts like the prehistoric tools with images of animals that had, beginning in 1840, been unearthed in France. His young

daughter wandered into the cave, and soon her cries were heard. When her anxious father entered, he found her excitedly pointing to images of bison—animals that had disappeared from Spain more than 12,000 years earlier—painted on the ceiling. Cave art had been discovered. But the paintings at Altamira would not be accepted as prehistoric until 1902; only after similar discoveries elsewhere would archaeologists accept the fact that such imagery and style could have been achieved by prehistoric people. Lascaux, the most impressive of these sites (see figs. 2-1–2-3), was not discovered until 1940, and new discoveries in the 1990s have continued to expand our knowledge of Paleolithic cave painting.

PALEOLITHIC ART

Near the entrance of the cave at Lascaux, in an area known as the rotunda (fig. 2-2), a grouping of bulls was painted on the cave walls. Our view (fig. 2-3) shows a detail of these bulls. The smaller one, the first to be painted, is represented in a quiet pose, as if grazing; its shape is created as a solid area of color. Painted over it at some later date is the outline that defines a large bull ambling to the left. Only a few details, such as the eye and shoulder vein (a target for the hunter?), are drawn within the contour lines. Both images were created by artists sensitive to the anatomy and liveliness of these wild animals.

Sometimes Paleolithic artists drew directly on the wall with chunks of red, yellow, brown, or black minerals or earth, but more often they created **pigments** by grinding minerals and mixing them with animal fat, vegetable oil, or bone marrow. They could apply these paints to the wall using a brush made of animal hair or a frayed stick; dots of color were sometimes pressed onto the wall with their fingers. Broader areas of color could be applied by blowing paint through a hollow reed or bone or by spitting the paint mixed with saliva against the wall. Whatever technique was employed, the skill was remarkable, not only in the fluid execution of the forms, but also in the exacting observation and memory of the artist, who reproduced these naturalistic animal forms—some seemingly in movement—by lamp or torchlight.

In Paleolithic cave art, painted or sculpted images of animals often make use of natural protrusions in the cave wall or floor. The human imagination was evidently inspired by areas of natural relief that suggested the forms of a particular animal; by adding paint or by carving, representational images were created. The theory that art originated in such an "image by chance" was stated in the West by the fifteenth-century artist and theoretician Leon Battista Alberti. In his book *On Sculpture*, Alberti writes about the birth of sculpture:

> I believe that the arts of those who attempt to create images and likenesses . . . originated in the following way. They probably observed in a tree-trunk or clod of earth and other similar inanimate objects certain outlines in which, with slight alterations, something very similar to . . . Nature was represented. They began . . . [to] take away or otherwise supply whatever seemed lacking to effect and complete the true likeness.

Alberti had not seen cave art, but recent archaeological discoveries have lent support to his suppositions. Alberti's desire to explain the goal of art as representational is related to western European attitudes about the visual arts. Where the attempt to create what might be termed "inner likenesses" dominates, as in China, Japan, Africa, Polynesia, and much of South and Southeast Asia, works are judged not on observational accuracy but on the ability to convey behavior, expression, or character.

In cave art, some animal images are shown pierced with spears or arrows, possibly as a practical demonstration to younger hunters. But the location of the paintings and the overpainting of images on successive occasions, perhaps hundreds or even thousands of years apart, suggest that they may have served a ritual purpose. The practice of re-creating the animals through representation may in some cases have been an attempt to capture their life spirits and thus help ensure a successful hunt. Whatever the function of the images, it seems to have been important that they be consistently lively and also identifiable by species. The rare occurrence of the human figure in Paleolithic art ranges from the representational to the schematic, but the majority are stick-like figures. Perhaps it was feared that too naturalistic a representation could capture the life spirit of the human being portrayed.

Of the sculptures that survive from the Paleolithic era, one type—involving about 150 sculptures from central Europe and Eurasia—poses unique problems of interpretation. Barely a few inches in height, these figures represent females whose breasts, abdomens, hips, and thighs have been emphasized (fig. 2-4). Traditionally these figures have been viewed as images of fertility, perhaps for use in a ritual dealing with childbearing, and the exaggeration of the parts of the body related to reproduction is sometimes assumed to be conscious abstractions by the artist. Scholars have also suggested that these figures represented the "ideal" Ice Age woman, with the fat accumulation desirable to conceive and bear healthy children during periods of food scarcity. Other explanations propose that these figures functioned as guardian figures or as dolls. Recent scholarship has demonstrated that as a group, they display various stages in a woman's life, from youth, maturity, and pregnancy to old age. Some archaeological evidence suggests that they were both made and used by women. Our uncertainty about the function of these sculptures is directly related to the limited evidence we have about Paleolithic life and culture.

THE NEOLITHIC PERIOD

The Ice Age that had dominated the life of Paleolithic peoples began to give way to a more moderate climate about 10,000 BCE in Europe. This warming trend in-

2-4. *Statuette of a Woman*, found at Willendorf, Austria. Paleolithic in Europe, c. 25,000–20,000 BCE. Stone, height 4³/8". Museum of Natural History, Vienna. Statuettes such as this one have been traditionally, but improperly, known as Venuses. Other similar figures are carved from mammoth ivory or modeled in clay. The navel of this figure is a natural indentation in the stone. Whether such works were made by particular artisans on demand or by individuals for their own use is unknown.

2-5. Pot, found in the River Thames near Hedsor, Buckinghamshire, England. Neolithic in Europe, c. 3100–2500 BCE. Terra-cotta, height 5". The British Museum, London. Whether such works were made by particular artisans on demand or by individuals for their own use is unknown.

creased the food supply for the hunter-gatherers. During the Mesolithic (Middle Stone Age), the transitional period that followed the Paleolithic era and lasted varying lengths of time in different parts of the world, techniques of gathering food became more efficient, and the cultivation of plants began. These developments led to the Neolithic era (New Stone Age) in about 8000 BCE in the Middle East, Africa, and Asia and about 5000 BCE in Europe. The Neolithic period is characterized by the domestication of plants and animals and the development of a sedentary life-style. The bands of hunter-gatherers settled into larger, kinship-based communities, probably as a result of several factors, including defense (scenes of human conflict are found in Mesolithic rock painting), economy, changing ecology, and religion. Job specialization developed at this time. Architecture of stone, mud bricks, and timber provided more permanent homes, and the development of pottery for storing and protecting food also contributed to a stabilized environment. In western Europe, Eurasia, Korea, Japan, and parts of Southeast Asia, Neolithic peoples raised large stone monuments, as at Stonehenge (see fig. 2-9).

NEOLITHIC ART AND ARCHITECTURE

A modest clay pot is evidence of one of the most consequential transitions in the development of humanity (fig. 2-5). Its design reveals its function as a container for food, and the twisted cord impressions suggest an aesthetic desire to make the object look pleasing. These designs, however, may also be explained as an aid in firing; they allowed heat to more thoroughly enter the body of the clay. Firing at high temperatures would make the pot water-tight. Pottery was important to the stabilized living environment of the Neolithic period because fired clay vessels were essential for cooking, transporting, and storing food.

The origins of pottery vessels are uncertain, but we now know that pots, first fashioned in the Mesolithic period, became a standardized production in the Neolithic. Early clay pots may have been molded over a round stone or hand-built by coiling (building up the walls of the vessel by successively adding long ropes of clay and then smoothing the joints). The pots were usually fired in open pits over fires of wood or dung, but soon special furnaces called kilns were developed for the firing of clay objects. The patterns on some early vessels may be adapted from weaving patterns. Perhaps wet clay was used to strengthen and waterproof woven baskets, and clay vessels were then made in imitation of the clay-impregnated baskets. By approximately 3000 BCE, the **potter's wheel**, a revolving stand for forming clay vessels, was in use throughout western Asia and in parts of China; it greatly increased productivity and encouraged

2-6. *Animal Hunt*, restoration of Shrine AIII.1, Çatal Hüyük (modern Turkey). Neolithic in the Middle East, c. 6000 BCE

2-7. Nok culture, Africa. *Head*. Prehistoric in Africa, c. 600 BCE–250 CE. Terra-cotta, height, 13¹/₂". The Cleveland Museum of Art, Cleveland, Ohio
1966, Andrew R. and Martha Holden Jennings Fund, 1995.21

the development of new modes of decoration. Pottery making also signaled economic changes, for the making of clay vessels apparently became a specialized activity of artists, who could trade their wares for other goods within their own community. Later, pottery was sometimes traded from one community to another.

Çatal Hüyük, a sophisticated settlement of about 10,000 people that prospered from approximately 6700 to 5700 BCE, has provided additional information about developments during the Neolithic period. Besides agriculture and animal breeding, Çatal Hüyük was also an important center for trade. One of the shrines excavated there contains a painting of a red bull surrounded by miniature human figures (fig. 2-6). Unlike Paleolithic cave paintings, which were executed directly on walls or ceilings, here a surface of white plaster was prepared first. If a new painting was required, another layer of plaster was laid over the previous painting to avoid the superimposition seen in some Paleolithic painting. The bull here probably relates to a religious ritual, for it was most likely a symbol of the male deity, embodying strength and fertility; bull skulls and horns were found in some shrines. The bull at Çatal Hüyük lacks the naturalism and vitality of its Paleolithic predecessors; it is less descriptive of a particular animal and more a diagrammatic symbol. This transformation might be the result of a different function for the image of the bull, or it might

also reflect an abstraction brought about by sequential repetitions of an earlier painting of a bull. This more schematic rendering of the animal and the increase in the number of human figures portrayed are characteristic of Mesolithic and Neolithic painting. But the treatment of human and animal figures varied considerably in different Neolithic communities.

In Nigeria, on the Jos Plateau, recent Neolithic finds have confirmed an early figurative sculpture tradition in sub-Saharan Africa. Among the most striking of these **terra-cotta** (fired clay) human and animal figures are the Nok heads (fig. 2-7), so called because of their initial discovery in the tin mines of the village of Nok. Apparently

2-8. Fort Ancient culture (?), North America. The Great Serpent Mound, Peebles, Adams County, Ohio. Prehistoric in the Americas, **c.** 1070 CE, length 1,254', average width 20', height approx. 4–5'. The "patron" would probably be the entire community, and perhaps everyone participated in the construction. The Fort Ancient culture was a Mississippian group that lived in the central Ohio Valley from c. 900 to c. 1600 CE.

these heads, distinguished by an emphatic facial realism, were once joined to fully modeled figures. Whether or not such descriptive heads were meant to be an early form of portraiture is unknown. Recent scholarship suggests that these works may have been made by women. As with most prehistoric art, more extensive archaeological investigation is needed in order to begin to interpret their use.

On the North American continent, the most conspicuous remains from the Neolithic period are giant earth mounds, such as the Great Serpent Mound in Ohio (fig. 2-8). One of a number of mounds in the forms of animals, the Great Serpent Mound consists of a low embankment, nearly a quarter of a mile long, which depicts a giant serpent uncoiling. Although the builders and purpose of this mound remain unknown, the Great Serpent Mound may have been associated with the nearby prehistoric Fort Ancient Amerindian culture.

In other known Mississippi River valley mounds, which were used for the placement of sacred objects or as burial sites, a superstructure was formed over a pit that was dug in what was to be the eventual shape of the mound. Clay or earth was then piled over this superstructure to complete the mound. Most earthworks are oriented toward the east, perhaps invoking a ritual of renewal involving the rising sun.

2-9. Stonehenge, Salisbury Plain, Wiltshire, England. Neolithic in Britain, c. 2750–1300 BCE. Earth markings and megaliths of gray sandstone and igneous bluestone; diameter of outer embankment about 300', diameter of outer circle of stones 106'; original height of tallest stone approx. 24'. Stonehenge was constructed in four stages between c. 2750 and 1300 BCE. Some of the megaliths were transported as far as 190 miles, probably by being dragged on sleds. They may have been raised using a series of levers. Earthen ramps were constructed to place the lintel stones. The entire community probably supported and participated in the construction.

During the Neolithic in western Europe, orientation toward the sun was also found at Stonehenge in England (figs. 2-9, 2-10), an extraordinary stone monument erected during this period. Among the common types of stone monuments erected during this period for burials and ritual spaces were stones weighing several tons that were raised upright. A single large block is known as a **megalith** or as a menhir when it is placed upright. When placed in a row, menhirs become a cromlech. Such monuments are not unique to Neolithic Europe but are also found across central Asia and into East and Southeast Asia during the Neolithic period.

The testimony of prehistoric monuments in Europe—remarkably later than elsewhere—is best evoked by the remains of Stonehenge, where an outermost ring of smaller stones set flush to the ground surrounds an inner ring, or cromlech. The innermost group of stones

is composed of pairs of stones with lintels (trilithons); they form a horseshoe that defines an axis within the circular plan. The axis at Stonehenge is oriented, through this horseshoe and the heel stone, toward the point on the eastern horizon where the sun rises on the dawn of the summer solstice. Other stones seem to have been aligned in relation to the setting sun on the winter solstice and various phases of the moonrise.

The arrangement of the stones at Stonehenge reveals the importance of celestial events for Neolithic peoples. The emphasis on the summer solstice implies that it was the most important of these events. The scale of the complex and the difficulty of construction suggest that Stonehenge was also a setting for religious rituals, again with the summer solstice as the major festival. This union of religion with celestial events is common in early belief systems. An understanding of the regular cycles of

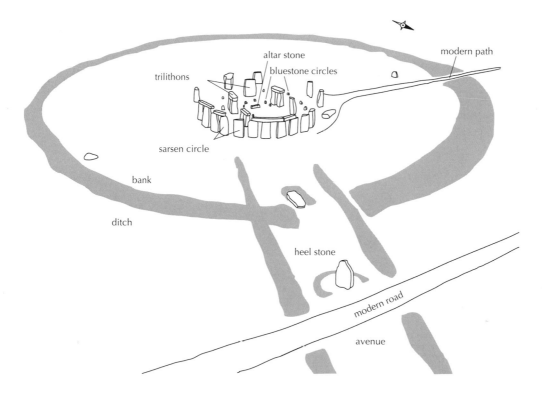

2-10. Diagram of Stonehenge site

the seasons based on celestial observation is intimately related to the planting and cultivation of crops, and both ritualistic and practical needs may have been served by Stonehenge.

PREHISTORIC ART AND THE PREHISTORIC ARTIST

Prehistoric art embraced a variety of forms and media. There were carvings in ivory and other materials, modeled clay figures, an array of tools and functional objects, such as sewing needles and spears, and even musical instruments. The earliest known flute, for example, was carved of bone about 30,000 BCE.

Study reveals that the efficiency of tools and instruments increased as civilization passed from the Paleolithic into the Neolithic era. Many of these tools had geometric designs or outlines of fish or other animals incised, or carved, into them.

If much prehistoric art was in fact involved with rituals, then the men and/or women who created the images may have been the individuals in the community who functioned as mediators with the spirit world. The ability to lead rituals and to create images may have been a specialized talent that was perpetuated through one or a few persons in each group. Perhaps they were recognized in their communities as having superhuman powers that would allow them to make efficacious images that could help lead the community to spiritual experience. If so, then it is possible that the images were produced in rituals observed by most or all of the community; they could thus be understood as public art in the most profound sense.

In settled Neolithic communities, the creation of pots, stone knives, and other objects was most likely bound to the developing division of labor. Artisans were specialists; they were potters, stone carvers, leather workers, and others whose works are lost to us because their materials were perishable. This early production must have been carried on both by specialists and by families. Pottery probably began as a family activity, but as the demand increased, the most skilled potters became specialists who were allowed to concentrate on production of pots instead of other tasks.

BCE	35,000	25,000	20,000	15,000
EUROPE ART		**c. 25,000–20,000 BCE** *WOMAN*, WILLENDORF, AUSTRIA		**c. 15,000–13,000 BCE** CAVE PAINTINGS, LASCAUX, FRANCE
HISTORY	**c. 35,000 BCE** Paleolithic period begins			
ASIA ART				
HISTORY	**c. 35,000 BCE** Paleolithic period begins			
THE AMERICAS ART				
HISTORY				
AFRICA ART				
HISTORY	**c. 35,000 BCE** Paleolithic period begins			
THE MIDDLE EAST ART				
HISTORY	**c. 35,000 BCE** Paleolithic period begins			

c. 3100 BCE
CLAY POTS,
ENGLAND

c. 2750–1300 BCE
STONEHENGE,
ENGLAND

c. 8000 BCE
Ice Age ends

c. 5000 BCE
Neolithic period begins

c. 5000 BCE
Plants, animals domesticated

c. 3000 BCE
POTTER'S WHEEL USED
IN CHINA

c. 8000 BCE
Neolithic period begins

c. 2200 BCE
Origins of ancient Indian culture

c. 8000 BCE
Plants, animals domesticated

c. 2000 BCE
Origins of ancient Chinese culture

c. 600 BCE–200 CE?
GREAT SERPENT
MOUND, OHIO

BEFORE 10,000 BCE
Paleolithic hunter-gatherers migrate
to American continents from Asia

c. 2000 BCE
Neolithic
period begins

c. 2500–1500 BCE
SAHARAN ROCK-ART
PAINTING

c. 600 BCE–250 CE
NOK CULTURE FIGURE
SCULPTURE

c. 8000 BCE
Neolithic period begins, earliest
settlements along Nile River

c. 4000 BCE
Plants, animals domesticated

c. 3200 BCE
Origins of ancient Egyptian culture

c. 6700–5700 BCE
PAINTINGS AT ÇATAL
HÜYÜK, TURKEY

c. 3000 BCE
POTTER'S WHEEL
USED

c. 8000 BCE
Neolithic period begins

c. 3200 BCE
Origins of ancient
Sumerian culture

c. 8000 BCE
Plants, animals domesticated

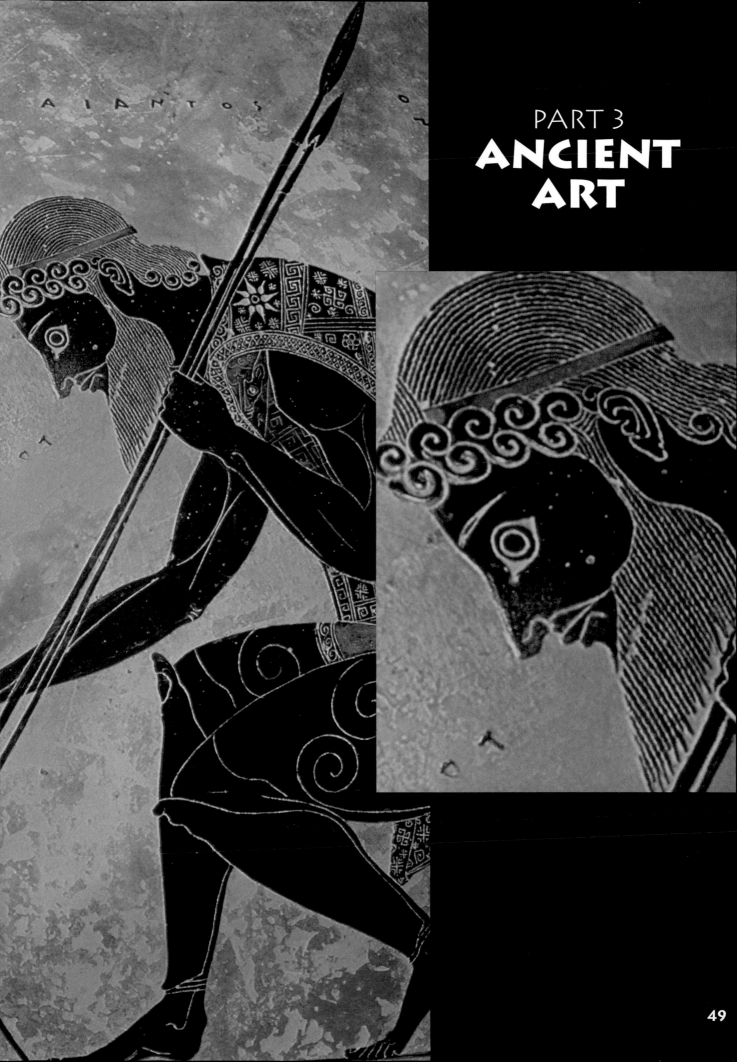

INTRODUCTION TO ANCIENT ART

The remarkable scene found on the back of this hand mirror (fig. 3-1)—a winged man huddled over an object on an altar—is unexpected, and at first it is enigmatic. But because our knowledge of ancient cultures is much greater than our understanding of prehistoric art, we know that this scene represents a practice that was common among ancient peoples. They believed widely that the interpretation of natural occurrences and objects provided omens that could predict the future. The flight patterns of birds, the position of lightning, the cracks on a bone thrown in a fire, or, as is depicted here, the "reading" of the spots on the liver of a sacrificed animal were important ways in which ancient peoples tried to understand the present and the future. The owner of this mirror would have been reassured by her faith in the power of divination to help determine decisions and choose appropriate behavior.

The increased information that characterizes the ancient world is the result of one of the most important developments in the history of humanity: the invention of writing. This historical beginning of the ancient period took place in different locations at different times. In Western terms, the ancient world is thought to end at the time of the decline of the Roman Empire, but a more positive demarcation for the end of the ancient period might be the beginning of the expansion of the living religions of Judaism, Christianity, and Buddhism, about 200 CE.

This emergence of writing in the ancient period enables us to know much about our mirror. It is the word *Calchas*, written in Etruscan script on the mirror, that identifies the diviner practicing here. The subject and style of the engraved design are drawn from the traditions of Greek mythology, which were popular with the people who created and used the mirror, who are known as Etruscans. Like many surviving ancient objects, Etruscan mirrors are most often excavated from tombs, where they were buried with their owners so that they could be used in the afterlife. And, like many objects that survive from the world's ancient cultures, this Etruscan mirror served both practical and religious purposes.

Beyond being an example of ancient art, the Etruscan

3-1. Etruscan. *Calchas Divining the Future.* c. 400 BCE. Bronze, engraved back of a mirror, diameter 6". Vatican Museums, Rome. The highly polished bronze surface of the reverse would have functioned as a mirror; the handle is lost.

mirror is also a reflection of the particular society that created and used it. The Etruscan civilization (see also pages 82–83) was a loosely bound federation of city-states in central Italy that paralleled the ancient Greek culture in time. Because their written language has yet to be translated, our knowledge of their beliefs and practices is largely derived from the archaeological evidence of their complex burial practices. They apparently believed in an afterlife that was a continuation of their earthly existence, and their grave goods, like this mirror, suggest that the deceased were commonly buried with virtually all the goods they used in life. The **naturalism** evident in the figure of the winged Calchas, the surrounding grapevine, the table, and the vase characterizes a style of representation often found in the ancient Western civilizations of Greece, Etruria, and Rome, but it is unlike the more abstracted styles practiced in ancient China and India.

Similar burial practices prevailed in China, where twentieth-century archaeological investigations have revealed a wealth of objects in grave settings. In clear contrast to the naturalism of the Etruscan mirror, ancient Chinese bronze vessels, like this *fang ding* (fig. 3-2), first attract our attention because of the combination of their powerful yet simple shapes with overall extravagant, abstracted patterning. Careful examination of the *fang ding* reveals that what at first seems to be nonrepresentational patterning is based on the forms of animals, parts of animals, or combinations of parts of beasts and/or birds. The main motif is the most famous pattern used on ancient Chinese bronzes, the **taotie**, or monster mask. The typical *taotie* is symmetrical, with each part repeated exactly across the central axis; eyes, ears, an open jaw, and feet are parts of all *taotie*. Sometimes the ears resemble those of oxen or cows; other times they appear to be closer to deer, moose, or elk. Why references to certain animals were made is not known, but the image always suggests power and presumably also shows considerable respect for the animal kingdom.

Vessels such as this one were created to hold sacrifi-

3-2. Chinese. *Fang ding*, from Tomb 1004, Houziazhuang, Anyang, Henan Province, China. Shang dynasty, c. 1150 BCE. Bronze, height 24¹/₂". Academia Sinica, Taipei, Taiwan, Republic of China. Commissioned by a member of the Shang imperial family

cial offerings of food and wine during ancient Chinese ceremonies dedicated to the veneration of ancestors. Sets of these containers were placed on family altars and were also buried in tombs of members of the ruling and aristocratic classes. These early bronze vessels sometimes had inscribed dedications to the deceased; beginning about 1000 BCE, inscriptions refer to historic events and legal transactions and are an important source of information about ancient Chinese life. The tombs where such vessels have been found also contained bronze weapons, some of which are inlaid with semiprecious stones, as well as ceramic vessels and objects carved from jade and other stones. These luxurious art objects were intended to confirm the political, military, and spiritual power of their patrons.

Anyang (see map, page 163), where this *fang ding* was excavated, was the last capital of the Shang dynasty (c. 1766–1122 BCE); the vessel's decoration also referred to the royal clan that ruled China during this period. The *taotie* on all four sides of the *fang ding,* for example, is thought to be the particular emblem of the Shang. The animal forms that create the vessel's patterns are believed to represent mediums through which earthly beings could communicate with the spirits of their ancestors. This idea is related to ancient shamanistic religious practices in China and elsewhere in which communication with the spirit world was aided by animals thought to have special powers of transcendence. A priest or holy person, often wearing a mask or ritual dress made up of animal parts (horns, feathers, skins), was understood to change not only appearance but also state of being, to transcend this world to that of the spirits; in some cultures these beliefs and practices have continued into the twentieth century

(see pages 592–93). The interrelationship between the spiritual and physical worlds demonstrated in many ancient objects studied here was an aspect that governed much of everyday life in ancient civilizations.

HISTORY

As husbandry, communal living, and the other distinguishing characteristics of Neolithic culture continued to emerge, some geographical areas gradually developed a more complex, urban existence. In fertile river valleys where abundant food was available—the Tigris and Euphrates in Mesopotamia, the Nile in Egypt, the Indus and Ganges in India, and the Huang Ho and Yangtze in China—large urban civilizations developed.

The first cities became administrative and/or religious centers for the surrounding territory, and many built monumental works of public architecture as symbols of their new central governing authority. As these cities and their territories grew in size and population, production became specialized and a division of labor developed, often reinforcing class distinctions. In some cultures, the administrative authority of the political/military and religious classes, which often existed in a symbiotic relationship, was supported by a system of taxation or tribute.

One key factor in the development of ancient civilization was the emergence of systems of writing and mathematics, which evolved in response to the needs of the new urban centers. The promulgation of laws and the keeping of records helped to provide order and continuity within the new complexity of urban life. Writing and mathematics also made possible the advent of literature and science.

These aspects of a more complex and interrelated urban life-style, or civilization, were present in different measures in societies beginning about 4000 BCE, but their development was not uniform. In Sumer and Egypt, they began about 4000 BCE; they date in India to about 2200 BCE and in China to 2000 BCE. In the Americas, settled life was known in the first millennium BCE. In western Europe, civilization emerged noticeably late, as is indicated by the realization that the prehistoric monument of Stonehenge (see fig. 2-9) dates from the same time as historical developments in Sumer and Egypt.

ART OF ANCIENT SOCIETIES

What we know about ancient civilizations most frequently comes from analyses of archaeological remains, artifacts produced by skilled artisans, and literature written by ancient authors. Literary remains are virtually nonexistent (or cannot be translated) for some ancient cultures, however, and most of the artifacts from archaeological investigations provide only a limited sample of evidence. Nevertheless, all early peoples produced materials that can help us understand their attitudes about spiritual as well as political, social, and economic matters.

Monumental architecture and public works such as temples, baths, amphitheaters, and granaries reflect societies that cared about issues of public as well as spiritual health. Many large-scale ancient architectural and sculptural monuments were dedicated to a combination of political and spiritual ideals, but in China spiritual and political power were more often expressed in ritual vessels and burial practices than by architecture. Although many ancient sculptures and paintings represented deities or leaders, some examples also recorded everyday activities.

Works of ancient art and architecture were made from a wide variety of enduring media, from common limestone to the most precious metals and gems, but the "perishable" arts, such as literature, dance, and music, are largely lost to us. In many cultures they may have been as significant as their more permanent visual counterparts, and our understanding of each ancient culture is in some way partial and incomplete. Nevertheless, study of the remains that have come to light provides clues to the common as well as the distinctive traits of human behavior worldwide.

The role of the arts is clearly reflected in new types of art objects that began to be produced in China from about the sixth century BCE onward. Sometimes these objects reveal new approaches to representation as well. One, the painted silk banner from the tomb of the so-called Lady from Dai (fig. 3-3), in south China, is an important early example of polychrome painting in China. Banners of this type, which were described in literary accounts, were probably carried in funerary processions before being buried with the deceased, and this one was found draped over the innermost of four coffins. Its iconography is descriptive and its presentation naturalistic in contrast to the geometricized patterns found on earlier ritual bronzes (see fig. 3-2). What is depicted on the banner is the path of souls after death, from the underworld to the earthly realm, and then to what is known as the Land of the Immortals. The underworld, or watery realm, is represented by the fish and deities of that world of darkness. The soul is then called back to earth, where it rejoins other souls and is feasted by the family of the deceased. The detail here portrays the Lady from Dai as she is feasted on earth. The top of the banner describes the Land of the Immortals, where creation tales are told.

This particular banner reflects two philosophies that arose in ancient China. As in many other ancient cultures, the preoccupation with the attainment of immortality characterizes most funerary art. The native Nature philosophy, of China, called Daoism, guided the selection of tombs' contents and their placement in the grave. At the same time, the naturalistic depictions of human beings reflect the impact of Confucianism, with its self-reflective attitudes toward human life. In the ancient world, as this banner shows, the arts could be a sensitive barometer of changes in social and intellectual order.

ART PAST/ART PRESENT   THE CONCEPT OF THE CLASSICAL

The terms *classic* and *classical* are widely used today, yet they have a number of different—and potentially confusing—meanings. In the context of ancient Greek art, for example, the term *Classical period* refers to a particular period within the development of Greek art (see pages 98–103); it received that name because in the nineteenth century it was seen as the high point of Greek art and culture. The term *classical*—with a small *c*—has a broader meaning, referring generally to the principles of order, harmony, balance, and clarity that are evident in much Greek and Roman art and architecture; this usage is based on the importance of these works during the Renaissance and later periods. An even broader usage is evident in the terms *classics* and *Classical World*, which are used today to refer to the study of the literary and other accomplishments of the Greeks and the Romans, and when we speak of something as a "classic," we are suggesting that it has a timeless significance.

3-3. Chinese. *Lady from Dai with Attendants*, detail of **T**-shaped banner found in the Dai Tomb, near Changsha, Hunan Province, China. Han dynasty, c. 180 BCE. Painted silk, 6'8³/₄" x 3' at top. Formerly Historical Museum, Beijing. Commissioned by Lady Dai or her family

THE ANCIENT ARTIST

In most ancient civilizations, artists—the men and women who created what we now commonly refer to as works of art—were counted among the ranks of laborers, and their products were seen as the result of manual effort. Most works of art were the product of a group of trained artists working together in a workshop, with various individuals undertaking differing aspects of the process of production. Apprentices in these workshops learned traditional forms and techniques, which ensured a continuity of artistic and iconographic formulas.

During the ancient period most works were commissioned by patrons, but because historical records are scarce, often we do not know their names. This does not mean that we should forget their important role in defining to the artist the kind of work they needed and how they felt it should function; in this period art was still very much a collaboration between the person(s) who commissioned the work and the artist and workshop that produced the finished product.

The role of rulers in ordering works of art to bolster their regime and express their wealth and beneficence was a common one during this period. Although rulers sometimes took pride in employing artists of significant talent, these instances did not contribute greatly to the social or economic prestige of the artist. In Greece, the personality and individual style of a number of artists are documented. Although these artists were personally admired, their profession was nevertheless viewed as lacking the philosophical and educational values of the liberal arts. Later Roman patrons valued Greek works of art as well as Greek artists, but Roman artists usually remained anonymous.

In China and India, embellished objects such as cast bronzes and stone carvings were designed and produced by craftspeople who usually worked together as a team; their specialized knowledge may have given them distinctive status in their communities. The creation and construction of the many vast ancient religious and urban complexes required cooperation, specialization, and overall coordination—prerequisites for ancient civilization. Although recognition of the role of the individual is extremely prominent in modern attitudes about art and artistic creation, it was not an important factor in most ancient societies.

BCE	4000	3000	2000	1000
EUROPE ART			**c. 1550–1450 BCE** PALACE AT KNOSSOS, CRETE **c. 1400 BCE** "TREASURY OF ATREUS," MYCENAE, GREECE **c. 1300–1200 BCE** LION GATE, MYCENAE, GREECE	**c. 900–700 BCE** GEOMETRIC STYLE, GREECE **c. 600–480 BCE** ARCHAIC STYLE, GREECE **c. 520–480 BCE** SEVERE STYLE, GREECE **c. 530 BCE** EXEKIAS'S *ACHILLES AND AJAX*, GREECE
HISTORY			**c. 2000–1450 BCE** Minoan civilization, Greece **c. 1400–1100 BCE** Mycenaean civilization, Greece **c. 1100 BCE** Dorians invade Mycenae	**776 BCE** 1st Olympian Games, Greece **8TH CENTURY BCE** Homer's *Iliad* and *Odyssey*, Greece **c. 700–509 BCE** Etruscan civilization **510–31 BCE** Roman Republic
ASIA ART		**c. 2500 BCE** MOHENJO-DARO SEALS, INDIA	**c. 1200 BCE** TOMB OF LADY HAO, CHINA	
HISTORY		**c. 2700–1500 BCE** Indus Valley civilization, India **c. 2200–2000 BCE** Urban centers develop in India, China	**c. 1766–1122 BCE** Shang dynasty, China	**563 BCE** Siddhartha Gautama, the Buddha, born, Nepal
THE AMERICAS ART				
HISTORY				
AFRICA ART	**c. 3150 BCE** *PALETTE OF KING NARMER*, EGYPT	**c. 2601–2515 BCE** GREAT PYRAMIDS, GIZA, EGYPT	**c. 1390–1212 BCE** GREAT TEMPLES, LUXOR, KARNAK, EGYPT **c. 1352–1336 BCE** AMARNA STYLE, EGYPT	
HISTORY	**c. 4000 BCE** Urban centers develop in Egypt **c. 3150 BCE** Lower and Upper Egypt united	**c. 3000 BCE** Hieroglyphic writing, Egypt **c. 2700–2190 BCE** Old Kingdom, Egypt **c. 2040–1674 BCE** Middle Kingdom, Egypt	**c. 1552–1069 BCE** New Kingdom, Egypt **c. 1390–1352 BCE** Amenhotep III rules Egypt **c. 1352–1336 BCE** Akhenaten rules Egypt	
THE MIDDLE EAST ART		**c. 3200–3000 BCE** VESSEL FROM URUK **c. 2100 BCE** ZIGGURAT AT UR, SUMERIA		**c. 720 BCE** *WINGED BULL*, ASSYRIA
HISTORY	**c. 4000 BCE** Urban centers develop in Sumeria **c. 3300–3000 BCE** Writing develops in Sumeria			

500	400	200	100 CE
c. 460 BCE *ZEUS,* GREECE	**c. 400–320 BCE** 4TH CENTURY STYLE, GREECE	**c. 180–160 BCE** *WINGED VICTORY OF SAMOTHRACE*	**72–96 CE** FLAVIAN AMPHITHEATER, ROME
c. 460 BCE SECOND TEMPLE OF HERA, PAESTUM, ITALY	**4TH CENTURY BCE** PRAXITELES' *APHRODITE OF KNIDOS,* GREECE	**c. 159 BCE** ALTAR OF ZEUS AND ATHENA, PERGAMON	**98–117 CE** BASILICA ULPIA, ROME
c. 450 BCE POLYKLEITOS'S *DORYPHOROS,* GREECE	**c. 320 BCE–30 CE** HELENISTIC STYLE	**c. 30 BCE** *BACCHIC MYSTERIES,* POMPEII, ITALY	**117–25 CE** PANTHEON, ROME
c. 450–400 BCE CLASSICAL STYLE, GREECE	**c. 230–220 BCE** *DYING TRUMPETER,* PERGAMON		**161–80 CE** EQUESTRIAN STATUE OF MARCUS AURELIUS
c. 447–438 BCE KALLIKRATES AND IKTINOS'S PARTHENON, ATHENS			**211–17 CE** BATHS OF CARACALLA, ROME
460–430 BCE Perikles rules Athens		**31 BCE–395 CE** Roman Empire	**79 CE** Eruption of Vesuvius buries Pompeii, Italy
431–404 BCE Peloponnesian War, Greece		**27 BCE–14 CE** Augustus is 1st Roman emperor	**313 CE** Emperor Constantine lifts ban on Christianity
		3TH CENTURY BCE GREAT STUPA, SANCHI, INDIA	**2ND CENTURY BCE** PAINTED SILK BANNERS, CHINA
	323–183 BCE Mauryan dynasty, India	**273–232 BCE** Asoka rules India	
		c. 100 BCE–750 CE PYRAMIDS AND TEMPLES, TEOTIHUACÁN	**c. 150–225 CE** PYRAMID OF THE MOON, TEOTIHUACÁN
		c. 100 BCE Urban centers develop	
c. 500 BCE PALACE OF DARIUS, PERSEPOLIS, PERSIA			

SUMERIAN ART

3-4. Vessel, found at Uruk (modern Iraq). c. 3200–3000 BCE. Alabaster, height 36". Iraq Museum, Baghdad. The reliefs celebrate the goddess of fertility through offerings of fruit.

3-5. *Worshipers and Deities,* found at the Temple of Abu in Tell Asmar (modern Iraq). c. 2750 BCE. Gypsum, height of tallest figure approx. 30". Iraq Museum, Baghdad, and The Oriental Institute, University of Chicago

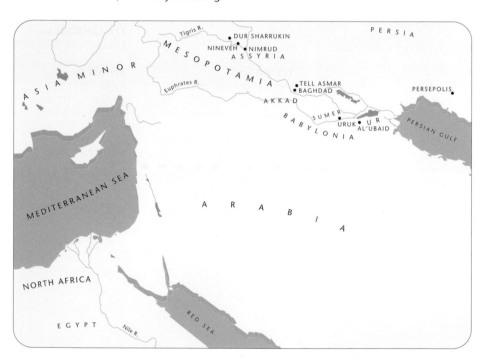

Our study of individual cultures of ancient art opens with an impressive large carved stone vessel more than 5,000 years old (fig. 3-4). Its **reliefs** of processions and offerings reveal the importance of ritual and ritual objects, while the clarity of representation that characterizes the figures and their gestures suggests the rigid repetition and controlled movements typical of a ritual intended to please or placate the god or gods that directed the community's destiny. The vessel is, however, only a reminder of what must have been a public event full of chants, music, movement, and perhaps incense.

In the Middle East, civilization began in Egypt and Mesopotamia at about the same time, between 4000 and 3000 BCE. Sumerian civilization was flourishing by about 3200 BCE, when the Sumerians brought the Tigris and Euphrates rivers under control for irrigation. At its height, the Sumerian civilization included more than a dozen loosely unified city-states fortified with walls, gates, and towers. Each had a population of between 10,000 and 50,000 inhabitants.

The Sumerians developed a flourishing agricultural economy, along with trade, commercial enterprise, and technological innovation, notably the invention of the wheel. The Sumerians also invented writing, when the system of pictographic signs that they had developed for record keeping evolved into a phonetically based system known as cuneiform. One scholar attributes a number of "firsts" to the Sumerians, including the first schools, the first historian, the first love song, and the first library catalogue. Sumerian developments in ethics, education, and written law were influential on later cultures. Sumerian literature too was noteworthy—the epic *Gilgamesh*, which tells how a king's quest for glory and immortality ends when he discovers that even the bravest heroes must face death, has been called the first great poem.

Sumerian religion was polytheistic, with more than 3,000 gods and goddesses. It was also animistic, encompassing virtually all aspects of nature. The divine, which was manifested in nature, was present in every object, and each city had a patron deity. Groups of standing Sumerian figures, found within shrines, are identified by inscriptions as representations of gods, priests, and individuals (fig. 3-5). They would have faced a cult statue of the main god or goddess, which may have had a more abstract form. The worshipers have rigidly clasped hands and large eyes inlaid with semiprecious blue lapis lazuli (imported from Afghanistan) or with shell. All wear a simple, skirtlike apron. The gods in the group are distinguished from the individuals by **hierarchical scale** (they are larger) and their enormous eyes. The statuettes of individuals would have served to present the life spirit of the donor in an attitude of continuous and vigilant prayer—a permanent and ever-alert substitute for the donor, who may not have been allowed to enter the sacred shrine.

The awe-inspiring sculpture shown in figure 3-6 presumably surmounted the entrance of a temple. The central figure—a threatening lioness-headed eagle with wings spread—is Imdugud, the force that exists within a storm cloud. This frontal deity with outstretched wings is framed by symmetrical stags,

3-6. *Storm God and Two Stags,* lintel from a temple at Al'Ubaid (modern Iraq). c. 2500 BCE. Copper sheets over wooden core (restored), length 7'10". The British Museum, London

3-7. Ziggurat, Ur (modern Iraq). c. 2100 BCE. Fired brick over mud-brick core, original height approx. 70', base 210 x 150'. Commissioned by several Sumerian rulers, including Ur-Nammu

which surely represent other natural forces, to create a composition that is commanding in its simplicity.

The most impressive structure of a Sumerian city—and of ancient Middle Eastern cities in general—was the **ziggurat** (from the Akkadian "pinnacle" or "mountaintop"), a high, terraced structure. The fifth-century BCE Greek historian Herodotus gave us a verbal picture of a ziggurat when he described the "Tower of Babel": it was 300 feet tall with, at its apex, a temple with a large couch and table of gold to be used by the god when he came down to earth. The best-preserved ziggurat is at Ur (fig. 3-7), the city thought to be the childhood home of the Old Testament figure Abraham. The structure was built on the ruins of earlier ziggurats by several Sumerian kings, including Ur-Nammu, who wrote one of the earliest

codes of law. It had a temple at the base and another, built entirely of blue enameled bricks, crowning the summit. This ziggurat's main deity was Ur's patron, the moon god Nanna-Sin. At the New Year festival, processions ascended the three staircases and proceeded through a ceremonial gateway to a brilliantly decorated temple with a cult statue and sacrificial altar at the top.

The Sumerian mother goddess was Ninhursag, the "Woman of the Mountain," and the mountains were the source of the water that nourished their country. As human-made sacred mountains, ziggurats enabled rulers and priests to ascend, during rituals, to the residence of the gods to ask for divine guidance in political and religious affairs. An early Mesopotamian text refers to a ziggurat as the "bond between heaven and earth."

ANCIENT EGYPTIAN ART

3-8. *Khafre.* Old Kingdom, c. 2570–2544 BCE. Diorite, height 5'6". Egyptian Museum, Cairo. This is one of a number of similar sculptures found in King Khafre's Valley Temple at Giza (see fig. 3-22), site of the three Great Pyramids from the Old Kingdom (see figs. 3-17, 3-19). The temple is located along the causeway that connects Khafre's pyramid with the colossal statue of Khafre as the god Hu, later known as the Great Sphinx (see fig. 3-18). Commissioned by Khafre

Egyptian sky god Horus, represented as a falcon, to symbolize the god's divine protection.

The statue, carved from an extremely hard stone and compactly composed, gives the appearance of being able to last forever. And, indeed, the solid, rigid character of this sculpture was the artist's way of meeting an extraordinary demand—that of creating a sculpture that to serve its purpose had to endure for eternity. The Egyptians believed that the *ka*, the part of the human spirit that defined a person's individuality and that would survive on earth after death, needed a physical dwelling place. The corpse of Khafre was mummified to provide this home, but if this mummy should decay or be destroyed, one or more sculptures of the deceased ruler could provide a home for the *ka*. The need to provide for the *ka*—as well as to accommodate other beliefs about death—underlay the creation of much of the surviving art and architecture from ancient Egypt.

HISTORY

The Nile River plays a central role in Egyptian geography, civilization, and art; the Greek historian Herodotus wrote that Egypt was the "gift of the river." The 900 miles of the river

The over-lifesize figure of Khafre, shown majestically seated on his throne (fig. 3-8), expresses the absolute authority of the Egyptian ruler. The idealized body is as architec-tonically rigid as the throne. There may be a hint of portraiture in the face, but the effect of the figure is grand and intimidating. Khafre's head is embraced by the wings of the sustained life in an otherwise arid desert region, and Neolithic settlements along its banks date from as early as 8000 BCE. The Nile, swollen by torrential rains, flooded its banks every summer and deposited fertile silt to support agricultural development. The flanking desert protected the rich Egyptian civilization from foreign invaders. The economy prospered, and crop production included flax for the making of linen and papyrus for paper and rope.

By the fifth millennium BCE, settlements along the Nile coalesced into distinct cultural areas. The northern area was known as Lower Egypt because of the flow of the Nile from the south to the Mediterranean in the north; Upper Egypt was to the south. Around 3150 BCE,♦ a legendary king now identified with Narmer (see pages 62–63) united Upper with Lower Egypt, establishing a political state that would endure almost continuously for more than 2,000 years.

This vast expanse of Egyptian history is subdivided into three major periods of political stability and cultural and economic growth known as the Old, Middle, and New Kingdoms. The Old Kingdom (c. 2700–2190 BCE) was characterized by an expansion of the central authority of the ruler, who oversaw Egypt's local administrative provinces. Its economic prosperity is evident in the funerary precinct near modern Cairo at Giza, which includes the three largest pyramids in Egypt (see fig. 3-17). Political unrest led to the end of the Old Kingdom when an economic depression, perhaps caused in part by lavish expenditures, was compounded by a famine, and local governors of the provinces broke the central authority of the ruler.

The Middle Kingdom (c. 2040–1674 BCE) saw a reunified Egypt.

♦ The dating system used is based on that established by the French Egyptologist Nicolas Grimal.

Sesostris III strengthened the central government, and new trade routes were established, stimulating the economy. The Middle Kingdom ended when a group of foreign settlers, the Hyksos, took advantage of a weakened government and of a new weapon—the horse-drawn chariot—to establish a separate kingdom.

Within a century, however, the Hyksos were expelled and Egypt entered a final period of cultural and economic prosperity, the New Kingdom (c. 1552–1069 BCE). The architectural remains of the New Kingdom reveal a vigorous economy, political stability, and the assured power of the ruler. This latter quality is reflected in the statue of the female ruler Hatshepsut (fig. 3-9).

There was an important, if short-lived, disruption in Egypt during the New Kingdom. The reign of Akhenaten (ruled 1352–1336 BCE), known as the Amarna period because his capital was located near present-day Tel el-Amarna, witnessed the transformation of many traditional cultural and artistic values. The relief of Akhenaten with Nefertiti and their children (fig. 3-10) retains some of the usual conventions of Egyptian art, such as the simultaneous combination of frontal and profile views (see page 63). But the artist has imparted a new naturalism to the figures. Unlike the earlier geometric treatment of the figure, the bodies of Akhenaten and his family are given sensuous curving forms that contribute to the relaxed intimacy of the scene. The fact that Akhenaten's queen is seen on the same scale as the ruler himself reveals the equality that characterized the Amarna period; in other Egyptian periods, women are usually shown as smaller in scale. After the Amarna period, the rigid conventions of older ways returned as the rulers established an authoritative continuity with their predecessors. The statues of Ramesses II (ruled 1279–1212 BCE) that flank the entrance to his mortuary temple at

3-9. *Hatshepsut.* New Kingdom, c. 1478–1458 BCE. Limestone, height 6'6". The Metropolitan Museum of Art, New York. Hatshepsut, Western history's first recorded female monarch, governed Egypt from about 1478 to 1458 BCE. Commissioned by Hatshepsut

Rogers Fund and Edward S. Harkness Gift, (29.3.2) 1929

3-10. *Akhenaten with Nefertiti and Their Children.* New Kingdom, c. 1348–1336/5 BCE. Limestone, 13 x 15". Staatliche Museen zu Berlin, Preussischer Kulturbesitz. Commissioned by Akhenaten and/or Nefertiti

3-11. Temple of Ramesses II, Abu Simbel. New Kingdom, c. 1279–1212 BCE. Height of sculpture approx. 67'. In 1968, these gigantic figures of sandstone, which had been cut directly into the cliff side, were disassembled and raised more than 200 feet to save them from being flooded by the lake created when the Aswan Dam was built. Originally commissioned by King Ramesses II, who dedicated the temple to himself as a god; the moving of the statues commissioned by the United Nations

Abu Simbel (fig. 3-11) recall the formal rigidity of the Old Kingdom statue of Khafre. But the colossal size of these sculptures reveals the grandeur typical of the New Kingdom. The Ramesses dynasty, which lasted until 1085 BCE, was the last significant dynastic family of the New Kingdom. During the following centuries, the power and splendor of the empire abated, and in 332 BCE Egypt was conquered by Alexander the Great.

RELIGION

Egyptian religion was a complex faith that included polytheism, magic, politics, and a steadfast belief in an afterlife. Wonder at the forces of nature and the spirit of animals led to the development of polytheism, with local gods or goddesses being affirmed in different communities. Early depictions of these deities include representations as animals, such as Horus (the sky god as a falcon), or as animal-headed humans, such as Anubis (a jackal-headed god associated with mummification).

For the Egyptians, whom Herodotus described as "religious to excess," magic was an important part of their religion. Believing that the spiritual world governed all aspects of life, the Egyptians even accompanied the commonplace practice of taking medicine with ritualistic incantations. Religion was also bound to politics. The ruler was viewed as a god who had absolute authority in secular and religious matters. During some reigns the god or goddess worshiped by the ruler would become the center of the state religion and be imposed over local religious practices.

Extensive religious ritual accompanied the belief in an afterlife, and the most important entity of the human soul to be served in the afterlife was the *ka*. The Egyptians believed that after death the *ka* would require an earthly abode. Thus, the body of the deceased should be preserved through mummification (the word *mummy* is from the Arabic *mumiya*, meaning "bitumen"—a petroleum substance mistakenly believed to have been used in mummification) and statues of the

deceased should also be provided in case of the accidental loss of the mummy. The process of mummification, strictly governed by religious ritual, took seventy days. The lungs, stomach, liver, and intestines were removed to separate containers called canopic jars, while the body was treated with chemical solutions to draw out moisture before being wrapped in as many as twenty layers of linen. The world of the afterlife was associated with the sunset and, therefore, the west; a song inscribed on an early tomb reveals the reward for the *ka*: "The span of earthly things is a dream, but a fair welcome is given him who has reached the West."

ART OF ANCIENT EGYPT

Providing service to the *ka* was a mainstay of artistic production in Egypt. Tomb walls were sculpted and/or painted with everyday scenes (see figs. 3-28, 3-29) to re-create a pleasant environment, and small servant figures were provided to perform common duties. Woodworkers constructed and artists decorated a series of coffins, which fit inside each other. Some were carved from stone (these are called **sarcophagi**, from the Greek *sarkophagos*, "flesh-eating stone").

In addition to the artistic preparations made especially for the use of the *ka* in the afterlife, jewelry and items of personal use were placed in the tomb. The throne of King Tutankhamen (fig. 3-12) displays the conspicuous wealth of the New Kingdom, while the relaxed figurative poses demonstrate influence from the Amarna period.

Although much of preserved Egyptian art relates to funerary practices, the desire to provide the *ka* with the means for enjoying life as it was experienced before death meant that this art also is an important record of everyday experience. Tomb paintings, for example, docu-

3-12. Throne of King Tutankhamen. New Kingdom, c. 1336/5–1327 BCE. Gold, silver, colored glass paste, glazed ceramic, and inlaid calcite, height 45". Egyptian Museum, Cairo. The top of the throne's footstool, a portion of which is glimpsed in the foreground, has a representation of defeated enemies. Tutankhamen, whom we popularly know as King Tut, was a ruler of relatively minor importance in Egyptian history. He succeeded to the throne following the rule of Akhenaten's son and died at an early age, perhaps violently. Tutankhamen's fame is primarily due to the fact that his tomb furnishings were largely intact when discovered by the British archaeologist Howard Carter in 1922. Commissioned by Tutankhamen

3-13. Diagram of the ancient Egyptian proportional system as reconstructed for the statue of *Hatshepsut* (see fig. 3-9). Egyptian workshops used a strict proportional scheme that allowed the efficient execution of painted and sculpted figures. A squared grid, drawn on the wall or on three sides of a block of stone, was used to demarcate the height and width of each figure's shoulders, waist, feet, and other body parts, following a standard formula. When applied to a block of stone, this system allowed unnecessary areas of the block to be chiseled away by unskilled assistants.

ment the labor of the lower classes as well as such festive occasions for the nobility as banquets with music and dancing. But even commonplace scenes often adhere to time-honored conventions of artistic practice. The strict grid of proportions followed (fig. 3-13) and the visually unnatural formula used to depict royalty and aristocrats—a combination of frontal with profile views (see fig. 3-15)—create a static figure typical of Egyptian art.

The relatively unchanging nature of Egyptian artistic practices reveals the stability of its civilization, yet artists were not slaves to formulas. Akhenaten caused a religious, political, and artistic revolution, but even before him, other currents brought degrees of diversity and vitality to Egyptian art, as is seen in the portrait bust of Ankhaf (fig. 3-14). The portrait bust as a type was related to funerary practices, probably as an additional home for the *ka*. The bust of Ankhaf displays a subtle and individualized surface anatomy: the

deep-set eyes, swelling of the cheeks, and diagonal lines from the nose to the corners of the mouth reveal an attentive sense of life akin to the naturalism observed in some tomb paintings. This bust contrasts with the authoritative power expressed in Egyptian royal portraiture.

THE EGYPTIAN ARTIST

In ancient Egypt, as in most early civilizations, no distinction was drawn between the artists who designed sculptures and paintings and the skilled laborers in workshops who brought their concepts into being. Artists labored as members of the lower classes. The exception was the architect, who enjoyed the status of a court official. Imhotep, the first recorded artist of Western history, designed the Old Kingdom funerary complex at Saqqara (see fig. 3-21). His fame was so great that by the New Kingdom he was deified as the god of learning and medicine.

3-14. *Ankhaf.* Old Kingdom, c. 2570–2544 BCE. Painted limestone, partially molded in plaster, height 22". Harvard–MFA Expedition, Courtesy, Museum of Fine Arts, Boston. This bust of Ankhaf, an official under Khafre buried at Giza, was found in his tomb. Commissioned by Ankhaf

ANCIENT EGYPTIAN ART: THE PALETTE OF NARMER

3-15. *Votive Palette of King Narmer* (side A). Old Kingdom, c. 3150–3125 BCE. Slate, height 25". Egyptian Museum, Cairo. The shieldlike shape and shallow indentation reveal that this is an enlarged, ceremonial version of an everyday object, a palette used for the grinding of pigments for eye shadow. This palette was found at Hierakonpolis, a sacred city of prehistoric Egypt. Probably commissioned by Narmer

3-16. *Votive Palette of King Narmer* (side B)

In the past, important historical developments often led to the creation of objects that commemorated or interpreted the event. One of the earliest surviving works of Egyptian art, the *Votive Palette of King Narmer*, was apparently created to mark the unification of Egypt. Narmer, who has been identified with Menes, the first king of the first Egyptian dynasty, appears three times. As the largest figure on side A (fig. 3-15), he wears the crown of Upper Egypt and brings under his control a figure who probably represents Lower Egypt. At the bottom of side A are two more defeated antagonists and small symbols of a fortified city and a gazelle trap that suggest victories in the city and countryside. The nearby human-headed figure with six papyrus blossoms, being held captive by the god Horus (shown as a falcon), almost certainly refers to the submission of

4000 BCE	Earth's population reaches about 85 million
3760 BCE	Earliest date in the traditional Jewish calendar
3500–3000 BCE	Wheeled vehicles in use
c. 3150–3125 BCE	***Votive Palette of King Narmer***
3000 BCE	Earth's population nears 100 million
c. 3000 BCE	Bronze is first produced

Lower Egypt to Upper Egypt. The use of symbols to represent complex ideas is an innovation that points to the later development of Egyptian hieroglyphs, in which figures or pictures signify words or sounds. At the bottom of side B (fig. 3-16), Narmer himself appears as a symbol—a horned bull, victorious over an enemy and the enemy's fortified city. Near the top of side B, Narmer, wearing the crown of Lower Egypt and accompanied by a processional retinue, views the decapitated corpses of enemies. The central symbol at the top of both sides represents Narmer's name and his palace. It is flanked by horned animals representing the sky mother, Hathor, to whose shrine the palette was probably offered. In addition to Narmer's assumption of the two crowns, the union of Egypt is also suggested by the joining of two fantastic, long-necked lionesses on side B, their serpentine necks intertwined to form the shallow indentation that refers to the function of the object as a palette.

A number of the most important surviving works of art from predynastic Egypt are similar palettes or fragments of palettes. The decoration is usually about political subjects. Apparently the larger versions of these palettes were displayed as **votives** (gifts made to a god or goddess), and they may also have been used to grind and mix the pigments that adorned the eyes of the cult statue of the deity. The *Votive Palette of King Narmer* probably had several functions: as an object to be used in a religious ritual; as a votive offering to the god or goddess (most likely Hathor); and as a commemoration of the military and territorial victories of Narmer. Such a union of political statement with religious ritual is typical of Egyptian art and culture.

Narmer is, in every case, represented as unnaturally larger than his subordinates and enemies through the use of hierarchical scale, which is common in Egyptian religious and political art. Narmer's large scale and the lucid design make the meaning of the palette more easily comprehensible. The human figures are presented in a design that clarifies the parts and their interrelationships—legs, head, and arms are seen in strict profile, while the torso and the eye are seen directly from the front. These renderings demonstrate the same clarity seen in the three-dimensional figure of Khafre (see fig. 3-8), but here they are united and suppressed into what is essentially a two-dimensional medium: **low relief** (see below). As unrealistic as this representation is, it is easily read and it emphasizes strength. This style of representing the figure would continue in Egyptian art for more than 3,000 years.

TECHNIQUE ▪ RELIEF SCULPTURE

The technique of sculpting figures or forms that are part of (or, less commonly, attached to) a background is known as **relief sculpture**. Because the figures are very flattened, the style of carving in the *Narmer* palette is known as **low relief**, or **bas-relief**. There is no differentiation in color, but light hitting the delicately varied levels of relief allows us to read the forms. This technique, difficult to perfect, was also practiced by later artists. The Egyptians also excelled at an unusual type of low relief known as **sunken relief**, in which the figures are recessed into the surface (see fig. 3-10). **High relief** is relief sculpture with forms that project substantially from their background (see fig. 3-82). In Egypt, as well as in later cultures, relief sculpture often has color added to support its design (see fig. 3-28).

THE EGYPTIAN PYRAMIDS

3-17. Great Pyramids at Giza. Old Kingdom, c. 2601–2515 BCE. Limestone and granite, original height of pyramid of Khufu 480', length of each side at base 755'. The three pyramids, from the left, were built by the Egyptian kings Menkaure (see fig. 1-2), Khafre (see fig. 3-8), and Khufu. The Great Pyramids were viewed as architectural wonders even in the ancient world; they are, in fact, the only surviving work from the list of "Seven Wonders of the World" compiled in antiquity. Constructed as royal tombs, they are the best known of more than eighty pyramids built in ancient Egypt. The pyramid of Khafre is the only one that preserves any of its outer dressed stone exterior. Many stones were taken from the site to build medieval and modern Cairo. Commissioned by Kings Menkaure, Khafre, and Khufu

3-18. King Khafre as the god Hu, later known as the "Great Sphinx," Giza. Old Kingdom, c. 2570–2544 BCE. Sandstone, height approx. 65'. Carved from sandstone on this site, the sphinx, with the pyramid of Khafre in the background, is part of the funerary precinct of Khafre, and its face bears his features, probably as Hu, the reincarnation of the sun god Re. The name *sphinx*, meaning stranger or mysterious person, was first used by the ancient Greeks; we do not know what name the Egyptians gave this monument. Commissioned by Khafre

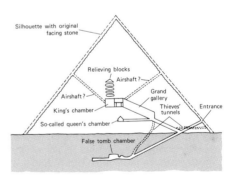

3-19. Section of the Great Pyramid of Khufu, Giza

Associating the transition to the afterlife with the sunset, the pyramids—the burial places of the rulers—were located on the western side of the Nile River (figs. 3-17, 3-18, 3-19). Today the desert area around the pyramids reveals little of the complex of funerary temples (see fig. 3-22) and other grave sites that once formed a huge necropolis ("city of the dead").

Grave sites in predynastic Egypt were usually shallow pits marked with mounds of sand near the edge of the desert. By about 2900 BCE, nobles were buried in underground chambers marked by mud-brick structures called **mastabas** (from the Arabic *mastabah*, "bench") with **battered** (sloped) **walls** (fig. 3-20). Mastabas contained offerings to the *ka* and chambers for a statue of the deceased.

About 2681 BCE, during the Old Kingdom, King Zoser commissioned Imhotep to design and construct a funerary complex at Saq- qara (fig. 3-21). The architectural climax was a large step pyramid, a solid structure that suggests the superimposition of progressively smaller mastabas.

It is not completely clear why the pyramidal form was used in this funerary context. One theory suggests that it is derived from the cult image of the sun god Re, a pyramidal stone that represented the rays of the sun descending to earth. A widely accepted view is that the pyramid fulfilled both practical and spiritual needs by offering a secure abode for the *ka* and by assisting the ruler's spirit in its ascent to heaven. A text found inside a pyramid states: "I have trodden these rays as ramps under my feet where I mount up to my mother Uraeus on the brow of Re."

The later complex at Giza was constructed between 2601 and 2515 BCE, and each pyramid took more than twenty years to build. Surveyors began the laborious and exacting process by observing a star in the northern sky, then orienting the square base so that each edge faced a cardinal direction—north, south, east, or west. Labor was supplied not by slaves but by the Egyptian people themselves, who gave their time during the three months of the summer flood, when their farmland was under water; records reveal that they were paid with food and drink. The high waters of the Nile facilitated the transport of granite from quarries miles away from Giza; much of the limestone used was quarried at the site, perhaps around the statue of the Great Sphinx. The stone blocks were transported, probably on a type of sled, up inclined ramps, and the capstone was polished or gilded to catch the first and last of the sun's rays. False passages were constructed to discourage grave robbers, but almost all Egyptian royal tombs were plundered in ancient times.

3-20. Reconstruction with section of mastabas. Old Kingdom

3-21. Model of the funerary district of Zoser, Saqqara. Old Kingdom, c. 2681–2662 BCE. Height of original stepped pyramid approx. 200'. The complex at Saqqara represents the earliest-known use of cut stone for architecture, and its architect, Imhotep, is the earliest-known named artist in world history. Commissioned by Zoser

ANCIENT ART: EGYPTIAN   **65**

THE EGYPTIAN TEMPLE

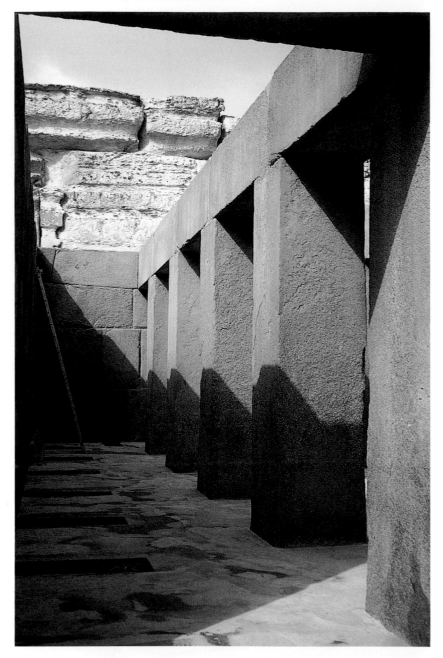

3-22. Valley Temple of Khafre, Giza. Old Kingdom, c. 2570–2544 BCE. Limestone and red granite. Post-and-lintel construction is exemplified in this temple, and it was here that twenty-three portrait statues of Khafre, including figure 3-8, were originally housed. The roof structure has collapsed. A causeway led from the temple to the pyramid of Khafre (see fig. 3-17) some 600 yards farther from the Nile. Commissioned by Khafre

This Old Kingdom Temple (fig. 3-22), composed of spaces defined by large, square columns, is quite simple, but over time the Egyptian temple evolved in response to the rituals enacted there (see figs. 3-22–3-27). Beginning with a long row of sphinxes flanking the avenue to the entrance, the organization of a New Kingdom temple is strictly axial, relating to the progress of the king's procession, and is characterized by **bilateral symmetry** (the forms are identical on both sides of the central axis). As the procession advanced, the king passed through a clear sequence of architectural spaces, beginning with the open road flanked by sphinxes, then moving into the sacred precinct through the pylon, whose broad sloping towers and flagpoles flank the central doorway. He then proceeded into one or more **colonnaded** courtyards open to the sky and framed on two or three sides by rows of **columns**. (Later kings often added courtyards, as at Luxor, fig. 3-26, where the latest open courtyard, built by Ramesses II, is out of alignment with the earlier structures.) Next he entered a large room filled with columns known as the **hypostyle** hall (see fig. 3-25). The only light here filtered down from the **clerestory**, the raised area along the central axis, where there are long vertical openings (for later examples of clerestories, see figures 4-12, 4-84). The final sequence of rooms, all fully enclosed, became progressively smaller, lower, and darker until the priest and/or the king entered the most sacred chamber, which contained the cult statue. The Temple at Luxor (see figs. 3-23, 3-26) was exceptional, for there were two sacred chambers; the one at the very back, which was entered directly from the exterior wall, was where the sacred boat of Amun was placed after carrying the king on the Nile from Karnak.

The enormous New Kingdom temples at Karnak and Luxor (see figs. 3-23, 3-25, 3-26, 3-27) are among the largest religious structures ever built. They played an important role in Egyptian religion and politics, especially the annual festival of Opet, a twenty-four-day celebration of the New Year, when

3-23. Courtyard built by Amenhotep III, Great Temple of Amun-Mut-Khonsu, Luxor. New Kingdom, c. 1390–1352 BCE. View of hypostyle hall from courtyard. The temple is dedicated to Amun, the sun god; his consort, Mut; and Khonsu, the moon god. Commissioned by Amenhotep III

the Nile was at full flood. At this time, the king and his family came to Karnak to participate in the procession that accompanied the golden statue of Amun, the chief Egyptian deity, to the shrine of his wife (the goddess Mut) and son (Khonsu, the moon god) at Luxor. The king, who was traditionally identified with Amun, emerged from the **pylon**, or entrance gate, at dawn, so that he was framed by the pylon's flanking towers while the sun rose behind him (fig. 3-24). Such ritual reinforced his identification with the sun god.

The hierarchical and exclusive quality of Egyptian society is expressed in these temples, for only a select few could follow the king into the courtyard, and fewer yet into the hypostyle hall. The enormous walls that enclose the sacred enclosure (more than a mile long at Karnak) excluded the multitudes and reminded them of their inferior social, political, and religious status, as did the overwhelming scale of the structures themselves.

3-24. Reconstruction drawing of a typical pylon gate, showing the rising sun emerging from the central doorway at dawn

Temple architecture stressed stability, weight, monumentality, and durability. These temples were meant to endure, and Amenhotep III (ruled 1390–1352 BCE) described a temple he had built at Thebes as

. . . an eternal, everlasting fortress of fine white sandstone, wrought with gold throughout; it is made very wide and large, and established forever.

The massive stone walls of Egyptian temples were solid, without windows; weight and stability were further expressed by the heavy cornices and battered walls of the pylon. Virtually all surfaces were covered with low or sunken relief carvings that emphasize the mass and weight of the stone. The hypostyle hall was a veritable forest of huge fat columns (at Karnak, the largest were 69 feet tall and 12 feet in diameter, with a circumference of almost 33 feet), and the effect was claustrophobic and intimidating. The solidity and austerity of these Egyptian temples directly reflect the stable and controlled civilization that created them.

3-25. Model of central section, hypostyle hall, Temple of Amun, Karnak. New Kingdom, c. 1294–1212 BCE. The Metropolitan Museum of Art, New York. The columns and capitals of this hypostyle are so large that dozens of people could stand on top of one of the capitals, and it takes at least eight people, holding hands, to span the circumference of a column near the base.

Levi Hale Willard Bequest. Purchase, 1890 (90.35.1)

The type of construction used for Egyptian colonnaded courtyards and hypostyle halls (see figs. 3-23, 3-25) is known as **post and lintel**, the post being the vertical supporting member, usually a cylindrical column, and the lintel being the horizontal member, often known as the **entablature** (see fig. 3-22). The only simpler types of construction are the wall and the mound. The engineering dynamics of post and lintel are straightforward—the weight of the lintel presses downward on the post, which must be strong enough to support the lintel's weight. If the lintel is too long or lacks sufficient **tensile strength** (longitudinal strength sufficient to support itself without breaking), it may collapse in the middle or shear and break where it meets the post. When columns are used, they are usually decorated, espe-cially at the top, or **capital**. In Egypt, the column and capital may resemble greatly enlarged papyrus, date palms, or bundled reeds (see figs. 3-23, 3-25)—forms that may derive from the use of bundled natural elements in early Egyptian architecture. Although the post-and-lintel system is simple, the rhythmic placement of the columns and the relationship of vertical to horizontal allow many architectural and aesthetic variations.

Egyptian builders were restricted by the available materials, which included vast amounts of stone but virtually no wood. The dense and brittle nature of the local stone kept the lintels short and the posts heavy and close together. The hypostyle hall was virtually the only large enclosed space that could be constructed.

3-26. Plan of the Temple of Khonsu, Karnak. New Kingdom, c. 1186–1154 BCE. Statistics for a much larger temple precinct at Karnak reveal the tremendous scale of some of these projects; The nearby Temple of Amun, for example is 1,220 feet long, and its sacred enclosure encompasses 62,000 acres.

The drawings of architecture in this book are meant to aid in your understanding of principles of design and construction. Some of these diagrams reveal how a building would look if it were sliced through, as in a **plan** (or **ground plan**; fig. 3-26), which shows the building as if cut off

approximately one foot above the floor level. In the plan, solid lines are structure, with openings indicating doors and windows; lighter lines indicate floor patterns; dotted or light lines are used to indicate the patterns of the ceiling (see fig. 4-82). A **cross section** shows the building sliced through from side to side (see fig. 3-116), while a **longitudinal section** slices the building from front to back (fig. 3-27). An **elevation** shows the exterior surfaces and their decoration diagrammatically, not as the human eye would see them (see fig. 6-28). A relatively recent kind of diagram is the **isometric projection**, which includes both a ground plan and a view of the exterior and/or interior from a specific point of view (fig. 3-27). Because of the artificial and two-dimensional nature of most of these diagrams, an understanding of any building usually requires an examination of several diagrams.

Today, buildings are erected using architect's diagrams similar to those discussed above, but we still do not know much about the use of drawings by architects, engineers, and construction crews in the past. The earliest surviving examples date from the Gothic period, in the thirteenth century. In some earlier periods, architects and engineers apparently laid out the plan of the building full scale on the ground, and then used pegs and string or vines in order to mark the edges.

3-27. Isometric projection with plan and longitudinal section of the Temple of Khonsu. Originally commissioned by Ramesses III and Ramesses IV, with later additions

EGYPTIAN TOMB PAINTINGS AND PAINTED RELIEFS

3-28. *Ti Watching a Hippopotamus Hunt*, in the Tomb of Ti, Saqqara. Old Kingdom, c. 2510–2460 BCE. Painted limestone, height approx. 46". On the wall opposite this painted relief are three small openings intended to allow three lifesize statues of Ti to gaze permanently at this hunting scene. Commissioned by Ti, overseer of the Sun Temples of Kings Neferikare and Nyuserre

The walls of Egyptian tombs were decorated with painted, low-relief sculptures or with paintings on plaster applied over the walls. The requirement that tomb decoration preserve pleasant everyday life for the delight of the *ka* throughout eternity means that these paintings tell us a great deal about ancient Egyptian life and customs and have a broad human interest and appeal.

The largest single scene among the hundreds of painted reliefs in the Old Kingdom tomb of a govern-ment official named Ti depicts a hippopotamus hunt, with Ti stand-ing in the boat (fig. 3-28). The emphasis on this particular scene suggests that it has a deep signifi-cance, and the hunt here probably refers not only to the general con-cept of victory but also specifically to Ti's victory over death. Ti is repre-sented in the typical Egyptian style, and the composition emphasizes clarity and repeated patterns. The Egyptian artist had to work within the strict limitations imposed by the function of the work; invention was not prized, and a new viewpoint or treatment might render the object or experience unavailable to the *ka* in the afterlife. This approach, which is not naturalistic, uses only frontal and profile viewpoints, the char-acteristic points of view in Egyptian art.

The zigzag pattern that repre-sents the water of the Nile is based on the hieroglyph for water, which is also the hieroglyph for the Nile itself; in Egypt the Nile was water, and water was the Nile. The parallel lines that create a foil for the organic shapes of the figures and animals indicate a setting deep in the marsh-es, for these are the stems of the same reeds that burst into leaf and blossom near the top of the relief. In this upper area, predators stalk birds, creating striking patterns against the geometric stalks as well as a metaphor for the hunt taking place below.

Pond in a Garden (fig. 3-29) from a New Kingdom tomb, with its rect-angular artificial pool with ducks, fish, and lotus blossoms surrounded on all sides by flowering and fruit-bearing trees, provides an interest-ing demonstration of the Egyptian

3-29. *Pond in a Garden*, fragment from the Tomb of Nebamun, Thebes. New Kingdom, c. 1400 BCE. Paint on plaster wall, 24 x 28". The British Museum, London. Commissioned by Nebamun, "scribe and counter of grain"

approach to representation. Completeness and clarity were demanded of the Egyptian painter, for anything not clearly included in the tomb painting would not be available to the *ka* in the afterlife. This explains why each object has to be shown in its most easily recognized view—the pond is represented as if seen from above, while everything else is in profile. The relationships among the objects in reality are also made clear in the representation: fish, ducks, and lotus are seen as within the pool, while the trees surround it. The trees are seen right side up and sideways, but not upside down—those at the bottom side of the pool are upright. Despite the lack of a consistent viewpoint for the scene and the flatness with which each object is rendered, we can still easily recognize that this is, indeed, a pond in a garden.

TECHNIQUE   FIGURE-GROUND RELATIONSHIPS

The distinct contrast that can be noted between forms and background in most works of art is called the **figure-ground relationship**. In *Ti Watching a Hippopotamus Hunt*, for example, we read the humans and the cat, birds, fish, foliage, and boat as "positive" elements—figures—isolated against "negative" backgrounds—the ground—behind them. A similar effect can be noted when works of sculpture and architecture are isolated and stand out against or within their surroundings. In analysis of works of art, the positive-negative, figure-ground relationship is always an important component. In some modern works, artists have achieved visual ambiguity by allowing the positive and negative forms to assume virtually equal importance in the composition.

THE INDUS VALLEY CIVILIZATION

3-30. Great Bath, granary, and houses, Mohenjo-Daro, Indus Valley (modern Pakistan). c. 2100–1750 BCE. Of the buildings excavated at Mohenjo-Daro, the most spectacular is the Great Bath, used for ritual bathing, which measures 40 by 30 feet and was sunk about 8 feet below the surface of the surrounding pavement. It was built from meticulously laid bricks set in gypsum plaster over a waterproof bitumen layer. A nearby well provided the water, which could be emptied through a massive drain. Excavation of Mohenjo-Daro, which is located northeast of present-day Karachi, Pakistan, was begun on a grand scale between 1922 and 1927 under John Marshall of the Archaeological Survey of India; since 1931, a number of other teams have worked at the site. Evidence suggests that Mohenjo-Daro, like other Indus Valley sites, was occupied from about 2700 to 1500 BCE; the stratified settlement debris investigated by archaeologists was 100 feet deep. The ancient center rises 40 feet above the surrounding plain; the highest point is formed by an artificial platform of mud and mud bricks.

At about the same time as the Old Kingdom in Egypt and Neolithic building activity at Stonehenge, the first civilization in South Asia arose at a group of sites in the Indus River Valley, in modern-day Pakistan and India. Many of these Indus Valley civilization sites are divided into two major areas—a lower, usually eastern, section of domestic buildings, craft workshops, and private shrines and an elevated section in the west containing public ritual buildings. A number of similarities among these sites—consistent use of a writing system, modular sizes of baked brick for houses and public buildings, settlement layouts, pottery styles, systems of weights and measures—suggest that a central administration controlled production and distribution of goods and services. Such a body probably controlled trade within the Indus Valley and outside at least as far as Mesopotamia (see map, page 163). There is evidence that they imported raw materials, exotic stones, gold, copper, and tin, but few manufactured or prestige goods from outside have been found.

What is surprising is that the Indus Valley sites lack royal burials, great funerary structures, monumental art, and other symbols of prestige and authority. The absence of larger, more ornate houses and exotic luxury goods suggests that there was no wealthy class. So it would seem that the usual model of a kingdom or empire, headed by a priest-king and supported by a royal clan holding authority through dynastic succession, did not apply here, as it did in the ancient palace-temple societies of Egypt, Mesopotamia, China, and Mesoamerica. In addition, there is little evidence of the military influence consistently found in other ancient empires. The raised platforms seem to define social and functional space and do not provide an area to defend citizens from external enemies.

Mohenjo-Daro (fig. 3-30) is the most interesting of the Indus Valley sites because of the age and scale of

c. 2100–1750 BCE   ***Seal with Ithyphallic Figure,* Mohenjo-Daro**
c. 2000 BCE   Systematic astronomy in Egypt, Babylon, India, and
                       China

the site and the richness of the finds, including numerous soapstone seals, the majority of which are engraved with an animal and a short inscription. That the most frequently represented animal is a profile view of a bull, the beast of burden revered in later Hindu India, suggests that there may be some connection between these early finds and later Indian religious developments. A similar conclusion is suggested by our example, with its depiction of a frontal male figure wearing buffalo horns and surrounded by animals (fig. 3-31). He is depicted ithyphallic (he is shown with an erect phallus) and is seated in the position of yogic meditation. The writing on the seal still defies translation, although nearly 4,000 different inscriptions have been identified. This exceptional figure may be an early rendering of the Hindu god **Siva**, the "Lord of the Animals," thought to have procreative powers, or it may be a representation of a chief with concerns for appeasing the wild kingdom. We do know that seals were used for administrative purposes, such as sealing bales of merchandise or marking storage boxes, and most inscriptions seem to record the names and administrative titles of their users.

Excavators have also found, inside many houses, a large number of small, elaborately dressed terracotta figures of women. These statuettes are thought to be part of private devotion to the powers of fertility, and, in fact, emphasis on the female procreative powers continues today in both Hindu and Buddhist iconography in Asia.

The lower, eastern part of Mohenjo-Daro had a grid of streets and lanes roughly oriented north-south and east-west, with blocks of houses

3-31. *Seal with Ithyphallic Figure,* found at Mohenjo-Daro, Indus Valley (modern Pakistan). c. 2100–1750 BCE. Steatite, height 1³/₈". National Museum, New Delhi, India. The seals found at Mohenjo-Daro are rectangular or square, unlike the cylindrical seals found in ancient Mesopotamian centers.

entered through narrow lanes. Although the houses varied in size, they all had rooms arranged around a central courtyard, usually with a well in a small room off the court and a bath and latrine draining through the wall, into either a soak pit or a covered drain under the street surface. Some two-story houses had brick stairs and tubular drainpipes extending from the upper story. Plumbing installations for the provision of water, bathrooms with polished brick floors, and the exterior drains found here are without parallel in other early historic societies.

Although there are public buildings on the raised platform that forms the highest part of the site, including a large granary and the Great Bath, no large community temple has so far been located at Mohenjo-Daro. The entire raised platform may have served as a ritual center, for at related sites, fire altars have been identified in the raised platform areas, as well as in private houses. The speculation about fire and water in ritual activity in the Indus Valley civilization is linked to their central role in the two major religions that emerged later in that region: Vedic Hinduism and Zoroastrianism.

The reason for the collapse of the Indus Valley civilization is not fully known, but it is often explained as a result of natural events such as earthquakes, which changed the course of the rivers, causing the population to desert its settlements.

AEGEAN ART: MINOAN AND MYCENAEAN

3-32. Minoan. *Bull Leaping*, from the palace at Knossos, Crete. c. 1750–1450 BCE. Fresco, height approx. 32" including borders. Archaeological Museum, Heraklion, Crete. The Greek myth of Theseus and the Minotaur may have been based on the bull-leaping ritual demonstrated here and the labyrinthine structure of the palace at Knossos (see fig. 3-34). Commissioned by a Minoan king

During the second millennium BCE, two distinct cultures flourished in the Aegean area (see map, page 84). As in many other early civilizations, the animal was an important motif in both cultures, as evidenced by the *Bull Leaping* fresco from Knossos (fig. 3-32) and the Lion Gate at Mycenae (see fig. 3-36). The contrast between the fluid movement of the jumping bull and the severe rigidity of the guardian lions, however, reflects the significant differences between these cultures.

The ancient Minoan civilization, named in modern times after King Minos from Greek mythology, flourished on the island of Crete. The origins of the Minoan civilization, which was based on agriculture and a wide seafaring trade, are unclear. Archaeological evidence has long been interpreted as showing that an

early culture, Minoan I, developed about 2000 BCE to 1700 BCE and was followed by Minoan II, which declined relatively abruptly after about 1450 BCE. Recent findings, however, indicate that a volcanic eruption, which is probably the cause of the rapid decline, occurred about 1620 BCE, thus throwing off previously accepted dating by several hundred years. Because the date question is still unresolved, we shall use broad dates for works of art for the Minoan culture. Natural catastrophes, perhaps volcanic eruptions with related

3-33. Minoan. *Snake Goddess* or *Priestess*, found at the palace at Knossos, Crete. c. 1800–1550 BCE. Faience, height 11⁵/₈". Archaeological Museum, Heraklion, Crete. The medium, faience, is a type of earthenware decorated with glazes that was used as early as the predynastic period in Egypt.

earthquakes and tidal waves, may have caused the end of Minoan culture—and may, in fact, be the historical explanation for the legend of the city of Atlantis, which is said to

c. 1750–1450 BCE	Minoan *Bull Leaping* fresco
c. 1700 BCE	Judaism is founded by Abraham
c. 1500 BCE	Silk is woven by the Chinese
c. 1300 BCE	Alphabetic script is developed in Mesopotamia
c. 1190 BCE	Troy is destroyed
c. 1122 BCE	Zhou dynasty founded in China

3-34. Minoan. Plan of palace at Knossos. c. 1800–1300 BCE. Commissioned by a series of Minoan kings

have disappeared beneath the sea.

The earliest Minoan artifacts exhibit a preference for abstract curvilinear designs that in the Minoan II culture were joined to representational forms to create dynamic and lively images, as in the *Bull Leaping* **fresco** (fig. 3-32). This fresco depicts a ritual or ceremonial event held in the central court of the palace at Knossos, in which trained athletes grasped the horns of a charging bull and vaulted over its back. An undulating rhythm defines the bull's forward motion; the line of its neck is continued in its elongated, curving body, lending a grace to what must have been a strenuous and dangerous activity. Bright, contrasting colors add to the vitality of the scene.

Excavations of the palace at Knossos have also brought to light statuettes related to Minoan religion. Although the Minoans' belief system remains mysterious, figures such as this small, snake-brandishing woman (fig. 3-33) may represent a goddess, perhaps the earth mother, or a devotee.

The remains of palaces indicate that the royal residences were combined with administrative offices,

3-35. Minoan. The Queen's Megaron, palace at Knossos, Crete. Partially reconstructed. c. 1700–1400 BCE. Commissioned by a Minoan king or queen

3-36. Mycenaean. Lion Gate, Mycenae, Greece. c. 1300–1200 BCE. Limestone, height of carved slab 9'6". This historic photograph shows Heinrich Schliemann, the director of the excavation, standing to the left of the gate. The woman seated to the right is his Greek wife, Sophia. The huge slab on which the lions are carved fills a triangular opening in the construction, which helps to relieve weight on the lintel. The missing heads were originally attached with dowels. It is possible that they were carved or cast from a different material, and they may have represented human heads.

Lion Gate (fig. 3-36). Atop the lintel, a relief sculpture displays symmetrical bodies of lions flanking a column that rests on altars. The scale of the relief and the stylized yet subtle animation of the lions' bodies proclaim the heraldry of royal power.

Homer's *Iliad*, the epic poem that tells of the war between the Trojans and the "Greeks" or Hellenes—a group that included the Mycenaeans—was long considered to be a product of human imagination, but its vividness intrigued Heinrich Schliemann, a German business executive and amateur archaeologist. In 1870, he began to excavate sites in Asia Minor, a peninsula between the Black Sea and the Mediterranean Sea, where he found the archaeological remains of Homer's Troy, and in Greece, where he excavated Mycenae. The investigations spurred by Schliemann's discoveries gave credence to the legends of ancient Greece and brought to light the robust activity of the ancient Aegean area.

The Mycenaeans were the descendants of Greek-speaking peoples who invaded the peninsula of Greece between about 2000 and 1700 BCE. They were active traders, especially with the Minoans, and Mycenaean goods have been exca-

servants' quarters, and ceremonial and storage rooms. At Knossos, these rooms are grouped around a central courtyard in a rambling, labyrinthine design that seems to have developed over time without a predetermined plan, rooms being added as they were needed (fig. 3-34).

The interior decorations of the palace exhibit the lively, rhythmic qualities common in Minoan art; brightly colored fresco paintings depict scenes of ceremony, ritual, and animal and marine life (fig. 3-35).

As the Minoan culture began to decline, the Mycenaean rose to supremacy in the Aegean area. This Bronze Age culture, which flourished about 1400–1100 BCE, was named for the walled city of Mycenae on the Greek mainland, which was known for its fortifications. It was the military force from this culture that, as the ancient Greek poet Homer wrote, "launched a thousand ships" to attack Troy.

The only entrance into Mycenae was through the monumental architectural gateway now known as the

3-37. Mycenaean. Plan and sections of the tholos tomb popularly known as the Treasury of Atreus, Mycenae (after A. W. Lawrence). c. 1300–1200 BCE. Stone, height approx. 45'. Because of their shape, such tholos ("round") tombs are also known as beehive tombs.

vated in Italy and Syria. Mycenae was only one of a number of fortified towns that shared a common culture and language, although each was ruled by an independent monarch. Mycenaean kings were buried in large round tholos tombs accompanied by their personal treasures, including weapons. The tomb shown here (fig. 3-37) is remarkable for its size and the precision of its cut stone blocks, some of which weigh several tons.

Two styles are found in Mycenaean art. One was inspired by the vivacity of Minoan art, but a second style, perhaps native to the Mycenaeans, offers a more abstract mode of representation. The gold funeral mask from a royal tomb excavated at Mycenae was once probably placed over the face of a deceased king (fig. 3-38). While offering some individual characteristics, such as the mustache and beard, the arched eyebrows and treatment of the ears display a more abstracted approach.

The Mycenaean culture ended when the Dorians entered the peninsula from the north about 1100 BCE and conquered the Mycenaeans, but their legacy and that of the Minoans nourished the evolution of later Greek culture.

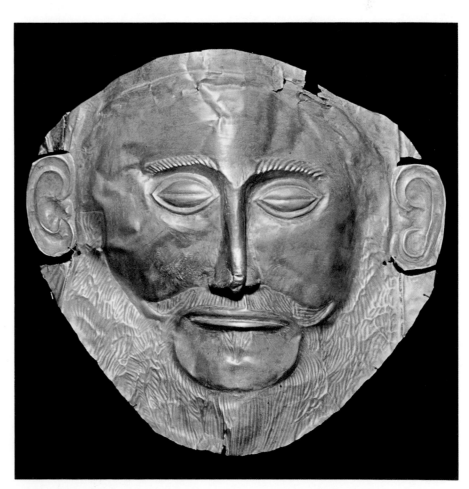

3-38. Mycenaean. Funerary mask, found at Mycenae. c. 1550–1500 BCE. Gold, height approx. 12". National Archaeological Museum, Athens

ANCIENT CHINA: THE SHANG DYNASTY

3-39. *Fang ding,* from the Tomb of Lady Hao, Anyang, Henan Province, China. Shang dynasty, c. 1200 BCE. Bronze, height 16³/4". Cultural Relics Bureau, Beijing. The Tomb of Lady Hao, excavated in 1976, was of modest scale compared to the royal tombs opened there in the late 1920s and 1930s, but its undisturbed chamber yielded a tremendous amount of magnificent tomb furniture, making it the best-preserved tomb ever excavated at Anyang, the last capital of the Shang dynasty, which was occupied c. 1300–1050 BCE. Our knowledge of ancient China has been greatly enriched by archaeological findings in the tombs of the Shang, the first documented historical Chinese dynasty (c. 1766–1122 BCE). The richest finds have been near modern Anyang, a ceremonial center for the Shang that included the royal burial grounds as well as official temples and palaces built on pounded-earth platforms. Some of the earliest examples of Chinese writing are Shang inscriptions on bronze vessels and on animal bones or turtle shells, used as oracles, that were excavated there. Commissioned by Lady Hao or her family

3-40. Pendant in the shape of a hawk, from the Tomb of Lady Hao, Anyang, Henan Province, China. Shang dynasty, c. 1200 BCE. Jade, height 2³/8". Cultural Relics Bureau, Beijing. Commissioned by Lady Hao or her family

The *fang ding* shown here (fig. 3-39) is from the Tomb of Lady Hao, which contained the largest and most intact group of Shang burial goods yet discovered. The tomb was an oblong shaft approximately 13' x 18'6". Along the eastern and western walls, at a depth of about 20 feet, were elongated niches with sacrifices: sixteen human be-

ings and six dogs. Tomb furniture was placed in eight layers both above and on the chamber top, in the chamber between its walls and the coffin, and inside the coffin itself. Of the total of 1,900 pieces, about 460 were sacred bronze vessels, tools, and weapons; almost 750 were jade; and about 560 were bone objects. There were also some

sculptures and ivory carvings and 5 pottery vessels. In addition to the 1,900 pieces, there were nearly 6,900 cowrie shells, presumably used as currency. The immense wealth of this tomb and others at Anyang (see map, page 163) indicates that the Shang had control of and created great resources.

More than 190 bronze vessels

c. 1766–1122 BCE	Shang dynasty in China
c. 1360 BCE	Population of Thebes, Egypt, is 100,000
c. 1200 BCE	***Fang ding* from the Tomb of Lady Hao**
c. 1200 BCE	Women are professional musicians in Egypt, Assyria, Babylon
c. 1100 BCE	Dorians enter Greek peninsula

from the tomb bear inscriptions that refer to Lady Hao and suggest her status and death date. A foreigner, she was a general who became the well-known consort of King Wu Ting. The materials found in her tomb confirm her acceptance into the Shang elite because she was allowed to use the clan emblem, the *taotie*. At the same time, she also seems to have retained cultural affiliation with her non-Shang parent culture, as evidenced by the jade hawk (fig. 3-40) and frontier-style bronze knives, horse gear, and mirrors also found in her tomb.

The Shang faith was **shamanistic**, which required offerings of food and entertainment to ancestors, to deceased great men, and to deities of rain, water, rivers, wind, and stars who could be appealed to but who also had to be appeased. The shamans, or *wu*, and their associates, diviners who predicted the future, served as mediums between the supernatural and human worlds. These ritual leaders, who could write and keep accounts, also served as archivists and historians.

Shamanism was reflected in the rituals and burial at Anyang, which paid homage to ancestors and to the spirits of the natural world. Many of the materials used at these ceremonies were decorated with the *taotie* mask that was the emblem of the ruling clan (see page 51). By claiming that communication with the spirit world, including ancestors, was only possible through the use of such vessels, the rulers and the elite may have been creating and maintaining their status separate from the masses. Because they controlled the production of bronze as well as the ceremonies that made use of bronze vessels and weapons, they demonstrated their dual power—access to the spirit world and military domination.

TECHNIQUE CHINESE PIECE-MOLD BRONZE CASTING

In ancient China, the industries involved in making sacred vessels and ritual implements were located in Anyang. The production of bronze, an alloy of copper, tin, and sometimes other minerals, was a sophisticated activity. It required a team of specialists—miners; refiners of ores for the alloy; designers; metallurgists to determine appropriate alloy makeup for the shapes and designs involved—all coordinated by a central authority. The process used was a sophisticated **piece-mold casting** method, which depended on knowledge of the properties of different clays. The designer produced an exact model of the desired final product in fine clay, complete with the incised designs on the surface. Heavy clay was packed around the model to create the mold. Once the model was removed, the distance between the model and mold was kept uniform by bronze spacers. The entire assemblage was packed in sand (not shown here) and heated, then molten bronze was poured into the opening to form the sacred vessel (fig. 3-41). After the casting cooled, details on the surface of the bronze were filed and polished to produce a clean-lined design and shiny surface.

3-41. The technique of bronze casting in ancient China

ASSYRIAN AND EARLY PERSIAN ART

3-42. Assyrian. *Human-Headed Winged Bull* (*Lamassu*), from the gateway of the Palace of Sargon II, Dur Sharrukin (modern Khorsabad, Iraq). c. 720 BCE. Limestone, height 14'. The Louvre, Paris. Commissioned by King Sargon II

The Assyrians and Persians successively controlled Mesopotamia. The Assyrians established a powerful kingdom in northern Mesopotamia from the ninth through the seventh centuries BCE, while the early, or Achaemenid, Persians were centered in southern Mesopotamia during the sixth and fifth centuries BCE (see map, page 56). Both cultures were known for their powerful kings, who tried to conquer and control vast territories. The Assyrians in particular were feared for their atrocities during war, but the Persians, who for a brief period even conquered Egypt, tried to establish a reputation for benevolent rule and had greater success in creating a huge empire.

Assyrian and early Persian palaces were similarly decorated, with low reliefs lining the palace rooms and passages. In Assyrian palaces, the themes were ritualistic, honorific, militaristic, or any subject that would impress the visitor with the unquestionable power and undeniable majesty of the royal personage. This sense of commanding omnipotence can also be seen in other palace sculptures, such as the *Lamassu* (fig. 3-42), which seems to have been intended to intimidate visitors—especially foreign ambassadors—before they entered into the presence of the Assyrian king. The threatening content is supported by the treatment of the stone; its high polish emphasizes its density, while the patterns and fine detail of the beard and wings stress the massive scale and powerful

1000–960 BCE	David rules as king of Israel
776 BCE	First Olympian Games, in Greece
c. 720 BCE	***Human-Headed Winged Bull**, Assyria*

3-43. Assyrian. *Dying Lioness*, from the North Palace of Ashurbanipal, Nineveh (modern Kuyunjik, Iraq). c. 645–635 BCE. Limestone, height of figure approx. 14". The British Museum, London. Commissioned by King Ashurbanipal

3-44. Early Persian. Royal audience hall (Apadana) and stairway of the Palace of Darius, Persepolis (modern Iran). c. 500 BCE. Commissioned by King Darius

3-45. Early Persian. Bull capital, from the Apadana, Palace of Darius, Persepolis (modern Iran). c. 500. Width 12'3". The Louvre, Paris

forms. The figure is given five legs to present a convincing stance from both the front view, on approach, and the side, in passing.

The Assyrian palace at Dur Sharrukin, where the *Lamassu* stood, covered more than 25 acres and had more than 200 courtyards and rooms. Here and at the ancient sites of Nimrud and Nineveh, continuous low reliefs depicted Assyrian military victories and the subsequent pillage and carnage. The reliefs emphasized the Assyrian king's strength in battle or in sport. In one series, he is shown engaged in a hunt in which lions were released from cages. The king is represented victorious in his chariot, surrounded by dead and dying animals. In the detail pictured (fig. 3-43), a lioness is shown in her death throes, dragging her paralyzed legs behind her and uttering a cry or moan of death.

The early Persian Palace of Darius at Persepolis (fig. 3-44) had grand staircases decorated with

reliefs. The reliefs depict seemingly endless processions and scenes in which, following an old Middle Eastern tradition, a fierce beast is represented attacking a domesticated animal. Such scenes are open to a number of levels of interpretation. On one level, they probably symbolize Persian power and victory, but they may also refer to political and even to cosmic conflict.

These imposing staircases led to a sequence of magnificent square throne rooms and ceremonial chambers filled with large columns. The largest was 250 feet square, with columns at least 40 feet high. The capitals—the decorated elements at the tops of the columns—are unusual and uniquely Persian, with gigantic figures of paired bulls (fig. 3-45). Stylistically, the debt of the Persians to Assyrian art is evident in the contrast between bold, simple masses and fine, abstract detail, but the Persian compositions have an increased refinement and elegance.

ETRUSCAN ART

3-46. Ash urn, found at Castiglione del Lago, Italy. c. 650–600 BCE. Terra-cotta, approx. 18¹/₂" high. Archaeological Museum, Florence, Italy. Etruscan burial practices, which varied widely from city to city, included cremation, as here, and inhumation. Probably commissioned by the family of the deceased

3-47. Sarcophagus with reclining couple, from Cerveteri, Tuscany, Italy. c. 525–500 BCE. Terra-cotta, length 6'7"; the figures are lifesize. Museo Nazionale di Villa Giulia, Rome. A similar sarcophagus in the Louvre in Paris has many traces of color, suggesting that this one may also have been naturalistically painted. Probably commissioned by the family of the deceased

The breasts and head that personalize this abstracted container (fig. 3-46) may have been enhanced by a wig made of real hair and by pieces of jewelry. As a container for the ashes of the deceased, it would have been placed in her tomb and surrounded by other possessions, which probably would have included a hand mirror (see fig. 3-1). The wig would most likely have been made from the hair of the deceased, and other personal details may have been added to the urn in paint. This type of ash urn is only one of the ways in which the Etruscans honored the dead.

The origin of the people we know as the Etruscans is debated, but by the eighth century BCE they had established themselves in a group of cities in Etruria (present-day Tuscany, in northern Italy) and were the most important power on the Italian peninsula (see map, page 114). These cities were fiercely independent and often had distinctive burial practices. During the seventh and sixth centuries BCE, Etruscans ruled as kings of Rome, and by the fifth century they controlled most of northern and central Italy. They were active traders, and their works in bronze, especially armor, were exported throughout the ancient world. During the fourth and third centuries BCE, the Etruscan cities were defeated and annexed by the Romans, and the Etruscan culture was absorbed into the Roman sphere.

Etruscan inscriptions have been translated, but there is no surviving body of Etruscan literature, so like other, earlier prehistoric civilizations, Etruscan civilization be studied primarily from archaeological remains. Like other early Mediterranean cultures, including Egypt, the Etruscans believed that the body or ashes of the deceased should be accompanied by household and other everyday objects to guarantee a satisfying afterlife. Thus, much of our knowledge of the Etruscans is based on their tombs, carved in rock and/or frescoed, and on the tomb furnishings, which included gold and bronze objects of superb artistry (see fig. 3-1) and fine imported goods, such as Greek vases. Needless to say, most of the evidence we have concerns the life-styles of the upper class.

On one Etruscan sarcophagus, a couple reclining on a banqueting

c. 650–600 BCE	**Ash urn, Castiglione del Lago, Italy**
625 BCE	Metal coins are introduced in Greece
597 BCE	Jerusalem falls to Nebuchadnezzar
c. 590 BCE	Greek poet Sappho is writing love poems
c. 550 BCE	Daoism is founded by the Chinese philosopher Laozi

3-48. Tomb of Hunting and Fishing, Tarquinia, Italy. c. 510–500 BCE. Fresco.
Probably commissioned by the family of the deceased

couch engages us with beguiling smiles (fig. 3-47). The construction of a terra-cotta group of this scale and complexity is an impressive technical accomplishment, but equally remarkable is the representation of their relaxed positions and their inner delight. That this work's original function was as a sarcophagus suggests the Etruscans' relatively content and reconciled outlook on death. Reclining in this manner is a Greek tradition, but the representation of a man and a woman reclining together is typically Etruscan. It suggests a respect for women that was unknown in Greece and was rare in other early cultures.

Many Etruscan works were inspired by Greek examples, but the Etruscans' style is generally bolder and simpler and displays little interest in the symmetry so favored by the Greeks. Much Etruscan iconography emphasizes everyday activities, but there are also frequent references to Greek myths, and it is clear that divination (see fig. 3-1) was an important Etruscan activity. Especially in such large-scale pieces as the sarcophagus and in figures and decoration used on architecture, Etruscans made important technical innovations in the use of terra-cotta, a fired clay. Most Etruscan artists did not sign their works; there seems to have been no cult of the artist, as there was in Greece.

Simple, bright colors, bold geometric and natural patterns, and clearly drawn figures combine in Etruscan tomb paintings to create a lively and vigorous effect. Typical Etruscan themes include banqueting figures—referring to the banquets that were part of the Etruscan funeral ritual—complete with the dancers and musicians that provided entertainment, as well as scenes of pleasurable daily life to be enjoyed by the deceased. In the Tomb of Hunting and Fishing (fig. 3-48), a profusion of wildlife guarantees success in the hunt; above, the deceased (and perhaps the living) are shown banqueting.

ANCIENT GREEK ART

3-49. Severe style. *Apollo and the Battle of the Lapiths and the Centaurs*, detail from the west pediment, Temple of Zeus, Olympia. 470–456 BCE. Marble, over-lifesize. Pausanias attributes the pediments at Olympia to the artists Alkamenes and Paionios. Archaeological Museum, Olympia

roof of the Temple of Zeus at Olympia. The composition is clear, the movement is bold and direct, and the details of anatomy and drapery are easily read by the viewer standing 50 or more feet below. The sculptures illustrate a mythological subject. Among the guests at a wedding feast are drunken centaurs (creatures who are half-human, half-horse), who attempt to abduct the Greek women; after a fierce battle they are subdued. This theme had an immediate significance for the Greeks of that time: their victory over the Persians in 479 BCE was symbolically expressed in the victory over the centaurs. On a more profound level, the calm presence of Apollo represents the mastery of reasoned order over brute force. The scene had a special meaning because of its location at Olympia, for during the famous Olympian Games, a truce was observed among the Greek city-states. The ideals exemplified by the myth and its representation at Olympia reveal attitudes that distinguish the Greeks from their neighbors in the ancient world.

In the midst of a chaotic combat (fig. 3-49), the over-lifesize figure of the Greek god Apollo majestically restores order. He occupies the axis of the composition, and his calm yet commanding presence contrasts with the outburst of surrounding activity. His idealized human physique and dignified bearing make him an appropriate introduction to the study of ancient Greek art.

This Apollo is part of a group of figures that originally decorated the triangular end (or **pediment**; see figs. 3-72, 3-74) of the **gable** (pitched)

HISTORY

About 1100 BCE, a people called the Dorians entered the Greek peninsula from the north and overwhelmed the Mycenaeans, who had ruled this area for 500 years. Gradually a new culture, historically known as the ancient Greek civilization, evolved. By the eighth century BCE, the two great Homeric poems, the *Iliad* and the *Odyssey*, had been composed, and Greece had evolved into a grouping of independent city-states. Each city-state (*polis*) commanded the loyalty of its citizens in religious, military, and economic matters, and their fierce independence prevented the political unification of Greece. In 776 BCE, the first Olympian Games were held. Called once every four years, they were held in honor of Zeus, ruler of the gods. Winners gained personal fame and were often honored in art. The winners of the footrace at similar games held in Athens, for example, were celebrated in such works of art as a victory vase, the **Panathenaic amphora** (fig. 3-50).

During the eighth century BCE, developing commerce among the city-states led to a prosperous economy. One of the major products was pottery, and a Geometric-style vase (fig. 3-51), with its bands of simple repeated patterns, demonstrates the artistic beginnings of the Greeks. The animals on the neck of the vase are arranged in a repeated rhythm. In the largest, central band are rather abstracted figures representing female mourners pulling their hair at a funeral; the deceased lies on his bier. The scene is related to the purpose of such vases, which was to mark a grave site and thus play an important role in honoring the dead. Oil, poured into the vases to commemorate the deceased, flowed through the open bottom and into the ground.

During what is known in art as the Archaic period, from the seventh to the early fifth century BCE,

3-50. Archaic style. *Panathenaic Amphora with Runners.* c. 520 BCE. Painted terracotta, height 24¹/₂". The Metropolitan Museum of Art, New York. The Panathenaic amphora was a large, specially decorated vessel given as a prize in the Panathenaic Games held in Athens, which were similar to the Olympian Games. It was filled with oil made from olives grown on special trees. Commissioned by the Panathenaic organizing committee
Rogers Fund, 1914 (14.130.12)

trade routes expanded, and the Greeks began to colonize areas of southern Italy and Asia Minor. At this time, the Greeks began to produce lifesize figurative sculpture and to construct marble temples.

The early fifth century BCE was a time of significant artistic and political changes. In both sculpture and painting, a more naturalistic rendering of the human figure emerged. In architecture, the forms of the Greek temple underwent a process of visual refinement that gave them a new sense of elegance.

In 490 BCE, the Persians invaded Greece. The city-states formed a defensive alliance and defeated the invasion force at Marathon, about 26 miles northeast of Athens. After the battle, a courier ran to Athens bringing news of the victory; he fell dead of exhaustion after exclaiming, "Rejoice, we conquer." His run is commemorated in today's 26-mile marathon races. Ten years

3-51. Geometric style. *Mourners around a Bier.* c. 750 BCE. Terra-cotta, height 5'1". National Archaeological Museum, Athens. The decorated pottery vessels of the Greeks, regardless of use, are traditionally known as vases. Vases such as this one are sometimes referred to as Dipylon vases because they were found at the Dipylon Cemetery in Athens. Probably commissioned by the family of the deceased

later, the Persians captured and sacked Athens, but in 479 BCE the Greeks again defeated the Persians, this time at the naval battle of Salamis. No peace treaty was signed until 449 BCE, and during the thirty years following the second Persian defeat, Athens, which had agreed to supply the navy for the Greek military alliance, continued to collect taxes from the other city-states. During this period, Athens became the preeminent political and economic center, but only at the cost of jealousy from the other city-states.

Although beset by internal political conflicts, the Greeks, who called themselves Hellenes, shared a common language and culture. They divided the world into two types of people: those whose native language was Greek, and others, who were called *barbaroi* ("barbarians").

3-52. Reconstruction model of the Acropolis, Athens. c. 400 BCE. Royal Ontario Museum, Toronto, and J. Walter Graham. The pedimented building in the right foreground was the only entrance to the Acropolis, and the building to its left is the earliest known example of a building built for the display of works of art; because art is inspired by the Muses, it was called a museum.

As a result of the Persian wars, the self-aware Greeks continued to define how their culture was distinct from that of the barbarians.

The mid-fifth century BCE in Greece is known as the Classical period of art and culture. Its center was Athens, where a politician named Pericles was chief general of the city from 460 to 430 BCE. The Athenian government is often cited as the first democracy in the Western world, although only free men were allowed to vote.

Pericles used the wealth of Athens and the taxes collected from other city-states for an ambitious campaign of renewal, including rebuilding the temples destroyed by the Persians on the Acropolis (from the Greek *akros*, "highest," and *polis*, "city"), an outcropping of rock that dominates the center of Athens (fig. 3-52). To the Greeks, it was the sacred location where Poseidon, god of the sea, and Athena, goddess of wisdom, had contested for control of the city. Poseidon caused salt water to flow from a spring, but Athena's gift of an olive tree was deemed more beneficial and the city was thus dedicated to her. As late as the second century CE, a salt-water spring and an olive tree could still be found on the Acropolis.

Pericles seems to have recognized the value of providing an intellectual, physically healthy, and aesthetically pleasing environment for the citizens of Athens. Later, when war had broken out in Greece, he offered a funeral oration for Athenian soldiers:

Our constitution is called a democracy because power is not in the hands of a few, but of the people. Our laws secure equal justice for all in their private disputes, and our public opinion welcomes and honors talent in every brace of achievement; what counts is not membership in a particular class, but the actual ability a man possesses.

Yet ours is no mere work-a-day city. No other provides so much recreation for the spirit—contests and sacrifices all the year round, and beauty in our public buildings to cheer the heart and delight the eye day by day.

We are lovers of the beautiful without being extravagant, and lovers of wisdom without being soft. We regard wealth as something to be used properly, rather than as something to boast about. . . . We decide and debate, carefully, and in person, all matters of policy, for we do not think there is an incompatibility between words and deeds.

Our city is an education to Greece.

As the political dominance of Athens grew, so did the resentment of the other city-states. The Peloponnesian War, which erupted in 431 BCE, plunged Greece into turmoil. When the war ended in 404 BCE, the power of Athens was broken, and Sparta and Corinth assumed a more prominent role in the political affairs of Greece. By the later fourth century BCE, however, a new force from the north commanded attention, and the next chapter of ancient Greek history was written by two Macedonian kings, Philip and Alexander (see pages 104–07).

INTELLECTUAL AND SCIENTIFIC ACTIVITIES

The love of wisdom Pericles described found expression in philosophy and science as well as in art. From the mid-fifth through the fourth centuries BCE, philosophy developed from the speculative questioning of Socrates and the ideal forms of Plato to the natural observations by Aristotle. The philosophical questioning of the Greeks, in fact, helps to explain why their artistic forms were constantly evolving.

The Hippocratic medical writings, by several authors, represent a diverse body of literature on healing practices and were the foundation of ancient medical study. The Greek pursuit of reason and speculative thought led to many practical inventions.

At the heart of the Greeks' world view was the belief that human reason—and especially mathematics—could understand and define the rational order inherent in the universe. In the sixth century BCE, Pythagoras wrote of the relationship between mathematics and musical harmony, noting that a stretched string, when plucked, produces a certain note by its vibration. When the string is measured and plucked at points that correspond to exact divisions by whole numbers—$1/2$, $1/3$, etc.—the vibrations produce a harmonious chord. If the string is plucked at any other interval, the sound seems discordant. To the Greeks, this discovery had a powerful impact. If the sounds of nature were governed by the order of mathematics, then the universe itself must obey the harmony of mathematical concurrences. This notion of a universal harmony that could be perceived by human reason came to govern the rules of art and architecture during the Classical period.

RELIGION

The Greeks worshiped numerous gods and goddesses, who ruled over all aspects of life and death. Leader among the gods was Zeus (see fig. 3-64); Hera, wife of Zeus, was queen of the gods and protector of women. Along with other deities, Zeus and Hera were believed to reside on Mount Olympus. Although some Egyptian gods had been represented in human form, it was the Greeks who fully anthropomorphized their deities, giving them both human form and human attributes. Numerous mythological tales speak of the exploits of gods and goddesses, who often deemed it necessary to alter human affairs.

Sacrifices to the gods were joined with great festivals that might include athletic games, such as the Olympian and other games, and theatrical productions. Greek theater developed from the rituals honoring Dionysos, an important, popular god and patron of drama and song. The Greek playwrights Æschylus, Sophocles, Euripides, and Aristophanes wrote plays to be performed during an annual Athenian festival honoring Dionysos. These plays are characterized by their pro-found and subtle expression of human motivation and behavior.

GREEK ART

The philosophical questioning that pervaded Greek intellectual life helps to explain why Greek art underwent a dramatic evolution of successive styles over a relatively short, 500-year period. The beginnings are represented in the Geometric phase (see fig. 3-51). The abstract features of Archaic period sculptures (see figs. 3-57, 3-58) were transformed into the Severe style (see figs. 3-49, 3-59, 3-64, 3-65) and then into the idealized representations of the Classical period (see figs. 3-67, 3-73–3-75), which sought to equate the perfection of art with the harmonies of the natural order. By the time of Alexander the Great (ruled 336–323 BCE), the realistic and emotionally dramatic representations of what is known as the Hellenistic style were common (see figs. 3-78, 3-81, 3-82). In painting, flat shapes (see fig. 3-51) gave way to elements of illusionism (see figs. 3-53 and 3-80; see page 105 for a discussion of a Greek painting competition), while in architecture proportions and decorative elements underwent a progressive transformation toward a more refined ideal (compare figs. 3-61 and 3-68, 3-69). The continuous process of revision characteristic of Greek art is only one manifestation of the questioning and philosophical Greek mind. Greek art and architecture had a profound impact on many later cultures, including our own in the twentieth century. The Romans copied famous Greek illusionistic paintings and mosaics—for example, the *Unswept Floor* by Sosos (fig. 3-53). And the Greek architectural orders, so popular in the Renaissance and later periods, have been revived again in the postmodern style.

THE GREEK ARTIST

The Greeks valued both intellectual and physical achievements, so it is

3-53. Heraclitus. *Unswept Floor*, fragment of a Roman mosaic copy of a Hellenistic mosaic by Sosos. 2nd century CE. Forms are lifesize. Vatican Museums, Rome

not surprising that they would begin to praise the artist as an individual with unique talents. An exceptional development in the seventh century BCE, with virtually no precedent in earlier cultures, occurred when artists began with regularity to sign their works. Such signatures are an indication of personal pride; they might also be an early form of advertising. Literary sources from both ancient Greece and ancient Rome offer descriptions and criticisms of works of art that were considered famous. By the fourth century BCE, such references begin to include comments on the personalities of specific artists and anecdotes about their lives. An ancient discussion of the fourth-century BCE painter Apelles, recorded by the Roman author Pliny, reveals the respect enjoyed by a successful artist:

> Nevertheless the painter who surpassed all those who were born before him and all those who came later was Apelles. . . . He produced volumes, which contain his doctrine. . . . He . . . was also gifted with a courteous nature and . . . was on quite good terms with Alexander the Great.

GREEK VASE PAINTING

3-54. Exekias. *Achilles and Ajax Playing Draughts,* detail of black-figure decoration on an amphora. c. 530 BCE. Painted terra-cotta, height 24". Vatican Museums, Rome. The stories represented on Archaic vases, which usually told of Greek mythological or historical events, were at first illustrated with black figures on a red background. Works in this style are known as black-figure vases. Exekias was both painter and potter of this vase.

During the Archaic period, the decorative bands prevalent on earlier Geometric vases (see fig. 3-51) were relegated to the base and neck, and increased surface area was given to figurative narration. This vase (fig. 3-54) depicts the Greek warriors Achilles and Ajax playing draughts (an ancient game related to checkers) during a lull in the Trojan War, which Greece waged against Troy after the Trojan Paris abducted Helen, wife of the king of the Greek city-state Sparta. The signature "Exekias painted me and made me" indicates an artist talented in both pottery and painting—a rarity in ancient Greece, where a division of labor was usually practiced in the production of vases. The composition, with its strong symmetry and the manner in which scene and decoration are related to the shape of the vase, reveals the Greek search for balance and harmony.

The various shapes of Greek vases developed according to both purpose and the Greek interest in aesthetic forms. By the Archaic period, specialized forms had become associated with specific functions (fig. 3-55).

After a vase was formed but before it was fired, the painter, using **slip** (a mixture of clay particles in water, sometimes combined with wood ash), painted black figures in silhouette. Details of the decoration and of the figures' anatomy, drapery, and armor were made by incising lines into the surface before firing. Working with a sharp pointed tool known to modern artists as a **burin**, the artist engraved lines through the slip, exposing the terracotta color beneath. As the vase was being fired, the air vents in the kiln were closed, causing the entire vase to turn black for a period as the red iron oxide of the terra-cotta was converted into black and magnetic iron oxides. When the air vents were again opened, the iron in the clay body returned to its red-orange color except in those areas covered by slip. In the firing, the slip had formed a glazed surface coating, sealing these areas from the air. They remained black, creating the black figures and decoration on the vase. On Archaic vases, the artist delighted in decorative geometric patterns that asserted the two-dimensional quality of the figures.

Around 530 BCE, a new technique that reversed the figure-ground colors was introduced, perhaps by a student of Exekias known as the Andokides Painter. This technique, the **red-figure style**, presents figures and objects silhouetted against the painted black background. Details of anatomy and costume are painted on, rather than incised into, the surface of the vase.

The vase with the *Death of Sarpedon,* signed by Euxitheos and Euphronios, was created shortly after the introduction of this new technique (fig. 3-56). The scene, described in Homer's *Iliad* (XVI, 426 ff.), depicts the body of Sarpedon, a fallen Trojan hero, being carried from the battlefield by personifications of Sleep and Death. The god Hermes, who will lead Sarpedon's soul to Hades, stands behind. The

| 580 BCE | Nebuchadnezzar begins building the Hanging Gardens of Babylon |
| **c. 530 BCE** | **Exekias, *Achilles and Ajax Playing Draughts*** |

amphora   Panathenaic amphora   calyx krater   volute krater   kylix   lekythos

3-55. Typical Greek vase shapes. The amphora and Panathenaic amphora are containers to store wine, olive oil, honey, or water. The calyx krater and volute krater are bowls for mixing wine with water, which was the Greek custom. The kylix is a drinking cup, and the lekythos is a container for olive oil.

3-56. Euphronios (painter) and Euxitheos (potter). *Death of Sarpedon during the Trojan War*, red-figure decoration on a calyx krater. c. 515 BCE. Painted terra-cotta, height 18". The Metropolitan Museum of Art, New York. Red-figure vases feature red figures against a black ground.

Bequest of Joseph H. Durkee, Gift of Darius Ogden Mills, and Gift of C. Ruxton Love, by exchange, 1972 (1972.11.10)

anatomy and drapery are more naturalistically rendered. Also, the rendering of some parts of the body as if seen in sharp recession is an early example of **foreshortening.** The greater naturalism is made possible by use of the brush, in contrast to the incising tool employed by the black-figure painter.

The level of artistry reached in these vases testifies to a refined understanding of both functional and visual values. The black-figure **amphora** has two handles for carrying and an opening large enough to admit a ladle. The broad opening of the red-figured **calyx krater** made possible the mixing of water and wine. In each of our examples, the painter has adapted the composition to the form of the vase. The arched backs of Achilles and Ajax echo the inward curvature of the amphora, while the composition on the calyx krater, with the horizontal body of Sarpedon balanced by the vertical pose of the attendants and the parenthetical effect of Sleep and Death, emphasizes the inverted trapezoidal form of the vase. It was this ability to join form, function, and decoration that made Greek vases so highly valued throughout the ancient world.

figures convey a physical and emotional presence that is new to Greek vase painting. Somber facial expressions betray the tragic loss. We sense the physical strain required to lift the body, while diagonal patterns of limbs and flowing blood pull the composition downward. Details of

GREEK SCULPTURE: ARCHAIC STYLE AND SEVERE STYLE

3-57. Archaic style. Kouros, from the Tomb of Kroisos, Anavysos, Greece. c. 520 BCE. Marble with red paint on the hair, headband, and pupils of the eyes, height 6'4". National Archaeological Museum, Athens. The inscription on the base reads: "Stop and grieve at the tomb of the dead Kroisos, slain by wild Ares in the front rank of battle." Commissioned by the family of Kroisos or his military comrades

The earliest large-scale Greek sculptures (c. 600 BCE) are indebted to Egyptian prototypes that were certainly known to the Greeks, who had a trading station in Egypt as early as the mid-seventh century BCE. But by about 520 BCE, when the kouros (youth) from Anavysos was created (fig. 3-57), the new direction Greek art would take was already evident. The Greek figure represents an athletic ideal and a new understanding of the organic nature of the human body. And although the Greek figure maintains a stance derived from Egyptian models (see fig. 1-2), with one leg advanced and hands clenched at the sides, the stone passages (which in Egyptian figures connect the forward to the rear leg and the arms to the torso) have been carved away. The Greek figure seems tense and prepared to take action, not frozen for all eternity. In contrast to Egyptian sculptures, most Greek male figures are nude. Greek athletes competed nude at the games held during religious festivals, but the nudity also demonstrates new Greek attitudes concerning the beauty and integrity of the human body. The slight smile, which suggests a confident assurance consistent with the buoyant energy of the body, recognizes the psychological and emotional aspect of human life in a manner foreign to most Egyptian art. These Greek nude male sculptures were set up as votive offerings at shrines and were used as grave monuments. The youthful figures sometimes marked the tombs of older men, which suggests that they represented a philosophical and aesthetic ideal, not specific individuals.

The style of Greek sculpture from about 650 to 480 BCE is usually referred to as Archaic. Figures from the first half of the fifth century BCE, which are now seen as moving toward the Classical style of the second half of the century, are usually designated Severe style (or Early Classical style or Transitional style, c. 480–450 BCE). These changes in style are the result of the constant questioning with which the Greeks examined all aspects of their culture.

The contemporary Archaic sculptures of female figures—the korai (maidens; singular, kore)—were used almost exclusively as votive figures. And they are always dressed (fig. 3-58); the female nude did not become common in Greek art until the fourth century BCE (see fig. 3-77). The gentle swelling of the body beneath the drapery suggests an interest in the organic qualities of the human fig-

3-58. Archaic style. Kore, from Chios (?). c. 510 BCE. Marble fragment with red, blue, and violet paint, height approx. 22". Acropolis Museum, Athens. Such Archaic sculptures of female figures are much rarer than their male counterparts.

3-59. Severe style. Kouros, also known as the *Kritian Boy*. c. 480 BCE. Marble fragment, originally with inlaid eyes, height 36". Acropolis Museum, Athens

ure, while rich visual patterns are offered by the subtle and varied textures of pleated drapery and plaited hair. This particular example preserves much of the color that was painted on the marble to enhance both its beauty and the lifelikeness of the sculpted figure.

The kouros known as the *Kritian Boy*, because it is similar to works attributed to the Greek sculptor Kritios, represents the figure in a position that combines flexed and relaxed muscles (fig. 3-59). Although the kouros's feet are lost, enough of the figure survives to reveal that it was represented in the relaxed and realistic position known since the Renaissance as **contrapposto**. The weight of the body is borne on one leg, while the other is relaxed. Contrapposto (from the Latin *contrapositio*, "counterpositioning") is related to a natural, relaxed stance; it has its basis in real life. Contrapposto affects the entire body, for the counterpositioning juxtaposes the forward, relaxed leg to the opposite shoulder, which also moves forward. The resulting figure seems to stand freely. Imaginary horizontal lines drawn through knees, pelvis, and shoulders will be seen to rotate around the figure's axis. More importantly, contrapposto suggests the potential for movement, making possible a figure that offers a new momentary quality. In addition, a sculpted figure standing in contrapposto becomes freestanding, a **sculpture in the round**, intended to be seen from many viewpoints. Contrapposto creates a unified figure standing in space, banishing the static Egyptian views (frontal, left profile, right profile) that had conditioned Greek sculpture at its origins.

To understand the revolutionary quality of this kouros, we must try to view it as would a Greek of the period. The pose, which must have seemed startlingly new and amazingly naturalistic, is enhanced by a softness and organic unity in the articulation of the muscles. The sculptor appears to have breathed life into the stone itself. Sculpture would never be the same.

Doric

Ionic

Corinthian

1 cornice
2 frieze
3 architrave
4 capital
5 column
6 entablature
7 stereobate
8 base
9 Doric echinus
10 Doric abacus
11 Doric triglyph
12 Doric metope
13 Ionic volute
14 continuous frieze

3-60. Diagram of Doric, Ionic, and Corinthian orders

An **order** gives aesthetic definition and decoration to the post-and-lintel system (see page 68). Between the seventh and fifth centuries BCE, the Greeks developed three architectural orders—the Doric, Ionic, and Corinthian—which have been in virtually continuous use up to the present day. The Greeks' invention and development of these orders (fig. 3-60) reveal a philosophical and analytical approach to architecture. An order establishes a group of specific architectural elements that are designed to integrate with each other and with the building as a whole. An order also dictates the proportional scheme governing the interrelationships of the parts. The elements of an order include the **column**, with its **capital**, and the **entablature**, composed of **architrave, frieze**, and **cornice**. A column can be decorated with vertical lines or raised areas, known as **flutes**, which accentuate its cylindrical and vertical quality.

The classical orders became the most basic design element for architecture. They were used not only as supports but also as decoration on buildings that were not post-and-lintel construction (for example, the Roman Colosseum; see fig. 3-108). Half-round decorative columns were often attached to a supporting or enclosing wall. These are known as **half columns** or **engaged columns**. When they are flattened, they are called **pilasters**.

An order, however, offers more than mere articulation and decoration, for it also carries the cultural significance of its origins in ancient Greece, and it can be used to impart to a building the dignity, harmony, and sense of philosophical reason that are part of the Western heritage from Greece. The orders are generally regular and predictable, and when the harmonious relationships and proportions are ignored, there is a strong sense of violation.

The **Doric order**, well established by 600 BCE, is vigorous and austere: its fluted columns are strong in appearance and stand directly on the **stereobate** (stepped platform), without a decorated base. The Doric **echinus** appears to be a resilient cushion tucked between the column and the square **abacus**, suggesting in a clear, visual manner the nature and even the idea of support. Together, echinus and abacus provide a simple and muscular transition from the vertical column to the horizontal superstructure. The Doric architrave is broad and simple, and the frieze area is decorated with **triglyphs**, which alternate with **metopes** (originally metopes seem to have been painted panels of terracotta; later they were sculpted). The first-century BCE Roman architect Vitruvius argued that the Doric order was originally derived from wooden architecture and that the tapering of the column was based on the use of tree trunks for early columns.

The **Ionic order**, which was first used in the sixth century BCE, is lighter in proportion and more elegant in detail than the Doric. Columns have richly decorated bases, and the Ionic capital is characterized by a scroll-like motif called a **volute**. Ionic temples often feature a continuous frieze in place of the triglyphs and metopes. The planar, frontal Ionic volutes created a problem at corners, which was solved by the development, during the fifth century BCE, of the **Corinthian order**, which employs a cylindrical capital decorated with acanthus leaves. The increasing elegance of the Greek orders is revealed by the constantly changing proportions of the column. In the Doric, the relationship of height to diameter is usually 4:1 to 6:1 or even 7:1. For Ionic, it is 7:1 to 8:1; Corinthian can be 8:1 to 9:1.

ART PAST/ART PRESENT   THE IMPACT OF THE ANCIENT GREEK ORDERS

The ancient world may be remote from us in time, but it still has an impact on our lives in many ways. One of the most obvious is the importance of the ancient Greek architectural orders on modern architecture and design. The Greeks developed a system of architectural decoration and proportion for columns in their structures (see pages 92–93) that was adapted, with very little change, by other ancient cultures—especially by the Romans (see figs. 3-88, 3-109, 3-111, 3-112). Many Christian churches during the medieval period, particularly in areas that had been colonized by the Greeks or the Romans, used variations on these orders (see figs. 4-55, 4-60, 4-63, 4-75, 4-81). During the Italian Renaissance, when many forms and subjects from antiquity were revived, the Greek orders became the dominant architectural decorative device. The orders continued to have an impact in subsequent centers, and in the postmodern style (see Part 10), when all historical architectural forms became open to revival, the Greek orders and other Greek forms became of major significance once again.

GREEK DORIC ARCHITECTURE

3-61. Second Temple of Hera (at right), Paestum, Italy. c. 460 BCE. At the left is the Temple of Athena (c. 530–520 BCE), which has lost its entablature. Southern Italy and Sicily were colonized by the Greeks beginning in the seventh century BCE (see map, page 114). The temples constructed in these colonies during the sixth and fifth centuries BCE are among the best-preserved examples of Greek architecture.

A Greek Doric temple (see figs. 3-61, 3-68, 3-70) is an imposing structure, an autonomous object that is complete within itself. The architectural forms are vigorous and assertive. The vertical fluting of the columns, reinforced by the triglyphs in the frieze above, produces an upward thrust that is held in balance by the horizontal articulation of the entablature and gable roof. The visual forces are in equilibrium, yet the temple is not static. Its massive forms communicate an almost muscular vitality.

The walled inner sanctuary, or **naos** (from the Greek "to dwell"), contained the cult statue (see fig. 3-71). On the exterior, the perimeter of the temple is surrounded by a **colonnade**, or continuous row of columns, called a **peristyle** (from *peri*, "around," and *style*, "column"); such temples are termed **peripteral** (fig. 3-62). It seems that only priests or priestesses and attendants were allowed inside the temple and that most rituals occurred outside, at an altar in front of the temple. The temple might thus be thought of as a sculptural background for the ritual.

A post-and-lintel system forms the peristyle, while walls enclose the naos. Columns support the entablature and roof. The pediments at each end of the gable roof are in some temples filled with sculpted figures. The roof was originally made of wood rafters covered with terra-cotta tiles.

The earliest Greek temples were small shrines containing a cult statue. During the eighth and early seventh centuries BCE, large wood temples with peristyles were built. By the later seventh century BCE, stone construction began to replace wood, partially as a practical response to the problem of supporting the heavy terra-cotta roof tiles. Stone construction, which coincides with the advent of monumental stone sculpture, reflects a confident

3-62. Plan of the Second Temple of Hera

c. 550 B.C.   c. 500 B.C.   c. 438 B.C.

3-63. Diagram of the evolution of Doric proportions to scale

new spirit, a spirit of permanence and achievement.

Once the design for a temple was determined, stonecutters began to cut marble at quarries. The blocks of stone, formed to specifications to reduce transportation weight, were moved to the construction site in specially designed carts pulled by teams of animals. After the temple's foundation had been built to the stylobate, the peristyle was set up. Columns were constructed of unfluted cylindrical units called **drums**, held in place by wood centering pins. The drums for the columns and the blocks of stone for the walls of the naos were lifted into

place with pulleys and cranes. No mortar was used to hold the stones in place. The blocks of the naos walls were secured by iron clamps encased in lead to prevent rusting. The roof was constructed of wood beams and rafters. A beam supported the apex of the gable roof, while additional support for the roof was provided by columns inside the naos. Finally, as the temple neared completion, the columns were fluted. The fluting disguised the joints of the drums and, by creating patterns of shadows, reinforced the three-dimensionality of the columns.

The changing proportions of the Doric order seen in the evolution of

the proportion of and relationship among column, capital, and entablature (fig. 3-63) reflect the search for an aesthetic harmony that was integral to Greek art. The diagram also reveals the increasing scale of the Doric temple over time.

GREEK SCULPTURE: SEVERE STYLE

3-64. *Zeus.* C. 460 BCE. Bronze with inlaid eyes, teeth, lips, and nipples, height 6'10". National Archaeological Museum, Athens. Lost in an ancient shipwreck at about the time of Christ, this sculpture was found in the sea near Cape Artemision in 1926–28. It is sometimes identified as representing Poseidon, god of the sea.

3-65. *Charioteer*, from a votive quadriga dedicated in the Sanctuary of Apollo, Delphi. c. 477 BCE. Bronze with inlaid stone and glass eyes, height 5'11". Archaeological Museum, Delphi. This figure and its quadriga were buried after they were damaged, perhaps in an earthquake. Only fragments of the horses and chariot survive. Commissioned by Polyzalos, Tyrant of Gela, to celebrate the victory of his quadriga in the Delphic Games

This larger-than-lifesize figure of Zeus originally held a lightning bolt, the god's symbol, in his right hand (fig. 3-64). His energetic movement is communicated by the tensed muscles of torso and abdomen, the distended veins, the buoyant position of the feet, and the arms, which are outstretched for balance and to help the god focus on his victim. The left foot is supported only on the heel and outside edge; the right touches only with the ball and toes. Three prongs in the soles held the figure in position on its base. Zeus's pose expresses the perfect physical development of the god and his complete physical control, and his severe facial expression complements the aggressive action.

Such a position would be impossible in marble, for marble's lack of tensile strength would not allow the outstretched arms, while the pose of feet and legs would not support the weight of the upper body. Because of its greater possibilities for both naturalistic effects and convincing movement, bronze was the favored sculptural medium of the Greeks after the Archaic period. But few ancient Greek bronzes have survived, because they could so easily be melted down and the bronze reused for weapons or other purposes. In this figure, the color of the bronze suggests a naturally sun-tanned, oiled body (the Greeks oiled their bodies when exercising), and the inlaid eyes and teeth, fringed sheet-bronze eyelashes, and inlaid colored lips and nipples reinforce the naturalistic impact.

The *Charioteer* (fig. 3-65) was originally part of a large votive monument that included a chariot and four horses, a grouping called a

quadriga. The patron, a tyrant from Sicily, commissioned the work as an offering to Apollo and a commemoration of the victory of his team and charioteer in the Delphic Games. The subtle and delicate pose evolves from a slight twist of the upper body. The figure wears the appropriate racing garment, and the artist has emphasized the subtle patterns of the delicate material as it is

caught and pleated by a belt and ribbons or straps. The head represents the ideal Greek type, with a strong nose that continues the line of the forehead, large eyes and ears, full jawline, broad cheeks, and prominent lips. The expression is alert and self-confident, with a hint of the pride that is appropriate to a winner in the games.

TECHNIQUE **GREEK LOST-WAX BRONZE CASTING**

The earliest-known bronze monumental sculptures in Greece date from the late sixth century BCE, but they were preceded by the casting of bronze body armor, which may have suggested and supported the development of bronze sculpture. Ancient Greek bronzes are hollow-cast of an alloy of copper and tin by what is known as the **lost-wax method** (fig. 3-66). A sculptor begins by forming a mass of clay (or some other malleable material) into the rough shape of the planned sculpture, but slightly smaller. This is covered with a layer of wax of the thickness desired for the finished bronze and modeled to approximate the surface finish of the planned sculpture. This wax coating is then encased in another layer of damp clay. When it has dried, the wax is melted away, leaving a hollow mold between core and exterior (supports hold the two in place). Molten bronze is poured into the mold. After it cools and hardens, the mold is broken or cut away, leaving bronze that has assumed the form first created in wax.

It is difficult to cast large figures in bronze, for the bronze can cool before it has reached the full extent of the mold. The ancient Greek bronzes discussed here were therefore cast in several sections. The *Charioteer*, for example, is composed of seven pieces and, as is common, pieces of different textures were cast individually—the figure's right arm was cast separately and is fitted into the opening left in the sleeve when the drapery was cast. Actual cloth, impregnated with wax, may have been used to help form the draped patterns of the costume, and it has also been suggested that the ancient Greek sculptors may have created body parts using clay molds made from living human figures.

▨ inner core of clay
☐ wax, later replaced with bronze
▨ outer mold of clay
━ metal pins that hold inner core in place when wax is melted out

3-66. Lost-wax bronze casting. Conjectural reconstruction of technique for right arm of figure 3-65.

After casting, the bronze was tooled and polished (worked with tools and an abrasive) to achieve the finished surface. Lips, nipples, and eyebrows were sometimes highlighted and given a realistic reddish cast by being overlaid with copper or with bronze of a high copper content. Fringed sheet-bronze eyelashes, inlaid stone and glass eyes, and teeth of silver, marble, or ivory were applied after the polishing of the bronze was complete. These additional colors and materials enhanced the beauty of the work, impressed the observer with the skill of the artists, and, most importantly, played a vital role in achieving the verisimilitude desired by the Greeks. They made these beautiful and ideal figures seem even more real.

GREEK CLASSICAL-STYLE SCULPTURE

3-67. Polykleitos. *Doryphoros* (*Spear Carrier*), Roman copy after a lost bronze original of c. 450 BCE. Marble, height 7'. National Archaeological Museum, Naples, Italy. This copy is generally considered to be the best version of Polykleitos's lost figure, but the spear that it once carried is missing, and the bronze original would not have had the tree trunk behind the right leg or the marble bar supporting the right arm.

Beauty . . . arises . . . in the commensurability [proportion] of the parts, such as that of finger to finger, and all of the forearm to the upper arm, and . . . of everything to everything else, just as it is written in the *Canon* of Polykleitos. For having taught us in that book all the proportions of the body, Polykleitos supported his treatise with a work; he made a statue according to the tenets of his treatise, and called the statue, like his book, the *Canon*.

Unfortunately, both Polykleitos's written text and his original bronze version of his demonstration piece—described here by Galen, a Greek physician, writing in the second century CE on Greek aesthetic theory—are lost. Nevertheless, the numerous surviving, more-or-less-complete marble copies of the original statue, which was made about 450 BCE, verify its significance in the classical world. Although Polykleitos called his example *The Canon* after the principles of proportion it was intended to demonstrate, the popular name, which we have inherited from antiquity, is the *Doryphoros* (*Spear Carrier*).

The specific subject of the *Doryphoros* (fig. 3-67) is probably an ideal Olympic athlete, but the statue was more importantly a demonstration of the system of perfect proportions that Polykleitos had perceived in the human body and established in his lost text. The *Doryphoros* was considered to be an ideal figure because its proportions adhered to common fractions (exact divisions by whole numbers) of the figure's height. Because Polykleitos's original figure and text are lost, the precise measurements of his canon remain undetermined, but the later Roman writer Vitruvius advocated a rule whereby the head (from the crown of the hair to the chin) was one-eighth of the total height, the width of the shoulders one-quarter the height, and so on, until every anatomical feature and the proportions among them were woven into a system of mathematical measurements. Such a demonstration of mathematical relationships could lead to a dull sculpture, but the *Doryphoros* exhibits a firm muscular structure that is enlivened by the contrapposto stance.

A century before the *Doryphoros* was created, the Greek philosopher and mathematician Pythagoras had presented mathematical proportion as the basis of musical harmony. Polykleitos's proportional system was, however, more than a set of abstract principles, for it bears an important relationship to the Greek belief in the agreement between natural and mathematical harmony, a belief that brought a new vitality to the human figure in sculpture and to the visual arts in general.

Vitruvius reported that the proportions governing the human figure in art also determined the proportions of Greek temples: "Further, it was from the members of the body that [the Greeks] derived the fundamental ideas of measures." Vitruvius defines proportion in a manner similar to our understanding of the Polykleitian canon as "a correspondence among the measure of an entire work, and of the whole to a certain part selected as a standard." Just as the Greeks gave human characteristics to their gods, they also humanized their architecture. The relative proportions, the capital as the head of the column, and the slight muscular swelling of a Doric column, or **entasis** (see page 101), all contribute to an empathetic understanding between us and the temple. This empathy was an extension of the Greeks' rational definition of their world.

TECHNIQUE   **CONTRAPPOSTO IN SCULPTURE**

The relaxed stance seen in the *Spear Carrier* was a recent development in Greek sculpture, but it had a powerful and long-lasting influence on later works. In the Italian Renaissance, when this stance was one of many features of ancient art that were revived, it became known by the term *contrapposto*. In ancient Greek art, contrapposto emerged tentatively during the period that art historians have named the Severe or Transitional period. One of the earliest surviving examples is the kouros known as the *Kritian Boy* (see fig. 3-59), but in that case the twisting of the figure in space—the natural outcome of balancing the body over one supporting leg—is only delicately suggested. With the *Spear Carrier*, the twisting of the body and the tilting of the pelvis are more evident.

The origin of this pose in ancient Greek sculpture can be understood as an outcome of the Greeks' interest in the ideal nude human body, in athletic achievement, and in understanding how the parts of the body work together organically. The development of contrapposto is also related to the development of **sculpture in the round**; the twisting of the body encourages us to view it from different viewpoints to fully understand the pose.

The ancient Romans adopted contrapposto along with many other Greek artistic ideas; the impact of the pose is evident in the *Augustus* (see fig. 3-92). But the interest in contrapposto did not last long after the rise of Christianity. Although contrapposto can still be seen in the Early Christian figure of the *Good Shepherd* (see fig. 4-9), the otherworldly ideals of Christianity eventually rendered the relaxation and informality of the contrapposto pose inappropriate (see, for example, the pose of the Gothic *Beau Dieu* from Amiens, figure 4-89).

Contrapposto reappears in the Italian Renaissance as a result of the joint interests in naturalism and ancient art. In *Saint Mark* (see fig. 5-9), the sculptor Donatello manipulates the drapery to emphasize the contrapposto, using fine, flutelike lines of material to emphasize the supporting leg and broader, draped patterns to accentuate the relaxation of the other leg. Notice how Saint Mark's right shoulder drops back in contrast to the forward position of his left knee. (For other Renaissance examples of contrapposto, see figures 5-10, 5-42, and 6-13.) Michelangelo sometimes exaggerated the twist of the contrapposto pose to achieve a dramatic, emotional effect, as in his *Saint Matthew* (see fig. 6-14); in the Renaissance, this pose was known as the *figura serpentinata*.

GREEK ARCHITECTURE: THE PARTHENON, ATHENS

3-68. Kallikrates and Iktinos. Parthenon, Acropolis, Athens. 447–438 BCE; sculpture completed by 432 BCE. Pentelic marble, 111 x 237' at base. The temple to Athena, goddess of wisdom and fierce protector of Athens, was built after the Persian wars, when Athens was controlled by Pericles, who insisted that the Athenians rebuild the temples the Persians had destroyed. The name *Parthenon* means "maiden," and the temple was dedicated to Athena, the maiden (*parthenon* was the name given to the room in a home where unmarried, virginal daughters lived). The Parthenon was the preeminent religious structure in Athens. It later served as a Christian church dedicated to Mary and, in the later Middle Ages, as the cathedral of Athens. After the conquest of Athens by the Turks, it served as a mosque. It was severely damaged in 1687, during a war between the Venetians and the Turks. Commissioned by Perikles, ruler of Athens

In the history of human accomplishment, the Parthenon on the Acropolis in Athens is one of the most famous monuments (see figs. 3-68–3-75). Its significance is not due to its basic form, which continues the Doric temple type developed more than a century earlier (see page 94). Rather, it is the harmony and grace of its proportions that make the Parthenon great. Its fame derives from its beauty.

The Parthenon was intended to be a home for the goddess Athena, but its grandeur made it a monument to the wealth, power, taste, and piety of Athens. It was entirely surfaced in white Pentelic marble, including even the roof. The interior has two chambers—a smaller one where the goddess's and city's treasures were stored, and the naos, where the colossal ivory-and-gold cult statue of Athena in military dress was enshrined (fig. 3-71). Although all people could look in from the door, it seems that only a few were allowed to enter these chambers. The rituals in honor of Athena were held outside, at a sacrificial altar to which the Parthenon was the backdrop.

The grace and beauty of the Parthenon are the culmination of a long Greek search for the ideal temple. The simple dynamics of the post-and-lintel system became a vehicle that encouraged Greek architects to attempt to achieve the most satisfying equipose. Compared to the Second Temple of Hera at Paestum (see fig. 3-61), the Parthenon offers a new grace and elegance.

There are a number of remarkable visual refinements in the Parthenon. All the horizontal lines—

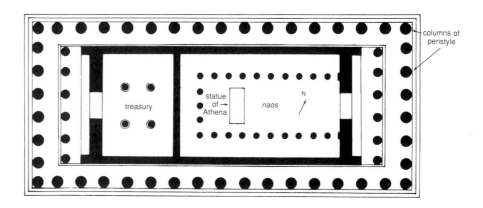

3-69. Plan of the Parthenon

3-70. Reconstruction model of the Parthenon. The Metropolitan Museum of Art, New York

Levi Hale Willard Bequest. Purchase, 1890 (90.35.2)

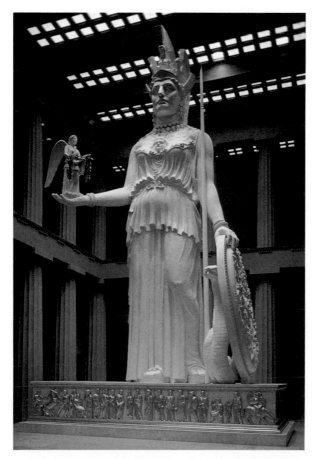

3-71. Reconstructed section of the naos, Parthenon, with the ivory-and-gold statue of Athena created by sculptor Alan Laquire. Nashville, Tennessee. The 40-foot statue was supported by a ship's mast; the flesh was composed of carved pieces of ivory, and the dress and armor were of sheets of gold. The section shows the gable roof construction and the superimposed columns of the naos.

steps, stylobate, stereobate, entablature—are raised slightly in the middle, ostensibly to correct the sag that the human eye imparts to a long horizontal (and also to add the practical advantage of helping rainwater to run off). Like the other optical refinements of the Parthenon, the lifting of the middle of the horizontals gives the building elasticity and a sense of life. Such adjustments made the structure more difficult to engineer and construct, for each block of marble had to be cut to fit its exact place. Other refinements include the tilting inward of the columns to enhance the effect of stability and compactness, and the placement of the three corner columns closer together to compensate for the dissolving effect of light at the corners; for the same reason, the corner columns were made slightly thicker than the others. The entire stylobate is tilted upward at the southwest corner to make the building more impressive both from the city below and from the entrance to the Acropolis.

Perhaps the single most revealing refinement is the **entasis** of the columns, which do not taper in a straight line but bulge outward about one-third of the way up from the base. The entasis creates an effect of muscular elasticity that helps give the Parthenon a human, organic quality. Later copies and variations often seem rigid and cold because they lack these refinements. The Parthenon is a monument that reveals the analytical quality of the human mind and the Greek search for the harmonious, the ideal, and the beautiful.

GREEK SCULPTURE: THE PARTHENON

3-72. Diagram of the Parthenon sculptures in their original positions. The sculpture is attributed to Phidias and his workshop.

The Parthenon's architectural beauty and richness were enhanced by the sculpture that was integrated into the Doric design (figs. 3-72–3-75). The pediments at both ends were filled with over-life-size figures; there were ninety-two metopes sculpted in high relief; and a continuous low-relief frieze, 550 feet long, encircled the outside of the naos wall. Like the edifice they adorn, these sculptures display an impressive mastery of form and technique. They were all completed in about twelve years, indicating that there must have been a large workshop of sculptors and assistants, but their general consistency of design suggests that a single sculptor was in charge. This sculptor most probably was Phidias (c. 490–430 BCE), who also designed the ivory-and-gold statue of Athena that stood in the naos (see fig. 3-71). The consistency of the sculptural conception suggests that Phidias provided drawings—perhaps on the stone itself—to guide the sculptors.

The iconographic themes are related to the dedication of the Parthenon to Athena, to the victories of the Greeks over their barbarians, and to Athens's political leadership among the city-states in Greece. The east pediment presented the *Birth of Athena* (fig. 3-73), the west the *Contest between Athena and Poseidon*. The metopes featured a series of battle scenes, including a battle between centaurs and men. Until recently, the continuous frieze had been thought to represent the procession of the Great Panathenaea, a celebration held every four years in honor of Athena, with musicians, elders, horsemen, chariots, and sacrificial cattle and sheep. A new interpretation—still controversial—relates the procession to an episode from the mythological history of Athens in which a daughter of the king offers to die to save the city; she is joined in a death pact by her two sisters. Whatever the actual subject, the frieze presents a vivid depiction of the participants in an ancient ritual procession.

On the east pediment the dramatic birth of Athena—who sprang full grown, wearing armor, from the head of her father, Zeus—is conveyed by figures who move outward from the central episode. There is a coherent unity of time and place similar to that which developed in contemporary Greek drama. The magnificent group of seated and

3-73. Reconstruction of the east pediment of the Parthenon, showing the *Birth of Athena* by Phidias and his workshop. The darkened figures show the original location of the *Three Goddesses* (see fig. 3-74). The darkened sections in the pediment indicate surviving fragments; the light lines are conjectural figures. The scenes in the metopes are extant.

3-74. Phidias and workshop. *Three Goddesses on Mount Olympus*, from the east pediment of the Parthenon, Athens. c. 438–432 BCE. Marble, height of center figure 5'; the figures are slightly over-lifesize. The British Museum, London. These three figures have been identified as Hestia, Dione, and Aphrodite. The Parthenon pediments were more than 90 feet long, and at the center they rose to a height of more than 11 feet. The platform on which the figures were placed was about 3 feet deep.

3-75. Phidias and workshop. *Horsemen*, from the frieze of the Parthenon. Marble, height approx. 43". The British Museum, London

reclining goddesses, for example (fig. 3-74), turn as they become aware of the birth. To compose within the sloping pedimental shape was a challenge for the Greek artist, but these goddesses, shown in graceful, natural poses and beautifully unified as a group, do not seem forced into the increasingly constricted space of the pediment. Their voluptuous bodies are clothed in clinging drapery that is gathered and folded into patterns emphasizing the sculptural presence of the figures. The clarity of the poses is remarkable, as is the graceful and flowing role they play within the triangular composition. Filling the outermost corners of the pediment are, on the left, the sun god's rising chariot to signify dawn and, on the right, the horses of the moon's chariot. These forms are cut off by the pediment, perhaps to suggest that the realm of the gods continues beyond any artificial restrictions.

The Parthenon frieze is a tour de force of low-relief carving that offers the illusion of as many as six figures and horses overlapping within a low relief that is no more than three inches deep (fig. 3-75). The relief is carved more deeply near the top as a concession to the placement of the frieze, high above the spectator's head. By thus giving the work greater readability, the Greek sculptor makes it clear that this frieze is for the enjoyment and enlightenment of the human spectator and is not merely a decoration added to the temple in honor of the goddess.

The Parthenon's sculptures had additions made of metal, some perhaps gilded, for the armor, straps, and other refinements. Many of the details of the figures were heightened by paint, although there is still controversy over the actual colors used. A bright blue has been proposed as the background for the pedimental figures, a red background for metopes and frieze. The hair of the figures may have been gilded; the drapery hems probably had painted patterns taken from actual Greek garments. Color would have enhanced the beauty of the marble figures and clarified the compositions for the Athenians, who saw the Parthenon as a monument to their success as well as to the generosity of their patron goddess.

GREEK SCULPTURE AND PAINTING: FOURTH CENTURY BCE

3-76. Praxiteles. *Hermes with the Child Dionysos*, 1st-century BCE copy after lost 4th-century BCE original. Marble, height 6'8". Archaeological Museum, Olympia. The lower left leg and foot of the figure have been restored.

Hermes may have held in his right hand. The articulation of muscles contrasts with that of the *Doryphoros* (see fig. 3-67). While the spear carrier's muscles were clearly defined, those of Hermes have a softer, more natural appearance. Hermes' stance reinforces this new organic unity, and the axis of the figure follows a shallow **S** curve, which adds to the sense of relaxation. What we can determine from this copy after Praxiteles (370–330 BCE), who was one of the dominant artists of the fourth century, indicates a continued evolution toward naturalism in Greek sculpture and a new, refined elegance.

Praxiteles also sculpted a statue of Aphrodite (Venus), the goddess of love and beauty, that was purchased by the city of Knidos, in Asia Minor, and installed in a temple there (fig. 3-77). This *Aphrodite* is the first monumental figure in Greek art to depict the female nude in three dimensions. Her nudity is explained by the vase and drapery under her left hand: she is represented either entering or leaving her bath. Lucian, a second-century BCE Greek rhetorician who saw the statue, observed:

> So strongly has the artist's art prevailed, that the recalcitrant and solid nature of the stone has been transformed in each limb. . . . [As we viewed the figure from behind], unforeseen amazement at the goddess' beauty seized us.

The *Aphrodite,* like the *Hermes,* is freestanding and is composed as sculpture in the round—the temple on Knidos was open on all sides so

Despite political instability in Greece after the Peloponnesian War ended in 404 BCE, the fourth century was a time of creativity and stylistic experimentation. We can see beginnings of stylistic change in *Hermes with the Child Dionysos* (fig. 3-76). As Hermes, messenger of the gods, holds him, the infant Dionysos, a god and patron of drama and song, reaches forward, probably to grasp a bunch of grapes that

3-77. Praxiteles. *Aphrodite of Knidos*, Roman copy after lost 4th-century BCE original. Marble, height 6'8". Vatican Museums, Rome. The first-century CE Roman writer Pliny tells us that Praxiteles made two similar statues, one clothed and one nude, and that the Knidians daringly bought the nude example.

that the statue could be appreciated from many different viewpoints. The diagonal movement of the right arm and hand and the slightly lifted left leg create an impelling motion across and, by implication, around the body. Unlike earlier Greek sculpture, which primarily has a frontal orientation, these works invite us to admire the sculptor's ability to create a complex, multifaceted composition in space.

We know from literary sources that the sense of drama and spatial involvement that characterized fourth-century sculpture was paralleled by advances in painting, but unfortunately no certain examples of fourth-century painting survive. Nevertheless, ancient literary sources offer accounts of accomplishments in perspective and illusionism that already astonished viewers by the beginning of this period The first-century CE writer Pliny the Elder reported, for example, on a contest between two late-fifth-century BCE artists:

[Parrhasios] entered a contest with Zeuxis, and when the latter depicted some grapes with such success that birds flew up to the [painting], Parrhasios then depicted a linen curtain with such verisimilitude that Zeuxis, puffed up with pride by the verdict of the birds, eventually requested that the curtain be removed and Parrhasios' picture shown . . . when Zeuxis understood his error, [he] conceded defeat . . . because he himself had only deceived birds, but Parrhasios had deceived him, an artist. It is said that afterward Zeuxis painted a picture of a boy carrying grapes, and when the birds flew up to them, he approached the work and, in irritation with it, said, "I have painted the grapes better than the boy, for if I had rendered him perfectly, the birds would have been afraid." (Pliny, *Natural History*, XXV)

The ability of painters to render the naturalism of appearance paralleled the subtle anatomical features, spontaneous attitudes, and increased spatial involvement of contemporary sculpture. These trends would develop as the influence of Greek culture spread throughout the eastern Mediterranean region.

HELLENISTIC ART

3-78. *Winged Victory of Samothrace*, from the Sanctuary of the Great Gods, Samothrace. c. 190 BCE. Marble, height 8'. The Louvre, Paris. This figure celebrates a naval victory, perhaps a victory of the navy of Rhodes at Side in 190 BCE. At Samothrace, the statue was erected on a darker gray marble base in the form of the prow of a ship, and to give the effect of a ship coming into harbor, statue and base were set in two pools, one with a rippled marble bottom and a second with huge boulders. Most likely commissioned by the victorious admiral or the ruler he represented

Despite the loss of head and arms, the *Winged Victory of Samothrace* expresses heroic triumph (fig. 3-78). The diagonal forward thrust of the body creates a dynamic effect of forward movement. The posture is strengthened by the complex and subtle patterns of drapery that envelop the figure, as well as the contrasting position of the unfurled wings. Effects of wind are felt as the drapery both presses against the body's surface and unfurls in vigorous forms that billow into space, echoing the movement of the wings. The dramatic spatial involvement and dynamic movement displayed by the *Winged Victory* are typical of the art of the Hellenistic period (c. 400–100 BCE).

HISTORY

In the late fourth century BCE, while the Greek city-states maintained a tenuous political stability, the hereditary kings of Macedonia, a kingdom to the north of Greece, strengthened their political power. Philip II, king of Macedonia, proposed a plan for the unification of Greece under his rule. In 338 BCE, while the Greeks debated his proposal, Philip defeated them. Philip's union of Greece with Macedonia was the initial step in a grand design to establish an empire that would include Persia. After Philip II was killed by an assassin in 336 BCE, his son Alexander, nineteen years old, ascended the throne. Following the vision of his father, he led a military campaign against Persia and defeated King Darius in 331 BCE (see figs. 3-80, 6-54). Later conquests extended the boundaries of his vast Hellenistic empire south through Egypt and east to the borders of India before the youthful Alexander died in 323 BCE.

225 BCE	Romans defeat the Celts
221 BCE	1st Chinese empire (Qin) established
215 BCE	Romans defeat Hannibal at Nola
c. 190 BCE	***Winged Victory of Samothrace***

Alexander had been educated by Greek standards, and his tutor was Aristotle, the philosopher and natural scientist. The young conqueror envisioned a unity between the Greeks and the Persians based on the cultural values of Hellenism, the ideas and ideals of Classical Greece. After his death, Alexander's dream of unity was fractured by the reality of political conflict among his own generals. Soon his empire was divided into smaller independent powers. Common to these diverse regions, however, was the unifying influence of Greek culture.

Alexandria, founded by Alexander in Egypt in 332 BCE, became a famous center of learning. The great library there may have contained as many as 500,000 volumes, representing the accumulated wealth of knowledge of the ancient world. The library was part of a complex known as the museum (from the Greek *mouseios*, "of the Muses," referring to the ancient Greek goddesses of art and music). The major centers of Hellenistic art production, which were founded outside the Greek mainland, included Alexandria, the island of Rhodes, and Pergamon in Asia Minor (see map, page 84).

ART OF THE HELLENISTIC PERIOD

The developing naturalism that characterized Greek fourth-century sculpture and painting deepened in the Hellenistic period and united with an interest in realism in subject matter. The appreciation of art was no longer restricted to the educated citizens of the city-states, however; the new empathetic and dramatic art appealed to a wider audience.

These displays of human emotion and drama in art paralleled the melodramatic staging of contemporary Greek theater.

Many portrait busts of Alexander were created to distribute throughout the empire and even beyond, images of the young man as a dynamic conqueror. They emphasize his mental and physical alertness through a combination of deeply set eyes, a furrowed brow, a naturalistically open mouth, and a strong twisting of the head on the neck. A similar emotional, inspired quality is evident in coins of Alexander that were created by his successors (fig. 3-79).

The Hellenistic emphasis on dramatic and emotional naturalism can be related to a changed philosophical outlook epitomized in the teachings of Aristotle (384–322 BCE). Aristotle's teacher, Plato, had viewed material objects as mere imperfect reflections of ideal forms. Aristotle, in contrast, stressed the roles of natural observation and experience in understanding reality. He sought to comprehend nature by perceiving its manifestations in the biological and earth sciences. The direction of Aristotle's philosophy, based on a penetrating observation of nature, parallels the dramatic naturalism of fourth-century and Hellenistic art.

HELLENISTIC PAINTING

As with Hellenistic sculpture, much of our knowledge of specific paintings is based on literary sources and/or Roman copies in fresco or in **mosaic**—designs composed of a number of small pieces (in various periods pebbles, stone, tile, and glass have been used for mosaics). The *Battle of Alexander the Great and*

3-79. *Alexander the Great with Amun Horns*, 4-drachma coin, issued by Lysimachus. c. 300 BCE. Silver, diameter 1¹/₈". Alexander was one of the earliest rulers to appear on coins; this example shows him with the horns of the Egyptian god Amun. Commissioned by the Hellenistic ruler Lysimachus, king of Lysimachia

King Darius (fig. 3-80), for example, is thought to preserve the composition of a Hellenistic painting mentioned in literary sources. The successful representation of vivid and energetic activity demonstrated in the mosaic testifies to the continuing advances in illusionism in Hellenistic painting. Alexander rides into the battle from the left, raising his spear; Darius anxiously looks back toward his pursuer. The foreshortening of the central horse and the frantic activity of the team pulling Darius's chariot add complexity to the tumult of the battle. Within the turbulent scene, the Hellenistic painter added a detail to demonstrate virtuosity: reflected in a Greek shield below Darius's chariot is the anguished face of a young Persian about to be crushed by the wheels of the chariot. The representation of suffering and death was a challenge

3-80. *Battle of Alexander the Great and King Darius of Persia*, Roman mosaic copy of a lost Hellenistic painting of c. 300 BCE. Stone and glass mosaic, height 10'6". National Museum, Naples. Found in the House of the Dancing Faun at Pompeii, this impressive mosaic uses more than a million small pieces of stone and glass to create the illusion of the battle. The lost Hellenistic original may have been by Philoxenos or Helena of Alexandria. Commissioned by the owner of the House of the Dancing Faun

to the Hellenistic artist (see figs. 3-81, 3-82), and here the horror reflected on the Persian's face dramatically communicates the personal reality of battle.

HELLENISTIC SCULPTURE IN PERGAMON

The *Dying Trumpeter* (fig. 3-81), one of a group depicting defeated Gauls from a large monument at Pergamon, displays the psychological and physical naturalism that characterizes Hellenistic art. Distinguished as one of the invaders from the north known as Gauls by his matted hair, his mustache, and the metal collar, or torque, around his neck, this soldier is shown pierced in the side; his blood spews from the wound. His face mirrors defeat, and we experience his last moments of life. Even in the marble copy, a keen observa-

tion of surface anatomy complements the psychological drama of impending death; both body and soul are rendered with unsparing reality.

During the mid-third century BCE, the Hellenistic kingdom of Pergamon became a major political power and art center. In 230 BCE, King Attalus I of Pergamon defeated an invasion by the Gauls, who had entered Asia Minor following their invasion of Greece in 279 BCE. In defeating the foreign invaders, Attalus I was able to establish his kingdom as the principal political force in the Middle East. By commissioning works that represent the noble deaths of the enemy, Attalus made his own victory seem even more impressive.

During the Hellenistic period, art no longer exclusively served the worship of the gods or the embellishment of the city-states; it could extol the exploits of a political leader and

so act to capture public support. This motive underlay construction of the great Altar of Zeus and Athena at Pergamon (fig. 3-82). The balance between theme and form demonstrated in the earlier *Dying Trumpeter*, however, gives way by the second century to an emphasis on drama that approaches the melodramatic.

The altar was raised on a platform about 20 feet high. Approaching the steps that lead to the altar, viewers encountered a dramatic frieze in such high relief that the sculpted figures seem to kneel and fall out onto the steps. The frieze depicts the Gigantomachy—a mythological battle between the giants and the Greek gods. At Pergamon, the overt display of emotion and the convulsive interlacing diagonals of the figural composition combine to create an overwhelmingly dramatic presentation and, thereby, a new level of expression in Western art.

3-81. *Dying Trumpeter*, Roman copy after a lost bronze original of c. 230–220 BCE from Pergamon. Marble, lifesize. Capitoline Museum, Rome. Commissioned by King Attalus I of Pergamon

3-82. Reconstructed Altar of Zeus and Athena, from Pergamon. c. 181–159 BCE. Marble, 120 x 113' at base; height of frieze 7'6"; the figures are well over lifesize. Staatliche Museen zu Berlin, Preussischer Kulturbesitz. Commissioned by King Eumenes II of Pergamon to commemorate the victory of King Attalus I over the Gauls

EARLY BUDDHIST ART

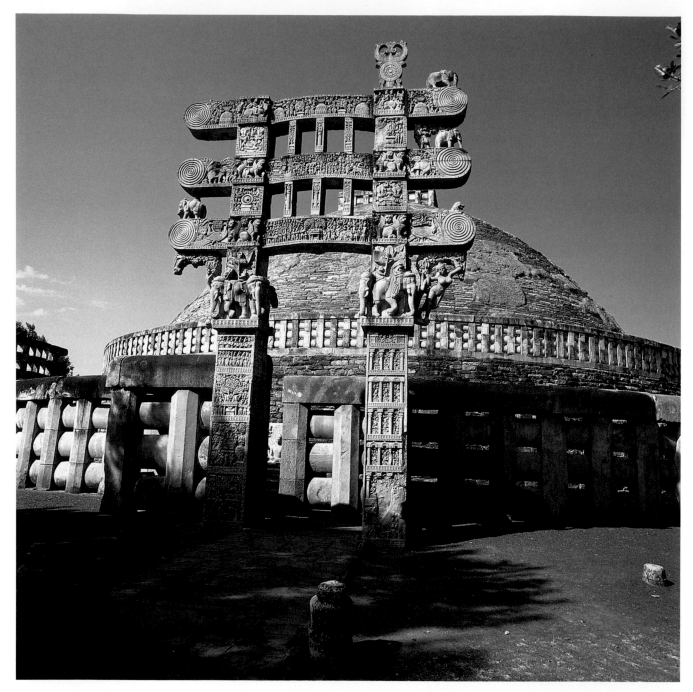

3-83. The Great Stupa and the East Torana, Sanchi, India. Begun 3rd century BCE, with later additions and enlargement. Brick and rubble originally faced with painted and gilded stucco, rails and gateways of yellow limestone; height of dome 54'. Stupas were the first sacred Buddhist buildings, and the Great Stupa at Sanchi is the oldest surviving example. The core of the structure probably originated in the third century BCE. Here, as in many Indian stupas, the original building was encased in a mass of earth and stone before it was enlarged, for it was considered a sacrilege to destroy any of the original monument. Originally commissioned by the Indian ruler Asoka; later supported by the lay community

3rd century BCE–1st century CE	The Great Stupa, Sanchi
221 BCE	Qin dynasty founded in China
191 BCE	Gaul (France) becomes a Roman province
101 BCE	Chinese ships reach India

The Great Stupa at Sanchi, on a hill rising out of the plain not far from modern Bhopal in central India (fig. 3-83), is a monumental burial mound known as a **stupa**, whose form dates back to prehistoric times. The stupa, as used for the burial of princes, had the shape of a large hemisphere. At an early date, this kind of tomb developed into a commemorative monument and was adopted by Buddhists as one of their main symbols and as the center of their religious compounds. The stupa could be an actual tomb, placed over remains of the Buddha or other holy Buddhist individuals, or it could act as a symbol to commemorate a sacred place, such as a site where an important event took place in the Buddha's life. The stupa played an important role in Buddhist beliefs, for it became the symbol of nirvana, or final enlightenment, the goal of Buddhism.

All such monuments follow a similar plan (fig. 3-84). They are solid mounds of rubble and brick, faced with stone; the upper parts are covered with white stucco that was originally decorated and partly gilded. The stupa is surmounted by a three- (or more) part "umbrella" symbolizing the three most basic aspects of Buddhism—the Buddha himself, the Buddha's law, and the monastic community. The rail around the umbrella shaft is thought to reflect the ancient concept of marking off the precinct around a sacred tree. The symbolic meaning of the stupa and its various elements are complex and multifaceted. The mound can refer to the World Mountain and also to the universe, while the umbrella shaft is sometimes interpreted as the axis of the universe.

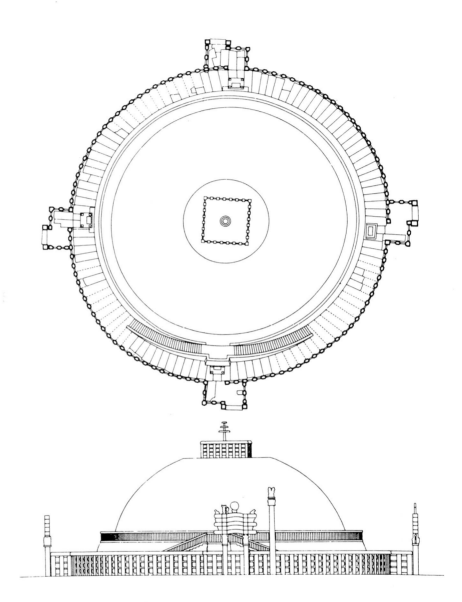

3-84. Plan and elevation of the Great Stupa

On the base around the hemispherical dome is a narrow path along which processions move. A second path is at ground level, where pilgrims can circumambulate clockwise, symbolic of walking the Path of Life around the World Mountain, following an ancient Indian rite of retracing the path of the sun while making offerings and ritual performances. The path is

enclosed within a tall stone railing, which isolates the sanctuary from the outside world. Access to it is gained through four monumental gateways (torana) 32 feet high, oriented to the cardinal directions. The uprights and crossbars are lavishly carved with stories from the life of the Buddha; with jataka tales, edifying legends in which the Buddha is shown as compassionate and

ANCIENT ART: BUDDHIST IN INDIA **111**

3-85. *Yakshi*, from the East Torana, Great Stupa. c. 10–30 CE

wise in previous lives; and with guardian figures called yakshas and yakshis (fig. 3-85), ancient gods and goddesses of fertility. These lively sculptures are a dramatic contrast to the massive character of the stupa and railing.

It is significant that the Buddha himself is not represented in figural form—a kind of symbolism called **aniconic**, or without image. His presence is suggested by symbols such as a wheel, footprints, a throne, or the Boh tree (pipal) where he received enlightenment (fig. 3-86), all important emblems of his life. At that time, it was thought to be impossible to represent the Buddha in human form because he had already passed into nirvana, an otherworldly state of being.

A richly decorated structure such as the Great Stupa took decades to complete. In its former splendor, it had smooth white or gaily colored plaster exteriors and sculpted decoration highlighted with polychrome painting. The sculpture depicted stories similar to folk tales that brought the life of the Buddha to visitors in familiar terms. The incorporation of the yakshas and yakshis was also a way to relate the monument to the people, for these sensuous deities had been worshiped as bearers of human and natural fertility long before Buddhism. The complicated but rhythmic pose of the voluptuous yakshi (see fig. 3-85) reveals the early importance of dance in Indian worship; it also refers to the legend that a yakshi could, with one touch of her heel, instantly bring a tree into full fruition.

The massive domes of stupas frequently enclose a system of concentric or radial supporting walls arranged by symbolic, rather than technical, considerations. They face the points of the compass and represent rays leading out from the center, a plan in the form of a **mandala**, or diagram of the cosmos (see fig. 5-3). This pattern is in no way perceptible from the exterior but was of crucial importance for the sacred substance of the monument. The profound importance of the mandala in Buddhist belief and practice is attested by its survival into the present day.

These early constructions celebrate the life of the historic Buddha (Sanskrit for "the Enlightened One"), a man called Siddhartha Gautama. Born about 563 BCE of a noble family living in the foothills of the Himalayas, he gave up his princely life to seek out the cause of the suffering that he discovered all around him. India of the sixth century BCE was undergoing rapid and violent political and social change. Like many of his contemporaries, Prince Gautama renounced his former life and, as an ascetic, contemplated and discussed the sorrows of the world with other learned recluses on the outskirts of villages. At age thirty-five, he sat under a large pipal tree in the town of Gaya and resolved not to leave his seat until the riddle of suffering was solved.

After hosts of temptations, he sank deeper and deeper into meditation, and at dawn on the forty-ninth day he knew the truth, the secret of suffering and how to overcome it—by releasing the mortal soul from the cycle of rebirth. He had reached nirvana. He remained seated under the Tree of Wisdom (the Boh tree), meditating on the truths he had found. He then journeyed to Deer Park (modern Sarnath) and preached his first sermon—in Buddhist phraseology, he "set the Wheel of the Law in motion." Soon he had a band of sixty ascetics who became his followers as he preached the Buddhist dharma (doctrine). For eight months of each year they wandered from place to place, but in the rainy

3-86. *Boh Tree*, detail on the south pillar of the East Torana, Great Stupa. c. 10–30 CE

season they stopped to live in huts at one of the parks given by wealthy lay followers. These were the first of the great Buddhist monasteries of later times.

The Buddha's quest was a personal one. He sought nirvana, a refined stage of enlightenment accepted by adherents of various religions of the time. Nirvana marked an end to the cycle of rebirth and was thought to be a state of enduring permanent bliss called the Supreme Truth or Reality. Buddhist dharma claims that there is no existence without suffering, that the cause of suffering is egocentric desire, and that the elimination of desire will end suffering.

After the Buddha's death at age eighty, in about 483 BCE, the religion grew and changed along with the political institutions of India. The third leader of the first great Indian empire, called the Mauryan dynasty

(322–183 BCE), was Asoka (ruled c. 273–232 BCE). He expanded Mauryan political influence over much of the Indian subcontinent. According to tradition, Asoka was moved to remorse and pity by the horrors of war and came to the conclusion that true power was realized through religion, not force. He became an active patron of Buddhism and supported the communities of monks. The political might of the Mauryans, as well as their patronage, brought the full institutionalization of Buddhism. A set of Buddhist religious offices (services) was created; numbers of monks occupied monasteries that acquired property; the canon of Buddhist texts was expanded, diversified, and refined. Asoka himself is said to have erected 84,000 stupas over the relics of the Buddha throughout the empire. Thus, the search for personal enlightenment by one man, the Bud-

dha, became an institution involving millions of people supported by one of the great ancient empires.

Stupas became the center of life in the monasteries, which included buildings used as lecture halls, kitchens, and hostels. Their locations and the lifeways of the monks were guided by recollections of the Buddha's life. These **chaityas** (sacred locations) were to a remarkable degree coincident with trade routes of the day, as the initial spread of religion under the state patronage of Asoka was linked to commerce. Because Buddhists enjoyed the protection of the state, traders associating with them came under the same protective umbrella. Monasteries were safe havens that received the financial support of their visitors. The symbiosis between monks and traders ultimately took this religion out of India and into China, Japan, and Southeast Asia.

THE ART OF THE ROMAN REPUBLIC

3-87. *Husband and Wife*, grave relief from the Via Statilia, Rome. 1st century BCE. Marble, height 6'. Capitoline Museum, Rome. Probably commissioned by the couple themselves or their family

This grave marker (fig. 3-87) exhibits the Roman continuation of the old Mediterranean practice of marking graves with images of the deceased, but the stern man and his dignified wife communicate the austere values and virtues of the Romans of the Republican period (c. 510–31 BCE), as they were defined by ancient writers: he seems sober and determined, demanding and uncompromising, while his wife appears dutiful and obedient, consistent with the prescribed role of women during the Republic. The

Romans of the early Republic were self-disciplined, devout, conservative, and supporters of traditional values. They admired military valor and prized family, heritage, and the state. They respected law and legal obligations. Their language, Latin, is remarkable for its lucid order and rigid rules.

The Romans of the Republican period showed little interest in art, and even later, during the Roman Empire, Romans seldom indulged in the philosophical debates about the nature of art that had been so

important for the Greeks. But a Roman strength that persisted into the Empire was their ability to absorb whatever was useful or good from other traditions. In art, the Romans owed a rich debt to the Etruscans and the Greeks. Only in a few areas did the Romans of the Republic make significant new contributions—most notably in architecture and engineering, especially in the use of concrete, the arch, and the vault (see pages 132–33).

The Romans' interest in and devotion to the family explains their interest in individual portraiture. It was traditional for patrician families to preserve wax, terra-cotta, or marble portrait heads of their male ancestors. These portraits were kept in "the most conspicuous position in the house, enclosed in a wooden shrine" and "when any distinguished member of the family dies they take [the busts] to the funeral," according to the first-century BCE historian Polybius. Roman portraits often emphasize the peculiarities of an individual (moles, wrinkles, large ears) in order to capture the uniqueness of the specific person. This respect for the individual—although usually limited, as

3-88. Temple of Portunus (formerly called Temple of Fortuna Virilis), Rome. Late 2nd century BCE

in most early cultures, to the male—can be related to Roman republicanism, for a system of government that encourages individual responsibility seems to lead to the development of naturalistic portraiture in art (for later examples, see seventeenth-century Holland, page 368, and early America, page 406).

HISTORY

In the eighth century BCE, the Romans had been only one of several groups of people living in villages along the Tiber River. But by the third century BCE, they governed a state that encompassed the Italian peninsula. In the subsequent two centuries they defeated Carthage in North Africa and annexed Greece, Spain, Asia Minor, and the south of France. The government developed as a republic, with rule by two consuls, a hierarchy of public officials, and a senate.

The early Romans had no defined policy of expansion, but their interest in commerce led them into contact with many of their neighbors. Eventually, the Romans were forced to protect their borders and guarantee their peace after attacks from the outside. In about 390 BCE, the Gauls sacked Rome, and later Carthage led Rome into war. The rapid growth of the city of Rome, which by 250 BCE had almost 100,000 residents, required an increasingly large territory to support it. The Romans were generally benevolent conquerors who absorbed rather than suppressed, offering citizenship to the conquered and acknowledging the significance of local traditions. Personal ambitions and the difficulties of governing vast territories and the huge city of Rome, however, led to administrative difficulties and eventually to civil wars and attempts by military figures to seize control. The Republic came to an end in 31 BCE, when Octavian, who later became the

3-89. Isometric projection with plan and longitudinal section of the House of Pansa, Pompeii, Italy. 2nd century BCE. There are shops on each side of the entrance. The women who died in this house during the Vesuvius disaster were wearing gold ear pendants, necklaces, and rings. When the eruption began, a sculpture of Bacchus was placed for safety in a copper kettle in the garden. Commissioned by the Samnites

garden

street

peristyle with pool

shops

atrium with pool

3-90. Atrium, House of Menander, Pompeii. c. 70 CE. The atrium is a feature well suited to the Mediterranean climate. The outer walls of the house were usually windowless, and the atrium allowed light and fresh air to enter, as well as rainwater, which was gathered in a central pool to flow into a cistern. The atrium functioned as a sitting room and usually contained the shrine for the household gods; on each side were small chambers for dining and sleeping. House built by Quintus Poppaeius, a relative of Poppeia, the wife of the Roman emperor Nero

emperor Augustus (see fig. 3-92), assumed power, and the Empire lasted from 31 BCE to about 400 CE.

REPUBLICAN ARCHITECTURAL DEVELOPMENTS

The Temple of Portunus in Rome (fig. 3-88) demonstrates the derivative nature of Republican religious architecture. The high podium, restriction of steps to the front, and deep porch are related to temples created by the Etruscans, while the suggestion of a peripteral colonnade is Greek. Note, however, that only the porch columns are freestanding; those of the sides and back are merely sculpted portions of the wall structure—engaged or half columns. The temple is, therefore, not peripteral but **pseudo-peripteral**. This design emphasizes the enclosed interior space, in contrast to the importance of the exterior in the Greek tradition. The columns provide a graceful rhythm and announce that this structure is a temple, but the pseudo-peripteral design reveals the Romans' lack of interest in the aesthetic unity and logic characteristic of their Greek source.

Architectural innovation during the Roman Republic appeared primarily in great public buildings and engineering projects. The Roman Forum (see figs. 3-95, 3-120) well illustrates several of these characteristics. Here, the arch and vault were combined with the new use of concrete (see pages 132–33) to make possible the relatively rapid construction of large, impressive complexes. Also, the **forum** design is a clear sequence of public and sacred spaces along an axis through which visitors moved. This molding of space and control of the observer's experience, as well as much more extensive development of Republican techniques and materials, would be important features of Roman imperial architecture.

THE ROMAN HOUSE AND VILLA

Most of our knowledge of Roman life is the result of materials preserved by the eruption of the volcano Vesuvius in 79 CE. Volcanic ash buried the seaside town of Pompeii, preserving shops, temples, houses, drainage and sewage systems, furnishings, food, and even the anguished positions of a number of victims. Although this event occurred during the period of the Roman Empire, the houses that were preserved there were little changed from their Republican antecedents. A letter by Pliny the Younger described the disaster:

> The buildings were now shaking with violent shocks. . . . Outside . . . there was the danger of falling pumice-stones. . . . As a protection against falling objects [the people] put pillows on their heads . . . they were still in darkness, blacker and denser than any ordinary night. . . . We also saw the sea sucked away and apparently forced back by the earthquake . . . a fearful black cloud was rent by forked and quivering bursts of flame, and parted to reveal great tongues of fire, like flashes of lightning magnified in size. . . . People bewailed their own fate or that of their relatives, and there were some who prayed for death in their terror of dying. Many besought the aid of the gods, but still more imagined there were no gods left, and that the universe was plunged into eternal darkness for evermore.

The houses and villas of middle- and upper-class Romans followed a regular plan, with rooms arranged along a longitudinal axis from entrance to garden (fig. 3-89). The plan is dominated by the **atrium**, an open courtyard (fig. 3-90). Rooms were decorated with richly patterned ceilings and wall paintings (fig. 3-91), but actual furnishings were minimal. Couches, used for resting, sleeping, studying, and dining while reclining in the Greek fashion, were usually the most elaborate pieces of furniture. Virtually all houses in Pompeii had water pipes with taps, as well as pipes leading to a sewer or trench.

The main rooms had mosaic floors, and the decoratively patterned floors of marble and stone in the richest homes copied famous Hellenistic paintings or patterns. One reproduction of a Hellenistic design featured the *Unswept Floor* (see fig. 3-53), a realistic depiction of the debris one might find underfoot after a banquet, complete with shadows to make it more realistic—pity the poor servant who had to clean such a design after a night of Roman revelry. Another mosaic was a copy of a famous Hellenistic painting, the *Battle of Alexander the* *Great and King Darius of Persia* (see fig. 3-80). Vestibule mosaics feature images of a chained dog and the words "Beware of the Dog" or a human skeleton and "Enjoy life while you have it."

The variation in design of the wall paintings at Pompeii reveals how fashions of decorating changed. Executed in a durable **fresco secco** technique (see page 128), these works were intended to transform the rooms into an elegant ambience for living and entertaining. The paintings are illusionistic. The simplest appear to be walls paneled in fine marbles, but in some the wall is "painted away" by an image that suggests continuous space. The subjects include realistic or fantastic views of architecture, landscapes, still lifes, portraits, and themes from Greek and Roman mythology and theater. The still lifes usually represent food—game, fruit, eggs—and may refer to the Roman custom of giving such food as gifts (see fig. 3-107).

3-91. Frescoed room from the House of the Vettii, Pompeii. 63–79 CE. Commissioned by the Vettius brothers, Conviva and Restitutus

THE ART OF THE ROMAN EMPIRE

3-92. *Emperor Augustus.* 15 CE. Marble, with traces of paint and perhaps also gilding, height 7'. Vatican Museums, Rome. This work, discovered at the villa of Augustus's wife, Livia, at Prima Porta (see fig. 3-105), 9 miles south of Rome, is sometimes known as the *Augustus Prima Porta*. The back is not complete, so the statue must have been intended for a niche. It may have been a cult statue, for after his death Livia was made the priestess in charge of the cult of the deified Augustus. Fragments of paint, such as reddish circles for the irises of the eyes, reveal that details were once painted. Perhaps commissioned by Augustus's wife, Livia

matic coup. These triumphs were also celebrated in poetry by the first-century BCE Roman poet Horace:

> Your age, Augustus, permitted the fields to bear rich harvests once more, and returned to the skies the battle standards, wrenched from the proud barbarians. (Horace, *Carmina*, IV, 15, 4–7)

The sculpture probably dates after Augustus's death, for it represents the emperor without boots, suggesting that he has been deified. The cupid (male baby angel) and dolphin by his right leg help support the figure and, as attributes of Venus, refer to Augustus's divine lineage as a descendant of Aeneas, son of Venus. The facial features identify the figure as Augustus, but they also represent an ideal, for Augustus was always shown in his early maturity, as here, although he was seventy-six when he died. In pose, the model was the Greek *Spear Carrier* (see fig. 3-67), which the Romans thought was a representation of another Trojan War hero, Achilles; a complimentary comparison between Augustus and Achilles was almost certainly intended. This sculpture, then, is an idealized portrait of a specific emperor; although it is based on classical Greek prototypes, its iconography and scale are specifically Roman, for they exalt the emperor and the Empire.

HISTORY

In 31 BCE, Octavian, grand-nephew and adopted son of Julius Caesar, became the sole ruler of Rome and all its territories; in 27 BCE, the Roman Senate named him *Augustus* ("noble, honored, consecrated one"), and after his death they declared him a god. Brilliant and resourceful, Augustus—who wrote that he "found Rome a city of brick and left it a city

> Remember thou, O Roman, to rule the nations with thy sway— these shall be thine arts—to crown peace with law, to spare the humbled, and to tame the proud in war. (Virgil, *Aeneid*, VI, 851–53)

The emperor Augustus, who commands our attention with his gesture in this over-lifesize statue (fig. 3-92), claimed descent from Aeneas, whose deeds are recounted in Virgil's epic poem *Aeneid*. Aeneas

was the legendary founder of the city of Rome, and Augustus was the founder of the Roman Empire, which lasted from 31 BCE to about 400 CE. Both statue and poem were intended to legitimize Augustus's rule and assert his imperial authority. Augustus wears parade armor decorated with reliefs of the Earth Mother with a cornucopia—symbolic of abundance—and of a Parthian, a Roman enemy, surrendering a battle standard in the presence of divinities, which refers to a major diplo-

3-93. Reconstruction of the Altar of Peace (Ara Pacis), Rome. 13–9 BCE. Marble, approx. 34'5" x 38' x 23'. Commissioned by the Roman Senate to mark Augustus's victorious return from Gaul and Spain in 13 BCE

of marble"—became the first emperor and ruled the Empire longer than any who followed him. He continued the expansion of the Roman state, as did his successors, and by the death of Trajan in 117 CE, Rome's population was about 750,000 and the Mediterranean had become a "Roman lake." The difficulties of governing this enormous area and its diverse population made the Romans experts at efficiency and organization. They had little time for or interest in the philosophical speculations that had formed Greek art and culture. Their most significant contributions are in world government and order, encompassing such diverse issues as legal codes and city planning.

The Romans had a strong sense of their historical importance and their contributions to world history: Julius Caesar wrote an account of the Gallic Wars; the emperor Claudius wrote two historical works now lost; and Augustus made a list of his accomplishments known as the *Res Gestae*. Roman attitudes toward history and art are expressed in the Altar of Peace, or Ara Pacis (fig. 3-93), in Rome. This monument commemorated the *Pax Romana* ("Roman Peace"), which had been declared by the Roman Senate in 13 BCE to express and celebrate the peace brought by Augustus to Italy and to the Roman state. Although they were aware of the significance of the *Pax Romana*, they could not know that never again would peace prevail for so many years over so vast an area. The Senate's declaration and the richly decorated altar were intended to bring recognition to this historic fact and to establish it as a Roman accomplishment and ideal. Augustus, accompanied by his family and friends, appears in the procession representing the altar's dedication. Although the stylistic sources for the reliefs lie in such Greek models as the Parthenon frieze (see fig. 3-75), Greek idealism is ignored in favor of documenting a specific historic moment and distinctive individuals. The presence of Augustus and other members of the imperial family at this sacrifice reveals piety and concord; the more important figures are in higher relief for emphasis and focus. Even the decorative motifs glorify the Empire and allude to its peace-giving role, for the garlands below refer to the abundance made possible by peace.

THE CITY OF ROME

Rome, which at its largest had a population of nearly a million, was in many ways similar to a modern city. It had impressive public spaces with state buildings and religious structures, as well as shopping areas, apartment buildings of five or six stories, and rooming houses. Most of the population lived in rental housing; a fourth-century CE document lists 46,602 apartment and rooming houses in the city and only 1,797 private homes. The apartment houses at Ostia (fig. 3-94), the port of Rome, were three or four stories high with an inner garden court and balconies, similar to late-twentieth-century apartment blocks.

The emperors kept the urban populace happy by providing food, facilities, and entertainment. Elaborate programs of building in the imperial forums (fig. 3-95) impressed the public with the power and magnificence of a specific emperor and of the state. Theaters and **amphi-**

3-94. Apartment house, Ostia. 2nd century CE

3-95. Reconstruction model of the Roman and Imperial Forums in Rome. Early 4th century CE. Museum of Roman Civilization, Rome. See figure 3-120 for plan. Originally commissioned by the Republican government of Rome; expanded by various Roman emperors

3-96. *Marcus Aurelius.* 161–80 CE. Bronze, over-lifesize. Now in the Capitoline Museum, Rome. Marcus Aurelius, who wrote the *Meditations*, has the longish hair and full beard that characterized the "poetic" emperor. The "military" emperor was clean-shaven and had short hair. The bronze statue is an impressive technical accomplishment, but it survived being melted down only because during the Middle Ages it was thought to represent Constantine, the fourth-century emperor who accepted Christianity. Commissioned by Marcus Aurelius

theaters provided places of entertainment for tens of thousands, and the public baths (see figs. 3-118, 3-119) offered facilities for communal bathing and exercise, as well as for social and intellectual gatherings.

ROMAN IMPERIAL ART

The size and diversity of the peoples within the Roman Empire meant that Roman imperial art encompassed a variety of types and styles, especially as local traditions were incorporated into works of art. Here we have chosen to limit our discussion almost exclusively to works of art created within the city of Rome and for its inhabitants. The majority of the artists employed by the Romans were of Greek ancestry. Greek artists were imported as early as 500 BCE, during the Republic, and works of art were also ordered from artists active in Greece. The demand for Greek works, new and old, accelerated after the Romans sacked Corinth in 146 BCE and brought a number of impressive Greek works to Italy.

Among the most characteristic monuments of Roman art are those that honor the Empire and emperor. They are often built on an enormous scale to communicate the size, power, and authority of the Empire and the specific ruler. Huge buildings and interrelated groups of buildings that express the grandiose aspirations of the Empire were made possible by the new techniques of construction that had been developed during the Roman Republic. The Empire's use of the arch, the vault, and concrete—devices that made feasible not only the large and magnificent monuments of ancient Rome, but also the powerful molding of space so important in Roman architecture—is among the most significant of all Roman accomplishments (see pages 132–33).

The creation of works of art honoring and commemorating an

3-97. Arch of Titus, Rome. 81 CE. Marble over concrete core. Commissioned by Titus

emperor's deeds and victories was a constant challenge to artists in the service of the Empire. One type of monument honoring emperors and generals was the equestrian monument, but the only surviving example is the *Marcus Aurelius* (fig. 3-96). This figure has the same commanding gesture as the *Augustus* (see fig. 3-92), but here his power is emphasized by his control over his lively and rather nervous horse. Originally, a figure of a defeated enemy was probably shown crouching under the horse's upraised hoof.

Another commemorative monument is the triumphal arch. Although its origins can be traced to the Republican period, the first to be called *arcus triumphalis* were the large and permanent triumphal arches erected during the reign of Augustus. Eventually there were more than fifty in Rome. The Arch of Titus (figs. 3-97, 3-98) memorializes Titus's suppression of a Jewish revolt and his capture of Jerusalem in 70–71 CE. The arch itself is simple

3-98. *Spoils of the Temple at Jerusalem Exhibited in Rome*, relief from the Arch of Titus (see fig. 3-97). Marble, height 6'7". Commissioned by Titus

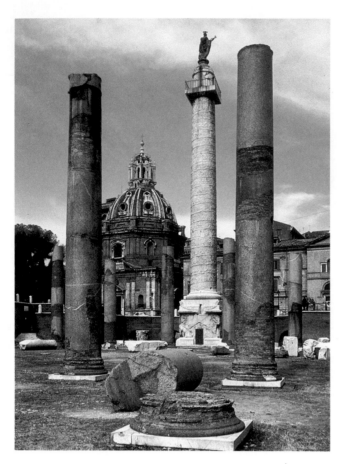

3-99. Column of Trajan, Rome. 113 CE. Marble, height originally 128'; length of frieze approx. 625'. Commissioned by Trajan as part of the Forum of Trajan

and handsome, with a compact and tightly knit composition of horizontal and vertical members enframing the tunnel vault. The simple basic form, an arch enclosed within a rectangle, is enlivened by architectural details, and originally the whole was surmounted by a huge bronze quadriga with the emperor. The reliefs under the arch represent, on one side, the triumph of Titus, who is shown riding in a chariot led by a personification of the goddess Roma. On the other side is the parading of the treasures of the Temple in Jerusalem—including the seven-branched menorah, the ceremonial candleholder—through the streets of Rome, where the procession is about to pass under a triumphal arch (see fig. 3-98). The deified Titus, who died shortly before the monument was completed, is shown in the center of the vault, being carried to

heaven on the back of an eagle.

Commemorating the emperor Trajan's early-second-century victories over the Dacians in eastern Europe is a huge freestanding column (fig. 3-99), as tall as a twelve-story building. It was originally topped with a monumental gilded bronze statue of the emperor, which has been replaced with a statue of Saint Peter. The column itself has a spiraling relief, carved in a lively and direct style, that tells in detail the episodes of Trajan's campaigns and victories. Although every detail of every scene is not visible to the viewer, the scale of the column and the length of the relief convey the extent and complexity of Trajan's exploits. Some of the upper scenes could have been read by people on the balconies of the courtyard of Trajan's library, which surrounded the column (see fig. 3-120). The

column and library were only part of Trajan's contributions to the imperial forums, which he, like other emperors, embellished as a way of asserting his presence and impressing the people with his magnificence.

TECHNOLOGY, ORGANIZATION, AND ENGINEERING

To run a large empire, to communicate and move supplies, and to feed the masses gathered in growing cities demanded important new developments in technology and organization. Innovations such as the arch, the vault, and concrete helped solve engineering and construction problems on a large scale; they ultimately affected the production and style of works of art. The celebrated Roman roads, bridges, and aqueducts were engineered to solve the particular problems of a specific area or terrain, and some are still in use today.

The Roman interest in order, efficiency, and organization is revealed by the Roman town plan (fig. 3-100), which was developed following Egyptian, Greek, and Hellenistic prototypes and which spread throughout the Roman world, from London to North Africa. Streets are laid out in a grid pattern within fortified walls, and the center of the town is marked by the intersection of the two main thoroughfares—the *cardo*, running north-south, and the *decumanus*, running east-west. Nearby is the forum—the social, political, and commercial heart of the city. The intersecting *cardo* and *decumanus* divide the city into quarters, each of which is further subdivided by streets meeting at right angles; only irregular or large buildings such as theaters or public baths disrupted this regular plan. The Roman solution to urban design is evident in major cities of the Western world, where avenues cross streets in grid patterns.

3-100. Plan of Thamugadis (Timgad), Algeria. Although most Roman town plans were laid out with main axes that were north-south and east-west, Thamugadis, founded c. 100 CE under the emperor Trajan, is slightly off-axis.

ROMAN RELIGION AND THE MYSTERY RELIGIONS

The more important official Roman deities were derived from the gods and goddesses of the Greeks, but their names were changed: Zeus became Jupiter, Aphrodite became Venus, and Dionysos became Bacchus, for example. But the number of Roman deities gradually expanded, for when the Romans conquered and annexed a new area, the local deities were usually added to the Roman hierarchy of gods. At the Pantheon in Rome (see fig. 3-117), there was even an altar dedicated to those gods whom the Romans had not yet discovered.

During the later Empire, the religious life of many Romans was dominated by participation in mystery religions, cults that centered on a savior who promised some kind of life after death. Their widespread popularity and the ultimate acceptance of Christianity as the official Roman religion have been seen as a reaction to the materialism and spir-

itual emptiness of ancient Roman life. Other mystery religions centered around the worship of Isis, an Egyptian goddess whose temple at Pompeii included a shrine with a reservoir of holy water from the Nile, and Cybele, the Great Mother (*Magna Mater*). An ancient Roman temple to Mithras, a militant god-hero who represented the victorious forces of light over darkness, was discovered in the remains of ancient Roman London during reconstruction after the bombings of World War II. Mithraism, an especially important late Roman cult, was widespread throughout the Empire as a result of its popularity with members of the army.

THE END OF ROME'S EMPIRE

Political, religious, and spiritual turmoil and threats from Northern barbarians characterize the later Empire. Diocletian (ruled 284–305) consolidated imperial rule, but he also banned and persecuted the Christians. Constantine lifted the ban on Christianity in 313 and later may have converted to the religion himself. But Rome lost much of its importance when Constantine shifted the imperial capital to Constantinople, which he had founded at a site on the Bosphorus named Byzantium (present-day Istanbul). In 395, at the time of the death of the emperor Theodosius I, the Empire was divided in half. But while the Eastern Empire centered around Constantinople enjoyed political stability, the Western Empire was beset with uprising from Germanic peoples, including the Visigoths, who captured and sacked Rome in 410.

LATE ROMAN SCULPTURE

Constantine's sculpted head (fig. 3-101) has a dramatic and intimidating impact, not just because of its enormous size, but also as a

result of the powerfully abstracted facial features. Portraiture has moved away from the highly realistic busts of Republican and early imperial Roman art. Although Constantine's head retains certain specific physical traits, such as the thick, muscular neck and the Roman nose known from his other portraits, these realistic features are joined with abstract patterns in the treatment of the hair over the forehead and the huge, staring eyes. The treatment of the eyes suggests Constantine's authoritarian power, his deified presence, and his ability to penetrate the world of the divine. There are indications from contemporary literary sources that the late Roman emperors, who were viewed as gods while they were living, were adorned like statues of gods and behaved in a manner that encouraged belief in their deified status.

It is difficult to determine why the new abstracted patterning occurs during the late Roman Empire, a period sometimes referred to as late antiquity. This innovation cannot be dismissed as a lack of technical ability on the part of the artist, for it seems to be used intentionally to promote such abstract concepts as imperial authority or divine power.

New spiritual attitudes are evident in late antiquity with the mystery cults and early Christianity. The most eloquent spokesperson for these values was Plotinus, a third-century philosopher. One of his pupils, Porphyry, wrote a biography of Plotinus in which he noted the difficulty of artists who wanted to create a portrait of the philosopher:

Plotinus . . . gave the impression of being ashamed that he dwelt in a body [and] he deemed it so degrading to submit himself to being a subject for a painter or sculptor that he said to Amelius, who asked him to permit his portrait to be made: "It is not sufficient just to carry around

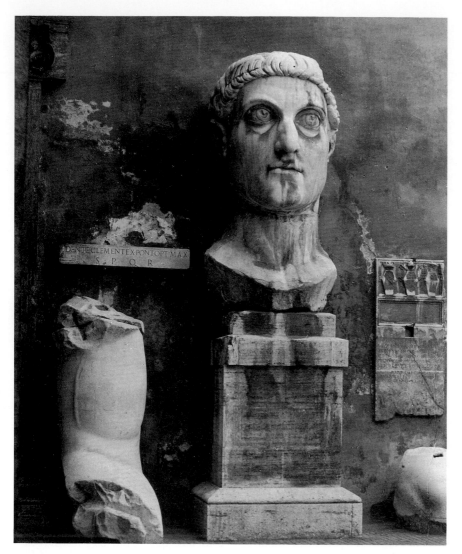

3-101. *Constantine*, from the Basilica of Maxentius and Constantine, Rome. Early 4th century CE. Marble, height of head 8'6". Palazzo dei Conservatori, Rome. These arm and head fragments are part of a colossal statue, originally about 30 feet tall, of the enthroned emperor Constantine initially placed in the apse of the basilica (see fig. 3-112). The head and limbs were carved from marble; the torso was fashioned of a brick core covered with wood and overlaid with bronze. The head once had a metal diadem. Commissioned by Constantine

that image which nature has imposed on us, without making concessions to it by deciding to leave behind a more lasting image of the image, as if it were one of those things which is particularly worth seeing."

The antiphysical attitude of Plotinus is in sharp contrast to the historical and naturalistic values that had been so prized in Roman figurative art. As in the colossal head of Constantine, inner spiritual life is deemed more significant than an exact portrait representation. We shall see in our examination of subsequent transformations that such an approach is consistent with the development of Early Christian art.

THE ROMAN ARTIST

In ancient Greece, artists had been famous and respected, but during both the Republic and the Empire, artists in the service of the Roman state became anonymous laborers once again. Few artists are known by name; not a single painting bears a signature, and only a few are documented as the work of a particular artist. In most cases, the large and elaborate programs of Roman art seem to have been accomplished by groups of artists working together, probably in well-organized workshops, and submerging their individuality in the concept of a unified project.

Most of the few names of artists that are recorded are Greek, and these are names of sculptors. Even during the Republic, it was recognized that Greek sculptors represented a long-standing tradition of excellence. The famous *Laocoön and His Sons* (fig. 3-102), once thought to be a work of the Greek Hellenistic period imported to Rome, is now believed to be a Roman work created by Greek sculptors working in a revival of the Hellenistic style for a Roman patron.

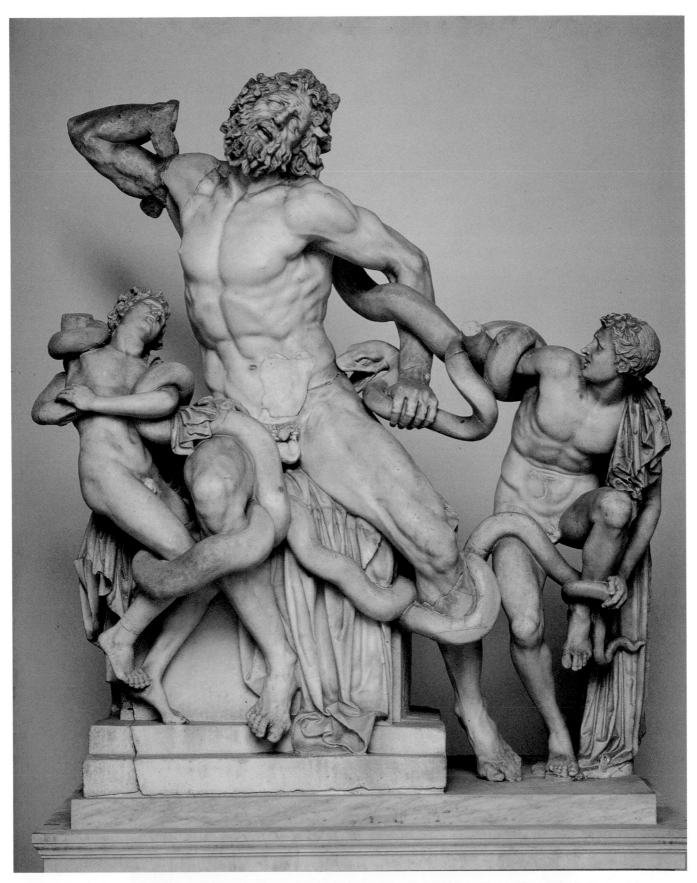

3-102. Hagesandros, Athenodoros, and Polydoros. *Laocoön and His Sons*. Early 1st century BCE(?). Marble, height 8'. Vatican Museums, Rome. This sculptural group was carved by three Greek sculptors from the island of Rhodes.

ROMAN FRESCOES AND ILLUSIONISM

3-103. *Bacchic Mysteries*, painting in the Villa of the Mysteries, Pompeii, Italy. c. 30 BCE. Fresco, room approx. 29 x 19'; height of figures approx. 5'. Whether these paintings, which are superb in quality, are original Roman works or copies of a lost Hellenistic painting from Pergamon is still debated by experts.

3-104. *Bacchic Mysteries*, detail of painting in the corner of the room in the Villa of the Mysteries, with a flagellation scene. Whipping in this context may be a ritual meant to ensure fertility.

3-105. *Garden*, painting from the Villa of Livia, wife of the emperor Augustus, at Prima Porta, near Rome. Late 1st century BCE. Fresco, height of wall 10'. Museo delle Terme, Rome. The statue of Augustus in fig. 3-92 was also discovered at Livia's villa. Commissioned by Livia

This room of frescoes (fig. 3-103) representing Bacchic (or Dionysiac) mysteries is exceptional in quality and subject, as well as in scale, for nearly lifesize figures such as these are rare in Roman painting. In addition, these frescoes are one of the first examples of **mural painting**—painted wall decoration that is integrated with the physical space and architecture of its setting.

The secret rites depicted here have not yet been fully explained, but this painting reveals the importance of the cult of Bacchus, god of wine and fertility, in Roman life. It has been proposed that the sequence of scenes, which seems to read from left to right, represents either the initiation of a new member into the cult or the transitions in the life of a young woman when she marries and becomes a Roman matron.

The central figures, badly damaged, represent the enthroned Ariadne, with Bacchus reclining on her chest. The initiate, or bride (not visible here), enters on the far left. She is enthroned as a matron on the far right (not visible in this view). In the interim, she encounters various trials and experiences. Among the dramatic episodes is the imminent unveiling of a large phallus to the right of the central figures of Ariadne and Bacchus. The regular, architectural rhythm of the paneling behind the figures sets off their poses, while the strong red background adds an element of drama appropriate for the subject.

The most dramatic episodes are represented at the two corners, where the artist took advantage of the walls meeting at 90-degree angles to represent interacting figures. At one corner, a fierce half-man, half-beast woods deity known as a silenus, who may be reading the young woman's fortune in the residue left in a wine cup, looks back at her as she flees in terror. At the other corner, a winged figure in a spiraling movement flogs the initiate or bride, who reclines on the lap of another woman (fig. 3-104).

One of the most enchanting of all Roman fresco decorations is the illusionistic painting that covered the four walls of a room in the Villa of Livia at Prima Porta (fig. 3-105). It represents a garden with fruit trees, flowers, and songbirds set off by a

Fresco painting (*fresco* is Italian for "fresh"), which involves painting directly on a plaster wall, was used by the Egyptians, Greeks, Romans, and later civilizations as well. When properly executed, it is durable, and when it is subtly related to its particular architectural setting, as in the cycle at the Villa of the Mysteries at Pompeii, it can be both decorative and dramatic. Generally, fresco painters have to cover large expanses of wall, and they often work quickly; the sketchy and suggestive quality of most Roman and later frescoes creates a lively and vivacious effect. (For a discussion of the somewhat more complex fresco technique that developed in Italy during the later Middle Ages and the Renaissance, see page 261.)

The Roman fresco painter began by applying two or three layers of fine plaster to the wall surface to be decorated. The background was painted on the top layer of plaster—sometimes while it was still moist—and left to dry. Each plaster patch (fig. 3-106) would reveal one day's work. Figures, ornaments, and architecture were usually added later. The natural pigments, which were made from earth, minerals, and animal or vegetable sources, were mixed with limewater. Glue and wax were sometimes added to create a hard and shiny surface. Painting onto wet plaster is called **buon fresco** (*buon* is Italian for "good" or "true") and painting on the already hardened dry plaster is known as **fresco secco** (in Italian *secco* means "dry").

3-106. Diagram of fresco patches at the Villa of the Mysteries. An examination of the surface of the frescoes reveals that they were painted in patches that follow the outlines of the figures. In later Italian fresco technique, each of these patches would be known as a *giornata* (Italian for "day")

background of sky. The fresco has all the freshness of nature's colors: the rich greens of the garden; the varied shades of fruit, flowers, and plumage; and a wonderful blue sky. All are executed with a light touch of the brush, as if the wind were just beginning to stir this idyllic environment.

3-107. *Still Life with Eggs and Thrushes,* painting from the House (or Villa) of Julia Felix, Pompeii. Before 79 CE. Fresco, 35 x 48". National Museum, Naples. The house where this fresco was found during excavations in 1755–57 is the largest yet discovered at Pompeii. The fresco shown here is one of a sequence of still-life paintings of food. Commissioned by the original owner of the house

Livia's garden room is more delightful and seductive than a framed painting of a garden, for it creates the illusion that we are in a natural setting. Such illusionism also played a role in *Still Life with Eggs and Thrushes* (fig. 3-107), for in both works the artists want to fool us into believing, albeit momentarily, that we are looking out into a real garden or at a real dish of eggs. This type of **illusionism**, which is also known by the French phrase *trompe l'oeil* ("fool the eye"), is a pleasant bit of trickery. Such paintings are meant to amuse and delight us, as was recognized by the Roman author Philostratus the Younger, writing about 300 CE:

> To confront objects which do not exist as though they existed and . . . to believe that they do exist, is not this, since no harm can come of it, a suitable and irreproachable means of providing entertainment?

The illusionism of Roman painting is inherited from an earlier tradition that developed in Greece (see page 87). The sense of pleasure in experiencing illusionism is not unique to the Greeks and Romans, as is revealed by the popularity of trompe l'oeil in later societies and even today.

There are several criteria for a successful illusionistic or trompe l'oeil painting. The objects in the painting should be represented in their natural scale in a clearly structured space, as is the case with both Livia's *Garden* and the *Still Life*. In the *Garden*, the artist has carefully developed the depicted space in overlapping levels within the painted illusion. **Cast shadows** define the placement of each object within the illusionistic space, as is especially evident in the *Still Life*, and the objects are naturalistically modeled with transitions from light to dark that indicate both the three-dimensionality of the objects and the source of the light (later, at the time of the Italian Renaissance, this treatment of shading will become known as **chiaroscuro**, from the Italian words for "light" and "dark"). Naturalistic lighting effects suggest the textures of the objects: note the different textures of the eggs and the metal vessels in the *Still Life*. Often, painters introduce an object in the immediate foreground that establishes the frontal plane of the illusionistic space; this form, known as a *repoussoir* (French, meaning "to push back"), can be noted in the low, open-work fence in the foreground of Livia's *Garden*.

The use of the *repoussoir* in the *Still Life* is especially interesting, for the illusionism is heightened by painting the bowl of eggs as if it extends *over* the frontal plane of the base—the *repoussoir*—to jut out into our space. To make the illusion convincing, the subject matter is usually everyday objects that need no explanation. The goals of such art are obvious, for the purpose, beyond Philostratus's "entertainment," is to impress us with the technical skill of the artist.

ROMAN ARCHITECTURE: THE FLAVIAN AMPHITHEATER

3-108. Flavian Amphitheater (Colosseum), Rome. Begun 72 CE; dedicated 80 CE; construction completed 96 CE. Approx. 615 x 510'. The building was damaged in later centuries, when much of the dressed stone of the outer surface was taken away to be used in the construction of other buildings. Commissioned by Vespasian; completed by his sons Domitian and Titus

3-109. Reconstruction model of the Flavian Amphitheater. Museum of Roman Civilization, Rome

Through the ages, the Flavian Amphitheater has conveyed the scale and strength of the Roman Empire (figs. 3-108, 3-109). Begun by Vespasian, an honored military leader and first emperor of the Flavian dynasty, it was built in part to reassure the Roman citizenry that the cruelty and self-indulgence of the reign of Nero, the last Julio-Claudian emperor, had ended; to establish a site for the amphitheater, Vespasian destroyed the lake and ostentatious pleasure gardens of Nero's house. The amphitheater was dedicated by Vespasian's son Titus with gladiatorial games that lasted more than a hundred days and featured a thousand gladiators and the deaths of thousands of animals.

43 CE	Roman London (Londinium) is founded
70 CE	Titus destroys Jerusalem
c. 70 CE	Writing of the Gospel of Saint Matthew
72 CE	**Flavian Amphitheater, Rome, begun**
73 CE	Fall of Masada

3-110. Isometric projection, with section, of the Flavian Amphitheater

The Roman **amphitheater**, or arena, was so well conceived that it has become the prototype for the modern sports stadium. The oval plan seems to have developed from the idea of facing and enclosing two theaters (*amphitheater* derives from the Greek *amphi*, "around," and *theatron*, "theater"). The Flavian Amphitheater, the largest amphitheater of the ancient Roman world, could hold about 50,000 spectators. They were sheltered from sun and rain by an awning rigged by sailors and supported by horizontal poles anchored in the top level. Eighty arched passageways on the ground floor provided entrance to a double row of **annular tunnel vaults** (fig. 3-110) encircling the arena, which led to interior stairs to vaulted passages on the upper levels. Such a plan permitted easy access and exit by the huge crowd of spectators.

Construction materials included travertine, brick, concrete, and tufa (see page 135). When finished, the exterior was faced with blocks of local travertine stone, held in place by iron clamps. The exterior design was unified by the repetition of arches flanked by half columns. The capitals on the three arched stories change from Doric below to Ionic and Corinthian for the second and third floors; Corinthian pilasters articulate the fourth level.

The amphitheater was an arena for displays of combat: gladiators battled both other gladiators and animals, while animals, especially lions and tigers brought from Africa, were pitted against one another. Women gladiators participated until 200 CE. The fight was usually to the death, a practice that may have evolved from an earlier Etruscan ritual in which a deceased relative was honored by a fight to the death between slaves. The floor of the Flavian Amphitheater was landscaped with trees and large rocks. Animals were raised by lifts from underground chambers, now visible after excavations. The amphitheater could be artificially flooded for contests mimicking naval battles. Although a few Romans denounced these games as bloody spectacles, most viewed them as displays of courage and virtue.

To the ruling families of Rome, the games also served a political purpose. At times, the unemployment rate reached approximately 15 percent, and, in addition to religious festivals, approximately 150 days each year were celebrated as holidays. Providing spectacular games became a political scheme to keep an often idle population entertained and content.

During the Early Christian era, some martyrdoms may have occurred here, but most public persecutions were held in the Roman circuses (arenas especially designed for chariot races). After Christianity was legally recognized by the emperor Constantine in 313 CE, growing numbers of Christians argued against the brutality of the games. Gladiatorial contests were banned in the early fifth century, but the animal games continued into the sixth century.

Until at least the mid-fourth century, a colossal (almost 100 feet tall) bronze statue of Nero as the sun god stood next to the Flavian Amphitheater. In the eighth century, a guidebook to Rome applied the term *Colosseum*, taken from the colossal sculpture, to the amphitheater itself, and ever since it has been known popularly by this name.

3-111. Reconstruction drawing of the interior of the Basilica Ulpia, Forum of Trajan, Rome (after Canina). c. 98–117 CE. For a plan of the Basilica Ulpia and its location within the Imperial Forums, see figure 3-120. Commissioned by the emperor Trajan as part of the Forum of Trajan

The dramatic contrast between the two ancient Roman interiors seen here is directly related to the materials and engineering used in their construction. The huge Basilica Ulpia from the Forum of Trajan (fig. 3-111) was based on post-and-lintel construction; the even larger and grander Basilica of Maxentius and Constantine (fig. 3-112), begun more than 200 years later, is built with rubble, brick, and concrete using a vaulting system based on the arch. When concrete hardens, it becomes monolithic, and today some of the huge vaults of the Basilica of Maxentius and Constantine are still standing in Rome. Not a column of the Basilica Ulpia is in place, in part because its great columns were reused in new construction during later centuries.

The arch was known to the peoples of the Middle East, as well as to the Egyptians, the Greeks, and the Etruscans, but it was the Romans, beginning in the Republic, who recognized its utility for engineering projects and its potential for spanning large spaces to create huge public buildings.

Post-and-lintel construction spans an opening with a flat beam of wood or stone, but an **arch** (fig. 3-113) is a means of construction by which an opening—usually semicircular—is spanned by a number of elements (stone or bricks) that are smaller than the opening itself; these elements are most often wedge-shaped blocks known as **voussoirs**. The central voussoir is called the **keystone**. All the vaults discussed below are based on the arch.

Arches and vaults are constructed upon a wooden support known as **centering**, which can be removed and reused. The point at which the arch or vault begins to curve inward and upward is known as the **springing**; the blocks immediately below the springing may jut out to support the centering (for an example of such blocks still in place, see fig. 3-114). The dynamics of the post-and-lintel system are relatively simple, with the **thrust** of the weight of the lintel pressing downward on the supporting posts. The dynamics of an arch or vault, however, create outward

3-112. Reconstruction view of the interior of the Basilica of Maxentius and Constantine, Rome, as planned by Maxentius. c. 306–313 CE. This basilica was begun by Maxentius and taken over by his rival Constantine, who completed it. The colossal head and arm of Constantine in fig. 3-101 were found here. Originally commissioned by Maxentius, completed by Constantine

diagonal thrusts that must be counteracted by **buttressing**, providing a masonry support that counteracts the thrust (as indicated by the arrows in fig. 3-113; for a later example, see fig. 4-84).

A **vault** is a structural system for a ceiling and/or roof that is based on the arch. The simplest type of vault is a **tunnel** (or **barrel**) **vault**, a deep, continuous arch that can cover a large area. Although light can enter at either end, the buttressing prohibits large openings along the sides. For a bridge and aqueduct such as the Pont du Gard (fig. 3-114), however, short tunnel vaults provide a solution. The lowest row is made up of tunnel vaults that are deep enough to support the road and protect the foundation against the force of the river during spring floods. An identically proportioned row of arches provides the extra height needed for the aqueduct at the top, which is raised on much smaller arches, four over the wider central arch and three over those to the sides. When tunnel vaults and

arches are placed in rows, each neutralizes the outward thrust of the adjacent member, but those on the ends must be well buttressed, a function here performed by the riverbanks to either side. The Pont du Gard is, however, more than a remarkable surviving example of Roman engineering skill; its simple design, handsome proportions, and rhythmic subtlety make it an impressive work of art. (For other structures that utilize the tunnel vault, see figs. 3-97, 4-60, 4-98, and 7-3.)

The three great square vaults that spanned the central area of the Basilica of Maxentius and Constantine (see fig. 3-112) were each formed by the intersection at right angles of two tunnel vaults; these are called **cross** (or **groin**) **vaults**. The outward thrusts of a cross vault are concentrated at the corners, and buttressing is only required at these points. When placed in a row, as here, or in groups, cross vaults can span vast areas and still permit large windows. (For other buildings with cross vaults, see figs. 3-108,

3-113. Diagrams of a round arch, an arch with centering, a tunnel (or barrel) vault, a cross (or groin) vault, a dome on pendentives, and a dome on squinches. The arrows suggest the general direction of the outward thrusts that must be buttressed, but only the drawing of the arch includes the buttressing that is essential in all vaulted systems.

keystone

voussoirs

springing

arch

keystone

centering

voussoirs

arch with centering

tunnel (or barrel) vault

cross (or groin) vault

bay

pendentive

dome

bay

dome on pendentives

dome

squinch

dome on squinches

3-109, 3-110; 3-118; 4-25, and 4-75) The vertical members that support a cross vault are known as **piers**. The area between each group of piers is known as a **bay**.

Series of vaults are usually arranged in straight lines, but sometimes the architectural needs demand another arrangement. When a tunnel vault is arranged in a curving or circular configuration, it is known as an **annular tunnel vault**; a series of cross vaults in a curving configuration are known as **annular cross vaults** (see figs. 4-61, 4-76, and 4-82).

A **dome** is a hemispherical structural system that can be understood as an arch rotated 180 degrees on its axis.

3-114. Pont du Gard (bridge and aqueduct), near Nîmes, France. Late 1st century BCE. Length 900'; height 162'. Commissioned by one of the Roman emperors, perhaps Augustus, to provide water to encourage the settlement of Nîmes

It must, therefore, be buttressed on all sides. The problem of light can be solved by opening the top of the dome with an **oculus**, as in the Pantheon (see fig. 3-117), by piercing the edges of the dome with small windows (see fig. 4-22) that are framed by heavy buttresses, or by raising the dome on arches or tunnel vaults (see fig. 6-27). To attain greater height, a dome may be raised upon a **drum**, a cylindrical or polygonal wall that provides continuous support (see figs. 5-37, 6-28).

When a dome is placed at the juncture of tunnel or barrel vaults, as occurs often in Christian church architecture (see figs. 5-35, 5-36), it must be located over a square base. The transition from the circular base of the dome to the piers or walls below has traditionally been handled in two ways. One method is the use of four **pendentives**; these are curving triangular segments of a larger dome that help create a visual and supportive transition from the four supporting piers to the dome above (see figs. 4-22, 4-68). The second system uses **squinches**: arches, lintels, or corbels that jut across the corners to create an octagonal base for the dome (fig. 4-43).

In many of the finest Roman buildings and engineering projects, such as the Pont du Gard, the material used was **dressed stone**: each piece was cut for its specific position and no mortar was employed. Repeated arches, such as those of the Pont du Gard, meant that a certain number of stones of regularized shape could be cut, and the structure could be fabricated at the site from stones cut and marked at the quarry to indicate their specific placement.

The most revolutionary Roman innovations in arches and vaulting occur in combination with the development of *opus caementicium*—cement (fast-drying, hardening volcanic sand) used to produce **concrete**. Roman construction methods were transformed when the Romans began to quarry large amounts of *pozzolana*, a silicate that functioned as a natural cement, near Naples in the second century BCE. The *pozzolana* was combined with broken pieces of stone and/or brick and water to provide a building material that hardened into a solid mass. Concrete was cheap, readily available, flexible, and fire-resistant. A lightweight stone was mixed with the cement for vaults, to lighten the weight and reduce the amount of buttressing needed. Cut stone and concrete were to remain the two most basic building materials of Western culture until the introduction of metal—iron and then steel—during the nineteenth century.

Other materials used by the Romans include brick, mud brick, and various stones that could be quarried nearby. Near Rome two kinds of stone were common—**travertine**, a kind of marble, and **tufa**, a soft volcanic rock that hardens on exposure to air. For the finished surface of their buildings, the Romans were not satisfied with concrete, which they usually covered with painted stucco, marble, or *opus incertum*, a facing of irregularly shaped small blocks of travertine or other stone.

The arch, vaults, and concrete were developed by the Romans precisely because they responded to the Roman demands for enormous scale, for efficiency and economy, and for flexibility. They helped to create and to convey the power and majesty of the Roman Empire.

ROMAN ARCHITECTURE: THE PANTHEON, ROME

3-115. Model/conjectural reconstruction of the Pantheon and its forecourt in ancient Roman times. Museum of Roman Civilization, Rome. The Roman Pantheon was dedicated to all the gods of the Roman religion; its name derives from the Greek *pan* ("every") and *theos* ("god"). An inscription on the exterior pediment ("Marcus Agrippa . . . built this") is misleading, for it refers to an earlier temple built on this site in 27 BCE. The gilding of the exterior dome further enhanced the references to the sun that are so important in this building. The current structure was erected by the emperor Hadrian, who, with characteristic modesty, copied the inscription from the earlier temple.

The Pantheon was regarded in ancient times as one of Rome's most important temples. It joins two disparate architectural designs, a Corinthian portico and a domed rotunda (figs. 3-115–3-117). Viewing the building from today's significantly raised street levels, the modern visitor is immediately aware of the cylindrical walls and dome, but they were not so visible in antiquity. A colonnaded forecourt and the portico, which was raised atop a flight of steps, masked these elements. The impressive entrance, with towering monolithic marble columns and huge bronze doors, gave no hint of the cylindrical walls of the rotunda; an ancient visitor who entered the structure must have been awestruck at the unexpected interior. The concrete dome, the largest built in Europe prior to the twentieth century, is perfectly hemispherical, and the distance from the floor to the top of the dome is the same as the diameter of the rotunda. The interior proportions, then, are governed by the geometrical purity of a sphere.

A series of transverse barrel

3-116. Cutaway of the Pantheon, showing the stepped buttressing that contains the outward thrust of the dome. 117–25 CE. Height of interior 144'. Commissioned by the emperor Hadrian

3-117. Interior of the Pantheon, as seen in an eighteenth-century painting of that name by Giovanni Panini in the National Gallery of Art, Washington, D.C.
Kress Collection

vaults hidden within the more than 20-foot-thick walls concentrates the weight of the dome on eight massive supports. The concrete of the dome must have been poured in sections over a huge mold supported by a centering structure so complex it would have made the interior look like a dense forest of hewn lumber. The weight of the dome is relieved by a series of **coffers** (the recessed panels—here square—that decorate the interior surface of a vault), which also add geometrical articulation to the hemisphere. The thickness of the dome decreases from 20 feet at the springing, where it is reinforced with stepped buttressing, to only 6 feet at the **oculus**, the circular opening 30 feet in diameter at the apex of the dome. The oculus allows adequate light, and the rain that enters is drained off by small, inconspicuous openings in the floor, which slopes slightly toward the center of the building.

In the Pantheon, Roman gods were represented by sculptures along the walls, while the dome assumed the symbolic significance of the heavens. Perhaps the most dramatic effect of the Pantheon is the harmony it demonstrates with the natural world. As the sun passes through the sky, a natural spotlight is cast into the rotunda, progressively illuminating the interior. To the Romans, the sun symbolized the eye of Jupiter, and its penetrating presence inside the temple seemed to make the deity manifest.

The Pantheon expresses the vision of the Roman Empire. It is a technological wonder of construction—like the vast network of highways, some still in use today, that were built to communicate with the corners of the Empire. The materials used in its construction and decoration, which were transported from lands as distant as Tunisia and Egypt, expressed the extent of Roman domination. The Pantheon relates the order of Roman rule to the Romans' reverence for a universal order.

ROMAN PUBLIC ARCHITECTURE

3-118. Central hall, Baths of Caracalla, Rome, as re-created in a rather imaginative nineteenth-century drawing by G. Abel Blonet. 211–17 CE. Commissioned by the emperor Caracalla

3-119. Plan of the Baths of Caracalla

passed to the pools in clay or lead pipes.

A visit to the bath usually began with physical exercise, followed by a stay in the steam room. In the calidarium, oil was used to cleanse the body. After cooling down in the tepidarium and frigidarium, a visitor received a massage, which completed the bath. The visitor might then take a walk in the gardens, study in the library, or attend lectures.

Lavish marble, stucco, and painted decoration embellished the interior surfaces. By the first century CE, the Roman political leader and author Seneca, recalling the austere values of the Roman Republic in his *Moral Epistles*, complained that new bath structures were too ornate:

The Roman taste for grand architecture found expression in two secular building types, the bath and the basilica. Visiting the bath, which was built at state expense and could be entered for a nominal fee, was a ritual of daily life for the Roman citizen, for the baths fostered both intellectual and social life. There were many baths throughout the Empire, but the most elaborate were those in Rome, built by the emperor Caracalla (ruled 211–17).

The Baths of Caracalla complex (figs. 3-118, 3-119) covered 50 acres and accommodated approximately 1,600 people at one time. Initially, mixed bathing was permitted, but later the sexes were segregated, with women and men bathing at different times. The plan was organized along a central axis; the tepidarium (warm-water pool), calidarium (hot-water pool, usually circular in shape), and frigidarium (cold-water pool) were all located on the axis. Gymnasia flanked the pools; and gardens, barber and hairdresser shops, libraries, and meeting rooms completed the complex. Water, transported by aqueducts from outside the city and heated by fires in basements, was

We think ourselves poor and mean if our walls are not resplendent with large and costly mirrors; if our marbles from Alexandria are not set off by mosaics . . . if our vaulted ceilings are not buried in glass; if our swimming pools are not lined with Thasian marble, once a rare and wonderful sight in any temple. . . . What a vast number of statues, of columns that support nothing, but are built for decoration, merely in order to spend money!

3-120. Plan of the Roman and Imperial Forums, Rome, with the Basilica Ulpia. Compare to the reconstruction in figure 3-95 and the reconstruction of the Basilica Ulpia in figure 3-111. Originally commissioned by the Republican government of Rome; expanded by various Roman emperors

Most Romans would not have agreed with Seneca, for they viewed the ritual of bathing and socializing within an opulent architectural environment as one of the joys of civilized life.

Another dramatic public space created by the Romans was the basilica (from the Greek *basilike*, "royal court"), a large building, often with an interior colonnade. Derived from earlier Greek buildings with colonnades, the basilica was entered on its longitudinal side. The interior was divided into three areas: two side areas known as **aisles** or **side aisles**, which flanked a large central axial hall called the **nave** (from the Latin *navis*, "ship," due to its resemblance to the upturned hold of a ship). Sometimes both ends of

the nave terminated with an **apse**, a large niche composed of a half cylinder surmounted by a half dome (see fig. 3-112).

The basilica served a variety of secular purposes for the Romans; business and administrative offices were located there, and law courts met there. Often, too, the apses contained shrines to deities. Basilicas usually adjoined a forum, the public square that was the center of commercial and social activity. The Roman Forum was developed beginning in the sixth century BCE. Later, imperial forums, built by different emperors, are unified along a longitudinal axis (see figs. 3-95, 3-120). At the northwestern end of this axis is the Forum of Trajan, with the Basilica Ulpia (see fig. 3-111; Ulpius was

Trajan's family name). The Basilica Ulpia adjoined libraries that flanked the Column of Trajan (see fig. 3-99). Given the Basilica's size—it is more than 400 feet long—the Roman architect was confronted with the problem of how to light the vast interior space. To solve this problem, the wooden gable roof of the nave was raised above the aisles to permit clerestory windows.

Roman baths, forums, and basilicas gave the Western world a heritage of architecture and ideas. Our spas and community centers reflect the public baths on a more modest scale, while the forum survives in Italian piazzas and in our own public squares. The basilica served as the prototype for Christian churches in western Europe.

MESOAMERICAN ART: TEOTIHUACÁN

3-121. Ceremonial plaza at Teotihuacán, Mexico. c. 100 BCE–750 CE. The complex covers 13 square miles. Photo taken from the top of the Pyramid of the Moon, facing south along the 3-mile-long Avenue of the Dead. The Pyramid of the Sun, in the upper left, faces west.

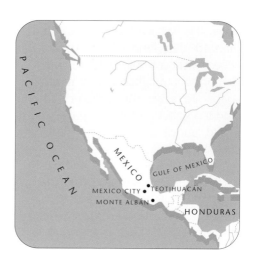

After 1,200 years, Teotihuacán stands today as mute testimony to the genius of unknown creators. Begun around 100 BCE on a dusty tableland north of modern Mexico City, it was both the first metropolis in the Americas and a remarkable example of city planning. At its height, Teotihuacán encompassed about 2,600 major structures, including markets and multifamily apartment compounds set along spacious esplanades. A city of temples, it was dominated by two majestic altars, each set atop a pyramid (see fig. 3-121). Its population was greater than Athens of Perikles, and its area was larger than Rome during the Empire. It exercised dominion over all of central Mexico and Honduras in the region known as Mesoamerica. In the middle of the eighth century, the people of Teotihuacán abandoned their capital. This site was so historically rich and impressive to the Aztecs that they called it Teotihuacán, or the "birthplace of the gods," when they built their capital there in the twelfth century. It is the Aztec names for this place and its gods that we use today.

Monumental architecture appeared at the site in the first century

c. 100 BCE–750 CE	Teotihuacán, Mexico
320 CE	Gupta dynasty begins to unify India
325 CE	Council at Nicea, first ecumenical council of the Christian Church
410 CE	City of Rome is sacked

CE with one of the most ambitious undertakings in all of Mesoamerica—the Pyramid of the Sun (fig. 3-121). Built over a cave held sacred since even earlier times, the Pyramid of the Sun (c. first century CE) retains the stepped outline of earlier pyramids in Mesoamerica, but here the scale is gigantic. The ground plan reveals a square base 738 feet across. The total height, including a temple that once stood on the upper platform, would have been about 246 feet.

Built in Teotihuacán somewhat later during the same period is the Pyramid of the Moon (c. 150–225 CE), whose structure is more sharply delineated on its surface and is of more modest size than its counterpart. The placement of the smaller pyramid in the northern part of the valley, on gradually rising terrain, brings the upper platform to roughly the same altitude as that of the Pyramid of the Sun. These two edifices, with their severe contours set against the mountainous landscape on the horizon, dictated the features of the city's growth. For example, the Pyramid of the Sun is oriented precisely at the point on the horizon where the sun sets over Teotihuacán the day it reaches its zenith at the summer solstice. Furthermore, the slightly later Avenue of the Dead, the city's main thoroughfare, runs strictly parallel to the main facade of the Pyramid of the Sun and is perfectly aligned with the axes of the Plaza of the Moon and the Pyramid of the Moon. With these pyramids completed, a gigantic urban plan began to emerge that reflected current ideas about astronomy and the desire to identify with the semiarid,

serene landscape of this central Mexican plateau.

The fundamentals of these urban complexes were set in Mesoamerica by earlier peoples. The use of truncated pyramids as a temple base, the careful placement of terraces, platforms, and temples to form plazas, and the skill at handling open spaces using fixed axes (probably set according to symbolic considerations) were constant from earlier periods. Such monuments as these pyramids are not strictly architectural since they do not function as enclosures of space; rather, they work as sculpture, with exterior space acting as a constructed, environmental art form.

Teotihuacán was the civic, religious, political, and economic center for the surrounding valleys. Also in the city were foreign enclaves, thousands of artisans in the market places, and a ritual center of monumental proportions. During religious festivals the city population would swell even more with pilgrims. At its peak in the second and third centuries CE, Teotihuacán attained a maximum population of about 200,000. At this time, a second stage of building reflected the abrupt spurt in urban growth. The Avenue of the Dead was laid out, and around it rose a number of ceremonial complexes. Residential sectors that were once mainly to the northwest of the two great pyramids began to grow in all directions—outward from the Avenue of the Dead and from the broad east and west avenues perpendicular to it.

During this period an important architectural refinement was initiated, the **tablero**, a heavy, projected,

rectangular molding outlined by a thick frame. This detail appeared on all religious structures, whether a simple altar, ceremonial platform, small temple, or majestic pyramid. Perhaps the most splendid example of the tablero is on the Temple of the Feathered Serpent (fig. 3-122). The meaning of feathered serpents is not clear, but they probably carried a double message—political and cosmic. They have been interpreted as symbols of rule, fertility, the calendar, and the beginning of time. The images were later given Aztec names, Quetzalcoatl (plumed serpent) and Tlaloc (deity associated with water). Aside from the symbolic and aesthetic appeal of the Temple of the Feathered Serpent, its structure reflects technological advances. The entire nucleus of the temple is reinforced with a skeleton of limestone. The colossal heads are deeply anchored into the core of the tableros and show great sophistication in the joining of stone, since use of hard metal tools was not known to these builders.

The plan of the entire city is noteworthy for the regularity of the city blocks and the density of residential sectors. The layout of the city was based on a module of 187 feet, which formed the standard blocks in residential areas. Multiples of the module apparently formed other compounds in the city as well and divided it into a grid, which suggests the existence of rigorous city planning as well as a centralized ruling group, both spiritual and temporal. Rivers were rechanneled, and the city at its height included large reservoirs, steam baths, specialized workshops, open-air markets,

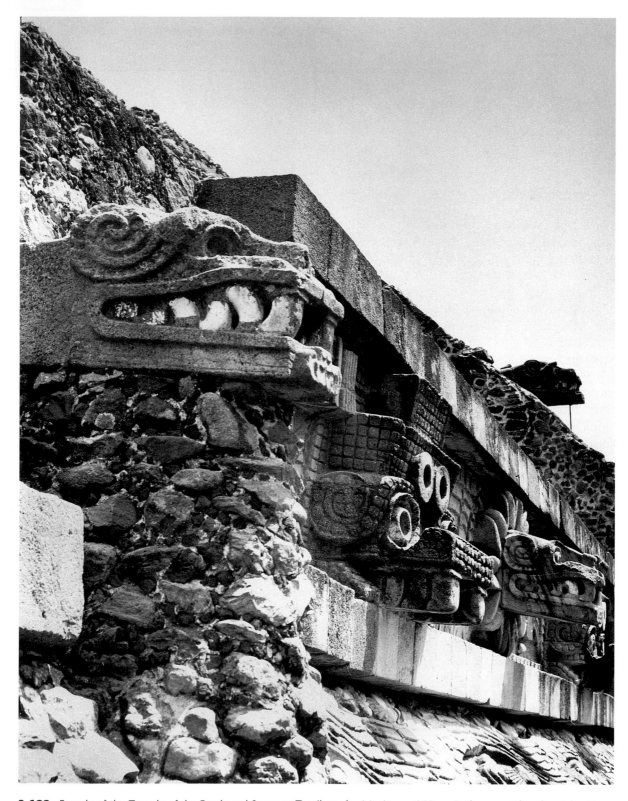

3-122. Facade of the Temple of the Feathered Serpent, Teotihuacán, Mexico. c. 150 CE. Each serpent head weighs 4 tons.

administrative buildings, theaters, and areas set aside for ball games and other public functions.

The Palace of Zacuala—an excellent example of what must have been the luxurious residence of a rich Teotihuacán merchant or high functionary—included a chapel decorated with brightly colored mural paintings depicting the storm god (fig. 3-123). In this painting, the storm god is casting seeds to the earth as if planting. A speech scroll issues from his mouth, ending in a sign symbolizing water and precious

3-123. Representation of Tlaloc (god of rain) c. 400–650 CE. Drawing from a fresco, palace wall of Zacuala, Teotihuacán

things. The deity is surrounded by a fringe of volutes representing waves and clouds. The composition refers to the water god in the guise of a patron of fertility and abundance. The opulence and spaciousness of the palace attest to the existence of a powerful upper class and to the importance of spiritual devotion in connection with that wealth.

Teotihuacán was apparently the most highly urbanized center of its time in the New World. The period of its life span, roughly from 100 BCE to 750 CE, was a spectacular one in Mesoamerica, with high points reached at Teotihuacán, at Monte Albán in Oaxaca, and in the Maya region. Each had a planned urban center with astronomical orientation for streets and buildings, monumental architecture, and in-

tellectual achievements such as the perfection of the calendar, mathematics, writing, and astronomy (the latter especially among the Maya). This was a splendid age of the arts and architecture, which was reflected in the pyramid-temples at Teotihuacán and Tikal, and in mural painting, ceramics, and mosaics. Professional people and artisans were organized into guilds. Traders were also well organized, and large and efficient markets offered goods from many regions. Merchants brought feathers from exotic tropical birds, cotton, cacao, jade, and turquoise into Teotihuacán for sale. The society was sharply stratified, militaristic, and theocratic. The predominance of religious representations in Teotihuacán as well as the presence of altars in the central courtyards of each house testify to

the importance of religion in this community. Religious, civic, and secular activities were joined in the centers, which supported priest-chieftains, nobles, merchants, poets, musicians, actors (who were highly respected and took part in religious and secular ceremonies), artists, laborers, farmers, servants, and slaves.

After a period of increased internal conflict, the city was attacked. Its palaces were burned and its temples were reduced to rubble. This was a process of ritual destruction and desacralization that was unprecedented in scope and scale in Mesoamerica. Temple and state were one; to destroy Teotihuacán politically was to destroy it ritually. The artistic legacy of its people, however, endured and was adapted in other times and places in Mesoamerica.

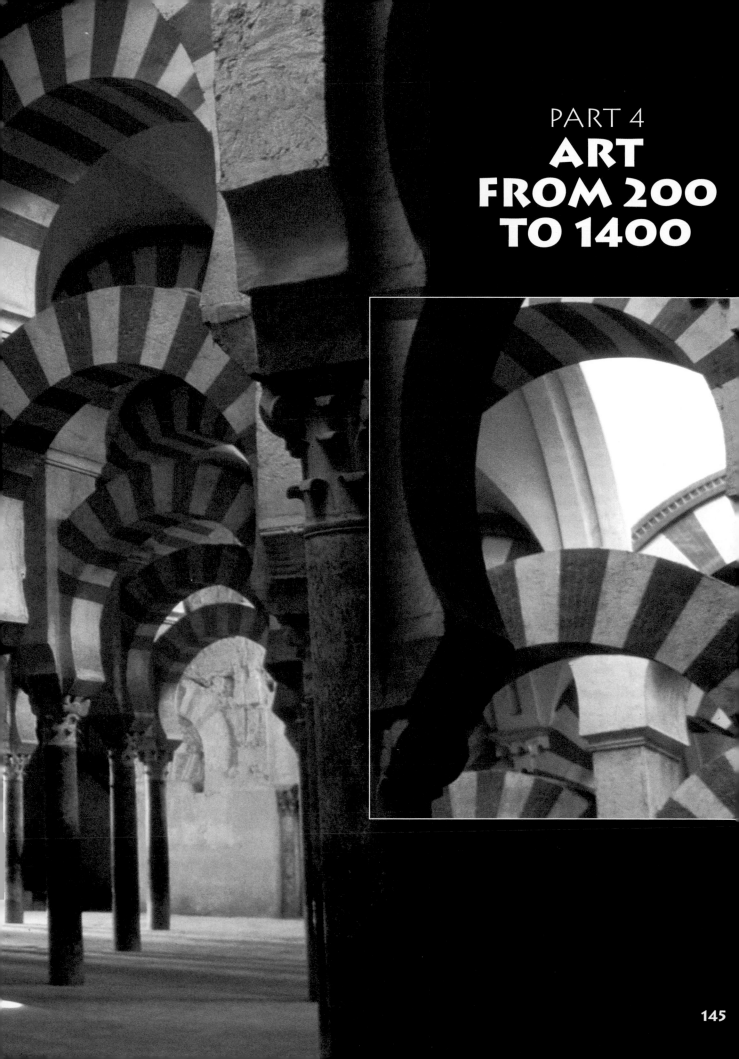

PART 4
ART FROM 200 TO 1400

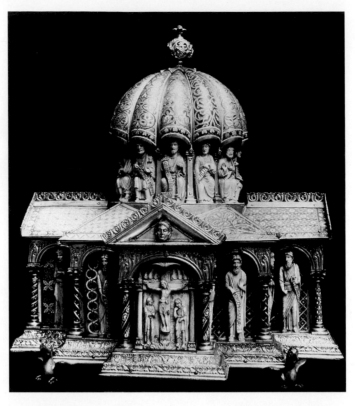

4-1. German Romanesque. Reliquary in the shape of a church, from the convent of Hochelten in the Lower Rhine region. c. 1170. Gilt cast bronze, enamel, and walrus ivory reliefs on a wooden core, height 21¹/₂". Victoria and Albert Museum, London. This reliquary was probably made by a workshop in Cologne, Germany.

INTRODUCTION TO ART FROM 200 TO 1400

The similarities and differences between a small Christian object shaped like a domed church (fig. 4-1) and a huge Hindu relief carved into the living rock (fig. 4-2) remind us that religious art and architecture can take many different forms. We can use these two works to begin to reveal some of the issues addressed by art during the long and complex period from 200 to 1400.

During this period, religions that continue to be important in today's world—Hinduism, Shintoism, Buddhism, Judaism, Christianity, and Islam—expanded beyond their places of origin and in several cases greatly increased their numbers of followers. New centers with monuments were dedicated to serve the needs of religious practitioners, including priests and other members of religious hierarchies and the common people. Art and architecture played important roles in supporting these developments. Although the function of religious art may seem self-evident, a study of objects and buildings created at different times and in different places reveals a wide variety of uses: to explain dogma, to confirm believers in the faith, to convert nonbelievers, and to connect religious beliefs to political leaders and institutions—these are only a few of the ways in which art and architecture are used during this period.

The miniature Christian church, for example, functioned as a **reliquary**—a container for the bones of a holy person or for objects associated with one or more such persons (see also fig. 4-57). Reliquaries were displayed to the faithful, who hoped to benefit from their proximity to such holy things. The specifically Christian content of this object is evident in the **iconography** of the **reliefs**, which feature Old Testament prophets, Christ, the apostles, and scenes from the life of Jesus, including the crucifixion.

To understand this work better, the spiritual content of Christianity, which played a crucial role in forming the

---

ART PAST/ART PRESENT   NAMING THE MIDDLE AGES

In Europe, the period between 200 and 1400 CE (and even later in northern Europe) is now known as the Middle Ages, or medieval period. The term *Middle Ages* was invented during the Italian Renaissance to suggest that this was an interim period between the "new" Renaissance age and the ancient civilizations of the Greeks and Romans. In the Renaissance, the Middle Ages were thought to be an interval of darkness and cultural inactivity, but historians today refute this characterization. The term *Middle Ages* has also been used by scholars, perhaps inappropriately, to describe certain contemporary phases of Indian and Chinese art.

4-2. Indian. *Descent of the Ganges*, Mahamallapuram, India. Middle Pallava period, c. 625–74. Carved on a granite cliff, height 20'. Commissioned by the Pallava king Mahendra-Varman I or his son King Mamalla

life and culture of the Middle Ages in Europe, must be examined. This is difficult to summarize, in part because of the many different interpretations of Christian belief that eventually developed. Christianity, a religion of salvation, emphasizes the inner, spiritual life, offering the promise of life after death for the soul in Paradise. Medieval Christianity emphasized belief in a single God understood as a Trinity, an indivisible unity of three persons: God the Father, the creator; Jesus Christ, his son, who assumed human form in what is known as the Incarnation; and the Holy Spirit, who is believed to be continuously active in the world. Jesus Christ is held to be the son of God, who was born to a pious woman known as the Virgin Mary. He died by crucifixion, as seen on the reliquary, after being charged with blasphemy. Medieval Christian art also often depicted the Last Judgment (see figs. 4-64, 4-65, 4-99), when Christ would come at the end of time to judge humanity and thereby determine who would enter Paradise. The richly colored enamels and carved panels of the reliquary may be an explicit reference to the gold-studded walls of the City of God mentioned in the Bible. This object was useful in confirming faith and in expressing the spiritual goals of Christianity; because important relics brought pilgrims to

a church and, therefore, wealth to the local community, there may also have been a commercial function.

In the Hindu relief at Mahamallapuram, it is again both form and iconography that express religious content. The site, in South India on the shores of the Indian Ocean (see map, page 163), was an important pilgrimage center for Hindu believers; it may have become identified with the holy because of the unusual rock formations that are found along the sandy beaches. On some outcroppings of granite, sculptors carved shrines and reliefs of immense proportions. The *Descent of the Ganges* is carved on the face of a cliff; above the relief is a natural pool. During the rainy season, the overflow cascades down the natural cleft to be collected in a pool at the base. Over millennia, this cleft had been smoothed by the flowing action of the water. This natural phenomenon may well have inspired carving the cliff with the story of the gift of holy water from the gods in heaven.

The Hindu religion developed a complex set of stories to explain the workings of nature, especially the fertility of crops and procreation. The traditions emphasize a single godhead that is capable of an infinite number of manifestations—assuming male, female, animal, and mixed animal and human forms—which helps to

4-3. Proto-Historic Japan. *Haniwa of a Warrior*. Kofun (Old Tomb) period, 3rd–6th century. Earthenware, height 47³/₈". Asian Art Museum of San Francisco, The Avery Brundage Collection, San Francisco, California. Hundreds of these earthenware figures of warriors, women, and animals—all known as *haniwa*—once encircled the huge mound tombs of the Japanese Yamato rulers, which were shaped like keyholes and surrounded by moats. Commissioned by a Yamato ruler

explain the great number of figures and animals in the relief. In personal terms, the most important aspect of Hinduism is the belief in reincarnation—every individual will return to life as another living creature, and good behavior in one life will lead to a higher state of existence in the next. The religion is thought to have combined ancient beliefs about fertility with ideas derived from such social customs as hierarchy and caste. The highest order of gods is a trinity: Brahmin the creator, Vishnu the preserver, and Siva the destroyer. Images of these deities and many others and their multitudinous activities were thought of as aids in contemplation and as a focus for identification. The southern Hindu tradition, as at Mahamallapuram, and its art forms were passed along the trade routes across the seas to Cambodia and Indonesia.

Although the iconography of some of the details in the *Descent of the Ganges* is still debated, the composition focuses attention on the cleft near the center. This water is usually identified with the Ganges, one of the three sacred rivers of India, and is thought to have life-giving powers. Representatives of all the living beings of the world—deities of the river, elephants, lions, gods, human beings, and even a cat and mice—are assembled here as the river is seen being given from heaven to earth. The god Siva, one of the major manifestations of the godhead in the Hindu religion, appears several times to express the destructive and creative aspects of nature. Because this monument was commissioned by the local rulers as they were establishing their kingdom, its large and impressive scale and the choice of subject may have been related to political needs as well.

HISTORY

The growth of powerful proselytizing religions was only one manifestation of worldwide change during this long period. A number of important political entities were established and flourished at this time, including the Gupta rule in India; the successive Han, Sui, Tang, and Song dynasties in China; the Maya and Aztec cultures in the Americas; and the Carolingian, Ottonian, and French Gothic cultures in Europe. The establishment of a national identity, the writing of history, and the creation of art forms that were peculiar to that culture were important factors in many cultures. This was the period, for example, when the Japanese state defined itself as a political institution—the name it gave itself was Yamato—and the *Haniwa of a Warrior* (fig. 4-3) is an example of the kind of art that was established within

4-4. Ni Zan. *Rongxi Studio.* 1372. Hanging scroll, ink on paper, height 29 3/8". National Palace Museum, Taiwan, Republic of China. For a portrait of Ni Zan, see figure 1-22.

this culture during the period of self-definition.

There was commercial, intellectual, cultural, scientific, and religious exchange on a large scale over great distances. Many Buddhists undertook pilgrimages from East Asia back to India, and the pilgrimage roads in Europe led the devout from northern Europe down to Spain and Italy. The Crusades, which were preached as "Holy Wars" against the Muslims, led to increased contact between the Christian West and Islam. This period saw the commercial silk routes flourish between East and West. The Venetian Marco Polo's travels from Baghdad to the China Sea between 1271 and 1295 are known through his book *The Description of the World,* which was spread through dozens of translations and hundreds of manuscripts. Polo studied not only China's natural environment but also its economy (which already used paper money), its architecture, its urban planning, and especially its industries, many of which were more advanced than those in Europe at the time. On his return home, he described additional observations and recorded stories he had heard about Java, India, and areas of Africa. His observations influenced Western perceptions of the East for centuries, while the success of his travels encouraged others interested in the trade in exotic goods to undertake similar explorations in hopes of commercial success. Ni Zan's painting of the *Rongxi Studio* (fig. 4-4) is the kind and style of Chinese painting that Marco Polo might well have seen at the home of the Chinese literati. In Japan in the sixth century, the Yamato rulers and the Shinto religion were already being challenged by the new religion of Buddhism, imported into Japan through Korea. The commercial, political, and religious travel that was undertaken meant that works of art, foreign styles, scientific inventions, and other intellectual developments were shared across the continents of Europe and Asia.

Islamic writers preserved much of ancient Greek and Roman literature and philosophy, then later reintroduced it back into European culture. Islamic science, mathematics, and medicine became well known in Europe at the same time. Scientific advances included astronomical investigations in India and Mesoamerica and the invention of gunpowder in China. Other inventions were the wheelbarrow, the compass, paper, and the spinning wheel. Practical, labor-saving inventions meant that there was less need for the slave labor that had characterized much of the ancient world. As large and powerful cultures and religious traditions developed, there was also contact through wars, including the religious and commercial wars in the eleventh, twelfth, and thirteenth

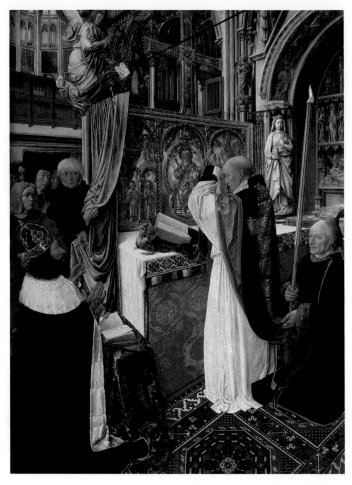

4-5. Master of Saint Giles. *The Mass of Saint Giles.* c. 1500. Oil on wood, 24¼ x 18". The National Gallery, London. A late-fifteenth-century painter here represents a ninth-century miracle taking place at an altar at the Royal Abbey Church of St.-Denis, near Paris.

centuries known as the Crusades. An increased awareness of diverse cultures was a hallmark during much of this period.

ART AND THE CHRISTIAN CHURCH

In much of Europe, the dominant medieval institution—culturally, educationally, spiritually, and often politically—was the Christian Church. In both East and West, some Christians withdrew from the world into monasteries and nunneries to follow a life of work and prayer. The Church developed a ruling hierarchy that was headed by the pope (the bishop of Rome, the first of whom had been Saint Peter) and local bishops and that included the heads of monasteries and nunneries. The expanding institutions and hierarchy of the Church created a great demand for works of art.

Christianity developed a series of rites and services known as the liturgy. The central Christian rite was the Mass, or Eucharist, a service at which the Last Supper was reenacted and salvation for repentant believers was

promised. By the early fourth century, this service was usually held in a church at an altar, which became the focus for the ritual and for works of Christian art. The painting shown in figure 4-5 demonstrates the rich decoration at a medieval altar. A priest, dressed in elaborately decorated vestments, stands at an altar with a bejeweled cross, a gold altarpiece, and a brocaded altar frontal. He raises the host, a consecrated piece of bread that stands for the body of Christ. (Missing from this representation is a chalice, the vessel that holds the wine standing for Christ's blood; see fig. 4-77.)

Although a unified style cannot be defined for all European medieval art, many works from this period, including Islamic works, offer a stylistic treatment that emphasizes spiritual values through an intentional denial of the ancient classical traditions of **naturalism**, individualism, and **illusionism**. This broad generalization offers some unity to the art produced in the diverse styles of the medieval period in Europe. Islamic motifs were sometimes borrowed from models known from Spain and western Asia. In addition, the majority of surviving European medieval works of art are directly related to and created for the rituals and practices of the Christian Church. The notion of the Church as an institution is suggested in the form taken by the reliquary (see fig. 4-1).

THE SCROLL AND BOOK

In the painting depicting the Christian Mass, the open book that is prominent on the altar suggests the importance of written texts during this period. Judaism, Christianity, and Islam are all religions with a holy book—a text that is at least in part believed to have been dictated to humanity by God. As a result, these texts are often highly decorated and enclosed in a rich and even bejeweled container. Lettering and decorating such texts were often considered to be acts of religious devotion.

The hand-lettered, decorated book or scroll played an important role in the artistic developments in all three of these religions. The Bible, for example, was held to be a compendium of divine proclamations and a record of God's actions in history. It has two sections: the Old Testament, which encompasses the books of the Jewish faith, and the New Testament, composed of four versions of the life of Jesus (the Gospels, written by the Evangelists—Matthew, Mark, Luke, and John) and other writings. Throughout the Middle Ages, Jewish Torah scrolls, Christian Bibles, Islamic Korans, service books, and private prayer books were written by hand—usually on treated animal skins (**vellum** or **parchment**). Because they represented the word of God, they were often richly adorned with fine materials, and many Christian books were also illustrated. Islamic culture avoided the representation of the human figure (see page 190), but copies of the Koran were decorated with spectacular calligraphic decorative patterns (for a later example, see fig. 6-59).

Handwritten, illustrated, and decorated manuscripts were also an important part of religious and secular traditions in other parts of the world. In the Far East, novels and religious tracts were printed in books or written on hand scrolls, which unrolled from right to left (see fig. 1-18). Readers held the scrolls in both hands, and only a small portion was visible at any one time. Vertical scrolls like the *Rongxi Studio* were also stored in boxes, but they could be hung on the wall for purposes of contemplation.

THE ARTIST

In Europe, there are few signed works of art during the medieval period before the fourteenth century. The individuality of the artist was not an issue during a period in which individuality generally was seen as unimportant; many medieval works were, in fact, produced by groups of artists and artisans working together. The artists of the Middle Ages included an important new class of artist: monks and nuns who, living within monastic communities, joined artistic productivity with the religious life. In Europe, the crafting of **manuscripts** and other liturgical objects was such an important activity that abbots of monasteries and even bishops continued to be active as artists after they had risen in the ecclesiastical hierarchy. But there were also lay artists, who lived in cities and were not connected to any religious order. There is evidence that by the tenth century these lay artists were organizing themselves into professional organizations, rather like trade unions, called **guilds**.

In most other cultures during this period, artists worked in groups, and the large endeavors required by religious practices were produced by workshops of artists and laborers. There are isolated instances of signed works, but these are not common. The main exception to this attitude toward the artist is in China, where the status of the artist as a scholar-intellectual, often working within the court, means that the majority of works are signed (see pages 34, 198–201).

CE	200	400	600	800
EUROPE ART	**150–400** EARLY CHRISTIAN ART PERIOD **333–90** OLD ST. PETER'S BUILT, ROME, ITALY	**c. 500–1453** BYZANTINE ART PERIOD **c. 547** MOSAICS AT SAN VITALE, RAVENNA, ITALY	**c. 620** SUTTON HOO PURSE COVER **c. 698** *LINDISFARNE GOSPELS*, ENGLAND **c. 771–c. 870** CAROLINGIAN ART PERIOD **786–87** MOSQUE AT CÓRDOBA, SPAIN	**816–23** *GOSPEL BOOK*, REIMS, FRANCE **c. 819** ST. GALL MONASTERY PLAN, SWITZERLAND **c. 936–1056** OTTONIAN ART PERIOD **10TH CENTURY–MID-12TH CENTURY** ROMANESQUE ART PERIOD
HISTORY	**313** Edict of Milan grants religious freedom to Christians **323** Constantinople becomes capital of Roman Empire	**410** Visigoths sack Rome **535** Benedict's rules for monks **527–65** Rule of Justinian	**756–1031** Islamic Umayad caliphs rule Córdoba, Spain **768–814** Rule of Charlemagne	**987–1328** Capetian rulers of France
ASIA ART		**c. 500** SHINTO SHRINE AT ISE, JAPAN **c. 525** XIE HE'S SIX CANONS OF PAINTING, CHINA	**607** HORYUJI FOUNDED, JAPAN **7TH–8TH CENTURY** CHANG'AN, CHINESE IMPERIAL CITY **c. 760–800** KAILASANTHA TEMPLE, INDIA	**835–60** BOROBUDUR TEMPLE, JAVA **c. 950** LI CHENG'S *BUDDHIST TEMPLE IN THE HILLS AFTER RAIN*, CHINA
HISTORY	**220–579** Six Dynasties period, China **320–500** Gupta dynasty, northern India **4TH–8TH CENTURY** Pallava dynasty, southern India	**MID-6TH CENTURY** Buddhism arrives in Japan from Korea	**618–907** Tang dynasty, China **646** 1st Japanese capital, Nara **794–1185** Heian period, Japan	**907–60** Five Dynasties period, China **960–1126** Northern Song dynasty, China
THE AMERICAS ART		**5TH CENTURY** MAYA COMPLEX AT TIKAL, GUATEMALA	**7TH CENTURY** MAYA COMPLEX AT PALENQUE, MEXICO	**900–1250** ANASAZI PUEBLO AT CHACO CANYON, UNITED STATES
HISTORY	**250–1500** Maya period in Mesoamerica		**750–1230** Anasazi in southwestern United States	**800–1500** Mississippian period, United States
AFRICA ART		**c.560** MOSAICS AT ST. CATHERINE, MOUNT SINAI, EGYPT		
HISTORY			**8TH CENTURY** Ife founded, Nigeria	**c. 800–1000** Benin culture urbanization
THE MIDDLE EAST ART	**150–400** EARLY CHRISTIAN ART PERIOD **244–45** SYNAGOGUE AT DURA EUROPOS, MESOPOTAMIA	**c. 500–1453** BYZANTINE ART PERIOD **532–37** HAGIA SOPHIA, CONSTANTINOPLE		
HISTORY		**570** Muhammad born at Mecca	**633–750** Early Islamic conquests	

1000	1100	1200	1300–1400
c. 1000 *GOSPEL BOOK OF OTTO III*, GERMANY	**12TH CENTURY** *VIRGIN OF VLADIMIR*, RUSSIA	**c. 1225–35** *BEAU DIEU*, AMIENS CATHEDRAL, FRANCE	**c. 1300** GIOTTO'S *MADONNA ENTHRONED*, ITALY
c. 1070–80 *BAYEUX TAPESTRY*, FRANCE	**c. 1120–32** TYMPANUM, VÉZELAY, FRANCE		**c. 1303–05** GIOTTO'S ARENA CHAPEL FRESCOES, PADUA, ITALY
c. 1080–1120 ABBEY CHURCH OF STE.-FOY, FRANCE	**1140** ABBOT SUGER BEGINS ST.-DENIS, FRANCE		**1339** *MADONNA OF JEANNE D'EVREUX*, FRANCE
	1140–1400 GOTHIC ART PERIOD		**1361–72** CHURCH OF ST. SEBALD, NUREMBERG, GERMANY, BUILT
	1194–1220 CATHEDRAL OF NÔTRE-DAME, CHARTRES, FRANCE, REBUILT		

1054 Eastern and Western Christian Churches split		**1236** Christians recapture Córdoba	
1066 Norman conquest of England		**1267–73** Thomas Aquinas publishes *Summa Theologica*, Italy	
1090–1291 Christian Crusades			

11TH–12TH CENTURY KHMER ART AT ANGKOR WAT, CAMBODIA	**1120–30** TAKAYOSHI'S *TALE OF GENJI* PAINTINGS, JAPAN		
	1180–1230 XIA GUI'S LANDSCAPE PAINTINGS, CHINA		

EARLY 11TH CENTURY Murasaki Shikibu's *The Tale of Genji*, Japan		**1271–95** Marco Polo visits China	
1127–1279 Southern Song dynasty, China			

11TH–15TH CENTURY IFE AND OWO SCULPTURE, NIGERIA		**13TH CENTURY** MOSQUE, DJENNÉ, MALI	**BEFORE 1400** CARVED MONOLITHS, GREAT ZIMBABWE

		1204 Constantinople sacked by Crusaders	

JEWISH ART: THE SYNAGOGUE AT DURA EUROPOS

4-6. Reconstruction of the west wall, with the Torah niche, of the synagogue, Dura Europos (modern Syria). 244/45. Tempera on plaster, length of wall approx. 40'. National Museum, Damascus. The Roman frontier city of Dura Europos, located in Mesopotamia, was a crossroads and minor trading center. It has provided rich archaeological information, especially in its several places of worship, which included a synagogue, a Christian site with a baptistery with frescoes, and temples to Bel, Zeus, and Mithras. The Torah niche in the synagogue is decorated with a shell, a motif taken from Roman art, where the shell is often used to signify a holy place. In this niche were placed scrolls that contain the first five books of the Bible, the sacred writings of Judaism. Attributed to Moses, these books contain the basic rules of the Jewish faith, including the Ten Commandments, which tradition holds were given to Moses by God on Mount Sinai.

Discovered in 1932, the synagogue at Dura Europos, in modern Syria (fig. 4-6), astonished archaeologists and scholars. Quite unexpectedly, its capacious house of assembly had figurative decoration: a complicated sequence of paintings of Old Testament scenes in bands around all four walls and a ceiling of tiles decorated with personifications, astrological subjects, animals, flowers, and other themes. Both scripture (the second of the Ten Commandments: "You shall not make for yourself a graven image [idol], or any likeness of anything that is in heaven above, or that is in the earth below, or that is in the water under the earth") and historical writings seem to imply that it is unlawful for Jews to make or have images. That this prohibition was not

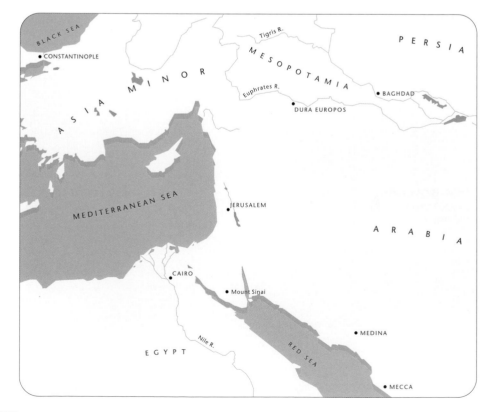

followed by all Jews is revealed by archaeological discoveries at Dura and elsewhere and by Jewish books from the Middle Ages, such as the many illustrated Passover Haggadahs. The cycle at the Dura synagogue includes such scenes as Solomon receiving the Queen of Sheba, David as King of Israel, Moses receiving the Law, the Consecration of the Temple, Moses leading the chosen people out of Egypt, Mordecai and Esther, Moses and the Burning Bush, Exodus and the Crossing of the Red Sea, and even a cityscape with a representation of Jerusalem and the Temple of Solomon.

The Jewish religion is monotheistic and is based on the worship of Yahweh, or God. The origins of Judaism are traced to a covenant made between God and Abraham, in which God promised Abraham that he would give him a mighty race of descendants and a Promised Land if his followers would stop worshiping idols. The emphasis in the services held in the synagogue and at home is on the telling of Jewish history, the reading of the laws, and the interpretation of those laws. Judaism has a strong scholarly tradition, and it is possible that the extensive narrative cycle in the synagogue at Dura Europos was used in part as an educational tool, to illustrate and teach the history and laws of the religion. The large number of competing religions practiced in Dura, each with its own sanctuary, may have encouraged the Jews there to decorate their synagogue.

In terms of art, Dura Europos was an unimportant provincial city, and the conventions of the figures and the use here of iconographic stereotypes and compositions known from other sites suggest that the Dura cycle was derived from a **pattern book**—a book of images, prepared as an artist's tool, that preserved a tradition of illustrated scenes, in this case from the Old Testament. In *Moses Giving Water to the Tribes* (fig. 4-7), Moses stands in a relaxed con-

4-7. *Moses Giving Water to the Tribes* and *Elijah Revives the Widow's Child*, detail of figure 4-6. The figures are smaller than lifesize. *Moses Giving Water to the Tribes* depicts Numbers 21:16–18, when a well was dug after God told Moses to "gather the people together, and I will give them water." In a continuous narrative that represents the widow twice and the child three times, *Elijah Revives the Widow's Child* shows the widow of Zarephath presenting her dead child to Elijah, Elijah resuscitating it, and the widow holding the revived child (I Kings 17:8–24).

trapposto position derived from ancient Greek and Roman art, but both the schematic nature of the composition—with smaller figures representing the tribes of Israel placed evenly around the edge of the scene—and the unrealistic way streams of water reach out to each tent are consistent with developments in Early Christian art. The Jews, a small minority at Dura, created an impressively decorated synagogue that expresses their piety and the dignity of their traditions.

EARLY CHRISTIAN ART

4-8. *The Three Hebrew Youths in the Fiery Furnace,* fresco in the Catacomb of Priscilla, Rome, Italy. Early 3rd century. Approx. 20 x 30"

The Three Hebrew Youths in the Fiery Furnace, from a Christian cemetery (fig. 4-8), represents the Christian use of the Old Testament story of three righteous Hebrew youths who were saved by God after being thrown into a furnace for refusing to worship idols. Three frontal figures, their arms raised in a position of prayer, stand amid flames. Their pleas for deliverance are answered, and a dove, symbolic of the Holy Spirit, descends bearing a branch symbolizing victory and/or peace. The message of the painting is direct: faith brings salvation.

Catacombs, underground burial complexes used by Romans, Jews, and Christians, were originally known by the Greek term *coemeteria* ("places of rest," from which we derive our word *cemetery*). Later,

the term *catacomba*, which initially referred to a specific cemetery in Rome, came into general use. The walls of the narrow, labyrinthine passages in the catacombs, cut from soft rock, had horizontal niches to hold the bodies of the deceased. Larger chambers, also underground, were used for funerary rites. Catacombs were not secret burial places, as legend has it, although they may have been used as hiding places during times of Christian persecution.

The painting of *The Three Hebrew Youths* expresses the faith of the early Christians by promising salvation in time of need and suffering. The Old Testament story was perceived as a precedent for New Testament teachings. Christians understood Christ as the Messiah who

fulfilled the prophecies of the Old Testament, and theologians and artists often associated the two religious traditions. The style of the painting is suggestive and animated, continuing a Roman manner of painting using fluid paint and flowing brushstrokes. Some modeling is used, but the strong outlines flatten and dematerialize the figures, and the emphasis on their large eyes enhances the spiritual intent.

HISTORY

A few years after Christ's death and resurrection, Paul (originally named Saul), a Jew who had persecuted Christians, was converted to the new faith (see fig. 7-14). He zealously preached the message of Christ and converted many to Christianity.

By about 40 CE, the term *Christian* was first used to designate these followers of Christ's teachings, and about 70–80 CE, when the Gospels of the New Testament were being written, Christianity broke decisively with Judaism.

By the early second century, an internal structure and hierarchy were being formed within the Church, and liturgical rites for worship were developed. Although subject to periodic and often vicious persecution, the new religion, with its emphasis on spiritual values, spread rapidly. In a letter written to the Roman emperor Trajan in 110, Pliny the Younger warned of this

extreme superstition. . . . Many of all ages, of all ranks, of both sexes, are being brought into danger, and will continue to be brought. The blight of this superstition has not been confined to towns and villages; it has even spread to the country.

ART

Early Christian art (c. 150–400 CE) developed gradually, in part because of intermittent persecution. Stylistically the new art was initially dependent on Roman and Hellenistic sources. In many cases, only the Christian subject matter indicates its religious function. Early Christian artists worked in a diverse range of media. Painters not only decorated church and catacomb walls but also created book illustrations. Sculptors made marble **sarcophagi** and ivory carvings. A favored medium for church decoration was **mosaic**.

One house at Dura Europos was converted for Christian services in 231. It included a baptistery with an image of the Good Shepherd (from the parable in Luke 15:3–7) above a scene of Adam and Eve in the garden. Here Old and New Testaments are intellectually related—

4-9. *Good Shepherd.* Late 3rd century. Marble (restored), height 39". Vatican Museums, Rome

the Good Shepherd becomes a reference to Christian redemption, overcoming the sin of Adam and Eve. The Good Shepherd image appears often on Early Christian sarcophagi and reliefs, and even as single figures (fig. 4-9), but it is uncertain whether these beardless youths represent Christ as the Good Shepherd or the more general concept of God caring for his flock. In any case, the humble modesty of the figure is consistent with the spirit of early Christianity.

Early Christian artists were challenged to express the promises and mysteries of their new faith. As in ancient Roman art and in most later medieval art, artists were laborers who worked in a communal situation, and their works are anonymous. They created the means to communicate the ideals of Christianity as it changed and became more public. These anonymous artists, at once conventional and innovative, helped effect a transition from the ancient to the medieval world.

CHRISTIANITY AND SYMBOLISM

4-10. *Passion Sarcophagus.* Second half of 4th century. Catacomb of Domitilla, Rome

The fish, as it appears in a number of Early Christian catacomb paintings

Peacocks, grapes and grape vines, and a form of the Chi-Rho monogram on a fourth-century sarcophagus made for a Christian

A plaque bearing the alpha and omega letters, a Chi-Rho, and a lamb—"the Lamb of God, which taketh away the sin of the world!" (John 1:19)

4-11. Early Christian symbols

From Judaism, Christianity inherited a disposition against representing the divinity, an **aniconic** attitude that was also supported by Christian criticism of the earlier practice of worshiping idols. As questions arose about the appropriateness of figurative art in the early Church, a vocabulary of symbols was developed to express abstractly the tenets of the new faith. One common Early Christian symbol is the so-called Chi-Rho, the combination of the first two letters of the Greek word for *Christ*, *X* and *P*, to form a monogram for Christ [☧], as seen at the top center of the sarcophagus (fig. 4-10); this symbol is related to the story of the dream of the Roman emperor Constantine, who had a vision that he would be victorious under this sign.

The Early Christian repertory of symbols was quite varied (fig. 4-11), but it seems unlikely that any were used as "secret" symbols for communication between members of this new and sometimes-persecuted religious group. Other Early Christian symbols include the anchor, referred to in Paul's letter to the Hebrews (6:19), which became a symbol of resolution and hope; and the fish, which became a symbol for Christ because the first letter of each word in the phrase "Jesus Christ, Son of God, Savior" forms the Greek word *ichthus*, "fish." Because ancient legend held that the flesh of the peacock was immune to decay and its feathers contained the complete spectrum of colors, the bird itself came to symbolize eternity. The A, alpha, and Ω, omega— first and last letters of the Greek alphabet—were adapted because Christ said, "I am Alpha and Omega, the beginning and the end" (Revelation 1:8). A curving vine and grapes refer both to God's relationship with his people ("I am the vine, you are the branches"; John 15:5) and to the wine used in the Mass.

With time, the use of symbols was gradually combined with that of narrative representation, as is seen in the so-called *Passion Sarcophagus* (see fig. 4-10). The narrative sequence is not the expected left-to-right development, and the culminating scenes of the sequence, Jesus' crucifixion and resurrection, are reserved for the central area, where they are given a highly symbolic treatment. In the earliest scene of the narrative sequence, to the right of center, we see the arrest of Jesus; this is then followed on the far right with the scene of Pilate washing his hands. The next scene, the mocking of Jesus, with a soldier crowning him with a crown of thorns, is to the immediate left of the center, while on the far left we see the fourth scene, Simon helping Jesus carry his cross. In the center, the crucifixion is referred to by the cross, while the subsequent resurrection, on Easter Sunday morning, is indicated by the elevated placement of the Chi-Rho enclosed in a triumphal wreath. The enclosing of the Chi-Rho within the wreath, an ancient Greek and Roman symbol that refers to victory, suggests the soul's desire to triumph over death. The sleeping soldiers below represent the Roman soldiers who fell asleep while guarding the tomb and who therefore did not witness the resurrection symbolized above, but they also symbolize those who deny Christ's resurrection. The doves perched on the cross are symbols of Christian souls and also of peace and purity.

EARLY CHRISTIAN ARCHITECTURE

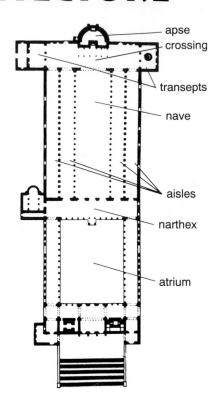

gable roof

clerestory

apse

nave   aisles

apse
crossing
transepts
nave
aisles
narthex
atrium

4-12. Reconstruction of the nave, Old St. Peter's Basilica, Rome. c. 333–90. Interior length approx. 368'. This basilica was demolished in the sixteenth century, when today's imposing edifice (see figs. 6-24–6-28, 7-22–7-23) was begun. The earlier church then became known as Old St. Peter's. Commissioned by the Roman emperor Constantine

4-13. Plan of Old St. Peter's Basilica

Old St. Peter's Basilica was a prototype for developments in Christian architecture (figs. 4-12, 4-13). The plan was initially adapted from the Roman **basilica** (see fig. 3-111), which was usually entered on its long side, but the Christian church was entered through an **atrium** and **narthex** (entrance hall) on its short side. This narthex was usually on the west, and the altar was toward the east, an orientation followed in most later medieval churches.

The interior division of space, with a **nave** flanked by side **aisles**, is similar to certain Roman basilicas. Old St. Peter's has **transepts** (from the Middle Latin *transseptum*, "transverse enclosure"), a feature that would become traditional in Christian churches. These architectural spaces, extensions to the north and south, meet the nave at the **crossing**. Transepts create a cross shape; the term *cruciform* (cross-like) *basilica* designates Early Christian churches with transepts. At St.

Peter's, as in many Roman basilicas, wooden beams supported a **gable roof**, and **clerestory** windows allowed light to illuminate the nave. Many of the **columns** used in building Old St. Peter's were taken from earlier Roman buildings; materials thus reused are known as *spolia* (Latin, "spoils"). The group of spiral columns that decorated the altar area at Old St. Peter's had a special significance, for they were thought to have been taken from the Temple of Solomon in Jerusalem.

The size of Old St. Peter's mirrors the triumphant attitude of Christianity following the Edict of Milan in 313, which granted religious freedom to the Christians. Constantine realized the unifying strength that the newly recognized religion could bring to his reign. Many privileges, including tax exemptions and donations of land and money, were granted the Church. Constantine personally contributed to the construction of St. John Lat-

eran in Rome (begun 313), which marks the first use of the basilica plan for Christian architecture. Constantine's support was further evidenced by his decision to build Old St. Peter's, which was both a martyrium (built over the grave site of Saint Peter, it marked and commemorated his martyrdom) and a basilica used for worship. It is believed that the development of the transept at St. Peter's derived from the need for additional space for worshipers and pilgrims around the shrine and a desire to separate Peter's grave from other tombs in the nave.

Old St. Peter's had a rather plain brick exterior, but the interior was adorned with precious materials, including marble Roman columns, mosaics, and frescoes. The decorated interior contrasted with the exterior, subtly reminding the visitor that the beauty of the inner spirit was more important than external, physical adornment. From the entrance, one's attention was focused on the high altar, set below an enormous arch on which a mosaic depicted Christ, Saint Peter, and the emperor Constantine with the inscription:

> Because under Your guidance the world rose triumphant to the skies, Constantine, himself a victor, built You this hall.

In the apse, where in a Roman basilica a statue of the emperor might be located (see fig. 3-101), another mosaic displayed an enthroned Christ flanked by Saints Peter and Paul. A reference to Christ as the supreme judge is thus found at a point where, in a Roman basilica, law had been dispensed. (In some churches, the cathedra, or throne, of the bishop was set in the apse. These churches, where bishops preside, are called **cathedrals**.) With the support of Constantine, who probably converted to Christianity near the time of his death, the flourishing Christian faith transformed the architectural forms and imperial symbolism of ancient Rome.

Another type of design adapted by the early Christians was the **centrally planned** structure, in which the main parts of a building radiate from a central point. It was used for baptisteries and mausoleums. Santa Costanza exemplifies the centrally planned structure (figs. 4-14, 4-15). Built about 354 as a mausoleum for Constantine's family, it features a central altar within a ring of paired columns that support the **dome** and clerestory. Between the columns and the outer wall is a circular corridor that at Santa Costanza is **barrel-vaulted** and decorated with mosaics; it is called the **ambulatory** (*ambulare*, "to walk"). Four large niches in the walls define the shape of a Greek cross (a cross with four equal arms). The cross circumscribed by the circular plan symbolized salvation and eternal life for the Christian and was thus an appropriate design for a Christian tomb.

4-14. Interior, Santa Costanza, Rome. c. 354. Commissioned by the Roman emperor Constantine for the members of his family

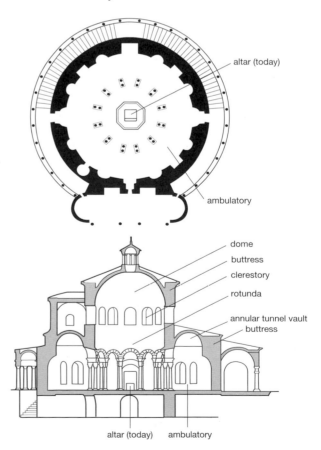

4-15. Plan of Santa Costanza

THE SHINTO SHRINE AT ISE, JAPAN

4-16. Naiku (Inner) Shrine complex, Shinto shrine, Ise, Japan. Late 5th–early 6th century. *Ise,* the name of the city in central Japan where the shrine is located, is used to refer to all the shrines collectively, as well as to the land on which they are situated. The original patron is unknown; the patron for rebuilding every twenty years is the Japanese ruling family and the nation of Japan

4-17. Plan of the Naiku Shrine buildings and the old shrine compound

Shinto, the indigenous religion of the Japanese people, has its origins in animism. The focus of Shinto is reverence for *kami*, the deities and supernatural qualities perceived in such natural objects as trees, rocks, waters, and mountains. The spirits of deceased emperors, heroes, and other famous persons are also revered as *kami. Kami* receive tribute at shrines in the form of food offerings, music, dance, and the performance of such traditional skills as archery and sumo wrestling.

The Ise complex includes the Naiku (Inner, western) Shrine (figs. 4-16, 4-17), which houses the sun goddess Amateratsu Omikami, the divine ancestor of the Japanese emperors, and the Geku (Outer, eastern) Shrine, which is dedicated to a local god. From prehistoric times, this area has been a sacred place and pilgrimage site. It is the recognized seat of the ancestral deities of the impe-

rial house, and in modern times, under State Shinto, it has become the shrine of the entire Japanese nation.

The initial construction of the Inner Shrine is thought to date from the late fifth to the mid-sixth century. Because only members of the imperial family worshiped there, Ise became the center for imperial rites. In the elaborate annual ritual calendar, the most important ceremonies were the Niiname-sai (first-fruits festival) and the Daijo-sai (enthronement ceremony), during both of which the emperor offered pure food to the deities and consumed a ceremonial meal that the deities were thought to share.

The *shoden* (fig. 4-18)—or main sanctuary of the Naiku complex—and other shrine buildings are erected in an ancient style of architecture using undecorated wooden members and a simple, thatched roof. They are raised above the

ground on wooden piles, a custom associated with the humid climate of Oceania, from which this style may have been derived. The natural, unadorned materials of the building are believed to represent a sympathetic association between nature and architecture. According to a tradition originating with the emperor Temmu (ruled 673–86), the shrines are rebuilt every twenty years in order to approximate the cycle of growth and decay in nature. Although the custom fell into disuse in the Middle Ages, the latest rebuilding at Ise took place in 1993 and repeats precisely the plan of the earliest documented structure of the *shoden*, dating from 690–97.

The Shinto complex at Ise has roots in prehistoric practices. The seasonal changes that had special significance for early cultivators greatly affected daily life. Farmers depended on *kami* to help them. They propitiated the *kami* to ensure

4-18. Front elevation of the *shoden* (main sanctuary). Earliest documented structure 690–97; rebuilt 1993

the success of their seasonal activities: sowing, planting, harvesting. A sacred annual cycle was observed, and the rituals of *kami* worship were the mainstay of everyday activity.

The earliest Shinto sanctuaries were simple piles of boulders or stones that marked the sacred dwelling places of the *kami*. In early Japan, the *kami* were regarded with awe and were segregated from the secular world. Their sanctuaries became hallowed ground, and access was forbidden except on ritual occasions. Priests could approach the *kami,* but only during special rites in which they acted as mediators between human beings and the *kami* world.

In order to make the domain sacred, the physical bounds of the sacred and profane had to be demonstrated. The stone monument in which *kami* were thought to dwell was first enclosed by a ring of rocks.

This "heart pillar" (*shin no mihashira*) lies buried deep in the ground at Ise and is dressed in the evergreen boughs sacred to Shintoism. These *sakaki* branches symbolize the tree where the divine mirror (the "literal" body of Amateratsu Omikami) was hung and where the sun goddess was enshrined. A later period saw the development of the **torii arch**, which marks the entrance to a Shinto sacred area.

Two occurrences led to the establishment of these sanctuaries as Shinto shrines. First, the introduction of Buddhism from China via Korea in the sixth century led the Japanese emperor to welcome Buddha as a great *kami* whose visible representation was housed in an impressive Buddhist temple. This had a profound influence on the development of Shinto shrines and on the emergence of permanent shrine sanctuaries in particular. Second, the

gradual deification of the emperor led to the establishment of an official Shinto shrine. At least as early as the late third and fourth centuries CE, Yamato rulers unified the competing clan lineages in the Yamato Plain under the aegis of their lineage, the sun line. The emperor came to be regarded as a living *kami*, with his divinity surpassing that of other *kami*. With this new status for the emperor, political and religious authority were joined. The union was sanctified at the Inner Shrine at Ise. The symbol of succession from the sun goddess to the sun line, the sacred necklace of *magatama* (jewels representing the soul spirit, which can enter the body of the possessor), is still the emblem of enthronement for the emperors of Japan and is kept at Ise, where Shinto doctrines were first systematically expounded. Today, the site is venerated, and pilgrimages there are an expression of patriotic sentiment.

BYZANTINE ART

4-19. *Transfiguration of Christ*, apse mosaic, Monastery of St. Catherine, Mount Sinai, Egypt. c. 560. The Monastery of St. Catherine is at the foot of Mount Sinai (see map, page 154), where, according to the Old Testament, God gave the Ten Commandments to Moses. Isolated in the Sinai Desert, the monastery, which has been in continuous use since the sixth century, is a repository of early manuscripts and other works of art (see fig. 4-21). Original patron of the monastery complex was the Byzantine emperor Justinian

In Christian tradition, the Transfiguration occurred when three apostles accompanied Christ to the top of a mountain. While they prayed, Christ was lifted up into the sky, surrounded by an aura of heavenly light, and appeared flanked by the Old Testament prophets Moses and Elijah (Matthew 17:1–13). The voice of God the Father was heard from a cloud: "This is my beloved Son: hear him." In the mosaic of the *Transfiguration of Christ* at the monastery at the base of Mount Sinai, Christ is represented on the axis surrounded by a **mandorla** (almond-shaped **halo**) of blue light, which emphasizes his resplendent white robes (fig. 4-19). Moses and Elijah symmetrically flank Christ, while the apostles below gesture with wondrous exclamation. The divinity of Christ is demonstrated in a scene with a spiritual emphasis that removes it from our physical world. No geographic details are given, and the event is bathed in a golden light symbolic of spiritual enlightenment. Although modeling is used, the shadows are linear patterns, denying the figures any illusion of weight or mass.

HISTORY

In 323, Constantine decided to move the capital of the Roman Empire from Rome to the eastern part of the Empire, to a historic trading center on the Bosphorus called Byzantium (from which we derive the name for the Byzantine civilization). The eastern provinces of the Empire, already strongly Christianized, had become increasingly more important, and the new capital was far from the political instability of Rome and the threats of barbarian invaders. The new capital, dedicated in 330, was named Constantinople.

Constantine's decision was a wise one. A port located at the center of regional trade routes and surrounded by rich timbered forests and agricultural fields, Constantinople developed rapidly as an economic and cultural center. This growth led to an increased military capability, and, during the reign of

the emperor Justinian (ruled 527–565), areas of the Empire that had been lost—Italy, southern Spain, and North Africa—were again brought under imperial rule. Under Justinian, an intelligent and efficient emperor, Byzantine civilization prospered. His wife, Theodora, a former circus performer, gave resolute counsel in assisting to govern the Empire. Justinian and Theodora shared a vision of reviving the grandeur of the Roman Empire while advancing the Christian faith (see figs. 4-25, 4-26).

But Justinian's military gains proved costly and short-lived. Later, the Empire was reduced through uprisings in western Europe and, beginning in the seventh century, through the rapid advance of the Islamic religion, which with zeal spread the ideals of the prophet Muhammad to Arabia, Persia, North Africa, and Spain. The location of Constantinople meant that the influence of Roman culture was gradually

supplanted by Greek taste and values, and Greek replaced Latin as the official language at court. Disagreements within the Church led to an official split in 1054 between the Western, or Roman, Church and the Byzantine, or Orthodox, Church, with its center in Constantinople. This split helps explain why the Christian Crusaders, on their way to fight the Muslims in 1204, diverted their campaign and captured and sacked Constantinople. They ruled the area for about fifty years. Cultural and political stability was later restored, but in 1453 Constantinople fell to the Ottoman Turks and was later renamed Istanbul.

ART

Many aspects of ancient Greek art and culture were preserved or revived during the long history of the Eastern, Byzantine Empire. The extensive revival of antiquity that occurred in the tenth century, for

4-20. *Prayer of Isaiah*, from the *Paris Psalter*. c. 900. Manuscript painting on vellum, 14 x 10^{1}/$_{4}$". Bibliothèque Nationale, Paris

example, can be seen in a manuscript painting from the *Paris Psalter* (a book of Psalms) in which Isaiah's prayers are met by a ray of light that extends from the hand of God (fig. 4-20). The figures on each side of Isaiah are classical personifications: Night is a female contrapposto figure wearing a Greek costume and with a veil of stars over her head, while Dawn is a boy with a lighted torch. The gold background is still dominant, as it was four centuries earlier in the *Transfiguration* at Mount Sinai, but elements of landscape recalling Hellenistic and early Roman painting have been revived. The classicizing influence is more strongly stated here than in comparable manuscript **illuminations** from western Europe.

THE ICON AND ICONOCLASM

One unique form of painting that developed in Orthodox Christianity was the **icon** (Greek for "image"). Used during religious services and to decorate churches, an icon is a consecrated religious painting that displays a holy person or event and is viewed as a vehicle to communicate with the spiritual world. Some icons were believed to date from the time of Jesus, and the most famous were thought to be of divine origin. The *Madonna and Child Enthroned with Saints Theodore and George and Angels* (fig. 4-21) is a rare surviving example of a sixth-century icon. The drapery patterns tend to flatten the figures, but the modeling and the slight contrapposto positions seen in the saints continue the classical interest in naturalism. Above the Virgin, two angels look sharply upward to God, whose hand descends into the pictorial space, emitting a strong ray of light. The static composition of the Virgin and saints, with their intense staring eyes, is characteristic of icon paintings. The medium is **encaustic** (from the Greek *enkaiein*, "to burn in"). It involves mixing dry pigments with hot wax, a technique that creates an effect that is both translucent and brilliant.

By the later sixth century, the faithful attributed miraculous powers to certain icons. Conservative factions, called iconoclasts (image destroyers), feared that icons had become objects of worship, which would be heretical; the divine nature of Christ, they argued, should not be represented, and to do so would encourage idolatry. They were countered by the iconodules (image venerators), who argued that

4-21. *Madonna and Child Enthroned with Saints Theodore and George and Angels.* 6th century. Encaustic on wood, 27 x 19^3/8". Monastery of St. Catherine, Mount Sinai

because Christ had become human (the doctrine of the Incarnation), it was permissible to depict him in his human form. The dispute erupted into open and at times bloody conflict between 726 and 843, a period in Byzantine history known as the iconoclastic controversy. During this period, icons and other religious images were damaged or destroyed, accounting for many losses of works of Early Christian and Byzantine art. A final victory for the iconodules occurred in 843; even today, one Sunday in the Orthodox Christian Church calendar celebrates the restoration of images.

THE BYZANTINE ARTIST

Byzantine artists, like their Roman predecessors, were trained and practiced in a workshop system. While they constructed and decorated public buildings and churches, the collective efforts of these artists in different media were coordinated by an official overseer. As is true of much of the Middle Ages, artists worked in anonymity.

Specialized workshops produced a variety of media, including mosaics, mural and icon paintings, manuscript illustrations, and small sculpture. Large-scale figurative sculpture, one of the cornerstones of Greek and Roman art, was seldom produced during the Byzantine era, perhaps out of fear that such works would have the connotations of earlier idols. Byzantine carvers produced sarcophagi reliefs and small, exquisitely refined ivories to adorn religious and secular objects.

HAGIA SOPHIA

4-22. Anthemius of Tralles and Isidorus of Miletus. Interior, Hagia Sophia (Holy Wisdom), Istanbul (Constantinople), Turkey. 532–37. Hagia Sophia, 270' in length, covers almost 1.5 acres, and the great central dome, 108' in diameter, crowns at a height of more than 185'. After the Ottoman Turks captured Constantinople in 1453, Hagia Sophia was converted to an Islamic mosque. Towering minarets, from which the faithful were called to prayer, were added to the exterior, while on the interior the Christian mosaics were covered and eight huge discs with sayings from the Koran and names of Muslim prophets were added. Hagia Sophia influenced later developments in Islamic mosque architecture (see figs. 6-60–6-62). Today, the former imperial church and mosque is a state museum. Commissioned by the Byzantine emperor Justinian

The interior of Hagia Sophia (fig. 4-22) offers a dramatic interplay of two crucial architectural elements: space and light. On entering, the visitor is astonished by the enormous interior space. Flanked by semi-domes on two sides, the central dome rests like a colossal canopy on four gigantic piers. The windows at the base of the dome create rays of light that dematerialize these supports. The high dome appears suspended, hovering in space above us.

Just as the drama of light at the Pantheon in Rome (see fig. 3-117) represents a metaphysical joining of the physical and spiritual worlds, so too was the amplitude of light within Hagia Sophia bound to the religious purpose of the building. Originally, the light was even more intense, for the windows around the dome were successively decreased when the dome was rebuilt three times due to structural damage from earthquakes, in 558, 989, and 1346. Light was an integral part of Hagia Sophia's effect, for when combined with the immense interior space and mosaics, the building created a powerful physical and spiritual experience, as recorded by Procopius, the court historian to Justinian, writing shortly after the church was decorated:

The sun's light and its shining rays fill the church. One would say that the space is not lit by the sun without, but that the source of light is to be found within, such is the abundance of light. . . . So light is the construction, the dome seems not to rest on a solid structure, but to cover the space with a sphere of gold suspended in the sky. . . . The scintillations of the light

4-23. Exterior, Hagia Sophia

forbid the spectator's gaze to linger on the details; each one attracts the eye and leads it on to the next. The circular motion of one's gaze reproduces itself to infinity. . . . The spirit rises toward God and floats in the air, certain that He is not far away, but loves to stay close to those whom He has chosen.

This remarkable synthesis of light and architectural form was conceived by Anthemius of Tralles, an artist and scientist, and Isidorus of Miletus, an architect and engineer. During a brief, six-week period, they evolved a new architectural plan that combined the longitudinal orientation of the basilica with the central plan (figs. 4-23, 4-24). Unlike Roman architects, who preferred to support a dome on a **drum**, Anthemius and Isidorus raised the central dome on **pendentives**, curving triangular seg-

4-24. Plan of Hagia Sophia

ments that provide the transition from the square plan of the piers to the circular base of the dome (see fig. 3-113), and flanked it with semi- or **half domes**. The huge piers reduced the load-bearing function of the walls, allowing for large amounts of window space (such nonsupporting walls are known as **screen walls**).

That Hagia Sophia was completed in just five years demonstrates the importance of the building in Justinian's plans. It is reported that at its dedication in 537, the emperor compared his accomplishment to that of Solomon, builder of the Temple in Jerusalem, when he proclaimed, "Solomon, I have outdone thee!"

SAN VITALE, RAVENNA

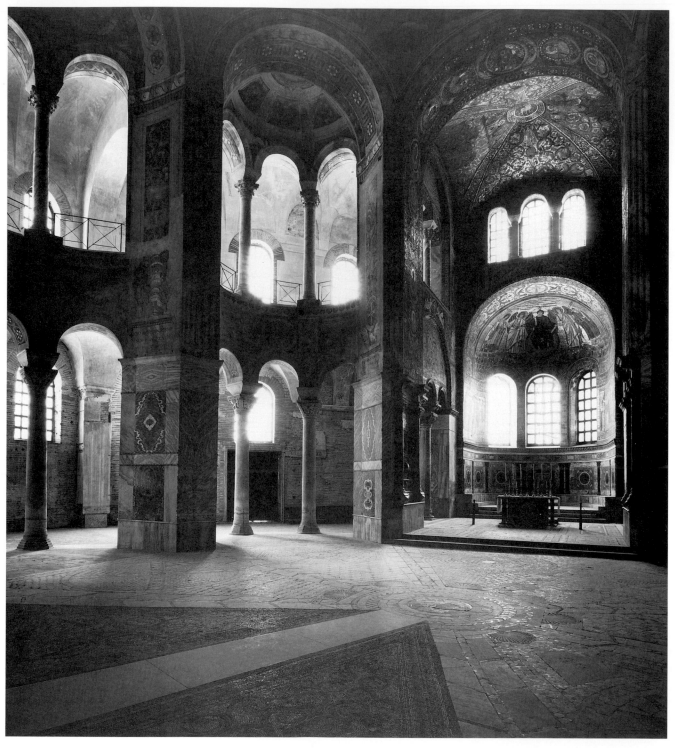

4-25. Interior, San Vitale, Ravenna, Italy. 526–47. Ravenna had been the capital city of the Ostrogoths, a Germanic people who conquered Italy by 493. In 540, the city was taken by Justinian's army and became a regional Italian capital and the local religious center of the Byzantine Empire. Commissioned by the Byzantine emperor Justinian and the local bishop, Maximianus

4-26. *(right)* Mosaics, San Vitale. c. 547. In the lunette, *Abraham Feeding the Three Angels* is represented. Between the columns is a glimpse of *Justinian, Bishop Maximianus, and Attendants* and the inlaid marble decoration below the mosaics.

The centrally planned church of San Vitale has the plain brick exterior that characterized much Early Christian and Byzantine architecture, but inside a comprehensive mosaic program synthesizes Christian iconography with imperial Byzantine politics (figs. 4-25, 4-26). It is a complex ideological program that joins Old and New Testament scenes, symbols, decorative patterns, and imperial portraiture. The unity of the mosaic program is defined by the axial placement of a number of images and symbols of Christ on, for example, the apex of the arch and at the center of the **groin vault**, where a lamb symbolizes Christ and his sacrifice. The monogram *Chi-Rho* [✶] leads to the most important of these references, the youthful Christ seated on the blue sphere of the universe in the apse. These align with the altar,

4-27. *Theodora and Attendants,* apse mosaic, San Vitale. c. 547

where Christ's sacrifice is reenacted during the Mass, reinforcing this programmatic unity.

The offering of bread and wine at the altar is prefigured by scenes from the Old Testament. In the semicircular area enclosed by the arch (**lunette**) to the left of the altar, Abraham is depicted offering hospitality to three angels symbolic of the Trinity (see fig. 4-26). To the right, Abraham is shown about to sacrifice his son Isaac, a narrative prophetic of Christ's sacrifice.

On the left wall of the apse, a rectangular mosaic depicts Justinian with ecclesiastical personnel on his left, including Maximianus, bishop of Ravenna, and civil and military personnel on his right (see fig. 4-26). Justinian carries the vessel that held the bread for the Mass; on the soldier's shield at the left border, a Chi-Rho monogram indicates the political importance Christianity had assumed within the Empire. Al-

though the figures are frontal, the manner in which they are lined up suggests a procession. Justinian never visited San Vitale, but his significance in this, his western capital, is implied by the mosaic.

Justinian's placement, flanked by ecclesiastical and civil representatives, communicates his position as head of both Church and State (in the Byzantine Empire, the emperor appointed the patriarch of Constantinople, the leader of the Eastern Christian Church). Individualized portraits are restricted to Justinian and his close associates. Although the figures overlap one another and some modeling is suggested, the scene, with its gold background, denies the illusion of real space. It is as if the earthly court of Justinian has been transfigured into a spiritual realm. As emperor, Justinian wears a jeweled crown, while as the earthly representative of God, he is shown with a halo. A decorative,

rainbowlike mosaic band rises vertically above his head to descend to the opposite mosaic of the empress Theodora, shown bringing the chalice of wine to the altar, and her attendants (fig. 4-27). The open passageway represented on the left of the mosaic is a subtle indication of the fact that Theodora and the other women are expected to observe the religious ceremonies at San Vitale from the galleries on the second floor.

In the semi-dome of the apse, the beardless Christ hands a crown to the Early Christian martyr Saint Vitalis, for whom the church was named. To Christ's left, Bishop Ecclesius, who laid the plans for the church, presents a model of the church. The complex ideological interrelationship of the mosaics is typical of Byzantine art, in which each figurative or decorative element is part of a comprehensive architectural and thematic unity.

4-28. *Justinian*, detail of figure 4-26. c. 547

The technique of mosaic seems to have developed from an earlier technique of pressing pebbles into plaster to form a durable and decorative floor covering. By the late fifth century BCE, Greek artists began arranging the pebbles into abstract and figurative designs. Soon, natural stones were replaced by cut pieces of colored stone, especially marble, called **tesserae** (singular: tessera, from the Greek *tesseres*, a square). The term *tesserae* is also used for the pieces of stone and glass in wall mosaics, as at Ravenna (fig. 4-28). At first, Roman mosaic was used primarily on the floors of private homes (see fig. 3-53), but occasionally it also decorated walls. Roman wall mosaics began to use glass tesserae in many colors, as well as gold tesserae, formed by sandwiching gold leaf between two layers of glass. The early Christians used mosaics to embellish the walls of their churches, but it was during the Byzantine era that the most splendid effects were achieved, as walls and vaults were covered with glass and marble mosaics enhanced by the predominant gold background.

In creating a mosaic, the image is first outlined on the floor, wall, or vault. Successive areas of this surface are then covered with fresh cement or plaster, and tesserae are placed into it, following the established design. As the cement or plaster hardens, the tesserae will be held firmly in place. When tesserae were set into walls and vaults, care was taken to adjust each so that its surface was at a slight angle to that of the neighboring tesserae. As the ever-changing light from the windows strikes the polished or glass tesserae, the changing angles of refraction create a shimmering and ethereal effect, a vision particularly suited to the mystical values of Christianity.

The figure of the *Pantocrator* at Daphni, Greece (see fig. 4-67), is an impressive example of fully mature Byzantine mosaic technique. The tesserae are arranged to reinforce the definition of an edge or surface; note, for example, how the curved patterns on Christ's forehead create a sense of plastic form while strengthening the vigorous facial expression. Except for the gold background, large areas of a single color are avoided. At Daphni, the highlighted area of Christ's brown robe contains gold and red tesserae to make it seem not merely lit, but radiant and, therefore, suffused with spiritual energy.

ANGLO-SAXON METALWORK

The abstract, heavily patterned style of the Sutton Hoo purse cover, found in a ship burial mound in England, is distinctive (fig. 4-29). In its use of valuable materials and in its emphasis on minute, fine craft, it continues the interest—typical of earlier pastoral peoples who lived in central and western Europe—in art that is valuable, portable, and a part of personal adornment. The most characteristic motif of Anglo-Saxon and Irish metalwork is the **interlace**, a complex pattern composed of a single line that intertwines and overlaps, filling completely the available space. This common motif can be found in small works made in pre-Roman Gaul (France) and in ancient Roman and Early Christian works as patterns of intertwining vines and plants. Here it has a strongly two-dimensional effect. In Anglo-Saxon art, the interlaced line is often given an animal head, the mouth of which bites down on its own tail. The legs and snouts of the four beasts at the top center of the Sutton Hoo purse cover also participate in the interlace pattern.

The discoveries at the Sutton Hoo mound confirmed the reports of rich possessions and similar burial practices found in the somewhat later Anglo-Saxon poem *Beowulf*:

> And there they brought the
> beloved body
> Of their ring-giving lord, and
> laid him near
> The mast. Next to that noble
> corpse
> They heaped up treasures,
> jeweled helmets,
> Hooked swords and coats of
> mail, armor
> Carried from the ends of the
> earth; no ship
> Had ever sailed so brightly
> fitted,
> No king sent forth more
> deeply mourned. . . .
> Take these treasures, earth,
> now that no one
> Living can enjoy them.

The Sutton Hoo treasury offers valuable evidence for a civilization about which we have little information. There are few written records and only limited monuments and archaeological remains. Many documented works were melted down, destroyed by fire, or lost during attacks and invasions. We do know that the Anglo-Saxons descended from Germanic peoples who emigrated to England in the fifth century.

Christianity, which had flourished in Roman Britain in the fourth century but then had waned, was strengthened in 597, when Pope Gregory the Great dispatched Augustine, later bishop of Canterbury, and forty missionaries to convert Ethelbert, king of Kent, and his court. Christianity and pre-Christian rituals existed side by side for a period; as late as the seventh century, an Anglo-Saxon king dedicated one altar to earlier gods and another to Christ.

The few fragments of Anglo-Saxon poetry and documentation that have survived reveal an aesthetic that delighted in luminous materials (especially gold) and in the color red. The interest in filling every available space with pattern or design seems to be related to the Anglo-Saxons' Germanic origin and traditions. The artists included monks, nuns, and laypeople. By the end of the Anglo-Saxon period, there is some evidence that craft guilds—medieval organizations of lay artists—were beginning to develop in England. When artists are mentioned, special attention is always given to the worker in precious metals, and it is on pieces of fine metalwork that we find the few artists' signatures of this period.

4-29. Sutton Hoo purse cover. c. 620. Gold with Indian garnets and cloisonné enamels, originally on an ivory or bone background (now lost), length 8". The British Museum, London. Found in 1939 in a ship–burial mound at Sutton Hoo, England, as part of the treasure of a king who probably died between 625 and 640, this purse lid of precious materials and exceptional technical proficiency once adorned a cloth or leather pouch. It would have been attached to the owner's belt by hinges. When placed in the burial mound, it contained gold coins and ingots. The huge ship, approximately 89 feet long, in which the treasure was buried, would have required thirty-eight rowers. The richness of the treasure, which included a helmet, shield, spears and a sword, bowls, drinking horns, remains of a musical instrument, and twenty-six pieces of gold jewelry, revealed the important status of the deceased, who is still not identified with certainty. With the spread of Christianity, the old tradition of ship burial, which provided the soul with a vehicle in which to travel to the next world, gradually declined, but some of the objects found suggest that the Sutton Hoo king may have been a convert to Christianity.

HIBERNO-SAXON MANUSCRIPT ILLUMINATION

4-30. Bishop Eadfrith. Carpet page, from the *Lindisfarne Gospels*. c. 698. Manuscript painting on vellum, $13^1/2$ x $9^3/4$". The British Library, London. The *Lindisfarne Gospels* contains a dedication to God and local saints that also identifies the artists involved: "Eadfrith, bishop of the church at Lindisfarne, originally wrote [lettered] this book for God and St. Cuthbert and—jointly—for all the saints whose relics are in the island. And Ethelwald, bishop of the Lindisfarne islanders . . . covered [bound] it . . . and Billfrith, the anchorite, . . . adorned it with gold and with gems . . . and Aldred, unworthy and most miserable priest, glossed [translated] it in English between the lines. . . . [They] made or, as the case may be, embellished this Gospel Book for God and Cuthbert." Eadfrith (bishop from 698 until his death, in 721) was both scribe and decorator. Another inscription reveals a typical medieval rationale for artistic creation: "Thou living God, be thou mindful of Eadfrith, Ethelwald, Billfrith, and Aldred a sinner; these four have, with God's help, been engaged upon this book."

The interleaf motif found in Anglo-Saxon metalwork (see fig. 4-29) was dramatically integrated into a Christian context in a series of manuscripts produced in Anglo-Saxon (English) and Irish monasteries between 600 and 800. Similarities in style and other interrelationships make it difficult to distinguish their production, which is perhaps best called Hiberno-Saxon (Hibernia was the ancient Latin name for Ireland). In some of these manuscripts, whole pages are devoted to abstract designs—now called **carpet pages** because of their resemblance to the complex patterns found in Turkish and other Islamic carpets. In this example, from the *Lindisfarne Gospels* (fig. 4-30), geometric panels are set within a surging sea of blue and red interlace. In the middle of each side are the confronted heads of two dogs or of two birds of prey. If we follow the patterns, we discover that the lines forming the outer borders of the decoration are their much-elongated bodies; at the corners, these lines are attached to a leg that is intertwined with the leg of a beast from the adjacent side.

The techniques used by the Hiberno-Saxon monks who made these manuscripts are difficult to reconstruct, and exactly how they

687   Venice elects first doge
c. 698   Carpet page, from the *Lindisfarne Gospels*
711   Moors invade the Iberian peninsula

accomplished such minuscule regular patterns without the aid of a magnifying glass is unknown. In one of the *Lindisfarne* carpet pages, the geometric pattern was first drawn on the back of the page using a ruler and compass, and the most important points of the design were then pricked through the vellum to provide a guide for the painter. The isolation of different types of decoration into geometric areas sets up maximum contrast between the widely varied patterns: fine and broad interlace, with and without animal-form additions, and swelling, swirling shapes. As a result, the interrelationship of the patterns as positive and negative forms and their placement in depth (which patterns are in front of or behind others) are tantalizingly difficult to decipher. The intensive and time-consuming nature of the design and execution is related to the austere and isolated nature of life in a Hiberno-Saxon monastery.

Monasticism flourished in Ireland earlier than in England, and Irish monastic **scriptoria** (halls where manuscripts were written and decorated) were producing important volumes by the middle of the sixth century. In England, the monastic tradition was established in the early seventh century, when King Oswald founded the monastery at Lindisfarne.

The earliest surviving Hiberno-Saxon religious manuscripts reveal an interest in decorating the letters themselves, a not surprising development when we remember that the words are believed to be proclamations of God. This tendency reaches its peak in the *Book of Kells* (fig. 4-31). When the text in the Gospel of Saint Matthew (1:22) reaches the crucial point where the

4-31. *Incarnation* page, from the *Book of Kells.* c. 800. Manuscript painting on vellum, 13 x 9^1/$_2$". Trinity College Library, Dublin

Incarnation of Christ is mentioned, the letters burst out in joyful, exuberant patterns. A whole page is devoted to the three words *Christi autem generatio* ("the birth of Christ"), with most of the page devoted to the first three letters of *Christi* (XPI). The X is the dominant form, and it surges outward in bold and varied curves to embrace Hiberno-Saxon whorl patterns. Free-form interlace fills other areas, and simple colored frames set off the large initials amid the consuming excitement. The human head that forms the end of the *P* also dots the *I*. Near the lower left base of the *X*, a small vignette shows cats watching while two mice fight over a round wafer similar to those used in the Mass—a scene surely of sym-

bolic intent, even if the exact meaning is lost to us today.

The pulsating vitality of the word of God and the exciting news of the impending birth of his son, Jesus Christ, are thus visually demonstrated. A twelfth-century writer who was shown a precious manuscript in Ireland—perhaps the *Book of Kells* itself—wrote:

> Look more keenly at it and you will penetrate to the very shrine of art. You will make out intricacies so delicate and subtle, so exact and compact, so full of knots and links, with colors so fresh and vivid, that you might say that all this was the work of an angel and not of a man.

THE CHINESE IMPERIAL CITY OF CHANG'AN

4-32. Plan of Chang'an (see map, page 163). Tang dynasty, 7th–8th century. The wall surrounding the city was almost 26 miles long, enclosing an area of almost 42 square miles. Chang'an, an ancient city in the Wei River valley, served as the capital of China during the powerful Han (206 BCE–220 CE) and Tang (618–907 CE) dynasties. It was the eastern terminus of the silk road, which joined China with the markets of western Asia and, as early as the second century, with Europe. Chang'an played an important role as a center for the transmission of the ideas and art forms that poured into China during the Tang dynasty. Commissioned by the imperial government

4-33. Zhang Xuan. *Court Ladies Preparing Newly Woven Silk,* detail of 12th-century copy attributed to Emperor Hui Zong, after 8th-century original hand scroll. Color on silk, 14^1/2 x 57^1/4". Chinese and Japanese Special Fund. Courtesy, Museum of Fine Arts, Boston. The copy shown here has been attributed to the twelfth-century emperor Hui Zong. Rich, glowing colors describe the scene, while a detailed precision embellishes the treatment of the fabric of the dresses worn by the women. Commissioned by the imperial academy

During the Tang dynasty (618–907), Chang'an became the cultural capital of all of East Asia (fig. 4-32). Laid out on a huge scale following important traditional practices, it was held in such esteem that it became a model for other contemporary capitals in Korea and Japan. It was by far the largest city in the world at that time; the present city on the site, Xi'an, occupies only about one-seventh the area of the Tang capital.

Production of different kinds of art in Chang'an reflects the city's importance as a Chinese capital as well as its position as an international center for trade. *Court Ladies Preparing Newly Woven Silk* (fig. 4-33) gives us an intimate view of aristocratic women; the ceramic *Camel* (fig. 4-34) represents the position of Chang'an as the terminus for the caravans across the silk route toward the west.

The city that was to become Chang'an began to take shape in the later sixth century, when a man rose to power in northwest China who reunified the traditional Chinese

7th–8th century

7th–8th century	Chinese Imperial City of Chang'an
642	Muslims conquer Egypt
c. 699	*Beowulf* is written
711	Muslims conquer Spain

4-34. *Bactrian Camel with Pack Saddle.* Tang dynasty, 1st half of 8th century. Earthenware with polychrome lead glaze, height 37". The Nelson-Atkins Museum of Art, Kansas City, Missouri. The Tang dynasty is notable in the history of Chinese ceramics for the dynamic beauty of its shapes, the development of colored glazes, and the perfection of porcelain. Fine white earthenware is often clothed in a polychrome glaze made by mixing copper, iron, or cobalt with a colorless lead silicate to produce a rich range of colors, from blue and green to yellow and brown. Both form and glaze convey a vigor that is true to most historians' view of life at the Tang court in the eighth century. This camel would have been placed in a tomb chamber.

Purchase: acquired through the generosity of numerous donors

lands after nearly four centuries of political instability and invasions from outside. In 581, he became Emperor Wen, the first ruler of the Sui dynasty, and he and his advisers were determined to build a capital city on a new and unprecedented scale at the site of the earlier Han dynasty (206 BCE–220 CE) capital. Their project for this "City of the Great Ascendancy" covered thirty-one square miles, but it was merely a skeleton when Wen took up residence in 583. With the founding of the Tang dynasty in 618, the city was expanded and renamed Chang'an—"City of Enduring Peace." At the height of the Tang, in the late seventh and eighth centuries, the city's population reached more than one million inside the walls, with probably another million in nearby satellite towns. Based on the principles of symmetry and axiality, Chang'an was the first totally planned Chinese city. The Tang leaders who conceived Chang'an intended to do more than create a city that would meet their practical needs. Such a city would dramatize their social order, express their hierarchy of values, and convey their view of the cosmos and their place in it.

First, to choose an auspicious site they turned to the ancient Chinese divination practice of *feng-sui,* which is still used today. Chang'an's location had been venerated for two millennia. Already, in the first century CE, a poet named Pan Gu had summed up its advantages in "Rhap-sody on the Western Capital," a poem included in a collection known as the *Wen Xuan*:

> In abundance of flowering plants and fruits
> it is the most fertile of the Nine Provinces
>
> In natural barriers for protection and defense
> it is the most impregnable refuge in heaven and earth
>
> This is why its influence has extended in six directions
> This is why it has thrice become the seat of imperial power.

As a perennial fulcrum of power—strong, fertile, and well populated—the site was practical as well as symbolic.

Second, the beginning of construction on the new Tang capital had to be properly timed. The most auspicious time and place to build were determined by centuries-old oracle-divination procedures similar to the divinatory and ritual-symbolic rites carried out by Greek, Etruscan, and Roman builders before embarking on the construction of new cities. Great importance was attached to the orientation of the city to ensure that it would be fully consonant with the natural order. Early descriptions of city planning (from the *Zhou li,* or *History of the*

4-35. Reconstruction of the Linde Hall of the Daming Palace, Chang'an. Tang dynasty, 7th century. The roof was made of ceramic tiles, and the tiles on the ridges and eave ends were glazed. Green and black tiles were excavated at the site, and we assume, based on textual evidence, that the exterior wall colors were primarily red and white with gold details, a striking combination with the black and green roofs. Commissioned by the imperial government

Zhou Dynasty, from the first millennium BCE) report that special officers took the shadow of the sun at noon and made observations of the North Star by night on successive days until they came to an accurate calculation of the four cardinal directions that would determine the city's orientation. No doubt, astronomers were also employed to assure that the orientation was attuned to the cosmic order.

Once properly sited and oriented, the city was surrounded by a rectangular wall of pounded earth (see fig. 4-32). There were gates in the outer walls except on the north, and broad north/south avenues led to each of the gates on the south wall. The city was subdivided into major zones. To the extreme north was the inner city, where the emperor held court, performed rituals of office, and resided with his harem. To the east and west of the avenue leading to the central southern gate were the imperial ancestral hall and the Altar of Earth.

In 634, the second Tang emperor, Taizong, expanded the city to the northeast of the inner city,

beyond the city walls, where he built a complex of palaces and other buildings that came to be known as the Daming Palace. Tang texts record that Hanyuan Hall, which has been excavated, was the site of ceremonies for the New Year and the winter solstice and that it was used for the investiture of new emperors, the changing of reign titles, and the inspection of troops and presentation of captives. Nearby was the Linde Hall (fig. 4-35), the other excavated Tang-period building of the Daming Palace, which was used by the emperor for feasting high officials. Both the Linde Hall and the Hanyuan Hall have similar architectural components, including covered **arcades** (or "flying galleries") that enclosed each building complex, side pavilions, and platforms that raised the entire building above ground level. Linde was a triple hall complex with a two-storied roof over the central building. The three halls lead directly from one to the next, without connecting arcades.

Beginning in the Han dynasty, ritual halls had weight-bearing walls at the sides and pillars that sup-

ported the main beams at the center. Reinforcing vertical struts that rested on the floor beams were fitted into the wall, while horizontal wooden pieces connected the struts. A wall beam was placed on top of the walls for added support. According to building regulations of the Tang, only the most important halls could have the **hipped roofs**, with their triangular, angled ends, seen in figure 4-35.

The remaining part of the city, known as the outer city, included 110 wards, most of which were predominantly residential; two were given over to marketplaces built and controlled by the government. The east market connected with the roads leading to the second Tang capital of Louyang, and the west market was the center of foreign trade and foreign residence. The ancient system of walled blocks was used for the whole outer city; the ward gates opened at sunup and closed at dusk, and it was a crime to be found on the streets after curfew. The residential wards were laid out on a grid pattern. The sides of these streets were lined with drainage ditches and planted with shade trees. The mansions of the aristocrats and officials were concentrated in wards near the Daming Palace and the east market, while those of commoners were found in the more densely populated area around the west market. Near the city parks at the extreme southeast corner of the outer city were a number of government-controlled entertainment districts. An elevated, covered roadway connected the parks so that the emperor could enjoy outings without being seen by his subjects.

Chang'an was an international capital, and the diplomatic envoys, religious missionaries, merchants, and students from many parts of the world who congregated there brought with them foreign religions, including Zoroastrianism, Manichaeanism, Judaism, Islam, and Nestorian Christianity. The most grand and numerous of the religious complexes in Chang'an were those of Buddhism and Daoism; some even occupied whole wards. The foreign goods brought by the city's exotic visitors were much sought after by the aristocracy, as well as the middle class.

The building of Chang'an was accomplished by able leadership in an era of peace and prosperity at home and enormous prestige abroad. In the early eighth century,

Ming Huang, a brilliant leader, took the throne. He cherished and upheld the Confucian order, and in 745 he founded the Imperial Academy of Letters (Han-lin Academy). Talent and wealth were concentrated in his court. His favorite scholars, poets, and painters, his schools of drama and music, his orchestras (two of which came from Central Asia), and his famous mistress, the beautiful Yang Guifei, were in attendance. Court painters and poets were kept busy by the emperor recording portraits and cultural and social events of court life.

During the reign of Ming Huang, the court painter Zhang Xuan was celebrated for his paintings of "young nobles, saddle horses, and women of rank." None of his work survives in the original, but one copy, *Court Ladies Preparing Newly Woven Silk*, is generally thought to illustrate the eighth-century Tang court tradition of scroll painting (see fig. 4-33). In the section reproduced here, court women of different ages are stretching and ironing a piece of newly woven silk. The dignified, realistic, and vigorous presentation is surely comparable to court life itself at that moment, even though only the barest essentials of the scene are recorded. The location of the women in space is carefully organized, but we are not told where they are, only what their rela-

tionship is to each other. Each woman refers to and is intimately connected to another through participation in the task itself and by gesture and location in space. This section of the scroll records an actual activity, but it may also refer to the broader theme of the maturation of court women from childhood (the small figure playing under the stretched silk), to adolescence, to the coming of age, to adulthood. Each step is distinguished by position, dress style, coiffure, size, and shape of figure.

The same realism that marks high court painting also characterizes the tomb figurines made during the Tang period. The presence of a ceramic camel in one's tomb must surely have referred to the importance of trade in the life of the deceased. The restrained energy and solidity of modeling found in the glazed ceramic camel illustrated here (see fig. 4-34) are typical of the best of this type of sculpture, which was made for the burials of both the aristocracy and the gentry.

Late in the ninth century, Chang'an fell victim to the ravages of a rebellion; in 904 many of its buildings were razed, and the royal court activities were transported to the second capital at Louyang. Although its political importance declined, it remained a bustling trading center.

BUDDHIST ART AT HORYUJI

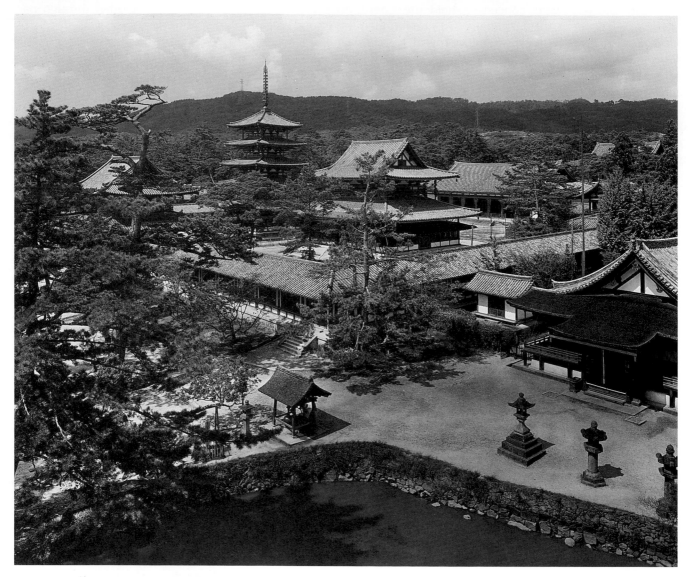

4-36. Horyuji complex, near Nara, Japan. Asuka period, 7th century. Stone, wood, plaster, and tile. Commissioned by Imperial Prince Shotoku

4-37. Plan of Horyuji

Horyuji is the oldest Buddhist temple in East Asia whose main parts have survived (figs. 4-36, 4-37); no earlier examples of Buddhist temples in China or Korea survive. Founded in 607, it is a treasure house of immense value for this phase of Buddhist development. One enters the temple-monastery complex through the **chumon**, the gate on the south face of the encircling **cloister**, and finds to the left (west) a **pagoda** and to the right (east) the main hall, or **kondo**, known as the Golden Hall. The pagoda and the *kondo* are equidistant from the *chumon* and are simultaneously visible as the worshiper enters. Instead of proceeding into the depths of the compound through a succession of buildings, as was the custom in China, the pilgrim makes a lateral turn. Lateral movement rather than linear penetration is repeatedly favored in Japanese spatial conceptions through history (see

TECHNIQUE   *TOU-KUNG* BRACKETING

At least as early as 1100 BCE in China, wooden blocks were added at the point where columns supported beams. They served as a type of cushioning that increased the surface of contact and thus reduced the span. Later, as in this Japanese example, cantilevered beams were projected outward from the top of eave columns to form a bracket arm.

These structural innovations allowed the deep eaves characteristic of this style of architecture. Eventually the blocks and the brackets were carved and painted, and elaborate *tou-kung* bracketing became an important part of the Japanese aesthetic.

Tou-kung eaves at the Horyuji *kondo*

fig. 4-16). Nevertheless, the individual buildings of Horyuji are typically continental—that is, Chinese or Korean—in style. They stand on raised stone bases and are built on a **bay** system, with post-and-lintel construction, tile roofs, and elaborate *tou-kung* bracketing (see above) designed to transmit the thrust and weight of the heavy tile roof down through the wooden members to the principal columns that support the structure.

The *kondo* is oriented to the four cardinal directions with a stairway on each side leading to a double door. Its interior is almost completely taken up by the platform and numerous statues. The main function of the *kondo* is to enclose them; it is a shrine rather than an assembly hall for a community (the *Kodo*, on the north end outside the cloister, was set aside for sermons and disputations). In the *kondo* are the images of the main statue of the Buddha in a triad (see fig. 4-38). This group is the spiritual center of the temple complex and is therefore most lavishly embellished: the posts and beams are painted and **gilded**; the ceiling, a canopy, represents Paradise or heaven. On each wall are paintings (damaged by fire in 1949) that represent the Buddha and the paradises of the cardinal directions. This program of statues and paintings in the *kondo* makes the temple a terrestrial representation of the Buddha's blissful realm. The sight of the gilded statues radiating the light of Buddha's wisdom and mercy is intended to inspire the believer. All the figures combine in a **mandala**, the center of which—the

HINDU ART AT ELLORA

4-39. Kailasantha Temple, Ellora, India. Rashtrakuta dynasty, c. 760–800, with later additions. Height 96'. The site at Ellora (see map, page 163) has thirty-four Hindu, Buddhist, and Jain rock-cut temples that date from the mid-sixth to the tenth century. The earliest temples are dedicated to the worship of the Hindu god Siva. They include elaborate pillared halls leading to shrines in the rear wall, which house *lingams* (stylized phallic symbols of Siva's procreative energies). By 600, the caves became a center for Buddhist worship, with Buddhist images carved both in the shrines of pillared halls and in the apsidal *chaitya* worship hall, where the Buddha is carved on the front of a monolithic stupa. Later, about 675 to 720, three-storied Buddhist caves focused worship on multiple Buddhas and other deities. A second wave of Siva worship in the eighth century included the building of this Hindu temple under the patronage of the Rashtrakutan monarch Krishna II (ruled 757–83).

The Kailasantha Temple (the name given to the entire eighth-century complex) is carved from a cliff to resemble a freestanding temple complex behind a high screen wall (figs. 4-39, 4-40). Although some sections are dedicated to different Hindu gods, the monument is literally a "magic mountain" in living rock where the theme of Mount Kailasa, the sacred mountain abode of Siva and his consort Parvati, is repeated several times. The artists, who wanted to represent the universe in this massive carving, oriented the structure to correspond to the four cardinal directions—the world compass. At the core of the temple is the place intended for individual worship in the Hindu faith; here was buried a box containing earth, stones, gems, herbs, roots, metals, and soils that was intended to tie the temple to ancient fertility

4-40. *(near left)* Plan of the Kailasantha Temple. The plan reveals the layout more clearly than any view. At the entrance, a large stone screen demarcates secular from religious space. Next is the Nandi shrine, flanked by the two towers. That small shrine is followed by three porches leading to a columned hall, which functioned as a gathering place, and to the shrine itself. Five subsidiary shrines on a second-story terrace outside the main sanctuary are dedicated to various deities associated with Siva. The sides of the tremendous pit created by the carving of the temple have secondary shrines in the vertical walls: the Shrine of Absolutions (or the Shrine of the Three Rivers), with representations of the three sacred rivers; a long series of sculptures at the rear; a second-story temple carved in the rock with a set of reliefs relating to Siva; a series of reliefs of avatars (incarnations) of Vishnu and aspects of Siva on the ground floor, surrounding the sides and completely enclosing the back wall; and a two-story complex on the right, once connected by a bridge to a porch, with representations of the Great Goddess (Devi) and the Seven Mothers. The large frieze sculptures that narrate the stories of the *Mahabharata* and the *Ramayana* on the south wall illustrate sacred literature. Numerous smaller shrines complete the group. Although the building of this great complex took place over a long period of time, it nevertheless represents a single architectural and sculptural conception.

beliefs and to emphasize the vitality of the religion.

The temple is an achievement of sculpture rather than architecture. It is composed of a court 276 feet long and 154 feet wide and a central tower 96 feet tall. The sheer physical problem of carving this tremendous temple from the living rock is awesome. Since the sculptors began working at a height above the tower, the total depth of the cut was about 120 feet—as high as a twelve-story building.

Upon entering this massive complex, one is aware of the contrast of the strong sunlight and deep blue shadows cast by the surrounding mountainside, which dramatizes the movement of space along the pathways and across the sculptural reliefs. The sculptural representations gesture wildly to enhance an overall sense of drama and exalta-tion for the believer. The boldness of conception and the skill in execution suggest centuries of tradition in which carving techniques and an understanding of the rock medium were developed, enabling craftworkers to push this southern Indian type of rock-cut temple to its limits.

Hinduism encompassed a broad variety of beliefs and practices; not all were shared by all Hindus, and some even contradicted each other. In fact, the religion is unusual in its tolerance of diversity. Completely decentralized, it has no hierarchy of clergy and no supreme authority—unlike Christianity, Islam, and Buddhism. The roots of the religion can be found 4,000 years ago in India, and as it developed it absorbed and reinterpreted the beliefs and practices of diverse groups of people. Assimilation occurred differently in various parts of India, and today, as in the past, the subcontinent is a repository of heterogeneous beliefs. That the worship of deities is a highly personal activity is reflected in the plan of Hindu temples, as well as in their sculptural reliefs. For instance, several of the shrines at the Kailasantha Temple do not have an interior sanctuary at all. (The Nandi shrine and the main shrine are open only on the second level.) Even when they are entered, the interior space is so small that an individual approach to the sacred images is required. Hinduism's personal approach to the gods is indicated in the thousands of different manifestations of the deity. Today this religion is vital to more than 750 million adherents in India, Sri Lanka, Pakistan, and East and South Africa, as well as on a number of islands in the Caribbean and Southeast Asian oceans.

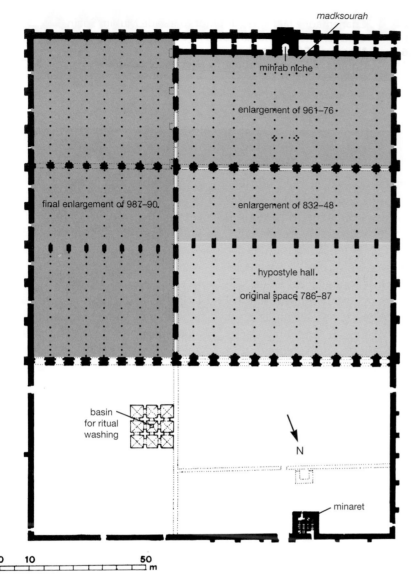

madksourah

mihrab niche

enlargement of 961–76

final enlargement of 987–90.

enlargement of 832–48

hypostyle hall.

original space 786–87

basin for ritual washing

N

minaret

0 10   50
m

4-42. Plan of the Mosque, Córdoba, 786–990. This plan shows the enlargements of 832–48, 961–76, and 987–90, the final expansion. The qibla and its mihrab at Córdoba do not literally face Mecca, but they do point in the same direction as the road that leaves Córdoba for that city.

taken by the Christians from earlier buildings. These columns and the arches above were incorporated into a new mosque that became famous for the placement of double rows of arches above columns. The superimposition of two tiers of arches gave added height and spaciousness, while the long rows of columns and arches helped direct the worshipers' attention toward the qibla and, thus, the road to Mecca. The superimposed arches over columns were repeated by a succession of rulers as they enlarged the mosque in 832–

48, 961, and 987, until it was converted back to Christian use after the reconquest of Córdoba in 1236. The first expansions enlarged the mosque in the original direction, but eventually the river that passes through Córdoba required an expansion to the side.

The interior "forest of columns" in the mosque emphasizes the democratic nature of Islam and the fact that Muslim worship stresses personal contact with Allah. Individual worshipers who entered the mosque for service would begin praying

at their own rate and not in concert with a leader or with other worshipers, as is the case in most other religions. Red-and-white horseshoe-shaped arches seem to extend endlessly to either side, but the view ahead, the direction toward Mecca, is open and direct. The overall plan is a traditional Muslim one (fig. 4-42). It has a crenelated, rectangular perimeter enclosing a forecourt with a basin for ritual ablution (washing). At one point, the qibla is hollowed out to form the sacred niche, or **mihrab**. Overlooking the courtyard is the **minaret**, the tower from which the muezzin ("crier") calls the faithful to prayer five times a day.

In 961–76, the caliph Al-Hakam II, mindful of his capital's prestige, built a superb, gleaming mihrab, preceded by a triple *madksourah*, or enclosure reserved only for the caliph. The enclosure is roofed by three ribbed domes, which rest on an unusual series of interweaving multilayered arches (fig. 4-43). All these interior areas are faced with mosaics against a background in gold.

Unlike Christianity or later Buddhism, the Islamic faith did not permit figurative representations of God or his prophets, and these mosaics, like most Islamic art, are stylized. No living creature is represented on Islamic religious structures, and the Koran is embellished with a luxurious, calligraphic version of Arabic lettering called **Kufic** (mistakenly named after the belief that the script originated in Kufa, in Iraq). Kufic script, complemented by abstract ornamental designs, became the main decoration in the form of inscriptions on mosques, secular buildings, and even utilitarian objects in metal, clay, and weavings in wool (for carpets, see fig. 6-62). This Islamic preference for linear surface decoration was used in the interior decoration of

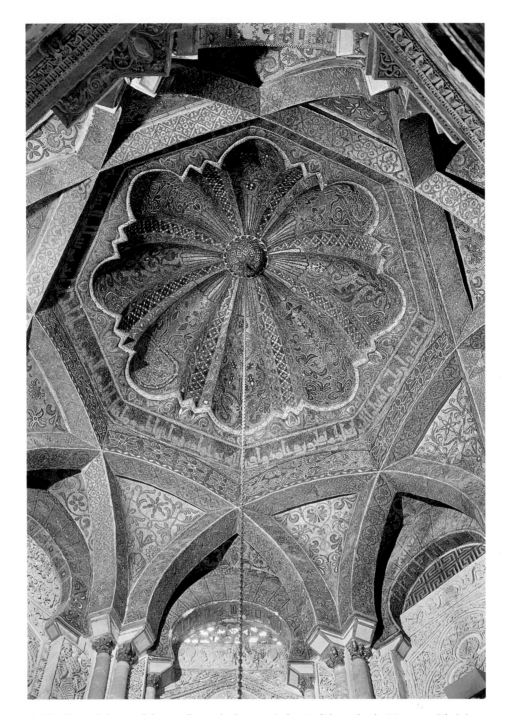

4-43. Central dome of the *madksourah,* the area in front of the mihrab, Mosque, Córdoba. 961–76. Colored stucco, tile, and glass mosaic. From the chain in the center of this dome was once suspended a silver lamp with 1,000 glass-cupped oil lamps. The ceiling of the small mihrab behind this is covered with a single large piece of stone, carved in the shape of a shell. Commissioned by Caliph Al-Hakam II

mosques. At Córdoba, the dome before the mihrab is typical, for it includes a stylized gold inscription in Kufic script at its base and a web of ornament above and below, made up of a variety of designs disciplined by symmetry, repetition, and rhythmic order.

Mosques serve both religious and secular functions. Following prayer in the mosque, the man who led the worship or his representative might speak on secular matters. This Arabic respect for learning contributed to advances in astronomy, mathematics, medicine, and optics through

centuries of support of its scholars. Such traditions continue in the modern world and predominate in Egypt and Syria, Saudi Arabia, Turkey, Albania, Iraq, Pakistan, Afghanistan, Iran, Yemen, Indonesia, Malaysia, Morocco, Tunisia, and Libya.

CAROLINGIAN ART

4-44. *Saint Matthew*, from the *Gospel Book of Archbishop Ebbo of Reims*, produced in Reims, France. 816–23. Manuscript painting on vellum, 10^{1}/4 x 8^{3}/4". Bibliothèque Municipale, Épernay, France. Commissioned for Archbishop Ebbo under the direction of Peter, abbot of the monastery of Hautvillers

During the reign of Charlemagne (also called Carolus, ruled 768–814), there was an interest in reviving the political unity and cultural ideals of the Roman world. This attraction can be seen in the image of Saint Matthew (fig. 4-44), which demonstrates how the art of this era—known as Carolingian art—could revive aspects of ancient classical style and yet remain true to medieval principles. Matthew wears a toga, and the modeling of the head, hands, and feet creates a sense of three-dimensional illusionism; the anonymous artist has clearly been inspired in part by a source imbued with the spirit of Hellenistic illusionism. In addition, the work shows the inspiration of Roman models in

the seemingly spontaneous technique, but here the fluid strokes of the brush—developed in Roman art to suggest movement—express a frenzy of divine inspiration that threatens to subsume both figure and landscape. Shimmering gold highlights on the toga, hair, and landscape heighten the liveliness, for they appear and disappear with changes in the reflected light.

The term *Carolingian* refers to the reigns of Charlemagne and his immediate successors, although in terms of art the particular qualities of Carolingian art did not endure long after his empire was divided by three grandsons in 843. Charlemagne, whose seal read *Renovatio Romani imperii* ("the revival of the

Roman Empire"), intended to create a Holy (that is, Christian) Roman Empire. He greatly expanded the Frankish kingdom he inherited, establishing a buffer between his kingdom and the Islamic threat in Spain and the East. On Christmas Day 800, Pope Leo III crowned Charlemagne emperor of Rome at St. Peter's Basilica.

Charlemagne's renewal included an interest in reform and education and a demand for order and efficiency. He codified law, issuing legal decrees from his capital at Aachen. He established a stable currency, ordered the creation of schools throughout his empire, reformed monastic life, corrected the calendar, established a large library, and encouraged the production of corrected copies of manuscripts, including the Bible. He required the use of a new, more easily readable style of lettering that is the basis of the typeface still used in most books. Literacy was a major goal, in part because it would enable people better to understand Christian doctrine and to participate in Church services. Charlemagne could read, but Einhard, his biographer, tells that he also wanted to learn to write and that he kept notebooks under his pillow, so that "he could try his hand at forming letters during his leisure moments."

Charlemagne's Palace at Aachen included a chapel (fig. 4-45), a centrally planned structure based on the most important church in the last Roman capital in the West, San Vitale in Ravenna (see fig. 4-25). Charlemagne received permission from the pope to remove columns and capitals from structures in Rome and Ravenna to incorporate into his palace complex. The large scale and simple forms of the building are an effort to relate it explicitly to the imperial style of ancient Rome

782   Arab forces attack Constantinople
814   Death of Charlemagne
816–23   *Gospel Book*, Reims

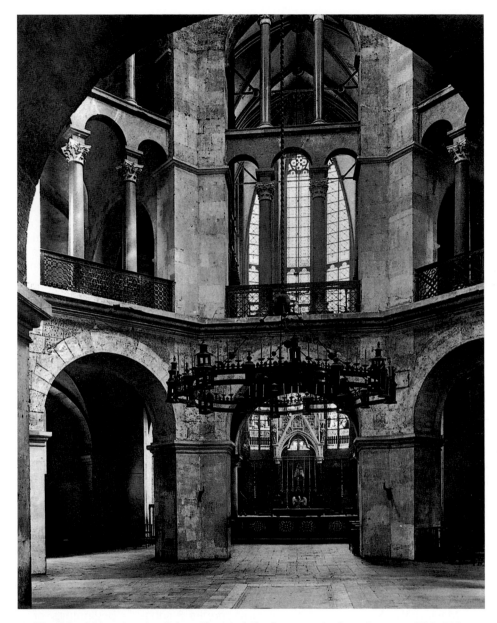

4-45. Odo of Metz. Interior, Palace Chapel of Charlemagne, Aachen, Germany. 792–805. Commissioned by Charlemagne

and to confirm Charlemagne's importance as the "Holy Roman Emperor." To emphasize the Christian nature of his rule, Charlemagne modeled his throne on that of Solomon, described in the Old Testament, and placed it in the Palace Chapel opposite the altar.

The Carolingian ideal of a world that would combine the greatness of the ancient past with the Christian vision is revealed in a letter that was sent to Charlemagne in 799:

If many people became imbued with your ideas a new Athens would be established in France—nay, an Athens fairer than the Athens of old, for it would be ennobled by the teachings of Christ, and ours would surpass all the wisdom of the ancient academy. For this had only for its instruction the disciples of Plato; yet, molded by the seven liberal arts, it shone with constant splendor. But ours would be endowed with the sevenfold fullness of the Holy Spirit, and would surpass all secular wisdom in dignity.

THE MONASTERY IN THE WEST

4-46. Plan of St. Gall Monastery. c. 819. Traced and drawn on five pieces of parchment sewn together, 44 x 30". Monastery Library, St. Gall, Switzerland. The St. Gall plan, traced from another plan now lost, represents an ideal formula to be adjusted for each particular site and needs. It even suggests the appropriate location of furnishings. Its orderly design may be related to the reforms of the monastic system within the Carolingian empire, discussed at meetings in Aachen, Germany, in 816 and 817. Not a document that normally would have been saved, it may have survived only because a life of Saint Martin was written on the back.

The monastery was perhaps the single most important institution in Europe during the medieval period. The St. Gall plan reveals the complex and varied needs of a monastic community (fig. 4-46). The central structure is the church itself, which has a basilical form following Early Christian models; the nave and side aisles provide additional altars needed because each priest was required to say Mass daily. At the western end of the church plan is a smaller apse with two towers forming an entrance facade known as a **westwork**. A Carolingian innovation in church design, the westwork helped to create an impressive entrance and was the source from which the traditional two-towered church **facade** would develop.

The subsidiary structures include a separate house for the abbot who ruled the monastery and, for the monks, a complex attached to the church that included a dormitory, latrine, bathhouse, and **refectory** (dining hall), as well as a cloister for walking and meditation. Outbuildings housed kitchen, mill, bakery, drying house, brew house, storerooms, barns, workrooms for artisans, and other facilities necessary for a self-sufficient community of approximately one hundred. There were also, set apart, a chapel and housing for those who were studying to become monks. A separate house, with its own kitchen, served special visitors. The services that the monastery provided the public included an infirmary, complete with herb garden, and a hospital for the poor. Usually there was a lodge for travelers. In an area adjacent to the main altar were the library and the scriptorium, where manuscripts were copied and illustrated. The orchard served as the monastic cemetery. The complex seen here would have been surrounded by vast fields worked by the monks and hired laborers.

Monasticism has its roots in the early days of Christianity in the Middle East and Egypt, when many Christians retreated into the desert or lived in caves in order to spend their lives praying, remote from the distractions and temptations of the world. Many chose to live a life of complete isolation, but some banded into communities that mark the beginnings of the monastic tradition. During the sixth century, Benedict of Nursia (later Saint Benedict) gathered so many followers that he wrote a rule (c. 535–40) for their behavior. This became the basis for later medieval monastic organization, in part because Charlemagne imposed it on all monasteries in his empire; by the seventh century, a variant of the Benedictine rule was in use for women. Benedict required that the monks remain within the monastery for life and that they observe poverty, chastity, and

4-47. Reconstruction of the Romanesque monastery and third church, Cluny, France.
c. 1157. The church and monastery were largely destroyed by Napoleonic edict in 1810.
Commissioned by the abbots of the monastery

obedience. A simple, humble garment and hairstyle were specified. The monks swore obedience to an elected abbot; daily life was a well-organized regimen of work, study, and prayer. There were at least eight daily services of psalms, hymns, and prayers. Work included all aspects of labor. Many monks and nuns became skilled in the arts, but Benedict's rule warns against the pride that could accompany artistic achievement:

> Let such craftsmen as be in the monastery ply their trade in all lowliness of mind if the abbot allow it. But if any be puffed up by his skill in his craft . . . such a one shall be shifted from his handicraft, and not attempt it again until such time as he has learnt a low opinion of himself, and the abbot bids him resume.

Through an emphasis on literacy and education, which were required to participate fully in the Christian life, the monasteries played a vital role in continuing and preserving the Western heritage. A number of ancient works of literature, science, and philosophy survive only in copies handwritten by monks and nuns.

In the course of the Middle Ages, there was a proliferation of monastic orders, but their rules were similar. Most were located in the country, away from the temptations of city life and far from other human beings. In the thirteenth century, two new orders, the Franciscans and the Dominicans, were approved by the pope. They emphasized public service in the urban environment, and their monasteries were established within the cities to serve the sick and the poor (see page 221).

No monastery was built that exactly followed the design of the St. Gall plan, in part because any complex of such scale would evolve slowly over time and in relationship to the peculiarities of the particular setting. The Romanesque monastery at Cluny, however, can be studied as an example of a fully developed medieval monastery (fig. 4-47).

Cluny, the mother church of a reformed Benedictine order that played an important role in monastic renewal during the eleventh and twelfth centuries, became one of the most important centers for learning and patronage of art in Europe. It was famous for the splendor and beauty of its services, and its third church, begun about 1085 and consecrated in 1131–32, was, with a length of 555 feet, the largest church in all Europe. The monastic complex at Cluny has virtually all the same facilities as the St. Gall plan; especially impressive is the amount of space given over to the huge infirmary.

BUDDHIST ART IN INDONESIA

4-48. Buddhist Temple of Borobudur, Java, Indonesia. Sailendra dynasty, 835–60. Lava stone; perimeter of lowest gallery 1,180'; diameter of crowning stupa 52'. Borobudur was rediscovered by Europeans in 1814, but few could understand it because of their inability to read Asian languages and the scripts in which Buddhist texts were written. Although the Javanese are predominantly Muslims today, they prize this monument and rescued it from neglect and severe water and atmospheric conditions through a ten-year restoration, which concluded in 1985. Now the structure is secure and its many reliefs can be properly seen again. Borobudur was built by a family of kings known as the Sailendras, or "Lords of the Mountains." The Buddhist ruler who started work on Borobudur was named Indra, after the god who lives on top of Mount Sumeru and who appears in several sculpted reliefs of the lower galleries.

The Buddhist temple called Borobudur (fig. 4-48) is situated on a hill above the fertile Kedu Plain in central Java (see map, page 163). The plain, covered with rice fields and coconut groves, is surrounded by high-peaked mountains. According to legend, Borobudur was designed by a divine architect named Gunadharma, whose profile is said to be visible in the outline of nearby mountains. Far from having been the work of a single designer, however, Borobudur was remodeled four times within its first century. Originally the site was recognized as sacred by the Hindus, who around

780 began to erect a structure on the hill. Workers cut terraces into the sides of the hills and erected a massive stone structure with three levels that correspond to the first three levels of the current monument. Such large human-made terraces have been found in other locations on Java and are thought to have been the sites of historical equivalents of the modern *punden*, rituals performed to obtain power from ancestors in order to purge evil influences.

The current stepped shape was built by the Buddhists partly to accommodate the earlier founda-

tion. The lowest part of what we see today is an undecorated base measuring 370 feet on each side. Originally, 160 relief panels illustrating Buddhist writings about heaven and hell adorned the base just above the ground. That base proved to be too narrow to support the monument and had to be rebuilt with the broader, unadorned base seen today.

From this base rise five square terraces with **balustraded** galleries. The inner and outer walls at each level are covered with carved panels illustrating the path toward enlightenment.

The three circular terraces hold seventy-two stone **stupas**, each about 12 feet high. The diamond-shaped perforations carved into the stupas on the two lower terraces express the idea of change and movement. On the top terrace, the openings are square and are thought to express calm and stillness. Each stupa contains a sculpted figure of the Buddha that is visible only as the monument is ascended. The entire monument is crowned with an enormous stupa containing an unfinished figure of the Buddha.

Borobudur is thought to have served many purposes, and it has been interpreted in many ways—as a visualization of the doctrine for the initiate; as a **mandala** for meditation (see fig. 5-3); as a symbolic mountain; and as a stupa that was a center of ritual activity in the ordered Buddhist world. Borobudur's design is most commonly compared to the Diamond World mandala, a type associated with the esoteric Tantric Buddhism practiced in Tibet and Nepal. Borobudur's form and hilltop location recall the setting of the jewel tower on Mount Sumeru (the World Mountain), where the Diamond World mandala was first described as being located in Tantric cosmology. We have no proof, however, that Borobudur was actually used as a mandala.

Borobudur's most convincing interpretation is as a stupa and/or symbolic mountain, an interpretation that combines both Javanese and Buddhist concepts. Some scholars argue that the main stupa on top of the monument originally contained a Buddhist relic. It seems that Javanese Buddhists came to Borobudur as pilgrims—to climb this holy, human-made mountain and thus to attain spiritual merit. This

4-49. *Prince Sudhana's Search for Enlightenment*, upper terrace of the Temple of Borobudur. 835–60. Lava stone, height 20"

stepped pyramid provided a place where Buddhists could physically and spiritually pass through the ten stages of development that could transform them into bodhisattvas, enlightened disciples of the Buddha.

As a symbolic mountain, this human-made holy monument can be understood as a continuation of the hill on which it sits. Mountains were important religious symbols in both pre-Buddhist Java and in the imagery of Mahayana Buddhism. The Javanese tradition of building terraced sanctuaries on high places, which continues today, began in prehistoric times; the upper stories are often built to evoke a holy mountain.

Mountains were equated with powerful spiritual forces, and as the pilgrims approached Borobudur all they could see were hundreds of statues gazing over the surrounding plain. In addition, the statues in niches suggest Javanese ascetics meditating in mountain caves as well as the gods who live in the caves on Mount Sumeru. The statues suggest that the pilgrim may have to endure self-denial and overcome physical

discomfort in order to gain the highest stage of development when reaching the stupa at the summit.

In order to follow the complete narrative sculpted in the reliefs, the pilgrim had to make ten circuits—four times around the first gallery and twice around each of the next three. While moving slowly upward, the pilgrim was symbolically retracing the steps of the bodhisattvas who attained enlightenment by successfully passing through all ten stages of existence. The 1,460 narrative panels on the monument were created to illustrate Buddhist scriptures: the *Vision of Worldly Desire*; the *Jataka Tales*, or the *Previous Lives of the Buddhas*; the *Life of the Gautama Buddha*. As the pilgrim circumambulated, the reliefs illustrated stories from these tales. Figure 4-49 illustrates a scene describing the young Prince Sudhana's search for enlightenment from the epic *Travels of a Young Man in Search of Wisdom*. The figure of the prince is sheltered by a royal umbrella, and his elaborate headdress sets him apart from the other figures.

CHINESE ART: LANDSCAPE PAINTING

4-50. Li Cheng (attributed). *Buddhist Temple in the Hills after Rain.* Five Dynasties/ Northern Song dynasty, c. 950. Hanging scroll, ink and slight color on silk, height 42". The Nelson-Atkins Museum of Art, Kansas City, Missouri. The authorship of few tenth-century landscape paintings is known with certainty. Descriptions of the work of these artists by critics of their own time make attributions such as this possible, however. Commissioned by the imperial court

Purchase: Nelson Trust

In this landscape attributed to Li Cheng (active from about 940 to 967), the autumn skies are clearing, leaving only mist in the low valleys and above the mountain pathways (fig. 4-50). In the immediate foreground are a group of huts and two pavilions built over water. The build- ings and figures are painted with such detail that we can distinguish peasants and courtiers at their meals in the rustic inn and scholars at the wine shops gazing off into the landscape from the pavilions. The temple that occupies the center of the painting is parallel to the peaks that dominate the distance. Such axially symmetrical monumental configurations of mountains and water came to be associated with the Chinese empire in the tenth cen- tury—grand, ordered, realistic, and powerful.

Li Cheng as a person was thought to represent the ideal Chi- nese painter—an artist who claimed descent from the imperial clan of the Tang dynasty (618–907), was educated in the humanities through study of the *Classic Books* (ancient texts on history, philosophy, and lit- erature), and was occupied with painting for his own delight without ambition for honors or advance- ment. A scholar and a gentleman, he enjoyed a quiet life devoted to the philosophic study of Nature as opposed to merely copying forms in the out-of-doors (nature). **Mono- chrome** ink paintings of landscape were the preferred type of art pro- duced by Li Cheng and his col- leagues.

Like many other landscape painters of the tenth century, Li Cheng had a preference for autum- nal or wintry scenes full of bleak,

c. 900   Vikings discover Greenland
c. 950   Li Cheng (attributed), *Buddhist Temple in the Hills after Rain*
988   Christianity introduced into Russia

4-51. *Buddhist Temple in the Hills after Rain*, detail

stony crags, gnarled trees with leafless crab-claw–shaped branches, and looming distant peaks. He shares with other landscapists of the period a preference for monochrome ink, laid on the silk in broad and jagged strokes, to describe the essential outlines of the rocks, trees, and buildings. These shapes are then broken up and modeled with **washes** of ink. On top of the washes are placed **cun**, small brushstrokes dabbed on quickly to create the sense of texture (fig. 4-51). Such paintings were then mounted on a vertical hanging or horizontal hand scroll. Closely associated with calligraphy, the brush paintings of China were produced for and by the intelligentsia, who painted as an avocation.

The Chinese doctrine of realism seen here aims for truth to natural appearance but not at the expense of a pictorial examination of how Nature operates. In Li Cheng's painting, the bent and twisted trees, for example, are organically constructed to expose their full skeletons— roots, trunk, branches, and even the dormant buds ready for spring awakening. This approach to realism

also explains the attitude behind **shifting perspective** in Chinese painting. In *Buddhist Temple* we are invited to "enter" the picture on the lower left and to explore as we move through the landscape. We can wander across the bridge, look down at rooftops, up at pavilions and the temple, and across to the towering peaks, but we cannot take a panoramic view from a single position outside (or inside) the painting, and the artist does not intend that we do so. Rather, little by little, Nature is revealed as if we were actually walking in the out-of-doors. In this sense, the Chinese landscape painter combines the element of time in much the same way as it is experienced in music. Shifting perspective allows for a journey and for a powerful personal impact on the individual participant. These paintings were meant to be visual exercises that allowed for examination of both the structure of nature or the universe and the contemplation of minute details. The power of these paintings is to take us out of ourselves and to provide spiritual solace and refreshment.

Guo Xi, a pupil of Li Cheng, declared in an essay that "the virtuous man above all delights in landscapes." The virtuous (or Confucian) man during this period accepted his civil responsibilities to society and to the state, which tied him to an urban life as an official, but he could nourish his spirit by taking imaginary trips into nature through viewing a landscape painting such as Guo Xi's *Early Spring* (see fig. 1-3).

There was important support for landscape painters during the Five Dynasties (907–60) and the Northern Song dynasty (960–1126). An important occurrence of the period was the initial printing of the *Classical Texts* in 953; for the first time, books became inexpensive and abundant. Scholars multiplied, and the knowledge of ancient literature was more widespread. The political consequences of the expansion of the literate class was manifest in the Song, the third centralized empire in Chinese history. The unification of the empire was the work of policy rather than conquest, a powerful submission of an aristocracy weary of disunion and

4-52. Xia Gui (attributed). *Sailboat in the Rain.* c. 1180. Fan-shaped album leaf, ink and light color on silk, 9³/8 x 9⁷/8". Chinese and Japanese Special Fund. Courtesy, Museum of Fine Arts, Boston. Commissioned by the imperial court

aware of its own cultural identity. The traditional civil service examination system returned civilians to positions of prestige and power in government that had been lost under previous military dictatorships. The prevailing pacifist policies and a series of enlightened sovereigns who were tolerant, humane, artistic, and intellectual provided substantial and consistent patronage for the arts. The collection of the Song emperor Hui Zong (ruled 1100–26; see fig. 4-33), for example, was said to include 159 paintings by Li Cheng. The Song period produced the first important academy of painting in the Far East; among the early members were the landscapists.

The Song dynasty was an age of many-sided intellectual activity—poetry, history, and, especially, phi-losophy. Characteristic of Song thought was the return to older Chinese sources, a conscious archaism and cultural introspection. The renaissance of classical literature branched off into the formation of a new system of philosophy called neo-Confucianism, which enveloped traditional moral and ethical teachings with Daoist thinking about nature and the cosmos, especially as presented in the *I-jing (Book of Changes)*. No distinction was made between the law of nature and moral law. The world was thought to be inspired by the "Supreme Ultimate" (or what the Daoists called the *dao*, or the Way); the neo-Confucianists referred to this as *li* (law), a moral law that was identical to the ethical code upon which human conduct should be modeled. These Song thinkers were also interested in correspondences in nature.

The manifestation of *li* in painting included faithfulness to nature as well as conventionalized symbols for representation of rocks, foliage, bark, water, and so forth. *Li* also governed the way a picture was put together.

Under pressure from the Jin Tartars on the northern borders of China, the Song court fled south in 1127. In 1135, a new capital was founded at Hangzhou (see map, page 163), where the academy of painting was reestablished under imperial patronage and every effort was made to assemble an imperial art collection equal to that of the Northern Song emperors. The Southern Song rulers were even more concerned with internal affairs than their predecessors, and a new mode of painting evolved that focused on depiction of what was nearby and up close.

Chinese painting is derived from the art of writing and is, therefore, a linear art. Its brushwork is imbued with calligraphic formulas. The highest aesthetic aim of the literati painters was to capture the spirit of what was depicted, rather than merely its appearance (see fig. 1-22). For these literati painters, the creative process embodied the *dao*, or Way of Nature, with its holistic vision of organic and metaphysical properties. In many Chinese paintings, idea and technique are one; the act of painting and the picture itself both carry meaning. Interestingly, these literati artists did not create sculpture or architecture, which were the work of highly skilled artisans.

Among the Chinese aristocracy, painting and calligraphy were revered media for examination and for the preservation of social, political, and aesthetic values. The earliest-known treatise on aesthetics was written in the second quarter of the sixth century by a man named Xie He (c. 500–c. 535). Called the *Gu hua pin lu (Classified Record of Ancient Painters)*, it graded earlier painters into six classes. What made the treatise so influential was its Preface, known as the Six Canons of Painting, which were used to judge painters and paintings. Because its language is filled with abstract philosophic thinking and presents generalized and theoretical prescriptions for painting, the canons have been translated and interpreted many times. An approximate translation of the Six Canons is:

1. A painting must have spirit or breath of life (*qi yun*).
2. The brushwork must be structurally sound.
3. The painting must faithfully portray forms.
4. A painting must have fidelity of color.
5. A painting must also be a properly planned composition.
6. A painting must transmit knowledge of past painting traditions.

The first canon, animation through spirit consonance, emphasizes the need for painting to have *qi yun*. **Qi** was thought to be the cosmic spirit that vitalized all things; to capture its essence was fundamental for "good" painting. Canons 2–5 clearly concentrate on technical matters, and canon 6 emphasizes the transmission of and reverence for tradition. Each generation of artists established a sense of external and internal reality in painting that could be challenged and reconsidered during the following period. Xie He's treatise remained the backbone of aesthetic criticism until the modern period in China, when its imperial, elitist roots were challenged by new socialist policies.

The ideals of painting of the tenth century were written down by a contemporary of Li Cheng named Ching Hao. In his essay *Record of Brush Methods*, or *Essay on Landscape Painting*, Ching Hao recorded his thoughts through a narrator, an old man whom he pretended to meet while wandering in the mountains. This wise man told him the six essentials of painting: spirit, rhythm, thought, scenery, brush, and ink. This logical system, based on Xie He, first lays down the concept of painting and then its expression. It distinguishes further between resemblance, which reproduces the formal, outward aspects of what is depicted, and truth (or spirit), which involves knowing and representing inner reality. Correct balance between representing visible forms of nature and their deeper significance was the goal of these Chinese painters.

Later Southern Song landscape painters such as Xia Gui (active 1180–1230) concentrated on rivers, lakes, and mists of south China (fig. 4-52). Xia Gui developed a shorthand manner in which forms are suggested rather than depicted, as they had been in the earlier style of Li Cheng and Guo Xi. His softer and less literal expression is organized asymmetrically, in a style called a "one-corner" composition by the Chinese. There is more mist than ink, and the subjective expression omits large sections of the landscape to concentrate on closer components. Xia Gui evokes a mood; he does not describe a particular place. He and other painters at court were associated with the politically weak and ineffectual court of the Southern Song in subsequent periods. For later Chinese critics, who commingled aesthetic and moral judgment, the Southern Song paintings were less highly valued than they were in Japan and the West.

OTTONIAN ART

4-53. *Christ Washing the Feet of Saint Peter,* from the *Gospel Book of Otto III.* c. 1000. Manuscript painting on vellum, 8 x 6". Bavarian State Library, Munich, Germany. This Gospel Book, created for the Ottonian emperor Otto III, is lavishly decorated with twenty-nine full-page illustrations of the life of Jesus Christ and a double-page portrait of the patron. Commissioned by Otto III

The bold exaggeration of the arm and hand of Christ in this manuscript painting (fig. 4-53) reveals the Ottonian artist's determination to create a representation that is simultaneously clear and dramatic. The emphasis is on Christ's divinity, as seen in the gesture of blessing, rather than on the mundane theme of the washing of feet. The placement of Christ's haloed head in the center of the composition, against an empty gold field, emphasizes his majesty. The complicated architectural forms, inconsistent in perspective and out of scale with the figures, are intended to inform the viewer that this is an indoor scene. The busy patterns of the drapery add energy, and the emphatic, staring eyes of the participants suggest that some-

4-54. Doors with scenes from the Old and New Testaments. c. 1015. Bronze, height approx. 15'. St. Michael's, Hildesheim, Lower Saxony, Germany. These doors and a huge bronze candlestick, 12'6" tall, were commissioned by Bishop Bernward (later Saint Bernward). The candlestick, decorated with scenes from the life of Jesus, is a Christianized version of ancient Roman imperial triumphal columns (see fig. 3-99). Commissioned by Bishop Bernward thing very significant is taking place. That Christ is clean-shaven reveals the influence of Early Christian or Byzantine models.

Like Charlemagne, the Saxon prince Otto I (ruled 936–73) wanted to revive the ancient Roman Empire, and he brought Germany and most of northern Italy, including Rome, under his control before being crowned emperor by the pope in 962. Otto established a centralized government, and his lineage—his son Otto II, who married a Byzantine princess, and his grandson Otto III—ruled until 1002. Their reforms in education and monasticism were similar to those of Charlemagne, and Ottonian art flourished until at least the middle of the eleventh century.

Ottonian patrons and artists continued elements of iconography and style from the Carolingian tradition, as well as from the ancient Roman, Early Christian, and Byzantine periods. There were some large-scale architectural projects and several active centers for manuscript illustration, ivory carving, and work in gold and bronze.

The imperial connotations of Ottonian rule are clear in the bronze candlestick and doors at St. Michael's, Hildesheim. The bronze doors (fig. 4-54), the first cast in Europe in centuries, have sources in both ancient Roman and Byzantine art. The figures have a lively intensity expressing strong emotions and psychological interaction; in the most famous of these scenes, fourth from the top on the left side of the door, an accusing God confronts Adam. Adam in turn points to Eve, who tries to put the blame on the dragonlike serpent crawling on the ground.

The **choir** area of St. Michael's is

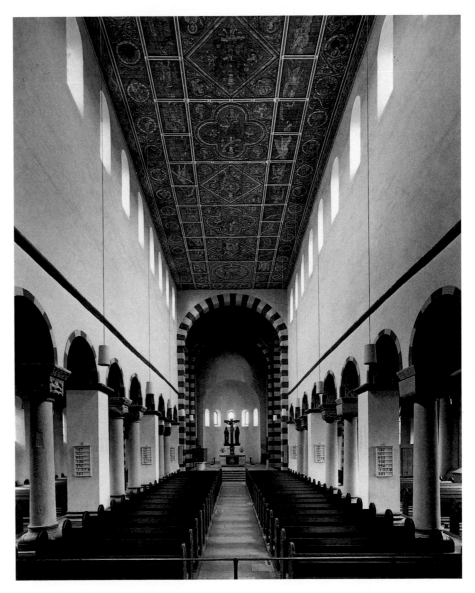

4-55. Interior, St. Michael's, Hildesheim. 1001–31. Badly damaged by bombing during World War II, St. Michael's has been restored. Commissioned by Bishop Bernward

raised so the monks can conduct their services while pilgrims continue to have access to the relics in a crypt below. The alternation of paired columns with **piers** in the **nave arcade** is new (fig. 4-55) and may be an attempt to divide the nave into more clearly defined units. The nave is higher and narrower than in earlier churches, creating a pronounced vertical emphasis. On the exterior, turrets at the **transepts** and two **crossing** towers create a fortresslike massing of monumental forms, pierced by small windows, that predicts the later developments of Romanesque art (see fig. 4-61). The Ottonian revival, as short-lived as Charlemagne's, demonstrates the importance of political and economic stability for the production of works of art and architecture.

ROMANESQUE ART

4-56. *Christ in Majesty with Angels, Symbols of the Evangelists, and Saints,* from San Clemente, Tahull, Spain. c. 1123. Apse fresco, diameter of apse approx. 13'. Museo de Arte de Cataluña, Barcelona

4-57. Sainte Foy reliquary. Later 10th century. Gold with filigree and precious stones over wooden core, height 33 1/2". Cathedral Treasury, Conques, Rouergue, France. The masklike face of this reliquary, which enshrines the bones of the saint, is made from an ancient Roman gold face guard and parade helmet to which inlaid enameled eyes have been added. The forearms and hands date from a post-Romanesque restoration. For the church at Conques that enshrined Sainte Foy's remains, see figures 4-60–4-62.

The term *Romanesque* ("Roman-like") was first applied in the nineteenth century to designate medieval art of the tenth to the mid-twelfth century, which is distinguished by a Europe-wide revival of monumental architecture, sculpture, and mural painting. In the Tahull apse painting, the enthroned Christ in Majesty, surrounded by a mandorla, is symmetrically flanked by angels and the symbols of the Evangelists (fig. 4-56). A row of standing saints below includes the Virgin Mary. The hierarchical presentation and the iconlike stare of the figures associate the painting with the Byzantine tradition (see fig.

4-27). But here the abstraction of earlier medieval art is intensified, and the drapery folds have a life of their own; instead of being used to reveal the body beneath the drapery, they flutter and fold in abstract patterns. Each body part is treated independently, with heads and hands exaggerated in scale. **Foreshortening** is avoided, as in the unnaturalistic rendering of Christ's book, with the inscription "I am the light of the world." The simple and direct presentation, harsh modeling, unnatural but bold colors, and frontal stiffness combine to create a commanding composition, representative of much Romanesque art.

HISTORY

During the tenth century, Europe stirred with revived economic, social, and cultural life. The wanderings and attacks of migrating peoples, a source of conflict and political unrest for centuries, abated, in part because of their conversion to Christianity. The 1054 split between the Western, or Roman, and the Byzantine, or Orthodox, branches of Christianity would never be resolved, despite efforts at reunion in later centuries. After the split, the Roman Church under the papacy consolidated its religious and political power in western Europe. England was united with much of France after the duke of Normandy's conquest in 1066, and Norman victories in southern Italy and Sicily freed those areas from Byzantine control. The new political stability fostered an expanded economy.

The Church gradually increased its influence in secular affairs, coming into conflict with the feudal nobility. The power and energy of the Church were manifested in the enormous undertaking of the Crusades, which began in the 1090s as an attempt to capture the "Holy Lands" from the Muslims and to establish commercial activity on a broader scale. The Reconquest, the war against the Muslims in Spain, led to the capture of Córdoba by Christian forces in 1236.

ART AND THE PILGRIM

The mainstays of earlier medieval workshop production—manuscript illumination, ivory carving, and metalwork—continued throughout the Romanesque period. More significant is the widespread revival of monumental architecture and art that distinguishes the eleventh century.

The pilgrimage, which earlier in the Middle Ages had been prescribed for the atonement of sin, became a regular feature of Chris-

4-58. *Saint Mark*, from a Gospel Book produced at Cambrai, Nord, France. Second half of the 11th century. Manuscript painting on vellum, $10^3/4$ x $7^7/8$". Bibliothèque Municipale, Amiens

tian life during the Romanesque period. Pilgrims traveled over defined routes, known as the pilgrimage roads, either to Rome or to Santiago de Compostela in western Spain. At St. Peter's in Rome or the Church of St. James in Santiago, pilgrims invoked God's intercession. To prepare spiritually for their destination at Santiago or Rome, pilgrims visited churches and monasteries along their routes, where they could pray before the relics of saints. These relics were usually encased in precious reliquaries such as that of Sainte Foy at Conques (fig. 4-57); many of the jewels that adorn her golden cloak were gifts from pilgrims. Pilgrims were sheltered in monasteries that since the earlier medieval period had functioned as centers of learning and hospitality. During this period, developments in Church architecture responded to the needs of both clergy and pilgrims.

MANUSCRIPT ILLUMINATION

The **illumination** (illustration and decoration) of manuscripts continued to be a significant medium of painting during the Romanesque period. The figure of Saint Mark in the Gospel Book (fig. 4-58), which displays the same intense color and bold outlines as the monumental apse painting from Tahull, is enlivened by an abstract curvilinear design. The saint, seated in his study, turns to grasp a scroll from his symbol, the lion. Framed within an arch, the scene is animated by the twisted body of the lion, whose contorted movement is echoed in the drapery around the arch and the diagonals of Mark's robe. The contrast between the stable framing of the scene and these lively patterns creates a dynamic interpretation of divine inspiration.

4-59. *King Harold Receiving a Messenger*, detail from the *Bayeux Tapestry*. c. 1070–80. Embroidered wool on linen, height 20"; total length 231'. Centre Guillaume Le Conquérant, Bayeux, Normandy, France. Despite the fact that the technique is embroidery, this work is traditionally known as the *Bayeux Tapestry*. It was probably executed by a group of women artists, who specialized in the needle arts. In more than seventy-five scenes accompanied by Latin inscriptions, the work tells the story of the victory of William the Conqueror over King Harold during the Norman conquest of England, in 1066. The embroidery, probably commissioned by Bishop Odo of Bayeux, half-brother of William, was intended for display in a great secular hall.

THE BAYEUX "TAPESTRY"

The unique embroidered narrative of the *Bayeux Tapestry* (fig. 4-59) depicts the events that led to the Norman invasion of England and the victory at Hastings in 1066. Our detail shows the English king, Harold, enthroned in his castle. A messenger informs the king that his rival, William, duke of Normandy, has ordered a fleet of ships to be built in order to cross the English Channel. In the sky to the left of the castle is Halley's Comet, which was visible in England in late April 1066; at the time, it was interpreted as a signal of impending disaster for Harold. The inscription reads: *Isti mirant[ur]stellam* ("These men marvel at the star").

The sequence of historical events is narrated in a lively, engaging manner. The curving axes of the figures of King Harold and the messenger animate the scene, while the abstract tree to the right, with its undulating

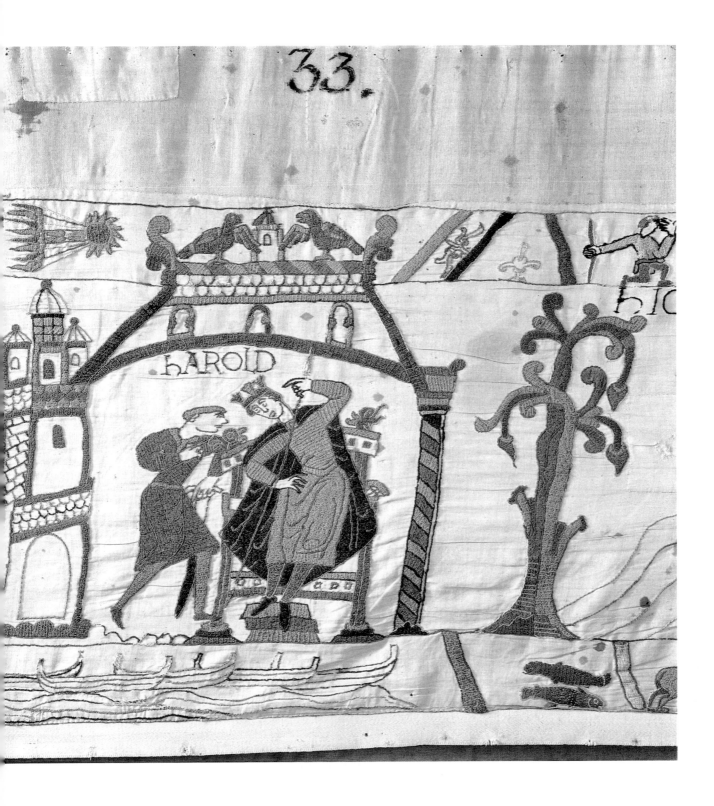

rhythm, demonstrates the continuation of Anglo-Saxon **interlace** motifs and asserts a vitality drawn from nature that permeates much of the work. The limited colors are used decoratively rather than descriptively, and the abstract rhythms of the composition enliven the historic narrative.

THE ROMANESQUE ARTIST

Artists, benefiting from the economic growth of the period, organized **guilds** to ensure quality and control in the production of art and the training of apprentices. Guilds offered protection for the artists as a group, encouraged a greater amount of self-regulation, and promoted an increased social prestige. Still, however, few works are signed and dated.

ROMANESQUE ARCHITECTURE AT CONQUES

4-60. Nave, Abbey Church of Ste.-Foy, Conques, Rouergue, France. c. 1080–1120. The monastic church of Ste.-Foy was located along one of the pilgrimage roads to Santiago de Compostela, Spain. The present Romanesque structure was built around an older church probably begun during the Carolingian period. Although located along pilgrimage routes, Conques later remained isolated from the urban development that affected many other medieval towns, and with the exception of two nineteenth-century towers, the church has been spared the restoration activity that so often transformed medieval architecture. The church is dedicated to a third-century virgin martyr, Sainte Foy (known in English as Saint Faith), whose relics were brought to Conques about 870 (for the reliquary preserved here, see figure 4-57). Originally commissioned by Abbot Odolric c. 1052; the cloister was begun by Abbot Begon

4-61. Abbey Church of Ste.-Foy, Conques. For the tympanum over the central doorway, see figure 4-64.

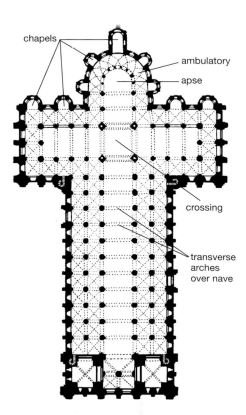

4-62. Plan of the Abbey Church of Ste.-Foy, Conques

Viewing the **crossing** and the **apse** of the Abbey Church of Ste.-Foy from the **nave** (fig. 4-60), we can immediately see why nineteenth-century historians coined the term *Romanesque* to describe this style of architecture. The use of round arches and stone vaults is reminiscent of ancient Roman building practice, and, like Roman architecture, the monumental scale establishes an austere, massive presence. The wooden truss roof common in Early Christian and Carolingian architecture has now given way to the favored construction feature of Roman architecture, the vault. At Ste.-Foy, the **barrel vault** of the nave is reinforced with **transverse arches** (arches that traverse the nave). On the exterior, vertical **buttresses** make the interior rhythm of the **bays** readable from outside (fig. 4-61). On exterior and interior, then, the articulation of the individual bays creates an order and unity characteristic of Romanesque architecture. The transverse arches also make it possible to construct a thinner barrel vault, allowing for larger windows. Romanesque stone vaulting also served other purposes, for it helped prevent the spread of fire, a prevalent threat with wooden truss-roof buildings, and it acoustically enhanced the liturgical chants of the monks.

Another feature of the Romanesque pilgrimage church was the use of a semicircular **ambulatory** (fig. 4-62). Adapted from ancient Roman and Early Christian centrally planned buildings, it is here used to solve a specific problem. At churches with monastic foundations, it was necessary that the monks occupy the area around the high altar for numerous services. The ambulatory connecting the side aisles in one continuous passageway allowed large numbers of pilgrims to move through the church, stopping to pray and venerate relics in the apsidal chapels without disturbing the monks.

ROMANESQUE SCULPTURE

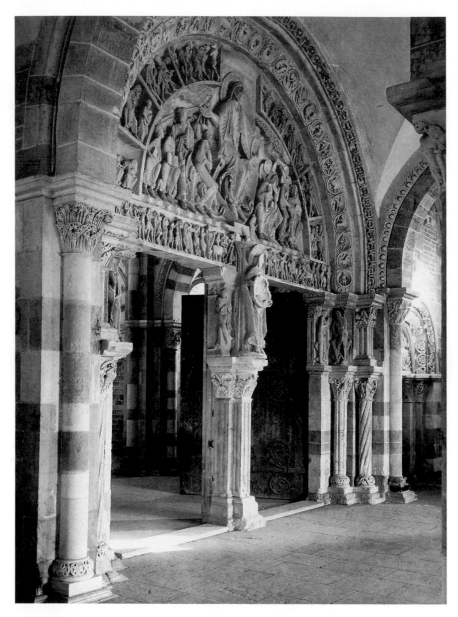

4-63. *Pentecost*, the *Peoples of the Earth*, and *Saint John the Baptist*, tympanum, lintel, and trumeau, central portal, Abbey Church of La Madeleine, Vézelay, Burgundy, France. 1120–32. Stone. Probably commissioned by Abbot Pontius

In the central **tympanum** (**lunette** above the door) at Vézelay, Christ is on the axis, enthroned in a mandorla with his arms outstretched (fig. 4-63). Axiality and hierarchical scale convey Christ's significance, while the angularity of his legs and the swirling drapery, similar to those in contemporary manuscript illumination (see fig. 4-58), animate his presence. Rays of illumination and inspiration, the gift of the Holy Spirit, flow from his hands (his left hand has been broken off) to the head of each apostle. Eight **archivolts** (arches of decorative and narrative motifs that enframe the tympanum) show the apostles preaching the Gospel and healing spiritual and physical ailments. In the outer archivolts, the zodiac symbols and representations of monthly labors signify that Christ is lord of all time and of everything in the world. On the sides of the doors (**jambs**) and on the central post (**trumeau**) are sculpted figures of saints and prophets.

The complex iconography of the Vézelay tympanum reveals the inspired spirituality of the later Middle

Ages. Representations of the human race from all over the world—some based on medieval legends of exotic peoples and therefore fantastically conceived—are shown in the compartments to the sides, while laborers and pilgrims appear in the **lintel**. John the Baptist, who predicted the coming of Christ, is placed on the trumeau in a position that visually and symbolically expresses his support of Christ.

Tympanum sculpture often spoke to the emotions of the people. The Last Judgment scenes at Conques and Autun emphasize the alternatives of eternal reward or everlasting punishment (figs. 4-64, 4-65). At Conques, Christ's judgment is reinforced by literary inscriptions. Axially positioned on the throne of justice, Christ announces to the saved: "Come, the blessed of my Father, take possession of the kingdom that has been readied for you." To the damned he proclaims: "Away from me, accursed ones."

At Autun, the events of the Last Judgment are dramatically portrayed. Across the lintel, humanity waits to be judged; the scales represent the weighing of souls to determine whether the evil a person has done outweighs the good. To Christ's right (our left), the blessed enjoy their reward in heaven; to his left, the damned begin an eternity of punishment at the hands of fantastic, demonic creatures. These horrific devils served as visual demonstrations of the punishment for sin, reinforcing the sermons preached inside the cathedral.

4-64. *Last Judgment*, tympanum and lintel, west portal, Abbey Church of Ste.-Foy, Conques, Rouergue, France. c. 1120. Stone, approx. 12 x 22'. Traces of paint remain on this tympanum, reminding us that color once played an important role in the total effect. Commissioned by the abbot of Conques

4-65. Gislebertus (?). *Last Judgment*, tympanum and lintel, west portal, Cathedral of St.-Lazare, Autun, Burgundy, France. c. 1125–35. Stone, approx. 12'6" x 22'. Probably commissioned by Abbot Étienne de Bâgé

LATER BYZANTINE ART

4-66. *Virgin of Vladimir.* 12th century. Tempera on wood, 31 x 21". Tretyakov Gallery, Moscow. This icon, which was probably created in Constantinople, was taken to the Russian city of Vladimir and then to Moscow, where Russians hoped it would ward off an attack by the Tartars. Only the faces date to the twelfth century, for, like many icons, the drapery has been repainted in a style similar to that of the original, but stiffer and more abstract.

4-67. *Pantocrator,* mosaic in central dome, Church of the Dormition, Daphni, Greece. c. 1100

Only a few types of Madonna and Child compositions were permitted in Byzantine art, and each was dependent on an old and venerated tradition. Invention and variation were discouraged, and the figures gradually became more stylized and remote from visual reality; perhaps as a result of the powerful control of the emperor, Byzantine art in general is more conservative and less open to innovation than is art in western Europe. The *Virgin of Vladimir* (fig. 4-66) is the type known as the *Glykophilousa* or *Eleousa* (the "affectionate, loving one"), which features the Christ Child pressing his cheek to his mother's. Mary looks out at us, with a solemn expression and large eyes that seem to convey an intense melancholy. Her delicate features—long thin nose, tiny mouth, and sharply defined eye sockets—remove her from the realm of the physical and sensuous. The shape of her veiled head, which is clearly drawn with a compass, is

4-68. Nave, San Marco, Venice, Italy. Begun 1063. San Marco functions as the palace chapel of the elected ruler of Venice, the doge, and is located next to the Doges' Palace. It enshrines the bones of the evangelist Saint Mark, Venice's patron saint, which two Venetian merchants stole from the original tomb in Alexandria, Egypt, and brought to Venice in 828. Commissioned by the Venetian doges

4-69. *Ascension,* mosaic in dome, San Marco. Late 12th century. Grouped below in a circular arrangement are the apostles, two angels, and the Virgin Mary, with palm trees to suggest a landscape setting. Between the windows are figures of Virtues. In the pendentives are the Evangelists, with settings of cities and rivers to suggest the worldwide influence of their works. Commissioned by the Venetian doges

geometric and two-dimensional.

Mosaics continued to be the primary medium of decoration in church architecture. The *Pantocrator* (from the Greek, "omnipotent") is an image of the triumphant Christ that was the usual theme for the dome or apse of a church (fig. 4-67). This figure forcefully communicates the concept of God's watch over the universe.

Close trade and diplomatic relations between the Republic of Venice in Italy and the Byzantine Empire also led to cultural and artistic influences. San Marco was rebuilt beginning in the eleventh century (fig. 4-68) on the model of a church built by Justinian that combined the domed **central plan** with the **Greek cross plan.** The splendid decoration of San Marco's interior—patterned marble floors and lower walls covered with slabs of veined marble, culminating in barrel vaults and domes covered with thousands of square feet of Byzantine-style gold mosaics—was so large a project that it was not fully completed until the seventeenth century. In the central dome, the story of Christ's ascension into heaven is represented (fig. 4-69), with Christ placed at the apex of the dome—the composition evolved in relationship to the shape and space of the dome. Nearby is a dome with the Pentecost, in which the Holy Spirit descends from heaven to inspire the apostles. In this dome, the design emphasizes the opposite movement—from the apex downward—as is fitting for a scene in which heavenly force descends in order to inspire the physical and intellectual world.

The exterior domes of San Marco are elevated high above the interior domes to create a festive and impressive design against the sky. Such picturesqueness, ultimately Byzantine in origin, is also seen in the later churches of eastern Europe, Greece, and Russia, as well as in the onion domes of Eastern-rite churches all over the United States.

ANGKOR WAT: CULT OF THE GOD-KING

4-70. Temple complex, Angkor Wat, Kampuchea (Cambodia). First half of 12th century. The inner wall of the temple measures 3,363 x 2,625'; the entrance building is 1,148' long. The site was rediscovered in the nineteenth century, and in the twentieth century modern archaeology and physical science retrieved it from the jungle and preserved it until it was ravaged again by neglect and the perils of war in the 1970s. At this time, there is yet another international effort to save this unique monument. Commissioned by Khmer rulers

The word *Angkor* (from *nokor*, Sanskrit for "city") means "the city," or "the capital," in the Khmer language of ancient Cambodia as well as in that of contemporary Kampuchea. Geographically, the term denotes about 75 square miles of fertile plain between the Kulen Hills and the lake of Tonle Sap where a dozen ninth–thirteenth century Khmer kings constructed capitals (see map, page 163). These centers encompassed a sophisticated irrigation system that controlled the vagaries of monsoon rains and drought so that enough rice could be grown to support about a million inhabitants. They also included major building complexes in brick, stone, and a reddish-pink stone called laterite. The temple that later became known as Angkor Wat is the largest and most artistically accomplished of this complex (fig. 4-70).

Altogether, these creations of conquerors and artisans embodied an integrated concept of the universe that was rooted in myth and deep religious belief. They express a combination of physical and spiritual grandeur similar to those found in Egypt and Greece, among the Maya and Aztecs in Mexico, and in the Gothic cathedrals of Europe.

The well-conceived and graceful monuments built at Angkor during the eleventh and twelfth centuries in particular testify to the creative ability of the Khmer civilization, which reached its zenith during this period. Established to the north and west of the floodplain of Kampuchea, the Khmer kingdom endured a sequence of quick rise and fall, of

prosperity and chaos, and of rapid changes in religious faith preferred by the kings. Greatly influenced by Indian culture, the Khmer kingdom began in the sixth century. Although there were more than thirty rulers in quick succession, of the twelve who ruled at Angkor, Yasovarman I (ruled 889–900), Suryavarman II (ruled 1113–50), and Jayavarman VII (ruled 1181–1219) are outstanding. They were devotees of Siva, Vishnu, and the Buddha, respectively, but their faith was eclectic and was not so much a devotion as a source of power. Through the newly designed cult of the *devaraja* (*deva*, "god," and *raja*, "ruler"), or god-king, the ruler derived both sanctity and power.

The emperors concentrated their building activity at Angkor, and each competed to outdo his predecessor. Suryavarman II constructed the temple at Angkor Wat in the first half of the twelfth century to house his mausoleum. He dedicated it to Vishnu, whose exploits are portrayed in virtually every sector of the temple (fig. 4-71), but Siva and the Buddha also appear at the site. The complex symbolically represents Mount Meru (Sumeru), the World Mountain and, traditionally, Vishnu's abode.

The simple plan of the temple approximates the World Mountain and embodies the ancient Khmer concept of the axis of the universe (fig. 4-72). The three concentric, consecutive galleries that rise toward the center are separated by paved courtyards. The highest gallery, at the center, is capped by a large central tower. Altogether, there are nine towers. The area covered

First half of 12th century	**Temple complex, Angkor Wat**
1100	Earliest recorded English mystery play
1122	Persian poet Omar Khayyam dies
1150	University of Paris has its beginnings

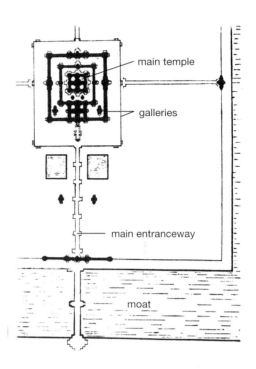

4-71. *Churning of the Sea of Milk,* sculptural relief, interior gallery wall, Angkor Wat. First half of 12th century. Stone. Almost the entire surface of the temple is chiseled with a variety of decorations, including bas-reliefs of Vaishaivite Indian myths and epics, historical triumphs, and dancing figures. More than 1,600 *apsaras* (celestial nymphs) in different moods and expressions are found at the corners and along the walls of the temple. In *Churning of the Sea of Milk*, Vishnu, the Hindu deity who is known as the Preserver, saves the universe from catastrophe by appearing in his avatar—a saving manifestation—as a tortoise. Hoping to obtain the Dew of Immortality, the gods and demons (*asuras*) made a truce so they could churn the Sea of Milk using a serpent wound around the World Mountain. When the mountain began to sink into the sea, Vishnu, in the guise of a tortoise, sat beneath it to support it. The sea gave forth delights, including the dew, which Vishnu obtained for the gods by assuming the form of a desirable woman, Mohini, who seduced the *asuras* into abandoning the elixirs. The gods defeated the demons, and Vishnu was credited with reconstituting the balance of good and evil. Carved in a style that is formal and that expresses a ranked order among the participants, the silhouetted and repeated forms resemble the rhythmic and measured ritual dances performed by the court dancers of ancient Cambodia. Commissioned by Khmer rulers

4-72. Plan of Angkor Wat

by the temple is surrounded by moats 623 feet wide. The causeway over the moat, paved in hard sandstone, leads directly to the central portico.

The temple at Angkor Wat shows clearly that the artists possessed a sound knowledge of three-dimensional geometry, which was necessary to create a perfect step pyramid. The rise of the terraces is so well calculated that all appear to be of equal height, without obscuring the view of the other terraces. Harmony of proportion is also displayed in the balance between vertical and horizontal forms.

These monuments of Khmer art were considered the embodiments, or continuations after death, of the kings and their world. The state cult of *devaraja* gave religious and secular power to the god-kings. Authority was concentrated in these leaders, and the architecture erected by them echoes their dominance over the land. After the thirteenth century and the demise of the Khmer kingdom, these buildings fell into neglect and were repossessed by nature.

THE JAPANESE NARRATIVE SCROLL

4-73. Takayoshi (attributed). Third illustration of the "Kashiwagi" chapter of *The Tale of Genji*. Late Heian period, c. 1120–30. Hand scroll, ink and color on paper, height 8¹/₂". Tokugawa Museum of Art, Nagoya, Japan

The "Kashiwagi" scene from *The Tale of Genji* illustrates one of the major concerns of the story (fig. 4-73). Prince Genji is playing out a theme that is closely linked to Buddhist concepts current in Japan in the eleventh and later centuries—that all acts have consequences. Good works will be rewarded by good fortune, sins will bring calamity, and there may be retribution for past deeds even in one's future life. Here he is declaring that the child in his arms is his, although the baby is actually the son of another.

The Tale of Genji survives in fifty-four chapters, although there may have been more. The story covers about seventy-five years, beginning with the birth of the hero, Genji, and concluding after his death. The principal setting for the novel is Kyoto (see map, page 163), then the capital of Japan, and much action occurs in the urban mansions and gardens of the aristocracy and royal family.

Genji, an imperial prince, was born to the favorite wife of the emperor, a woman too low in rank for him to inherit the throne. A handsome, cultured, and sensitive man, he had many romances. His intrigues and affairs take up two-thirds of the novel, leaving the last

third to tell of the loves and lives of two young men, Genji's heirs in Kyoto. The scene in figure 4-73 explores the effect on Genji of committing a great sin against his father. In his youth, Genji fell in love with his father's youngest wife, Fujitsubo, a woman whom he was encouraged to see because she looked so much like his birth mother, who died when he was an infant. This liaison produced a son, a child who was passed off as the emperor's own and who eventually succeeded to the throne. Fujitsubo, the beloved consort of the emperor, was so tormented by guilt that she became a nun to expiate her sin. The full consequence of this past deed came to Genji, however, only in middle age, when his youngest wife had an extramarital affair that resulted in a son whom Genji had to publicly avow as his own, just as his father had done with Genji's son.

The ceremony acknowledging this son, illustrated here, is depicted in the first known illustrated version of the novel. As the scroll is unrolled and read from right to left, the brown surface of the courtyard—originally silver—and a verandah placed at a sharp angle come into view. The roof and interior walls of the building have been removed

and replaced by bamboo blinds and curtains of state—white cloth curtains with loose black ties hang from horizontal poles. At the base of the curtain appears the bottom of a twelve-layered robe, the garment of a lady-in-waiting. Above, red and black lacquered plates are heaped with food. The colors of the garments and the careful placement of the food dishes indicate that a ceremony is in progress. Two-thirds of the way across the scene, figures appear: Genji at the top with the baby in his arms, ladies-in-waiting below. In the extreme upper left of the illustration, the child's mother is indicated by a mound of fabric.

The text accompanying this scene describes Genji's thoughts as he goes through the painful ritual. He knows that the attendants realize that he is not the father. The artist suggests his emotional discomfort by the physical awkwardness of his placement at the top of the sharply slanting floor, where the space is so cramped that he cannot even raise his head. Architecture plays an important role in the telling of this episode—it interrupts the leftward motion of the illustration and shields the figures from view, thus playing out the theme of retribution.

Despite the title of her novel and the centrality of the hero, Genji, Murasaki Shikibu took interest in exploring the lives and characters of many noblewomen. Genji's greatest love, Murasaki, is introduced in the novel as a child, and the reader can follow her as she matures and finally dies. Few women enjoy thoroughly happy lives in this novel, for the point is made over and over that in a polygamous society delicate distinctions of status often dictate behavior. Murasaki, for instance, is beautiful, talented, and witty, and she is perceived by Genji and her readers alike as the focus of Genji's life. Even so, she is constantly afraid of losing his affection. She suffers two humiliations. First, she is unable to provide him with a child and is therefore charged with raising his daughter by another woman. Second, because of her relatively low status and lack of powerful relatives, she is disqualified as his principal wife, an honor given instead to a woman described as a vapid and childish princess.

Another of the main themes of the novel for both male and female characters is the pathos in and transient quality of experience, illustrated with high emotional intensity. The scattered placement of the women in figure 4-74 and the slightly opened door give ample indication of the potential of the past and future moment in that scene. This picture depicts a group of women and their maids as heads and hands emerging from masses of drapery. Naka no Kimi is having her hair combed after washing. Her half-sister, Ukifune, faces her and looks at a picture scroll while a maid reads from a text. The tension and dismay that Ukifune felt because of an attempted seduction only hours before is described in the text and is subtly indicated here by the tension between her half-hidden figure and the mundane setting of the scene.

The creation of the *Genji* scrolls must have been a monumental project. The novel in English translation is nearly 1,000 pages long. Only twenty pictures from this early illustrated version survive, but it must have originally included one or more illustrations for each of the fifty-four chapters. Most estimate that there were ten scrolls in all.

Scholars trying to determine how the scrolls were made conclude that there were five teams who worked on the project. Each team included a nobleman noted for his calligraphy and his cultural sophistication, a group of painters, including a principal artist (the *sumigaki*, or painter who draws in black ink), and specialists in the application of

c. 1120–30 Takayoshi, *The Tale of Genji* illustrations
1189   Third Crusade to the Holy Land

4-74. Takayoshi (attributed). First illustration of the "Azumaya" chapter of *The Tale of Genji* by Murasaki Shikibu. Late Heian period, c. 1120–30. Hand scroll, ink and color on paper, height 8^1/2". Tokugawa Museum of Art, Nagoya, Japan. *Genji monogatari* (*The Tale of Genji*) is a long work of prose fiction written, probably in the early eleventh century, by Murasaki Shikibu (978?–1031?), a lady-in-waiting at the court of Emperor Ichijo (ruled 986–1011). Often called the world's first novel, *The Tale of Genji* was an immediate and lasting success, revolutionizing the art of prose fiction in Japan. Nothing like it had been written before, and both the content and the romantic mood of *Genji* inspired generations of poets. Well-known themes and episodes from *Genji* also appear in No plays from the fourteenth century through the Edo-period (1615–1868) puppet and Kabuki theater into modern plays and film. Over the centuries, chapter titles and memorable episodes from the novel became popularized as the subjects of parlor games, depictions on folding screens, and in illustrated scrolls, books, and woodblock prints. The palace architecture described in the text became an inspiration for later imperial structures (see figs. 1-5, 7-6, 7-7).

traditional pigments. Once a particular episode was chosen, the *sumigaki* planned the composition and sketched it on the scroll in fine black lines. Then the pigment specialists applied layer upon layer of paint within the lines. The *sumigaki* returned to paint in the details of the faces—tiny red mouths, narrow eyes, noses of a single hooked line, thin mustaches, short beards. The painting technique used in the *Genji* pictures, the application of layers of paint over an underdrawing, is called *tsukuri-e* ("constructed" or "built up"). The technique and style of the *Genji* and other illustrated narrative scrolls dating from this period came to be known as the *yamato-e* style, or "Japanese pictures."

The Tale of Genji lent itself well to the horizontal illustrated scroll, the *emakimono*, a uniquely East Asian format. Both Chinese and Japanese languages were traditionally written in vertical lines from right to left, so the horizontal format of the *emakimono*, laid out and unrolled from right to left, provided a familiar way to relate text and image. The juxtaposition of textual passages of varying lengths with pictorial images was a potent format for many centuries and was translated in modern times into the medium of film with ease, for instance. The preference for highly formalized compositions and stylized depictions of figures carries over with little variation into single frames of twentieth century films directed by Ozu and Kurosawa, among others.

GOTHIC ART

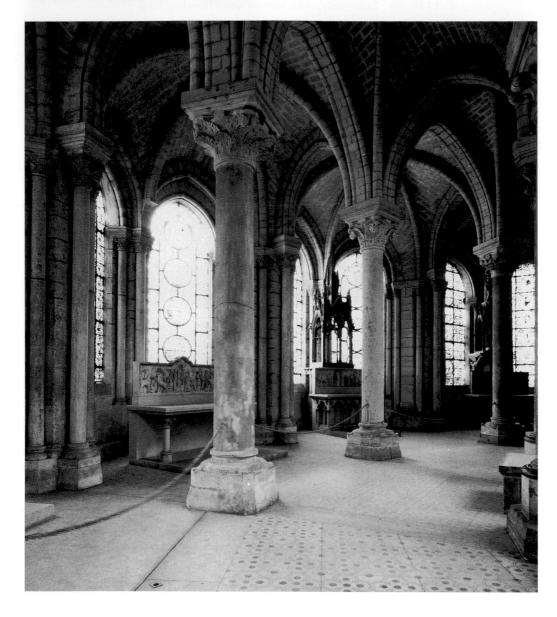

4-75. Interior, the Royal Abbey Church of St.-Denis, near Paris, Île-de-France, France. 1140–44. This view shows the ambulatory and radiating chapels. Here, where Gothic architecture was invented, we see the distinctive attributes of the style in the union of pointed arches, ribbed groin vaults, and large stained-glass windows. Commissioned by Abbot Suger

The Gothic style, the preeminent style in Europe from about 1140 to 1400, was first defined in architecture, and architectural motifs appear throughout Gothic painting, sculpture, and decorative arts. Gothic is easily identifiable because of its unique vocabulary: pointed arches, ribbed cross vaults, flying buttresses, cluster piers, and glowing stained-glass windows. Gothic architecture seems to have been invented by Abbot Suger (1081–1151), friend and adviser to the French kings Louis VI and VII, when he rebuilt the facade, ambulatory, and radiating chapels of the Royal Abbey Church of St.-Denis (figs. 4-75, 4-76). The beauty of the Gothic style and the importance of St.-Denis, the royal French church where the coronation regalia were stored and kings and queens were buried, helped to popularize the new style throughout France. The brilliant colors of the large stained-glass windows of chapels and ambulatory were designed to lead the sensitive observer to imagine the glories of the Heavenly Jerusalem, the holy "City of God" in Paradise. In other words, the architecture was intended to help the worshiper rise from the physical, material world to an immaterial, spiritual realm. Suger wrote about how his new architecture created a "crown of light"—a frequent metaphor for the divine:

For bright is that which is
    brightly coupled with the
    bright,
And bright is the noble edi-
    fice which is pervaded by
    the new light;
Which stands enlarged in our
    time,
I, who was Suger, being the
    leader while it was being
    accomplished.

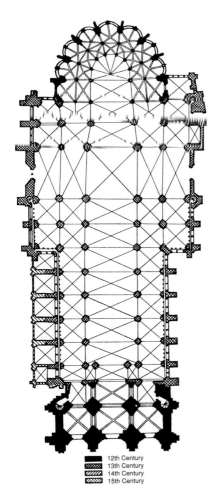

4-76. Plan of the Royal Abbey Church of St.-Denis as it exists today, showing the various building campaigns. Abbot Suger rebuilt the facade (consecrated 1140) and the chapels and ambulatory (1140–44); from 1231 to 1281, the old Carolingian nave and upper choir were rebuilt in the mature Gothic style.

ABBOT SUGER

In an inscription over the west portal of the facade, Abbot Suger gives himself credit for the rebuilding of St.-Denis; no artists' or architects' names are mentioned. His new vision of architecture is based on his belief that the material beauty and splendor of the church would lead worshipers to a new understanding of God and the spiritual realm, as is further clarified in an inscription once on the golden doors of the west facade of the abbey:

> Marvel not at the gold and
> the expense but at the
> craftsmanship of the
> work.
> Bright is the noble work; but,
> being nobly bright, the
> work
> Should brighten the minds,
> so that they may travel,
> through the true lights,
> To the True Light where
> Christ is the true door.

Suger specifically compared the church at St.-Denis to the Holy Jerusalem, the City of God: St.-Denis and other, later Gothic cathedrals are intended to suggest the Paradise that awaits the pious Christian.

HISTORY

Growth during the Gothic period and financial and social developments meant that life changed dramatically for much of the population. The development of international banking was centered in rapidly growing cities. Paris was the mercantile hub of Europe, and its popular annual trade fairs brought together Europeans of many cultures. Among the merchandise bought and sold were works of art. The complex life in the cities led to better-educated administrators and bureaucrats.

That France was preeminent in the arts in Europe during the later Middle Ages is not unexpected, for in the twelfth and thirteenth centuries Paris was the leading intellectual center in Europe and the capital of a strong monarchy (the Capetian line of French kings ruled from 987 to 1328). The University of Paris, the model for late-medieval universities, including Oxford, Cambridge, and Padua, became the focus for a new rational approach to philosophy and theology known as Scholasticism, which examined, questioned, clarified, and codified Christian dogma and practice. Thomas Aquinas, a professor at the University of Paris, wrote the *Summa Theologica* (1267–73), an encyclopedia that set out to systematize and encompass all knowledge on theology and the world.

The Crusades, which had begun in the late eleventh century, continued into the Gothic era, but with little political or military success. They were a significant financial and human drain on western Europe, but they encouraged the development of banking, new methods of taxation, and a more complex money economy. In western Europe, many scientific and philosophical developments resulted from contact with the Islamic culture.

ART

The term *Gothic* originally had a pejorative connotation. It was coined during the Italian Renaissance to refer to the whole of medieval art, which, from the perspective of the Renaissance, seemed crude and without reason. Judged to be the work of barbarians, medieval art was called Gothic after the Visigoths, an early Germanic people who sacked Rome in 410. During the Gothic period itself, the new architecture was known as *opus modernum* ("modern architecture"), *opere francigena* ("French architecture"), or pointed architecture.

Gothic art is elegant, highly decorated, and characterized by the use of sumptuous, colorful materials. Architecture included churches, urban monastic complexes, and castles. Sculpture was focused on church portals and on elaborate tombs with architectural frames. Painting was largely limited to manuscript illuminations. The decorative arts—secular and liturgical—encompassed works in gold and other fine materials (fig. 4-77), including ivory and precious gems. Increasing personal wealth meant that secular works—personal jewelry, tapestries, ivory boxes, and mirror backs—became more common.

The figural pose that characterizes Gothic art is revealed in the

4-77. *Abbot Suger's Chalice.* c. 1140; reworked later. Silver gilt and agate, with jewels, height 8". National Gallery of Art, Washington, D.C. The beauty of Suger's architecture is reflected in the costly vessels he had made for liturgical use. This chalice was created by adding a rim, foot, and handles to an ancient agate cup made in Alexandria in the second century BCE. It was originally inscribed *Suger Abbas* ("Abbot Suger"). For a view of equally rich objects on an altar at the church of St.-Denis, see figure 4-5. Commissioned by Abbot Suger

Widener Collection

4-78. *Madonna of Jeanne d'Evreux.* 1339. Silver gilt with enamel, height 27". The Louvre, Paris. This work was presented to the abbey of St.-Denis in 1339 by the French queen Jeanne d'Evreux. The stylized iris held by the Madonna is the fleur-de-lis, the symbol of French royalty. Commissioned by Jeanne d'Evreux

Madonna of Jeanne d'Evreux (fig. 4-78). The Madonna stands in the Gothic "hip-shot" position, in which one hip juts out to support the Christ Child; the effect is less naturalistic than elegant, giving the body a flowing **S**-curve shape. The small head of the Madonna is also a Late Gothic mannerism. In typical Gothic fashion, the body is completely covered by heavy drapery. The small scale of this statuette, its precious materials, and its delicate figure type and flowing drapery patterns reveal the sophistication and elegance of the fully developed Gothic style.

The *Annunciation* page from a Parisian **book of hours** (fig. 4-79) reveals the elaboration of decoration common in Gothic art. The *Annunciation* was traditionally one of the most ornate of all pages, for it is the moment of the Incarnation, when the seed of God was placed in the womb of the Virgin Mary and Christ was conceived and became flesh. In prayer books, it is represented before the texts for matins, the first service of the day, and therefore serves as a frontispiece not only to that important service but also to the whole of the book. Here the artist sets the scene in an elaborate churchlike structure, com-

plete with altar and **altarpiece**; all the architectural motifs are Gothic. Although Gabriel holds a scroll bearing his message, Mary looks upward toward God, and it is from his figure that the dove of the Holy Spirit emerges. Old Testament prophets, whose writings were believed to predict the virgin birth and the coming of Christ, appear in the upper stories of the Gothic structure, while baby angels playing musical instruments populate the elaborate floral motifs of the borders. Typical of the growing interest in symbolism is the use of a number of complex symbols that elaborate on the content of the narrative. The caged bird behind Mary, for example, which at first seems to be merely a household decoration, is a symbol for Christ's Incarnation, when his soul was "caged" within a physical body while the mating birds in the border refer by contrast to the nonsexual manner by which God's seed found its way to Mary's womb. The spider and ladybug may refer to the devil, who was understood as ever-present.

THE GOTHIC ARTIST

During the Gothic period, the vast majority of works of art were not signed, but we begin to find references to specific artists in a few documents and inventories, where named artists are praised for their skill. A number of the architects/contractors who designed and constructed the cathedrals are known from inscriptions and documents. Some traveled widely: the Frenchman William of Sens was called to England to rebuild Canterbury Cathedral, and Villard de Honnecourt went to Hungary and Switzerland. Several artists are noted as active in more than one medium; André Beauneveu, for example, who was working for Charles V of France in 1364, was a painter, sculptor, designer of tapestries, and consultant to architectural projects. Nevertheless, the majority of Gothic artists were anonymous. Later, during the Italian Renaissance, the art historian Giorgio Vasari would be puzzled by the Gothic artist's "indifference to fame."

THE FRANCISCANS

The urbanization of Europe was accompanied by significant developments in monasticism that shifted the emphasis from rural retreats of work, prayer, and meditation to large complexes within cities, where the monks could serve the poor and sick and preach the word of God in

4-79. *Annunciation,* from the *London Hours,* created in Paris by an Italian artist. c. 1400–10. Manuscript painting on vellum, 9 x 6". The British Library, London. This book of hours was made for the Parisian market, for it features the particular devotions and saints common in Paris. The coat of arms at the bottom of each page was left blank in order to be painted later with the arms of the purchaser, revealing that this book was a commercial production made for the art market and was not commissioned by a specific patron. This late phase of Gothic is sometimes called the International Gothic style because it was pervasive throughout Europe during the period c. 1400–25.

the language of the people. In the early thirteenth century, Francis of Assisi founded a popular new mendicant (begging) order, the Franciscans, which emphasized poverty and humility. The sermons and writings of his followers reveal a new emphasis on human emotion in interpreting the lives of Jesus and the saints. Legend tells us that Francis developed the tradition of the Christmas pageant to make Christianity more immediate and meaningful for the populace. This innovation is related to the rapid and widespread development of religious drama—mystery plays—during this period. A Franciscan

monk, writing in the late thirteenth century about the birth of Jesus, urges a special kind of imaginary participation. He speaks directly to the reader, advising:

> You too . . . kneel and adore your Lord God and then His mother, and reverently greet the saintly old Joseph . . . beg His mother to offer to let you hold [the baby Jesus] a while. Pick Him up and hold Him in your arms. Gaze on His face with devotion and reverently kiss Him and delight in Him. (*Meditations on the Life of Christ*)

THE GOTHIC CATHEDRAL: CHARTRES

4-80. Nave, Cathedral of Nôtre-Dame, Chartres, Île-de-France, France. 1194–1220. Chartres Cathedral is the most memorable of French Gothic cathedrals, not only for the superb quality of its architecture and sculpture but also because it alone preserves virtually all its original stained-glass windows. Begun again after a fire in 1194 destroyed the earlier cathedral (except for the west facade, with its sculpture [see fig. 4-91], the crypt, and some of the stained glass, including *"Nôtre Dame de la Belle Verrière,"* fig. 4-93), the new construction was largely completed by 1220. Commissioned by the bishops of Chartres

Entering a great Gothic cathedral is a thrilling, emotional, and—many would say—spiritual experience. The emphatic verticality of a Gothic **nave** urges us upward, and it is easy to experience a sense of weightlessness and immateriality, a physical condition that can be related to spiritual enlightenment (figs. 4-80, 4-81). Space seems to expand not only upward but also outward to the sides as we look both upward and through the nave **arcade** into the side aisles. Space is also a dominant experience in such earlier architecture as the ancient

Roman Pantheon (see fig. 3-117), but the simple, monumental union of dome and cylinder of the Pantheon is in sharp contrast to the complex interrelationships and forms of varied sizes of the Chartres interior. In the Gothic structure, the experience of space is much less lucid, and the ultimate effect, a combination of height, dark corners, and glowing **stained-glass windows**, is mystical and otherworldly.

From its foundations, sunk 25 feet or more into the earth, to the height of its vaults and roof (at Beauvais, the tallest of all cathedrals, the vaults peak at 157 feet over the floor and the roof reaches 223 feet above the street), the Gothic cathedral is a monument to the determination, engineering daring, and physical energies of patrons, architects, and builders. Despite construction campaigns that lasted over decades and even centuries, not one of the great French Gothic cathedrals was ever fully completed; the vision of patrons and architects was too ambitious—too glorious—to be realized.

The high, narrow nave of the Gothic cathedral is the climax of a long tradition in Christian art in which architects tried to create a physical space that would express the spiritual goals of the Christian religion. The Gothic interest in ever-increasing height, lightness, and

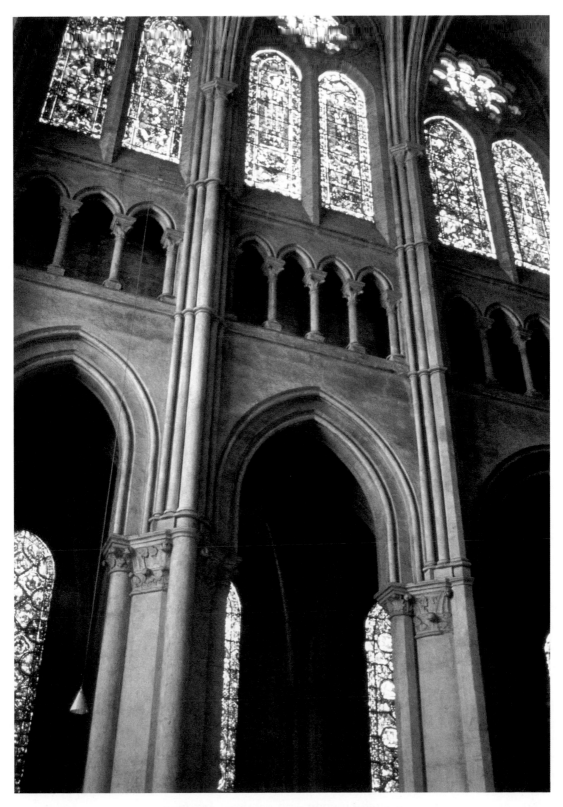

4-81. View of the nave wall, Chartres Cathedral

TECHNIQUE	Proportions of Gothic Cathedrals, 1160–1230		
	APPROX. HEIGHT OF THE NAVE VAULTS	APPROX. WIDTH OF THE NAVE	PROPORTION OF NAVE HEIGHT TO WIDTH
Laon, Cathedral 1160–1205	80'	37'6"	2.13:1
Paris, Nôtre-Dame 1163–96	115'	40'	2.88:1
Chartres, Nôtre-Dame 1194–1220	120'	45'6"	2.64:1
Bourges, St.-Étienne 1195–c. 1270/80	117'	44'	2.66:1
Reims, Nôtre-Dame designed 1210	125'	46'	2.72:1
Amiens, Nôtre-Dame designed 1220	144'	48'	3:1
Beauvais, Cathedral (vaults before apse) designed 1230s	157'	47'	3.36:1

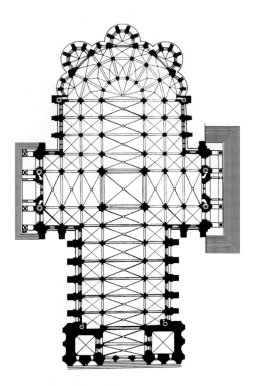

4-82. Plan of Chartres Cathedral

slenderness of proportion is evidenced by the statistics, arranged chronologically above.

A tall church was thought to please God. In addition, it could fuel the rivalry between neighbors, for during the Middle Ages the local cathedral was the emblem not only of the sanctity of the town's population but also of their wealth, power, and pride.

A unique combination of **pointed arch, ribbed groin vault,** and **flying buttress** (see page 226) defines Gothic architecture. Although each of these elements had been used earlier elsewhere, it is their combination into a coherent and rational system that is new in the Gothic period. The pointed arch, seen everywhere in Chartres's interior (see fig. 4-81), continuously directs our attention upward. The ribs of the vaults help define the parts of the architectural structure and also create a series of lines that keep the eye moving. The ground plan of Chartres (fig. 4-82) is not remarkably different from earlier Christian traditions; the new statement is in the construction and decoration. The rational basis of Gothic architecture demands that each element be explicable and interrelated (as in the Gothic philosophical system known as Scholasticism), and each vault is related to and visually supported by a **colonnette** (a thin column) that begins at floor level. Groups of colonnettes turn the supporting **piers** into **cluster piers.** The interior elevation (see fig. 4-84) is composed of a nave arcade, a **triforium** (a narrow gallery that opens the structure where normally there would be an expanse of wall), and an enormous, window-filled **clerestory.**

In most structures, we are aware of a continuous and relatively dense wall surface punctured and punctuated by doors and windows, but in the Gothic cathedral there is so little wall—and what remains is so dissolved or disguised by the linear patterns of ribs and colonnettes—that windows and wall are no longer alternatives. They are unified into an energetic skeleton with huge openings filled with vibrantly colored stained-glass windows. The flying buttresses—hidden from an interior view by the stained-glass windows— are clearly visible on the exterior and add lightness and visual energy to the exterior (see fig. 4-86).

The ideal Gothic church would have had seven spired towers—a twin-towered western facade (a development from the Carolingian westwork; fig. 4-83), a tower at the **crossing,** and twin towers at both north and south **transepts.** Such a massing of vertical forms pointing upward suggests the dissolution of the mass of the structure and a denial of gravity consistent with the motivations and aspirations of the cathedral builders.

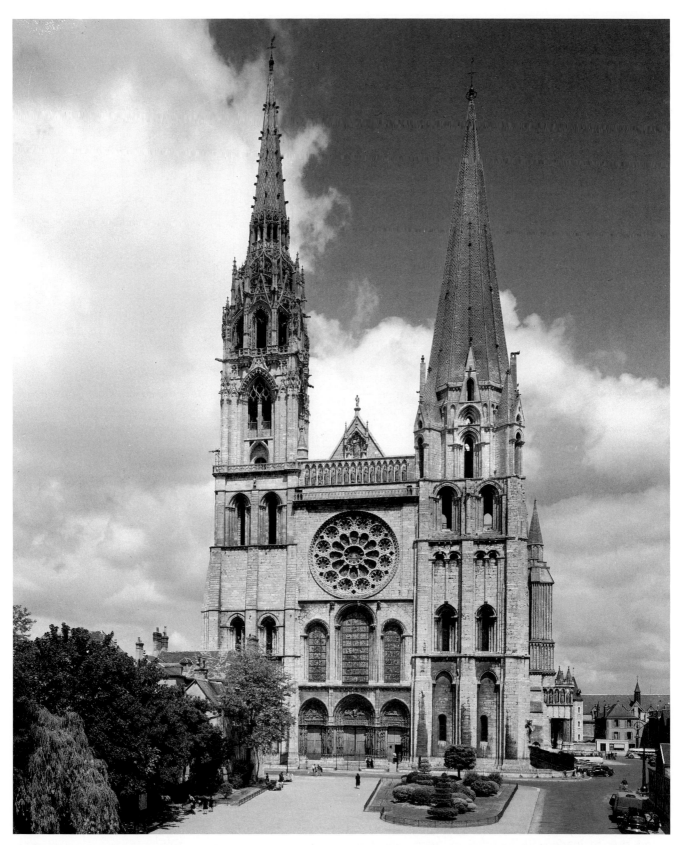

4-83. West facade, Chartres Cathedral. The mismatched towers of the Chartres facade give it a distinctive personality and reveal the changing nature of the Gothic style. The shorter, transitional Romanesque-Gothic tower was completed before the fire of 1194; the elaborately decorated, fully Gothic example was not begun until 1507. For sculptures from the facade, see figure 4-91.

The Gothic cathedral is based on complex engineering principles (fig. 4-84). It is founded on the dynamic interaction/equilibrium between the outward **thrust** of the high cross vaults and the flying buttresses that contain this thrust. The desire for both height and maximum window openings led to the creation of a structure aptly described as "skeletal"; every element is manipulated to help meet these goals.

The Gothic cathedral is the result of the union of three distinct constructional elements:

Pointed arch: its design achieves a vertical emphasis, and the angle at which the sides meet at the apex focuses attention at the point of its greatest height. The pointed arch makes possible the unity of space characteristic of a Gothic structure. Since a pointed arch can rise to any height (fig. 4-85) despite its width (unlike a round arch), it can vault a **bay** of virtually any shape—such as those of Abbot Suger's ambulatory (see fig. 4-75). In addition, the outward thrust of a pointed arch is reduced, because it is more vertical than that of a rounded arch. Thus, lighter buttresses are required and larger areas of wall can be replaced with stained-glass windows.

Ribs of the vault: these not only make the vaults appear lighter, they allow for a physically lighter structure. The ribs were constructed first, and because of their weight-bearing potential, the surfaces of the vault can be composed of lighter materials. These surfaces, sometimes called the **web**, or infilling, seem stretched, like a fabric or skin, between the linear, skeletal supports of the ribs.

Flying buttress: this development, by transferring the thrust and weight to an exterior support some distance from the wall, permits a lighter structure and a greater expanse of windows. In earlier architecture, the heavy buttresses, created by greatly thickening parts of the wall surface, cut down on the amount of light that reached the windows and gave the structure a ponderous exterior appearance.

The structural dynamics of the Gothic cathedral—which today we can analyze with computers and study through models—were explored by Gothic architects by building three-dimensional models of arches and buttresses. At times, the Gothic desire for height and lightened structure led to difficulties. At Beauvais Cathedral, the choir vaults peak at 157 feet above the floor, making the interior of the church as tall as a fifteen-story building; they collapsed due to inadequate foundations, piers, and buttressing and were rebuilt with additional supports and buttresses. A huge crossing tower—perhaps 500 feet tall—was then built, but when it collapsed, work stopped, and Beauvais today consists of little more than an apse.

1. bay
2. nave
3. aisle
4. nave arcade
5. clerestory
6. cluster pier with colonnettes
7. triforium
8. buttress
9. flying buttress
10. wooden roof

4-84. Isometric projection and cross section showing the structure and parts of Chartres Cathedral

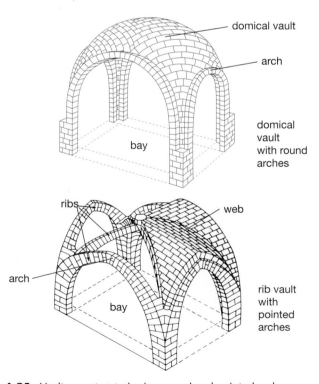

domical vault

arch

domical vault with round arches

ribs

web

arch

bay

rib vault with pointed arches

4-85. Vaults constructed using round and pointed arches. The pointed arches enable the openings on each side and the center to reach a unified height over a rectangular bay.

The French Gothic style spread rapidly, and by the mid-thirteenth century, buildings all across Europe demonstrated Gothic qualities. But local traditions, native artistic practices, and regional cultural factors often meant that these buildings also had individual characteristics. The ability of Gothic architecture to express late-medieval attitudes is revealed by its pervasive popularity as an architectural style. This is especially remarkable in light of the political connotations expressed by the Gothic style because of its origins at the French Royal Abbey Church of St.-Denis.

In England, the emphasis in religious architecture is on length rather than height, and at Salisbury (fig. 4-86) the nave, which is only 81 feet tall, is 449 feet long; on the interior a strong cornice enhances the effect of horizontality. Salisbury's nave is crossed by two transepts, a typical English development, and the climax behind the high altar is not the French polygonal apse with radiating chapels but a flat wall surface pierced by Gothic pointed windows. On the exterior, the facade is lower and broader, and the emphasis is on the central crossing tower rather than on the two-towered western facade seen in France (see fig. 4-83).

In Italy, the Gothic arch was used for doors and windows, and the pointed, ribbed cross vault was common, but at San Francesco (fig. 4-87) the small windows and the emphasis on a continuous wall surface seem diametrically opposed to the diaphanous window walls of the French examples. Rather than the shallow rectangular bays of the French Gothic, Italian churches often feature square or nearly square bays, and the triforium is often eliminated. Clarity replaces complexity, and there is a feeling of solid physical presence and massive bulk.

Typical of Late Gothic developments in Germany is the hall church (fig. 4-88). The aisles often reach the same height as the nave, and the piers can seem thin and insubstantial in the midst of the open and airy surrounding spaces.

None of the developments of Gothic architecture outside France has the same emphasis on engineering and structural complexity seen in the French sources; in fact, most Gothic churches outside France lack flying buttresses, and seldom do their patrons and architects desire to attain either the height or the narrowness of proportion of the French examples.

4-86. English Gothic. Exterior, Salisbury Cathedral, Salisbury, Wiltshire, England. 1220–70. The high crossing tower and the flying buttresses were added in the fourteenth century. Commissioned by the bishops of Salisbury

4-87. Italian Gothic. Nave, San Francesco, Assisi, Umbria, Italy. 1228–53. The Church of San Francesco was begun in 1228, as soon as Saint Francis, who had died in 1226, was canonized. The walls are covered with fresco cycles of the Old and New Testaments and, on the lowest level, the life of Saint Francis. Commissioned by the Franciscan friars of Assisi

4-88. German Gothic. Nave and choir, St. Sebald, Nuremberg, Franconia, Germany. 1361–72

GOTHIC SCULPTURE

4-89. *Beau Dieu,* trumeau, central portal, west facade, Cathedral of Nôtre-Dame, Amiens, Île-de-France, France. c. 1225–35. Stone. The popular name for this rather severe figure of the blessing Christ is the *Beau Dieu,* the "Beautiful Lord." Like most Romanesque and Gothic portal sculpture, this figure was originally polychromed. Commissioned by the bishops of Amiens

As in Romanesque church facades, sculpted figures populate the exterior of Gothic churches, not only on the three western portals but also on as many as six transept entrances as well. The west facade at Amiens reveals how the number of figurative sculptures and the extent of applied decoration have increased (fig. 4-90). The deep porches contain rows of **jamb** and **archivolt** figures; narrative reliefs decorate many other areas. The sculptures represent figures and scenes from the Bible, including both Old and New Testaments, as well as more secular themes, such as the signs of the zodiac and the labors that the Middle Ages thought were characteristic of each month of the year. The facade as a whole is intended to represent all God's creation. Its order, as commanded by the axial figure of Christ on the trumeau, reflects the divine order of the Christian world.

The earliest Gothic portal sculptures, the *Ancestors of Christ* at Chartres (fig. 4-91), already display significant differences from their Romanesque predecessors. The elongated figures are columnar, for their restricted poses reflect the vertical columns behind them. Drapery folds fall in abstract, linear patterns unrelated to underlying anatomical structure. But these drapery patterns are unlike those of Romanesque figures, which are lively and expressive; at Chartres the drapery quietly reinforces the figures' verticality. The faces of the Chartres jamb figures, while still somewhat stylized, convey a softer and more naturalistic quality than, for example, the severe face of Christ in the tympanum at Vézelay (see fig. 4-63).

As portal sculpture developed through the Gothic period, especially during the early thirteenth century, the figures began to be realized in higher and higher relief and

As they entered the main, western door of the Amiens Cathedral, the faithful were greeted by the **trumeau** sculpture of Christ holding a book and making a gesture of blessing (fig. 4-89). The book, probably the Gospels, symbolizes Christ's words and deeds, but this image of the teaching Christ is also combined with the victorious Christ, as represented in the lion and the dragon trampled under his feet. In Christian tradition, the dragon symbolized the Devil, and in this context the lion was understood as a symbol of the Antichrist. Unlike Romanesque trumeau figures, with their lively abstract patterns, the Amiens Christ is not only naturalistic but also has a quiet and stately presence. The simple verticality of the figure echoes the inherent architectonic role of the trumeau, the drapery falls in a naturalistic manner, and Christ's face has been given a human, solemn dignity.

1222   University of Padua is founded
c. 1225–35   *Beau Dieu*, **Amiens Cathedral**

4-90. West facade, Amiens Cathedral. c. 1225–35. Commissioned by the bishops of Amiens

4-91. *Ancestors of Christ*, column figures, right jamb, central door (royal portal), west facade, Cathedral of Nôtre-Dame, Chartres, Île-de-France, France. c. 1145–55. Stone. Commissioned by the bishops of Chartres

4-92. *Vierge Dorée*, trumeau figure, south portal, Amiens Cathedral. c. 1250. Stone. This sculpture is popularly known as the *Vierge Dorée* ("Gilded Virgin") because parts of the figure were originally decorated with applied gold leaf. Commissioned by the bishops of Amiens

began to lose their columnar emphasis. The Amiens Christ exemplifies the increasing naturalism of early-thirteenth-century Gothic sculpture, while retaining the serious dignity that characterized the jamb figures at Chartres from about eighty years earlier.

The *Vierge Dorée* at Amiens (fig. 4-92) dates about twenty years later than the Amiens Christ. Now a new, relaxed elegance characterizes the sculpture. The figural proportions are elongated, and Mary's body follows an exaggerated curve created by the tilt of the hip to support the arm holding the Christ Child. The drapery, falling in broad folds, contributes to the statue's elegance and emphasizes her sophisticated pose. A warm, affectionate smile plays across Mary's delicate face as she gazes at the child. The reverent dignity of the *Beau Dieu* and the human charm of the *Vierge Dorée* express the diverse vitality that occurs in the development of Gothic sculpture. The figures that decorate Gothic portals reintroduced monumental figural sculpture to western Europe.

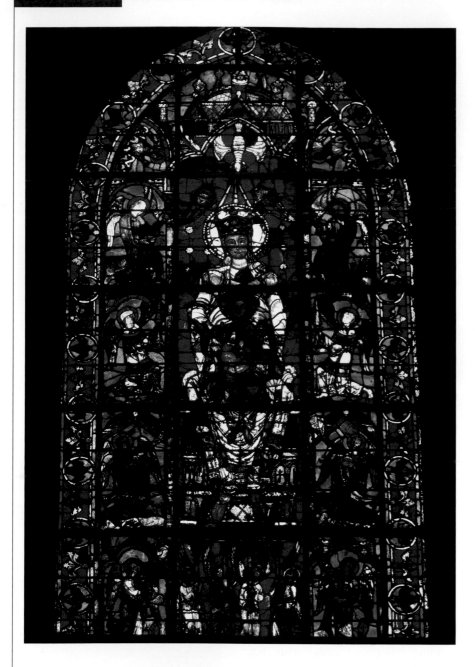

4-93. *"Nôtre Dame de la Belle Verrière,"* Cathedral of Nôtre-Dame, Chartres, Île-de-France, France. 12th century (central portion); 13th century (surrounding angels). Stained glass, approx. 16' x 7'6". This venerated window is known as *"Nôtre Dame de la Belle Verrière"* ("Our Lady of the Beautiful Window"). The *Enthroned Virgin and Child* section that forms the central portion was saved when Chartres Cathedral burned in 1194. As the cathedral was being rebuilt in the new Gothic style of the thirteenth century, the earlier window was flanked by panels with angels in a more fully Gothic style.

The brilliant contrast between the blues and reds of *"La Belle Verrière"* establishes a dynamic equilibrium, and the other colors and the black paint used to define faces, drapery, and other details enrich and dramatize the window (fig. 4-93). The glowing, gemlike windows that decorate a Gothic structure help create the ideal of the church as a metaphor for the Heavenly Jerusalem, which was described in the Bible as having foundations composed of precious stones (Revelation 21:19).

"La Belle Verrière" exemplifies two styles—the transitional style between Romanesque and Gothic and the fully mature Gothic style. The rigid axiality of Mary and the Christ Child (whose faces have been restored) is eased only slightly by the tilt of Mary's head. In contrast, the angels in the side panels are more animated, and the pieces of colored glass used to form the image have bolder, more varied colors.

Like the exterior sculptural program of a Gothic church, the figurative imagery of a stained-glass window instructed the people through symbolic imagery and narratives from the Old and New Testaments. But with stained glass, this instructive purpose was joined with a spiritual, almost mystical, effect. On an average day, the light level outside has

4-94. A craftsperson, making a stained-glass window, is fitting the lead strips, which in section are shaped like a sideways **H** around the glass. The original design, used to determine the shapes of the glass pieces, is visible in the foreground.

been measured as approximately 9,000 lumens, but the reading for the interior space of Chartres is only a few lumens; in other words, there is 1,000 times more light outside than inside. As our eyes adjust to the dark, cavernous space, a radiance of light seems to burst from the windows, where images executed in stained glass appear suspended in an aura of colored light. As light passes through these windows, it causes them to glow with a radiant richness and to cast beams and spots of color throughout the interior.

Abbot Suger wrote about how the sumptuous quality of Gothic objects brought him into the mystical presence of the divine:

> Thus, when—out of my delight in the beauty of the house of God—the loveliness of the many-colored gems has called me away from external cares, and worthy meditation has induced me to reflect, transferring that which is material to that which is immaterial, on the diversity of the sacred virtues: then it seems to me that I see myself dwelling, as it were, in some strange region of the universe which neither exists entirely in the slime of the earth nor entirely in the purity of Heaven; and that, by the grace of God, I can be transported from this inferior to that higher world in an anagogical manner.

STAINED-GLASS TECHNIQUE

The origins of stained-glass windows, which are composed of pieces of colored glass joined by lead strips (fig. 4-94), are uncertain. Colored-glass windows and windows made of thin stone through which light could filter were already in use in Early Christian and Byzantine churches, and although stained-glass windows became more common during the Romanesque period, it was only during the Gothic that they became a crucial and integral part of the architecture and a major means of artistic expression.

The colored glass is produced by adding metallic oxides to the molten glass (pot metal glass) or by fusing a layer of colored glass onto clear glass (flashed glass). During the late Middle Ages, the design for a window would be drawn in chalk on a flat table, then pieces of glass were cut to fit each small shape or area of the design. The details of faces and drapery were added by painting in black enamel, which was then fused to the glass by firing. The fragments of glass were assembled, with lead strips bonding them in place, over the design. Because these glass-and-lead designs were heavy, armatures of iron bands were used to strengthen and support the windows when they were installed in the church. Stained glass is one of the most radiant and vibrant media in the history of human expression.

EARLY ITALIAN PAINTING

4-95. Giotto. *Madonna Enthroned with Angels and Saints*, from the Church of Ognissanti, Florence, Tuscany, Italy. c. 1300. Tempera on wood, 10'8" x 6'8^{1}/^{4}". Uffizi Gallery, Florence. Originally commissioned by an unknown patron for the Church of Ognissanti (All Saints) in Florence, this panel is sometimes called the *Ognissanti Madonna*.

Once Cimabue thought that
   in painting
He commanded the field,
   and now Giotto has the
   acclaim.

As this quotation from Dante's *Divine Comedy* reveals, Cimabue (c. 1251–1302) was once the most important painter in Florence. His style represented a final statement of the Byzantine influence in Italy. Dante wrote that it was soon superseded by the revolutionary style of Giotto (1266/7– or 1276–1337), an assessment that we share with Giotto's contemporaries. A comparison between their compositions of the Madonna and Child reveals the significance of Giotto's innovations (figs. 4-95, 4-96). The scale and simple composition of Cimabue's painting create an impressive and severe effect consistent with the expressions of the faces. In his work, Giotto reestablishes the connection between the art of painting and the nature of objective reality, an attitude not evident in painting since ancient Roman illusionism. Giotto's figures are represented as massive, weighty forms that seem to exist within a spatial continuum in which gravity is an inescapable factor. These large, bulky figures have strongly modeled, naturalistic drapery, as seen in the flowing folds of the angels kneeling in the foreground (unfortunately, the darkening of the blue of the Madonna's robe and the repainting of her knees and lap have deprived the central figure of some of its original sense of weight and presence).

The heavy marble throne of Giotto's *Madonna* seems solidly fixed in space; Cimabue's wooden throne is lighter and less rational (there are no back legs). In both Cimabue's and Giotto's panels, the figures to the sides overlap, but in Giotto's they seem to stand solidly on the ground; Cimabue's angels seem to be floating in an abstract decorative pattern. The placement of Giotto's figures in space is clearly structured: the kneeling angels overlap the standing angels, who in turn overlap the throne; in the grouping of saints, Giotto lets some of the haloes overlap shoulders and even faces. Giotto surrounds the Madonna and Child with figures placed to create a natural, believable effect, with no loss of dignity or emphasis.

Equally important for Giotto's revolution is the new responsiveness of the figures, which even in this traditional subject is of such intensity that a dramatic effect is created. The angels respond to the impressive presence of the Madonna and Child with spontaneous expressions of awe. The Madonna and Child have neither the remoteness nor the insubstantiality seen in Byzantine art, and their parted lips and direct gazes convey a significant human presence.

Giotto's painting, with its recognition of both the physical and the psychological natures of human activity, is in direct contrast to the schematic composition and expressionless figures of Cimabue's panel. Giotto transformed the art of painting; by emphasizing the concept of the "painting as a window," he established an approach that would endure until the revolutionary experiments of Cézanne and the Cubists in the late nineteenth and early twentieth centuries.

4-96. Cimabue. *Madonna Enthroned with Angels and Prophets*, from the high altar of Santa Trinita, Florence. c. 1285. Tempera on wood, 11'7" x 7'4". Uffizi Gallery, Florence. Tradition has it that Cimabue was the teacher of Giotto. The two Florentine painters are used by Dante to elucidate the fleeting nature of fame.

GIOTTO, THE ARENA CHAPEL FRESCOES

4-97. Giotto. *Lamentation*, fresco in the Arena Chapel, Padua, Italy. c. 1303–05. Approx. 6' x 6'6". The Arena Chapel was built and decorated for Enrico Scrovegni, a wealthy Paduan businessperson. It was attached to the Scrovegni Palace, which had been built on the site of the ancient Roman arena of Padua, hence the name Arena Chapel. Commissioned by Enrico Scrovegni

4-98. Giotto. Frescoes, Arena Chapel. The Arena Chapel has windows on only the right-hand wall, as seen in this view; the left is completely filled with the bands of narratives. Below are figures of the Virtues and Vices. High on the triumphal arch is a fresco of God sending Gabriel to earth; below, to either side, are the kneeling figures of Gabriel and the Virgin at the moment of the Annunciation and Incarnation. The vault above is decorated with blue sky, gold stars, and holy figures appearing in circular, windowlike frames.

As in his *Madonna* (see fig. 4-95), the figures in Giotto's *Lamentation* (fig. 4-97) offer an illusion of weight and mass not seen in painting since antiquity. At the same time, they convey a convincing drama and expression of emotion. Through gesture and placement, the composition, with its simple friezelike arrangement and sloping hillside setting, focuses attention on the dramatic core of the narrative, the heads of the Virgin and Jesus in the lower left corner. Two heavy figures seen from the back enframe this tender and private moment and communicate the tragic loss and mute pain appropriate to the agonized farewell

4-99. Giotto. *Last Judgment*, fresco in the Arena Chapel. c. 1303–05. Approx. 33' x 27'6". Filling the inside of the entrance wall, and therefore the last thing viewers see as they leave, is a panoramic representation of the Last Judgment.

of a mother to her son. The simple landscape of barren hill and dead tree supports the expressive figures. The Lamentation and the related theme of the **Pietà**, which are not mentioned in the Bible, are subjects that emerged with the demand for a more emotional religious art in the late-medieval period.

Giotto's *Lamentation* cannot be understood as an isolated composition and must be examined in relation to its context. In the Arena Chapel (fig. 4-98), Giotto painted a continuous cycle of thirty-eight scenes from the lives of the Virgin and Jesus that starts at the top and, reading left to right, spirals around to culminate in six final scenes on the left wall. The cycle as a whole has a continuous left-to-right development, and this last section begins with an exceptionally strong left-to-right movement in a representation of Jesus carrying the cross. This movement is halted by the centralized composition of the *Crucifixion*, but in the subsequent *Lamentation*, Giotto forces our attention backward and downward to the conjunction of the heads of the Virgin and Jesus. Giotto demands that we stop and concentrate on the *Lamentation*. The impact of the event is

conveyed to us not only by the variety of human emotions expressed by Jesus' followers as they gather around his body but also by the reflection of these emotions in the angels who flood the sky with grief. Such a strong emphasis on experience and empathy is surely related to the preachings and writings of the followers of Saint Francis.

In the *Last Judgment*, Christ appears in the center, flanked by saints and angels; below, on his right hand, are the blessed, while to our right are the damned (fig. 4-99). Near the center, to the left of the cross that marks the dividing line between Paradise and eternal damnation, is a representation of Enrico Scrovegni offering his chapel, represented as a model held by a monk, to the Virgin. Scrovegni's purpose in having the

chapel erected and painted is thus clarified, for in making this offering he hoped to atone for the sins of his father, who had accumulated a fortune by charging exorbitant rates of interest, a sin called usury that the Church condemned.

There are references to virtues and vices in other areas of the chapel. They appear as figures in **grisaille** (gray and white, simulating sculpture), which alternate with illusionistic marble panels.

The Renaissance artist Lorenzo Ghiberti said the Arena Chapel was "one of the glories of the earth," and the modern artist Henri Matisse announced that, on looking at a scene in the Arena Chapel, "I understood at once the feeling which radiates from it, and which is instinct in the line, the composition, the color."

4-100. Schematic diagrams of a section of a typical late-medieval tempera painting. Tempera is opaque, and the arrow (right) suggests that light penetrates only the translucent varnish layer on the surface of the tempera (section B enlarged, far right). Notice how the frame is integral to the initial construction and not something that is added later (above).

During the fourteenth and fifteenth centuries, Giotto, Masaccio, Piero della Francesca, Mantegna, Botticelli, and other Italian artists created paintings in **tempera** and in **fresco**, two techniques that were as distinctive in appearance as they were in execution. Fresco (see pages 128–29) and tempera both have their origins in antiquity; in fourteenth-century Europe, they were well established as alternative techniques understood and used by the same artist but often for different settings and purposes.

The use of tempera paint dates back to the Egyptians. The support for tempera paint is usually wood (fig. 4-100), and large panels such as those of Giotto and Cimabue (see figs. 4-95, 4-96) are composed of planks glued together, with an integral frame constructed at the same time. To provide an appropriate surface for the paint, the wood panel was covered with linen or canvas and several layers of gesso. Onto this surface the painter drew preliminary designs, probably with charcoal. The final design was scratched into the plaster surface, following the outlines of the forms to be painted. Thin sheets of gold leaf were applied, using red glue, to the background areas. The paint used was composed of ground pigments combined with egg and perhaps a little vinegar. The paint, which dried quickly, was applied methodically in numerous thin coats to prevent flaking.

The finished paintings are characterized by rich colors against a luminous gold ground. Many later painters enhanced their work by elaborately decorating the gold background. Using delicate carving tools, they impressed floral and Gothic decorative patterns into the surface of the gold to create borders and halo designs that caught the light and shimmered on the reflective surface.

As in tempera painting, the creation of a fresco de-manded a number of sequential steps (fig. 4-101). The work would be commissioned and a legal contract drawn up. At this point, the painter probably was advanced money to pay for the purchase of necessary materials. Small drawings might be prepared to show to the patron for approval before the contract was signed. After the contract was signed, scaffolding was erected, and a layer of rough plaster (*arriccio*) was applied over the brick or stone wall surface. To mark the subdivisions, a string soaked in red color was held up to the surface and then snapped to create horizontal and vertical guidelines. The artist then made preliminary charcoal drawings on the *arriccio*. These drawings were reinforced with pale ocher paint and the charcoal erased. The ocher painting was reinforced in *sinopia* (red paint); such full-scale compositional drawings are called *sinopie*. At this point the *sinopie* could be viewed and approved by the patron. The final layer of fine plaster (*intonaco*) was then applied.

In the true fresco technique (**buon fresco**), a patch of plaster large enough to be completed the next day is applied at the end of a day's work. Each daily patch is known as a **giornata** (Italian for "day"). The patches are usually applied in sequence, beginning with the upper left area of the wall, then moving across the top, and ending with the lower right (see fig. 5-17).

The wetness of the plaster, which changes over the course of the day, has to be taken into account by the painter. When the plaster is quite wet, the paint sinks into the plaster surface (up to 1/4 inch) and bleaches slightly. If the artist is painting a large passage of drapery beginning in the morning and ending in the afternoon, during the later part of the day a little water must be added to the paint so that the last areas to be painted will not be darker

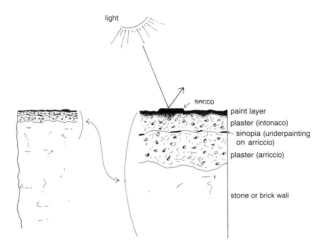

4-101. Schematic diagram of sections of a typical late-medieval fresco painting. The arrow suggests how light does not penetrate the surface of a fresco painting.

Labels in diagram:
light
secco
paint layer
plaster (intonaco)
sinopia (underpainting on arriccio)
plaster (arriccio)
stone or brick wall

in hue. As the plaster dries, a chemical reaction takes place: the carbon dioxide of the air combines with the calcium hydrate in the plaster, producing calcium carbonate. After all the *giornate* are painted, haloes are gilded. ***Fresco secco*** (color with glue in the **vehicle**—egg white or lime) is used for some details. Blue is usually applied in this fashion.

The process and the end results of fresco and tempera are different. Fresco, for example, is faster than tempera. No wooden frame has to be built and covered with fine layers of plaster, and the artist works on a large scale with a bigger brush and with a relatively thin paint that applies easily. This technique is also much cheaper than tempera, partly because of the speed involved in its execution and the fact that the materials with which the painter works are less expensive. Tempera is slower because it is a finer technique, meant to be seen close up. Because the colors dry rapidly, only one thin coat can be applied at a time, and each color must be built up in layers. Tempera works were painted in the *bottega* (shop), but frescoes had to be painted directly on the wall, where both the artist and the patron assumed they would be forever. This concept of painting in place meant that the painter frequently took into consideration the architecture and lighting of the setting.

Tempera paintings are usually brilliant in color, with deeply saturated hues, while frescoes tend to be slightly washed out, of **higher value**, and less deeply saturated because the pigment sinks into the plaster. Brighter colors are used for tempera paintings because finer pigments are employed in this medium and they are meant to be seen close up; in fresco, cheaper, more earthy pigments are used, partly because large quantities are necessary.

Tempera is more conservative; it discourages experi-

mentation because the entire conception must be worked out before the carpenter begins to construct the panel. Fresco encourages experimentation because it is easily corrected if the artist's first effort is not acceptable: the still-damp plaster can be scraped off and the artist can start again the next day. While fresco invites spontaneity, tempera is so methodical that the artist is encouraged to be very precise. Fine detail can be emphasized, whereas frescoes are frequently high on the wall and forms are therefore suggested rather than spelled out in detail (see fig. 5-18). The fresco technique favors a broad style of painting, which is more exciting than the accuracy and precision of the tempera technique. The distance between the viewer and the painted wall also allows fresco painters to be more dramatic and to use a few prominent gestures to communicate ideas and expression. Frescoes are generally larger, the figures are usually about lifesize, and the style is often illusionistic.

Both media are durable, partly because of the care with which they are executed. Both represent careful refinements of experiments over many years, and they are sound technically. However, frescoes deteriorate if moisture seeps through from behind, and the wood support of the tempera panel can warp, crack, or rot. Another common difficulty with frescoes is that fine details painted in the *fresco secco* technique can flake away.

One motivation for an artist to work in both media is the fact that fresco painting is not feasible in the winter, when the increased humidity in Italian churches meant that the plaster did not dry quickly enough (documents survive that tell us about frescoes that grew moldy rather than drying). During the winter the painter could be busy in the *bottega*, making tempera paintings.

THE ROYAL ART OF AFRICAN KINGDOMS

4-102. Ife culture. *Head of Queen Olokun*, from the Ife kingdom, Nigeria. 11th–15th century. Brass, height to top of ornament approx. 36". The British Museum, London. The metal used to cast the heads found at Ife is often called bronze, but as an alloy of copper and zinc, it is more properly classified as brass. Commissioned by an Ife ruler

4-103. Edo culture. Altar head, from the Benin kingdom, Nigeria. 17th century. Cast alloy of copper and iron, height 8³/4". National Museum of African Art, Smithsonian Institution, Washington, D.C. This head once supported a decorated tusk, as in figure 4-104. Commissioned by a Benin ruler

4-104. Benin culture. Royal Ancestral Shrine, Benin kingdom, Nigeria. Ancestral shrines for Benin kings in the present-day palace compound display brass commemorative heads that support elaborately carved ivory tusks. Ivory was precious, its whiteness symbolizing purity and peace. The monarch, or *oba*, received one tusk from every elephant killed in the kingdom. Carved tusks, some as long as 6 feet, were also a symbol of longevity. Numerous other ritual objects rested on the altars, including cast brass bells and figurative sculpture. Commissioned by various Benin rulers

The main subject of Ife art is the human head, rendered realistically but with the regularized features of an idealized portrait (fig. 4-102). The *Head of Queen Olokun* is presented with a serene and regal countenance that comes from a sculptural tradition known first in clay and then in metal. The more than 15 million Yoruba-speaking people who now live in Nigeria and the Popular Republic of Benin are the descendants of the makers of this head. They have a long history in West Africa. They were, and continue to be, one of the largest and most prolific art-producing groups of Africa.

Their urbanism is ancient and legendary, probably dating from as early as 800–1000 CE, according to excavations at two sites, Owo and Ife. These were only two of numerous city-states headed by sacred rulers (both men and women) and councils of elders and chiefs. The city-states best known for their sculpture and cultural life were Ife, Benin, and Owo. Ife is regarded by the Yoruba as the place of origin of life itself and of human civilization, and the dynasty of kings there remains unbroken to the present day. It is probably the oldest continuous kingship in the world.

Ife, situated in the southwest of what is now Nigeria, is the oldest of these city-states. Its first settlement dates from the eighth century, but little is known about its rise to power. By 1100, artists at Ife had already developed a refined and highly naturalistic sculptural tradition in terra-cotta and stone, which was soon followed by works in copper, brass, and bronze. The terra-cotta heads and works cast in brass found at Ife are known to date between the eleventh and sixteenth centuries.

11th–15th century	Head of Queen Oluhun
1167	Founding of Oxford University
1220	First giraffe is shown in Europe
1364	Aztecs build Tenochtitlán in Mexico

4-105. Yoruba culture. *Head of a Woman*, from Ugba' Laja site, Owo, Nigeria. 15th century. Terra-cotta, height 6 7/8". Nigeria National Museum, Ile-Ifer

South of Ife was the kingdom of Benin, which built its capital at Benin City. When the Portuguese arrived there in 1485, the highly organized Benin society was headed by a wealthy and militarily powerful monarch called the *oba*. He lived in a large city with a regular grid pattern of tree-lined avenues. The *oba* was supported by a large aristocracy and an efficient group of bureaucrats. Artists and crafts-workers, including metal casters and ivory carvers, were organized into guilds, worked exclusively for the king, and lived in special compounds in the city. The system was maintained until 1897, when a British expedition sacked and destroyed the city. The British soldiers went to Benin City to avenge the death of an English consul who was killed when he entered the city in violation of the orders of the *oba*. The Benin leader had forbidden the visit of foreigners because he was absorbed in rituals in honor of his ancestors. The thousands of works of art taken as booty were sold in London to cover the cost of the expedition and are now in the major

museums of Europe.

The art of Benin is court art, the principal aim of which was the glorification of the ruler. Each newly enthroned *oba* ordered brass memorial heads to be cast in honor of his father (fig. 4-103). These heads are not individualized portraits intended to portray a particular monarch, but rather their function is to memorialize both one *oba* and all *obas*. They are testimonies to royal descent and were one of the six essential items (the others include wooden heads, the royal sword, brass bells, sculpted leopards, and carved ivories) to sit on the ancestral altar of the palace to emphasize the king's prestige and power (fig. 4-104). As commemorative images, they represented the enduring power of inherited leadership.

The *obas* were believed to have both divine and Edo (the local ethnic group) lineage, and all beings, whether living or spiritual, were thought to possess life force, or *ase*. Priests, initiates, diviners, rulers, and elders could learn to use *ase* for the benefit of themselves and those around them. The tangible world of

the living (*aye*) interacted with the invisible realm of the spiritual forces (*orun*), which included gods, ancestors, and spirits. The tangible and spiritual aspects of all *obas* were meant to be realized in the brass heads.

Another kingdom, Owo, maintained close ties to Ife and also experienced the powerful artistic and cultural influences of Benin City. Excavations at Ugba' Laja uncovered the ruins of a thatched-roof mudhouse, thought to be a shrine, that contained objects associated with rites of sacrifice—terra-cotta heads (fig. 4-105), incomplete small figures, fragments of larger figures and groups, ceramic pots, iron implements, and polished stone axes. In technical execution and style, the head from Ugba' Laja falls within the naturalistic tradition also characteristic of the art of their neighbors, the Ife. The vertical striations that line the face represent the scarification that was performed to signify the rite of passage to adult life. The heirs of this sculptural tradition remain active and influential as artists in West Africa today.

5-1. Piero della Francesca. *Resurrection*. c. 1460. Fresco, approx. 8' x 6'6"; the figures are approx. lifesize. Pinacoteca, Sansepolcro, Italy. Commissioned by the chief magistrates of Sansepolcro for their state chamber

INTRODUCTION TO FIFTEENTH-CENTURY ART

Many of the artistic developments in European art that occurred in the fifteenth century in Italy and Flanders can be seen in *Resurrection* (fig. 5-1) by Piero della Francesca (c. 1420–92) and *Deposition* (fig. 5-2) by Rogier van der Weyden (1399?–1464). Both are large, with lifesize figures, and offer a **naturalism** not seen in painting since the time of the ancient Romans. The figures are realistically proportioned, seem to have weight and to occupy illusionistic space, and suggest the potential for movement. In addi-

tion, they are charged with emotional and psychological tensions that demand a response from the viewer. Piero's resurrected Christ fixes us with a compelling gaze, while in Rogier's painting waves of emotion sweep through the followers as they receive the body being lowered from the cross. They weep, convulse, and faint.

Nevertheless, significant differences between the two works suggest the artistic and cultural distinctions between Italy and Flanders at this time; it is during the fifteenth century that we begin to find the development of sharply different traditions within Europe. Piero's Christ is like a Greek god—his handsome musculature

5-2. Rogier van der Weyden. *Deposition*. c. 1435–38. Oil on wood, 7'2⅝" x 8'7⅛". Prado, Madrid. The symbol of the commissioning guild, the crossbow, is used for a decoration in the side spandrels. Commissioned by the Crossbowmen's Guild of Louvain for the Church of Nôtre-Dame hors-les-murs

and dignified bearing can be compared to the Apollo from Olympia (see fig. 3-49). Such an interest in classical motifs and types is seldom found in Flemish painting. Piero's forceful triangular composition, with Christ's head at the apex and the sleeping soldiers grouped below, reveals the Italian concern with harmony and order. Rogier's composition is much more visually complex, and its flowing forms weave a pattern of pathos and despair. This concentration is reinforced by Rogier's Flemish attention to precise detail, made possible by new developments in oil painting (see pages 272–73).

FIFTEENTH-CENTURY DEVELOPMENTS

In fifteenth-century Europe, the foundations were being laid for many of the developments that help explain later Western attitudes. In fact, the fifteenth through seventeenth century has been called the "Early Modern" period in the study of Western history. Because so much of the Western world view has its origins then, European artistic developments of this time must be discussed in some detail.

There were continuing developments in—and increasingly important contacts among—all parts of the world in the fifteenth century. The explosion of publications in the West (the first printed edition of Marco Polo's *Description of the World* was published in Germany in 1477) inspired interest in other cultures, and Columbus's explorations in 1492 were to lead to extensive contacts between Europe and the Americas in the sixteenth century.

While western Europe was undergoing rapid developments and changes in the form and content of its art, Asian art is characterized by the continuation of earlier forms, especially within the Buddhist tradition that had, by this time, spread from its origins in India throughout most of Asia. The form of the fifteenth-century *Mandala of Jnanadakini* from Tibet (fig. 5-3), for example, follows that of centuries-old examples, but the use of brilliant color is typical of Tibetan art in the fifteenth century. *Mandala* means "circle," and this Buddhist symbol for the structure of the universe was used for meditation and to introduce devotees to a higher spiritual order. A mandala can be painted, as here, or made in colored sand, or used as the basis for Buddhist temple design, as in the substructure of the stupa at Sanchi (see fig. 3-83) or as at Borobudur, in Java (see fig. 4-48). In this Tibetan example,

5-3. Tibet, School of the Ngor Monastery. *Mandala of Jnanadakini*. Late 15th century. Opaque watercolor on cloth, 33$^1/4$ x 28$^7/8$". The Metropolitan Museum of Art, New York

Purchase, Lita Annenberg Hazen Charitable Trust Gift, 1987 (1987.16)

the center is controlled by a *dakini*, a female demigod who represents the absolute principle in Buddhist cosmology. The four quadrants represent the four directions; four cosmic Buddhas, each a different color, preside over the four quadrants. The geometric harmony of this Tibetan mandala has formal similarities with the design of many Italian works of the fifteenth century, creating an unexpected aesthetic parallel between works created in two diverse, unrelated cultures.

In East Asia during this period, China under the Ming dynasty (1368–1644) was the most stable political entity. The arts were used to revive and reassert the stability of Chinese traditions. Early in the century, architects designed much of the layout of Beijing, including the Temples of Heaven and Earth and the palace known as the Forbidden City. The symmetry and balance of these plans reveal the stability and power of the Chinese imperial authority at this time, while the design also communicates a cosmological order traditional in China. In Japan, the fifteenth century was a period of constant warfare and absence of central authority, although the trades and arts continued to flourish during these troubled times. It was during this period that Zen Buddhism became dominant in Japanese religious and intellectual life. There was a renewed interest by the Japanese in Chinese culture, perhaps because of the stability that China represented in Asia.

THE IDEA OF A RENAISSANCE

Our use of the term *Renaissance* (French for "rebirth") is drawn from a conception of history found in the writings of the sixteenth-century Italian painter, architect, and writer Giorgio Vasari, whose historical fame rests primarily on his *Lives of the Most Eminent Painters, Sculptors, and Architects* (1550, 1568), a history of Italian art and artists. Vasari champions the works of ancient Greece and Rome, describing medieval art as a "disastrous decline," and argues that in Italy during the fifteenth and sixteenth centuries "art has been reborn and reached perfection in our own times." Vasari's concept influenced the French historian Jules Michelet, who in 1855 gave the title *La Renaissance* to a volume of his *Histoire de France* and thereby extended the idea of the Renaissance to embrace a cultural phenomenon that included northern Europe. Michelet's Renaissance was characterized by "the discovery of the world and the discovery of man." The reasons behind the appeal of antiquity in this period are not easy to define; the richness and splendor of antique monuments, even in ruins, had had an impact throughout the Middle Ages, and as society and economic life blossomed at the end of the medieval period, such monuments provided appropriate models for new construction. The new self-confidence expressed in politics, business, and learning in the fifteenth century found important models and inspiration not only in ancient texts but also in ancient sculpture, especially the Greek emphasis on the dignity and beauty of the human figure and the Roman ability to capture the individual in portraiture.

For Italian Renaissance artists, the models of classical antiquity provided an impetus for artistic transformation, but it would be a mistake to view these artists as merely copying ancient works of art. They adapted the classical aesthetic to the attitudes of their own times, creating works of art distinctly different from those of antiquity. This "rebirth" of the antique encompassed not only works of art, but also the recovery of ancient texts and classical literary style. Leonardo Bruni, a diplomat and scholar versed in Latin and Greek (see fig. 5-4), is characteristic of the new scholarship in his careful reading of antique texts and his application of ancient civic values to his own time, which led to a new historical consciousness fundamental to the growth of Renaissance humanism (see below).

NAMING THE STYLES

The transition from the late Middle Ages to the Renaissance in the cosmopolitan European centers of Flanders and Italy was a gradual one, and many aspects of Renaissance society and art evolved slowly from medieval traditions. Historians still debate if fifteenth-century Flemish painting is best understood as a late manifestation of the Gothic or as a Northern version of the Renaissance. Because neither *Gothic* nor *Renaissance* is a completely appropriate stylistic term for these Flemish works, they are here identified under an independent designation: fifteenth-century Flemish painting. In Italy, and especially in Florence, new Renaissance ideas dominate the production of art during most of the fifteenth century. This period is generally known as the Early Renaissance, to distinguish it from the late fifteenth and early sixteenth centuries, when the culmination of earlier ideas resulted in the period called the High Renaissance (see pages 298–300).

HISTORY

As our introductory paintings reveal, much of the artistic activity of western Europe during the fifteenth century was centered in Florence and Flanders. Scholar Leonardo Bruni praised Florence as "the new Athens on the Arno." He likened the civic values of his time to those fostered in democratic Athens and in Rome during the Republic. Although Bruni praised Florentine republicanism, contrasting it to the despotic rule in other Italian city-states, in actuality Florence was led by an oligarchy of commercial interests. The Florentine government was eventually dominated by the Medici family, whose wealth was derived from banking and commerce. Beginning with Cosimo de' Medici, the family consolidated the reins of power behind a facade of republicanism. His descendants firmly tightened their political control, and Lorenzo ("Lorenzo the Magnificent") ultimately ruled as a benevolent tyrant. Toward the end of the century, the domination of the Medici and the conspicuous wealth and humanist interests of the Florentine citizenry were challenged by the fiery sermons of the Dominican friar Girolamo Savonarola. Following the exile of the Medici in 1494, Savonarola assisted in restoring a more representative form of government. But as Savonarola continued to act as the harsh conscience of Florence, the Church and some of the citizenry turned against him, and he was executed for heresy in 1498. Florence maintained her republic until 1512, when the Medici again regained control.

In Flanders, an area roughly equivalent to present-day Belgium, a prosperous new merchant society based on the wool trade and banking was established during the fourteenth and fifteenth centuries. The flourishing city of Bruges was the most important center, and the

5-4. Bernardo Rossellino. Tomb of Leonardo Bruni. c. 1445. Marble with traces of paint and gilding, height to top of arch 20'. Santa Croce, Florence, Italy. Commissioned by the Signoria of Florence or the College and Council of Arezzo

presence of foreign bankers, such as the Medici from Florence, made it the banking capital of northern Europe. Other important centers included Ghent and Tournai. As in Italy, trade **guilds** controlled manufacturing, as well as the production of works of art.

Flanders was distinguished by a rich and diverse culture, which included a revolutionary school of composers that dominated European musical developments throughout the century. Northern intellectuals, however, were not very interested in the revival of the forms and subject matter of ancient Greece and Rome that were so important to the Italians, and in Flanders some arts, especially architecture and the decorative arts, remained Gothic well into the sixteenth century.

ITALIAN RENAISSANCE HUMANISM

The Renaissance concept of humanism (as distinct from the modern concepts of humanitarianism and secular humanism) had a profound philosophical foundation. The title *humanist* was originally applied to a teacher of humanistic studies, a curriculum that included rhetoric, grammar, poetry, history, and moral philosophy; at the base of many of these disciplines was the study of ancient texts on these topics in Latin and, eventually, in Greek as well. Already in the fourteenth century, scholars and writers had been inspired by the ideas they found in ancient Greek and Roman texts, which confirmed their new intellectual and scientific interest in understanding the world. The praise for the deeds of great figures from antiquity that the humanists found in Greek and Roman texts supported the notions of pride and fame that were

becoming important in a society whose major figures were successful business entrepreneurs and bankers. During this period, humanism was, with some effort, integrated with Christianity; it sought to supplement faith by insisting on the dignity of the individual and the human potential for achievement. Although the development of humanism was centered in Florence, by mid-century most of the important courts in northern Italy had been significantly influenced by humanism.

Humanist values are visually exemplified on the Tomb of Leonardo Bruni (fig. 5-4), the Florentine diplomat and champion of humanist education. An effigy of the deceased Bruni rests atop a bier supported by two eagles, standards of ancient Rome. Crowned with laurel, the ancient symbol of honor and victory, and with his hands embracing the book he wrote, *History of the Florentine People*, Bruni lies eternally in state. On the sarcophagus below is a Latin inscription in classical lettering: "At Leonardo's passing, history grieves, eloquence is mute, and it is said that the Muses, Greek and Latin alike, cannot hold back their tears." These antique literary references are reinforced by the classicizing architecture of the tomb. The **Corinthian pilasters** and round **arch** may refer to the ancient Roman **triumphal arch** (see fig. 3-97). Over the arch, two **putti** hold aloft Bruni's coat of arms. The **relief** of the Virgin and Child within the arch is the only reference to Christianity. Such a union of ancient traditions and Christian theology was one of the primary goals of humanism. It had an influence on many works of art, including Botticelli's *Birth of Venus* (see fig. 5-56).

ITALIAN RENAISSANCE ART THEORY

Humanism played an important role in the development of **art theory**. Leon Battista Alberti, well educated in humanistic studies, was attracted to the new work of such Florentine artists as Filippo Brunelleschi, Donatello, and Masaccio. He noted that these artists revived classical art, and using a literary approach that joined his knowledge of the principles of classical poetry and rhetoric, he wrote about the new art in *De pictura* (*On Painting*) in 1435. This cornerstone of Western art theory discusses the noble purpose of painting, the painter as an educated professional, and the use of mathematical principles, including scientific perspective (see pages 262–63), in painting. *On Painting* gave art and artists a new dignity and opened the way for a new level of literary discussions on art.

THE UNION OF THE CLASSICAL AND THE NATURAL

Natural observation, an important feature of fifteenth-century art, was addressed by the late medieval artist Cennino Cennini in his practical manual for painters, *The Craftsman's Handbook*, written c. 1400. He recommended learning to draw from the works of recognized masters:

> Now you must forge ahead again, so that you may pursue the course of this theory. . . . Having first practiced drawing for a while . . . take pains and pleasure in constantly copying the best things which you can find done by the hand of the great masters.

Having established the importance of studying great works, Cennini turned to nature:

> Mind you, the most perfect steersman that you can have, and the best helm, lie in . . . copying from nature. And this outdoes all other models; and always rely on this with a stout heart, especially as you begin to gain some judgment in draftsmanship.

5-5. Donatello. Equestrian monument of Erasmo da Narni (*Gattamelata*). c. 1445–53. Bronze, originally with gilded details, height 12'2". Piazza del Santo, Padua. Erasmo da Narni was a famous mercenary general who was employed by the Venetian government to raise and lead its armies; his nickname, Gattamelata, means "honeyed cat." Commissioned by the Venetian Senate

To the Renaissance artist, copying from nature led not only to the heightened perception gained from meticulous observation but also to an attempt to understand the principles that govern the order and processes of nature. This sympathy with the natural world was a decisive aspect of Renaissance art.

The equestrian monument *Gattamelata* (fig. 5-5), by Donatello (c.1386/90–1466), combines naturalistic observation with a well-known antique type, as exemplified by the *Marcus Aurelius* (see fig. 3-96). An ambitious feat of bronze casting, it was the largest sculpture cast in bronze since antiquity. With the bronze *David* (see fig. 5-42), probably commissioned for the Medici Palace courtyard (see fig. 5-38), Donatello revived the lifesize, freestanding, nude figure. The acceptance of nudity in art is related to the humanist insistence on the dignity of the individual and the view that the human figure is a microcosm of the macrocosm, a smaller, symbolic reflection of the larger universe.

5-6. Piero della Francesca. *Battista Sforza* and *Federigo da Montefeltro*. 1474. Oil and tempera on wood, each 18$^1/2$ x 13". Galleria degli Uffizi, Florence. Federigo da Montefeltro ruled Urbino from 1444 until 1482. His wife, Battista Sforza, bore him eight daughters and one son. Federigo was a soldier and a prolific patron of artists and architects. Probably commissioned by Federigo da Montefeltro

EUROPEAN INTELLECTUAL AND SCIENTIFIC ACTIVITY

The Gutenberg Bible—the first complete book to be printed using independent, movable type—was made between 1450 and 1456. By 1460, woodcuts were being used for illustrations in books; as an inexpensive method of producing illustrated books in large quantity, they contributed to the development of the sciences. Knowledge was more easily shared when a printed illustration could offer an exactly repeatable image, unchanged by the hand of a copyist. Through the medium of printing, knowledge reached a level of circulation only recently surpassed by modern media, including the computer.

CHANGING PATTERNS OF PATRONAGE IN EUROPE

During the fifteenth century, artists and workshops received a variety of secular and religious commissions. Rulers continued to employ works of art for the tradi-tional purposes of exalting and consolidating their power, but now their imagery more often had an ancient basis and/or was inspired by models from antiquity. A relatively new development is patronage by city govern-ments in the Italian communes and patronage by the mercantile class in Flanders and Italy; based on the writ-ings of the humanists, patronage was now viewed as an important activity of the responsible and enlightened cit-izen. While devotional images were produced in increasing numbers to adorn the family chapels and the bedrooms of the expanding middle class, new types of art—portraits, mythological subjects, and secular deco-rations—were commissioned by individuals to adorn their private palaces, town houses, or country villas. In many instances, patrons and family members were rep-resented in the wings or at the sides of works they com-missioned (see fig. 5-13).

In Florence, Cosimo de' Medici was generous in his support of libraries. He took an avid interest in the art of Donatello, and his patronage of scholars helped support the formulation of Neoplatonism, a complex humanist philosophy that sought to fuse Plato's ideals with Christian thinking by emphasizing how the spiritual aspects of life can overcome physical limitations. Cosimo's grandson, Lorenzo the Magnificent, collected antique works of art and encouraged commissions for Florentine artists; he was also a friend and supporter of the young Michelangelo. Such involvement with the arts was not solely altruistic, for support of humanist scholarship and the arts demonstrated benevolence and was useful in forming public opinion and securing fame. Moreover, given the political intrigue and conflict of the time, it was an advantage for rulers to surround themselves with intellectuals as advisers.

Rulers often commissioned portraits. Piero della Francesca gave his patrons, the rulers of Urbino (fig. 5-6), an almost omnipotent presence. They seem elevated above everyday affairs, and the broad landscape backgrounds suggest the extent of ducal power. On the reverse, they are shown on triumphal carts surrounded by allegorical figures that represent Virtues (his more active, hers more contemplative) that are based on antique and medieval writings. The combination of such allegorical figures with the commitment to naturalism so apparent in the unidealized representation of Federigo's profile, which was disfigured in a tournament, is typical of much of fifteenth-century art.

THE FIFTEENTH-CENTURY ARTIST IN EUROPE

The dignity of the individual and the new self-consciousness promoted by the humanists had an important influence on attitudes about artists. In contrast to the prevalent medieval attitude that the artist was a humble craftsperson serving God, some Renaissance artists were viewed as trained intellectuals, versed in the classics and geometry. Artists became famous; in 1481, for example, an author named Cristoforo Landino made a list of Italian and Flemish artists and praised them for their skill and innovations; he even suggested that Donatello could be "counted among" the ancient masters—the highest praise possible at the time. Artists began to sign their works with more frequency, and one artist, Lorenzo Ghiberti, wrote his autobiography. The modern ideal of the artist as a genius has its origins in these developments in the fifteenth century.

During the first half of the fifteenth century, Flemish and Italian artists began to create self-portraits, a sure indication of their new status. In 1433, Jan van Eyck depicted himself wearing a fantastic headdress—a tour de force of painting—and looking out at us with a penetrating gaze (fig. 5-7). On the frame are van Eyck's motto ("The best I can do") and the date. Artists even began to include self-portraits within their works. Lorenzo Ghiberti's "Gates of Paradise" (see fig. 5-28) have both a self-

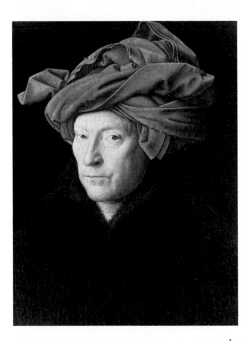

5-7. Jan van Eyck. *Self-Portrait*. 1433. Oil on wood, 10^1/4 x 7^1/2". The National Gallery, London. Because of the acute gaze and the motto on the frame, this painting has been identified as the artist's self-portrait.

5-8. Lorenzo Ghiberti. *Self-Portrait*, from the East Doors of the Baptistery (see fig. 5-28), Florence. 1425–52. Gilded bronze, approx. height 3". Museo dell' Opera del Duomo, Florence. Commissioned by the Opera of the Baptistery and the Arte di Calimala

portrait (fig. 5-8) and a self-promoting Latin inscription that praises the "marvelous art" with which Ghiberti made the work. The development of self-portraiture may have played an important role in constructing new attitudes about the artist during this formative period. The new dignity accorded the artist in the fifteenth century is a foundation upon which the later conception of the artist as an inspired genius is based.

CE	1400	1420	

EUROPE ART

c. 1411–15
DONATELLO'S *SAINT MARK*

c. 1415
BRUNELLESCHI DEMONSTRATES SCIENTIFIC PERSPECTIVE

1420–36
BRUNELLESCHI'S DOME FOR FLORENCE CATHEDRAL

c. 1425–30
CAMPIN'S *ANNUNCIATION*

c. 1425–28
MASACCIO'S *THE TRINITY*

1425–52
GHIBERTI'S EAST DOORS OF THE FLORENCE BAPTISTERY

1432
VAN EYCKS' *THE ALTARPIECE OF THE LAMB* COMPLETED

1434
VAN EYCK'S *PORTRAIT*

1436
BRUNELLESCHI'S SANTO SPIRITO

HISTORY

ASIA ART

1402–24
BEIJING TEMPLES AND PALACE LAID OUT

1423
JAPANESE ARTISTS VISIT KOREA

HISTORY

1368–1644
Ming dynasty in China

1403
Completion of Chinese encyclopedia in 22,937 volumes

THE AMERICAS ART

c. 1400
MOUND BUILDERS ACTIVE IN NORTH AMERICA

c. 1400–1521
AZTEC CODEX PAINTINGS

HISTORY

1427
Aztec empire expands in Mexico

1438
Inka empire established in Peru

AFRICA ART

c. 1400–1550
BENIN EARLY PERIOD

HISTORY

1405–33
Chinese Admiral Zeng visits African coast

1418
Portuguese explore African coast

THE MIDDLE EAST ART

HISTORY

1400–02
Tamerlane's conquests of Syria, Baghdad, Anatolia

1440	**1460**	**1480**

c. 1445–53
DONATELLO'S *GATTAMELATA*

1445–59
MICHELOZZI'S MEDICI PALACE

c. 1465
BALDOVINETTI'S *PORTRAIT OF A YOUNG WOMAN*

1465–74
MANTEGNA'S CAMERA PICTA

c. 1478–80
LEONARDO'S *MADONNA AND CHILD WITH CAT*

c. 1482
BOTTICELLI'S *REALM OF VENUS*

1483–85
LEONARDO'S *MADONNA OF THE ROCKS*

c. 1484–86
BOTTICELLI'S *BIRTH OF VENUS*

c. 1495–98
LEONARDO'S *THE LAST SUPPER*

1498–99
MICHELANGELO'S ROME *PIETÀ*

1441
Portuguese begin Atlantic slave trade

1450–56
Gutenberg Bible printed

1477
Marco Polo's *Description of the World* printed

1498
Savonarola executed for heresy

1492–96
Columbus's voyages

1480
RYOANJI GARDEN, KYOTO, JAPAN

c. 1447
1st Dalai Lama appointed ruler of Tibet

1467
Start of civil wars in Japan

1476–1520
AZTEC ROCK-CARVED TEMPLES, MEXICO

15TH CENTURY
INKA TEMPLE OF THE SUN, CUZCO, PERU

15TH CENTURY
AZTEC MOTHER GODDESS FIGURES, MEXICO

1492
Inka empire at its height

1492–96
Columbus explores Caribbean islands

BEFORE 1450
CONICAL TOWERS OF GREAT ZIMBABWE

1455
Venetian navigator Cadamosto explores the Senegal River

c. 1450
The Arabian Nights compiled

1453
Ottoman Turks conquer Constantinople

EARLY RENAISSANCE SCULPTURE IN FLORENCE

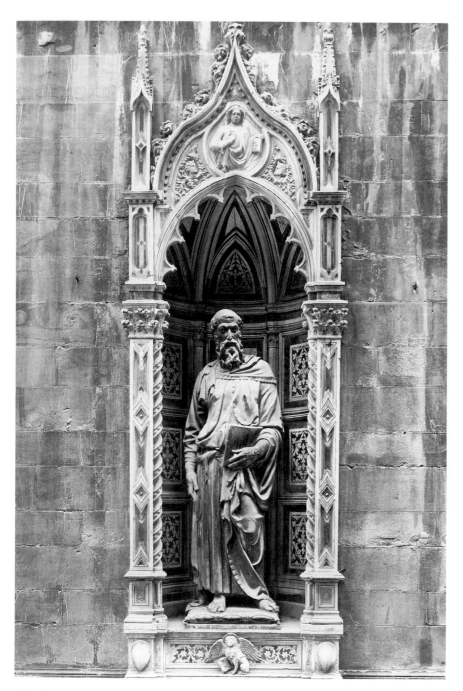

5-9. Donatello. *Saint Mark*, from Orsanmichele, Florence. c. 1411–15. Marble, originally with some polychromy and metal details, height 7'10". This statue of the Evangelist is shown in its original Gothic setting in the Guild of Linen Weavers and Peddlers' niche—one of fourteen niches assigned to Florentine trade guilds—on the civic granary and shrine of Orsanmichele. Commissioned by the Guild of Linen Weavers and Peddlers

Donatello's *Saint Mark* (fig. 5-9) overlooked a Florentine street, surveying the urban scene with an expression that conveys a questioning intelligence. It is reported that when Michelangelo saw the work, he proclaimed "that he had never seen a figure which had more the air of a good man than this one, and that if Saint Mark were such a man, one could believe what he had written." In other words, for Michelangelo the *Saint Mark* expressed integrity. In medieval art, the Evangelists had been depicted as figures receiving divine inspiration (see fig. 4-44). Donatello's Renaissance interpretation emphasizes the more human attributes of wisdom and reason. In addition, Donatello's *Saint Mark* attains the dignity we accord an individual, for in physiognomy and body type he suggests a specific, compelling personality. The revival of antiquity, so important for the Italian Renaissance, is readily apparent, for *Saint Mark* is closer to ancient Greek and Roman figures than any figure created during the long interval of the Middle Ages. The emphatic **contrapposto** of the saint, which helps establish his naturalism, was influenced by ancient examples (see fig. 3-67).

1394–97	Manuel Chrysoloras teaches Greek in Florence
1405	Florence buys Pisa
1410	Ptolemy's *Geography* is translated into Latin
c. 1411–15	**Donatello, *Saint Mark***
1415	Jan Hus is burned at the stake for heresy

The *Four Saints* (fig. 5-10), on the same civic structure as *Saint Mark*, represents Christian stone carvers who, during the late Roman Empire, were put to death when they refused to make an idol of a Roman god. Their serious demeanor and the open mouth and oratorical gesture of the figure on the right suggest that their sculptor, Nanni di Banco (c. 1385–1421), has depicted the moment in their legend when they debate whether to compromise their religious beliefs or to submit to death. Nanni's inspiration from ancient Roman models is obvious in the heads, one of which has a stubbly beard carved in a Roman manner, and in the drapery folds of the togas. Although such an interest is consistent with Renaissance attitudes, Nanni's antique references could also be viewed as part of his effort to establish historical veracity. What could be more appropriate than to emulate ancient Roman models when creating representations of figures who had lived in the late antique period? The new Renaissance respect for historical accuracy may thus have played a role in the conception of this sculptural group.

5-10. Nanni di Banco. *Four Saints*. c. 1410s. Marble, height 6'. Orsanmichele, Florence. Commissioned by the Guild of Sculptors and Stone Masons for its niche at Orsanmichele

FLEMISH PAINTING: THE LIMBOURG BROTHERS

5-11. The Limbourg Brothers. *February*, calendar page from the *Très Riches Heures du Duc de Berry*. Before 1416. Manuscript painting on vellum, 11³/8 x 8¹/4". Musée Condé, Chantilly, France. This manuscript is listed in an early inventory as "The Very Rich Hours of the Duke of Berry." The patron was John, duke of Berry (and brother of Charles V of France), whose library included more than 300 manuscripts. The artists were three brothers—Pol, Herman, and Jean Limbourg. The calendar pages, which traditionally accompany the listing of saints' feast days, include the labors of the month and zodiac signs with various astrological calculations. Commissioned by John, duke of Berry

5-12. The Limbourg Brothers. *Crucifixion in the Darkness of the Eclipse,* from the *Très Riches Heures du Duc de Berry*. Before 1416. Manuscript painting on vellum, 11³/8 x 8¹/4". Musée Condé, Chantilly, France

The puff of frosty breath from the mouth of the figure hurrying across the farmyard and the smoke curling from the chimney are the kinds of subtle details that characterize the comprehensive realism developing in Flemish painting at the beginning of the fifteenth century (fig. 5-11). The traditional calendar page for February showed people sitting by a fire, but the Limbourg brothers' representation encompasses a modest farm, complete with dovecote, beehives, and sheepfold, set within a vast snowy landscape with a distant village. Several figures reveal the peasants' restricted winter activities. The sky is no longer merely a flat blue background, but offers atmospheric midwinter effects that reveal the Limbourgs' study of natural phenomena.

The Limbourgs' attention to naturalistic effects also extends to biblical stories. Taking inspiration from the passage in Matthew's Gospel that, at the time of the crucifixion, "there was darkness over all the land" (27:45), they created a panoramic crucifixion scene in tones of gray that suggest the naturalistic effects of an eclipse (fig. 5-12). In a blaze of gold, blue, and red, God the Father appears to bless his dying son. In the top right roundel, an astronomer surveys the heavens, searching for an explanation for this unexpected phenomenon.

The *Très Riches Heures* marks a final phase in the development of manuscript painting in the North (for earlier examples of medieval manuscripts, see figs. 4-20, 4-30, 4-31, 4-44, 4-53). This sumptuous manuscript, with 130 illustrations, includes devotions for different periods of the day in a format that is called a book of hours, thus the book's name. The heightened interest in representing naturalistic lighting effects, panoramic landscapes, and precise details explains why this manuscript has been so admired and its compositions so often copied by later artists.

FLEMISH PAINTING: ROBERT CAMPIN

5-13. Robert Campin. *Annunciation with Patrons* and *Saint Joseph in His Workshop*. c. 1425–30. Oil on wood, 25^1/4 x 24^7/8" (center); 25^1/4 x 10^3/4" (each wing). The Metropolitan Museum of Art, New York The Cloisters Collection, 1956. The patron who commissioned this work is represented kneeling in the left wing; his wife, beside him, has been painted over the green grass, suggesting that she was added after the picture was finished, probably at the time of their marriage. It was perhaps at this same time that Campin made the work even more realistic by painting over the gold leaf that had originally filled the central windows, substituting sky, clouds, and coats of arms in stained-glass windows indicating that the patron was a member of the Ingelbrechts family. This work is often referred to as the *Mérode Altarpiece* because it was owned by the Mérode family during the nineteenth century. Robert Campin is sometimes known as the Master of Flémalle. Commissioned by a member of the Ingelbrechts family

This folding **triptych**, or three-part altarpiece or devotional picture (fig. 5-13), represents a further development of the revolutionary new qualities evident in Flemish manuscript painting at the beginning of the fifteenth century (see figs. 5-11, 5-12). Perhaps most startling is the precision with which its artist, Robert Campin (documented from 1406, died 1444), rendered objects and figures. Naturally lit, they are modeled with subtle transi-tions from light to shadow that make them seem three-dimensional and weighty. This naturalism results from the union of the fine detail of oil paint with a revolutionary preci-sion of observation on the part of the artist (see page 272–73). It almost seems as if no artist had ever seen shadows with such clarity before—certainly no artist had ever rendered them so precisely. Such naturalism demands intense concentration in both vision and technique.

Accompanying this naturalism of representation is the realistic de-piction of the subject, for a biblical event from the distant past is set in a fifteenth-century Flemish house. Gabriel enters to announce to a dis-tinctly Flemish Mary that she will be the mother of the Son of God, while Mary's husband, Joseph, a carpen-ter, is shown in a fifteenth-century workshop in the right wing. Cam-pin's depiction of this setting offers valuable evidence about wood-

1422	England resumes war with France
c. 1425–30	**Campin, *Annunciation***
1427	Thomas à Kempis, *The Imitation of Christ*

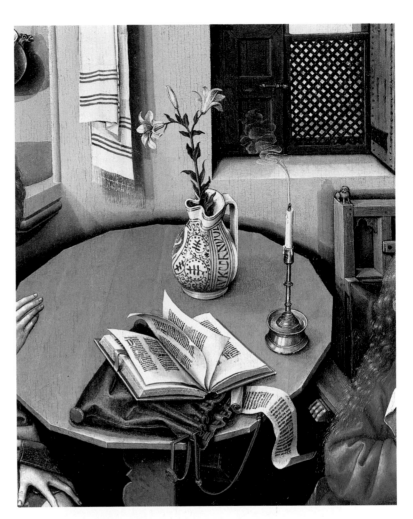

5-14. Robert Campin. *Annunciation*, detail

workers' shops and tools, including a folding shelf on which Joseph offers a mousetrap for sale directly from his shop. As secular as this may seem, locating the Annunciation within a contemporary setting is intended to make the sacred events more comprehensible and meaningful. Such an approach to religious **iconography** is paralleled in popular devotional literature and is probably also related to the representation of such subjects in contemporary religious theater.

To understand Campin's interpretation, we must look beyond the dazzling surface realism, since a pervasive symbolism (sometimes called disguised symbolism) gives a religious content to virtually every object in the painting. The three lilies on a single stalk that decorate the Virgin's table, for example, refer to the Christian Trinity; the bud is Christ. An especially intriguing symbol is Joseph's mousetrap, for it expresses the late-medieval notion that God married the Virgin to a devout older man to prevent the Devil from discovering that her child was the Son of God; in such an explanation Joseph became a "mousetrap" set by God.

The candle on the Virgin's table (fig. 5-14), just extinguished, releases a puff of smoke that suggests that the painting represents a precise moment in time. Light is a common metaphor for divinity, and the light of the Virgin's candle is extinguished because of the entry into the room (and into the world) of divine light in the person of Christ, who appears as a minuscule baby entering on rays of light through a round window on the left. The candle might also refer to the late-medieval custom of

the bridal candle, which was extinguished when the marriage was consummated, or to the symbolism of the extinguished candle as an indication that a vow has been fulfilled. The blowing out of the candle and the presence of Christ within the Virgin's chamber would then express the moment of the Incarnation. Notice that this religious content is expressed by everyday objects and that, in keeping with his naturalistic bias, Campin has not used haloes for his figures.

Robert Campin's style is known from a small number of paintings, all of which are similar in their use of ordinary people as models, their

depiction of drapery with sharp, rather abstract folds, and their crowded compositions, which avoid empty spaces (*horror vacui*). The use of ordinary people and an everyday setting is related to a revolution in 1423 in Tournai, where Campin lived. A new democratic government, led by representatives of the craft guilds, was established. This democratic, mercantile culture helps to explain the middle-class setting and virtues of Campin's Annunciation triptych, with its delight in a typical household and the inclusion of Joseph as a hardworking husband and father.

ITALIAN RENAISSANCE PAINTING: MASACCIO

5-15. Masaccio. *The Trinity with the Virgin Mary, Saint John, and Two Donors*, fresco in Santa Maria Novella, Florence. c. 1425–28. 21'10^{1}/2" x 10'5"; the figures are approximately lifesize. On the vertical axis, God the Father holds the cross, presenting his crucified son to us. A flying dove, symbol of the Holy Spirit, hovers between their heads. At the foot of the cross stand Mary and John the Evangelist; Mary's gesture and outward glance engage our attention. The kneeling profile figures are the donors who commissioned the painting. Their identity remains uncertain, although he wears the red robe of a Florentine official. The bottom portion of the painting contains a skeleton resting on a ledge. Above the skeleton, an inscription in classical lettering reads: "I was once what you are; what I am, you will be." The inclusion of the skeleton and the inscription add a *memento mori* (a reminder that all must die) context to the theme. Such references to human mortality were popular in the fourteenth and fifteenth centuries, when plagues often ravaged the populace.

The triangle, symbol of the Trinity, becomes the unifying compositional form in *The Trinity with the Virgin Mary, Saint John, and Two Donors* (fig. 5-15) by Masaccio (1401–28). With the head of God the Father forming the apex and the donors comprising the base, the triangular composition, popular in the Early Renaissance, is visually clear and easy to read. This clarity is supported by the illusionary space created by the use of **scientific perspective** (see pages 262–63). To the viewer positioned in front of the painting, the effect is of an actual chapel with real figures. The architectural forms are closely related to the Renaissance architecture being developed by Filippo Brunelleschi at this time (see figs. 5-35, 5-36). He may well have assisted Masaccio with this aspect of the painting. The clarity of the composition is combined with boldly three-dimensional figures recalling those painted by Giotto. Masaccio here has advanced the innovations of Giotto by combining them with the coherent illusory space that distinguishes Renaissance painting.

5-16. Left and portion of rear walls of Brancacci Chapel, Santa Maria del Carmine, Florence, with frescoes by Masaccio (c. 1425–28), Masolino (c. 1425–28), and Filippino Lippi (1484). Height of each register 8'. Scenes shown here include *The Expulsion of Adam and Eve* and *The Tribute Money* by Masaccio (top register, left wall); *Preaching of Saint Peter* by Masolino (top register, back wall); *Saint Peter in Prison* by Filippino Lippi (lower register, left scene on left wall); *Resurrection of the Son of Theophilus and the Chairing of Saint Peter* by Masaccio and Filippino Lippi (lower register, main scene on left wall); and *Saint Peter Healing with His Shadow* by Masaccio and Masolino (lower register, back wall). Commissioned by a member of the Brancacci family

A short time before he was commissioned to paint *The Trinity*, Masaccio was employed with another artist, Masolino (c. 1400–40/47), in decorating the Brancacci Chapel with scenes primarily from the life of Saint Peter. In *The Tribute Money* (based on Matthew 17:24–27), Jesus and his apostles are confronted by a tax collector who requests that a temple tax be paid (fig. 5-16). Jesus instructs Peter to go to the edge of the sea, to our left, where he finds the necessary coin

of tribute in the mouth of a fish. To the right, Peter pays the tax collector, an act prophetic of Jesus' words "Pay to the emperor what belongs to him, and pay to God what belongs to God" (Matthew 22:15–22). Because three different episodes take place within the unified space of the composition, *The Tribute Money* exemplifies continuous narration, a thematic device that had been used in ancient Roman painting and sculpture (see fig. 3-99).

The perspective of *The Tribute Money* contributes to a unity of organization, while the boldly modeled figures reveal a light source that corresponds to the real light that falls into the chapel from a single window on the altar wall. The building at the right, which obeys the laws of scientific perspective, draws our attention to the head of Jesus, while **atmospheric perspective** envelops the trees and hills of the background. Within the logic of this spatial illusionism, Masaccio's figures

FIFTEENTH-CENTURY ART   **259**

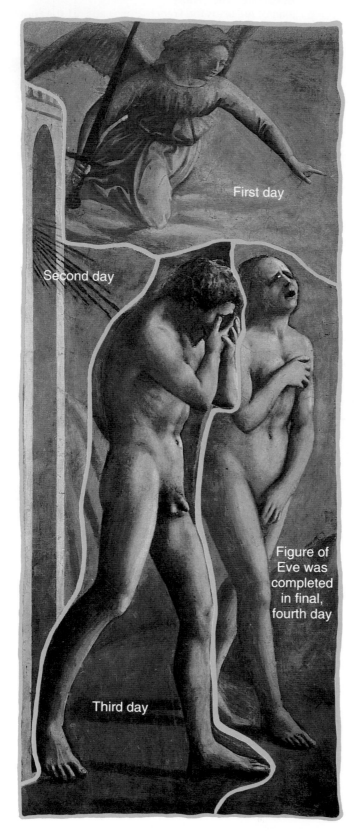

First day

Second day

Figure of Eve was completed in final, fourth day

Third day

5-17. *Giornata* diagram for *The Expulsion of Adam and Eve*

act out the story with simple, direct, and dignified movements.

Masaccio's sculpturesque modeling and bold figurative presentation are especially evident in *The Expulsion of Adam and Eve* on the same wall. Having disobeyed God, Adam and Eve are driven by guilt and shame. In Masaccio's interpretation, Adam hides his face in his hands, leaving his genitals uncovered. Masaccio thus emphasizes the psychological rather than the physical nature of Adam's shame. The figure of Eve, which was inspired by an ancient sculpture of the Modest Venus, conceals her nakedness but throws her head back in a moan as she bewails their fate.

Masaccio's figures, instilled with psychological presence, recall the human gravity of Donatello's sculpture, while the classicizing architecture and use of scientific perspective reveal his relationship with Brunelleschi. Although he died in his twenties, Masaccio translated into paint the Renaissance innovations of Donatello and Brunelleschi, and he influenced later generations of Renaissance artists, including Michelangelo. An epitaph, composed in

5-18. Head of apostle, detail from Masaccio's *The Tribute Money* (see fig. 5-16). Fresco

5-19. Head of Adam, detail from Jan van Eyck's *The Altarpiece of the Lamb* (see fig. 5-25). Oil on panel

5-20. Head of Mercury, detail from Botticelli's *Realm of Venus* (see fig. 5-55). Tempera on panel with oil glazes

To understand the three different painting techniques—**fresco**, **oil**, and **tempera**—available to fifteenth-century European painters, we can compare Masaccio's fresco head (fig. 5-18) with the head of Adam, painted in oil by Jan van Eyck (fig. 5-19), and the head of Mercury, painted in tempera with oil glazes, by Botticelli (fig. 5-20). Although each head offers its own distinctive reality, the bold masses of Masaccio's head contrast with the finer detail that characterizes the other two heads. Masaccio's apostle, rendered in fresco, is broadly and quickly painted with strong contrasts of light and dark to create a powerfully modeled form.

Van Eyck's head of Adam, painted in oils, shows the artist's interest in representing surface texture: notice the cracked lips, the wrinkles of the forehead, and the masses of curls that make up the mustache, beard, and hair and that seem to be composed of individually painted hairs. Botticelli's Mercury is painted with tempera with some use of oil glazes; here the artist is less interested than Masaccio or van Eyck in modeling to create an effect of mass, but his drawing of the head, tilted back into space and slightly foreshortened, is very convincing. Using oil glazes, Botticelli captures the translucency of the human eye when it is struck by light.

the sixteenth century, recognized Masaccio's contribution: "I painted, and my picture was lifelike; I gave my figures movement, passion, soul: they breathed" (Annibale Caro, as cited in Vasari's *Life of Masaccio*).

The speed of Masaccio's execution is indicated in the *giornata* diagram for *The Expulsion of Adam and Eve* (fig. 5-17), which indicates that it was completed in only four days. The breadth and simplicity of Ma-

saccio's painting technique are also revealed in the classically inspired head of an apostle from *The Tribute Money* (see fig. 5-18).

5-21. Paolo Uccello. Perspective drawing. c. 1430–40. Pen and ink on paper, 13³/₈ x 9¹/₂". Gabinetto dei Disegni, Galleria degli Uffizi, Florence. Vasari tells us that Uccello delighted in making such complex studies and that he often worked late into the night, "seeking to solve the problems of perspective." When called to bed by his wife, Uccello would reply, "Oh, what a sweet thing is this perspective!"

5-22. Diagram of Perugino's *Christ Giving the Keys to Saint Peter* (see fig. 1-15) showing the orthogonals and transversals of the scientific perspective scheme. The gradually shaded areas in the background indicate the blurring and color modulations characteristic of atmospheric perspective.

The perspective drawing by Paolo Uccello (1397–1475) is a virtuoso rendering of a geometricized chalice that is at least partially transparent (fig. 5-21). The geometricized rings at the top and base are derived from Uccello's studies of a wire- or wicker-frame construction (*mazzocchio*) that was wrapped with cloth to create a type of male headgear popular in the fifteenth century. Perhaps it was the faceting of the skeletal structure of this headdress that led Uccello to study the chalice with a similar geometric, linear emphasis.

The study of perspective, the rendering of figures or objects in illusory space, was an important innovation in Renaissance art. Perspective had been a conscious development in ancient Greek painting, and many examples of Roman art attest to the accomplished use of perspective in antiquity. During the Middle Ages, however, pictorial reproduction of the physical world became less significant within a culture that emphasized spiritual and otherworldly values. Perspective gradually became valued in the later Middle Ages, but a coherent system allowing artists to determine the relative diminution of size of figures and objects was lacking.

That problem was solved by Filippo Brunelleschi (1377–1446), the Early Renaissance architect (see page 274). Around 1415, Brunelleschi demonstrated a **scientific perspective** system (also called **linear** and **vanishing-point perspective**) in two lost paintings. His new perspective system was incorporated in works by other artists, including Perugino in *Christ Giving the Keys to Saint Peter* (see figs. 1-15, 5-22); Donatello in *Feast of Herod* (figs. 5-23, 5-24); as well as Ghiberti and Leonardo (see figs. 5-27 and 5-60).

Within the complex architectural structure of the *Feast*

5-23. Donatello. *Feast of Herod*, from the Siena baptismal font. c. 1425. Gilded bronze, 23¹/₂" square. Baptistery, Siena, Tuscany, Italy. Donatello uses continuous narration to depict the story of the beheading of John the Baptist. Within the distant arch in the left background, the just-severed head is given to a servant; in the left foreground, it is presented to Herod, who recoils in horror. In the right foreground, Salome still sways with the rhythms of her dance. Commissioned by the Cathedral Administration of Siena

5-24. Diagram of the orthogonals and transversals of the perspective scheme of Donatello's *Feast of Herod*

of Herod, Donatello narrates the dramatic events surrounding the beheading of Saint John the Baptist. His use of scientific perspective assists in visually unifying these events. The diagonal lines created by the recession of architectural elements parallel to each other, such as those of the floor in the foreground, converge at a vanishing point. The convergence of these diagonal lines, which are called **orthogonals**, helps Donatello determine the exact diminution of figures and architecture.

Scientific perspective is based on the assumption that parallel lines receding from us seem to converge at a point on the horizon. This is the basis for the meeting of the orthogonals at the vanishing point. Scientific perspective also assumes that the diminution in size of objects is in direct proportion to their distance from us and that space is, therefore, quantifiably measurable.

What Brunelleschi arrived at through empirical study, Alberti stated with theoretical reasoning in his book *On Painting*. By constructing orthogonal lines crossed by **transversals** (lines that recede parallel to the **picture plane**) on the planar surface of a painting or relief, a receding modular grid pattern is created. This pattern establishes a coherent, mathematically measurable illusory space within which the artist can determine the proportional diminution of objects distant from the viewer. In a fully developed example of Renaissance illusionistic painting, such as Perugino's *Christ Giving the Keys to Saint Peter* (see figs. 1-15, 5-22), scientific perspective is combined with **atmospheric perspective** for a unified effect that encompasses vast spaces, correctly proportioned figures, and the subtle qualities of the sky and distant landscape as they appear to the eye.

FLEMISH PAINTING: HUBERT AND JAN VAN EYCK

5-25. Hubert and Jan van Eyck. *The Altarpiece of the Lamb* (interior). Completed 1432. Oil on wood, 11'5³/4" x 15'1¹/2". Cathedral of St. Bavo, Ghent, Belgium. This work is also known as *The Ghent Altarpiece.* An inscription on the frame identifies the patron as Jodocus Vijd, the date of completion as 1432, and the painters as Hubert and Jan van Eyck. Hubert died before September 18, 1426, and the role each brother played in the conception and execution of the many panels has been much debated. Scholars today generally agree that the altarpiece includes a number of works by Hubert, some of which may have been left unfinished at his death, which Jan combined into a totality, adding works conceived by Jan (in particular, the figures of Adam and Eve) to complete the altarpiece. This may explain the juxtapositions in figural scale between the parts of the altarpiece. The luminous technique and fine detail that unify the painting are considered to be the work of Jan, who by the sixteenth century had been credited with the invention of oil painting.

The iconography is complex. The lower panels represent the Triumph of the Lamb of God, with crowds of saints pressing inward to worship the symbolic lamb on the altar. The upper panels include God the Father in the center flanked by the Virgin Mary and Saint John the Baptist, musical angels, and Adam and Eve. Above Adam and Eve are small grisaille scenes of the story of Cain and Abel.

Adam and Eve were among the few subjects that permitted Northern artists to represent the nude, but Jan's virtually lifesize figures are unprecedented. Jan's commitment to realism here confronts traditional restrictions, for although the figure of Adam is clearly based on a nude model (notice the sunburned face, neck, and hands; see fig. 5-19), Eve is an imaginative re-creation based on contemporary ideals rather than on observation of a live model. The small, high breasts and bulbous abdomen are Gothic stylizations. The emphasis on the large abdomen stresses the role of childbearer assigned to women in the fifteenth century. Commissioned by Jodocus Vijd, a wealthy landowner and member of the Ghent city government, and his wife, Isabel Borluut

5-26. Hubert and Jan van Eyck. *The Altarpiece of the Lamb* (exterior). Oil on wood, 11'5³/4" x 7'6³/4". The donors of the altarpiece, Jodocus Vijd and Isabel Borluut, are shown in the lower panels, kneeling before Saints John the Baptist and John the Evangelist, patrons of the city of Ghent. In the upper register is a scene of the Annunciation; the topmost panels show representations of the Old Testament prophets Zachariah and Micah and two sibyls.

I n scale and wealth of detail, *The Altarpiece of the Lamb* (*The Ghent Altarpiece*), a large, hinged **polyptych** (multipaneled **altarpiece**), is an overwhelming accomplishment—the work of years and the most impressive of all early Flemish paintings (figs. 5-25, 5-26). The diverse scale and size of the panels and the variety of subjects represented allowed Hubert van Eyck (1370–1426) and Jan van Eyck (before 1390–1441) to paint Flemish interiors, vast landscapes, illusionistic sculpture, portraits of living donors, the male and female nude, elaborate brocades, bejeweled and gold-embroidered borders, and musical instruments. Jan van Eyck's ability to re-create the visual world in oil paint is staggering, but among the wealth of details offered by *The Ghent Altarpiece*, the most unforgettable may be the artist's self-portrait in the studio, which is reflected in one of the innumerable pearls in the papal crown worn by God the Father, the central figure of the interior. This tour de force of painting is one of several "reflected" self-portraits found in the work of Jan van Eyck (see also fig. 5-32). Jan's pride in his accomplishments is also evident in his *Self-Portrait* (see fig. 5-7), one of the first independent self-portraits in the history of art.

Jan van Eyck's ability to represent textures as if they were real is based on his acute examination of light and how it reacts differently when it strikes and reflects from various surfaces. He composed his paintings to emphasize this phenomenon, juxtaposing materials to contrast textures and heighten his illusion. Jan's figures seldom express strong or dramatic emotions. The wonder that his paintings generate comes from his ability to observe reality and to convey in oil paints the excitement of vision.

FIFTEENTH-CENTURY ART   **265**

ITALIAN RENAISSANCE SCULPTURE: LORENZO GHIBERTI

5-27. Lorenzo Ghiberti. *Story of Jacob and Esau*, from the East Doors of the Baptistery, Florence. c. 1429–37. Gilded bronze, 31¹/₄" square. Museo dell' Opera del Duomo, Florence. The story of Jacob and Esau, from the Old Testament book of Genesis (25:19–28:5), tells how Jacob and his mother, Rebecca, conspired to steal the birthright of Jacob's twin but slightly older brother, Esau, by deceiving the boys' father, the old and nearly blind Isaac, into giving his blessing to Jacob instead of Esau. In Ghiberti's representation, the scene of the arranged blessing of Isaac is shown at the right, with Rebecca looking on, while the central figures represent the moment when Isaac and Esau discover the deception. Commissioned by the Opera of the Baptistery and the Arte di Calimala

Lorenzo Ghiberti (1378–1455) represents the *Story of Jacob and Esau* with grand, classicizing architecture and graceful figures gathered into beautiful groupings (fig. 5-27). His ideal and orderly Renaissance world makes no reference to the treachery and emotional trauma inherent in the Old Testament narrative. Ghiberti chose to subordinate these unpleasant realities to his Renaissance interest in harmony. The fifteenth-century concern for fine detail and exquisite finish is obvious in every area of the relief, from the delicate Corinthian **capitals** of the architecture to the shaggy fur of Esau's dogs in the foreground. The regular recession of the Brunelleschian scientific perspective (see pages 262–63) and the subtle diminution in the height of the relief, from the virtually three-dimensional figures of the left foreground to the low-relief figure of Rebecca praying in the upper right corner, create a convincing, controlled illusion. The four female figures in the left foreground, who pose with such exquisite grace, play no role in advancing the narrative and have been added by Ghiberti to enhance the beauty of the work of art.

In his autobiography, Ghiberti states that when he was offered the commission for the doors (fig. 5-28), "I was given a free hand to execute it in whatever way I thought would turn out most perfect and most ornate and richest." In this he seems to be following the precepts of the theorist Leon Battista Alberti, who, in *On Painting*, had defined the qualities of the perfect narrative painting (*istoria* or *historia*) in the following manner:

> The first thing that gives pleasure in a "historia" is a plentiful variety. Just as with food and music, novel and extraordinary things delight us for various reasons but especially because they are different from the old ones we are used to, so with everything the mind takes great pleasure in variety and abundance. . . . I would say a picture was richly varied if it contained a properly arranged mixture of old men, youths, boys, matrons, maidens, children, domestic animals, dogs, birds, horses, sheep, buildings and provinces.

5-28. Lorenzo Ghiberti. East Doors of the Baptistery (also known as the Gates of Paradise). 1425–52. Bronze and gilded bronze, 18'6" x 12'. Museo dell' Opera del Duomo, Florence. Ghiberti's doors are the last of three sets of doors made for the portals of the Florentine Baptistery. His themes are drawn from the Old Testament. The doors were commissioned in 1425 and erected in 1452. The creation of wax models for the ten narratives has been dated 1429 to 1437, and the finishing of the details consumed most of the 1440s. Ghiberti employed a large workshop of assistants and apprentices to help him with the doors, which were by far the most expensive sculptural work produced in Florence during the fifteenth century. Most of the individual panels represent several scenes of a continuous narrative within a single architectural or landscape setting. For Ghiberti's self-portrait on the doors and a reference to the Latin inscription, see page 249. The area between a baptistery and a cathedral was known as the *paradiso*, which helps to explain the name attributed to Michelangelo, who supposedly said that Ghiberti's doors were worthy to serve as the Gates of Paradise.

The technique of wood carving is what is known as a **subtractive technique**, in which the artist or artists start with a solid piece of material and create the work by gradually removing areas and pieces of the material (for marble carving, also subtractive, see page 305). This is a technique that does not tolerate mistakes; once a piece is removed, it cannot be readhered.

The traditional techniques of working in wood pose special problems for the sculptor. A variety of metal gouges, chisels, and knives are employed, but particular care is a constant requirement lest the wood fiber split. Some gouges are struck with a wooden mallet; others, in a more delicate but firm manner, can be pushed by hand. Restrictions are imposed by the size of a log; large wooden sculptures often have to be composed of a number of pieces joined together. Because wood expands and contracts during changes in temperature and humidity, care must be taken during the carving process to prevent the wood from cracking later.

Donatello's *Penitent Magdalene* (see figs. 5-29, 5-30) was carved from a single piece of wood, and its technique represents a distinctive break from earlier figurative wood carving. Previous to Donatello, sculpted wood figures usually had a broad expanse of drapery across the front to hide the large hollow space that had to be carved from the rear of the statue to prevent splitting as the wood dried. This limited the sculpture to a frontal viewpoint but ensured minimal surface cracking because most of the expansion and contraction of the wood was contained by the hollow area in the back. The *Penitent Magdalene*, with its subtle contrapposto pose, is more nearly a sculpture in the round. The hollowed gap between the legs allows for the expansion and contraction of the wood while visually contributing to the naturalism of the figure.

Virtually all medieval and Renaissance wood figures are polychromed to increase their naturalism, and many have gilded details. A thin coat of fine plaster, called **gesso**, was applied over the wood to provide a neutral base for the paint, and a range of naturalistic color would be painted on the figure. In this case, gold tint was added to the brown of the hair to refer to the traditional red hair of the Magdalene.

Donatello's lifesize, naturalistically **polychromed** wood sculpture of *Penitent Magdalene* (figs. 5-29, 5-30) is an

5-29. Donatello. *Penitent Magdalene.* Late 1430s–1450s? Wood with polychromy and gilding, height 6'2". Museo dell' Opera del Duomo, Florence

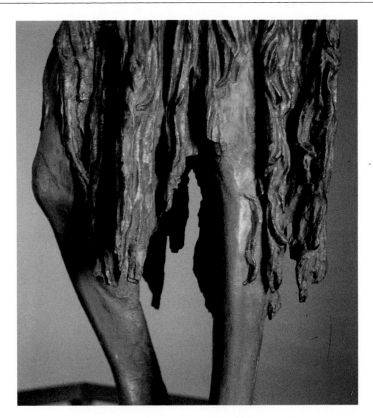

5-30. Donatello. *Penitent Magdalene*, detail

example of a type of sculpture commonly used for popular devotion during the Middle Ages and Renaissance. Such sculptures, sometimes wearing real clothing, still adorn altars or are carried in religious processions in some areas of Europe; for an earlier example, see the polychromed wood German Gothic *Pietà* (see fig. 5-63).

By Donatello's day, the legend of Saint Mary Magdalene identified her as a beautiful prostitute who repented when she was forgiven by Jesus; she became one of his most devout followers. Because she was thought to be the woman who used her hair to anoint Jesus' feet, long hair became one of her attributes. She was present at the Crucifixion, where she is often identifiable because of her beauty and her long flowing red hair, and it was to the Magdalene that Christ first appeared on Easter morning, after his Resurrection. After the Crucifixion, she lived a life of penance in the wilderness, eating little (one legend has it that she was fed by angels) and clothed only in her own long hair. Because of her history, the Magdalene became the patron saint for fallen women and widows.

Donatello's patrons apparently requested that he represent her at the end of a long period of penance, when fasting and living in the desert have reduced her to an old, virtually starving woman. There is still a memory of her former beauty in her refined bone structure and her elegant, **contrapposto** stance, white intense devotion is conveyed by the upward tilt of her head and the trembling manner in which her hands are raised in prayer.

FLEMISH PAINTING: JAN VAN EYCK

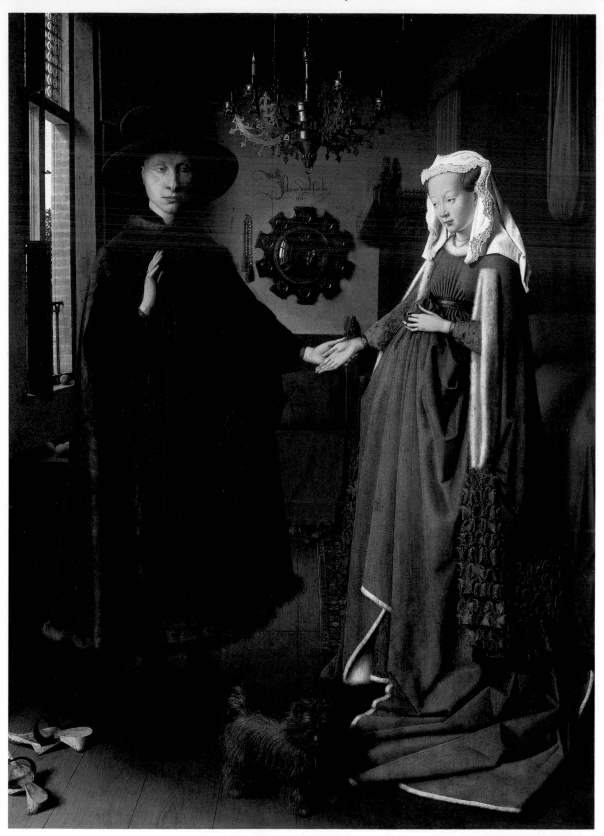

This tantalizing and unparalleled image (fig. 5-31) is one of the enigmas of art history. With its compelling characters, its puzzlelike combination of objects, and the truly breathtaking detail of its execution, it demands an explanation. But extensive research, numerous articles, and several books examining betrothal and marriage practices and other social behavior have failed to provide an identification for

5-31. (opposite) Jan van Eyck. *Portrait of Giovanni Arnolfini and Giovanna Cenami* (?). 1434. Oil on wood, 32^{1}/4 x 23^{1}/2". The National Gallery, London. The identification of the figures is not certain but is based on an early inventory that names them as "Hernoul le Sin with his wife"; a later inventory states that the panel had wooden shutters, painted to resemble jasper, and that the gilded frame had verses from the writings of the Roman poet Ovid. Giovanni Arnolfini was a successful Italian cloth merchant and money lender from Lucca who lived in Flanders; Giovanna Cenami, who was Giovanni's widow when he died in 1472, also came from a wealthy Lucchese family active in Paris and Flanders. Probably commissioned by Giovanni Arnolfini and Giovanna Cenami, if these are indeed the two figures represented in the painting

the couple and what it is, exactly, that they are doing in the image; the motivation behind the commissioning of this painting thus remains uncertain. For the purposes of clarity here, we will examine the picture in some detail and include some of the questions and theories about it in parentheses.

The couple, probably Giovanni Arnolfini and Giovanna Cenami, is shown standing in elegant dress in a well-appointed bedchamber (Is this a portrait of a real room?). The positions of their hands seem to indicate that an oath is being taken, suggesting that the painting might have functioned as a kind of legal document (Does the picture represent their betrothal or their marriage?). The function of the painting as a document is supported by the unusual wording accompanying the painter's name above the mirror: "Jan van Eyck was here, 1434" (Is the florid decoration of the first letter related to similar decoration found in signatures on contemporary legal documents?). Two figures standing in the doorway of the room are reflected in the mirror (Is one the painter? Were both required to be present as witnesses?).

The man's huge hat (Is this another suggestion that this is an important, formal occasion—or merely a reference to the fact that Giovanni once sold hats?) and fur-trimmed cape suggest his wealth and status, as do the many yards of material in the woman's train, which she holds up in a pose that emphasizes her abdomen (To stress

the idea that she is ready to bear children?). Her hair is forced into nets to create the fashionable "horns" of the period, and her head covering is trimmed with elaborate ruffles. The fact that both have covered their heads seems important (Is this a sign of respect and sanctity, perhaps because they are participating in the sacrament of marriage?). Both have removed the sandals that they would have worn in the dirty streets outside (Is this an example of their cleanliness, or might it refer to the sacramental nature of marriage, based on the fact that Moses removed his sandals when he met God in the burning bush on Mount Sinai; Exodus 3:1–10?).

Wealth and a high standard of living seem evident. The elaborate chandelier is brilliantly polished, but its single burning candle seems unnecessary on such a bright day (Could the candle represent the divine presence of Christ, or is it an indication that the vow being taken is as yet not final—or could it even be an erotic symbol?). The large, expensive mirror is decorated with scenes of Christ's passion; next to it hangs a glass rosary (Is this another indication of piety, or perhaps, because light can pass through glass without changing it, a symbol of the bride's virginity?). The oranges, imported from Spain, would have been rare in northern Europe at this time (Are they another symbol of virginity?). The alert dog in the foreground stands between us and them and almost seems to be pro-

tecting them (Is the dog a symbol of fidelity—Fides, the origin for the popular nickname "Fido"—or of erotic desire?). That the dog might be symbolic is suggested by the fact that he is not reflected in the mirror, surely not an accidental omission on the part of this precision-minded artist. The bed might be a dowry present from the groom, and the chair beside it has a statuette of Saint Margaret emerging triumphant from the dragon; because of this miracle, Margaret is one of the patron saints of women in childbirth. Jan van Eyck's simple symmetrical composition stresses the individuality of the figures although the woman is shown, as is traditional, as more passive in contrast to the activity suggested by the man's raised hand.

Because there is no similar portrait in all of Italian or Flemish fifteenth-century painting, it seems unlikely that the purpose of this work was simply to record their betrothal or marriage. There must have been something special about the relationship between these two individuals that demanded this representation. A recent theory proposed that Giovanna's dowry might have been paid to Giovanni when she was still too young to be given over to him; the painting might thus have been for her, still living in her father's house, a promise of her future role and prosperity. A related lost painting by van Eyck that represented a nude woman in this same room (Giovanna?) does not seem to be of much help in interpreting this painting. The inscription on the frame of the portrait, which is reported to have referred to how the couple deceive each other, adds another level of mystery. Whatever the function of this portrait, the desire of this couple to record their relationship has given them immortality.

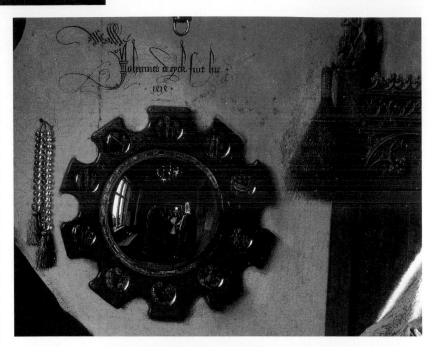

5-32. Jan van Eyck. *Arnolfini* (?) portrait, details

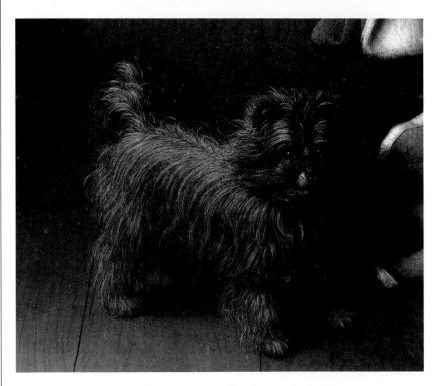

5-33. Jan van Eyck. *Arnolfini* (?) portrait, details

The details from Jan van Eyck's *Arnolfini* (?) portrait display impressive virtuosity (figs. 5-32, 5-33). The contrasting textures of the various materials are convincingly illusionistic. Such precise detail is made possible not only by the artist's acute perception but also by the development of oil paint as a primary vehicle, a step that revolutionized Flemish painting in the early years of the fifteenth century.

None of the materials used here (fig. 5-34) is new. The support was similar to that used for tempera painting (see fig. 5-20), a wooden panel covered with a layer of fine white plaster (gesso), sometimes with a layer of canvas or linen between the wood and the plaster. Van Eyck probably explored compositional ideas by drawing on the plaster with charcoal and "erasing" unsuccessful designs with a feather. He would then have reinforced a satisfactory composition with fine lines created with a brush dipped into tempera paint. The pigments used to create the color are the same powdered materials used by artists working in tempera (see pages 236–37). Oil as a drying vehicle had been known and used since ancient times. During the medieval period, oil was the final layer

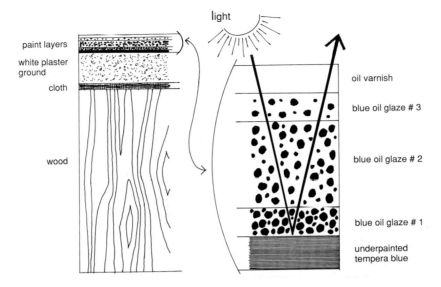

paint layers
white plaster ground
cloth
wood

light
oil varnish
blue oil glaze # 3
blue oil glaze # 2
blue oil glaze # 1
underpainted tempera blue

5-34. Schematic diagram of a section of a Flemish fifteenth-century oil painting, demonstrating the luminosity of the medium. The arrow suggests how light penetrates translucent oil glazes.

given a tempera painting to create a luminous surface finish. Here it is used as the primary vehicle.

Oil is a translucent vehicle; in making oil paint, particles of powdered pigment are suspended in this translucent vehicle, as shown in the diagram of a section of a Flemish panel painting. When it is applied in many thin layers (**glazes**), light will penetrate the layers and be reflected, creating a gemlike brilliance of color. This new resonant richness makes Flemish oil paintings such as those of van Eyck and Campin distinctly different in appearance from their tempera antecedents.

Oil dries more slowly than tempera, and its speed of drying can be further slowed by adding turpentine, permitting the artist to blend colors to create the subtle tonal modulations that help suggest light falling on an object. Van Eyck's fine detail is accomplished by using oil and soft, fine brushes, and the resulting imperceptible transitions from color to color and the smooth surface finish offer virtually no hint of the artist's brushstrokes.

The greater resonance of color and the new realism of Flemish paintings are also due to the changed **color palette**. In tempera painting, a particular **hue**, such as red, would be mixed with white to achieve the transitions from shadow (red) to highlight (white). In the oil technique, the same red would usually be mixed with black to accomplish the change from highlight (red) to shadow (black). In tempera paintings, then, colors are modeled upward toward white, while in oil paintings most colors are modeled downward toward black. The greatest intensity of a hue in

tempera painting is in the shadows, while in oil it occurs between shadow and highlight. Most importantly, the scheme used in oil paintings is closer to what we observe in reality. Flemish painters learned this laborious craft as apprentices. Only years of watching and practice could prepare a young artist for a career working in such a painstaking and methodical technique. The results of their fine and patient work are evident in the superb condition of many of these paintings today.

To learn how to paint like Campin and van Eyck took more than technical skill, however, for the artist had to learn how to see—how to distinguish the distinct patterns of light and shadow observable on such different surfaces as velvet, wood, brass, and glass in various lighting conditions. In the work of these two artists, the precision of depiction is intimately related to the fact that all these objects are mirrors of religious truths. A candle is not just a candle and a triple lily is more than a floral oddity. Like other techniques, the development of the fine oil technique of the Flemish painters was a response to a distinct need: they created a technique that would allow them to endow objects with a magical potency—a dazzling realism—that could suggest the deeper meanings that lie behind observation. Their new style is rooted in the complexities of medieval symbolism and theology, but it contains a seed of the new Renaissance concern with the individual and the world. It is no surprise that the motto of Jan van Eyck, painted on the frame of his *Self-Portrait* (see fig. 5-7), is *Als ich can* ("The best I can do").

ITALIAN RENAISSANCE ARCHITECTURE: BRUNELLESCHI

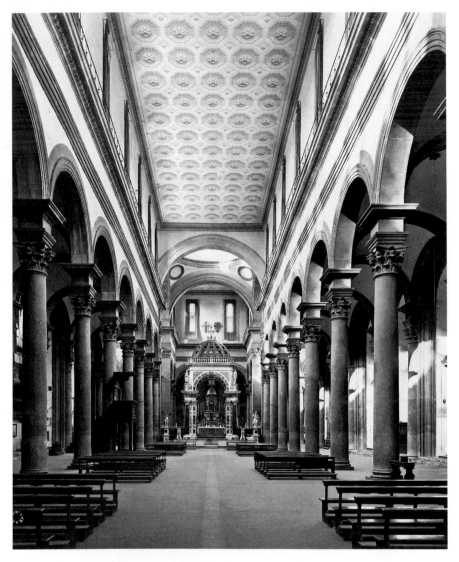

5-35. Filippo Brunelleschi. Nave, Church of Santo Spirito, Florence. Begun 1436. In this view, we are looking toward the crossing and high altar; the elaborate canopy over the altar is a later, obtrusive addition. Commissioned by the abbot of the Monastery of Santo Spirito

5-36. Filippo Brunelleschi. Plan of the Church of Santo Spirito

The interior of the Church of Santo Spirito (fig. 5-35) provides a conspicuous contrast to Gothic architecture, which overwhelms us with its towering vertical emphasis (see fig. 4-80). In Brunelleschi's light-filled Renaissance church, on the other hand, we perceive a measured order and harmony. Here the human reason of the architect and faith in a rational God and universe create architecture that is an alternative to the spiritual striving of the Gothic.

The satisfying regularity of Santo Spirito is derived from the use of simple proportional schemes similar to those used in ancient Greek and Roman architecture. The plan (fig. 5-36) makes it clear that each of the square **bays** of the **aisle** or the **ambulatory** can be understood as a basic module. With this in mind, it can be demonstrated that the relationships that govern the interior design of Santo Spirito are few and simple: 1:1, 1:2, 1:4, and 1:8. The square **crossing**, under the **dome**, is four times as large in area as the basic module, as are the **altar** and

5-37. Filippo Brunelleschi. Dome, Florence Cathedral. 1420–36. Commissioned by the Wool Guild and the Cathedral Administration

transept areas that surround it (1:4). The nave is twice as wide as the module (1:2). An elevation or a view inside the church reveals how this proportional system continues in the three-dimensional structure. The bays of the aisles and ambulatory are four times as tall as they are wide (1:4), and the nave is twice as tall as the aisles and ambulatory (4:8). The nave is composed of an **arcade** (a series of arches supported by **columns** or **piers**) and of the **clerestory** above it. Each of these elements is as high as the nave is wide. This proportional approach is combined with the use of **round arches** and **capitals** based on ancient models. The result is an architecture that revives both the principles and the forms of classical antiquity. The regular placement of windows and the avoidance of both the stained-glass windows of French Gothic and the frescoes of Italian Gothic mean that the rational order of Brunelleschi's church is well illuminated and clear, free of shadows and mysterious height.

Brunelleschi secured his fame as an architect and engineer by designing the enormous dome for the cathedral in Florence and engineering its construction (fig. 5-37). The Florence Cathedral, begun in 1296 to replace an earlier church, is a Gothic structure, but from its inception a dome over the crossing was intended. The difficulties of constructing such an immense dome—the largest in Europe since antiquity—were solved by Brunelleschi in the early fifteenth century with a design that was responsive to and harmonious with the original Gothic design. The pointed profile, with eight external **ribs**, is more Gothic than Renaissance, yet the eloquence of its grand scale and simple harmony express the clarity characteristic of the new Renaissance architecture. The cathedral dome was an architectural, engineering, and psychological feat. That so large a dome could be constructed without **centering** (see fig. 3-113; Brunelleschi designed a self-supporting system) was a technological achievement. In this joining of scale, design, and technology, the Florentine people found a source of civic as well as religious pride. Brunelleschi's dome continues to dominate the skyline of Florence, a visual expression of a domineering spirit in the arts.

THE ITALIAN RENAISSANCE PALACE

5-38. Michelozzo. Courtyard, Medici Palace, Florence. 1445–59

5-39. Exterior, Medici Palace. This early print shows the palace before later extensions and changes. Unlike medieval castles, the Renaissance palazzo is found within the city, and its owner was as likely to be a merchant or a banker as a noble. Such palaces housed the entire family, including married children and grandchildren. The Medici, who were bankers, were among the richest families in Florence. In the course of the fifteenth century, they gradually assumed control of the Florentine government. Commissioned by Cosimo de' Medici

The Medici Palace presents a departure in domestic architecture (figs. 5-38, 5-39). The centralized courtyard is decorated with a classical-style arcade reminiscent of the **atrium** or garden **peristyle** of an ancient Roman house (see fig. 3-90). In his references to antiquity and lucid regularity in the courtyard, Michelozzo (1396–1472) reveals the new attitudes of the Renaissance. As a composition, the palace is a three-story masonry block, with regularly spaced windows and a large **cornice**, which projects out from the roof. The **rustication** (use of roughly carved blocks) of the street-level story is gradually reduced on the upper two floors, and the heights of the floors are equally decreased. Lucid regularity is also demonstrated in the plan. It has been suggested that the regularity of the Medici Palace was inspired by the description of ancient Roman houses given by Vitruvius, the first century BCE architect and theorist. The decoration of the palace included portrait busts of the Medici (see fig. 5-46), likewise based on ancient sculptural models.

Many of the paintings and sculptures in the Medici Palace had distinctive secular themes. The bedroom of Lorenzo de' Medici was decorated with panels by Uccello representing the Battle of San Romano, a victory credited to Niccolò da Tolentino, a friend and supporter of Cosimo de' Medici (fig. 5-40). Tolentino died later in an accident perhaps arranged by Cosimo's enemies, and his victory at San Romano may have been commemorated at the palace in order to suggest that he was a Medici martyr.

Small bronze sculptures could be found throughout the palace. Antonio Pollaiuolo (1429?–98) exemplifies an episode from the adventures of Hercules in a powerful bronze statuette (fig. 5-41). Hercules was the mythological founder of Florence, and the use of the Hercules theme at the Medici Palace may have been a way of identifying the Medici with the city and its traditional founders and heroes. This also explains the presence of a statue of Donatello's *David* (fig. 5-42) in the Medici courtyard, for the youthful David was also a symbol of the city.

1441	Africans are sold as slaves in the markets of Lisbon
1445–59	**Michelozzo, Courtyard, Medici Palace**
1453	End of the Byzantine Empire

5-40. Paolo Uccello. *Niccolò da Tolentino Directing the Attack*, from a series of three paintings illustrating the Battle of San Romano. c. 1450s. Tempera and silver foil on wood, 5'11¹/₂" x 10'6". The National Gallery, London. Originally the three panels decorated the bedroom of Lorenzo the Magnificent. Their combined length was more than 34 feet. Commissioned by a member of the Medici family, perhaps Cosimo de' Medici

5-42. Donatello. *David*. 1440s? Bronze with gilded details, height 5'2¹/₄". Museo Nazionale del Bargello, Florence. David is documented in the courtyard of the Medici Palace. Donatello's representation of the Old Testament hero is consistent with the biblical story (I Samuel 17:38– 51). The broad shepherd's hat would have cast David's face into shadow, leaving his expression enigmatic. This is the first lifesize nude sculpture in the round since antiquity. Probably commissioned by Cosimo de' Medici

5-41. Antonio Pollaiuolo. *Hercules and Antaeus*. c. 1470s. Bronze, height 18". Museo Nazionale del Bargello, Florence. Antaeus was the son of Mother Earth, and to defeat him, Hercules had to lift him up and crush him while he was separated from his maternal source of power. Probably commissioned by a member of the Medici family

THE BEGINNINGS OF PORTRAITURE IN EUROPE

5-43. Alesso Baldovinetti. *Portrait of a Young Woman.* c. 1465. Tempera on wood, 25 x 16". The National Gallery, London. The elaborate hairstyle and high, plucked forehead are typical of Renaissance fashion. Among the most expensive and elaborate parts of a Renaissance woman's costume were her detachable sleeves; here, the decoration on the sleeves may be a reference to her name or family.

5-44. Domenico Ghirlandaio. *Portrait of a Man and a Boy.* c. 1480. Tempera and oil on wood, 24³/₈ x 18¹/₈". The Louvre, Paris. The artist has used the man's disfiguring disease as an aesthetic device, repeating similarly rounded forms for the boy's curls and the trees.

5-45. Domenico Ghirlandaio. *Portrait of a Man on His Deathbed.* c. 1480. Silverpoint and point of the brush, heightened with white on pink prepared paper, 11⁵/₈ x 12⁵/₈". Nationalmuseum, Stockholm. This is a preparatory drawing for figure 5-44.

c. 1465

1457	"Futeball" and "golfe" are forbidden by Scotland's Parliament
1464	Royal postal service is established in France
c. 1465	**Baldovinetti, *Portrait of a Young Woman***

5-46. Mino da Fiesole. *Portrait of Piero de' Medici*. 1453. Marble, height 18". Museo Nazionale del Bargello, Florence. An inscription on the work identifies the artist, sitter, and date, as is common in male busts of this type. Probably commissioned by Piero de' Medici

5-47. Hans Memling. *Madonna and Child with Martin van Nieuwenhove*. 1487. Oil on wood, each 17³/8 x 13". Hospital of St. John, Bruges, Flanders (Belgium). The inscriptions across the bottom date the work, identify the patron, and state that he was twenty-three years old. A merchant, Martin van Nieuwenhove later served as mayor of Bruges. Commissioned by Martin van Nieuwenhove

The silhouette or profile portrait (fig. 5-43) immediately reveals variations in individual physiognomy. Portraiture was revived in the fifteenth century, and Alesso Baldovinetti (c. 1425–99) used the profile formula of the earliest Renaissance portraits. It was quickly superseded by three-quarter or full-view portraits and sculpted portraits. By the time of Leonardo da Vinci's *"Mona Lisa"* (see fig. 6-16), portraiture was a well-established subject, and it continued to provide an important means of support for artists until the advent of photography in the nineteenth century.

The precise function of the earliest portraits is not certain, and it is possible that Baldovinetti's sitter died young and the portrait was commissioned as a remembrance after her death. Such is certainly the case with the *Portrait of a Man and a Boy*, for the drawing Domenico Ghirlandaio (1449–94) made from the man's corpse survives (figs. 5-44, 5-45). The delicate and beautiful face of the child, unmarked by time, looks up with respect and love toward the old man.

The bust-length portrait sculpture became popular in the mid-fifteenth century in Florence, partly in response to ancient Roman sculptural precedents. These portraits were sometimes placed over the doorways of Renaissance palaces. The earliest surviving marble bust represents a member of the Medici family, the richest and most politically important family in the city (fig. 5-46).

The simultaneous evolution of painted portraits in Flanders during the fifteenth century included a devotional type that represented an individual in an attitude of prayer with an image of the Madonna and Child (fig. 5-47). These **diptychs**, which served as private devotional images, were hinged so they could travel easily and be self-supporting when opened. In the example by Hans Memling (c. 1430–94), the donor's natural three-quarter view contrasts with the frontal placement of the Madonna; the architectural setting suggests a Flemish room. The realistically depicted stained-glass window behind the donor represents Saint Martin, the patron's name saint, and the donor's place in heaven seems assured by the inclusion of his coat of arms in the window behind the Madonna. The mirror, a symbol of virginity, reflects the foreground figures, confirming an intimate relationship between the real and sacred worlds.

FIFTEENTH-CENTURY ART **279**

ITALIAN RENAISSANCE PAINTING: ANDREA MANTEGNA

5-48. Andrea Mantegna. Camera Picta, Ducal Palace, Mantua, Lombardy, Italy. 1465–74. Frescoes, wall with fireplace 19'6" x 26'6". The room is approximately 26'6" square. The figures over the fireplace represent Mantegna's patron, Lodovico Gonzaga, duke of Mantua, with his family and retinue, and the scene to the left depicts a meeting between Cardinal Francesco Gonzaga and his father, Lodovico. The ceiling decoration has illusionistic insets suggesting relief portraits of ancient Roman rulers. The side walls are painted with balustrades and pilasters.

5-49. Andrea Mantegna. Camera Picta, detail of illusionistic balcony with women and putti. Diameter of balcony 5'. This room is now popularly known by a later name, the Camera degli Sposi ("Room of the Married Couple"), in reference to the patron and his wife, who are shown seated in the fresco over the fireplace. Commissioned by Duke Lodovico Gonzaga

The Camera Picta ("Painted Room") is a dazzling and witty tour de force of illusionism that proves the brilliance of both the artist, Andrea Mantegna (1431–1506), and his patron, Lodovico Gonzaga, duke of Mantua (figs. 5-48, 5-49). The magnificence of a Renaissance prince or princess was in part determined by the abilities of the artists at their court. The painted illusion created by Mantegna and his workshop at the Ducal Palace in Mantua completely covers the vaulted ceiling and two walls. Most of the vault is painted with **grisaille** and gold decorative patterns in a classical style that simulate stucco relief decoration. This design emphasizes the ceiling's flat surface and serves as a foil for the central area, with its unexpected illusion of a circular opening with a balcony and a view up to the sky and clouds. The painted figures around the **balustrade** seem to interact with us and with each other, and a huge pot of plants, precariously supported on a pole, threatens to fall into the room. This fictive space is populated with imaginary figures, baby angels derived from ancient Roman precedents and known in Italian art as putti. One is struggling, for he has caught his head in one of the round openings of the balustrade.

TECHNIQUE   FORESHORTENING

Mantegna's putti in the Camera Picta, represented as if seen from below, are rendered in a technique known as **foreshortening**. This technique involves representing a figure or object as if seen in sharp recession.

Mantegna's *Christ*, however, demonstrates how easily we accept an unrealistic representation (fig. 5-50). If we were to look at a corpse from this sharp angle, we would not see it as Mantegna painted it but with larger feet and a somewhat smaller head. Mantegna's treatment, however, serves to pull us into his composition and to fix our attention on the wounds.

Dürer's woodcut (fig. 5-51) is less a demonstration of an actual technique used by artists than an illustration of the principles of foreshortening and how the technique can be studied (and illustrated in a book). The line of sight of the observer is represented by the cord fastened to the wall on the right. A piece of paper that can be swung aside has been placed in an upright frame. After the end of the cord is held on a place on the lute, the point where the cord passes through the frame is marked by the intersection of two movable threads. The paper is then swung back into place and the point transferred to the paper. The connect-the-dots diagram that results provides an accurate image of a lute seen in sharp foreshortening, as is evident in the illustration.

5-50. Andrea Mantegna. *A Foreshortened Christ.* c. 1466. Tempera on canvas, 26³/4 x 31⁷/8". Brera Gallery, Milan, Italy. This painting, sometimes called *Lamentation over the Dead Christ,* is almost certainly identical with the painting listed in Mantegna's house as *A Foreshortened Christ.* It may have been painted by the artist for his personal devotion.

5-51. Albrecht Dürer. *Artist Drawing a Lute with the Help of a Mechanical Device.* 1525. Woodcut, 5¹/8 x 7¹/4". This woodcut was designed as an illustration for Dürer's treatise *A Course in the Art of Measurement with Compass and Ruler,* published in Germany in 1525.

5-52. Leonardo da Vinci. *Madonna and Child with Cat.* c. 1478–80. Pen and ink, $5^{1}/8$ x $3^{3}/4$". The British Museum, London

5-53. Leonardo da Vinci. *Drawing of a Flying Machine*, from the *Codex Atlanticus*. c. 1490. Pen and ink. Biblioteca Ambrosiana, Milan

Leonardo's pen-and-ink study of the *Madonna and Child* is a spontaneous, animated drawing in which Mary greets the Christ Child's attempt to embrace a struggling cat with tender approval (fig. 5-52). Quick and repetitive lines impart a pulsating energy to the theme. This rapidly executed design represents a revolutionary approach to the use of preliminary compositional studies.

Previous to Leonardo (1452–1519), drawings by artists were often characterized by meticulous execution,

not only because such precision was part of the Early Renaissance aesthetic but also because they were done on an expensive surface such as vellum. By the mid-fifteenth century, the availability of cheap paper (a development in response to the demands of the new publishing industry) meant that drawing could become more common and more spontaneous. Leonardo was a decisive influence in developing the quick artist's sketch, which is so much a part of artists' work even today. He wrote:

5-54. Leonardo da Vinci. *Study of the Spine.* c. 1510. Pen, brown ink, and wash over traces of black chalk, 11¼ x 7⅞". Royal Library, Windsor Castle, Berkshire, England

You will first attempt in a drawing to give to the eye an indication of the intention and the invention which you first made in your imagination, then proceed to take away and add until you are satisfied.

After determining a basic composition, a Renaissance artist would make drawings studying the various elements within the composition. Leonardo's *Study for the Head of Judas* (see fig. 5-61) reveals the exacting interplay between his observing eye and talented hand. All these studies were then joined in a final, full-scale preparatory drawing known as a **cartoon** (from the Italian *cartone,* which refers to the thick paper used for this purpose).

For Leonardo, drawing was not restricted to studies for works of art. "Art," he wrote, "truly is a science," and his remarkable examination of subjects ranging from engineering to the earth sciences found expression in more than 3,500 surviving pages of his notebooks. Numerous drawings, such as his projected flying machine (fig. 5-53), make visible Leonardo's powers of observation and imagination. Other investigations probed the physical sciences, includinganatomy. His drawing of a spine from front, side, and back views—a didactic device still used in modern anatomy textbooks—demonstrates a knowledge of anatomical structures far in advance of that available to the medical profession at that time (fig. 5-54).

ITALIAN RENAISSANCE PAINTING: SANDRO BOTTICELLI

5-55. Sandro Botticelli. *Realm of Venus* (or *Primavera*). c. 1482. Tempera on wood with oil glazes, 6'8" x 10'4". Galleria degli Uffizi, Florence. This painting is first documented in 1498 in the Florentine palace of Lorenzo di Pierfrancesco de' Medici and Giovanni di Pierfrancesco de' Medici. The former, a cousin of Lorenzo the Magnificent who married in May 1482, was most likely the patron.

Realm of Venus and *Birth of Venus*, by Sandro Botticelli (1445–1510), are among the first large-scale paintings to be devoted to mythological themes since antiquity. Botticelli's figures are otherworldly deities who do not belong to the realm of the real. Their exquisite beauty asserts their divine nature.

The *Realm of Venus* (fig. 5-55) represents Venus reigning in a garden where it is always spring. The citrus fruit shown here was sacred to her. On the left, Mercury drives away clouds. Venus reigns as goddess of love and marriage, and Botticelli's painting may be a decoration made to celebrate a marriage. The unpredictable nature of love is suggested by the blindfolded Cupid, son of Venus, who shoots an arrow at her attendants. The physical nature of love is suggested by Zephyr, on the far right, who has the nymph Chloris in his arms. After seducing and marrying her, he returns her to the garden, where we witness her transmogrification into the goddess Flora, who strews flowers. Flora is the goddess of spring (*primavera* in Italian). Her festival, Floralia, was celebrated in April and May, months ruled by the astrological deities Venus and Mercury.

Botticelli's *Birth of Venus* (fig. 5-56) celebrates the legend that Venus was born full grown. Here she is blown ashore in a storm of roses by Zephyr and Chloris, to be received by one of her attendants. Her pose is based on ancient sculptures, but she is hardly sculptural. The elegance of

5-56. Sandro Botticelli. *Birth of Venus*. c. 1484–86. Tempera on canvas, 5'9" x 9'2". Galleria degli Uffizi, Florence. Who commissioned this secular, mythological painting is unknown, but most likely the patron chose the subject and suggested the particular interpretation. The most popular previous secular decorations for Florentine palaces had been Flemish tapestries, and the patterns, colors, and gold highlights of Botticelli's painting may be an attempt to relate to and even rival tapestries. The unusual fact that this is painted on canvas suggests that it may originally have functioned as a processional banner. Most likely commissioned by a member of the Medici family

the figure is set off by the intertwining patterns of Venus's hair. The enframing figures enhance her unexpectedly introspective quality. The *Birth of Venus* is strongly reminiscent of a passage in Alberti's *On Painting*:

> Let [hair] wind itself into a coil as if desiring to knot itself and let it wave in the air like unto flames. . . . Let no part of the drapery be free from movement. . . . it will be well to put into the painting the

face of the wind Zephyr or Auster blowing among the clouds, showing why the drapery flutters.

Humanist philosophy in Florence during the later fifteenth century was dominated by Neoplatonism, and in Neoplatonic terms, Venus personified beauty, and beauty equaled truth. The Neoplatonic philosopher Marsilio Ficino wrote in a letter:

> Venus [is] Humanitas. . . . Her

soul and mind are Love and Charity, her eyes Dignity and Magnanimity. . . . The whole, then, is Temperance and Honesty, Charm and Splendor. . . . How beautiful to behold!

The Neoplatonists went even further and equated Venus, source of divine love, with the Virgin Mary. Such an approach to ancient themes may explain why, in the final analysis, Botticelli's figures of Venus both seem to be so meditative.

ITALIAN RENAISSANCE PAINTING: LEONARDO DA VINCI

5-57. Leonardo da Vinci. *Madonna of the Rocks.* 1483–85. Oil on wood, transferred to canvas, 6'2¹/₂" x 48". The Louvre, Paris. A second version of this painting is in the National Gallery, London. The interpretation of Leonardo's painting remains mysterious and elusive, with the holy group set within a darkened cave. Detailed foreground naturalism is combined with a background that seems to belong to a primitive world, where the forces of nature are still carving the mountainous landscape. Commissioned by the Confraternity of the Immaculate Conception for their chapel in San Francesco Grande, Milan

In his *Lives of the Artists*, Vasari viewed the High Renaissance of the late fifteenth and early sixteenth centuries as the perfection and culmination of all the investigation and experimentation that had characterized Early Renaissance art, and he rightly argued that the transition to the High Renaissance occurred with the art of Leonardo da Vinci. One aspect of this transition took place when Leonardo developed a new unified composition in which he grouped figures to suggest a solid geometric form, such as a pyramid or cone. In Leonardo's *Madonna of the Rocks*, the figures are related to each other to form a pyramid (fig. 5-57). Mary's head forms the apex; her right arm extends to grasp the infant Saint John the Baptist, who is worshiping the Christ Child. To our right, the angel's head and billowing red cloak define another side of the triangle, while the Christ Child, who blesses the Baptist, extends the triangle forward, anchoring the py-

1483–85   **Leonardo, *Madonna of the Rocks***
1484   Pope Innocent VII issues a proclamation against sorcery and witchcraft
1489   First epidemic of typhus in Europe

5-58. Leonardo da Vinci. *Vitruvian Man.* c. 1485–90. Pen and ink, 13 1/2 x 9 5/8". Galleria dell' Accademia, Venice, Italy

5-59. Leonardo da Vinci. View and plan of a centrally planned church. c. 1489. Pen and ink, 9 1/16 x 6 5/16". Institut de France, Paris. No patron, but perhaps related to churches commissioned for Milan by Duke Lodovico Sforza

ramid. In a splendid example of foreshortening, Mary extends her left hand out over the Christ Child, as if to offer protection and blessing. For Leonardo, the achievement of a unified composition did not mean a static presentation—the language of gesture in the *Madonna of the Rocks*, for example, is varied and complex.

Leonardo's use of the pyramidal composition has multiple meanings. As a compositional scheme, the pyramidal grouping offers visual unity and stability, while it also carries the religious association of the Christian Trinity. As a geometric form, the pyramid relates to the Renaissance macrocosmic/microcosmic tradition, based in antiquity, which held that everything in the universe is governed by the order and precision of geometry. This tradition equated the human figure, or microcosm (small world), to the universe, the macrocosm. This complex philosophical notion found expression in a number of drawings

known as the *Vitruvian Man*, the most familiar of which is by Leonardo (fig. 5-58). The image of a human figure with arms and legs outstretched to touch both a circle and a square is based on a passage from the ancient Roman writer Vitruvius, who suggested that there is a consonance between the human body and the perfection of geometry that related the body to the mathematical systems inherent in the universe. This fundamental belief in macrocosmic/microcosmic analogy influenced Italian artists to compose figures in geometric configurations, thus creating a visual harmony alluding to the ideal harmony of the universe. Leonardo experimented with the unified composition in many studies, always seeking to incorporate a variety of poses to reflect the vitality of life.

In the 1480s, Leonardo began to design a series of **centrally planned churches** (fig. 5-59). These drawings, which evolve from simple to

more complex structures, were probably intended for a treatise on architecture. None of Leonardo's designs was built. His involvement with centrally planned structures may have been in part inspired by Alberti's book *On Architecture*, which dates from about 1450. Alberti, citing the common appearance of the circle in bird nests and other forms in nature, recommended the central plan as an ideal one for church architecture. Theologically, the circle, without beginning or end, was considered symbolic of the perfection of God. Leonardo's conceptions of centrally planned churches as embodied in his drawings often combined exterior views with sections and/or plans. Drawn while Leonardo was working in Milan, they influenced Donato Bramante, who would later develop the centrally planned structure for St. Peter's in Rome (see figs. 6-24–6-28).

ITALIAN RENAISSANCE PAINTING: LEONARDO'S *THE LAST SUPPER*

5-60. Leonardo da Vinci. *The Last Supper*, wall painting in the Refectory, Santa Maria delle Grazie, Milan. c. 1495–98. Oil, tempera, and varnish, 14' x 28'10^{1}/$_{2}$"; the figures are over-lifesize. The Dominican monastery of Santa Maria delle Grazie was patronized by Lodovico Sforza, duke and ruler of Milan, who commissioned Leonardo to paint *The Last Supper*. This view shows the painting in the course of the recent restoration, which has brought to light subtle details of facial expressions and radiant colors that had been covered by earlier restorers, who repainted rather than cleaned the surface.

According to Leonardo da Vinci, "Painted figures ought to be done in such a way that those who see them will be able to easily recognize from their attitudes the thoughts of their minds." Leonardo's *The Last Supper*, painted in the dining hall of a monastery, exemplifies his maxim that figures should express emotional and psychological realism (fig. 5-60). The stable and calm figure of Jesus, who is both on the axis and at the focal point of the scientific perspective construction, forms a triangle that, while symbolic of the Trinity, also gives visual stability to the composition and contrasts with the activity of the apostles who flank him. The apostles are composed in four groups of three figures each.

The agitated movement of the apostles reveals their psychological turmoil in reaction to Jesus' declaration, "I say unto you, that one of you shall betray me" (Matthew 26:21). The impact of these words on the apostles is understandable when we realize that they had left their families, friends, and professions to follow him. Now, when celebrating a Passover meal, Jesus announces that one of them will be a betrayer. The apostles' reactions are shown in different physical attitudes that reveal such psychological responses

1492	Christopher Columbus lands at San Salvador and Cuba
1492	Death of Lorenzo the Magnificent
1492	First known reference to smoking tobacco
c. 1495–98	**Leonardo, _The Last Supper_**

5-61. Leonardo da Vinci. _Study for the Head of Judas_, preparatory drawing for _The Last Supper_. 1495–97. Red chalk on red prepared paper, 7 1/8 x 5 7/8". Royal Library, Windsor Castle, Berkshire, England. Leonardo draws attention to the figure's neck in reference to Judas' suicide by hanging after his betrayal. No patron, but related to Leonardo's work for Duke Lodovico Sforza

as surprise, piety, uncertainty, and faithfulness.

The powerful emotional drama that we perceive in _The Last Supper_ is but one level of meaning in Leonardo's complex painting. In earlier Last Supper paintings, Judas had been shown on our side of the table, removed from the space occupied by Jesus and his apostles. Leonardo, however, kept Judas with his fellow apostles. The fourth figure from the left, he is shown recoiling from Jesus. Judas is the only figure whose face is lost in shadow, a subtle indication that he is lost from the light of Jesus.

Leonardo has joined the depiction of these two different, yet active, episodes with a third. The hands of Jesus are directed toward the bread and wine on the table, suggesting the institution of the Eucharist.

The activity of these dramas is contained within an impressive organization. Light from the upper left (following the placement of windows in the hall) defines the figures. The grouping of the apostles on each side of Christ provides symmetry, while the positioning of the apostles in four groups of three each discloses the numerical symbolism of the spiritual (3 is the number of the Trinity) and material (4 is the number of the elements) components of creation. This expression of universality, contained in number symbolism, is also apparent in the number 12: in keeping Judas with the eleven faithful apostles, Leonardo retains the integrity of the number 12, which refers not only to the apostles but also to the months of the year and the hours of day and of night, extending the numerical

symbolism to include the cycles of time.

It is now difficult to discern the subtle details that Leonardo intended, for in an attempt to achieve a new subtlety in mural painting, Leonardo, always the inventor, mixed his pigments with a combination of oil, tempera, and varnish, producing a paint that proved disastrous almost from the start. Later attempts at restoration have even further dimmed our vision of this masterpiece. However, we can glean some sense of its intended effect from surviving preliminary drawings. The study for the head of Judas exhibits an acute understanding of anatomy and physiognomy (fig. 5-61). Such detailed, descriptive observation, found in numerous studies, was joined to a unified, yet complex narrative interpretation.

ITALIAN RENAISSANCE SCULPTURE: MICHELANGELO'S ST. PETER'S *PIETÀ*

5-62. Michelangelo Buonarroti. *Pietà.* 1498–99. Marble, height 5'8^1/2"; the figures are over-lifesize. St. Peter's Basilica, Vatican, Rome, Italy. On August 27, 1498, a twenty-three-year-old sculptor from Florence, Michelangelo Buonarroti, signed a contract in Rome for a Pietà, intended as a tomb sculpture. The contract was repeating tradition when it stated that the completed group should be the "most beautiful work of marble in Rome," but the work Michelangelo created within about a year and a half fulfilled the terms of the contract in a new and unparalleled way. Commissioned by the French Cardinal Jean de Bilhères Lagraulas for the chapel where he planned to be buried at Old St. Peter's in Rome

The Rome *Pietà* by Michelangelo Buonarroti (1475–1564) demonstrates a command of concept and tragic expression, drawn with consummate skill from an inert block of marble (fig. 5-62). The Virgin Mary, seated on a rock, cradles the lifeless body of her son, which has just been taken down from the cross. With the open gesture of her left hand, she presents her son's sacrifice to us. The design of the sculpture, with its sweeping passages of drapery and angular arrangement of limbs, is coherently resolved into a pyramidal composition.

The theme that we call the Pietà (Italian for "pity" and "piety") is not found in the Bible. The image first appears in northern European Gothic sculptures in which anatomical details are exaggerated to emphasize Jesus' suffering and death. The German Gothic *Pietà* illustrated here demands an immediate and powerful devotional response from the viewer (fig. 5-63).

Michelangelo's biographer Ascanio Condivi, writing in 1553, recorded that with the St. Peter's *Pietà* the sculptor wanted to show "that the Son of God truly assumed human form," so that his physical suffering could be easily understood. But Michelangelo's conception of humanity is also rooted in the idealism of the Italian Renaissance, and he avoided the distortions of earlier Northern Pietà images in favor of an interpretation that conveyed his views on the integrity and beauty of the body. While still a young man in Florence, Michelangelo had studied human anatomy,

and from early dissection practice he learned the structure of the human body. His authority over anatomy is displayed here in the figure of Jesus. In a more subtle way than with earlier Pietàs, we can identify with Jesus' humanity and better understand his suffering and death. Unlike the wailing mother of the Gothic *Pietà*, Michelangelo's youthful and beautiful Mary bears her sorrowful burden with quiet, meditative resignation. Michelangelo here suggests an inner suffering restrained by dignity.

In describing the St. Peter's *Pietà*, Vasari, in his book *Lives of the Artists*, observed the beauty and technical achievement of the sculpture:

> Among the lovely things to be seen in the work, to say nothing of the divinely beautiful draperies, is the body of Christ; nor let anyone think to see a greater beauty of members or more mastery of art in any body, or a nude with more detail in the muscles, veins and nerves over the framework of the bones, nor yet a corpse more similar than this to a real corpse. Here is perfect sweetness in the expression of the head, harmony in the joints and attachments of the arms, legs, and trunk, and the pulses and veins so wrought, that in truth Wonder herself must marvel that the hand of a craftsman should have been able to execute so divinely and so perfectly, in

5-63. German Gothic. *Pietà*. Early 14th century. Polychromed wood, height 34^1/2". Provinzialmuseum, Bonn, Germany

> so short a time, a work so admirable; and it is certainly a miracle that a stone without any shape at the beginning should ever have been reduced to such perfection as Nature is scarcely able to create in the flesh.

The sculpture was an astounding success in Rome. Vasari goes on to report, however, that when the *Pietà* was newly finished, questions arose as to the identity of the artist. To end any doubts, Michelangelo carved his signature on the ribbon that crosses Mary's torso. The Rome *Pietà* is the only work Michelangelo ever signed.

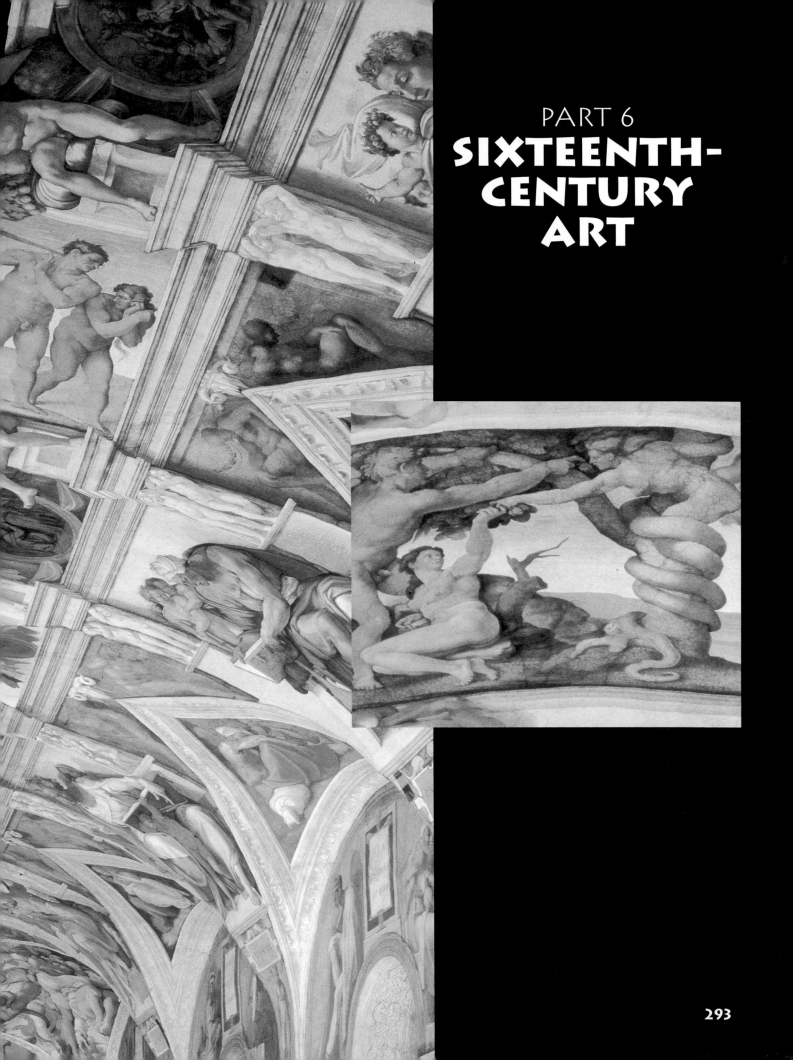

PART 6
SIXTEENTH-CENTURY ART

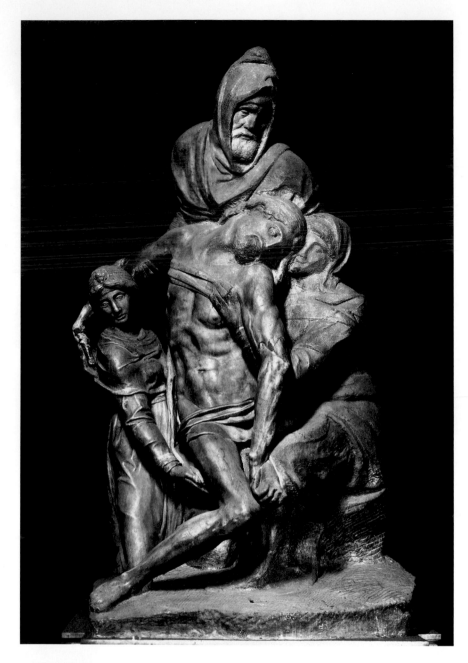

6-1. Michelangelo Buonarroti. *Pietà*. c. 1547–55. Marble, height 7'8". Museo dell' Opera del Duomo, Florence, Tuscury, Italy. After working on this sculpture for almost a decade, Michelangelo smashed it in anger, leaving it seriously damaged. He presented the damaged work to a pupil, who repaired it and laboriously finished the figure of Mary Magdalene on our left. Although based on Michelangelo's design, she is now too small for the composition and no longer seems to be supporting Jesus' right arm. Jesus' left leg, which was once positioned over Mary's, is completely lost. Theories have been advanced as to why Michelangelo attacked the work. Giorgio Vasari, writing in 1568, stated that the artist discovered that the marble was flawed.

INTRODUCTION TO SIXTEENTH-CENTURY ART

By the middle of the sixteenth century, when Michelangelo's Florence *Pietà* was created, the optimism that had characterized so much of fifteenth- and early-sixteenth-century Italian Renaissance art had evaporated. This new pessimistic mood is conveyed by Michelangelo's *Pietà* (fig. 6-1). We sense the dead weight of Jesus' body in the angular arrangement of limbs, the head collapsed to one side, and the efforts needed to support the body. To our right, the Virgin tenderly presses her face against her son's head. Behind, the towering figure of Nicodemus, a follower of Jesus, compassionately helps support his dead master.

Although the legacy of the High Renaissance is evident in the musculature of the body of the central figure, the elongated figures and angular composition break the norm of Renaissance harmony. Emotional grief has seized the participants, and this emotional impact is reinforced when we realize that Nicodemus is a self-portrait of Michelangelo himself. Michelangelo (1475–1564), who was about seventy-two years old when he began carving the Florence *Pietà*, intended it to be placed over his tomb. Its unsettling emotional content reflects his personal psychological condition and may also be related to the tumultuous conflicts of sixteenth-century Europe.

HISTORY

The extent and importance of contacts between widespread and highly diverse cultures that had so long been a feature of global history were expanded in the six-

6-2. Porcelain dish decorated with chrysanthemum patterns. Ming dynasty, Hung Wu period, 1369–98. Underglaze blue on porcelain, diameter 18". Östasiatiska Museet, Stockholm, Sweden

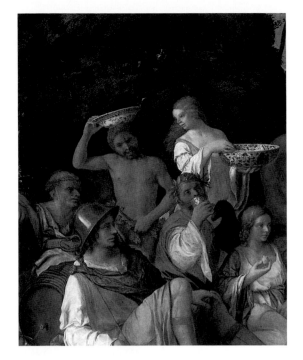

6-3. Giovanni Bellini. *Feast of the Gods*, detail showing Chinese Ming porcelains. 1514. Oil on canvas, 5'7" x 7'2". National Gallery of Art, Washington, D.C. Commissioned by Alfonso d'Este for his Studiolo in the Castle of Ferrara
Widener Collection

teenth century, especially through the dramatic increase in traffic on the high seas, new explorations, and new interest in mapping the globe. The precious objects and fine goods (such as spices) of one culture were exchanged for the luxury goods of another culture. The high-quality porcelains of the Ming dynasty (fig. 6-2), for example, found their way to the West, where they were greatly prized. Only after centuries of experimentation could the West begin to approximate the fine quality of these Chinese wares, and it is no accident that we still refer to our finest dishes as "china." One of the earliest representations of such china in European

painting is in the *Feast of the Gods* (fig. 6-3) by Giovanni Bellini (1430–1516); the context makes it clear that such dishes were thought to be the appropriate vessels for deities. One of the great surviving collections of Chinese and later Japanese porcelains was ordered by the Turkish sultans and is now on display in Istanbul.

Other contacts were less commercial. In 1582, a Jesuit priest named Matteo Ricci arrived in China and

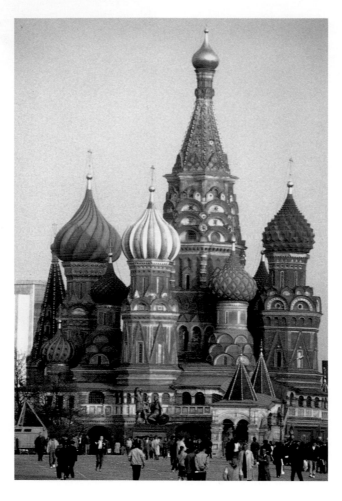

6-4. Postnik and Barma (?). Cathedral of St. Basil the Blessed, Moscow, Russia. 1554–60 and later. No other work of architecture by either of these men is known; the names may be legendary or Barma ("mumble") may be Postnik's nick-name. The structure was initially dedicated to the Virgin Mary, but it became known as St. Basil's when a holy man of that name was buried there in the 1550s. Commissioned by Tsar Ivan IV, the Terrible

established a sinicized Jesuit Order in Guangzhou (Canton). He presented the emperor with a mechanical clock, the first in China, and guaranteed his continuing presence there as the only person who could keep it in working order. The underlying purpose of his mission was to establish a long-standing Christian base in one of the world's most populous, non-Christian nations.

In 1526, the Mughal empire, which would last until 1756, was established in India. The Muslim emperor Akbar (ruled 1556–1605) attempted to reconcile Muslim, Hindu, and Christian thought. In this philosophy of reconciliation, Mughal artists incorporated European elements, such as scientific perspective and atmospheric effects, into their paintings. Akbar and the two emperors who succeeded him were avid patrons of the arts.

The main political protagonists of the European sixteenth century—a period convulsed by shifting alliances—were the popes in Rome and the rulers of northern Europe. Pope Julius II succeeded in establishing the papacy as a major political power early in the century, but the newly strengthened Church conflicted with the expansive plans of secular rulers in the North, where the strife between Emperor Charles V of the Hapsburg line and Francis I, king of France, affected many aspects of sixteenth-century life. In 1520, Charles V was crowned Holy Roman Emperor, a position that Francis I had also

sought. The territories ruled by Charles V were vast; they encompassed Spain, the Netherlands, and parts of northern Italy, Germany, and central and northern Europe. France was effectively isolated, but even a brief imprisonment did not deter Francis from his conflict with the emperor. Charles was usually aligned with the pope, but a significant break in this alliance occurred in 1527, after Pope Clement VII backed Francis I in an attempt to check the increasing power of the emperor. Charles V's troops entered and pillaged Rome and even imprisoned the pope. But the attention of Charles V was also directed toward the East, where he attempted to counter the expansion of the Ottoman Turks under Suleiman the Magnificent, who had extended his empire into eastern Europe and North Africa.

In areas that remained isolated, the local traditions sometimes became gradually more extreme and individualized. Russia, Christianized in 988, had adapted Byzantine forms—especially the multidomed, centrally planned church. Over time in Russia, however, the drums that supported the domes were heightened and the domes themselves took on a helmet shape, with a point at the top, and eventually they became "onion" domes, with heightened curves dominating the shape. The most extreme example of this trend came in the sixteenth century, when Ivan the Terrible commissioned a nine-domed church to commemorate his victory over the Tartars at Kazan. St. Basil's, next to the Kremlin on Red Square in Moscow, has become a symbol of Russia precisely because its forms are unparalleled in other cultures (fig. 6-4). The exotic Russian quality of the structure may have been intentional on Ivan's part, for he might well have wanted a structure that would give a new and distinct identity to his capital in Moscow. The later, seventeenth-century decoration of the domes with the forms and colors of Russian folk traditions has given the monument an even more Russian flavor.

Throughout the century, expansion across the Atlantic continued. The Spanish were particularly active in colonizing. In 1513, Vasco Núñez de Balboa crossed Panama to reach and name the Pacific Ocean, and Juan Ponce de León established a settlement in Florida. In the late fifteenth and early sixteenth centuries, a Florentine merchant and seafarer, Amerigo Vespucci, charted eastern coastline areas of South America. In 1507, the mapmaker Martin Waldseemüller, drawing on Vespucci's information, demonstrated that Vespucci had reached land masses separate from Asia and suggested that they be named after Vespucci; hence they came to be called the Americas.

6-5. Lucas Cranach the Elder. *Portrait of Martin Luther.* 1533. Oil on wood, 8^{1}/4 x 5^{7}/8". Germanisches Nationalmuseum, Nuremberg, Germany. This is one of some fifty portraits of Luther painted by Cranach and his workshop.

INTELLECTUAL AND SCIENTIFIC DEVELOPMENTS IN EUROPE

Although the vast majority of Europeans still felt bound to the scientific beliefs and superstitions that had guided life for centuries, important discoveries in the sixteenth century laid the foundation for the modern development of science. These discoveries were aided, in part, by the tremendously expanded publication of books. By 1600, about 2,000 books per year were being produced, a rate double that of a century earlier.

In 1543, two publications appeared that began to overturn many incorrect beliefs about human anatomy and the universe that had been based on the writings of ancient authors. *De humani corporis fabrica* (*On the Fabric of the Human Body*), written by Andreas Vesalius, a twenty-eight-year-old surgeon/anatomist, began to clear away traditional misconceptions about anatomy and provided a base for later advances in medicine. Also in 1543, the Polish astronomer Nicolaus Copernicus, in *De revolutionibus orbium coelestium* (*On the Revolution of the Celestial Spheres*), asserted his theory of a heliocentric universe, in which the planets revolve around the sun. This "modern" view of the universe, which had been held by a minority of philosophers since antiquity, was later popularized by Galileo Galilei, whose teachings, challenged by the Catholic Church, demonstrated the conflict between the new scientific reason and traditional religious authority.

THE PROTESTANT REFORMATION

The most significant religious event of the sixteenth century—one that would forever change the history of Christianity—was the Reformation. Over the centuries, the Catholic Church had become increasingly materialistic. The rebuilding of St. Peter's in Rome (see pages 312–13) and the construction of a new papal palace there led to the expansion of such unscrupulous practices as the selling of indulgences. According to Catholic belief, before gaining access to heaven, souls had to enter purgatory to suffer for their earthly sins. An indulgence allowed a person to "buy" a soul out of purgatory by the payment of a "donation." The proceeds of this expedient were shared by the local Catholic hierarchy and the papacy. Indulgences were especially solicited in Germany, leading to disillusionment within the local clergy.

A German Augustinian monk, Martin Luther (fig. 6-5), publicly questioned these practices, arguing that faith alone could "buy" salvation, in opposition to the Church's position that faith needed to be combined with good works. Aiming at reform from within, Luther drafted ninety-five theses, which he nailed to the doors of Wittenberg Cathedral on October 31, 1517. Among his theses, he argued:

27. There is no divine authority for preaching that the soul flies out of purgatory as soon as the money clinks in the bottom of the chest. . . .

50. Christians should be taught that, if the pope knew the exactions of the indulgence-preachers, he would rather the church of Saint Peter were reduced to ashes than be built with the skin, flesh, and bones of his sheep.

Luther called on German rulers to assist in promoting reform within the Church, but when he repudiated papal supremacy, Church authorities ruled that he was no longer a member—they excommunicated him.

The Reformation was soon bound to political realities. Most of the German princes were glad to restrict the power of the Church, which was draining their territories of wealth. Luther was given protection by Northern rulers, who were grasping the opportunity to counter Church authority and seize Church property. In 1529, Charles V ordered that measures be taken against those who dissented from the Catholic faith. The Lutheran princes who protested the emperor's order became known as Protestants. The open conflict that erupted in 1546 ended in 1555 with an agreement known as the Peace of Augsburg, which declared that the religion of a ruler determined the religion of that area. It was a victory for the Protestants.

Protestantism spread, with different groups developing in different areas of Europe. In England, Henry VIII requested that Pope Clement VII annul his marriage. Papal refusal led to the 1534 Act of Supremacy, which made the English sovereign the head of the English (Anglican) Church. In Switzerland, another Protestant movement flourished under John Calvin. Calvinism stressed the supremacy of the Bible as a guide for moral conduct.

By the end of the century, approximately one-fourth of western Europe's population was Protestant. England, Scotland, Denmark, and Sweden had become Protestant nations, while Protestants in the Netherlands were fighting to obtain their independence from Catholic Spain. In Germany, almost one-half of the population had become Protestant. The ramifications of these developments for art became obvious in the course of the seventeenth century and later.

THE COUNTER-REFORMATION

The response of the Roman Catholic Church to the Reformation is usually known as the Counter-Reformation. Voices calling for reform had been heard within the Catholic Church even before the Lutheran challenge, but the rapid growth of Protestantism led the Church to call a major council at Trent, in north Italy. Between 1545 and 1563, the Council of Trent established policies for internal reform and planned a strategy to combat the spread of Protestantism, which was viewed as a heresy.

The council affirmed the traditional belief that both faith and good works were the means to salvation, emphasizing the Bible and the "sacred tradition" as sources for doctrine (belief) and practice. It also enacted policies that would lead to a better-educated priesthood. Enforcement of the Church's beliefs and policies was given to the Inquisition, an ecclesiastical court established in the late Middle Ages to punish heretics.

Calls for an educated priesthood were met by a new order of priests founded by Ignatius of Loyola in 1534. Loyola, from Spain, had been a soldier in the armies of Charles V. While recovering from a leg wound, he read the lives of Christ and the saints and determined to devote his life to Christ and the defense of the Church. He founded the Society of Jesus, commonly referred to as the Jesuits, which was distinguished by its missionary zeal, preaching, and scholarly interests. As teachers, Jesuits founded many influential schools. Jesuits were counted among the intellectual leaders of the time. Their achievements contributed greatly to a restored respect for the Catholic Church.

At the final session of the Council of Trent, the Church reaffirmed the value of art in promoting religious education. According to the council, religious art should appeal to the emotions, be morally acceptable, and use clear compositions. Accuracy in theology was required; failure to meet these requirements made the artist answerable to the Inquisition. The impact of this policy contributed to new directions in art and was of significance for artistic and iconographic developments in the seventeenth century.

EUROPEAN SIXTEENTH-CENTURY ART

During the sixteenth century in Italy, three successive styles can be deduced: High Renaissance, Mannerism, and early Baroque; because of the importance of Italy as an artistic center, these styles would have an important impact on the rest of Europe in the sixteenth century and into the seventeenth. Three paintings with a similar theme demonstrate the visual characteristics of each style.

Madonna and Child with Saint John the Baptist by Raphael (1483–1520) exemplifies the union of ideality and naturalism that characterizes the High Renaissance (fig. 6-6). Bathed in soft gold light, the seated Madonna tenderly embraces the Christ Child. The relaxed pose of the child lends a note of informality. The flowers and plants are painted with precise observation, and naturalism is also evident in the modeling of the figures and in the atmospheric perspective of the distant landscape. Such naturalistic details, however, are part of an idealized composition seen in the pyramidal grouping. In Raphael's painting, the world as it is seen is joined to ideals

6-6. Raphael. *Madonna and Child with Saint John the Baptist* (also known as *La Belle Jardinière*). 1508. Oil on wood, 48 x 31$^{1}/2$". The Louvre, Paris. The infant John the Baptist, kneeling in the foreground, holds a cross and wears an animal skin to refer to the time he will spend in the wilderness. Commissioned by Filippo Sergardi

6-7. Parmigianino. *Madonna and Child with Angels and a Prophet* (known as the *Madonna with the Long Neck*). 1534–40 (unfinished). Oil on wood, 7'1" x 4'4". Galleria degli Uffizi, Florence. Commissioned by Elena Baiardi for the Church of the Servites, Parma, Italy

of perfection. A divergent branch of High Renaissance art would develop in Venice, with greater experimentation with colors, broader brushstrokes, and more dynamic compositions.

Madonna and Child with Angels and a Prophet (fig. 6-7) by Parmigianino (1503–40) was painted about thirty years after Raphael's *Madonna*. This Mannerist painting exhibits an aristocratic elegance: elongated figural proportions are evident (note especially the fingers of Mary's right hand), while the languid body of the Christ Child, the prominent leg of the angel, and the drapery clinging to Mary's torso create a distinctly sensual effect. The illusion of space is consciously disjointed, with columns (unfinished) in the background that rise to gigantic proportions. Derived from the Italian term *maniera*—meaning "style" in the sense of sophistication, elegance,

and poise—Mannerist art moved away from the classical values of the High Renaissance. Mannerist artists sought to create an artificial and complex construction to demonstrate their intellectual and technical virtuosity and the sophistication of their patrons.

The *Madonna degli Scalzi* (fig. 6-8) by Ludovico Carracci (1555–1619) might be seen as a reaction against the visual complexity of Mannerist painting. Dating from late in the century, it can be considered an early Baroque work, as the painting displays many of those features that will characterize Baroque art as it develops in the seventeenth century. The figures are rendered with an easily understood naturalism. Mary, raised on the axis on a crescent moon, holds a lively Christ Child. Christ extends his hand to Saint Francis, on our right, while Saint Jerome, with his symbolic lion, looks attentively

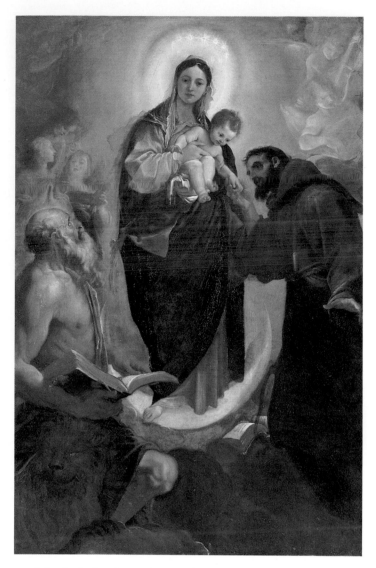

6-8. Ludovico Carracci. *Madonna and Child with Saints Jerome and Francis* (or *Madonna degli Scalzi*). 1590–93. Oil on canvas, 7 x 5'. Pinacoteca Nazionale, Bologna, Italy. Commissioned by a member of the Bentivoglio family for their chapel in the Chiesa della Madonna degli Scalzi, Bologna

from the left. A halo of golden light surrounds Mary's head. The light reflects on a host of angels joyously playing musical instruments. Carracci's emphasis on religious expression, visualized in a direct, simple, yet forceful composition, has an emotional appeal well suited to communicate the aims of the Counter-Reformation Church.

In northern Europe, the ideality of the Italian High Renaissance art affected many artists, especially Albrecht Dürer (1471–1528). Much of Northern painting, however, continued an adherence to a strict naturalism that can be related to the developments of Flemish painting during the fifteenth century (see pages 254–57, 264–65, 268–71). Dürer's drawing of *Praying Hands* (fig. 6-9), for example, demonstrates the continuing commitment to naturalistic observation and fine detail by Northern artists.

6-9. Albrecht Dürer. *Praying Hands*. 1508–09. Brush, heightened with white, on blue-grounded paper, $11^1/2$ x $7^3/4"$. Albertina, Vienna, Austria. This is among a number of surviving drawings for one of Dürer's most famous works, the *Heller Altarpiece*, which was commissioned by Jacob Heller, a merchant of Frankfurt.

Late in the century, many Northern artists adopted the affectations of Mannerism, while others, Pieter Bruegel (1564–1638) in particular, emphasized the Northern landscape and Northern traditions in paintings that laid the foundation for developments in the new republic of the Netherlands in the seventeenth century.

THE SIXTEENTH-CENTURY ARTIST IN EUROPE

The new respect for the artist as an intellectual, which had developed in the fifteenth century (see page 249), made impressive gains during the sixteenth century. In Italy, both Michelangelo and Raphael earned the nickname *il divino* ("the divine one"), surely a sign that the artist was now being viewed as an almost godlike creator. Artists continued to make self-portraits throughout the century. Parmigianino's unusual *Self-Portrait in a Convex Mirror* (fig. 6-10) reflects intellectual conceits associated with Mannerist art.

Art theory continued to evolve within an intellectual climate that nourished it, and other types of writings contributed to the elevated social status of the artist. Baldassare Castiglione, an Italian diplomat and literary figure, included witticisms and more serious discussions on art in his *Book of the Courtier*. Benvenuto Cellini's fame as an artist was buttressed by his theoretical writings and a roguish *Autobiography* that still enjoys great popularity.

6-10. Parmigianino. *Self-Portrait in a Convex Mirror*. 1524. Oil on wood, diameter 9⁵/₈". Kunsthistorisches Museum, Vienna. Parmigianino's *Self-Portrait* is actually painted on a convex wooden panel to heighten the illusionism.

6-11. Sophonisba Anguissola. *Portrait of the Artist's Three Sisters with Their Governess*. 1555. Oil on canvas, 27⁹/₁₆ x 37". Narodowe Museum, Potsdam, Germany. Sophonisba Anguissola, who was also trained in music, languages, and literature, is the first nationally recognized woman artist of whom we have any certain knowledge. She is credited with inventing a new type of group portraiture in which the sitters are shown in lively activity and psychological interaction rather than being merely aligned and accompanied by conventional props. Here she shows her sisters during a game of chess, an intellectual activity usually restricted to men at this time. The picture thus makes an important point about the capabilities of young women during this period, in which so many restrictions on female behavior were accepted. At the same time, it demonstrates the artist's interest in capturing complex personal interrelationships through gesture and expression.

Giorgio Vasari, an artist active at the Medici court in Florence, published his *Lives of the Most Eminent Painters, Sculptors, and Architects* in 1550 and revised it for a second edition in 1568. Vasari viewed Renaissance art as an evolutionary progression (see page 245). Beginning with Giotto in the fourteenth century, he argued, Italian art had been rescued from the "dark ages" to be restored in the light of classical eloquence. Each generation of artists built upon the foundation set by the previous generation until perfection was reached with the High Renaissance. Throughout the *Lives*, Vasari noted the regard in which great rulers held artists, enjoying their friendship and advice.

When Vasari wrote the *Lives*, he had more in mind than just art history. He was promoting the establishment of an art academy. His efforts assisted in founding the Florentine Accademia del Disegno (Academy of Design) in 1563. In this academy, and in many other academies that followed, artists were educated within a broad liberal-arts context. This enhanced education made it more possible for at least some artists to mingle with the higher social ranks. The artistic, intellectual, and social gains made by artists during the sixteenth century gave us a new concept of the artist, that of an inspired genius.

One benefit of these social changes for the artist was that the profession began to open its ranks, however slowly at first, to women. During the Middle Ages, women artists had been active primarily as embroiderers and manuscript illuminators. By the sixteenth century, women were becoming established as painters as well. In Italy, both Sophonisba Anguissola (fig. 6-11) and Lavinia Fontana (fig. 6-12) developed very high reputations.

6-12. Lavinia Fontana. *Self-Portrait*. c. 1577. Oil on copper, diameter 6". Galleria degli Uffizi, Florence. This self-portrait, which shows the artist in her studio, captures the confident elegance of Mannerist portraiture. Lavinia Fontana, from Bologna, was the daughter of a painter. She married a fellow student in her father's studio on the condition that she be free to follow her career. Her husband apparently assisted her by painting frames or by painting the clothing in some of her portraits. A portrait medal of 1611 shows her painting in an attitude that suggests that she, like Michelangleo, was divinely inspired.

CE	1500		1520

EUROPE
ART

1501–04
MICHELANGELO'S *DAVID*

c. 1503–05
LEONARDO'S *MONA LISA*

1504
DÜRER'S *ADAM AND EVE*

1506
BRAMANTE'S DESIGN FOR NEW
ST. PETER'S, ROME

1508–12
MICHELANGELO'S SISTINE CHAPEL
CEILING FRESCOES

1509–11
RAPHAEL'S STANZA DELLA SEGNATURA
FRESCOES

c. 1510
GIORGIONE'S *SLEEPING VENUS*

c. 1510–15
BOSCH'S *GARDEN OF EARTHLY DELIGHTS*
TRIPTYCH

c. 1512–15
GRÜNEWALD'S *ISENHEIM ALTARPIECE*

1519–26
TITIAN'S PESARO *MADONNA*

1524–34
MICHELANGELO'S MEDICI CHAPEL
SCULPTURE

1538
TITIAN'S *VENUS OF URBINO*

HISTORY

1517
Luther's 95 Theses begin the
Reformation

1520
Charles V crowned Holy Roman Emperor

1527
Sack of Rome by the troops of Charles V

1534
Act of Supremacy makes English ruler
head of Anglican Church

ASIA
ART

c. 1500
SESSHU'S *WINTER LANDSCAPE*

EARLY 16TH CENTURY
SOAMI'S GARDEN AT DAITOKUJI,
KYOTO, JAPAN

HISTORY

1368–1644
Ming dynasty in China

1500
Beijing (population c. 672,000) is world's
largest city

THE AMERICAS
ART

15TH –16TH CENTURY
INKA COMPLEX AT MACHU PICCHU,
PERU

16TH CENTURY
AZTEC CODEX PAINTINGS

HISTORY

EARLY 16TH CENTURY
Vespucci charts eastern coastline of South
America

1501
First slaves brought to Americas
(Santo Domingo)

1513
Balboa crosses Panama to Pacific

1513
Ponce de León establishes settlement in
Florida

1521
Cortés conquers Aztecs, makes Mexico
Spanish colony

1533
Pizarro conquers Inkas, takes Cuzco, Peru

1539
Spain annexes Cuba

AFRICA
ART

HISTORY

1517
Turks conquer Egypt, control Arabia

THE MIDDLE EAST
ART

SECOND HALF OF 16TH CENTURY
GARDENS OF PARADISE PRAYER RUG

HISTORY

1520–66
Sultan Suleiman I rules Ottoman Empire

c. 1545
BRONZINO'S *ALLEGORY OF TIME AND LUST*

1546–64
MICHELANGELO'S PLANS FOR NEW ST. PETER'S, ROME

c. 1547–55
MICHELANGELO'S FLORENCE *PIETÀ*

1554–60
POSTNIK AND BARMA'S ST. BASIL'S, MOSCOW

1565
BRUEGEL'S *DECEMBER LANDSCAPE*

1566
PALLADIO'S SAN GIORGIO, VENICE, BEGUN

1566
BRUEGEL'S *PEASANT WEDDING FEAST*

1573
VERONESE'S *LAST SUPPER/FEAST IN THE HOUSE OF LEVI*

1542
Pope Paul III establishes the universal Inquisition

1545–63
Council of Trent establishes Counter-Reformation policies

1550, 1568
Vasari's *Lives of the Artists*

1558
Queen Elizabeth I crowned in England

1563
Academy of Design founded in Florence, Italy

1568
Protestant Netherlands revolt against Catholic Spain

1600
2,000 books per year produced

1556
AKBAR ESTABLISHES ROYAL WORKSHOPS FOR PAINTERS IN INDIA

LATE 16TH CENTURY
SEN NO RIKYU PERFECTS THE TEA CEREMONY IN JAPAN

1526
Mughal empire established in India

1568–1603
Momoyama period in Japan

1570
Japan begins to admit foreign ships

1577
Akbar unifies northern India

1582
Jesuit Order established in China

1590
Hideyoshi unifies Japan

1541
De Soto discovers the Mississippi River

1550
BENIN EARLY PERIOD ENDS

16TH CENTURY
Turunku Bakwa is the Hausa queen in West Africa

1551–58
SINAN'S SULEIMANIYE COMPLEX

ITALIAN RENAISSANCE SCULPTURE: MICHELANGELO

6-13. Michelangelo Buonarroti. *David*. 1501–04. Marble, height 14'3". Galleria dell' Accademia, Florence. In 1873, the statue was moved from its original location, at the entrance of the Palazzo della Signoria, to the Accademia, where a special setting had been constructed for it. The medium is white marble from Carrara, near Pisa. These quarries still yield vast quantities of fine-quality marble for artistic and architectural use. On a sheet of paper with drawings for the right arm of *David* and for a bronze statue of the same subject, Michelangelo wrote a couplet: "David with his sling / and I with my bow / Michelangelo." These lines have been interpreted with reference to Michelangelo's psychological state as he was about to carve the *David*. Just as David had the most meager of weapons, a sling, with which to battle Goliath, Michelangelo had only a simple sculptor's bow with which to attack the huge block of marble already misshapen by earlier attempts to carve it. For Michelangelo, the bow was a sculptor's drill, used for boring into the marble. It was one of the limited number of traditional sculptor's tools used by his predecessors. The drill is still an important tool in certain kinds of sculpture. Commissioned by the Cathedral Administration to be placed on a buttress below the dome of Florence Cathedral (see fig. 5-37)

Michelangelo's huge sculpture of the Old Testament hero David is a stirring embodiment of physical and psychological strength (fig. 6-13). Michelangelo chose an unusual moment to represent, for he shows David before his battle with the enemy Goliath. The sling is over his shoulder and the stone rests in his right hand, but his muscles are taut and a defiant scowl seizes his face. The figure pulls powerfully to the left, away from the implied enemy, and David's apprehension is further indicated in the swelling veins in his hand and the sucking in of breath revealed in the tensed muscles of the abdomen. In Michelangelo's interpretation, David has become human. In his *Lives*, Vasari, referring to the huge block of white marble from which Michelangelo carved the *David*, said that the sculptor had brought "to life a thing that was dead."

In saying that Michelangelo had given life to the stone, Vasari alluded not only to his artistic accomplishment but also to the history of the block of marble from which the *David* was carved. Quarried in 1464, before Michelangelo's birth, the enormous block was brought to Florence to be carved, perhaps under the supervision of the aging Donatello, as a *David*, one of a series of Old Testament prophets to be placed high above street level on the buttresses of the cathedral. The stone, partially carved, languished in the courtyard of the cathedral workshop for decades.

We do not know to what extent the stone had been carved before Michelangelo received the commission to finish the statue in 1501 and cannot, therefore, judge the difficulties he had to overcome. We do know that it was decided not to hoist the completed sculpture into position on the cathedral buttress. Perhaps there was fear that the sculpture might be damaged, or the work may have been too impressive to be removed from close public attention. A committee that included Leonardo da Vinci and Botticelli decided to place the *David* at the entrance to the Palazzo della Signoria, the center of Florence's civic government. That decision was significant, for the meaning of the *David* gained an enhanced political impact.

Michelangelo's *David* was carved after the expulsion of the Medici, when the republican traditions of Florence had been reasserted. The Medici would again rule the city in 1512, but at the time of the *David*, the democracy and liberty of the old Florentine republic reigned, and Michelangelo's sculpture was seen as a manifestation of those civic virtues. Just as the biblical David had triumphed against the physical power of Goliath, so too had the Florentine people courageously restored their republic. The *David* symbolized the Florentines' defiance of tyranny.

Fulfilling its new role as a political symbol, the *David* partook of the Renaissance in yet another way. While conforming to the designation *statua*, as public sculpture had been explained by the ancient writer Pliny the Elder, Michelangelo's

David also elevated *statua* to a grand and heroic scale. With the *David,* Vasari proclaimed that even the cherished art of ancient Greece and Rome had been surpassed:

1494   Sebastian Brandt, *The Ship of Fools*
1495   *Everyman*, morality play, is performed
1501   Amerigo Vespucci's second voyage to the Americas
1501–04   **Michelangelo, *David***

> Without any doubt this figure has put in the shade every other statue, ancient or modern, Greek or Roman . . . such were the satisfying proportions and the beauty of the finished work. . . . To be sure, anyone who has seen Michelangelo's *David* has no need to see anything else by any other sculptor, living or dead.

6-15. Michelangelo Buonarroti. *Saint Matthew,* detail

TECHNIQUE   STONE SCULPTURE

6-14. Michelangelo Buonarroti. *Saint Matthew.* 1504–08. Marble, height 8'10". Galleria dell' Accademia, Florence. This is the only figure of a series of twelve apostles originally commissioned from Michelangelo for Florence Cathedral. The project was abandoned when Michelangelo was called away to work for Pope Julius II. Commissioned by the Cathedral Administration

Like carving in wood (see page 269), working in marble is a **subtractive** technique. An important source for understanding traditional methods of carving is Benvenuto Cellini's sixteenth-century *Treatise on Sculpture.* Trained as a goldsmith, Cellini worked on both a miniature and a monumental scale. Cellini prescribes that, after the clay model for a sculpture is completed,

> you draw the principal views of your statue onto the stone . . . The best method I ever saw was the one that Michelangelo used; when you have drawn on your principal view you begin to chisel it round as if you wanted to work a half relief, and thus gradually it comes to be cut out.

This half-relief effect is evident in the *Saint Matthew* (fig. 6-14), which is carved back from one face of the block, with the result that large areas of marble still fill the background. Cellini also describes the chisels used to work from the outside of the marble block to the "skin" of the figure. Excess stone was removed with a pointed chisel, while toothed or clawed chisels were employed as the sculptor neared the surface of the figure. Marks from the toothed chisel are visible in the detail of the *Saint Matthew* (fig. 6-15). Work with a flat chisel would then remove the ridges left by the toothed chisels, and a series of files would be used to finish the surface. Drills were utilized for areas of deep undercuts, and polishing was achieved with a close-grained pumice stone.

Even today, centuries later, sculptors continue to work with traditional chisels like those used by Michelangelo. Only the electric drill has eased the physically demanding process of carving a figure in stone.

ITALIAN HIGH RENAISSANCE PORTRAITURE

6-16. Leonardo da Vinci. *Portrait of a Woman* (known as the *Mona Lisa*). c. 1503–05. Oil on wood, 30¼ x 21" (cut down). The Louvre, Paris. The sitter is unknown, despite the traditional title. Vasari said that she was the wife of Francesco del Gioconda, which led to the popular name *La Gioconda* for the painting. Vasari also tells the unforgettable tale that Leonardo employed musicians or jesters during the sittings for the portrait to keep her full of merriment and to chase away any trace of melancholy that might arise from the boredom of sitting quietly posed, repeatedly, for long hours. Leonardo, who seems to have worked on the painting over a number of years, took it with him when he went to France, where he died in 1519. After Leonardo's death, the painting was owned by Francis I of France. In the early nineteenth century, Napoleon kept the portrait in his bedroom. The painting has been cut down; it was once wider, and the figure was shown enframed by columns on each side. Today, only the column bases survive. Commissioned by her husband, Francesco del Gioconda?

The *Mona Lisa,* probably the most widely known portrait and perhaps even the best-known painting in the history of art, is difficult to appreciate today (fig. 6-16). Covered by layers of yellowing varnish and a protective sheet of thick glass, the painting seems to have none of the naturalistic effects reported by Vasari in the sixteenth century:

> The nose, with its beautiful nostrils, rosy and tender, seemed to be alive. The opening of the mouth, united by the red of the lips to the flesh tones of the face, seemed not to be colored but to be living flesh.

Leonardo became famous for his ability to create soft shadows and to create a sense of mystery by gently modeling forms through a careful blending of tones, and while these effects survive in the *Mona Lisa*, the freshness of his color and observation is obscured. What remains clear is Leonardo's composition, which became a model for many later Renaissance portraits. As in his earlier religious works (see figs. 5-57, 5-60), the basic form is a pyramidal shape. Leonardo successfully and naturally integrates the hands into his portrait, adding yet another vehicle for the expression of personality into the tradition of portraiture.

Even in the Renaissance, the mystery of the sitter must have excited the imagination of the viewer. The androgynous quality—neither

c. 1503–05	**Leonardo, *Portrait of a Woman***
1506	Machiavelli establishes a citizen militia in Florence
1511	Pocket watch is first mentioned

6-17. Raphael. *Portrait of a Woman* (now known as *Donna Velata*). c. 1513. Oil on canvas, 33¹/2 x 23¹/2". Pitti Gallery, Florence. It is suspected that the beautiful sitter for this portrait was Raphael's beloved, the baker's daughter (*la fornarina*) mentioned by Vasari.

fully female nor fully male—and the self-satisfied expression, created by the blurring of the corners of the mouth and eyes, are tantalizing. Our uneasiness is in part created by the unexpected appearance of a figure with the plucked eyebrows and forehead fashionable in the Renaissance. Also disturbing is the fantastic mountainous landscape setting. Note that the horizon lines of the landscapes are clearly on different levels. Perhaps the most remarkable single aspect of the painting when it was created is the manner in which this woman looks directly into the viewer's eyes; for a Renaissance man this would have

been an unsettling and unexpected experience, for Renaissance etiquette books warned women that they should never look directly at a man. Whoever she is, the *Mona Lisa* continues to project and protect her mysterious secret.

In Raphael's *Donna Velata (Veiled Woman)*, the natural beauty of the woman and the High Renaissance style are mutually compatible (fig. 6-17). The woman appears to be a specific individual, and her expression can be interpreted as conveying warmth, gentleness, and intelligence. The High Renaissance demand for unity is evident in the sweep of her veil, which unites

myriad complex forms into the favored conical composition. The beautifully rounded forms of her head and eyes are repeated in the necklace and again in its individual stones, as well as in the curves of the neckline and bodice; the pearl set against her dark hair is a microcosm of the whole composition. The costume is a coloristic symphony in shades of gold and white, a scheme that emphasizes the flesh tones and draws attention to the compelling dark eyes and enframing hair. The elaborate sleeve, a painter's triumph, enhances the elegance of his sitter and confirms Raphael's technical skill.

GERMAN PRINTMAKING: ALBRECHT DÜRER

6-18. Albrecht Dürer. *Adam and Eve.* 1504. Engraving, 9⁷/₈ x 7⁵/₈" (for a detail, see figure 6-21). Dürer, one of the first artists to sign and date his works, may have done so because of the lively business in forgeries of his prints. No patron; made as part of a commercial endeavor

The increasing contact between Italian and Northern artistic traditions is demonstrated in Dürer's *Adam and Eve* (fig. 6-18). The precise detail of the heavily wooded background reflects Northern tradition, while the use of antique models for the figures reveals Dürer's contact with Italian Renaissance art (Dürer went to Italy twice, in 1494–95 and 1505–07). Dürer's difficulty in blending these two distinct styles is evident, for the figures resemble sculptures rather than living beings and seem out of place in this dense forest setting. Nevertheless, they are striking in their classical elegance— which is not surprising, for Dürer studied proportional systems for the human body from nature and from classical and Italian Renaissance sources, and he completed two volumes of a proposed four-volume *Treatise on Human Proportions.* The diverse animals in the background bear an important relationship to the figures, for they symbolize the various "humors," fluids within the body that were believed to control personality. The rabbit stands for the lust or lechery of humanity, which will become active as soon as Adam takes a bite of the apple held by Eve.

This blending of Northern and Renaissance is also seen in Dürer's *Knight, Death, and the Devil* (fig. 6-19). The central figure, dressed as a Renaissance knight, is an allegorical representation of the Christian soul. He is every human being, riding through life, which is shown as a landscape filled with terrors. The Devil is a hideous horned monster, and Death, his crown entwined with serpents, brandishes an hourglass as a reminder of the inevitability of death. These imaginative creations belong to a Northern tradition, but the knight and his sturdy mount are inspired by classical and Renaissance works Dürer had seen in Italy.

Dürer's prints brought him international fame. During his lifetime, he was internationally recognized as the leading German artist. When Dürer was in Venice, the Senate offered him a regular salary if he would become a citizen there, and he was also employed by Maximilian I, the Holy Roman Emperor. Dürer loved to travel, and in 1520–21, in the Netherlands, he saw a room full of Aztec gold treasures sent back by Hernán Cortés. He praised these exotic objects, writ-

1504 **Dürer, *Adam and Eve***
1504 Columbus returns from his final voyage
1504 Erasmus, *Instructions for the Christian Soldier*

6-19. Albrecht Dürer. *Knight, Death, and the Devil*. 1513. Engraving, 9⅝ x 7½". Dürer called this print *The Rider*, but scholars have related the symbolism to Erasmus's handbook, *Instructions for the Christian Soldier*, published in 1504. The initials, with the *A* encompassing the *D*, create a unique monogram, an indication of Dürer's pride in his work. No patron; made as part of a commercial endeavor

6-20. Albrecht Dürer. *Four Horsemen of the Apocalypse*. c. 1497–98. Woodcut, 15½ x 11" (for a detail, see figure 6-22). The *Apocalypse* series, of which this is a part, was based on the Book of Revelation in the Bible. It consisted of fifteen prints with relevant texts on the back in German or Latin. No patron; made as part of a commercial endeavor

ing, "I have seen nothing that rejoiced my heart so much as these things, for . . . I marveled at the subtle ingenuity of men in foreign lands."

Dürer's impressive engravings were intended for a sophisticated audience of wealthy print collectors, but he also produced more reasonably priced and easily understood prints in series for a popular audience—the *"Small" Life of the Virgin Mary*, the *"Large"* and *"Small" Passions*, and the *Apocalypse*. These

works, executed in the bolder and more direct medium of woodcut, were printed in large quantities to be sold at fairs and carnivals, as well as by Dürer and his agents. The subject matter is both more traditional and more direct, as in the *Four Horsemen of the Apocalypse* (fig. 6-20), drawn from Revelation 6:1–8. Death ("on a pale horse") in the foreground and the other riders follow Revelations' description: Famine has a pair of scales, War a sword, and "the conqueror" (Pestilence, or the Plague)

carries a bow. Dürer's powerful patterns reinforce the relentless motion of the horsemen as they ravage humanity. The Apocalypse and Last Judgment were popular themes just before 1500, when it was feared time would end and Christ would appear to judge humanity.

Dürer had sympathies with the Protestant movement, and when he heard a rumor that Luther had been murdered, he wrote, "If Luther is dead, who will explain the Gospel to us now?"

6-21. Albrecht Dürer. *Adam and Eve*, enlarged detail of figure 6-18. Engraving

Enlarged details from an **engraving** and a **woodcut** by Dürer reveal his acute vision and the technical accomplishment and expression he achieved in these two media (figs. 6-21, 6-22). They are especially impressive given the distinctive technique of these two major types of printmaking. In the engraved head, multiple fine lines, often placed parallel (**hatching**) and perpendicular (**cross-hatching**) to each other, create highlights, modeling, and subtle pockets of shadow. In addition, these lines suggest the illusion of specific textures. In the woodcut head, the effect is more linear, and the sharp distinctions between light and dark patterns add drama and movement to the work. In woodcuts, the defining lines either follow the naturalistic shapes or are grouped parallel to each other.

The **printmaking** processes involve pressing a piece of paper (or, rarely, some other absorbent material, such as **vellum** or silk) against a surface to which ink has been applied (technically known as the **print form**). When the paper is removed, a reversed impression adheres to it; this is known as a **print**. In most print media, the surface of the print form can be re-inked and a number of additional prints (an **edition**) produced. The development of this relatively cheap means of mass-producing an image, which was related to improvements in the quality of paper and a tremendous decrease in its price, had a dramatic impact on western European culture. Now avidly collected by museums and collectors, most of the earliest prints were simple book illustrations or modest, inexpensive religious images intended for popular consumption. In the hands of such skilled artists as Dürer, however, the techniques

6-22. Albrecht Dürer. *Four Horsemen of the Apocalypse,* enlarged detail of figure 6-20. Woodcut

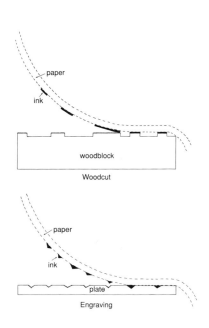

6-23. These diagrams of the woodcut and engraving techniques show schematically the moment when the paper is being lifted from the woodblock or the plate at the completion of the printing process. Note how the ink is transferred from the print form to the print.

became sophisticated, their expression more subtle, and the iconography more complex.

The woodcut was first developed in China in the late ninth century; the earliest European examples date from the late fourteenth century. Woodcut is called a **relief process** because the lines and surfaces to which the ink adheres are higher than the parts that are not to be printed. To create a woodcut, the artist draws the design on a piece of wood sawed lengthwise along the grain (fig. 6-23). Using a knife or chisel, he or she then cuts away the background areas, leaving the raised design. When the woodblock is inked, the ink adheres to the raised surfaces. Dampened paper is applied, and the print can be made by hand or in a printing press. Approximately a thousand good prints can be made before the prints reveal that the block is showing signs of wear. Our understanding of the woodcut technique makes Dürer's accomplishment even more impressive, for, unlike earlier harsh and simple images, his designs suggest the illu-

sion of three-dimensional forms with light playing over them.

Engraving is known as an **intaglio process** (from the Italian *intagliare,* "to carve" or "to cut") because the lines that print are incised into the surface of the print form. In engraving, the print form is a thin metallic plate, usually of copper. With a sharply pointed steel instrument called a **burin,** the artist incises grooves in the surface of the plate. The plate is then inked with a heavy, viscous ink and wiped with a rag (or the palm of the hand), leaving the ink in the grooves. The paper used for printing an engraving is slightly moistened before being applied to the inked plate. Plate and paper are then run through a printing press, which can apply the sufficient pressure (more than is needed to print a woodcut) to force the paper to pick up the ink in the grooves. The printed lines that result are sharply defined and slightly raised. Several hundred high-quality prints can be made before weak lines on the print reveal that the copper plate is wearing down.

6-24. Donato Bramante. Medal showing Bramante's design for the new St. Peter's, Rome. 1506. The British Museum, London, England. Bramante's design was commissioned by Pope Julius II. Twelve impressions of this commemorative medal by Caradossa were enclosed in the cornerstone of the new St. Peter's. Commissioned by Pope Julius II

On April 18, 1506, Pope Julius II, who was aggressive in both religious and political matters, laid the foundation stone for a new St. Peter's. As part of a campaign to restore Rome so that it would be worthy of its status as the capital of Christendom, he commissioned Donato Bramante (1444–1514) to rebuild the structure, an event commemorated in a medal issued that year (fig. 6-24). Since the late fourteenth century, St. Peter's and the Vatican had been home to the popes, and although Old St. Peter's (see fig. 4-12) was one of the most revered churches in Christendom, it had fallen into disrepair and no longer seemed grand enough to serve as the church that marked the burial spot of the first pope and, now, the religious center for the papacy.

Bramante's design (fig. 6-25), never completed, would have replaced the Early Christian **basilica** with a **centrally planned** church, a plan appropriate to St. Peter's function as a martyrium and consistent with Renaissance philosophical ideals (see fig. 5-59). Four equal arms, terminating in **apses**, radiate from a central **crossing** crowned with an immense dome surrounded by smaller domes. The underlying geometry of the design is simple, producing a monumental effect not unlike the unified compositions offered in painting and sculpture by Leonardo, Raphael, and Michelangelo.

The boldest aspect of Bramante's conception is its colossal scale. Bramante set out to surpass the monumental architectural remains of ancient Rome, creating a structure that would dominate all Rome. Bramante is reported to have stated that he was inspired to "place the Pantheon on top of the Basilica of Constantine" (the diameter of the dome of St. Peter's is 138 feet, only about 6 feet smaller than that of the Pantheon).

Before journeying to Rome, Bramante had known Leonardo in Milan in the 1480s and 1490s and had experimented with centrally planned church designs. For St. Peter's, Bramante joined the central plan, thought to be symbolic of God's perfection, with a **Greek cross** pattern. The spaces between the cross arms enclose this central plan within a square. Unlike the **cruciform basilica** plan of Old St. Peter's, where the cross shape emphasized salvation, Bramante's central plan expressed the universal harmony of God's created world.

The new St. Peter's was not consecrated until November 18, 1626, more than 120 years after Bramante's reconstruction was begun. The work encompassed the reigns of twenty popes and the efforts of fourteen architects, including Raphael, Michelangelo, and Bernini. Each succeeding architect had to contend with Bramante's original

1506	**Bramante, new St. Peter's basilica**
1513	Late Gothic tower of Chartres Cathedral is finished
1513	Machiavelli, *The Prince*

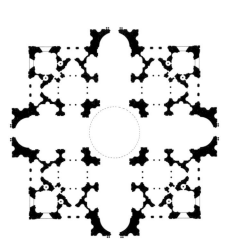

6-25. Donato Bramante. Plan of new St. Peter's, Rome. 1506. Commissioned by Pope Julius II

6-26. Michelangelo Buonarroti. Plan of new St. Peter's, Rome. 1546–64. Pope Paul III appointed Michelangelo chief architect of St. Peter's. The artist, burdened by his advancing age and numerous other artistic projects, took charge of the construction of St. Peter's without pay and for the "salvation of his soul," as he expressed it. Late in the sixteenth century, an argument developed over whether the design of St. Peter's should be limited to Bramante's and Michelangelo's central plan or whether a nave should be added to create the more traditional axial composition that dates back to Old St. Peter's (see fig. 4-13). In the early seventeenth century, a nave was added by Carlo Maderno (see fig. 7-23) that, from both the outside and the inside, obscures the view of the great dome that Bramante and Michelangelo planned would be the central and unifying feature of the church. Commissioned by Pope Paul III

plan, as well as the advancing construction of the building under successive architects. Michelangelo took charge of construction in 1546, noting that "every architect who has departed from Bramante's plan . . . has departed from the right way." Michelangelo's plan (fig. 6-26) retains the integrity of Bramante's central plan, but it achieves a more cohesive unity by simplifying it, giving a new lucidity to the exterior form and the interior spaces. This unity is further expressed in the use of the **giant order** (**pilasters** or **columns** that span more than one story of the structure) on both the exterior and the interior. On the exterior, Michelangelo's wall design is more varied than Bramante's, sheathing the building like muscle and flesh over bone and creating an external vitality enveloping the inner, structural core (figs. 6-27, 6-28).

The commanding dome of St. Peter's, also based on a design by Michelangelo, was erected by Giacomo della Porta (c. 1540–1602) between 1588 and 1591. Structural reasons dictated that it be slightly more pointed, to exert less thrust, than Michelangelo's original design. The dome retains Michelangelo's grand scale and articulation and is a worthy climax to Bramante's earlier vision.

6-27. Michelangelo Buonarroti. Longitudinal section of St. Peter's (engraving by Dupérac, 1569)

6-28. Michelangelo Buonarroti. Longitudinal elevation of St. Peter's (engraving by Dupérac, 1569)

MICHELANGELO, SISTINE CHAPEL CEILING

6-29. Michelangelo Buonarroti. *Creation of Adam*, detail of frescoes (after completion of cleaning in 1990) on the Sistine Chapel ceiling, Vatican, Rome. 1508–12. Commissioned by Pope Julius II

6-30. *(right)* Michelangelo Buonarroti. Sistine Chapel ceiling frescoes (after completion of cleaning in 1990), Vatican, Rome. The Sistine Chapel, named after its builder, Pope Sixtus IV, was constructed in the late 1470s. The walls were decorated by such leading artists as Perugino (see fig. 1-15), Botticelli, and Ghirlandaio with scenes from the lives of Moses and Christ. Originally the vault was simply decorated with gold stars on a blue ground.

He who made everything,
   made every part,
And then chose what was
   most beautiful,
To reveal on earth the
   excellence of His creation,
And the divine art with
   which He made it.

(Michelangelo, "Sonnet,"
   c. 1510)

In the gap between Adam's listless hand and God's commanding gesture, the energy of creation is concentrated (fig. 6-29). Seldom in the history of art has such a small segment of pictorial space been endowed with such powerful meaning. God the Father, his thrusting, forward movement intensified by his billowing cloak, sweeps dramatically toward Adam. A host of putti accompanies God, who with his left arm embraces a female figure who may represent Eve or the Virgin Mary. Adam reclines in a barren landscape, his arm supported by his upraised knee. His figure is so powerfully muscled that even in repose we sense immediately the energy that will be released once God touches him and endows him with a soul, with life.

Following his triumph in Florence with the colossal *David* (see fig. 6-13), Michelangelo was called to Rome in 1506 by Pope Julius II, nephew of Sixtus IV. At first Julius asked Michelangelo to design and execute a grand papal tomb for himself, but by 1508 he had commissioned him to paint the ceiling of the Sistine Chapel, where fifteenth-century artists had decorated the walls with frescoes (fig. 6-30). Michel-

6-31. Michelangelo Buonarroti. Sonnet with a caricature of the artist standing, painting a figure on the ceiling over his head. c. 1510. Pen and ink, 11 x 7". Casa Buonarroti, Florence. In the sonnet, Michelangelo complains of the physical difficulties of painting the Sistine Chapel ceiling in terms that reveal he worked standing, not lying down.

angelo accepted the task grudgingly; as he describes in a sonnet (fig. 6-31), painting the ceiling was a demanding physical labor:

I've got myself a goiter from
   this strain . . .
My beard toward Heaven, I
   feel the back of my brain
Upon my neck, I grow the
   breast of a Harpy;
My brush, above my face
   continually,
Makes it a splendid floor by
   dripping down. . . .
Pointless the unseeing steps
   I go.
In front of me, my skin is
   being stretched
While it folds up behind and
   forms a knot,
And I am bending like a
   Syrian bow. . . .

Although the scheme is often discussed as if Michelangelo were his own iconographer, the complexity of the cycle suggests that the ceiling's intricate iconography was developed in consultation with his patron and one or more theologians. Our first impression of the ceiling is of a maze of complexly posed human figures that have to be seen from different viewpoints (see fig. 6-30). Order, however, is created by the painted architectural framework. The central spine of the ceiling has a sequence of nine scenes, alternating in size from small to large, from passages in Genesis (1:1–9:27).

To see the figures along the side walls, the viewer must turn 90 degrees to the left or right. The largest figures are the Old Testament prophets and ancient Sibyls, who, possessed by the spirit of God, foretold the coming of Christ. In the window **lunettes** and **spandrels**, Michelangelo portrayed the ancestors of Christ.

Another level of figures, nude, males called *ignudi* ("nudes"), are seated in poses that vary from the decorative to the energetic. They support painted bronze medallions decorated with scenes from the Old Testament that refer to wise and just rule. Garlands of oak leaves and acorns, emblems of Julius II's family, are held by some of the *ignudi*, but their primary role is to embellish Michelangelo's cycle.

As our eyes ascend from the first level of ancestral figures toward the histories, the figures in each horizontal level are distinguished by an increasing freedom of movement. In Neoplatonic philosophy (see pages 248–49), unrestricted figural movement was symbolic of the freedom of the human soul to ascend to the divine, for as the soul ascended, it

was believed to be less and less restricted by the bonds of earthly matter: the eloquent movement displayed by the *ignudi* is a metaphor for the freedom of the soul.

The symbolism of our aspiration to join God is conveyed by the central histories, which relate God's love in the acts of creation and in the story of Noah. The cycle runs backward in time, but it has an internal logic. Michelangelo begins with the sin and disobedience of Noah, the most righteous man God could find on earth, to stress the sinfulness of all humanity. What redeems this human sin is the love of God, with which the cycle concludes in the first moment of the Creation. God's initial act of love, dividing Light from Darkness, is painted directly over the altar.

RAPHAEL, STANZA DELLA SEGNATURA

6-32. Raphael. *Philosophy* (popularly known as *The School of Athens*), fresco in the Stanza della Segnatura, Vatican, Rome. 1509–11. 19 x 27'. Commissioned by Pope Julius II

Raphael's *Philosophy* has long been viewed as the ideal of High Renaissance painting (fig. 6-32). Figures that represent venerated ancient philosophers in a consummate variety of postures are composed within a classicizing architectural setting. The use of **scientific perspective**, within a lucid and impressive setting, directs our attention to the two main figures in the center. The **coffered vaults** and the niches with sculpture remind us of the decoration of the baths of ancient Rome (see fig. 3-118) and of Bramante's new church of St.

Peter's (see fig. 6-24), being erected nearby at that very moment by the same patron.

The philosophers in the center are the gray-haired Plato, holding his *Timaeus*, a book on the origin of the universe, and Aristotle, who holds his *Nicomachean Ethics*. Plato points heavenward to indicate his philosophical approach to the world of ideas, while Aristotle gestures over the earth to suggest that the universal can only be understood through examining the natural world. Other philosophers can be identified by their attributes. Euclid,

the geometrician, seen bending over a compass and board in the right foreground, has the features of Bramante, a close friend of Raphael who secured this commission for the young painter from Pope Julius II. Vasari suggests that Bramante designed the architectural setting of this particular scene for his friend. Plato bears a resemblance to the elderly Leonardo, who was in Rome at this time. Raphael himself engages our attention, for in his self-portrait near the right border he looks out at us. By portraying the historical personalities from antiq-

1509–11	**Raphael, frescoes, Stanza della Segnatura**
1514	Papal proclamation against slavery and the slave trade
1515	Thomas More, *Utopia*

6-33. Raphael. Stanza della Segnatura. 1509–11. *Theology*, known as the *Disputà*, is on the wall opposite *Philosophy*, and in the lunette over the window are three Virtues. The room originally functioned as Julius II's study and personal library; only later did it receive the name by which it is known today. The themes chosen for the walls—Philosophy, Theology, Justice, and Poetry—relate to its use as a library. The ability of the High Renaissance to simplify and clarify is evident in this program, which encompasses the four basic realms of scholarship and literature. It has also been suggested that the four themes refer to the pope's interest in Truth (Philosophy and Theology), Goodness (Justice), and Beauty (Poetry). Early sources reveal that Pope Julius II himself designed this impressive program.

uity with the visages of contemporary people, Raphael gave personal meaning to the ideal of the Renaissance as a revival of classical values.

Another portrait is the brooding, melancholic figure in the left central foreground who, pen in hand, appears self-absorbed. His inclusion was an afterthought, for he was painted on a fresh patch of plaster. The figure represents the ancient philosopher Heraclitus, who expressed the solitary, pensive nature of the creative temperament. In pose, the figure recalls the prophets from the Sistine ceiling, while the face suggests that it is a portrait of Michelangelo. Raphael added the figure in homage to the older master, probably after the partially completed Sistine ceiling was unveiled in August 1511.

Theology presents groupings of saints in heaven and theologians on earth, all gathered around a central axis, which descends from God the Father, Jesus Christ, and the Holy Spirit to the bread of the Eucharist displayed on the altar (fig. 6-33). Raphael's composition suggests an apse, and the fresco visually embodies the concept that it is persons—in heaven and on earth—who make up the Church. *Philosophy* and *Theology* face each other in the Stanza della Segnatura, expressing the union that the Renaissance forged between Christian theological values and the classical philosophical tradition.

HIGH RENAISSANCE PAINTING IN VENICE

6-34. Giorgione (completed by Titian). *Sleeping Venus*. c. 1510. Oil on canvas, 3'6³/4" x 5'9"; the figure is lifesize. Staatliche Gemäldegalerie, Dresden, Germany. The painting was apparently damaged at an early date and a kneeling cupid near the feet of the figure, which is the attribute which identified the main figure as Venus, was painted over. An early source suggests that Titian completed both the cupid and the landscape. Giorgione, who died in the great plague of 1510, may have left the work unfinished. The face of Venus has been repainted, probably in the nineteenth century.

6-35. Titian. *Venus of Urbino*. 1538. Oil on canvas, 3'11" x 5'5". Galleria degli Uffizi, Florence. The work was painted for Guidobaldo II della Rovere of Urbino. Although a letter from Guidobaldo to his agent refers to the painting not as Venus, but as *la donna nuda* ("the nude woman"), the roses in her hand and the myrtle, a symbol of Venus, growing in the pot in the background, support an identification with Venus. The dog at her feet has been recognized as an emblem of marital fidelity. Commissioned by Duke Guidobaldo II della Rovere of Urbino

Giorgione's *Sleeping Venus* helped establish the reclining female nude as a standard type in the history of European art (fig. 6-34; for a later example, see fig. 9-48). This subject is obviously erotic, and Giorgione's composition accentuates the sensuous quality of the female body by contrasting the swelling forms of the upper contour—head, breast, abdomen, and wrist—with the long curve of the bottom edge of the figure. The elegant slenderness of Venus's body is emphasized by her pose, with the right arm raised and the right ankle and foot hidden behind the left. The shimmering white drapery and deep red pillow accentuate and enhance the warm flesh tones of the body, isolating the figure in a verdant green landscape with a luminous Venetian sky and clouds. Giorgione established a new oil-painting technique in which the forms are rendered without detail (see page 328). In *Sleeping Venus*, the technique emphasizes the delicacy and softness of the body. The landscape setting removes the figure from the more erotic setting

6-36. Giorgione. *Tempestuous Landscape with a Gypsy and a Soldier* (traditionally known as *The Tempest*). c. 1505–10. Oil on canvas, 30¹/₄ x 28³/₄". Galleria dell' Accademia, Venice. A reference to the painting in 1530 calls it "the little landscape on canvas with the tempest [and] gypsy and soldier."

of a bed, and by representing Venus with her eyes closed, as if asleep, Giorgione encouraged the male patron and his friends to observe her beauty without embarrassment. At the same time, such a pose establishes a certain distance and restraint, and the kneeling cupid may have served as a guardian figure. The ultimate effect is of a slender figure dreaming in a warm Italian landscape.

It is not surprising that one of the first paintings of the sensuous nude was created in Renaissance Venice. Venice, "Queen of the Adriatic," had for centuries been the major trading center between Europe and Asia, and it cultivated its reputation as the most cosmopolitan city in Europe with exotic buildings, fine food, and beautiful courtesans.

Titian's painting (fig. 6-35) was modeled on Giorgione's, perhaps at the request of the patron. The same red, white, and green tones enhance the flesh of the painted figure, but now the setting is an interior, complete with a bed with rumpled sheets and bed curtains. Now the nude is awake: she looks directly at us, posing without embarrassment. Titian's ability to suggest texture is especially evident in the locks of wavy red hair that flow onto her shoulders. The maids in the background are gathering her garments from a Renaissance chest.

Giorgione's *Tempestuous Landscape with a Gypsy and a Soldier* is a difficult work, and scholars have long debated its specific iconographic meaning (fig. 6-36). A young man and a nude woman nursing a child occupy the foreground; their relationship is inexplicable, but the "soldier" seems to be watching over the "gypsy." The landscape that dominates the composition offers both ruins and contemporary buildings. A lightning bolt crosses the background, and the trees are dramatically silhouetted against the eerie light of the stormy sky. The main purpose of this painting may be to set a mood rather than to tell a story, and perhaps we appreciate it best by surrendering logic to feeling. That an emotional sensation should be the main purpose of a work of art is a new idea in the history of art, but one that seems consistent with the Venetian interest in the suggestive and poetic.

HIERONYMUS BOSCH, "GARDEN OF EARTHLY DELIGHTS" TRIPTYCH

6-37. Hieronymus Bosch. *Creation of Eve in the Garden of Eden*; *"Garden of Earthly Delights"*; *Hell* (interior of the *"Garden of Earthly Delights"* triptych). c. 1510–15. Oil on wood, 7'2 5/8" x 6'4 3/4" (center); 7'2 5/8" x 38 1/4" (each wing); the figures in the foreground of the central panel are approximately 10–14 inches tall. Prado, Madrid, Spain. The iconography of the work has been much debated, and there is no general agreement as to its meaning or exact purpose; one suggested interpretation relates it to the contemporary interest in alchemy, a subject investigated in some of Bosch's other works. The work may have been commissioned by Hendrik III of Nassau for the palace of the House of Nassau in Brussels, where it was hanging in 1517. In this setting, the painting must have been a novel secular decoration and a focus for intellectual discussions. Perhaps commissioned by Hendrik III

The left and right wings of the interior of Bosch's **triptych** represent traditional Christian subjects (fig. 6-37). The left wing shows the Garden of Eden, with God the Father creating Eve as Adam looks on, while the right wing presents a vision of the devastation of hell after the Last Judgment. Placed between these views of humanity's past and future is the central panel, which has been interpreted as representing the present, when humanity indulges the sins, begun in the Garden of Eden, that will lead to hell.

Bosch's moral stance seems evident, and few of the hundreds of naked figures cavorting in the expansive garden of the central panel express even momentary delight. In the central section of the detail (fig. 6-38), a man looks up guiltily as he embraces a woman, while nearby figures greedily gather around a giant floating berry. A pearl seeps from between the legs of a couple lying within a giant shell carried by another man. Hundreds of unexpected episodes and surprising details capture our admiration for the

painter's imagination in expressing humanity's determined perversity. In the landscape are real and imaginary birds and beasts, including the owl, symbol of perverted wisdom (it can see only in the dark), and huge raspberries, strawberries, and other fruits, whose multiple seeds hint at rampant promiscuity. The work is executed in seductive pastels. It has been suggested that the theme here is humanity before the great flood, when God, grieving "that he had made man on the earth," destroyed all but Noah and his family (Genesis

1509   Erasmus, *In Praise of Folly*
c. 1510–15   Bosch, *"Garden of Earthly Delights"* triptych
1517   Luther's Ninety-five Theses

6-38. Hieronymus Bosch. *"Garden of Earthly Delights,"* detail of central panel

6:5–6; 6:11–13). Whatever the exact theme, seldom in the history of humanity has the role of evil in the world been more astonishingly and unexpectedly depicted.

In light of the iconography of the main panel, a reexamination of the wings reveals unusual details. The birds, beasts, and plants that inhabit the Garden of Eden include composite creatures that suggest that even in Eden unnatural cross-fertilization has taken place. Life in God's creation is violent: the animals and birds of Paradise already stalk and devour each other. The delighted expression on Adam's face as he ogles the newly created Eve suggests that, in Bosch's interpretation, sexual pleasure is the first thought of the first man.

The devils that populate Bosch's *Hell* provide further evidence that he is the first great artist of the fantastic. The ponds in the left and center panels give way in *Hell* to a wasteland, above which rises an edifice created by a combination of a dead tree and a man that represents the "tavern of lost souls." The Devil is enthroned as a frog with a bird's head who endlessly devours sinners. They are excreted only to face further torment. Although the triptych as a whole is related to Last Judgment paintings, it offers no view of souls in Paradise. In this world, there is no redemption.

Details about Bosch's life help little in clarifying his art. His grandfather and father were both painters. Bosch himself seems to have had a successful life. He was a member of the Brotherhood of Our Lady, a pious religious group, and through his wife he owned a large estate. Internationally known, he received commissions from the archduke of Austria, and his works were collected by important connoisseurs. It has been suggested that the tree-man in the center of *Hell* is a self-portrait. The face, which is in sharp contrast to the other, generalized figures, looks askance at the suffering around him. Bosch has been claimed by the twentieth-century Surrealists as their true ancestor (see page 544).

SIXTEENTH-CENTURY ART   **323**

GERMAN PAINTING: MATTHIAS GRÜNEWALD, *ISENHEIM ALTARPIECE*

6-39. Matthias Grünewald. *Saint Anthony*; *Crucifixion*; *Saint Sebastian*; with the *Lamentation* below, exterior of the *Isenheim Altarpiece*. c. 1512–15. Oil on wood, 9'9$^{1}/2$" x 10'9" (center); 8'2$^{1}/2$" x 3'$^{1}/2$" (each wing); 2'5$^{1}/2$" x 11'2" (base). Musée d'Unterlinden, Colmar, France. The altarpiece was painted for the chapel of the monastic Hospital of St. Anthony at Isenheim, near Colmar. The hospital specialized in treating patients with skin diseases, including leprosy and syphilis, and the monastery chapel was a pilgrimage shrine for those suffering from such diseases. Given the mission of the hospital, the scars and sores on Jesus' body are poignant and appropriate. In the late medieval period, it was believed that all physical illness was a manifestation of spiritual illness, and the first step in treating patients at the Hospital of St. Anthony was to bring them before this *Crucifixion* to pray. Grünewald's representation of Jesus was created so that patients could identify with his sufferings. Probably commissioned by the abbot of the monastery

The monumental *Crucifixion* by Matthias Grünewald (1455–1528) depicts all the gruesome details with unsparing realism (fig. 6-39). Jesus is dead: his head falls dramatically to the side, the blood pouring from the wound in his side begins to congeal, and his body is covered with wounds from the flagellation. The weight of his body pulls down on the crossbar, and the torture wrought by the nails in his hands and feet is painful to see. The lower abdomen is violently compressed, while the rib cage almost bursts through the skin as a result of the anguished death by suffocation brought about by crucifixion. As the Bible relates, darkness envelops the scene. The painting also emphasizes the suffering of the Virgin Mary and Saint John the Evangelist and Mary Magdalene. Saint John the Baptist points to the figure on the cross, stating, "He must become more important, while I must become less important" (John 3:30).

c. 1512–15	**Grünewald**, *Isenheim Altarpiece*
1513	Ponce de León plants orange and lemon trees in Florida
1513	Balboa discovers the Pacific Ocean
1513	First European ship lands in China
1519	Leonardo da Vinci dies in France
1520	Raphael dies in Rome

6-40. Matthias Grünewald. *Annunciation; Mystical Nativity with Musical Angels; Resurrection, Isenheim Altarpiece*, with the outer set of wings open. When the wings seen here were opened, the innermost figures, depicted in sculpture, and two painted wings were visible. For a detail of the Madonna and Child in the *Mystical Nativity*, see figure 6-45.

The dark sky and red garments add drama.

The choice of subjects and their interpretation can be directly related to the position and role of Grünewald's altarpiece within the monastic and hospital complex at Isenheim. Usually the wings were kept closed to emphasize the Crucifixion and Saint Sebastian, invoked by sufferers of the plague and other diseases, and Saint Anthony, patron saint of the monastery. When the *Crucifixion* panel was opened (notice that Grünewald has painted Jesus' body to the right of the opening), the joyful scenes of the *Annunciation*, *Mystical Nativity*, and *Resurrection*, painted with vivid, luminous colors, became visible (fig. 6-40). Certainly these inner panels would have been shown on the feast days of the subjects celebrated here—the Annunciation, Christmas, and Easter. And since Christ's resurrection is celebrated every Sunday, they would most likely have been visible on a weekly basis as well. The innermost decoration, with sculpted figures and two scenes from the life of Anthony, would have been shown on Saint Anthony's feast day.

The contrasts between the various layers of the altarpiece are explicit. In the *Resurrection*, an immediate contrast to the grisly *Crucifixion*, Christ's body is healed and his wounds have become glowing, rubylike jewels. He rises weightless and triumphant while the soldiers guarding the grave fall helplessly in confusion below. The restored beauty of Christ's body would have encouraged hope on the part of the hospital's patients. Even in the joyful scenes, however, a sense of the crucifixion as Christ's destiny is found, for the cloth in which Mary holds the Christ Child in the *Mystical Nativity* (see fig. 6-45) is the same tattered fabric that serves as his loincloth when he is crucified.

TITIAN'S ALTARPIECES

6-41. Titian. *Madonna of the Pesaro Family*. 1519–26. Oil on canvas, 16' x 18'10"; the figures are approximately lifesize. Santa Maria Gloriosa dei Frari, Venice, Italy. The main patron was Jacopo Pesaro, who led papal troops to victory over the Turks in 1502. The armored figure with the banner and the turbaned Turkish prisoner allude to Pesaro's victory. Commissioned by Jacopo Pesaro

6-42. Titian. *Madonna of the Pesaro Family* as seen in situ in its original frame in the Church of Santa Maria Gloriosa dei Frari, Venice. Titian's painting was created to be placed here, in the left side aisle, and his asymmetrical composition is in part inspired by the viewpoint from which one approaches the altar. Titian's huge columns are related to those of the nave of the Gothic structure. X-rays have revealed that Titian tried several solutions to the painting's architectural setting, including one that continued the architectural forms of the painting's frame, before deciding to use dramatic columns to relate his painting to its largest architectural context.

Titian's Pesaro *Madonna* pioneered a dynamic new compositional mode that was championed by Venetian painters during the sixteenth century (figs. 6-41, 6-42). Nothing in earlier Renaissance art prepares us for this asymmetrical composition, with the Madonna set off to one side before grandiose columns seen in diagonal recession.

The six male members of the Pesaro family who gather below, the patron Jacopo on the left and five others to the right, are introduced to the Madonna and Child by Saints Peter and Francis. The movement inherent in Titian's composition is also found in the twisting figure of Saint Peter at the center and in the Madonna and Child, who direct their

attention in opposing directions. The chubby Christ Child kicks his foot and plays with his mother's veil with a liveliness unusual in religious art (see fig. 6-44).

Titian's *Assumption and Coronation of the Virgin* maintains the symmetrical, triangular Renaissance composition, but it accomplishes an effect of dynamic spontaneity

1517	Cairo is sacked by the Turks
1519–26	**Titian, *Madonna of the Pesaro Family***
1521	Martin Luther is condemned by an edict passed at Worms, Germany
1523	Turkeys are introduced into Europe
1529	Martin Luther writes hymns "Away in a Manger" and "A Mighty Fortress Is Our God"

6-43. Titian. *Assumption and Coronation of the Virgin.* c. 1516–18. Oil on wood, 22'6" x 11'10"; the figures are over-lifesize. Santa Maria Gloriosa dei Frari, Venice. This huge altarpiece is still in situ in its original Renaissance frame on the main altar of the Frari in Venice. Despite the rivalry of the light that flows in from the Gothic apse windows, the painting's composition is even discernible from the entrance to the church, some 300 feet away. Commissioned by Germano da Caiole, the abbot of the Monastery of the Frari

through movement, strong color, and painterly brushstrokes (fig. 6-43). The composition is like a target, with the standing figure of the Virgin Mary placed within a circle created by the semicircular frame and a ring of clouds and flying putti below. Above, God the Father sweeps in with open arms to welcome and crown her. The main figures of God the Father and the Virgin wear garments of a brilliant red, and the Virgin's dominance is enhanced by the strong blue cloak that enfolds her. Titian's triad of primary colors is consistent with High Renaissance practices in Rome. Before a realistic blue sky below, two apostles stand out in the group due to their red garments and eloquent gestures. They create the base of Titian's compositional triangle. The combination of rich color with a simple composition is perfect for the altarpiece's position, which demands that it be legible from the main entrance of the church. The ultimate effect is of grandeur and visual richness.

6-44. Venetian. Titian. *Madonna of the Pesaro Family,* detail of figure 6-41

6-45. German. Matthias Grünewald. *Mystical Nativity with Musical Angels,* detail of figure 6-40

This detail from Titian's Pesaro *Madonna,* although substantially reduced in size, reveals the new style of painting pioneered in Venice during the first years of the sixteenth century (fig. 6-44). The traditional techniques of Renaissance painting—tempera on wooden panel and fresco—had proved unsatisfactory in the humid Venetian climate, and by about 1500 oil painting on canvas was becoming the accepted medium. The development of a new technique for painting in oils began with Giorgione (see figs. 6-34, 6-36), who softened his forms and blurred their edges, partly as a result of the influence of Leonardo da Vinci, who visited Venice in 1500. Titian, Giorgione's pupil and friend, went further to develop a style using bold, large strokes that had a profound impact not only on later Venetian painters but also on many other artists in later centuries, including Rubens and Velázquez. Titian's lively, broad brushstrokes have what is known as a **painterly** quality because the motion of his hand is so evident; these

painterly brushstrokes are consistent with his interest in movement and asymmetrical compositions.

In creating a large painting such as the Pesaro *Madonna,* Titian would first paint or stain the canvas a medium brownish-red. He would then boldly outline his forms in dark paint and reinforce them by modeling them in monochrome, from white to black. After this underpainting dried, Titian would add layers and layers of colored translucent oil **glazes** (varnish, often with a small amount of color), building up a rich, sonorous color through their superimposition. Tradition has it that Titian once exclaimed that he used "glazes, thirty or forty!" to achieve this rich effect.

Titian's looser painting technique, as seen in the detail from the *Madonna of the Pesaro Family,* gives pictorial unity because of the continuous texture of brushstrokes. In contrast, the detail from the painting by Grünewald (fig. 6-45) demonstrates hidden brushstrokes, an emphasis on precise detail, and the creation of the illusion of varying textures.

6-46. Titian. *Rape of Europa.* c. 1559–62. Oil on canvas, 6'1" x 6'9". Isabella Stewart Gardner Museum, Boston, Massachusetts. One of a series of *poesie* (poetic mythological themes) painted for Philip II of Spain, this picture depicts the moment when Zeus, having disguised himself as a bull, abducts a beautiful princess. Titian was inspired by the story as it is told in Ovid's *Metamorphoses* (II, 870–75). The unexpected nature of the abduction is expressed in the awkward position of Europa, who seems about to slip off the back of the bull/Zeus. Commissioned by Philip II of Spain

6-47. Titian. *Rape of Europa,* detail

Grünewald's style represents a continuation of the oil technique first developed by Robert Campin and Jan van Eyck (see pages 256–57, 264–65, 270–71).

Later in Titian's life, his brushstrokes became even more bold, and he used large, thick strokes (**impasto**), often of pure color, to define form. In the *Rape of Europa,* (figs. 6–46, 6–47), impasto is evident in the scales of the fish in the foreground, the feathers of the cupids flying at the top, the mountains, and the quickly sketched figures of Europa's abandoned friends, waving from the distant shore. The shape and direction of the brushstroke reinforce the movement of the figures and the directional patterns of the composition. While Titian's rich strokes and bold color accentuate the painting's surface, the diminution of the distant figures and the solidly depicted Europa produce a dramatic effect of space enhanced by the apricot and purple sky in the distance.

LATER MICHELANGELO AND THE DEVELOPMENT OF MANNERISM

6-48. Michelangelo Buonarroti. Medici Chapel, including the Tomb of Giuliano de' Medici and the altar wall. 1524–34. Marble, size of entire bay 23 x 15'; length of reclining figures approx. 7'. New Sacristy, San Lorenzo, Florence. The Giuliano de' Medici commemorated here was the son of Lorenzo the Magnificent and brother of Pope Leo X, who in part sponsored Michelangelo's work at San Lorenzo, the Medici family church in Florence. Michelangelo never saw the Medici Chapel sculptural and architectural ensemble as we see it today; it was assembled by assistants following his designs and instructions. On the wall opposite the Tomb of Giuliano, Michelangelo designed a similar tomb for Lorenzo, the grandson of Lorenzo the Magnificent. Lorenzo is depicted as Contemplative Life, with allegories of Dusk and Dawn beneath his idealized portrait. Commissioned by Cardinal Giulio de' Medici, who later became Pope Clement VII

Michelangelo's Medici Chapel introduces a new vitality and complexity to the interrelationship between sculpture and architecture in sixteenth-century art (fig. 6-48). In the Tomb of Giuliano de' Medici, an idealized portrait of Giuliano as Active Life is seated, clad in ancient Roman armor. Resting atop the sarcophagus are allegories, the female Night and the male Day. Michelangelo's plan called for two allegories of rivers, to be placed on a platform below.

The allegories of the times of day symbolize the passage of time as it consumes mortal life, while the river allegories were perhaps intended to represent the Arno and Tiber to refer to Medici power in Florence and Rome. In his position above, Giuliano transcends both time and matter, fulfilling the spiritual ascent emphasized by the Neoplatonic philosophers (see pages 248–49) and the resurrection to eternal life celebrated in Masses for the dead (a fresco of Christ's resurrection was intended for the altar wall).

The figures of Night and Day are twisted in a manner related to contrapposto, but with a more extreme twisting of the body parts. This type of posture became known later in the century as the *figura serpentinata* ("serpentine figure"). Although developed during the High Renaissance, this pose became a hallmark of Mannerist art.

In the Medici Chapel, the poses are further enlivened by the visual activity of the walls, which give way to planes that articulate different levels of surfaces. The **cornice** is segmented to extend forward into the space of the chapel. The "movement" of these architectural forms establishes a vibrant interplay between the architecture, the sculpture, and the space of the chapel.

1524–34	**Michelangelo, Medici Chapel**
1534	Henry VIII breaks with the Roman Church
1534	Ignatius of Loyola founds the Jesuit Order
1534	Thomas More is beheaded

The visual energy and artistic license exhibited here characterize Mannerism (see pages 332–333), a style that followed and countered the classical idealism of the High Renaissance. Michelanglo's freedom of expression was viewed by younger artists as a force of liberation; at the end of his discussion of the Medici Chapel, Vasari wrote, "Thus all artists are under a great and permanent obligation to Michelangelo, seeing that he broke the bonds and chains that had previously confined them to the creation of traditional forms."

In 1534, Michelangelo left Florence for Rome, never to return. Rome at midcentury was a changed city. The sack of Rome in 1527 by the imperial troops under Charles V, to punish the pope for siding with Charles's enemy, Francis I of France, had been brutal. The impact felt from the Reformation caused further turmoil. The psychological climate was leaden.

Michelangelo was commissioned to paint *The Last Judgment* in the Sistine Chapel, where he had painted the ceiling earlier. Although the ceiling expressed God's love and the promise of salvation (see fig. 6-30), now pessimism broods (fig. 6-49). Christ, on the axis and surrounded by an aura of light, looks toward hell and raises his right hand against the wicked. Mary recoils next to him, "slightly timid in appearance and almost as if uncertain of the wrath and mystery of God," wrote the artist's friend and biographer, Ascanio Condivi, in 1553. Angels blow trumpets to announce the day and awaken the dead.

In the bottom register, to our left, the dead rise, some being pulled from their graves. To our right, the damned are being dragged down to eternal torment. Above, figures ascend to heaven, where the elect flank Christ. In the semicircular lunettes at the top, angels wrestle with the instruments of Christ's pas-

6-49. Michelangelo Buonarroti. *The Last Judgment.* 1534–41. Fresco, 48 x 44'. Sistine Chapel, Vatican, Rome. Originally, many of the figures in *The Last Judgment* were nude, but in the climate of the Counter-Reformation, some observers found nudity offensive in a papal chapel. Between 1559 and 1565, drapery was added to many of the figures and most of these were not removed during the recent restoration. Commissioned by Pope Paul III

sion. Around Christ, martyrs brandish the weapons used to torture and kill them.

To the right of Christ, Saint Bartholomew, who was flayed, looks to Christ. He holds a knife in his right hand, while his flayed skin hangs from his left hand. The face on the skin was identified as Michelangelo's self-portrait only in 1925.

The anguished facial features, which reflect Michelangelo's tortured spirit, add a highly personal message to the painting.

Of Michelangelo's *Last Judgment*, Condivi wrote: "In this work Michelangelo expressed all that the art of painting can do with the human figure, leaving out no attitude or gesture."

MANNERISM

6-50. Bronzino. *The Allegory of Time and Lust*. c. 1545. Oil on wood, 5'1" x 4'8³/4". The National Gallery, London. Much about this painting remains a mystery to us. Although the circumstances of its commission are unknown, it may have been made for the Medici to give to Francis I of France. Probably commissioned by Duke Cosimo de' Medici

The Allegory of Time and Lust, by Bronzino (1503–72), is a visually and iconographically complex painting (fig. 6-50). At the top, allegories of Time and Fraud pull back a blue curtain, revealing the central figure of Venus, who, exposed by a cool, harsh light, is being caressed by her son, Cupid. Additional allegorical figures, including Deceit, to the right, behind the putto, and Jealousy (recently interpreted as representing Syphilis), demonstrate the results of lust. The precise iconography of the work is still debated; this difficulty of interpretation reveals the complex intellectual themes of Mannerist art. The crowded figures and exceptionally varied poses address a new style of highly artificial composition and unusual spatial effects.

Mannerism often invited the knowledgeable viewer to appreciate the subtle and hidden conceits of the work. Mannerist art was not intended to appeal to a mass audience. The works of Michelangelo and Raphael provided a starting point for the Mannerists, who developed selected ideas and forms to achieve a stylized, artificial elegance.

These traits are immediately evident in Cellini's *Saltcellar of Francis I*, which reveals the artist's delight in demonstrating both technical ac-

6-51. Benvenuto Cellini. *Saltcellar of Francis I*. 1543. Gold and enamel, 10$^{1/4}$ x 13$^{1/8}$". Kunsthistorisches Museum, Vienna. Cellini's saltcellar (a receptacle for table salt) was commissioned by the French king Francis I

6-52. Giambologna. *Rape of the Sabine Woman*. Completed 1583. Marble, height 13'6". Loggia dei Lanzi, Florence. The theme is drawn from an event that occurred in the early years of ancient Rome, when the Romans abducted Sabine women as wives. No patron, but purchased by Duke Cosimo de' Medici

complishment and artistic invention (fig. 6-51). In its graceful refinement, the *Saltcellar* reflects the conspicuous wealth and manner of sixteenth-century European courts. In its decorative treatment of counterbalanced nude figures and complex iconographic details, it demonstrates the visual and thematic complexities that occur in Mannerist art. The work was created to delight both the eye and the mind.

Rape of the Sabine Woman, by Giambologna (1524–1608), with its twisting, spiraling, upward movement, was titled only after its completion (fig. 6-52). Contemporary sources reveal that the artist was initially inspired not by a subject but by the challenge to compose a group of multiple interlocking fig-ures in dynamic movement. Giambologna's solution, based on a use of the *figura serpentinata,* offers effective and varied visual expressions when viewed from different positions. The rhythmic interplay of the figurative forms, emphatically stressed along diagonals, contributes to the work's dynamism, while the spiraling movement compels us to walk around the sculpture to view its varied presentations. This complex and energetic spatial involvement is a characteristic of late-sixteenth-century sculpture; it continues the course set earlier by Michelangelo's exaggerated figural style. But whether the sculpture is monumental or more intimate, the dazzling display of the artist as virtuoso performer is apparent.

EARLY LANDSCAPE PAINTING

6-53. Pieter Bruegel the Elder. *December Landscape* (commonly known as *Hunters in the Snow*). 1565. Oil and tempera on wood, 3'10¹/8" x 5'3³/4". Kunsthistorisches Museum, Vienna. This landscape is part of a series of six that represented different times of the year; five survive today. They probably were originally displayed in the home of a wealthy Antwerp banker.

December Landscape (fig. 6-53), by Pieter Bruegel the Elder (1525/30–69), emphasizes nature not only by the vast sweep of the terrain but also by the manner in which the season—as expressed by the landscape—dominates and controls the activities of the peasants. Trudging peasants with a pack of motley dogs lead us into a village scene with skaters in the middle ground. The landscape culminates with distant, atmospheric peaks reminiscent of the Alps, which Bruegel crossed on a trip to Italy. The leaden

gray-green of the sky and its subtle transformation in the colors of the frozen ponds, in combination with the stark, silhouetted trees and birds, evoke the time of year, the kind of day, and even the temperature of the moment.

In earlier periods, landscape was often viewed as an adversary, a frightening and unpredictable element populated with thieves and the unknown. With the exception of some ancient Roman frescoes and mosaics, landscape as a theme developed only late in the history of

art. These examples from the sixteenth century are some of the first paintings to convey appreciation for landscape.

One of the first artists to show an interest in the expressive power of landscape was the German painter Albrecht Altdorfer (1480–1538). His *Battle of Alexander and Darius* is both landscape and history painting (fig. 6-54; for an earlier representation of the same subject, see figure 3-80). The global scope of the landscape is tied to Altdorfer's historical narrative, for he wants to

1565

1558–1603　Queen Elizabeth reigns in England
1565　　　**Pieter Bruegel the Elder,** *December Landscape*
1569　　　The Mercator projection map of the world is published in
　　　　　Flanders

6-54. Albrecht Altdorfer. *Battle of Alexander and Darius*. 1529. Oil on wood, 5'2^{1}/$_{4}$" x 3'11^{1}/$_{4}$". Alte Pinakothek, Munich, Germany. Altdorfer's panoramic landscape combines natural observation with historical fantasy. Its ostensible subject is the famous ancient battle at Issus, where Alexander the Great defeated the Persian king Darius in 331 BCE. This historical theme almost certainly refers to the sixteenth-century hope that German troops would be able to stop the advance of the Ottoman Turks (see page 296) into Europe. Commissioned by the city of Regensburg at the request of Duke Wilhelm of Bavaria

6-55. El Greco. *Toledo*. c. 1600–10. Oil on canvas, 47^{3}/4 x 42^{3}/4". The Metropolitan Museum of Art, New York. El Greco, who was born on the island of Crete and who studied in Venice, lived in Toledo, Spain, from about 1575 until his death in 1614.

H. O. Havemeyer Collection. Bequest of Mrs. H. O. Havemeyer, 1929 (29.100.16)

suggest that the battle at Issus was a struggle for control of the known world. This earthly conflict seems to take on an even cosmic significance, for Altdorfer presents a struggle between the setting sun and the rising moon as they vie for superiority in the background.

Dramatic landscape also marks the work of El Greco (1541–1614). The configuration of hills, valleys, and monuments in this painting identifies the city as Toledo (fig. 6-55), but both the natural forms and the city's structures have been stretched and verticalized to create a nervous effect that is heightened by the somber colors and stormy sky. Along the banks of the river and on the hillsides are tiny human figures, who are dominated and threatened by the landscape. El Greco's vision of the city where he lived is less a portrait than a vehicle to convey a mood of drama and, perhaps, religious ecstasy.

PIETER BRUEGEL THE ELDER

6-56. Pieter Bruegel the Elder. *Peasant Wedding Feast*. c. 1566. Oil on wood, 3'8⁷/₈" x 5'4¹/₈". Kunsthistorisches Museum, Vienna. The bride is the smug woman seated in front of the suspended cloth with a crown above her head. To either side are the groom and the couple's parents. To the right, a priest is in conversation with a distinguished-looking man who probably represents the landowner for whom these peasants worked.

In his *Peasant Wedding Feast*, Bruegel emphasizes the rustic nature of peasant life (figs. 6-56, 6-57). The huge, grain-filled barn of a prosperous landowner is the site where a wedding feast is being celebrated. In the right foreground, two men carry food on a huge makeshift tray composed of a door balanced on two sticks. A guest reaches eagerly to pass the plates. The composition is based on the strong right-to-left diagonal recession of the table, which is opposed by the movement of the figures carrying the food. The lower right corner offers a glimpse of a chair; the left has a figure pouring beer into a miscellany of jugs and a child licking his fingers. Bruegel's palette, with simple browns set off by white, red, and the abundant gold of the grain, suggests the rich simplicity of peasant life.

For the twentieth-century observer, Bruegel's paintings of peasant life provide a fascinating source of knowledge about lower-class life, but the function of these paintings for Bruegel and his contemporaries is uncertain. Details of the present picture suggest some criticism of peasant life: the smugness of the bride, the gluttony of the participants, the fact that the priest and the landowner have withdrawn from the rest of the crowd. In the

1565	Tobacco is introduced into Britain
c. 1566	**Pieter Bruegel the Elder, *Peasant Wedding Feast***
1578	China's population reaches 60 million

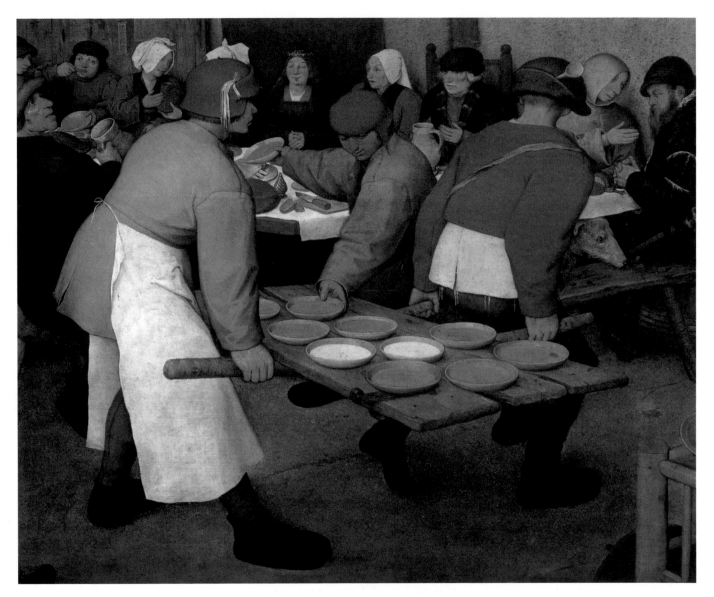

6-57. Pieter Bruegel the Elder. *Peasant Wedding Feast*, detail

absence of evidence to the contrary, however, it is reasonable to suggest that Bruegel was recording, not condescending. He may have decided to capture the local traditions that enrich daily life specifically because they represent the actual and expected.

Bruegel was a friend of intellectuals, and his works were collected by connoisseurs. He also designed prints, including copies after works by Bosch and works in Bosch's style. Bruegel traveled as far as Italy. He died, only in his late thirties or early forties, in 1569. During Bruegel's lifetime, the Netherlands was engaged in a long battle for independence against foreign overlords. Some of his paintings representing the horrors of war refer to this conflict, and in some, specific details convey the dignity of the local populace and the oppression of the Spanish. In this light, it is tempting to question whether Bruegel's emphasis on local traditions in the peasant paintings could also have a patriotic connotation. The peasant pictures represent the vitality of Northern life, but without any obvious reference to the Spanish overlords who governed the subservient nation.

ISLAMIC ART OF THE OTTOMANS

6-58. Prayer rug. Second half of 16th century. Silk warp and weft with cotton and wool pile, 5'8" x 4'2". The Metropolitan Museum of Art, New York. The composition symbolizes the gardens of Paradise. In the central compartment hangs a mosque lamp designating a mihrab. The four hexagonal buildings above the central niche represent heavenly pavilions, perhaps the domiciles of the souls of the righteous.

The James F. Ballard Collection, Gift of James F. Ballard, 1922 (22.100.51)

6-59. Illuminated frontispiece of a Koran. Transcribed by Ahmed Karahisari in 953; illuminated edition for Suleiman I, 1546–47. Gold marginal drawings, watercolors on folios, each 11⁷/16 x 7⁵/16". Topkopi Sarayi Museum, Istanbul, Turkey. The Ottomans, like other Islamic societies, regarded calligraphy as the noblest of the arts. To copy the holy book, the Koran, was considered an act of piety and devotion. Commissioned by Sultan Suleiman I the Magnificent

6-60. Sinan. Suleimaniye complex, Istanbul. 1551–58. Commissioned by Sultan Suleiman I the Magnificent

During the mid-sixteenth century, the Ottoman Empire (1299–1922) under the leadership of Sultan Suleiman I (1520–66) extended in the west to Greece, Albania, and Yugoslavia; into central Europe; across North Africa; to the central, historic Islamic lands of Saudi Arabia and the regions along the Arabian Gulf and the Red Sea. The Ottoman sultan—the central political leader, chief military officer, and protector of Islam—was also guardian of Mecca, Medina, and Jerusalem, the holy cities of the Islamic world, and ruled over the cultural centers of Damascus and Cairo.

The centralized administrative structure of the Ottoman state was also applied to artistic production. Societies of artists—including calligraphers, painters, bookbinders, jewelers, metalsmiths, woodworkers, tailors, hatmakers, and bootmakers—were created to respond to the needs of the palace. Each society had a chief, a deputy chief, master workers, and apprentices. All were paid daily wages by the state. The most influential of these groups was the *nakkashane* (imperial painting studio), which formulated the decorative themes and designs that were eventually transmitted to various court arts, from architectural decoration and furnishings to metalwork, textiles, ceramics, and rugs (fig. 6–58) but were first employed in manuscripts, such as the pages of the Koran illustrated here (fig. 6-59). The *nakkashane* was the creative source for the Ottoman court style. Its influence could be felt in all parts of the empire.

The most conspicuous feature of Ottoman court art of this period is the representation of nature in depictions of flora in perpetual growth. This theme, executed in styles that reflected both mystical and naturalistic approaches, was meant to highlight the essence of nature: beauty and perpetuity. Objects produced in the imperial workshops re-created an enchanted forest inhabited by mythical creatures and naturalistic flora.

Suleiman's court architect, Sinan (c. 1491–1588), was responsible for all construction throughout the empire, including roads, bridges, and waterworks. On top of the highest hill in the imperial Ottoman capital of Istanbul, Sinan designed a huge mosque complex (*kulliÿe*) for Suleiman (figs. 6-59–6-61), which included four colleges, a Koranic school, baths, a hospital, a market street, an inn for travelers, a soup kitchen, and, in the adjoining cemeteries, tombs for Suleiman and his wife Roxelana. The purpose of such a complex was to fulfill Islam's requirement that all Muslims practice charity, but the design of the mosque had its roots in Byzantine architecture. When the Ottoman Turks captured Constantinople in 1453, one of Mehmet the Conqueror's first acts was to declare that Hagia Sophia (see figs. 4-22–4-24), the Byzantine palace chapel and coronation church, should become a mosque. The enormous scale of this domed building and its connection to the Byzantine palace meant that it had a political content that Mehmet intended to neutralize. At the same time, Hagia Sophia's grand but ethereal unified space also meant that it would be appropriate for the worship of the single god, Allah, of Islam. Later Ottoman mosques were inspired by Hagia Sophia, and Suleiman apparently gave Sinan the challenge of creating a rival to the older structure in the Suleimaniye. Sinan followed the basic design of the Byzantine church, but his space is even more centralized and simplified. He indicates the **qibla** and the **mihrab** by a sophisti-

6-61. Dome, Suleimaniye complex

6-62. Plan of Suleimaniye complex

cated use of marble, stained glass with calligraphic designs, and wood, ivory, and mother-of-pearl–decorated doors and shutters. The view of the mosque from the entrance to the arcaded courtyard is a skillful massing of domes and half domes.

Originally the mosque at the Suleimaniye was filled with prayer rugs, or *seccades*. Characterized by

their small size and stylized decor (see fig. 6-58), these rugs were meant to be used by one person in private devotion or at the mosque as part of a group. Each *seccade* includes a depiction of a mihrab (see pages 190–91), identified by arches supported by columns. The niche oriented the *seccade*—and the worshiper—toward Mecca.

LATE-SIXTEENTH-CENTURY ARCHITECTURE

6-63. Palladio. San Giorgio Maggiore, Venice. Begun 1566. Andrea di Pietro della Gondola was given the nickname "Palladio," an allusion to Pallas Athena, the Greek goddess of wisdom. Commissioned by the monastery's abbot, Andrea Pampuro da Asolo

6-64. Interior, San Giorgio Maggiore, Venice

The church of San Giorgio Maggiore, with its white marble **facade** radiant against the blue sky and water, is built on an island just across the lagoon from the main public square of Venice (fig. 6-63). Renaissance architects had long wrestled with one major problem of facade design for **basilica** churches: how to reconcile the different roof heights of the **nave** and side **aisles** within a visually coherent design. Palladio's novel solution was to superimpose one classical temple front, reaching the height of the nave, over another, broader temple front, spanning the width of the side aisles. The use of the **giant order** unifies the double-tiered arrangement, while the **pediments** create a dynamic, axial accent. The facade is vigorous and simple. Its commanding scale and Renaissance harmony carry especially well from the public square near San Marco.

The articulation of the facade design is carried through the interior (fig. 6-64). Shorter **pilasters**, corresponding to those on the lower, broader temple front on the exterior, face the side aisles, while a giant order of pilasters and **engaged columns** face the nave, **crossing**, and **apse**.

Palladio's designs, whether for ecclesiastical or secular architecture, such as the Villa Rotonda (see fig. 1-7), express visual harmony. Palladio's proportional systems were derived from musical scales, and they governed the interrelationship of all of the parts of a building as a totality.

Palladio had an incalculable influence on later developments in Western architecture because his ideas were published in editions illustrated with ground plans, sections, and elevations of his buildings. Palladio's *Four Books on Architecture*, first published in 1570, found their way into many great European and American libraries, including those of Robert Adam (see fig. 8-3) and Thomas Jefferson (see figs. 8-19–8-21).

The concerns of the Counter-Reformation and the Council of Trent found an important architectural expression in Il Gesù, the main church of the Jesuit Order in Rome (figs. 6-65–6-67). The design, by Giacomo da Vignola (1507–73), emphasizes the importance of having a unified congregation during services. The side aisles are transformed into chapels that open off the nave, and the **transepts** have been shortened, creating a monumental interior space that is both compact and unified.

The classical vocabulary of columns, **entablatures**, and pediments on the facade (see fig. 6-67) has its roots in Renaissance designs, but della Porta's combination offers a new sense of drama. The pilasters and engaged columns create a sequence that builds, visually and literally, toward a climax at the central door, which is framed by both a rounded and a triangular pediment and is emphasized by a cornice that, instead of being flat, is thick-

6-65. Giacomo da Vignola. Plan of Il Gesù, Rome. 1568. Commissioned by the Jesuit Order

6-66. Giacomo da Vignola. Interior, Il Gesù, as represented in a 1639–41 painting by Andrea Sacchi and Jan Miel, which shows a visit to the church by Pope Urban VIII. The painting is now in the Galleria Nazionale d'Arte Antica, Rome. Between 1672 and 1685, Gaulli and Bernini decorated the nave ceiling with the *Triumph of the Name of Jesus* (see fig. 7-5).

6-67. Giacomo della Porta. Facade, Il Gesù, Rome. c. 1575–84. Although Vignola had submitted a design for the facade, the Jesuit who was in charge of the church's construction, Father Giovanni Tristano, chose della Porta's design instead. Commissioned by the Jesuit Order and Father Giovanni Tristano

ened at certain points to emphasize the architectural rhythms of the pilasters and columns below; this is called a **broken cornice**. On the upper story, a temple facade has a similar effect. The design, created by the dynamic interplay of architectural elements, will be further developed by Baroque architects in the seventeenth century.

VERONESE AND THE IMPACT OF THE COUNTER-REFORMATION

6-68. Paolo Veronese. *Last Supper/Feast in the House of Levi*. 1573. Oil on canvas, 18'3" x 42'. Galleria dell' Accademia, Venice. Veronese continued to paint in the Venetian High Renaissance style. Probably commissioned by Andrea Buono, a friar in the monastery

At first glance, this huge and sumptuous painting by Paolo Veronese (1528–88) seems to represent a secular banquet (fig. 6-68). The setting is a palatial loggia, and the figures at the table are surrounded by richly costumed servants. However, Veronese created this work in response to a commission to paint a Last Supper for the refectory of the monastery of Santi Giovanni e Paolo in Venice. His interpretation of the Last Supper was questioned by the patron, at which point Veronese was called before one of the Inquisition tribunals established by the Catholic Church (see page 298). The transcript from his trial survives, giving us rare insight into a confrontation between the needs of the Counter-Reformation Church and the nature of artistic freedom in Italy during the Renaissance:

INQUISITIONER: What is the significance of those armed men dressed as Germans, each with a halberd [battle weapon] in his hand?

VERONESE: We painters take the same license the poets and jesters take. . . . They are placed here so that they might be of service because it seemed to me fitting that the master of the house, who was great and rich, should have such servants.

INQUISITIONER: And that man dressed as a buffoon with a parrot on his wrist, for what purpose did you paint him on that canvas?

VERONESE: For ornament, as is customary. . . .

INQUISITIONER: Did anyone commission you to paint Germans, buffoons, and similar things in that picture?

VERONESE: No, milords, but I received the commission to decorate the picture as I saw fit. It is large and, it seemed to me, it could hold many figures.

INQUISITIONER: Are not the decorations which you painters are accustomed to add to paintings or pictures supposed to be suitable and proper to the subject . . . ? Does it seem fitting at the Last Supper of the Lord to paint buffoons, drunkards, Germans, dwarfs and similar vulgarities?

VERONESE: No, milords.

INQUISITIONER: Do you not know that in Germany and in other places infected with heresy [Protestantism]

6-69. Jacopo Tintoretto. *Last Supper*. 1592–94. Oil on canvas, 12' x 18'8". San Giorgio Maggiore, Venice (see page 340 for a discussion of San Giorgio Maggiore). Tintoretto's painting is stylistically related to Mannerist developments. Probably commissioned by Michele Alabardi, prior of San Giorgio Maggiore

it is customary with various pictures . . . to mock . . . and scorn the things of the Holy Catholic Church in order to teach bad doctrines to foolish and ignorant people? . . .

VERONESE: Illustrious Lords, I do not want to defend it, but I thought I was doing right. I did not consider so many things and I did not intend to confuse anyone.

The tribunal contended that Veronese's *Last Supper* lacked decorum because the inclusion of so many extra figures was inappropriate to the subject. It was suggested that the secular elements could be viewed as an attempt to confuse and belittle the Church's authority. Veronese's additional figures should be understood as a reflection of the extrava-gances of Venetian society rather than the ideas of the Reformation, and the artist based his defense on artistic license. He argued that artists should have the right to adorn and decorate their work as they saw fit. Ultimately he satisfied the tribunal by changing the name of the painting to suggest that it represented another New Testament story, the feast in the house of Levi (Luke 5:29–39), in which Jesus dined with tax collectors.

The *Last Supper* (fig. 6-69) by Jacopo Tintoretto (1518–94) shares elements with Veronese's painting, such as the inclusion of a number of servant figures and animals, but it offers an emphasis on the mystical content of this subject that is in keeping with the attitudes of the Counter-Reformation Church. The strong diagonal of the table is a departure from the traditional Last Supper format, in which the table was placed parallel to the picture plane (see fig. 5-60). The powerful thrust of the table into space creates a visual tension that complements Tintoretto's dynamic treatment of the theme. Jesus rises, his head surrounded by an intense glowing halo, to offer the bread, predicting the Eucharist, to the apostles. The space of the room is energized and spiritualized by ethereal angels, whose transparent, swirling forms emphasize the spirituality of this moment. The visual drama of the painting demands an emotional response from the viewer, while its didactic role promotes the Counter-Reformation ideal of the Church as the path to salvation.

THE ART OF ZEN BUDDHISM IN JAPAN

6-70. Teahouse, Japan. Momoyama period, c. 1573–1615. Hara Collection, Yokohama, Japan. The teahouse, usually small and humble in appearance, was designed out of natural materials in order to blend with its setting. The interior, where the tea ceremony took place, was entered through an entrance that was usually so small that guests had to bend low or even crawl through its opening. This gesture was presumably symbolic of shedding one's status. In the soft interior light, guests were to admire the painting or calligraphy hanging before them and eat the sweets and sip the tea prepared for them by the host and tea master.

6-71. Cold water jar *(mizusashi)*. Momoyama period, late 16th century. Shino ware, stoneware with feldspathic glaze over painted iron-oxide decoration, height 7". Seattle Art Museum, Seattle, Washington

Eugene Fuller Memorial Collection

6-72. Sesshu. *Winter Landscape.* Ashikaga period, c. 1500. Hanging scroll, ink and slight color on paper, height 18$^{1/4}$". Tokyo National Museum, Tokyo, Japan. In 1431, at age eleven, Sesshu entered a Zen monastery and was ordained early as a priest. He became a student of Zen priest-painters, and in 1468 he went to China for a year, where he studied Chinese landscape painting and was honored as a Zen priest. From 1481 to 1484, he made pilgrimages all over Japan to study landscape. His paintings, which gained him a wide reputation in Japan, were intentionally different in temperament and effect from the Chinese paintings that he knew so well (compare fig. 4-50). Sesshu's paintings, spontaneous and natural, deemphasize complexity; *Winter Landscape* is both direct and simple. His brushstrokes, firm and bold, are thought to be animated with the spirit of transience because they are executed rapidly and spontaneously. These qualities are essential to the Zen conception of the transience of the spirit and of life. Probably commissioned by the Ouchi family, rulers of Yamaguchi, Honshu's westernmost province

During the fifteenth and sixteenth centuries, a period of civil disorder in Japan, islands of repose and tranquillity could be found in many bustling urban centers. The gate into the precinct of a temple or teahouse (fig. 6-70) led from the ordinary world into a realm devoted to repose and beauty. At the teahouse, the host invited friends of like artistic tastes not only to share tea but also to enjoy an inspired choice of art objects. The ceramic (fig. 6-71) and **lacquer** wares used for serving the tea, the particular scroll painting chosen for that day (fig. 6-72), and the garden (fig. 6-73) all contributed to the harmony of the experience. With the changing seasons and moods, this experience could never be recaptured in quite the same way again.

The animating spirit of the age was Zen, a meditative sect of Buddhism (see page 185). It was the religion of the samurai, who were the patrons of the arts associated with *cha no yu*—the art of tea. The Zen sensibility is primarily concerned with inner rather than outer form. Thus, each object was intended to speak directly to the heart or fulfill

c. 1573–1615	**Teahouse, Japan**
1578	Catacombs of Rome are discovered
1581	Russian conquest of Siberia
1592	Pompeii is discovered
1607	Monteverdi writes *Orfeo*, considered the first opera

the spirit. Recognition of inward form required mental discipline that was based on the ephemeral, the transience of life. Zen taught that there was no Buddha except the Buddha in your own nature and that only through meditation could you realize your own Buddha nature. You achieved enlightenment—an intuitive identification of spirit and object—when you realized unity with yourself and with all things. Zen doctrine, simple and direct, had an immediate appeal to the pragmatic, military samurai. The arts were inspired by the Zen apprehension of the spiritual identity of all things, by an appreciation of direct, intuitive perception, and by aesthetic standards that stressed subtlety, allusiveness, and restraint.

Tea was brought to prominence by monks who went to China to study Zen Buddhism in the twelfth century. Tea functioned as a stimulant to aid their study and meditation and was considered a medicinal beverage. Tea made its way into the society through the teachings of Zen to become the focus of gatherings of the nobility and the samurai and, eventually, the common people.

The most famous and revered Zen tea master, Sen no Rikyu, lived in the sixteenth century. He developed a set of aesthetic ideals that became the basis for Japanese etiquette and taste as part of the tea ceremony. The ceremony had four requirements: harmony, respect, purity, and tranquillity. Two all-important tea ceremony qualities were *sabi* (studied nonchalance)

6-73. Soami (attributed). Dry garden of the Daisenin of Daitokuji, Kyoto, Japan. Ashikaga period, early 16th century. The garden is sited on a small space on the east side of the building. Its depth from the edge of the veranda, where one would meditate upon it, to the clay wall opposite is no more than 10 feet.

and *wabi* (quiet simplicity). The choice of unadorned, unpretentious tea utensils represented a pursuit of these qualities in material form. The goal was to recognize and appreciate (or create) with discriminating taste the inherent characteristics of all things associated with tea.

Japanese gardens, which were attached to private homes as well as monasteries, were planned to correspond to the essentials of Zen beliefs. Because they were a means for Zen self-examination, spiritual refinement, and ultimate enlightenment, they were not created for idle viewing or simple pleasure. Zen qualities are unmistakable in the dry garden at Daisenin, a temple at Daitokuji in Kyoto, attributed to Soami—a painter, poet, and practitioner of broad aesthetic knowledge and talent. Here, stones and gravel

represent a course of water falling over a waterfall (to the right), racing along a mountain riverbed, and finally flowing into a broad river (at the bottom). It was thought to preserve an individual, spontaneous expression and could, therefore, never be copied or even approximated. It was an object of meditation.

The gardens associated with homes and areas surrounding the teahouses are usually "wet" gardens. Guests could wander through them, appreciating the qualities of nature emphasized in the design before eventually arriving at the rustic, intimate house where tea would be served. Zen objects and practices required an expression of restraint, vitality, and intimacy that was intended to capture the "inner form" of life's spirit so essential to the core of Zen thought.

PART 7
SEVENTEENTH-CENTURY ART

7-1. Gianlorenzo Bernini. *David*. 1623. Marble, height 5'5". Galleria Borghese, Rome, Italy. Commissioned by Cardinal Scipione Borghese

INTRODUCTION TO SEVENTEENTH-CENTURY ART

In their exuberant representation of vivacious movement and in the ways they engage our attention, Bernini's *David* and Hals's *Merry Drinker* (figs. 7-1, 7-2) are characteristic of much of the art produced during the seventeenth century in Europe. In his depiction of the Old Testament hero David, Bernini (1598–1680) has caught the figure coiled in space like a taut spring, about to sling the stone at the giant Goliath. His bursting energy urges us to move out of the line of fire. In the painting by Frans Hals (c. 1581–1666), a man invites us to join him in a drink: we impulsively want to reach out and grab the glass he holds so precariously. The loose brushstrokes and warm, golden color enhance the movement and naturalism of the painting.

In creating his tour de force, Bernini, an Italian, was certainly aware that his work would be compared to the sculptures of David by his two great predecessors, Donatello and Michelangelo (see figs. 5-42, 6-13). He rivals their accomplishments by representing a new moment in the David narrative. His choice of the instant of greatest action is consistent with much of European seventeenth-century art. Hals's painting is a work virtually without precedent, in part because it is the product of a new kind of society— the mercantile, bourgeois, Protestant nation established in the Netherlands in the seventeenth century. Despite significant differences in medium, size, and function, these works are similar in the artists' determination to involve us in the action they represent and in their emphasis on depicting arrested motion.

The art of the seventeenth century, however, is not this simple. The two qualities cited above, which are part of a movement within the century known as the European

7-2. Frans Hals. *Merry Drinker*. 1628–30. Oil on canvas, 31⁷/₈ x 26¹/₄". Rijksmuseum, Amsterdam, Netherlands

Baroque (see below), are not shared by all seventeenth-century European works, in part because of increasingly complex and diverse developments in history.

HISTORY

Europe had become steadily more prosperous in the course of the sixteenth century, partly as a result of the influx of wealth from the Americas and the development of new markets there. European wealth continued to increase in the seventeenth century, especially in areas with stable governments and strong commercial and trading interests. The centers of European financial power gradually shifted northward, to the rapidly growing cities of Amsterdam, Paris, and London.

Much of the pluralism of seventeenth-century art can be related to historical developments, for it is during this century that many of the national identities recognized today were consolidated as the map of Europe assumed territorial divisions similar to those of the twentieth century. New, or newly powerful, national entities had a profound influence on artistic developments.

The establishment of the new republic of the Netherlands was perhaps the most dramatic historical development of the seventeenth century in Europe. By 1609, the rebels from the northern Netherlands won their independence after a decades-long war against Spanish Catholic overlords. The new nation was unlike any other in Europe, for it was a true republic, with no traditional hereditary aristocracy. It was governed by merchants, who quickly developed a sound commercial basis for the economy. By providing goods at more reasonable prices, they developed markets all over Europe and the Americas. Although the Netherlands became largely middle class, a number of successful business entrepreneurs achieved great wealth. Amsterdam became the fastest-growing city in Europe, and the Netherlands soon had a more highly urbanized population than any other European country. In addition, it became Europe's leading maritime power, establishing the East and West India Companies and taking control of much of international commerce, including a monopoly on the spice and the slave trades. The Dutch were both Protestant and tolerant, and Jews who fled Poland, Spain, and Portugal during this period largely settled in the Netherlands. Amsterdam also became a lively intellectual community and the most important book-publishing center in Europe. It was in the Netherlands that the new theories of the French philosopher René Descartes, which were founded on the principle of universal doubt, were published. It should be no surprise that important new developments in art occurred here.

By the end of the seventeenth century, France, with a population of approximately 19 million, was the largest nation in Europe and the strongest and wealthiest. Reunited by Henry IV at the beginning of the century, the monarchy consolidated its power under a series of energetic and able administrators—Richelieu, Mazarin, and Colbert—during the reigns of Louis XIII and Louis XIV. Under Louis XIV, the Sun King, who ruled until 1715, the centralization of power and wealth under the monarchy was completed. The power of the traditional nobility in France was broken, and the king governed as a supreme and autocratic ruler. By the end of the century, France had an army of 150,000 that was feared throughout Europe.

The decline of Spain as a European power, which had begun in the sixteenth century, continued. Spain's economy was stagnant, despite its important territories. It still controlled the southern Netherlands (or Flanders, roughly equivalent to today's Belgium) and all of Italy south of Rome, including the huge shipping port of Naples. But the conservative rigidity of the Spanish court restricted growth. The Spanish Netherlands remained Catholic and under the control of a traditional aristocracy, but it had been substantially weakened by its foreign overlords, and the country's outstanding Baroque artist, Peter Paul Rubens, found his most important commissions outside his homeland.

The central and northern portions of the Italian peninsula were still controlled by local city-states, the largest of which were Milan and Venice. Here, too, the economy stagnated, with Venice gradually losing its traditional maritime supremacy in the Mediterranean to English and Dutch shippers, whose prices were substantially lower. The most powerful political force in Italy was the papacy in Rome, which during the seventeenth century flourished under dynamic and ambitious popes. They rebuilt Rome with glorious Baroque monuments, fought Protestantism, and reasserted the authority of the Catholic Church.

Germany was devastated by the Thirty Years' War (1618–48), which destroyed the power of the Holy Roman Empire and killed at least one-third of its population. Political turmoil consumed energies in England, where Charles I, important collector and art patron, was overthrown and beheaded in 1649.

In 1644, the Ming dynasty in China, which had ruled since 1368, fell as a result of an economic depression, governmental incompetence and corruption, and factionalism. It was succeeded by the Qing (Manchu) dynasty, a group of outsiders who would rule until 1912. The Manchu emperors quickly adopted Chinese ways, supporting literature and the arts in ways such as collecting earlier Chinese art and commissioning works in a traditional Chinese style.

Edo (Tokyo) continued to be the capital of Japan during this period. The elegance of the Momoyama period (1573–1615) was replaced by the so-called Edo period (1615–1868), a time of military dictatorship. Samurai—warrior aristocrats—and an expanded mercantile class were important patrons of the arts, and following their interests, the developing arts were sometimes secular in tone and content. European traders and missionaries were expelled in 1638, and Japan remained almost totally isolated until the nineteenth century.

In India, the Mughals continued to extend their authority—and Islam—over North India, which was largely unified as the Mughal empire under Shah Jahan. It was this Mughal ruler who brought in international craftspeople, including stonecutters from Italy, to design and build one of the most famous of Mughal monuments, the Taj Mahal in Agra, India (c. 1632–48), as a tomb and shrine for his beloved wife, Mumtaz-i-Mahal.

INTELLECTUAL AND SCIENTIFIC ACTIVITY IN EUROPE

The explosion of printed information that followed the invention of movable type in the fifteenth century led to

7-3. Annibale Carracci. Ceiling fresco, Farnese Gallery, Farnese Palace, Rome. c. 1597–1604. 67 x 20'. Commissioned by Cardinal Odoardo Farnese

greatly increasing levels of literacy. By the end of the seventeenth century, almost half of the adult male population of Europe was literate. In addition, scientific questioning, which had been made more possible after the Reformation, led to important advances in medicine and the other sciences by such major figures in scientific theory and invention as Bacon, Galileo, Newton, Harvey, Hobbes, Kepler, Locke, Leeuwenhoek, Descartes, and Pascal. Many of the European capitals developed academies and learned institutions in science and in other areas, which began publishing scholarly periodicals to promote the advancement of knowledge. In literature, poetry and drama found a new, more vivid and emotional expressiveness in the works of Milton, Corneille, Molière, Racine, and Shakespeare. The caricature, a humorous or critical portrait based on exaggeration, had been invented earlier, but in the seventeenth century it was popularized and developed by Bernini and Annibale Carracci. At the end of the century in Florence, a group interested in reviving ancient Greek drama offered musical presentations that led directly to the development of opera. One of the first of these compositions was Jacopo Peri's *Euridice*, which was performed at the marriage by proxy of Marie de' Medici to Henry IV of France in 1600 (see page 364). One of the guests was the artist Rubens.

THE STYLES OF SEVENTEENTH-CENTURY EUROPEAN ART

Given the complexity of the historical and intellectual developments of this period, it should not be a surprise to learn that seventeenth-century art encompasses a number of different styles. The most typical style is known as the Baroque, a term sometimes confusingly applied to all art produced in the seventeenth century. In painting, this style is characterized by asymmetrical compositions, powerful effects of movement, and strong lighting in combination with dramatic interpretations of subject matter. Similar effects in sculpture are accomplished, often with rich materials and surprising light sources from hidden windows. In Baroque architecture,

the classical orders continue to be used as vocabulary, but they are arranged in new patterns that are dynamic and energetic. The Baroque is a style that was especially suited to the goals of autocratic rulers of the Counter-Reformation Catholic Church. The origins of the word *baroque* are uncertain, although some have traced it to the Portuguese word *barroco*, meaning an irregularly shaped pearl; in any case, the term *baroque* seems to have first been used to describe works of art in the eighteenth century, when it became a derogatory term for works that were considered strange, irregular, and irrational.

During the seventeenth century, there was also interest in continuing the classicism of the High Renaissance, although with a greater complexity of composition and in a grander and more highly decorative manner. These stylistic qualities were usually reserved for subjects drawn from classical mythology or history. This style can be called Baroque Classicism. A typical example is Annibale Carracci's ceiling fresco decoration for the Farnese Palace in Rome (fig. 7-3). The theme is mythological (the loves of the ancient gods) and his sources of inspiration include Michelangelo, Raphael, and classical sculpture; compared to these earlier works, however, the ceiling decoration is

7-4. Gianlorenzo Bernini. Fountain of the Four Rivers. 1648–51. Marble and travertine, with Egyptian-style obelisk. Piazza Navona, Rome. The obelisk recycled here, long thought to be an ancient Egyptian original, is in reality an imitation commissioned by the emperor Domitian in the first century CE for the circus (a racetrack and site for other games) that he built in Rome at this location. Commissioned by Pope Innocent X Pamphili

more complex and ornate. Examples of Baroque Classicism in architecture are Versailles (see fig. 7-43) and Christopher Wren's St. Paul's Cathedral in London.

A third style, the Dutch Baroque, is limited to painting. This style is represented by thousands of Dutch paintings of Dutch subjects, characterized by their realism and naturalism. Although some of these paintings can be shown to have certain elements in common with Baroque works elsewhere (as was demonstrated with Hals's *Merry Drinker*), Dutch Baroque paintings are noted for their relatively small scale and their choice of Dutch subjects. Mythological and religious paintings were usually avoided. The exception is the work of Rembrandt

(1606–69), who cannot be characterized as a Dutch Baroque artist (as the style has been defined above) and whose style at different times in his life has affinities both with the Baroque and with Baroque Classicism.

Some seventeenth-century works overlap categories, and some fall outside the three that have been defined here (as do those of the Spanish painter Velázquez). The stylistic distinctions drawn here are merely an aid in understanding the complex art of this century. These distinctions will be refined and expanded in subsequent discussions of individual works, but in the final analysis it must be admitted that seventeenth-century works of art cannot be easily categorized.

7-5. Giovanni Battista Gaulli (assisted by Gianlorenzo Bernini). *Triumph of the Name of Jesus,* ceiling fresco with gilded stucco surround and white stucco angels by Antonio Raggi, Il Gesù, Rome. 1672–85. Gaulli is also known by the nickname "Baciccio." This decoration fills the blank ceiling seen in figure 6-66. Commissioned by Father Oliva, Father General of the Society of Jesus

SEVENTEENTH-CENTURY EUROPEAN ART

In Italy, Flanders, and Spain—countries that remained Catholic—the Counter-Reformation (see page 298) led to the production of dramatic Baroque religious images, especially of subjects that fostered and supported Catholic beliefs: the lives of Jesus and the Virgin Mary, the miracles and martyrdoms of saints, and the lives of monks, nuns, and priests. Elaborate cycles of paintings of religious subjects and dramatic sculptural groupings were produced for churches throughout the Catholic world. Architecture in these areas generally followed the same enthusiastic Baroque style.

In the Netherlands, the prevailing religion of Calvinism, which forbade the representation of God or Christ, led to a virtual moratorium on the production of religious subjects (again, Rembrandt stands as a distinct exception). At the same time, the absence of aristocratic or royal patronage meant a decline in interest in mythological subjects. The lively artistic production in the Netherlands specialized in naturalistic paintings of Dutch subjects—landscapes, **genre** themes (the representation of scenes of everyday life), still lifes, portraits—for the home. There was little interest in grand architectural or sculptural projects.

In the countries that had a strong court and aristocracy—France, Flanders, Spain—and in the Italian cities of Florence, Naples, Rome, and Venice, the production of portraits and history paintings continued to provide an important livelihood for painters. Royalty, such as Charles I of England or Marie de' Medici, queen of France, the noble families of Rome, and members of the clergy, not to mention the papacy, provided lucrative commissions for artists. France offered the most extensive development of art and architecture in the service of autocracy since the ancient Roman Empire.

Although fountains had played a role in urban planning and garden decoration since ancient Roman times, new possibilities in fountain design were explored by that inventive Baroque genius Bernini. His most triumphal fountain, in the Piazza Navona in Rome (fig. 7-4), has an Egyptian-style obelisk raised over a rocky landscape with four monumental figures—each as big as

Michelangelo's *David.* They symbolize what at the time were considered to be the four main rivers of the world: the Danube, Nile, Rio della Plata, and Ganges. The theme of the fountain, a papal commission, is consistent with the Counter-Reformation, which suggests that all the peoples of the world will be converted to Catholicism through the efforts of an energetic papacy and the revived Church of the Counter-Reformation. Bernini forces the water of the fountain to cascade in sheets to create the maximum noise and splash. The water, integral to his conception, is incorporated into both design and theme. He even incorporates the drain into his design, for a smiling, cavorting fish "swallows" the water, adding yet another sound to this lively complex. The fountain has a new excitement and energetic dynamism consistent with Baroque attitudes.

One of the most dramatic expressions of the Baroque aesthetic and Counter-Reformation ideals is Baroque ceiling painting. The figures in Gaulli and Bernini's *Triumph of the Name of Jesus* (fig. 7-5), which is set off by a wide gilded frame held by angels in relief, seem to come to life. Struggling, suffering figures appear to fall down toward us, into the space of the church, while at a vast distance high in the sky, the monogram of Christ (*IHS*) glows with an unearthly intensity. The painting offers a view of heaven, with angels and ranks of the faithful adoring Christ's name, while the rays of light that flow downward force disbelievers away from this mystic vision, into a realm of shadowy darkness. With a touch of wit, Gaulli here heightens his illusion by interrelating the painted figures with the three-dimensional stucco forms: the foot of one of the stucco angels who surround the frame gives an extra push to one of the sinful figures being cast out of Paradise. A great deal of the success of the illusion painted on the vault of the church of Il Gesù is due to the gilded stucco frame and ceiling coffering, which establish a point of reference for the spatial development. The progressive diminution of the figures is joined with gradually intensifying light to lead us past the frame, beyond the limits of the architecture, while the clouds and figures that overlap the frame seem to be emerging into our space. Their position within the church seems confirmed by the shadows they cast on the coffering. This ensemble seems to fulfill the tenets of the Council of Trent of more than a century earlier. With vigor and enthusiasm, it seduces and overwhelms us in an attempt to convince us of the truth of what we see.

THE SEVENTEENTH-CENTURY ARTIST

Seventeenth-century European artists were willing to undertake huge projects, and the most successful were entrepreneurs like Bernini and Peter Paul Rubens (1577–1640), who managed large workshops of assistants and apprentices. Only with such help could they have carried out gargantuan projects like Rubens's Marie de' Medici cycle and Bernini's sequence of works for St. Peter's (see pages 366 and 367). The Baroque is also the period of the virtuoso, in art no less than in drama and music. Artists enjoyed demonstrating their creative powers to enthusiastic patrons, and a typical Baroque work was an incredible tour de force. In Bernini's *Apollo and Daphne* (see fig. 1-4), marble has been transformed to suggest textures that convey the mythological miracle: hair becomes leaves and toes take root as bark encompasses the instantaneously frozen figure of Daphne.

Another important development, new in the history of art, took place in the Netherlands in the seventeenth century, where there was such a demand for paintings that a free market in works of art developed. Rather than waiting for a commission to work on a specific project for a specific patron, Dutch artists made more general works for a wide and popular audience. These works were bought not only by citizens but also by art dealers, who established shops selling art. For the first time, the relationship between the artist and the public began to

7-6. Peter Paul Rubens. *Self-Portrait with Isabella Brandt.* 1609–10. Oil on canvas, 5'9" x 4'5^{1}/2". Alte Pinakothek, Munich, Germany. This double portrait was painted at the time of the couple's marriage, apparently for Rubens's own collection. The studied informality of the pose is unexpected, but the elegance of the costumes reveals Rubens's aristocratic aspirations.

approach the situation we know today. Speculation in works of art became a part of the commercial activity of the Netherlands. In fact, there was so much activity that artists could support themselves working as specialists in a single category, such as marine painting, flower painting, or genre painting.

In France, where the king and his ministers controlled all aspects of culture, artists were less free than elsewhere. An academy determined production and through lectures and publications enforced the state-favored style of Baroque Classicism. In most of Europe, the Renaissance tradition of the artist as a respected intellectual continued to develop in the seventeenth century, aided by the explosion in art criticism and in writing about art that was a part of the enormous increase in publishing during the century.

With the exception of the Netherlands, patronage in Europe during this period was still quite traditional. Rulers and popes continued to commission grand projects, and the aristocracy built and decorated palaces and commissioned paintings from well-known artists that would enhance their reputation as sophisticated and knowledgeable individuals. Because of the growing respect for artists, patrons often allowed them more freedom in selecting subject matter and determining its interpretation; in other words, the concept of artistic "genius" led not only to greater respect for the artist, but

7-7. Artemisia Gentileschi. *Self-Portrait as the Allegory of Painting.* 1630. Oil on canvas, 38 x 29". The Royal Collection, Great Britain. In this unusual allegorical portrait, Artemisia Gentileschi reveals a special identification with her profession. Her unruly hair suggests the divine frenzy that was held to be an important indication of genius during this period.

7-8. Judith Leyster. *Self-Portrait at the Easel.* c. 1635. Oil on canvas, $29^3/8$ x $25^5/8$". National Gallery of Art, Washington, D.C. Gift of Mr. and Mrs. Robert Woods Bliss, 1949

also to greater independence. As mentioned above, in the Netherlands the growing art market meant that most artists painted general works for the market and did not work on commission; it is this exceptional circumstance that helps explain Rembrandt's remarkable career and his selection, in later years, of themes that he found psychologically and artistically challenging (see figs. 7-31, 7-32). The relative cheapness of canvas meant that artists could take a chance on a little-known subject or that they could even produce paintings for their own collections, as is the case with Rubens's painting of his country house (see fig. 7-50). Where patrons are known for the works in this section, they are listed in the captions; where no patron is listed, this means that either the patron is unknown, the work was created for the market, or the work was produced for the artist's own satisfaction. The latter case is true only for a very few works during the seventeenth century, but by the nineteenth century, it is perhaps fair to say that most of the works that we con-

sider to be of exceptional interest were created to satisfy the personal needs of the artist.

The public's interest in the artist and the artist's new self-confidence are expressed in the increasing number of self-portraits. In the two preceding centuries, the self-portrait was exceptional, but a much larger percentage of seventeenth-century artists have left us self-portraits, and it was during this period that the Medici of Florence began a collection of self-portraits. Among the most impressive self-portraits of the period is Rubens's charming *Self-Portrait with Isabella Brandt* (fig. 7-6).

The interest in self-portraits by women artists that we noted in the sixteenth century continued in the seventeenth. Perhaps the most remarkable is Artemisia Gentileschi's *Self-Portrait as the Allegory of Painting* (fig. 7-7), a representation in which the painter says, in essence, "I am painting." The Dutch artist Judith Leyster represents herself informally at the easel, smiling out at us with ease and a typical Dutch familiarity (fig. 7-8).

	CE	1600		1620

EUROPE
ART

1603–04
CARAVAGGIO'S *ENTOMBMENT OF CHRIST*

c. 1619
VELÁZQUEZ'S *WATER CARRIER*

1621–25
RUBENS'S *ARRIVAL AND RECEPTION OF MARIE DE' MEDICI*

1624–33
BERNINI'S *BALDACCHINO*

c. 1625
GENTILESCHI'S *JUDITH AND HER MAIDSERVANT*

1627
HALS'S *BANQUET OF THE OFFICERS OF THE CIVIC GUARD OF ST. GEORGE*

1638–41
BORROMINI'S SAN CARLO ALLE QUATTRO FONTANE, ROME

HISTORY

1609
Galileo invents the telescope

1609
Large groups of Muslims expelled from Spain

1611
King James Bible published, England

1633
Inquisition forces Galileo to retract theses

ASIA
ART

17TH CENTURY
ROYAL MUGHAL ART WORKSHOPS, INDIA

17TH CENTURY
SOTATSU'S *MATSUSHIMA SCREENS*

c. 1604
SIKH GOLDEN TEMPLE BUILT AT AMRITSAR, INDIA

1608
HIMEJI CASTLE COMPLETED, JAPAN

1620–63
KATSURA IMPERIAL VILLA, KYOTO, JAPAN

c. 1632–48
TAJ MAHAL, AGRA, INDIA

HISTORY

1615
Edo period begins, Japan

1628–58
Shah Jahan rules Mughal empire, India

THE AMERICAS
ART

HISTORY

1607
Jamestown, Virginia, established as first permanent English colony in North America

1608
Champlain establishes French colony of Quebec

1619
First African slaves arrive in Virginia

1620
Mayflower Pilgrims land at Plymouth Rock, Massachusetts

1636
Harvard College is founded, Massachusetts

AFRICA
ART

17TH CENTURY
BENIN ARTS PEAK

17TH CENTURY
EKOI ANCESTOR FIGURES

17TH CENTURY
BUSHONGO ROYAL FIGURES

HISTORY

1631
Rebellion against Portuguese in Mombasa, Kenya

THE MIDDLE EAST
ART

1609–16
BLUE MOSQUE IS BUILT IN ISTANBUL, TURKEY

1612–20
GREAT MOSQUE OF SHAH ABBAS IS BUILT IN ISFAHAN, PERSIA

HISTORY

1602–12
Turkey and Persia at war

1623–38
Persians take Baghdad away from Ottoman Turks and hold city

1642
REMBRANDT'S *MILITIA COMPANY OF CAPTAIN FRANS BANNING COCQ*

1645–52
BERNINI'S *ECSTASY OF SAINT TERESA*

1654
REMBRANDT'S *BATHSHEBA WITH KING DAVID'S LETTER*

1656
BERNINI'S COLONNADE AT ST. PETER'S BEGUN, ROME

1656
VELÁZQUEZ'S *LAS MENINAS*

c. 1660
VERMEER'S *MAIDSERVANT POURING MILK*

c. 1660
POUSSIN'S *ARCADIAN SHEPHERDS*

1668
VAN OOSTERWYCK'S *STILL LIFE WITH A VANITAS THEME*

1669
LE VAU AND HARDOUIN MANSART'S VERSAILLES PALACE BEGUN, FRANCE

c. 1670
VAN RUISDAEL'S *DUTCH LANDSCAPE*

1648
Thirty Years' War ends

1649
Charles I beheaded, England

1664–75
More than 70,000 die of plague in London

1666
Great Fire of London

1683–99
European war against Turks

1644–1912
Qing Dynasty, China

1680
Pueblo uprising against Spanish in New Mexico

1682
La Salle explores Mississippi River

1661
British establish first permanent settlement in Africa

1687
Turks revolt against Ottoman sultan Mohammed IV

CARAVAGGIO AND HIS INFLUENCE

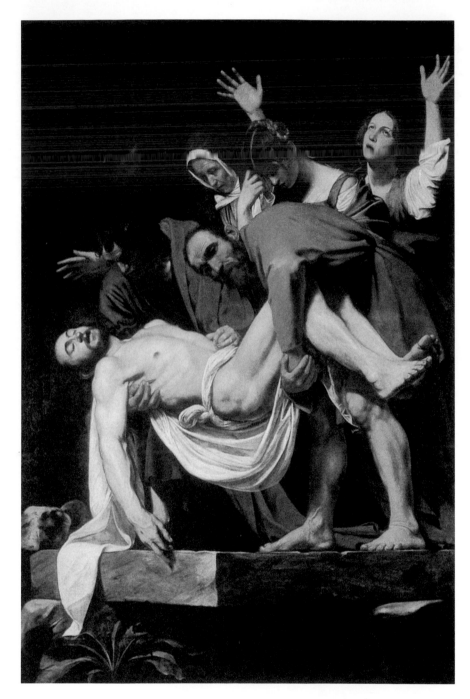

7-9. Caravaggio. *Entombment of Christ*. 1603–04. Oil on canvas, 9'10¹/₄" x 6'8"; the figures are over-lifesize. Vatican Museums, Rome. In 1642, this painting was listed as being Caravaggio's greatest work. Commissioned with funds left by Pietro Vittrice for his chapel at Santa Maria in Vallicella in Rome

*E*ntombment of Christ, by Caravaggio (1573–1610), is an arresting painting (fig. 7-9), for it seems as if we are really there—the figures are naturalistic, the strong light gives them a sharp physical presence, and their actions and emotions are convincing. The figures stand on a great tomb slab that seems to jut out of the picture into our space. This intrusion into our space commands that we participate in the experience, as does the gaze of Nicodemus, the old man who looks out at us with a troubled, weary expression. We seem to be below, in a dark and empty space. Caravaggio may be suggesting that we are standing in the tomb of Jesus. The figural composition flows downward from the upper right, beginning with the dramatic gesture of one of the Marys, who raises her hands in supplication, and concludes with the descending dead weight of the body of Jesus. The painting is clear, direct, and moving.

Two particular qualities characterize this powerful painting as the work of Caravaggio: the strong lighting and the inclusion of lower-class figure types. The light enters in a bold flash, creating strong highlights and deep pockets of shadow. It seems like a sudden illumination in a world full of darkness. The figures, modestly dressed, range in age from the youthful women to the old, tired figure of the Virgin Mary. Their wrinkles and bare feet are only two of the obvious means by which Caravaggio gives his figures a striking actuality.

Our participation in a dramatic religious event is demanded by

7-10. Caravaggio. *Christ with the Doubting Thomas*. c. 1602–03. Oil on canvas, 42^{1}/8 x 57^{1}/2". Neues Palast, Potsdam, Germany. Commissioned by Vincenzo Giustiniani, an important collector of Caravaggio's work

Christ with the Doubting Thomas (fig. 7-10). The lifesize figures are half-length, and our presence as spectators, standing before the picture, fulfills the semicircular grouping of Christ and the apostles. The composition seems to need us to be complete. In the biblical story, Thomas doubts that the figure appearing to the apostles is Christ. Christ tells him that for proof he should stick his finger in the wound in his side. The text implies that Thomas did not do this, but Caravaggio has chosen to represent Christ forcing Thomas's finger into the wound. Such a shocking, physical emphasis is not uncommon in Caravaggio's works. Although the Bible stresses the humble origins of the apostles, Caravaggio is one of the few artists who gives them a compelling reality and dignity.

Not everyone appreciated Caravaggio's vigorous realism. A seventeenth-century critic said that one of his paintings lacked "proper decorum, grace, and devotion." But Caravaggio's art was revolutionary precisely because it was not ennobled by a concept of beauty and because he did not adhere to the idealistic theories of art that had evolved during the Renaissance.

Caravaggio's mastery at depicting internal emotion is evident in his representation of the conversion of Saint Paul (fig. 7-11). In the biblical story (Acts 9:1–9), the Roman Saul

7-11. Caravaggio. *Conversion of Saint Paul*. c. 1601. Oil on canvas, 7'6^{1}/2" x 5'10". Santa Maria del Popolo, Rome. Commissioned by Tiberio Cerasi, general papal treasurer under Pope Clement VIII

7-12. Artemisia Gentileschi. *Judith and Her Maidservant with the Head of Holofernes*. c. 1625. Oil on canvas, 6'1/2" x 4'7³/4"; the figures are over-lifesize. The Detroit Institute of Arts. The story of Judith and Holofernes is told in the biblical Old Testament Apocrypha. Judith was a virtuous Jewish widow who saved her people during a siege. Entering the Assyrian camp, she captured the attention of the enemy general Holofernes and, after he became intoxicated at a banquet, beheaded him. She became a symbol of Fortitude and, because she played a role in saving her people, is often seen as a prototype for the Virgin Mary.

Gift of Mr. Leslie H. Green

was traveling toward Damascus to persecute Christians when "suddenly a light flashed from the sky all around him," and he fell to the ground. He heard a voice saying, "Saul, Saul, why do you persecute me?" When Saul asked, "Tell me, Lord, who you are," the reply was, "I am Jesus, whom you are persecuting." Saul, who was blinded by the "brilliance of the light"

for three days, was converted to Christianity and baptized with the new name of Paul.

Divine revelations and mystical conversions were common themes in the art of the Counter-Reformation. In Caravaggio's painting, the powerful light comes from almost directly overhead, and Caravaggio suggests that the force of the light

has thrust Paul to the ground. Paul reaches out to embrace the light in a natural gesture that is both supplicating and receptive.

Although Caravaggio seems to have had no direct pupils, his art had a potent impact on Italian art and on the many foreigners studying and working in Rome. His close followers are known as Caravaggisti. The Cara-

7-13. Judith Leyster. *Gay Cavaliers* (also known as *The Last Drop*). c. 1628–29. Oil on canvas, 35⅛ x 29". Philadelphia Museum of Art. Leyster was a teacher (in 1635 she had three male students) and a successful, independent artist who painted genre pictures, portraits, and still lifes. Her production diminished after she married a fellow artist and had three children.

Johnson Collection

vaggesque movement became international when French, German, Spanish, Flemish, and Dutch artists returned home from Italy to teach and work. Prints after works by Caravaggio and his followers also had an impact on these developments, and artists who never visited Rome and probably never saw an original painting by Caravaggio knew and were inspired by the great Italian painter's innovations.

In the monumental *Judith and Her Maidservant,* by Artemisia Gentileschi (c. 1597–after 1651), we are intruders—walking in on an episode charged with excitement and fear (fig. 7-12). The Caravaggesque qualities are evident in the dramatic tension, powerful light, and realistic figures. Holofernes has been decapitated and the head is being wrapped for their escape when

Judith hears an unexpected sound. The momentary effect achieved as the nervous women look up is dramatized by the light. The painting communicates a mood of tension and emotional drama that few of Caravaggio's followers could match. Artemisia, daughter of the painter Orazio Gentileschi, specialized in large-scale paintings of biblical or mythological subjects, often choosing themes that featured female heroes. She was proud of her accomplishments, and after finishing a painting for one patron declared: "This will show your Lordship what a woman can do."

Caravaggio never included a source for the strong light that illuminated his subjects, realizing the mystery and drama that an unknown light source can convey. But his followers often chose to intro-

duce the light source into the painting, as is the case with Artemisia Gentileschi's *Judith*. The addition of the light source opens up new possibilities of expression, as seen in Artemisia's painting: when Judith holds up her hand to shield her vision from the candle's glare, the strong shadow cast on her face adds an additional element of suspense.

In Judith Leyster's *Gay Cavaliers* (fig. 7-13), the illumination once again emanates from a candle. The figures are posed to catch the light from different angles, enhancing the composition's lively, momentary effect. Their abandoned gestures of delight in the intoxication of alcohol and tobacco (a new vice in the seventeenth century) are naturalistic, but we are uncertain whether or not Leyster intended any critical comment.

BAROQUE GENRE PAINTING

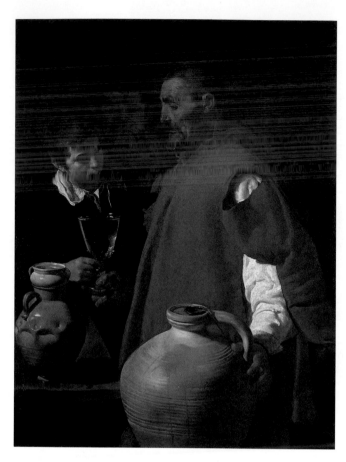

7-14. Diego Velázquez. *Water Carrier*. c. 1619. Oil on canvas, 41¹/₂ x 31¹/₂". Wellington Museum, London. This is an early work by Velázquez, painted when he was only about twenty. He painted this genre painting to be presented to the king of Spain as a demonstration of his skill.

In the *Water Carrier*, by Diego Velázquez (1599–1660), the simple act of offering, accepting, and consuming a glass of water gains dignity and import (fig. 7-14). The old water seller, who has brought a jug of fresh spring water from the mountains to the city, offers a youth a goblet of water sweetened with a fresh fig. In the shadowy background, a man is drinking. Both the heat of the day and the coolness of the water are revealed in the rivulets of condensation that run down the earthenware jug in the immediate foreground.

The influence of Caravaggio is evident in the half-length, lifesize figures, dark background, and strong light, as well as in the impressive dignity with which these individuals are represented. The composition is simple and pyramidal, focusing attention on the expressions: the downcast, sober eyes of the old man, who is seen in profile; the hesitation in the three-quarter face of the boy; the meditation of the central figure, shown frontally. The somber mood suggests that this scene of everyday life has a deeper significance. The old man seems to be passing on the gift of life to the shy boy. The mood has been described as "sacramental."

Velázquez's profound interpretation of a genre subject is not unique in the seventeenth century, for there are many genre paintings by other European painters that communicate the dignity and seriousness of everyday life. At the same time that Caravaggio gave a new profundity to his religious subjects by infusing them with reality (see fig. 7-10), genre themes were being given a new seriousness as patrons and painters found the sacred and the holy in the everyday.

An equally serious quality is found in *Peasant Family* (fig. 7-15), by Louis Le Nain (1593?–1648). The somewhat awkward composition lends reality to this quiet gathering, while the figures display an impressive dignity. The generally drab colors of their home and clothing are relieved by the warm tones of the fire and by the deep ruby red of the glass of wine, which is held as if in preparation for a visitor. We find this and similar paintings by Louis Le Nain and his brothers impressive, but we do not easily understand their function within the elegant, court-oriented culture of seventeenth-century France.

Genre had its greatest popularity in the Netherlands, where straightforward representations of Dutch home and tavern life were especially popular. In contrast to the works of Velázquez and Le Nain discussed here, most Dutch genre paintings emphasize a pleasing and homey domesticity. The greatest of the Dutch genre painters was Jan Vermeer (1632–75), who produced only about forty paintings in his life-

1611	University of Rome is founded
1615	Cervantes, *Don Quixote*
c. 1619	**Velázquez, *Water Carrier***

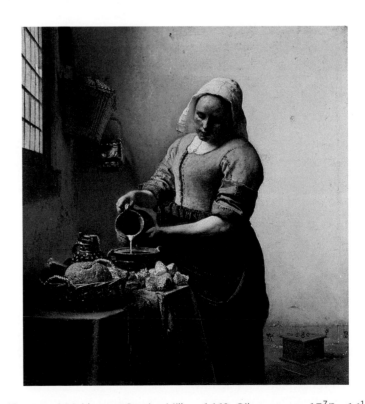

7-15. Louis Le Nain. *Peasant Family*. c. 1640. Oil on canvas, 44^{1}/2 x 62^{1}/2". The Louvre, Paris

time. *A Maidservant Pouring Milk* (fig. 7-16) is typical in its subject: a single woman is shown in the corner of a room, with light coming from a window in the left wall. The setting offers typical objects from a Dutch kitchen, including a footwarmer on the floor and a border of Dutch blue-and-white tiles. It is Vermeer's depiction of light that elevates this humble subject to the status of a masterpiece. Dots of paint make the objects sparkle and glow. It is as if we sense for the first time the beauty inherent in everyday things. Evidence in this and other paintings suggests that Vermeer studied his subjects through a **camera obscura**, an apparatus for projecting an image onto an interior screen of a darkened box, lit only by a small hole, so that the image could be traced (see also page 456). Vermeer's use of the camera obscura explains the slight abstraction in the treatment of light in his work, which heightens its impact. Like other Baroque painters, Vermeer owes a debt to Caravaggio, whose interest in and emphasis on light sensitized the artists of the entire century.

Vermeer most often used models in elegant contemporary clothing, and his focus on a humble subject here may have a specific iconographic meaning. The bread and milk provide the basic nourishment necessary for human life, and by portraying the clean kitchen and humble, hardworking maid, Vermeer may be making a statement about the virtues of domestic life.

7-16. Jan Vermeer. *A Maidservant Pouring Milk*. c. 1660. Oil on canvas, 17^{7}/8 x 16^{1}/8". Rijksmuseum, Amsterdam

SEVENTEENTH-CENTURY ART **363**

PETER PAUL RUBENS

7-17. Peter Paul Rubens and workshop. *Arrival and Reception of Marie de' Medici at Marseilles*. 1621–25. Oil on canvas, 13 x 10'. The Louvre, Paris. This is one of a series of twenty-one huge paintings celebrating Marie de' Medici's life that she commissioned from Rubens for the newly completed Luxembourg Palace in Paris.

In Rubens's painting of Marie de' Medici (fig. 7-17), we are thrust into a world of fantasy, where jubilant mermaids and a bare-breasted allegorical flying figure celebrate the arrival on French soil of the new wife of the king. The scene represents a historical event, but it has been transformed to express what the patron felt was the underlying meaning of the event. Marie, who had been married by proxy to Henry IV of France, was not met by her husband, who, history reveals, was at a hunting lodge with his favorite mistress. Rubens has painted Marie being welcomed by the personification of France. Above, Fame trumpets Marie's arrival. Marie's crossing had been rough, and Neptune, mythological god of the seas, and his mermaids jubilantly cele-

brate her safe arrival. By allegory, vivid colors, and lively movement, Rubens has created a pageant to satisfy the aspirations of his royal client.

Rubens was one of the best-educated and most-intellectual artists of the seventeenth century. He was certainly the only artist of the period to receive an honorary degree from Cambridge University. He served as court painter and ambassador for the rulers of the Spanish Netherlands and was as active as a diplomat as he was as an artist. He counted many members of the royalty and nobility among his friends. He was widely traveled, and his influence helped to make the Baroque an international style.

As a diplomat, Rubens worked tirelessly to promote peace in Europe. One of his most profound allegorical paintings conveys his opinions on the meaning of war for

7-18. Peter Paul Rubens and workshop. *Allegory of the Outbreak of War.* 1638. Oil on canvas, 6'9" x 11'3⁷/8". Pitti Gallery, Florence, Italy. Commissioned by Ferdinando II, Grand Duke of Tuscany

humanity (fig. 7-18). Rubens himself explained the content in a letter:

The principal figure is Mars, who has left the temple of Janus open (which according to Roman custom remained closed in time of peace) and struts with his shield and his bloodstained sword, threatening all peoples with disaster; he pays little attention to Venus, his lady, who, surrounded by her little love-gods, tries in vain to hold him back with caresses and embraces. On the opposite side, Mars is pulled forward by the Fury Alecto with a torch in her hand. There are also monsters signifying plague and famine, the inseparable companions of war. Thrown to the ground is a woman with a broken lute, as a symbol that harmony cannot exist beside the discord of war; likewise a mother with a child in her arms indicates that fertility, procreation, and tenderness are opposed by war, which breaks into and destroys everything. There is furthermore an architect fallen backwards, with his tools in his hands, to express the idea that what is built in peace for the benefit and ornament of cities is laid in ruin and razed by the forces of arms . . . you will also find on the ground, beneath the feet of Mars, a book and a drawing on paper, to indicate that he tramples on literature and other refinements. . . . The sorrowing woman . . . clothed in black with a torn veil, and deprived of all her jewels and ornaments is unhappy Europe, which for so many years has suffered pillage, degradation, and misery affecting all of us so deeply that it is useless to say more about them.

This passage reveals the intellect of Rubens and his knowledge of traditional subject matter and history.

BERNINI'S WORKS FOR ST. PETER'S

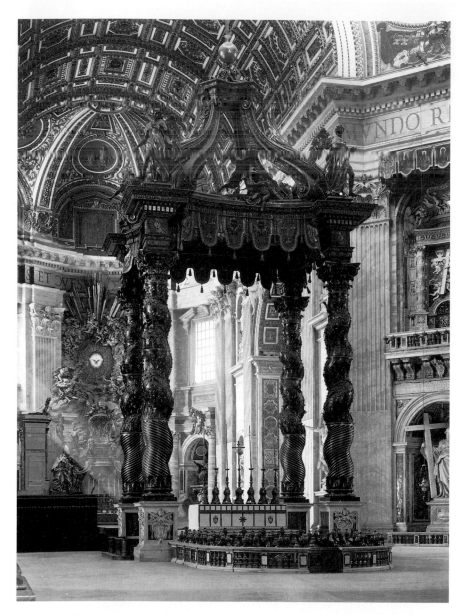

7-19. Gianlorenzo Bernini. *Baldacchino.* 1624–33. Bronze with gilding, height 93'6".
Cathedra Petri. 1656–66. Marble, bronze with gilding, stucco, alabaster, and stained glass.
St. Peter's Basilica, Vatican, Rome. Bernini's use of twisted columns was inspired by a series
of ancient twisted columns, once in Old St. Peter's, which were thought to have decorated
the great Temple of Solomon in Jerusalem. Commissioned by Popes Urban VIII Barberini
and Alexander VII Chigi

As a glowing dove of the Holy Spirit descends, angels and golden rays fill the apse of St. Peter's, and the columns of the **baldacchino** (canopy) over the high altar appear to writhe with excitement (fig. 7-19). We seem to be witnessing a miracle.

Bernini's *Baldacchino* solved some important problems. It provided a focal point for the vast interior by marking the burial spot of Saint Peter and the high altar of the **basilica**, without blocking the view to the **apse** or overwhelming the interior. The dark bronze and gilded highlights stand out against the white marble of the basilica's architecture, as do the dynamic spiral columns and the beautiful angels, curving **volutes**, and the flaps decorated with tassels—all emulating temporary cloth baldacchinos—on the top. Later, Bernini's *Baldacchino* became a frame for the *Cathedra Petri*, a multimedia climax at the end of St. Peter's that enshrines, like a huge reliquary, a wooden and ivory chair thought to be the papal throne used by Saint Peter. Four figures of early theologians—Saints Ambrose, Athanasius, John Chrysostom, and Augustine—support the reliquary just as they had approved the primacy of Saint Peter and the Roman Church in their writings. One of Michelangelo's windows has been changed by the addition of a stained-glass, alabaster, and gilded stucco representation of the Holy Spirit surrounded by golden rays and radiant putti, which sweep out with Baroque splendor to dominate

1624–33   **Bernini, *Baldacchino***
1626   Purchase of Manhattan island
1628   Harvey publishes on the circulation of the blood

7-20. Gianlorenzo Bernini. Colonnade, St. Peter's, Rome. Begun 1656. Travertine, longitudinal axis approx. 800'. A drawing reveals that Bernini conceived of the sides of the colonnade as a representation of the embracing arms of the pope and, therefore, of the Catholic Church as an institution. Commissioned by Pope Alexander VII Chigi

Michelangelo's Renaissance apse.

Bernini's **colonnade**, which shapes the piazza in front of St. Peter's, is more than just an impressive entrance to the basilica, for it also serves to define the space where the faithful gather to receive the papal blessing (fig. 7-20). Bernini's design is based on an oval with a width of almost 800 feet. As we enter this huge and richly decorated space, the broad axis creates a dynamic effect, and space seems to expand to either side. When Bernini built the piazza,

the area was surrounded by medieval houses and narrow, winding streets, an approach that would have rendered the spatial explosion of the piazza even more impressive. Huge travertine columns—284 placed in rows of 4—define the piazza without closing it off from the surrounding areas. As a result, it can be quickly emptied when a crowd wants to disperse.

Bernini, who was appointed main architect for St. Peter's in 1637, worked on the building and

its decoration for forty-two years, until his death. Among his other works are two papal tombs, another tomb, the altar decoration of the Chapel of the Holy Sacrament, and the nave decorations. From the ancient Roman bridge that was the ceremonial entrance to the Vatican, which Bernini and his assistants adorned with statues of angels in the 1660s, to the dramatic *Cathedra Petri*, works by Bernini transformed St. Peter's from a Renaissance structure into a Baroque experience.

THE DUTCH BAROQUE GROUP PORTRAIT

7-21. Frans Hals. *Banquet of the Officers of the Civic Guard of St. George.* 1627. Oil on canvas, 5'10$^{1/2}$" x 8'5$^{1/2}$". Frans Halsmuseum, Haarlem, Netherlands. The Dutch civic militia groups of the first half of the seventeenth century descend from groups that played a crucial role in gaining the independence of the Netherlands. They continued to have important functions, including guarding the cities and keeping order, and it became traditional that they have their portraits painted. Often, as here, they are shown at the annual banquet given them by the city. Commissioned by the Civic Guard of St. George

The boisterous members of Frans Hals's militia seem to be inviting us to join their celebration in the *Banquet of the Officers of the Civic Guard of St. George* (fig. 7-21). Just to the right of center, a man holds his glass upside down; he was a brewer, and the artist suggests that he is more than slightly inebriated. The vivacious activity of Hals's lifesize figures as they turn, converse, and gesture seems completely spontaneous. Hands are raised, mouths are open, and figures glance in various directions. The suggestion of movement is enhanced by the diagonals in the composition, by re-

peated strokes of strong color, and by the use of bold diagonal brushstrokes.

The group portrait had its first important development in the democratic, bourgeois Netherlands, and its first great artist was Frans Hals, who overcame the inherent repetitiveness of this subject, in which a painter had to represent a group of individuals, all about the same age and all of whom were similarly dressed. The democratic traditions of the Netherlands demanded that the individuals be shown as equals, and usually each paid the painter an identical amount to be included. Hals is able to capture

the individuality of each member, as well as the exuberant union that joins the group into a whole.

Rembrandt's *"Night Watch"* is surely the most famous painting known by a completely misleading name. The scene is not represented taking place at night, and the correct title is *Militia Company of Captain Frans Banning Cocq* (fig. 7-22). Rembrandt's dramatically composed and lit portrait of the members of this Amsterdam militia company offers a radical solution to the problems of the militia portrait. Rembrandt subordinates the democratic ideal to pictorial drama and focus, creating a sense of unified action. The moment chosen is not the indulgent banquet, but the captain and lieutenant ordering the militia to march. The other members of the company, as well as certain additional figures—a young woman with a dressed bird hanging from her belt (the bird's claws were the emblem of the militia guild), a boy firing a rifle, and others—are gathered in seemingly spontaneous groupings. Bold light and lightly colored costumes emphasize the main figures and give focus to the composition. A number of subordinate figures are virtually lost in shadow. They were added by Rembrandt to create variety; they were not militia members who had paid to be included for posterity. The composition, rich and complex, is truly

1627	**Hals, *Banquet of the Officers of the Civic Guard of St. George***
1630	Bubonic plague kills 500,000 Venetians
1633	The Inquisition forces Galileo to retract his defense of the Copernican system
1636	"Haarlem" is founded by Dutch settlers on Manhattan island

7-22. Rembrandt. *Militia Company of Captain Frans Banning Cocq.* 1642. Oil on canvas, 12'2" x 14'7". Rijksmuseum, Amsterdam. This group portrait, Rembrandt's largest surviving work, is usually known, inaccurately, as *"The Night Watch"* because layers of dirty varnish once made it seem like a night scene. The painting was part of a series of group portraits of militia companies that decorated a great hall in the headquarters of the Amsterdam civic guard. The patrons were members of Cocq's company, each of whom paid a sum consistent with his prominence in the painting. In the eighteenth century, the painting was cut down, and as a result, the composition was transformed. Rembrandt's group portrait was commissioned for a specific position. To reconstruct the angled view that a spectator would have had when approaching the work from the only doorway in the room, hold this book at an angle so that the painting is to your right and sharply receding. This clarifies a number of elements in Rembrandt's composition, including the glance and gesture of Captain Cocq, who, it can now be understood, was looking toward the spectator. Rembrandt adjusted his composition to gain maximum effectiveness, given the intended location of his painting. The other civic militia portraits in the same hall included the artist's self-portrait, and Rembrandt, with wit, represented himself in the back of the crowd. All we see is an eye, part of his nose and forehead, and a painter's beret. Commissioned by Captain Frans Banning Cocq and the members of his militia company

Baroque. The figural composition is set off by the off-center gateway—a reference to an ancient triumphal arch—in the background.

No sound evidence supports the often repeated story that the members of the company themselves were unhappy with Rembrandt's brilliant and unexpected solution to the problem of the group portrait. The painting was praised in the seventeenth century; one of Rembrandt's pupils wrote:

> It will outlast all its competitors, being so artistic in conception, so ingenious in the varied placement of figures, and so powerful that, according to some, it makes all the other pieces there look like decks of playing cards.

Rembrandt was the most famous Dutch artist of the seventeenth century and virtually the only one with an international reputation. As a young man, he had hoped to be a history painter, but his earliest success came as a painter of group and individual portraits. In 1642, the year of this group portrait, his wife, Saskia, died, leaving him with an infant son to raise. His art had already shown signs of change, and after 1642 he sought subjects and techniques that would satisfy a personal need for profundity and emotional depth (see figs. 7-31, 7-32).

BAROQUE ARCHITECTURE: FRANCESCO BORROMINI

7-23. Francesco Borromini. Dome, San Carlo alle Quattro Fontane, Rome. 1638–41. Dedicated to a recently canonized saint, Carlo Borromeo, this church is also named after its location at an intersection with four fountains (*quattro fontane*) representing the four seasons, one on each corner. Commissioned by the Spanish Discalced Trinitarians

This dome by Francesco Borromini (1599–1677) almost appears to be a hallucination (fig. 7-23). The hovering oval form, with its elastic **coffers**, seems to bear no relation to the heavy, solid stuff of architecture. If we blink, will it disappear, descend, or snap back into a circular shape with regular coffering? Startling and unbelievable architecture is typical of the works of Borromini. His Baroque monuments tantalize us with their energy, complexity, and tension. The oval form used here is one that has an inherent dynamism, for an oval establishes an axial direction and presents a variation in curvature, but Borromini also exaggerates the diminution of the coffering to suggest that the dome is larger than reality, and by adding hidden windows at the base of the dome, he creates a floating, levitating sensation. The excitement generated by the dome at San Carlo is resolved by the circle in the middle of the lantern, which is decorated with a triangle, symbol of the Trinity and emblem of the Trinitarian Order, which commissioned the church.

The demand that we be involved, the effect of captured movement, and the dramatic lighting of this architecture are consistent with the Baroque innovations examined in the paintings of Caravaggio and his followers. This small church is only one example of Borromini's brilliant inventiveness in creating new and exciting experiences within the classical vocabulary of architecture.

1638–41

1635	Boston's public Latin School opens
1638–41	**Borromini, Dome, San Carlo alle Quattro Fontane**
1639	Smithfield hams from Virginia are sold in London
1643	Death of Louis XIII

7-24. Francesco Borromini. Plan of San Carlo alle Quattro Fontane. 1638–41. Note how Borromini has located his church within the irregular space available to him.

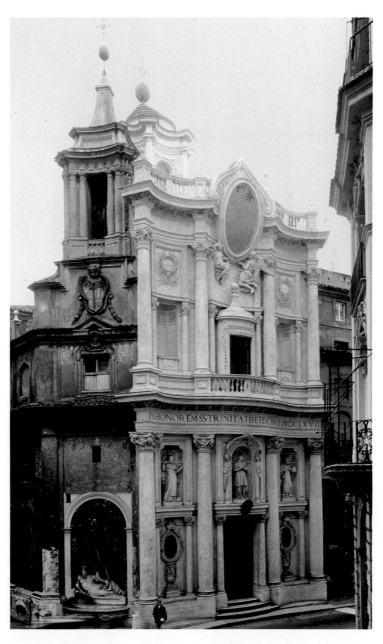

7-25. Francesco Borromini. Facade, San Carlo alle Quattro Fontane. 1665–67. Although the facade was completed long after the rest of the church, it is probably based on plans that Borromini had drawn earlier.

The complexity that characterizes the interior of San Carlo (fig. 7-24) rivets our attention as we try to discern the logic and order we expect in a building based on the classical orders. The **entablature** is composed of contrasting flat and concave sections that surge around the small interior, while the patterns of columns and of triangular and semicircular **pediments** create two overlapping and interlocked systems. The design is both logical and brilliantly complex. Architectural historians have analyzed the mathematical formulas on which Borromini based his structures. In this case, he evolved his design from the triangle, symbolic of the Trinitarian Order. At its most basic level, then, the shape of San Carlo alle Quattro Fontane has a form and an iconographic content that can be related to both a particular religious order and the Christian religion in general.

The facade predicts the interior in the grouping of four evenly spaced columns, in the undulation of the surging entablature, and in the scale of the lower story of columns (fig. 7-25). When one is standing in the narrow street before the church, however, the complex energies of contrasting concave and convex forms overwhelm any sense of logic. The upper row of columns completely masks the dome, making it a total surprise for the unsuspecting observer entering the church.

BERNINI, *ECSTASY OF SAINT TERESA*

7-26. Gianlorenzo Bernini and workshop. *Ecstasy of Saint Teresa*. 1645–52. Marble and bronze, height approx. 11'6"; the figures are over-lifesize. Cornaro Chapel, Santa Maria della Vittoria, Rome. Teresa, a sixteenth-century nun and a leading personality in the Counter-Reformation Church in Spain, founded a new, stricter reformed group of Carmelite nuns known as the barefoot Carmelites. For this reason, she is represented as barefoot in Bernini's sculpture. She wrote a number of works about the mystical life, including a popular and widely read *Autobiography* in which she detailed the visions and ecstasies she experienced. Commissioned by the Venetian Cardinal Federigo Cornaro as part of a burial chapel for his family

It pleased the Lord that I should sometimes see the following vision. I would see beside me . . . an angel in bodily form. . . . He was . . . short and very beautiful, his face so aflame that he appeared to be . . . all afire. . . . In his hands I saw a long golden spear and at the end of the iron tip I seemed to see a point of fire. With this he seemed to pierce my heart several times . . . he left me completely afire with a great love for God. The pain was so sharp that it made me utter several moans; and so excessive was the sweetness caused me by this intense pain that one can never wish to lose it, nor will one's soul be content with anything less than God. It is not bodily pain, but spiritual, though the body has a share in it—indeed a great share. (Teresa of Ávila, *Autobiography*)

1645–52	**Bernini, _Ecstasy of Saint Teresa_**
1648	Taj Mahal is completed in India
1648	End of the Thirty Years' War in Germany
1649	Charles I of England is beheaded

7-27. The Cornaro Chapel as seen in an eighteenth-century painting. Staatliches Museum, Schwerin, Germany

Bernini has visualized Teresa's words and experience in his sculpted altarpiece (fig. 7-26), capturing in the saint's pose and facial expression the combination of "sweetness" and pain she describes so vividly and physically. Her figure seems to convulse, her arm is limp, and her head slumps back, her mouth open and her eyes half-closed. The figure of the angel smiles radiantly, and its drapery ripples with flamelike folds that evoke Teresa's words.

Bernini's interpretation, however, encompassed more than just Teresa's description of this single ecstasy. It relates this experience to other aspects and events of her life and to contemporary attitudes about ecstasies and saints. Teresa's miraculous death, as described by those who witnessed it, is evident here in the beauty Bernini gives the saint. Although her homeliness is documented, at the moment of her death, when she was in her sixties, witnesses testified that she became youthful and beautiful and that she died while in a state of ecstatic love for God. The relationship between ecstasy, death, and fervent love of God and the ideal of the marriage of the soul with the divine are revered parts of the mystical tradition that has its roots in the Old Testament love poetry of the Song of Songs. Teresa herself had written a commentary on the Song of Songs, in which she related Christian death and ecstasy to the soul's desire to expire in the anguish of divine love. Bernini shows the saint levitating, transported off the ground by heavenly clouds. Levitation is described by Teresa in the context of other ecstasies she experienced after attending Mass. By levitating the figure, Bernini makes his sculptural group more impressive and its effect more momentary, while in the context of Teresa's life he also refers to her devotion to the Eucharist, an appropriate emphasis in an altarpiece.

Bernini's representation of the ecstasy of Teresa is itself a miraculous apparition, for the large white figures of the angel and the saint float above the altar. Originally they must have glowed in a gentle, mysterious light that flowed dimly down on golden rays from a window filled with stained glass. Today, electric lights have been added, which make the lighting more dramatic than Bernini intended.

The vision of the miraculous ecstasy is enhanced by the enshrinement of the altarpiece group in a pedimented tabernacle. This niche, made of brilliant multicolored marble, is the centerpiece of a visually sumptuous chapel complex, every detail of which was designed by Bernini (fig. 7-27). The back wall is covered with marble paneling that is broken by the surging pediment above the niche, which undulates outward and upward. The ceiling is frescoed with a burst of heavenly light, and angels seem to pour down into the chapel, accompanying the angel in Teresa's ecstasy. The front of the altar is decorated with a gilded bronze and lapis lazuli relief of the Last Supper, while the floor tombs are decorated with inlaid figures of gesticulating skeletons in foreshortening, as if those buried below were being resurrected by the saint's ecstasy.

Bernini unites painting, sculpture, and architecture in a beautiful totality, one that breaks down the barriers between the world in which we live and the work of art. The tabernacle and figures invade our space, demanding that we become involved. A text on a banner held by angels on the entrance arch offers words that, Teresa wrote, were spoken to her by Christ during one of her visions: "If I had not already created heaven I would create it for you alone."

7-28. Rembrandt. *A Man Rowing a Boat on the Bullewyk.* c. 1650. Quill pen and brown wash heightened with white, 5^{1}/4 x 7^{7}/8". Devonshire Collection, Chatsworth, Derbyshire, England. The location is a tributary of the Amstel River, near Amsterdam, with the spire of the Ouderkerk (Old Church) in the background. The white used here is an opaque paint that allowed Rembrandt to suggest white highlights.

The freshness of nature is captured in Rembrandt's spontaneous drawing of a still tributary near Amsterdam (fig. 7-28). A few quick pen strokes capture the wind as it riffles the leaves of the trees around the cottage. Rembrandt applied **wash** (ink thinned with water) with a brush to achieve the darker shadows that give weight to the mass of the cottage and create the reflection of the trees and cottage on the surface of the water. A thin wash at the top suggests the sky, and a bold, dark mass in the lower left corner establishes the *repoussoir*. Rembrandt's economy of means captures the flux of nature.

Throughout the centuries, artists have made and used drawings for a great variety of purposes (see page 282). We normally think of drawings as being preparatory—studies made in the process of creating a larger, more finished work in another medium—and such is often the case. Although almost all drawings created before the Renaissance are lost, this does not mean that artists in earlier periods did not use preparatory drawings. Egyptian and Greek stonecarvers,

for example, probably drew guidelines on the four sides of their blocks of stone before they began carving, and their contemporaries surely made some kind of sketch or drawing prior to beginning to paint or to build a building. Many later paintings are based on drawings on the plaster or canvas surface (known as **underdrawings** because of their position under the finished work). Artists have also made drawings as records of completed works, often as a means of documenting their production. Finely finished drawings were sometimes made to be presented to collectors and friends. These are known as **presentation drawings**. Drawings were first systematically collected during the Renaissance, when the artist was recognized as a genius whose every creative effort was worth preserving.

There are many media in which drawings have been executed: charcoal, lead pencil, pen and ink, chalk in various colors, **pastel**, and points made of silver, gold, or other metals. Wash, **watercolor**, and **gouache** (see page 471) are also considered drawing techniques, even though they

7-29. Rembrandt. *Saskia in a Straw Hat.* 1633. Silverpoint drawing on white prepared vellum, 7¹/8 x 4¹/8". Staatliche Museen zu Berlin, Preussischer Kultur-besitz, Kupferstichkabinett. The drawing is inscribed: "This is drawn after my wife, when she was 21 years old, the third day after we were engaged— 8 June 1633." Rembrandt and Saskia were married in 1634.

7-30. Rembrandt. *Two Women Teaching a Child to Walk.* c. 1637. Red chalk drawing on rough grayish paper, 4¹/8 x 5". The British Museum, London

are liquid media applied with a brush. Although paper is the most widely accepted support for drawings, artists have also used **vellum**, **parchment**, and other materials.

Hundreds of drawings were executed by Rembrandt in virtually every drawing medium that was available to him. Although some can be identified as studies for paintings or **etchings**, the majority are sketches of **genre** scenes, land-scapes, and animals. All the evidence suggests that Rem-brandt made his drawing of *A Man Rowing* for his own pleasure, for none of his landscape paintings are endowed with this kind of naturalism. We know from an inventory of his possessions that Rembrandt sorted his drawings and stored them by subject. The implication is that when he began a new painting or etching, he could look through his drawings for inspiration drawn from life.

When Rembrandt made a drawing of his fiancée, Saskia, shortly after they became engaged, he chose the difficult technique of **silverpoint** on specially prepared vellum (fig. 7-29). During the fifteenth and sixteenth cen-turies, drawing with sharpened points of silver (or gold) on specially prepared paper or vellum had been common, but by the seventeenth century, this medium was rare. The virtue of this particular technique is that it creates a very fine line. It was especially favored by artists interested in preci-sion, such as van Eyck, Dürer, and Leonardo. Silverpoint and goldpoint demand a special proficiency, for the drawn lines cannot be erased or changed. Before the silver oxi-dizes and darkens, the shimmering lines have a sumptuous effect. Rembrandt has chosen the perfect medium to cap-ture forever the face of his fiancée.

In a drawing executed with soft red chalk, Rembrandt has, with incredible economy, captured a hesitant child, wearing a padded hat for protection, in the process of learning to walk (fig. 7-30). The child is encouraged by two women, one of whom, on our right, betrays her age by her stiffness. There is no setting, nor is there a single extraneous detail. It is a tiny drawing of the utmost simplicity, but the moment of life that it captures is precious.

REMBRANDT: LATE PAINTINGS

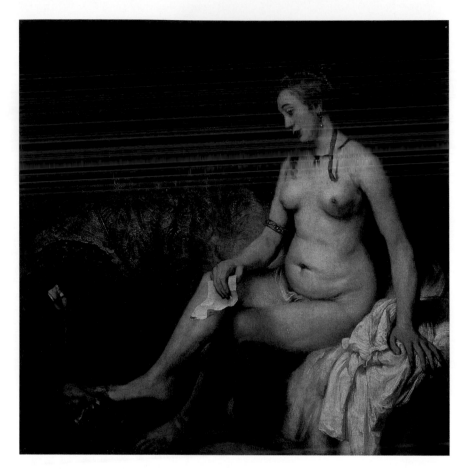

7-31. Rembrandt. *Bathsheba with King David's Letter*. 1654. Oil on canvas, 55⁷/8 x 55⁷/8". The Louvre, Paris. A repeated motif in the Old and New Testaments is the sinfulness of humanity; the Old Testament king David, slayer of Goliath and the author of the Psalms, is no exception. After David had forced a married woman, Bathsheba, into his bed, he connived to have her husband, Uriah, killed in battle so he could marry her. In Rembrandt's painting, Bathsheba holds the message from David, who has summoned her to the palace, while her maid prepares her for this first meeting with the king.

Rembrandt's later works are characterized by subjects of universal human significance, as in this example of the story of Bathsheba (fig. 7-31). The main subject here is the female nude, but the interpretation emphasizes her inner emotions and meditation. Rembrandt has overturned tradition by painting a nude figure that is more emotional than physical, more thoughtful than sensuous. In keeping with the Dutch interest in naturalism, his model is a mature and dignified woman, one who is capable of understanding the profound implications of the king's demands. Despite the secondary figure at her feet, Bathsheba is alone in her predicament.

Dutch artists in general avoided emotionally complex themes, but the restriction on religious subjects and the general disinterest in historical and mythological themes in the Netherlands were irrelevant to Rembrandt, who, perhaps in reaction to the unemotional art being created by other Dutch artists, chose to probe deeply into human life for subject matter and to paint religious subjects

1650 World population is about 500 million
1652 War is declared between England and Holland
1654 Rembrandt, *Bathsheba with King David's Letter*

7-32. Rembrandt. *Return of the Prodigal Son.* c. 1662–68. Oil on canvas, 8'8" x 6'8". Hermitage Museum, St. Petersburg, Russia. Jesus' parable of the prodigal son (Luke 15:11–32) was popular with the followers of Caravaggio, and especially with the Dutch Caravaggisti. Here Rembrandt represents the most profound moment in the story: the son, reduced to poverty, returns home to discover that his father, who still loves him, will forgive him.

if their emotional content interested him. Rembrandt's works often have a direct and sympathetic correlation with the events of his life and the people whom he loved. The model for Bathsheba is probably Hendrickje Stoffels, Rembrandt's second, common-law wife, whom he was unable to marry because of financial restrictions in the will of his deceased wife, Saskia. In 1654, the same year that Rembrandt painted Bathsheba, Hendrickje was called before the council of the Reformed Church and barred from receiving communion

because she was living with a man to whom she was not married. The connection between Hendrickje's difficulties and the Bathsheba story is indirect, but the human predicament is related.

The *Return of the Prodigal Son* is Rembrandt's largest history painting (fig. 7-32). The impressive figures are over-lifesize. The son, in rags and worn-out shoes, has thrown himself to his knees to indicate his repentance. The aged father bends over him, pulling the young man toward him with stiff hands. The

son gently lays his head on his father's chest and closes his eyes. Time seems to stop. The richness of their inner experience is in part expressed abstractly by the textures of the **impasto** (raised brushstrokes of thick paint) with which Rembrandt paints their garments and by the warm, sonorous colors. Jesus' parable used the human story to illustrate a moral: God will forgive sinners who repent. Rembrandt uses the same story to emphasize a human experience—the forgiving love of a parent for a child.

7-33. Rembrandt. *Christ Preaching.* c. 1652. Etching with drypoint and burin, 6$^1/8$ x 8$^1/8$". Rembrandt was internationally famous as a printmaker during his own lifetime, and his prints regularly sold for high prices. Less than twenty years after Rembrandt's death, the Florentine art historian Filippo Baldinucci would write: "This artist truly distinguished himself . . . in a certain most bizarre manner which he invented for etching on copper plates. This manner too was entirely his own, neither used by others nor seen again; with certain scratches of varying strength and irregular and isolated strokes, he produced a deep chiaroscuro of great strength."

Etching   Drypoint

7-34. Diagrams of the etching and drypoint techniques. The more blurred lines of the drypoint technique are the result of the burr of the drypoint line.

Rembrandt presents us not with a specific biblical subject but with an interpretation of Jesus as a humble and gentle teacher who stands within the crowd in a city street to preach (fig. 7-33). He is surrounded by people of all ages, rich and poor, and in Rembrandt's representation they react as individuals to Jesus' words. Some ponder his meaning, but others seem uninterested. A child busies himself drawing in the dust in the foreground.

Rembrandt's technique is **etching**, and this is one of a number of prints produced from the same plate for collectors of prints. It is the etching technique that permits the creation of blurred lines and a soft, atmospheric quality not possible in **woodcut** or **engraving**. Etching is not a new technique—Dürer and other printmakers had experimented with its possibilities—but it was Rembrandt who first realized its potential for expression.

Etching is an **intaglio** technique (see page 311), and the same thin copper plate used for engraving functions as the

print form (fig. 7-34). To create an etching, one must cover the plate with an **etching ground**, an acid-resistant, resinous mixture. The artist scratches through this ground with a steel **etching needle**, creating lines that expose the copper. When the design is completed (or when the artist wants to test the progress of the composition), diluted acid (nitric, iron chloride, or hydrochloric) is poured over the plate or the plate is dipped into an acid bath. The acid eats into the copper, creating grooves where the needle has scratched through the ground. The ground is then cleaned off and the plate is inked and printed, as in the process for printing an engraving. If the results are unsatisfactory or incomplete, the ground can be reapplied, the design can be strengthened or completed with the needle, and the acid bath can be used again. Another alternative is to strengthen the lines by using the **burin** (as in engraving) and/or drypoint (see below). Only about 50 excellent and 200 reasonably good prints can be made from an etched plate.

7-35. Rembrandt. *Three Crosses*. 1653. Drypoint and burin (first state), 15^1/$_4$ x 17^3/$_4$". Rembrandt made successive changes to the plate in producing later states of this print.

An eighteenth-century development in the etching process was the soft-ground etching, which uses a greater percentage of tallow or wax in the ground. A thin sheet of paper is laid over the ground, and a drawing is made on the paper. When the paper is lifted, a soft, grainy impression is left on the plate. The plate is then etched, using a weak acid bath.

The etching technique encouraged freedom and spontaneity, for the etching needle moves easily through the ground to scratch the plate (unlike the concentrated pressure needed to push the burin through the resistant copper to create an engraving). Although an etched line lacks the sharp and precise quality of an engraved line, its blurriness creates the atmospheric effect that we admire in Rembrandt's work. Rembrandt's earliest printed works were pure etchings, sometimes with the use of the burin for strengthening. Later, to achieve an even greater effect of atmosphere, he began to add lines in drypoint, as is the case in *Christ Preaching*.

Drypoint is the technique of scratching directly into the copper plate with the etching needle (see fig. 7-34). This method creates grooves that have tiny raised ridges of copper, known as the **burr**, to either side, where the expelled material is forced by the needle. These drypoint ridges catch the ink and create rich areas of deep, soft shadow. The necessary pressure applied by the press during printing will wear down the burr rather quickly, and only about ten good and twenty reasonably good impres-

sions can be made. In *Christ Preaching*, drypoint lines are visible in the beard and hair of Jesus and in the deep shadows of his drapery.

A few of Rembrandt's last prints are executed entirely in drypoint, with an additional use of the burin for certain sharp details. Rembrandt's last print was probably the large *Three Crosses* (fig. 7-35), which he worked on over a period of years. He created three successive stages, known as **states**, in 1653 by reworking the plate and a final, almost completely reworked fourth state in the early 1660s. It is a profoundly moving personal interpretation of the Crucifixion based on the text in Luke 23:44–47:

> And it was about the sixth hour, and there was a darkness over all the earth until the ninth hour. And the sun was darkened, and the veil of the temple was rent in the midst. And when Jesus had cried with a loud voice, he said, Father, into thy hands I commend my spirit: and having said thus, he gave up the ghost. Now when the centurion saw what was done, he glorified God, saying, "Certainly this was a righteous man."

The centurion is kneeling, to suggest that Rembrandt is representing the very moment of the death of Jesus. The powerful shaft of light is a momentary blaze, a heavenly response to Jesus' words and his death. In this late work, Rembrandt avoids painstaking detail to emphasize powerful emotional experiences.

DIEGO VELÁZQUEZ

7-37. Diego Velázquez. *Las Meninas*, detail of Princess Margarita

7-36. Diego Velázquez. *Las Meninas* (*The Maids of Honor*). 1656. Oil on canvas, 10'5" x 9'; the figures are lifesize. Prado, Madrid. The cross on Velázquez's chest indicates that he has been made a Knight of the Order of Santiago. As Velázquez did not receive this honor until 1659, three years after the painting was dated, the cross must have been added later. Probably commissioned by Philip IV of Spain

For just a moment, Velázquez's painting convinces us that the little princess and her attendants—including dwarfs and a large dog—are posing just for us (fig. 7-36). Although *Las Meninas* is a large picture, its subject seems intimate and even casual. We glimpse a large dark room in the palace, where the painter is at work on a huge canvas. He looks out and leans back, raising his brush as he prepares to apply a stroke of paint. In the foreground is the five-year-old Margarita, daughter of Philip IV, surrounded by her maids (*las meninas*) and the dwarfs and developmentally disabled people who were a traditional part of life at the Spanish court. With the exception of the princess, all these figures are represented in the midst of movement, as is Velázquez. Note especially the figure to the right who, one hand raised, awakens the dog, which slowly raises its head. Velázquez's illusionism, which is supported by his loose brushstroke and the blurred edges of the forms (fig. 7-37), attempts to convince us that we are seeing reality.

But is the princess posing for us? The shimmering surface on the back wall is a mirror that reflects the figures of King Philip and Queen Mariana. A real mirror would have reflected the whole room, but Velázquez, with artistic license, includes this reference to his royal patrons as the sole element that reminds us

1656

1656	**Velázquez, *Las Meninas***
1656	Pendulum clock is invented
1657	London's first chocolate shop opens

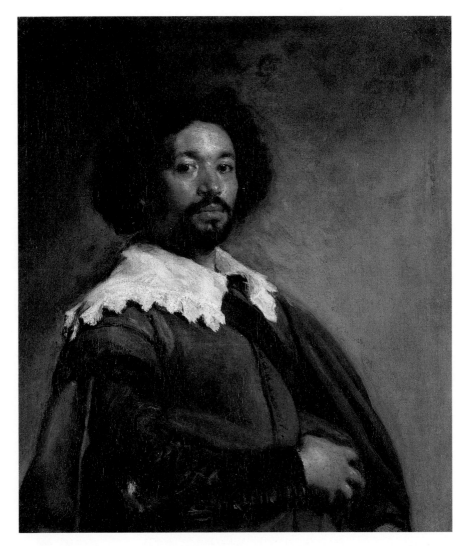

7-38. Diego Velázquez. *Portrait of Juan de Pareja*. 1650. Oil on canvas, 32 x 27^1/2". The Metropolitan Museum of Art, New York

Fletcher Fund, Rogers Fund, and Bequest of Miss Adelaide Milton de Groot (1876–1967), by exchange, supplemented by gifts from friends of the Museum, 1971 (1971.86)

that what we are looking at is indeed a painting.

In Velázquez's *Portrait of Juan de Pareja* (fig. 7-38), the sitter looks out with calm and assured dignity. Velázquez's loose brushstroke and subtle light create an effect of immediacy and, again, reality. The painting is a coloristic triumph, for within a restricted palette of white, black, grays, and beiges, Velázquez creates an impressive variety of tones. The restriction of color is no

accident, for this portrait of one of Velázquez's assistants was a practice piece. Velázquez was in Rome, buying paintings and ancient sculptures for King Philip, when he received the commission to paint a portrait of Pope Innocent X. This particular portrait was a difficult task, for the pope, who had a ruddy complexion, had to be painted wearing red papal garments, seated in a red chair in a setting dominated by red hangings.

To prepare himself for this challenge, Velázquez posed a similar problem by painting Juan de Pareja, who was of Moorish descent, using a restricted color palette based on his flesh tones. The picture was a sensational success. After it was exhibited at the Pantheon, Velázquez was elected to the Rome Academy. One contemporary remarked that although all the other paintings in the exhibition were art, "this alone was truth."

BAROQUE CLASSICISM: NICOLAS POUSSIN

7-39. Nicolas Poussin. *Arcadian Shepherds*. c. 1660. Oil on canvas, 34¹/₄ x 47¹/₄". The Louvre, Paris. The inscription on the tomb is *Et in Arcadia Ego* ("Even in Arcadia I [Death] am to be found"). Painted for Cardinal Rospigliosi and bought by Louis XIV in 1685

The idealized painting of Nicolas Poussin (1594–1665) transports us to remote antiquity, where we stand with shepherds and a shepherdess by a monumental tomb (fig. 7-39). Arcadia is an idyllic region in Greece where, during the ancient golden age, it was believed that humanity had lived peacefully and harmoniously with nature. To the shepherds who lived there, life seemed perfect until they discovered a tomb and realized that death is a reality that they will someday have to confront. Despite the dramatic implications of the subject, the mood of the painting is calm and contemplative. In Poussin's approach, even death becomes philosophical.

Poussin's style is consistent with his intellectual interpretation of the subject. The composition is lucid and the poses of the figures are clearly articulated and interrelated. To assure satisfying compositions, Poussin worked them out by arranging miniature wax figures on a stage in a small box until he was pleased with their disposition. The colors are cool and simple, the light regular and undramatic, and the brushstroke controlled. The influence of

7-40. Nicolas Poussin. *Landscape with the Body of Phocion Carried out of Athens*. 1648. Oil on canvas, 47 x 70^1/$_2$". Phocion was a loyal Athenian general whose character was in many ways like that of Poussin: he was stern, prized economy, and was dedicated to truth. His austerity and moral rectitude, however, made him hated by the popular faction in Athens, who, when it gained power, had Phocion executed on a false charge of treason and decreed that his body had to be carried outside the city for burial. This is the event shown in Poussin's painting. Later Phocion was given an honorable burial in Athens. Commissioned by Serisier, a Lyons silk merchant. National Museum and Gallery, Cardiff, Wales, on loan from the Earl of Plymouth

the High Renaissance style of Raphael is evident, and the costumes and facial types reveal Poussin's careful study of ancient art. Poussin's paintings are among the finest examples of Baroque Classicism. The landscape is based on the area around Rome, which Poussin knew well.

Nicolas Poussin was probably the most classical, intellectual, and philosophical painter of the seventeenth century. Although born in France, he spent most of his mature life in Rome. A close circle of similarly minded French friends there and in Paris were the patrons for his well-studied, thoughtful compositions. He preferred heroic or stoic themes from antiquity.

Poussin's landscapes always include a narrative subject, usually one drawn from antiquity. In *Landscape with the Body of Phocion Carried out of Athens*, the landscape setting is clearly not taken from nature (fig. 7-40). Poussin has rearranged nature to provide the properly sober, clear, and balanced setting for his profound theme.

DUTCH STILL-LIFE PAINTING

7-41. Maria van Oosterwyck. *Still Life with a Vanitas Theme.* 1668. Oil on canvas, 29 x 35". Kunsthistorisches Museum, Vienna. Maria van Oosterwyck did not come from an artistic family, but tradition tells us that she was determined to become a still-life painter. She developed an international reputation and produced works for Louis XIV of France and the members of other European royal houses.

Realistic still-life painting is a democratic art—one needs no background in aesthetics or art theory to appreciate the ability of Maria van Oosterwyck (1630–93) to render the butterfly that lights on the book or the mouse nibbling at the grain, not to mention the fresh flowers, skull, and globe (fig. 7-41). There is even a fly on a book to the right and a self-portrait of the artist reflected in the flask to the left. It was in the democratic Netherlands that such still lifes were most fully appreciated, and the market for pictures such as this one was so large that artists could become specialists in still-life painting and hone their skills so as to produce increasingly more brilliant depictions of objects in ever more elaborate profusion.

Sixteenth- and seventeenth-century art theorists, however, largely ignored still-life painting, as they also neglected the painting of landscape, genre, and portraits. These types of art were considered unimportant because they were merely copies from nature. A painter's most significant accomplishment, they argued, was a history painting, the conception, design, and execution of which demanded intellectual prowess and academic training. The painter of histories also needed an understanding of anatomy and experience in drawing the male nude. Still-life, landscape, portrait, and genre paintings were considered to be much less valuable than history paintings and generally sold at much lower prices.

During the seventeenth century, a number of women artists excelled at still-life painting, in part, perhaps, because this was a category of art in which they could succeed without threatening the long-established dominance of male artists. Because at this time women were not admitted to the academies, they hardly had the option of receiving training in creating history paintings. The two artists examined here were both products of the more liberal Dutch culture, but during the sixteenth and seventeenth centuries there are documented French, Flemish, and Italian women still-life artists as well.

The theorists underestimated still-life painting. To select the forms of a still-life painting and arrange them into a satisfying composition, with coordinating and contrasting patterns of textures and colors, demand different skills from those required of the history painter. And still-life paintings are not always purely decorative displays, devoid of any deeper meaning. The title of Van Oosterwyck's painting reveals that it forms part of a distinguished tradition of seventeenth-century paintings on the theme of Vanity, one of the minor vices, that expressed the transience of the things of the world and the inevitability of death. Such paintings were especially popular in the Netherlands, where the tradition of complex symbolism goes back to Van Eyck (see page 271). In the most impressive of these compositions, of which Van Oosterwyck's is an example, each element contributes its own special content to the meaning of the whole. The hourglass, for example, refers to the inexorable passage of time. The fly is a symbol of sin, ever present in the world, and the mouse symbolizes evil. The large book is labeled "Reckoning. We live in order to die. We die in order to live."

An early source tells us that Van Oosterwyck was pious, and the underlying Christian hope of her still-life painting is expressed in these words and in the butterfly, symbol of the resurrection of Christ and the salvation of humanity. Although the skull is an obvious reference to death, when it is wreathed in ivy, as here, it refers to life after death. All these objects and symbols are united in a skillful composition that takes maximum advantage of contrasting forms, colors, and textures.

Flower Still Life by Rachel Ruysch (1663–1750) is arranged along a prominent diagonal that is enhanced by the curving stems of the blossoms at the upper right and lower left (fig. 7-42). The simple centrality of the vase and niche is enlivened by the diagonal recession of the table and by the contrast in light to either side. On the right, a

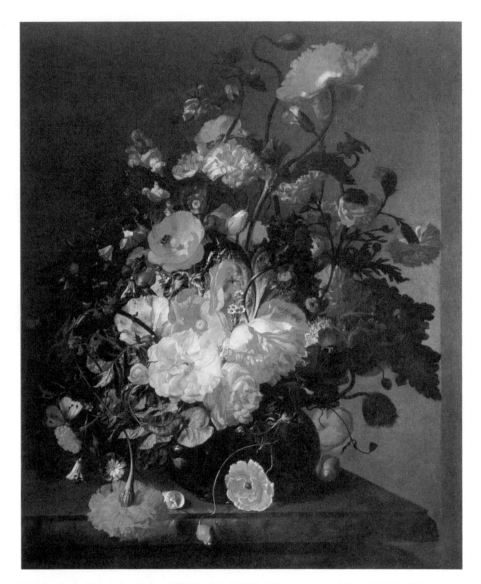

7-42. Rachel Ruysch. *Flower Still Life.* After 1700. Oil on canvas, 30 x 24". The Toledo Museum of Art, Toledo, Ohio. Rachel Ruysch is ranked among the greatest still-life painters in the Netherlands, and her international reputation continued after her death. She was apprenticed to an important still-life painter at the age of fifteen and by eighteen was active as a painter in the same genre. From 1708 to 1716, she was court painter to the elector Palatine in Düsseldorf, Germany.

light area silhouettes the forms and emphasizes their irregularity, while on the left a completely different effect is accomplished by setting off the complexity of many small blossoms against the dark background. Ruysch's father was professor of anatomy and botany, and his collec-

tion of scientific specimens may have inspired her inclusion of the insects found so often in her paintings. She depicts them with impressive accuracy, a technical precision that reveals her participation in the new scientific interests and investigations of the seventeenth century.

THE PALACE AT VERSAILLES

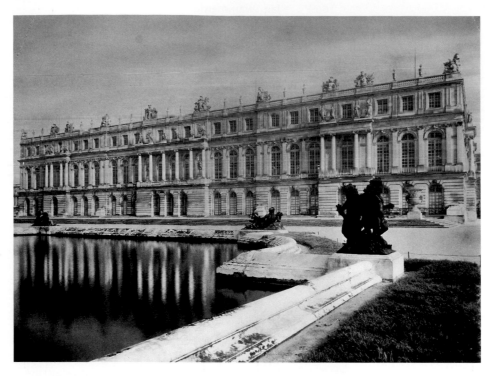

7-43. Louis Le Vau and Jules Hardouin Mansart. Garden facade, Palace of Versailles, France. 1669–85. Begun by Louis XIV, who decided to enlarge a royal hunting lodge eleven miles southwest of Paris, Versailles officially became not only the main royal residence in 1682 but also the governmental seat. The administrator J.-B. Colbert, who also advised Louis on political, economic, and religious matters, and the painter Charles Lebrun were in charge of the artists and workers—sometimes as many as 30,000 at one time—who created the buildings and grounds. At its height, the palace served a court that totaled almost 20,000 people, including 9,000 soldiers quartered in the town and about 4,000 servants who lived within the palace itself. Commissioned by Louis XIV

The palace of the French kings at Versailles is the largest and most emulated royal residence in the world (fig. 7-43); as it stands today, it is largely the work of two architects, Louis Le Vau (1612–70) and Jules Hardouin Mansart (1646–1708).

The palace has hundreds of rooms, and its facade is almost a half mile long; the garden encompasses 250 acres. Its impressive scale actually made a political statement, for it was intended to assert for the French populace and nobility, as well as for foreigners, the power of the French monarch. In some ways, the very creation of Versailles may have played a role in establishing and perpetuating that power.

The expansive length of the garden facade itself makes a powerful architectural statement, but the architects faced the problem of how to articulate such a long structure. They decided not to break the mass in any dramatic way and chose to emphasize the horizontal sweep by articulating the second floor with **pilasters**. They created punctuation points with columned pavilions that jut out only slightly from the mass of the structure, with sculpture decorating their **cornices**. The design and ornament are completely classical, in keeping with the French interest in drawing a relationship between the principles of order and control and the rule of the French monarchy.

The Salon de la Guerre offers a rich scheme of multimedia Baroque decoration (fig. 7-44). A huge oval stucco relief over the fireplace with a monumental equestrian figure of Louis XIV immediately draws our attention. Below, dark bronze reliefs represent prisoners in chains, while above, gilt stucco angels trumpet his fame and offer him the hero's crown. The relief in the fireplace shows the muse of history, Clio, recording Louis's triumphs. The combination of materials—stucco, bronze, gilded stucco, and marble—and the parquet floors, mirrors, paintings on the ceiling, and a crystal-and-gold chandelier testify to the wealth of the king, while the iconography emphasizes his imperialistic ambitions. Such a

1669

1669	**Le Vau and Hardouin Mansart, Versailles begun**
1669	Antonio Stradivari makes violins in Cremona, Italy
1670	Molière, *Le Bourgeois Gentilhomme*

7-44. Jules Hardouin Mansart, Charles Lebrun, and Antoine Coysevox. Salon de la Guerre (Room of War), Palace of Versailles. Begun 1678. This room, at one end of the Hall of Mirrors, is a pendant to the Room of Peace at the opposite end; the decoration of these rooms celebrated recent French victories. The sculptor Coysevox is responsible for the huge stucco relief of *Louis XIV on Horseback* over the fireplace. The painted ceiling, the theme of which is France at war, is by Lebrun. The Hall of Mirrors was named for the large mirrors opposite the arched garden windows. As decoration, this room had bejeweled trees and gold and silver furniture, but these were melted down in 1689 and 1709 to help pay for French wars. Commissioned by Louis XIV

7-45. André Le Nôtre. Plan of the gardens and park, Versailles (17th-century engraving). Designed 1661–68; executed 1662–90. Note that the main streets of the town of Versailles, at the bottom of the map, converge on the palace to emphasize its significance. André Le Nôtre, son of a royal gardener, became the greatest designer of formal gardens and parks in seventeenth-century Europe. The layout of the garden uses radiating diagonals and dramatic long vistas. Commissioned by Louis XIV

room was primarily a setting for court ritual and would be in use especially on those occasions when its particular iconography would be most effective.

In the great park, ponds and pathways seem infinite, and at each crossroad there are several choices of direction in which to proceed (fig. 7-45). The vistas and paths offer sur-prises: fountains, basins, terraces, flights of steps, sculptural groups, flowerbeds, hedges, and even small architectural monuments. Nature on a vast scale has been tamed and ordered, to provide a place of pleasure for the king and his court. Although the most basic purpose of the park is the same as that of the palace—to reflect the glory of the French monarchy and the king's centralized authority—André Le Nôtre (1613–1700) has also been sensitive to the delights of nature that such a park can offer to the observer. The plan informs us of the general layout, but Le Nôtre's park was not designed to be seen from above, but by the human spectator, walking, choosing pathways and vistas.

JAPANESE ART

7-46. Sotatsu. Pair of six-panel *byobu*, known as the *Matsushima Screens*. 17th century. Ink, color, and gold leaf on paper; each screen 4'9⁷/₈" x 11'8¹/₂". Freer Gallery of Art, Smithsonian Institution, Washington, D.C.

The highly decorative mode of painting that flourished in the seventeenth century in Japan characterizes native Japanese taste. Painting was executed on large-scale surfaces: sliding door panels (*fusuma*) or folding screens (*byobu*), usually executed in pairs. The style is characterized by the use of bold colors with gold leaf and by the use of stylized motifs for the houses of royalty, the aristocracy, and commoners. The most popular themes demonstrate a revival of the basic Japanese concerns with the natural world and with people and their activities, including such genre themes as horse races, theatrical performances, bathhouse prostitutes, and even Westerners. One pair of *byobu* (fig. 7-46) by Sotatsu (active 1600–40) are called the *Matsushima Screens* because they are thought by some scholars to depict Matsushima, one of the *sankai*, or three most beautiful landscapes in Japan. This bay near Sendai, far to the north of Kyoto, is dotted with small pine-capped islands. Other scholars argue that these *byobu* are not specific and only represent exceptionally beautiful passages of landscape. Still others argue that because the islands in the pictures resemble rocky configurations along the shore near Ise, these *byobu* illustrate a poem from *The Tales of Ise* that deals with the feelings of a man who, banished from the capital, gazes at the surf and white-capped water as he crosses a beach; because the twelfth-century illustrators of *The Tale of Genji* used natural elements to reflect human emotions, there is historical precedent for this interpretation. Whatever the subject, there is no question that the artist's vision has distorted reality, as is evident in the passage in which gold clouds turn into rocky shores where pine trees cling and grow.

One of the favorite books of Imperial Prince Toshihito (1579–1629) was *The Tale of Genji* (see pages 216–17), and many of the details of the Imperial Villa he commissioned at Katsura (see figs. 1-5, 7-47, 7-48), southwest of Kyoto, were inspired by this tenth-century novel. The last palace built by the novel's main character, Genji, was called Katsura, and it too was located along the Katsura River. As described in the novel, it was subdued and relatively unostentatious. It contained a large lake with several artificial islands, a rustic fishing pavilion, and a lodge next to the racetrack for the games that were held there in conjunction with festivals at the Kamo shrine in Kyoto. Toshihito's new royal seventeenth-century residence consisted of a main *shoin* (a large residence) with a bamboo-floored moon-viewing platform, a smaller *shoin*, and a music room placed in a garden, all set out in accordance with descriptions in *The Tale of Genji*.

One of the imperial family's important symbolic roles was to maintain traditional Japanese culture, which was accomplished at Katsura Villa by retaining native choices in design and in decorative styles. Traditional Japanese aesthetic expression is recalled in all

17th century	**Sotatsu, *Matsushima Screens***
1670	Minute hands are first used on watches
1670	André Le Nôtre lays out the Champs-Elysées in Paris

7-47. General view of *shoin*, Katsura Imperial Villa, Kyoto, Japan. 1620–63. For an interior view, see figure 1-5. Commissioned by Prince Hachijo Toshihito and his son Toshitada

1 old *shoin*	4 narrow veranda
2 middle *shoin*	5 visitors carriage rest
3 moon-viewing platform	6 vestibule

7-48. Plan of *shoin*, Katsura Imperial Villa

elements of the house—the use of natural wood structural members (fig. 7-47), irregular and asymmetrical planning of room sizes and their positions (fig. 7-48), sliding paper doors as illustrated in *Genji* manuscripts (see fig. 4-73), and the abrupt contrasts of textures in the rocks, plants, water, and dry areas of the gardens.

At other villas of the period, the rank of individuals, so important in the samurai culture of this period, were emphasized through different floor levels or by the placement of connotative images in the *tokonoma,* a shallow, recessed platform where paintings and flower arrangements or objects of value were placed. Because Katsura Villa was designed for the imperial family as a place where they could put aside issues of class in a relaxed atmosphere, there are no such provisions for emphasizing rank. This less formal character is consistent with *The Tale of Genji.*

Seventeenth-century art in Japan was dominated by a spirit of reflection and a return to established traditions. The standard set by the nobility focused on the art of tea and on such classics of Japanese literature as *The Tale of Genji* and *The Tales of Ise.* Japanese aristocrats were expected to know *The Tales of Ise* by heart. The Katsura Villa and the screens by Sotatsu are characterized by the self-assuredness and return to historical precedent so important in this period of political stability and economic prosperity.

LANDSCAPE PAINTING

7-49. Jacob van Ruisdael. *Dutch Landscape from the Dunes at Overveen*. c. 1670. Oil on canvas, 21⁷/₈ x 24³/₈". Mauritshuis, The Hague, The Netherlands

During the seventeenth century, the flat expanses of the Netherlands, reclaimed from the sea and wrested from Spanish domination, were painted thousands of times by Dutch painters. These paintings were avidly collected by the proud and patriotic citizens of the new nation. Although there had been a sporadic interest in landscape among Northern painters during the six-

teenth century, now, for the first time in the history of Western art, landscape became a truly popular theme. In the seventeenth century, the Netherlands was more highly urbanized than any other European nation, and the nostalgia felt by city dwellers for open countryside may have been an additional factor in explaining the popularity of landscape painting.

Despite its relatively small size, *Dutch Landscape from the Dunes at Overveen*, by Jacob van Ruisdael (1628/29–82), captures the salient features of the Dutch countryside: land, sky, and a changing relationship between light and shade (fig. 7-49). More than two-thirds of the canvas is given over to the clouded sky, which is the dominant feature of the Dutch countryside. The sky becomes the

c. 1670	**Van Ruisdael, _Dutch Landscape_**
1675	Native American population drops to about 20,000
1675	Antonie van Leeuwenhoek invents the microscope

7-50. Peter Paul Rubens. _Landscape with Het Steen._ c. 1636. Oil on panel, 51^5/$_8$" x 7'6^1/$_4$". The National Gallery, London. This view of Het Steen, the country estate Rubens bought in 1635, remained in his possession during his lifetime.

mediator by which we perceive the land as well. As the clouds rush by, the earth is intermittently revealed by patches of bright light.

Ruisdael's landscape is precisely identifiable, for the Gothic church that rises among red tile roofs in the background is St. Bavo in Haarlem. The ubiquitous Dutch windmills, so necessary to keep the land drained of excess water, dot the countryside; in the foreground, small figures stretch linen to be bleached, a proud reference to the prosperous Haarlem linen industry. The function of this realistic image is clear: to represent and exalt the local countryside and its livelihood.

Although other seventeenth-century painters occasionally demonstrate an interest in landscape—Poussin with his classical land-

scapes (see fig. 7-40) and Rubens with his views of the Flemish countryside—these are exceptions, and only in the Netherlands did a truly national school of landscape painters develop.

Although the Dutch seem to have preferred realistic views of local scenery, Dutch painters also produced a variety of other types of landscape painting, including seascapes with Dutch vessels and rather fantastic views of wild scenery. A number of Dutch artists settled in Rome, where they painted views of the sun-drenched Italian countryside that were popular back home.

The sixteenth-century Flemish interest in landscape found a worthy successor in Rubens, whose landscapes have the same tumultuous

vitality and visual excitement as his religious, mythological, and allegorical pictures. In his landscapes, Rubens puts us in contact with the growth and energies of the world of nature. In his _Landscape with Het Steen_ (fig. 7-50), the rising sun is a shimmering silver-yellow disk near the right edge of the painting. A hunter and his dog in the foreground draw our eyes to a stump, which in turn leads us to an undulating row of trees that surge into the landscape toward the fresh, glowing morning sky. Simultaneously, a peasant family that is going to market in the shadowy left foreground draws our attention to the opposite direction. Rubens's personal energies and his understanding of the dynamic and ever-changing nature of landscape are here united.

8-1. Germain Boffrand. Salon de la Princesse, Hôtel de Soubise, Paris. 1736–39. The term *hôtel* in this context refers to the lavishly adorned town houses of the French aristocracy. Commissioned by François de Rohan, Prince de Soubise

INTRODUCTION TO EIGHTEENTH-CENTURY ART

This interior design for the Princess's Salon (fig. 8-1), by Germain Boffrand (1667–1754), exemplifies the decorative exuberance of the Rococo style, which in the eighteenth century succeeded the Baroque. The decoration of the oval room is animated with carved and painted woodwork, stucco, and a series of integral paintings depicting the tale of the mythological lovers Cupid and Psyche. The web of gold woodwork and stucco ornament creates a light, airy sensation that seems to transform the white walls into thin screens, while the undulating movement of the curving **cornice** joins the rhythm of the delicate arches to further enliven the interior. The effect is elegant and ebullient.

Some similar aesthetic qualities are apparent in the beautiful wooden synagogue of Wolpa, Poland (fig. 8-2), but here the effect is dependent solely on architectural form and definition of space rather than on richness of materials and refinement of decorative patterns. This and the other wooden synagogues of this period in Poland, all destroyed in the Holocaust, provide an important example of how a period style—in this case, the Rococo—could be combined with local folk art traditions to serve a particular need. Here the local eastern European tradition of wooden architecture has been transformed to produce a large religious structure of great sophistication in design. The unknown architects have simultaneously combined a series of balconies, intended for use by the women of the congregation, with elegant curving forms that pull our eyes upward. The four great columns—here timber **piers**—that support the structure were traditional in synagogue design and are a reference to the destroyed Temple of Solomon in Jerusalem.

Just slightly more than twenty years after the Rococo elegance of the Princess's Salon, the English architect Robert Adam (1728–92) began remodeling Osterley Park House. The fireplace niche in the entrance hall (fig. 8-3) demonstrates Adam's use of an alternate eighteenth-century style, Neoclassicism, in which the ornamentation is based on antique prototypes, from the **pilasters** and **coffered half dome** to the wall moldings. The axis is visually reinforced by the Neoclassical relief set over the fireplace, while the flanking niches with their antique sculptures balance the composition and add further references to the cultures of classical antiquity. In contrast to Boffrand's Rococo interior and the Wolpa synagogue's exuberant spatial effects, Adam's Neoclassical design is disciplined and controlled. The antithesis between these designs reflects the enormous artistic contrasts of the eighteenth century.

HISTORY

The eighteenth century was a period when the differences between the West and the rest of the world became even more pronounced. During this period, traditional values dominated most of the countries of Asia. Both Japan during the Edo period (1615–1868) and China during the Qing dynasty (1644–1912) continued

8-2. Synagogue, Wolpa, Poland (now destroyed). 18th century. Wood. The wooden synagogues in Poland were systematically destroyed during the Holocaust, but fortunately they had been well documented in photographs and drawings.

8-3. Robert Adam. Fireplace niche, Entrance Hall, Osterley Park House, Middlesex (London), England. Begun 1761. Adam's adaptation of classical architectural forms was so successful that one phase of the English Neoclassical style is known as the Adamesque. Commissioned by Francis Child

to be almost exclusively concerned with internal affairs. Both demonstrated a concern with understanding and continuing their own traditions and excluding Western influence. Japan remained closed to the West during this period. In northern India, the Mughal empire was in decline, but in art there was a continuation of traditional values and ideas. During the eighteenth century, Russia and Austria made important gains against the Ottoman

Turks, although the Ottoman empire would last until 1918. It was in the West in the eighteenth century, however, that the revolutionary currents of democracy began to rewrite the face of politics, of social structure, and of art.

The memorable opening lines from Dickens's novel about the French Revolution can describe the European eighteenth century as a whole:

> It was the best of times, it was the worst of times, it was the age of wisdom, it was the age of foolishness, it was the epoch of belief, it was the epoch of incredulity, it was the season of Light, it was the season of Darkness. (Charles Dickens, *A Tale of Two Cities*, first published 1859)

8-4. Hyacinthe Rigaud. *Portrait of King Louis XIV of France.* 1701. Oil on canvas, 9 x 6'. The Louvre, Paris. Commissioned by Louis XIV

It was a century of social, cultural, and artistic contrasts, prodigious scientific and technological advances, and sweeping political changes. Historians often refer to the close of this century as the period that marks the beginning of the modern Western world.

Politically, the century opened with the dominance of France under Louis XIV. The Baroque portrait by Hyacinthe Rigaud (1659–1743) conveys the solemn majesty of his authority and the opulence with which the French monarchs were surrounded (fig. 8-4). After Louis XIV's death in 1715, however, France's military and political influence began to abate. Frederick the Great, who came to the throne in Prussia in 1740, seized opportunities to expand and establish the German states as the premier military power on the Continent. To check Prussia's growing political and military strength, France and Austria entered an alliance. In the resulting conflict, known as the Seven Years' War (1756–63), Prussia was victorious. France's holdings and influence in the Americas were diminished when Quebec surrendered to the English in 1759 (see fig. 8-24), effectively ending the French and Indian War in North America. Austria was defeated in the Seven Years' War but prospered in the latter part of the century, under Maria Theresa and her son, Joseph II, to become one of Europe's most distinguished cultural centers.

England's economic stability and political importance grew steadily through the century. By the 1750s, England was established as an important maritime power, and the victory over the French in North America gave the English command of much of that continent. By the close of the century, England enjoyed the highest per capita income in western Europe as the new industrial economy took root. London's population grew to more than 1 million, the first modern city to reach that size. At the same time, George III, who ruled from 1760 to 1820, saw the power of the monarchy wrested away by Parliament. Increased taxation led the American colonies to declare independence in 1776; and, with French assistance, the colonies defeated the British at Yorktown in 1781. A peace treaty was signed between England and the new American nation in 1783.

The growing desire for self-rule, one of the features of the philosophy of the Enlightenment (see below) in response to the authoritarian rule of Europe's traditional absolute monarchs, also affected developments in France. During the reign of Louis XVI and his wife, Marie Antoinette, lavish government expenditures led to economic depression. As relations between the French aristocracy and the people deteriorated, the National Assembly was formed in 1789 to compose a written constitution for France. During the French Revolution, a constitutional monarchy was established, but internal political factions and outside military pressure threatened the new government. Within France, hostility against the aristocracy rose to a fever pitch by 1792, and in the bloody executions that followed, even Louis XVI and his queen were guillotined. Within this context of domestic uncertainty and foreign wars, a young military commander, Napoleon Bonaparte, rose in power and, at the age of thirty in 1799, was made first consul of the French Republic.

INTELLECTUAL AND SCIENTIFIC ACTIVITY IN EUROPE

The eighteenth century has been called the Age of Enlightenment. The influence of the Catholic Church declined, and philosophical investigations were directed less to theological than to secular and scientific issues. Descartes's belief in the supremacy of human reason and the centrality of the natural sciences, which dates from the seventeenth century, was inherited and advanced by eighteenth-century philosophers. The Enlightenment was marked by faith in human reason, natural human rights, science, and progress toward a utopian society. This joining of the natural sciences with philosophical questioning strengthened the belief in empiricism, a view that human knowledge was pragmatically gained from experience and sensation. The foremost proponent of empiricism from the late seventeenth century was the English writer John Locke. Locke's treatises on government, based on his experience with the rise of parliamentary government in England, avowed that a nation's power derived from its people. The people

8-5. Elizabeth Vigée-Lebrun. *Portrait of Marie Gabrielle de Gramont, Duchesse de Caderousse.* 1784. Oil on wood, 41³/₈ x 29⁷/₈". The Nelson-Atkins Museum of Art, Kansas City, Missouri. Elizabeth Vigée-Lebrun was one of the foremost artists of Louis XVI's court. In her memoirs, Vigée-Lebrun wrote: ". . . I could not endure powder. I persuaded the handsome Duchess de Gramont-Caderousse to put none on for her sittings. Her hair was ebony black, and I divided it in the forehead, disposing it in irregular curls. After the sitting, which ended at the dinner hour, the Duchess would not change her headdress but go to the theatre as she was. A woman of such good looks would, of course, set a fashion: indeed, this mode of doing the hair soon found imitators, and then gradually became general. This reminds me that in 1786, when I was painting the Queen, I begged her to use no powder, and to part her hair on the forehead. 'I should be the last to follow that fashion,' said the Queen, laughing; 'I do not want people to say that I adopted it to hide my large forehead.'"

Purchase: acquired through the generosity of numerous donors

entered into a social contract with their government and retained the right to dissent and withdraw support if their government proved no longer responsive to their will and needs. Locke's political philosophy guided the American Revolution and the drafting of the U.S. Constitution and, through Voltaire, assisted in fomenting the French Revolution.

Empiricism also fertilized the growth of the natural sciences. Building on Isaac Newton's observations and discoveries, advances continued in physics, mathematics, and astronomy. In 1759, Edmund Halley's name was given to the comet that returns every seventy-six years. Zoology, botany, and mineralogy were established as scientific disciplines. The chemist Antoine Lavoisier was the first to demonstrate correctly the process of combustion; he later named the reactive element, essential for life, oxygen. Constant improvements in such devices as the telescope, microscope, barometer, and thermometer allowed for greater accuracy in scientific observation.

8-6. Thomas Chippendale (probably). Bed. 1750–54. Wood, japanned in red and gilt. Victoria and Albert Museum, London

Technology benefited from this increasing scientific knowledge. New processes in metallurgy contributed to the use of iron as a building material, and the perfection of the steam engine by James Watt in 1769 brought Europe closer to the momentous and far-reaching economic and social changes of the Industrial Revolution.

EIGHTEENTH-CENTURY ART IN EUROPE

The Rococo and Neoclassical styles dominated the visual arts in Europe during the eighteenth century. The term *Rococo,* derived from the French *rocaille* (literally "rock-work" or "rubble"), was first used to designate a style of French art associated with the reign of Louis XV. In early-eighteenth-century France, charm and finesse were the hallmarks of an artificial code of social behavior. The Rococo's light, ornamental elegance, as exemplified in the portrait (fig. 8-5) by Elizabeth Vigée-Lebrun (1755–1842), complemented the artificiality of aristocratic values and tastes.

The contact with other cultures that brought new styles and aesthetic ideas into European art reveals not only an interest in new and exotic ideas but also a typical European superficiality in response to outside cultures and influences. The bed illustrated here (fig. 8-6), probably by the famous English furniture maker Thomas Chippendale (1718–79), was inspired by the elegant forms of Chinese architecture, especially the pagoda roof. In Europe, this style, known as *chinoiserie,* was popular for chairs, tables, wallpaper, porcelain, clocks, and other decorative arts. Pieces of Chinese porcelain of elegant simplicity were enshrined in elaborate Rococo mounts. Although Europeans in general made little attempt to understand the Chinese civilization, there were few European eighteenth-century palaces that did not have a room decorated in this style. This approach to foreign cultures—borrowing without understanding—reveals the attitudes typical of Westerners during much of the early modern period.

The Neoclassical style, first named in the mid-nineteenth century, developed as an alternative to the Rococo in the eighteenth. Fueling the Neoclassical style at mid-century was a reawakened interest in classical antiquity spurred by the rediscovery of two Roman cities that had been buried by the first-century eruption of Mount Vesuvius: Herculaneum was found in 1738 and Pompeii in 1748. The revival movement of Neoclassicism is the first in a series of revivals—some nostalgic, some ideological—that would flourish in the nineteenth century, and because of this, Neoclassicism is sometimes understood as the first step in the development of the broader movement known as Romanticism (see page 422).

The most eloquent spokesperson for Neoclassical taste was the German art historian Johann Winckelmann, who had his portrait painted by Angelica Kauffmann (1741–1807), one of the most famous artists of the period. He viewed the rationality and ideality of classical art as the summit of artistic achievement. In his influential *Thoughts on the Imitation of Greek Art in Painting and Sculpture* of 1755, Winckelmann wrote:

> Good taste, which is spreading more and more throughout the world, had its beginning under a Greek sky. . . . To take the ancients for models is our only way to become great, yes, unsurpassable if we can. As someone has said of Homer: he who learns to admire him, learns to understand him; the same is true of the art works of the ancients, especially the Greeks.

Neoclassical art was well suited to the changing political realities of the late eighteenth century. Compared to the lighthearted and aristocratic elegance of Rococo art, the Neoclassical style offered a restrained, solemn design that was intended to convey a moral dignity. As ancient classical edifices first bore witness to the representative governments of Athens and Rome, what better style was there to emulate during the new age, which asserted that each individual had natural rights—or, in the words of the Declaration of Independence, "inalienable rights"—and that among these was a voice in government? To the Neoclassicists, the art and history of the classical world offered models to be used as guides for human behavior and achievement.

THE EIGHTEENTH-CENTURY ARTIST IN EUROPE

The education of artists in academies (see pages 33–34) was now firmly established in Europe. The Royal Academy of Painting and Sculpture in Paris, founded in 1648, flourished, sending promising students to Rome to study classical art. Its primacy was gradually challenged by the Royal Academy of Arts, founded in London in 1768, which also championed Neoclassicism. The guiding spirit of England's Royal Academy was Joshua Reynolds (1723–92), a painter who had spent two years in Italy studying both ancient and Renaissance arts (see fig. 8-17). As the Royal Academy's first president, Reynolds delivered fifteen *Discourses,* which expressed his views on learning the "grand style" of art and outlined an education based on imitating the perfection of nature as revealed through classical and High Renaissance art:

> The moderns are not less convinced than the ancients of [the] superior power existing in art; nor less sensible of its effects. . . . The *gusto grande* of the Italians, the *beau ideal* of the French, and the great style, genius, and taste among the English, are but different appellations of the same thing. It is this intellectual dignity . . . that ennobles the painter's art . . . we must have recourse to the ancients as instructors . . . they will suggest many observations, which would probably escape you, if your study were confined to nature alone.

Reynolds also recommended the study of the "great masters" of the Italian Renaissance:

> I would chiefly recommend, that an implicit obedience to the Rules of Art, as established by the practice of the great masters, should be exacted from the young students. That those models, which have passed through the approbation of ages, should be considered by them as perfect and infallible guides; as subjects for their imitation, not their criticism.

Although the Royal Academy was founded to raise the status of both the arts and the artists, its conservative dogmatism, as revealed by Reynolds's preemptory language, began to be viewed by some as a constrictive environment. The tradition of the academy, which in the later sixteenth century had begun as part of a liberating ambiance for the artist, was now becoming a conservative cloak, dictating proprieties in subject matter and form. One academic priority was history painting, which was promoted as the most noble of artistic expressions. History painting drew its iconography from the classical past and, less often, the more recent past. Themes were

8-7. Adélaide Labille-Guiard. *Self-Portrait with Two Pupils.* 1785. Oil on canvas, 6'10³/4" x 4'11⁷/8". The Metropolitan Museum of Art, New York. Labille-Guiard was instrumental in convincing the French Academy to lift its quota on women members, who had been limited to four, and to allow women professors.

Gift of Julia A. Berwind, 1953 (53.225.5)

8-8. Angelica Kauffmann. *Self-Portrait Hesitating between the Arts of Music and Painting.* 1791. Oil on canvas, 4'10" x 7'2". Nostell Priory, Yorkshire, England

selected that could be interpreted on several levels. Academic history painters most often picked themes that exemplified an elevated code of human behavior. Such themes were considered appropriate for the "grand style" or the "grand manner" in art.

To truly understand the "grand style," every artist who aspired to gain professional fame felt compelled to make a tour of the antiquities of Italy. We can understand the importance of viewing the actual artistic remains of the classical and Renaissance past from the letters of Benjamin West (see page 411), an American painter who, en route to London, traveled from 1760 to 1763 through Italy. West later wrote to another American artist, John Singleton Copley, advising him on what to see in Italy:

> In regard to your studies in Italy my advice is as follows: That you pursue the higher Excellences in the Art, and for the obtaining of which I recommend to your attention the works of Ancient Sculptors, Raphael, Michelangelo, Correggio, and Titian, as the Source from which true taste in the arts have flowed.

In terms of patronage, little changed in the eighteenth century. The grandest projects were those commissioned by royalty, nobility, and the Church, but in a democratic society like America the state also began to become an important patron, as revealed in Thomas Jefferson's Capitol for the State of Virginia (see fig. 8-19). Portraits were staple product for both painters and sculptors. The growing importance of academies and their exhibitions and competitions (such as the Prize of Rome) meant, however, that artists were encouraged to develop large display pieces with a subject of their own choosing. Some artists, such as Hogarth (see fig. 8-11) and David (see fig. 8-22), created works that make a powerful personal statement intended for the public; their belief that art can change or reform society led to some of the most idealistic art of this period and has had an impact on our belief in the power of art to the present day.

Eighteenth-century artists' self-portraits reflect the vitality of the different art styles that characterized the Age of Enlightenment. Adélaide Labille-Guiard (1749–1803) continued the Rococo style into the latter years of the century. Noted for her abilities as both an artist and a teacher, she depicted herself, in elegant dress, at her easel with two attentive students (fig. 8-7). An early self-portrait by Angelica Kauffmann (fig. 8-8) shows the young artist between figures representing the classical allegories of Music and Painting. Kauffmann, who was an accomplished musician, here adapted the Neoclassical style to demonstrate her dilemma at having to choose between music and painting as a career.

CE	1700		1720
EUROPE ART	**1717** WATTEAU'S *PILGRIMAGE TO THE ISLAND OF CYTHERA*		**1735–44** NEUMANN'S KAISERSAAL
HISTORY	**1707** United Kingdom of Great Britain formed **1715** Death of Louis XIV, France		
ASIA ART	**c. 1700** SHITAO'S LANDSCAPE PAINTINGS, CHINA	**18TH CENTURY** MARUYAMA-SHIJO SCHOOL OF PAINTING, JAPAN	**18TH CENTURY** HAKUIN EKAKU'S ZEN PAINTINGS, JAPAN
HISTORY	**c. 1525–18TH CENTURY** Mughal empire in India **1615–1868** Edo period in Japan **1644–1912** Qing dynasty in China		**1724** State of Hyderbad in India achieves independence from Mughal empire **1724** Chinese take control of Tibet **1739** Nadir Shah sacks Delhi
THE AMERICAS ART	**c. 1700** TAOS PUEBLO BUILT, NEW MEXICO		
HISTORY			
AFRICA ART	**18TH CENTURY** EKOI ANCESTOR FIGURES	**18TH CENTURY** BENIN ROYAL ART	**18TH CENTURY** BUSHONGO ROYAL FIGURES
HISTORY	**18TH CENTURY** Ottoman Turks expand power in North Africa	**1713** Asiento Treaty starts most active period of British slave trade **1715** French take Mauritius	**c. 1730–50** Awura Pokou rules as queen of the Baule people
THE MIDDLE EAST ART			
HISTORY	**18TH CENTURY** Ottoman Turks rule lands of former Mesopotamia		**1722** Afghans overthrow Safavid dynasty, Iran **1736** Nadir Shah establishes Afshar dynasty, Iran

1740	**1760**	**1780**

1787
DAVID'S *DEATH OF SOCRATES*

1740
Frederick the Great ascends throne of Prussia

1756–63
Seven Years' War

1760–1820
Rule of George III of England

1769
James Watt perfects steam engine, Scotland

1789–99
French Revolution

1791
Olympe de Gouges's *Declaration of the Rights of Women and Female Citizens*

1799
Napoleon Bonaparte becomes first consul of French Republic

MID-18TH CENTURY
UKIYO-E PAINTINGS, JAPAN

1757
British Rule established in India

1777
Christianity introduced into Korea

1787
Rice riots in Edo, Japan

1796
British conquer Ceylon from Dutch

c. 1768–70
COPLEY'S *PORTRAIT OF PAUL REVERE*

1785–89
JEFFERSON'S VIRGINIA STATE CAPITOL

1756–63
French and Indian War

1759
British defeat French at Quebec

1774
First Continental Congress of American colonies

1775–83
American Revolution

1775
Second Continental Congress of American colonies

1776
Declaration of Independence of American colonies

1781
Colonies defeat British at Yorktown, winning the Revolutionary War

1787
U.S. Constitution signed

1789
George Washington elected president of the United States

1791
 U.S. ratifies Bill of Rights

1768–73
James Bruce reaches the source of the Blue Nile in Abyssinia

1792
Denmark is first nation to prohibit slave trade

1799
Bonaparte leads French army into Egypt

LATE 18TH CENTURY
ZAND DYNASTY ARCHITECTURE FOR CAPITAL AT SHIRAZ

1787–92
Austria and Russia combine to fight the Ottoman Turks

1799
Bonaparte invades Syria

EIGHTEENTH-CENTURY PAINTING IN EUROPE

8-9. Antoine Watteau. *A Pilgrimage to the Island of Cythera*. 1717. Oil on canvas, 4'3" x 6'4¹/₂". The Louvre, Paris. As Watteau's reception piece for the French Royal Academy, this painting was listed as *"une fête galante,"* a new category of painting in which elegant aristocratic men and women are represented partying in a landscape setting.

8-10. Jean-Honoré Fragonard. *Happy Accidents of the Swing*. 1767. Oil on canvas, 31⁷/₈ x 25³/₈". Wallace Collection, London. Commissioned by Baron de Saint-Julien, Receveur général des biens du clergé

A Pilgrimage to the Island of Cythera, by Antoine Watteau (1684–1721), combines reality and fantasy to express the transitory nature of romantic love (fig. 8-9). Delicately scaled couples in eighteenth-century dress move slowly toward a fanciful ship that will return them from the island of Cythera, mythical home of Venus, goddess of love. The statue of Venus at the right has been adorned with garlands by these pensive lovers, who came to worship at her shrine and engage in the rituals of her cult. Their reluctance to leave pleasure behind is expressed in their gestures and poses, while the muted colors and light brushstroke express the transience of love. The composition moves from the statue of Venus to the vessel of departure, reversing our normal reading direction and heightening the bittersweet nature of the departure. Watteau simultaneously conveyed the poetry of love and suggested how remote it is from everyday reality. Romantic love survives only in the world of the imagination.

Fragonard's painting, on the other hand, reaffirms the pleasures of lovers' games (fig. 8-10). Jean-Honoré Fragonard (1732–1806) received the commission for the painting from Baron de Saint-Julien, who specified the details of the subject. His mistress is in a swing pushed by a bishop so high that her slipper falls off the tip of her foot and her skirt shoots upward for the delight of the indiscreet eyes of a charming youth reclining among the flowers beneath her; happily there hovers above him a cupid whose gesture enjoins him to keep the secret of what he has seen.

The theme incorporates an obvious pun, for the baron served as the government representative who collected the taxes paid by the Church. His title was *Receveur général des biens du clergé* ("Receiver general of the 'goods' offered by the clergy"). Fragonard's pastel palette, which centers around the pink dress and the blue-green trees, and the delicate lightness of his brushstroke help to underline the frivolity of the subject.

The qualities seen in these two works help to define Rococo painting. The colors are unusually light,

8-11. William Hogarth. *Marriage à la Mode, Scene II*. 1743. Oil on canvas, 27½ x 35¾". The National Gallery, London. This is the second scene in a series of six. To Hogarth's contemporaries, *"à la mode"* implied something fashionable but cheap and short-lived. The series was subtitled *Modern Occurrences in High Life*. Hogarth's painted series on moral subjects was reproduced as popular engravings. The artist compared himself to dramatists and novelists, saying that he "considered subjects as writers do," adding, "My picture was my stage and men and women my actors." The inspiration of contemporary English theater (Gay) and literature (Fielding, Defoe) on Hogarth is well documented. In two earlier series, Hogarth chronicled *A Harlot's Progress* (1728–30), which follows an attractive young girl from her arrival in London, where she is discovered by a procuress, to her death, and *A Rake's Progress* (1735), in which a weak young man wastes his father's fortune, ending up in an asylum, probably the infamous English Bedlam.

and the thin paint is delicately brushed onto the surface. The figures are generally small and delicate in proportion, and the composition creates a flowing, idyllic movement. Themes are superficial scenes from court life, especially romance.

A series of paintings done by William Hogarth (1697–1764), *Marriage à la Mode*, presents a satirical view of modern life and exposes the difficulties of a loveless "city" marriage of convenience (fig. 8-11). The serious nature of Hogarth's social criticism of both the nouveau riche and the nobility is evident throughout the series, which begins with the signing of the marriage contract between the daughter of a rich, social-climbing merchant and an impoverished nobleman (Count Squanderfield). In a sequence of six scenes,

their debauchery progresses through adultery, the murder of the husband by the wife's lover (Silvertongue), and her death by suicide, leaving their only child an orphan. Our scene shows the husband returning at 1:20 P.M. with a hangover after a night on the town. The dog sniffs at a woman's cap hanging from his pocket. His pose is meant to suggest sexual exhaustion. The wife's pose and the overturned chair and scattered music suggest that her lover is the music teacher, who seems to have departed quickly. Extravagance is evident in the ugly mantelpiece, with its ostentatious display of bric-a-brac, and the stack of bills held by the clerk. The painting over the mantel features a figure of Cupid, Venus's son and assistant, blowing a bagpipe—an inharmonious phallic

symbol—amid ruins. The venereal disease that will ultimately infect the couple's child is already evident in the black spot on the husband's neck. In style, the looseness of Hogarth's brushstrokes in the original paintings is indebted to the example of contemporary French painting.

Romantic love—its dreams and disappointments, pleasures and pains, realities and fantasies—becomes a central theme in Rococo art. The variety of interpretation, demonstrated in these three examples, and the probing character of the representations reveal important changes as the themes of art are broadened, revealing an expanded interest in the psychological and emotional states that affect people in their everyday lives.

ROCOCO ARCHITECTURE AND SCULPTURE

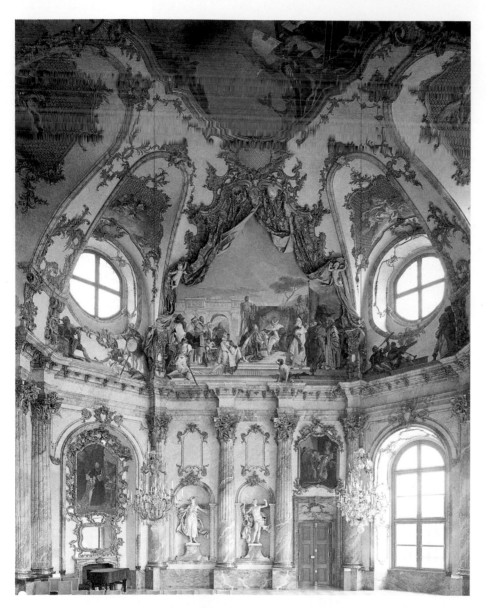

8-12. Johann Balthasar Neumann, Giambattist Tiepolo, and Antonio Bossi. Kaisersaal (Imperial Hall), Episcopal Palace, Würzburg, Germany. 1735–44. The 1751–52 frescoes by Tiepolo represent scenes glorifying the twelfth-century German emperor Frederick Barbarossa and the bishop of Würzburg. The stucco work is by Antonio Bossi. The Italian painter Tiepolo spent three years in Würzburg decorating this official residence of the prince-bishops of Würzburg. Commissioned by the Prince-Bishop of Würzburg

The Kaisersaal documents the life of the aristocracy in the eighteenth century (fig. 8-12). One must imagine it filled with the elaborate furniture of the period, its crystal chandeliers lit with flickering candles. The shape of this elegant salon is too complicated to be either an oval or an octagon, but it is surmounted by a high oval dome pierced by windows. The columns seem to be a beautiful pink marble, but like most such columns in Rococo buildings, they are stucco painted and polished to give the illusion of marble. The lightness of the architecture is enhanced by the large irregular frescoed oval and by two scenes enframed by elaborate, gilded curtains. Painted figures and animals by Giambattist Tiepolo (1696–1770) wander out onto the entablature to chat, sit, and look down at us.

The Rococo style in architecture developed in France at Versailles about 1700 and flourished in southern Germany in part because of political connections. The palace at Würzburg was built by a family of local hereditary prince-bishops who set out to surpass Versailles (see fig. 7-43). The Rococo style is perhaps at its most exuberant here, where all restraint seems to evaporate in gilded decoration, fake marble columns, and an indissoluble union of painting and architecture. Although it owes its origins to the classical vocabulary of the Renaissance, the Rococo offers a new lightness of color and of movement and a new delicate scale of ornament, which are in contrast to the more ponderous forms and colors of Baroque architecture.

Equally exuberant is the church nicknamed Die Wies near Munich

1721	J. S. Bach, Brandenburg Concertos
1724	Convent of Corpus Christi for Native American women founded, Mexico
1728	Gay, *The Beggar's Opera*
1732	Benjamin Franklin's *Poor Richard's Almanack* is issued
1735–44	**Neumann, Kaisersaal**
1739	John Wesley founds the Methodist movement
1741	Handel, *The Messiah*
1748	Fielding, *Tom Jones*

8-13. Dominikus Zimmerman. Interior, Die Wies, Germany. 1745–54. The frescoed vault and stucco decoration are probably by Johann Baptist Zimmerman, the architect's brother. The exterior of this structure is rather plain, and the contrast between exterior and interior is an important part of the architectural experience. Commissioned by the local bishop

8-14. Egid Quirin Asam. *Assumption of the Virgin*, detail. 1721–23. Painted and gilded stucco and stained glass. Monastery Church, Rohr, Germany

(fig. 8-13). Here Rococo architecture and decoration become a visionary premonition of the heavenly Jerusalem. Die Wies is a pilgrimage center where devout Catholics of all classes worship at the shrine of a miraculous statue of Christ. Virtually every surface is decorated—this is architecture that does not let the eye rest—and like the French Gothic style (see fig. 4-81), its celestial metaphor is in part accomplished by an attempt to deny visually the weight of architectural forms. The white gilded stucco **capitals** have a flamelike movement, and irregularly shaped windows pierce the walls. The openness and lightness of the oval "nave" area contrast with the colors of the architectural climax at the altar, where the statue is en-

closed within a shrine of red and white columns. The vault is pierced with curving, Rococo openings that let light in from windows in the outer wall. This denial of the principles of vaulted architecture makes Die Wies seem like an apparition not dependent on normal structural systems. Nor is it subject to the force of gravity. The exuberance of Catholic Rococo architecture may be in part a reaction to the severity characteristic of contemporary Protestant architecture.

At the Monastery Church of Rohr, a light-filled white and gold nave directs attention to the richer colors of the columns behind the high altar that enframe a monumental sculptural group (fig. 8-14). While gesticulating apostles sur-

round a Rococo sarcophagus, we gasp as we seem to witness the Virgin being carried to heaven by angels. The architecture seems to open, and a golden stained-glass window offers a portal to heaven. Since the Renaissance, religious drama had used special effects of lighting (candles, torches, fireworks) and theatrical machinery to make transcendent miraculous events seem more realistic and more dramatic, and one of the most successful Counter-Reformation tools employed by the Jesuits in southern Germany was the use of sacred theater as a teaching device. This *Assumption*, by Egid Quirin Asam (1692–1750), is a permanent version of one of these theatrical representations.

EIGHTEENTH-CENTURY PORTRAITURE

8-15. John Singleton Copley. *Portrait of Paul Revere.* c. 1768–70. Oil on canvas, 34⁷/8 x 28¹/2". Courtesy, Museum of Fine Arts, Boston. Paul Revere was a political activist in Boston. His famous night ride to warn Bostonians of the advance of the British army occurred on April 18, 1775. Copley's family was sympathetic to the British, and the artist left the colonies forever on the eve of the Revolution. Commissioned by Paul Revere

Gift of Joseph W. Revere, William B. Revere, and Edward H. R. Revere

The honest and informal portrait of the Boston silversmith and engraver Paul Revere by John Singleton Copley (1738–1815) represents both the New England work ethic and Copley's artistic joy in rendering exact visual detail (fig. 8-15). The darkened background focuses our attention on Revere and the tools and products of his trade in the foreground. He wears the simple work clothes of an artisan. Such a straightforward approach, which dignifies labor and craft, was in keeping with Puritan values. Copley convincingly portrays a sense of immediacy between Revere and ourselves. It is as though we have discovered Revere deep in thought, almost as if he has forgotten the engraving of the teapot and is now engrossed in the contemplation of more difficult issues. Revere's eyes meet ours, and his raised right eyebrow seems to signify an acknowledgment of our presence. It is clear that Copley delighted in the naturalistic representation of figures and objects. Note how the sharp, detailed reflection of Revere's fingers in the silver teapot contrasts with the diffused reflection of his shirt on the polished wooden worktop.

Copley and Benjamin West (see fig. 8-24) are acknowledged as America's first significant artists. Copley's fame in the colonies was established primarily by his ability as a portraitist. His sensitive observation and carefully developed talent earned him a distinguished reputation and a significant financial income, both in the colonies and in his later career in Britain. Although portrait painting ranked behind his-

tory and religious painting in the academic classification of subject matter, it was an economic mainstay for many artists.

Rosalba Carriera (1675–1757), in her painting of France's young king Louis XV (fig. 8-16), demonstrates the elegant grace of Rococo portraiture. The soft, delicate effect is achieved not only by the blending of high-valued colors but also by the use of **pastel** as a medium. Carriera, a Venetian artist, became famous for her ability to render portraits in pastel. Her influence in France and Italy popularized the medium in the eighteenth century.

In England, two competing artists excelled in portraiture: Joshua Reynolds, president of London's Royal Academy, and Thomas Gainsborough (1727–88). Our two portraits, which display the abilities and different approaches of these two artists, both represent Sarah Kemble Siddons, a popular and accomplished actress of the period (figs. 8-17, 8-18).

True to his philosophy that painting should aspire to the "grand style," Reynolds chose to depict Siddons as a classical allegorical figure, the muse of tragic drama. She sits on a throne, head and eyes raised as if in response to divine, creative inspiration. Behind her are figures symbolizing Pity and Terror, the attributes of tragic drama. Reynolds's composition directly recalls Michelangelo's figures of prophets and Sibyls on the Sistine Chapel ceiling (see fig. 6-30) in order to demonstrate his ability to adapt and update the Renaissance style.

When Gainsborough painted the

8-16. Rosalba Carriera. *Portrait of Louis XV as a Young Man.* 1720–21. Pastel on paper, 18¹/2 x 14". Courtesy, Museum of Fine Arts, Boston. Most likely commissioned by Louis XIV or Louis XV

The Forsyth Wickes Collection

1750	World population is about 750 million
1760	Population of American colonies is about 1.6 million
1762	Catherine the Great becomes czarina of Russia
1764	Mozart, age eight, writes his first symphony
1762	Jean-Jacques Rousseau's *Social Contract* published
c. 1768–70	**Copley, *Portrait of Paul Revere***
1770	Boston Massacre
1773	Boston Tea Party
1772	Joseph Priestley and Daniel Rutherford separately discover nitrogen

8-17. Joshua Reynolds. *Allegorical Portrait of Sarah Siddons as the Tragic Muse.* 1784. Oil on canvas, 7'9" x 4'9¹/2". Henry E. Huntington Library and Art Gallery, San Marino, California. Reynolds painted two versions of this portrait; the second, painted in 1789, was intended for his agent, Desensans.

8-18. Thomas Gainsborough. *Portrait of Sarah Siddons.* 1783–85. Oil on canvas, 49³/4 x 39¹/4". The National Gallery, London

same celebrated actress, he chose to portray her as an elegantly dressed, confident woman. The painting, which recalls the tradition of Venetian and Baroque portrai-ture, is a sumptuous treat for our eyes. The blues and whites of her dress enhance the warm, golden tones of her shawl and muff, while the magnificent black hat is silhou-etted against a deep red curtain. Gainsborough's painterly technique and luxurious colors create an impressive portrait of a dynamic woman.

EIGHTEENTH-CENTURY ART   **407**

THOMAS JEFFERSON AND NEOCLASSICAL ARCHITECTURE IN THE UNITED STATES

8-19. Thomas Jefferson. State Capitol, Richmond, Virginia. 1785–89. Photo taken in 1865 by Mathew Brady. Commissioned by the State of Virginia

8-20. Thomas Jefferson. University of Virginia, Charlottesville. 1817–26

You see I am an enthusiast in the subject of the arts. But it is an enthusiasm of which I am not ashamed, as its object is to improve the taste of my countrymen, to increase their reputation, to reconcile them to the respect of the world, and procure them its praise. (Thomas Jefferson, in a letter to James Madison, 1785)

Jefferson's Virginia State Capitol (fig. 8-19) must have surprised many Richmond residents (see map, page 440), for it was the first public building in the youthful American republic to be modeled on the classical temple form. Thomas Jefferson (1743–1826) designed the building while he was serving as U.S. minister to France,

where he was inspired by both French architects already working in the Neoclassical style and the ruins of the ancient Roman civilization in Gaul. He was especially influenced by a Roman temple at Nîmes, in southern France, which is similar to the Temple of Portunus (see fig. 3-88) in Rome. Jefferson wrote in a letter that he had gazed at the temple for hours, "like a lover at his mistress." While maintaining its basic design, he greatly enlarged it for the Virginia State Capitol. The resulting structure, with its Ionic portico, pediment, and classical proportions, confers a solemn, dignified appearance—appropriate, as Jefferson himself believed, to the ideals of a young democratic nation.

Although the Neoclassical architectural style flourished throughout the Western world, it was particu-

larly meaningful in the United States, as the nation adopted a democratic form of government following the Revolution. The emulation of Roman buildings was viewed as an appropriate vehicle to express architectural dignity and command public respect. For Jefferson, public architecture demanded a moral content. The nobility of the Neoclassical edifice would serve as a guide to the behavior and aspirations of the young republic. The Neoclassical architectural style in the United States is also known as the Federal style because of its prominent use for government buildings.

In 1817, Jefferson, now a former president, began planning the first state university in the United States. His design for the University of Virginia, in Charlottesville, harmonizes the stateliness of the

1783	First successful hot-air balloon flight
1784	Steam is first used to power textile machinery
1785–89	**Jefferson, Virginia State Capitol**
1786	Mozart, *Marriage of Figaro*
1787	U. S. Constitution is signed
1790	Washington, D.C., is founded
1790	U.S. population is almost 4 million

8-21. Thomas Jefferson. Monticello, Charlottesville, Virginia. 1768–82; remodeled 1796–1809. The Italian name *Monticello* ("Little Mountain") was adopted by Jefferson because of the hilltop setting of his home.

Federal style with the practical needs of an educational community (fig. 8-20). The mall is dominated by the Rotunda, an adaptation of the ancient Pantheon in Rome (see fig. 3-115). The Rotunda contained the library; the individual pavilions along the mall each housed a different academic discipline, including living quarters for the faculty and classrooms.

Jefferson's design for his country home, Monticello, demonstrates the adaptability of Neoclassical architectural features to domestic buildings (fig. 8-21). The use of antique architectural elements is evident, but Jefferson's sources for the composition here are also drawn from the Renaissance, particularly the villas of Palladio. The Villa Rotonda (see fig. 1-7) and others inspired the

main block, with its domed ballroom, while other Palladian villas in the countryside around Venice were the source for the wings that reach out to embrace the landscape and unify the house with the farms and countryside that support the estate. Soon houses throughout the United States would sport Doric, Ionic, and Corinthian porticoes as an indication of American democratic ideals.

NEOCLASSICAL PAINTING

8-22. Jacques-Louis David. *Death of Socrates*. 1787. Oil on canvas, 4'3" x 6'6". The Metropolitan Museum of Art, New York. The liberal philosophy of Socrates, the fifth-century BCE Athenian philosopher, stressed the worth of the individual over that of the state in a manner that upset Athenian officials. Because he could not be brought to trial for his philosophical beliefs, he was tried for "impiety," found guilty, and ultimately sentenced to death. It was clear that he could have gone free if he had renounced his teachings, but Socrates himself pointed out that death had been the verdict of a legitimate court. Following Athenian practice, he drank hemlock. Commissioned by Charles-Michel Trudaine, a lawyer at the French Parliament

Catharine Lorillard Wolfe Collection, Wolfe Fund, 1931 (31.45)

Heroic suicide may seem to be a contradiction in terms, but the purpose of David's theme (fig. 8-22), painted in the unsettled years in France before the Revolution, was to demonstrate the need to live by principles and the heroism of the stoic virtue of absolute self-sacrifice. Jacques-Louis David (1748–1825) depicted a heroic, muscular Socrates reaching for the cup of poisonous hemlock held by a distraught disciple. With an exclamatory gesture, Socrates points upward, insisting on the truth of his ideals. On viewing the painting, one contemporary observer remarked, "This is the triumph of virtue which is raised higher than all other things by a heroic courage and an inspired soul."

Although the theme of the death of Socrates is taken from the classical past, David's choice and interpreta-tion of subject are strictly contempo-rary, and within the cultural context of late-eighteenth-century France, they would have been easily under-stood. In 1758, the philosopher and writer Denis Diderot had detailed a proposed drama on Socrates' death that popularized the theme with artists and writers. Socrates' unwa-vering devotion to his ideals provides the theme for this history painting. Both the lesson and David's repre-sentation were acclaimed by critics and the public. The work offered a guide for moral behavior in the trou-bled social climate of France. David became a supporter of the French Revolution, and the *Death of Socrates* illustrates his belief that paintings "of heroism and civic virtue offered the eyes of the people [will] electrify its soul, and plant the seed of glory and devotion to the fatherland." The

crisp modeling of the figures creates precise, linear, sculptural forms, revealing David's academic training and approach, while the planar space of the painting suggests that ancient relief sculpture may have been one of David's inspirations.

The Swiss painter Angelica Kauff-mann (see fig. 8-8) also championed the virtues of history painting. The theme of Kauffmann's *Cornelia* (fig. 8-23) is drawn from Roman antiq-uity. Cornelia was renowned as a devoted mother. When a friend who had just displayed her own jewelry asked to see Cornelia's gems, Cor-nelia presented her two sons. The personal and emotional implications of the theme are clear, and it should perhaps be pointed out that Kauff-mann selected and successfully rep-resented a subject that would be recognized as revealing a particular

1787 **David, *Death of Socrates***
1787 Dollar currency is introduced in the United States
1788 *The Times* of London begins publication
1798 Omiki-san Nakayama, a Japanese woman, founds Tenri Kyo, a major Shinto sect; her writings become the sect's scriptures

8-23. Angelica Kauffmann. *Cornelia, Mother of the Gracchi*. 1785. Oil on canvas, 40 x 50". Virginia Museum of Fine Arts, Richmond. Purchased by George Bowles of Wanstead, Essex, who was an important collector of Kauffmann's works
Williams Fund, 1975

8-24. Benjamin West. *Death of General Wolfe*. 1770. Oil on canvas, 4'11¹/2" x 7'. The National Gallery of Canada, Ottawa. The story of the death of the British commander James Wolfe on the battlefield at Quebec in 1759 was inspirational. After three months of stalemate, Wolfe had led his troops to victory over a much larger French force, but mortally wounded, he died in the arms of his officers at the moment of victory. George III commissioned a replica of this painting from West
Gift of the Duke of Westminster

feminine insight. Kauffmann's elegant, yet disciplined Neoclassical compositions gained her an international reputation.

In *Death of General Wolfe* (fig. 8-24), Benjamin West (1738–1820) popularized a new concept within the category of history painting, for West represented the figures in contemporary costume, avoiding the antique clothing and setting that, according to traditional academic rules, could elevate a subject to its universal significance. West's earliest biographer recounted the report that Joshua Reynolds, president of the Royal Academy, had advised West to "adopt the classic costume of antiquity, as much more becoming the inherent greatness of . . . [the] subject than the modern garb of war," and that West had replied:

The event intended to be commemorated took place on the 13th of September, 175[9], in a region of the world unknown to the Greeks and Romans, and at a period of time when no such nations, nor heroes in their costume, any longer existed. The subject I have to represent is the conquest of a great province of America by the British troops. . . . If, instead of the facts of the transaction, I represent classical fictions, how shall I be understood by posterity! . . . I want to mark the date, the place, and the parties engaged in the event; and if I am not able to dispose of the circumstances in a picturesque manner, no academic distribution of Greek or Roman costume will enable me to do justice to the subject.

West's composition was stimulated by a serious study of classical sculpture and of the works of Renaissance and Baroque artists, and his painting, a popular success, pioneered an important change in the representation of contemporary history. Although he avoided classical costume, West did refer to tradition by including the Native American as a personification of America. The painting successfully communicates the tragedy of the death of Wolfe, an event that inherently demonstrated the universal values of self-sacrifice, courage, and patriotism. George III commissioned a copy of West's painting and made him the official history painter at the court.

9-1. Eugène Delacroix. *Liberty Leading the People*. 1830. Oil on canvas, 8'6³/8" x 10'8". The Louvre, Paris

INTRODUCTION TO NINETEENTH-CENTURY ART

The ideal of revolution, so important for the development of the modern world and so central to the history, ideology, and art of the European nineteenth century, is expressed in two paintings by Eugène Delacroix (1798–1863) and Claude Monet (1840–1926). Delacroix's subject (fig. 9-1) celebrates the July Revolution of 1830, when an uprising of Parisians mounted a revolutionary red, white, and blue flag—the tricolor—on the spires of Nôtre-Dame Cathedral and forced the abdication of Charles X, as well as the adoption of a new charter that doubled the number of citizens who elected the legislative chamber. This was a modest but important triumph for the liberals, lower bourgeoisie, and skilled workers who had led the revolt. In Delacroix's painting, the personification of Liberty, holding the tricolor, leads an army of Parisian rebels over the bodies of their dead comrades toward victory. Delacroix's technique, too, is revolutionary, for in reaction to the sharp linearity of the prevailing Neoclassical style (see pages 428–29), he introduces blurred edges, strong colors, and loose brushstrokes in an active style appropriate to his modern subject. Of Delacroix's significance, the later painter Paul Cézanne would say, "We all paint differently because of him."

From later in the century, Monet's revolutionary painting (fig. 9-2) expresses Impressionist ideals. In defiance of the criteria that had been taught in European art academies since the Renaissance, the Impressionists challenged the emphasis given to traditional subject matter and exalted the importance of the momentary glimpse of a real scene. Monet chose this particular cityscape not in response to patriotic fervor, for example, but because he was challenged by the problem of how to represent the visual effect of the brilliant colors and the ever-changing movement offered by the flags. Monet's goal was to capture a visual "impression" of what the eye sees, regardless of subject. Traditional critics were as upset by this attitude about subject matter as they were by his loose brushstrokes.

9-2. Claude Monet. *Rue St.-Denis Festivities on June 30, 1878*. 1878. Oil on canvas, 29^7/8 x 20^1/2". Musée des Beaux-Arts, Rouen, France

HISTORY

Economic, technological, and political revolutions dominate the history of the nineteenth century in Europe and the United States. The Industrial Revolution, with its mechanization of production in factories, transformed life for a large percentage of the population in the West. The rapidly expanding lower and middle classes, concentrated in the cities near their factory jobs, organized to demand democracy and more humane treatment. The spirit of reform that began in the nineteenth century extended into the twentieth, eventually leading to universal suffrage in much of the world. The institutions,

life-styles, and class structures that resulted had an important impact on art.

During the nineteenth century, the world seemed to become a smaller place as steam-powered trains and ships led to increased world trade. The expansion of communications with the establishment of inexpensive newspapers and periodicals, printed on high-speed printing presses, and the development of the telegraph and telephone led to greater international awareness. An interconnected world gradually evolved, prompted by world trade and centered around the great international fairs held in the second half of the century. The establishment of European colonies in Africa, Asia, and

Australia brought Western culture into contact and conflict with local traditions and beliefs. More and more artists traveled from America, China, Japan and elsewhere to study in France and Germany, and soon even painters from Pittsburgh were submitting works to the Salon in Paris and the Royal Academy exhibitions in London. Inexpensive reproductions of works of art were widely distributed.

Napoleon dominated European history in the first decade of the nineteenth century, leading French armies to victory until he controlled all of Europe. Only Britain, which defeated Napoleon's navy at Trafalgar, was able to repel the French. Napoleon was proclaimed emperor of France in 1804 and king of Italy in 1805. Determined to break the traditional and historic power of the Catholic Church and its clergy, Napoleon closed monasteries and destroyed symbols of ecclesiastical and monastic power. To enlarge his own private collections and those of the French state, he appropriated many works of art. He attacked Russia in 1812 and took Moscow, but in retreat his army was virtually annihilated. Napoleon abdicated in 1814, returned briefly to power in 1815, and was defeated by the English at Waterloo. The new European borders set at the Congress of Vienna in 1815, after Napoleon's defeat, established a balance of power that endured until World War I.

The French Revolution and later revolutionary uprisings in France in 1830 and 1848, as well as the success of the new democracy in the United States, gave impetus to other revolutionary movements. Throughout Europe there was an increased demand for "liberty, equality, and fraternity [nationalism]"—there were eleven revolutionary uprisings in major European cities in 1848–49.

The nineteenth-century demands for revolution, however, would reach their most profound outcome with the Russian Revolution of 1917. Great Britain remained stable, and the British Empire underwent tremendous expansion accompanied by an astonishing economic development—the result of peace, industrialization, and the world market provided by the empire. The power of the British naval and merchant marine was unrivaled. In the United States, rapid expansion and industrialization led to prosperity and optimism, but this mood was dissipated by the divisive Civil War (1861–65), and after the war American culture became increasingly dependent on conservative European models. By the end of the nineteenth century, nationalistic desires for unification in Italy and in Germany had succeeded.

The British Empire brought the English language and the British bureaucratic system to many different regions of the world; the largest and most dramatic of these was India. India had played an important role in trade since the seventeenth century, when British, Dutch, French, and other European traders had arrived there in search of luxury goods in demand in Europe: spices, fine cottons, silk, opium, and indigo, among others. India prospered from this trade, which was conducted by trading companies that held monopolies; the most important of these was the British East India Company, which also acted as a political and military force, helping to secure British rule in India by the mid-nineteenth century. British officials were in charge of virtually all of India, but there was no single central authority. By the end of the century, India had become a part of the world economy, and, based on the British example, a modern bureaucratic system had been established. Interest among

9-3. Kunisada. *A Woman Frightened by Thunder.* 1849–53. Woodblock print, 14^1/2 x 10^1/8". This print was part of a large collection of more than 200 Japanese prints owned by the Post-Impressionist painter Vincent van Gogh; the artist owned 165 prints by Kunisada alone. Japanese prints were a formative influence on many French nineteenth-century painters, especially Manet, Monet, Degas, Toulouse-Lautrec, and Van Gogh. The bold silhouetting and complex patterning of their designs (especially evident here in the pattern of the mosquito netting over the designs of the woman's costume), the truncation of the forms (note the flying reed shade in the upper right corner and the lightning bolt that flashes into the room), the high viewpoint, and the diagonal recession of the architectural settings were all characteristic of Japanese art, and all had an effect on the development of modern French painting.

Indian artists in European painting and architecture was another result of the British colonization of India.

During the nineteenth century, Japan was gradually opened to the West. In 1804, a representative of the czar of Russia arrived, and in 1846 and 1853, respectively, Commodores Biddle and Perry of the United States were received. The treaties that were negotiated between Japan and the Western powers led to increased communication, and the delegates who left Japan to take up posts in the Western world returned with news of Western industrial progress. Japanese students began to go to Europe to study. By 1889, the new Meiji Constitution was in place, and in the next twenty years Japan waged wars against China and Russia; by the end of the nineteenth century, Japan also had become an "imperial" power.

Asian works of art were imported into Europe and collected by individuals and museums, and by the end of the century, the collecting of works from Africa was well under way, aided by European colonization of the continent and the attempt to suppress local traditions.

Although Asian works had a significant impact on the development of art (for example, Impressionism; see page 460) and on popular taste and collecting (fig. 9-3) during the nineteenth century, the impact of the African works was not felt until the twentieth century. European-style painting was known in Asia, primarily through the works of Japanese artists returning from Europe and from reproductions in Chinese and Japanese journals, and by the end of the nineteenth century there was a widespread interest in western European art.

It would be oversimplifying to draw direct relationships between each of the global historical events summarized above and the developments in art with which this part deals, but our study of earlier art has often demonstrated the intimate connection between historical events that affected the lives and attitudes of large groups of people and the art that was produced at the same time. As both the world and art have become more complicated and interrelated, we must continue to try to grasp the role of historical change in new developments in art. We also must not neglect the role that art may have played in defining and transforming history.

THE INDUSTRIAL REVOLUTION

By the mid-nineteenth century, Britain led the world in the mechanized production of inexpensive goods for mass public consumption. Such production became the financial base for England's expansion during the century. Simultaneously, the Industrial Revolution spread through much of Europe and into America, and there was fierce competition for the global markets for mass-produced goods. When power-driven machinery revolutionized the production of textiles, entrepreneurs established huge mills in which hundreds of workers manufactured vast amounts of cheap fabric. Factory-made nails and milled lumber, produced by the power-driven sawmill, revolutionized the housing industry in America. The rapid spread of the railroads transformed transportation, the delivery of merchandise, and communications.

The new industrial production was celebrated in a series of international exhibitions, beginning with the Great Exhibition of the Works of Industry of All Nations at the Crystal Palace in London in 1851 (see fig. 9-39). This exhibition was intended to emphasize England's role as the world's greatest manufacturing center, but it also became a challenge to other countries to compete with England's commercial successes. By bringing together handicrafts and manufactured goods from all over the world, the exhibition introduced new styles and techniques into the prevailing Victorian taste.

The Industrial Revolution raised standards of living for large groups of people, but it also created unsafe

9-4. Édouard Manet. *A Bar at the Folies-Bergère.* 1881–82. Oil on canvas, 37¹/₂ x 51". Courtauld Institute Galleries, Home House Trustees, London. Many of the barmaids who worked at the Folies-Bergère were also prostitutes. Manet's presentation of this woman is as a commodity that is as readily available as the goods on the bar. At the same time, however, her expression creates a strong sense of the woman as an individual with a personal emotional life. In Manet's oil sketch for the painting, the background is more easily read as a mirror reflection; in the final version, the reflection of the woman and her customer is changed to emphasize the flatness of the pictorial surface and the unreal aspect of the painting. In describing the painting while it was in the studio, Georges Jeanniot, one of Manet's friends, noted that "he did not copy nature at all closely; I noted his masterly simplification. . . . Everything was abbreviated." This painting was exhibited at the Paris Salon in 1882.

working conditions and led to unemployment. The difficulties of urban life were documented in contemporary novels by Charles Dickens (*Oliver Twist,* 1838) and Victor Hugo (*Les Misérables,* 1862). The issue of the isolation and alienation of the individual in a modern, urban society is expressed by Édouard Manet (1832–83) in his depiction of the barmaid, who probably also worked as a prostitute, in *A Bar at the Folies-Bergère* (fig. 9-4). The Industrial Revolution also transformed art, for the mass production of cheap prints developed a new audience for art. Reproductions of paintings were available virtually everywhere. Illustration flourished, led by such entrepreneurs as Currier & Ives in the United States. The mass production of furniture and other household goods led to a reaction in the second half of the century, when the finely finished works of the individual craftsperson were exalted in the Arts and Crafts and Art Nouveau (see fig. 10-8) movements.

EUROPEAN INTELLECTUAL AND SCIENTIFIC ACTIVITIES

In Europe, the social and financial inequities that were amplified by industrialism led to a number of responses—socialism, anarchism, utopian movements, and revolutionary communism. The latter was explicitly defined by Karl Marx and Friedrich Engels in the *Communist Manifesto*, published in 1848. Similar sentiments about inequity led to revolutions in China, Russia, and India in the twentieth century.

Intimately connected with industrialization were advances in science, engineering, and technology. Science replaced philosophy as the most influential university discipline. New scientific theories, especially Charles Darwin's *The Origin of Species* (1859), with its message of the "survival of the fittest," deeply affected attitudes about religion and the meaning of life.

The explosion of activity in the fields of literature and music makes it impossible to mention all the important figures at work during the nineteenth century. Some of the artistic movements had parallel developments in literature and music. Romanticism, for example, was expressed in literature in poetry, historical novels, fantasy and horror tales, and romance and adventure stories by such figures as Lord Byron in England, Johann Goethe in Germany, Victor Hugo in France, and Aleksander Pushkin in Russia. Romanticism and Realism are united in the works of Dickens. The Romantic movement in music includes Frédéric Chopin (who even wrote a piece called "Revolutionary Étude"), Johannes Brahms, Richard Wagner, and Pëtr Tchaikovsky. Impressionism is paralleled in music in the compositions of Claude Debussy. Art criti-

9-5. Henri de Toulouse-Lautrec. *At the Moulin Rouge.* 1892. Oil on canvas, 48³/₈ x 55¹/₄". The Art Institute of Chicago. The dramatic lighting of the face in the foreground, which reflects the strong color of the cabaret's gas lighting, reveals the Impressionists' interest in representing the effect of light on their subjects.

Helen Birch Bartlett Memorial Collection

cism flourished, and partisans of both conservative and "modern" art developed.

ART

Communication and interrelationships between parts of the world increased rapidly and dramatically in the course of the nineteenth century, and the chronological structure of this book becomes both more revealing and more logical as we examine the art of this period. In earlier centuries, the chronological organization allowed us to demonstrate the simultaneity of distinctly different developments in art in various parts of the globe and to study broader trends, such as the spread of world religions, in their widest historical context without isolating, for example, Christianity, Islam, and Buddhism. In the nineteenth century, the chronological structure emphasizes the interrelationships that evolved as the world shrank. We can, for example, see how art in Asia began to have an important effect on art in Europe and understand the impact of European developments on art in the United States and Asia. During this period, Japanese prints responded to Western ideas about illusionism and perspective, for example, while at the same time some Japanese aesthetic qualities seen in the prints helped to transform European and, subsequently, American paint-

ing. Thomas Eakins certainly knew the paintings of the Realist Courbet and of the Impressionists, although the Impressionists seem to have had less impact than Courbet; Eakins's student Tanner, however, felt more strongly the influence of the Impressionists.

No brief survey of global art can encompass or even refer to every development in every nation. In surveying the nineteenth century, we shall focus on French developments because they had such a potent impact on art and on attitudes about art and the artist in the nineteenth and also in the twentieth century. Many of our current popular attitudes about art have their sources in French nineteenth-century developments. We also shall explore extensively American art and architecture during this century because they provide an excellent example of both the dependence of American art on European innovations and a certain independence that leads into American twentieth-century developments.

The subjects of nineteenth-century European and American painters ranged from historical, mythological, and religious themes to scenes of the everyday life of the working classes. By the end of the century, even the vulgar characters and activities of a popular dance hall had become acceptable as a theme for art (fig. 9-5). The development of exhibitions, such as those at the Parisian Salon and London's Royal Academy, and of art galleries

9-6. Frédéric-Auguste Bartholdi. *Liberty Enlightening the World* (now known as the *Statue of Liberty*). 1870–86. Hammered copper over wrought-iron pylon designed by Gustave Eiffel; height from base to top of torch 111'6". New York Harbor. Commissioned by the French American Union

9-7. Gustave Eiffel. Diagram of the construction of the *Statue of Liberty*

in every major city in Europe and the United States meant that more and more painters and sculptors were producing works for exhibition and for the general art market. As the percentage of commissioned works declined, there was a growing division between artist and public, and the gulf between conservative and revolutionary artists, who assumed the title of **avant-garde**, gradually became wider. Although the development of photography robbed painters of a traditional means of support, the elite continued to commission painted portraits. Landscape became a particularly popular subject, perhaps because it was such a good vehicle for expressing aesthetic theories (see page 434). Despite the significance of the Industrial Revolution, scenes of industry were relatively rare.

The popular print developed with the growth of newspapers and periodicals to become a prominent vehicle for social protest (see page 438). The photograph, invented in the nineteenth century, was used both as a journalistic and as a documentary tool. In sculpture, the heroic monument dominated the century and was considered to be the primary challenge of the sculptor (see figs. 9-6, 9-7, 9-12), but the diversity of the century is

seen in examples of traditional architectural sculpture and in works that demonstrate revolutionary attitudes about sculpture (see fig. 9-55). In architecture, new forms were demanded by the dramatically increasing pressure of population and business crowded in great urban centers. Impressive technological and engineering advances made possible the skyscraper, the railroad station, and the great bridges (see fig. 9-40) and monuments (figs. 9-6, 9-7) of the later nineteenth century.

In other parts of the world during the nineteenth century, the idea of modernism, so important in the West, was seldom an important issue. In India, China, Japan, the continent of Africa, and elsewhere, local traditions in art continued with little transformation. In the Melanesian island nation known as New Ireland, for example, the masks used in traditional island rituals (fig. 9-8) were not changed by contact with European culture. Similar to the ritual practices in Africa (see pages 504–05) and else-

9-8. Malanggan. Tableau, New Ireland. 19th–20th century. Bamboo, palm and croton leaves, painted wood, approx. 8' high. Museum für Völkerkund, Basel, Switzerland

where, dancers wore these intricate masks for rituals that commemorated ancestors and initiated youths into adulthood in villages throughout the South Pacific islands. Most of these masks were carved from a single piece of wood; the generous use of openwork, sliverlike projections, and overpainting subdivides the objects into minute geometric patterns that create an elaborate, fragmented appearance. When they were not in ritual use, the pieces were set up in a tableau at a special house, where they could be seen by Western visitors. Only in the twentieth century did such objects command the attention of Western artists for their brilliant and complicated abstracted designs.

Global communication and contacts, however, meant that there was an increasing awareness of developments everywhere, and some art students from Asia studied in Paris and other Western centers and quickly introduced into their own cultures an interest in the latest Western styles. When Impressionism was introduced into Japan it was equated with modernism, and it thereby won approval from some industrialized and political leaders who were seeking economic parity with the West. In general, however, Western styles had little impact on the well-established local traditions, which were closely attached to notions of Japanese cultural identity. Like the importation of Japanese style into the West, in most cases the Japanese interest in Western style was purely aesthetic. The democratic principles that underlay Impressionism, for example, were not brought into Japan by Japanese artists who had worked in Paris.

THE PRIMACY OF FRANCE IN WORLD ART

Not all the great works of art produced during the nineteenth century were made by French artists, but it was developments in France that gave names to the revolutionary nineteenth-century movements in modern art, and much of the new art created in Europe and the United States reflected the latest French styles. The sequence of movements in France was watched with interest, enthusiasm, and, occasionally, dismay, and in the rest of the world it was the French styles that were considered to be "modern." The annual art exhibitions of the French Salon were world-famous and were the ones in which virtually all serious European and American

9-9. Henri Rousseau. *The Sleeping Gypsy.* 1897. Oil on canvas, 4'3" x 6'7".
The Museum of Modern Art, New York

Gift of Mrs. Simon Guggenheim

artists desired to be included. To be represented in a Salon could make one's reputation.

Conservative interests dominated the Salon exhibitions, however, and when the Salon jury of 1863 rejected a number of works that we would consider modern (for example, see figure 9-47), there was such an outcry that a special exhibition of the rejected works, known as the Salon des Refusés, was established:

Numerous complaints have reached the Emperor on the subject of works of art which have been refused by the jury of the exhibition. His Majesty, wishing to let the public judge the legitimacy of these complaints, has decided that the rejected works of art are to be exhibited in another part of the Palace of Industry. This exhibition will be voluntary, and artists who may not wish to participate need only inform the administration, which will hasten to return their works to them. This exhibition will open on May 15. Artists have until May 7 to withdraw their works. After this date their pictures will be considered not withdrawn and will be placed in the galleries. (Proclamation of the Salon des Refusés, 1863)

THE STYLES OF NINETEENTH-CENTURY ART IN THE WEST

The basic styles defined in this century receive their names from terms applied to paintings—to French paintings in particular. The new style at the end of the eighteenth century, Neoclassicism, continued in popularity well into the nineteenth century, especially in the arts of architecture and sculpture (see page 428). It received a special impetus from Napoleon's enthusiastic support for a variation of Neoclassicism known as Empire, which supported his new status as emperor. Soon, however, the rational and lucid order of the Neoclassical style and its belief that art should express universal truths were challenged by a style that might be considered its antithesis, Romanticism. This style, with its expression of spontaneous, strong, and even violent individual feelings, is in part based on a new distrust of rationalism. In architecture, Romanticism, in combination with a new interest in history and historical precedent, helps explain the interest in reviving earlier styles, especially the Gothic Revival (see page 440), so important in American and European architecture. Some critics have included the Neoclassical style within the general category of Romanticism because of the nostalgic manner in which Neoclassical artists looked back to the past.

In France, Romanticism was challenged by two styles: Academic Art and Realism. *Academic Art* is the term applied to the conservative and even reactionary art—heroic, moral themes rendered in exact verisimilitude—that prevailed in the French Salon exhibitions and in the French academies. Realism encompasses everyday subjects rendered with emphatic boldness. By denying to art the exalted mission preached in the academies, Realism was considered to be revolutionary. Realist attitudes about subject matter and technique influenced the Impressionists, who set out to represent a momentary impression of light, color, and atmosphere in paintings of contemporary subjects. A number of painters who went through an Impressionist phase but later moved on to other styles are known as Post-Impressionists. The end of the century saw the beginnings of new qualities that would lead to the development of expressionist trends in the twentieth century. In addition, there were styles in architecture and the decorative arts that can be subsumed in the general category of Victorian, which implies a heavy, elaborately decorated style of sumptuous materials, complex silhouettes, and varied textures and colors. In reaction to the Victorian style and to the industrialization of the arts were the utopian style of the Arts and Crafts Movement as developed by William Morris and the effulgent Art Nouveau style (see fig. 10-8).

Amid the eclecticism and variety of late-nineteenth-century art, some uniquely personal styles emerged that would deeply affect the course of early modern art, including those of the Post-Impressionists and of the self-taught artist Henri Rousseau (1844–1910). Rousseau was working as a toll collector (hence his nickname, "Le Douanier," or "customs officer") when, in his early forties, he retired to devote himself to painting. Such works as *The Sleeping Gypsy* (fig. 9-9) are a synthesis of artistic naïveté, innocent vision, and serious intent. Although *The Sleeping Gypsy* recalls the exoticism of Romantic artists, the direct rendering of the forms, the sparse and planar landscape, and the naive foreshortening create an almost hallucinatory scene. Rousseau insisted that he painted images "from life," but his fantastic scenes appealed to Picasso and the avant-garde of Paris, who befriended Rousseau in 1908. The author Guillaume Apollinaire expressed the modernist attitude toward Rousseau when he observed:

> His paintings were made without method, system, or mannerisms. From this comes the variety of his work. He did not distrust his imagination any more than he did his head. From this came the grace and richness of his decorative compositions.

THE NINETEENTH-CENTURY ARTIST

During the nineteenth century in Europe and America, the individuality of the artist as a creative and expressive personality took on an even greater importance. One logical outcome of this inclination was more personalized and revealing self-portraits, as in the portrait Francisco Goya (1746–1828) painted of himself on the verge of death (fig. 9-10). By the end of the century, the revealing personal drama evident in the self-portraits of Vincent van Gogh (1853–1890) is not unexpected, although his particularly dramatic evolution from Impressionism could not have been predicted (fig. 9-11). The modern Western conception of the artist as a political and social

9-10. Francisco Goya. *Self-Portrait Being Attended by Dr. Arrieta*. 1820. Oil on canvas, 45$^{1}/_{2}$ x 31$^{1}/_{8}$". The Minneapolis Institute of Arts. The inscription at the bottom of this painting reads: "Goya, in gratitude, to his friend Arrieta, for the skill and care with which he saved his life in his acute and dangerous illness, suffered at the end of 1819 at the age of 73. Painted in 1820."
The Ethel M. Van Derlip Fund, 1952

9-11. Vincent van Gogh. *Self-Portrait with Bandaged Ear and Pipe*. 1889. Oil on canvas, 20$^{1}/_{8}$ x 17$^{3}/_{4}$". Private collection

9-12. Photograph of Harriet Hosmer in Rome, at work on the clay model for her statue of *Senator Thomas Hart Benton,* c. 1862. The completed work in bronze was the first public sculpture in the state of Missouri. It was placed in Lafayette Park, St. Louis, Missouri, and dedicated in the spring of 1868. Commissioned by a committee appointed by the Missouri Legislature

9-13. Edmonia Lewis. *Forever Free.* 1867. Marble, height 41$^1/4$". The Howard University Gallery of Art, Washington, D.C.

liberal and a revolutionary is largely a product of such nineteenth-century personalities as Théodore Géricault, Gustave Courbet, and James McNeill Whistler. In the Renaissance, artists had worked hard to convince their upper-class and noble patrons that they were individuals worthy of recognition and status. In the nineteenth century, artists began to emphasize their bonds to the middle and lower classes. Georges Seurat planned to write a book about his principles and techniques that would enable anyone to paint a masterpiece.

The change in the status and attitude of the artist is also related to the change in the relationship between the artist and the patron. By the beginning of the nineteenth century, there were probably as many artists painting works for their personal satisfaction and for exhibition as there were artists painting particular works on commission from influential and demanding patrons. The one exception to this generalization might be portraiture, but during the second half of this century the development of the photographic portrait (and the portrait painted *over* a photograph) meant that only a few artists could

hope to earn their living painting portraits. The new democratic ideals so important for nineteenth-century developments encouraged a broader clientele in Europe, America, and Japan to begin collecting art, and artists responded to this climate by an increasing interest in everyday subject matter. Consequently, most of the works listed in Part 9 will not have any indication of patronage in the caption.

Throughout the nineteenth century, the educational and professional opportunities that were opening for women, however slowly, increased the ranks of women artists. The number of women whose works were exhibited in the annual French Salon swelled from fewer than 30 early in the century to almost 800 in just over seventy-five years. As was true of the eighteenth century (see page 399), many American artists studied and worked in Europe. Among them was a group of women sculptors whom the writer Henry James collectively named "the white marmorean flock." James identified the leader of this group as Harriet Hosmer (1830–1908). A friend of Hosmer's described the artist as a woman who, "at the very outset of her life, refused to have her feet cramped by the little Chinese shoes, which society places on us all, then misnames our feeble tottering, feminine grace." Hosmer, known for her vigorous and independent personality, journeyed to Rome in 1852 to study the revered arts of antiquity and the Renaissance and to be part of an international community of artists. By the end of the decade, her studio was an established part of the European art scene, and she enjoyed a range of patrons from Europe, England, and America.

As a sculptor, Hosmer struggled to cast aside stereotypical and sexist attitudes toward women artists. Her Neoclassical sculptures of women offered nineteenth-century audiences representations of feminine strength, and when she received the commission from the state of Missouri for a colossal statue of Thomas Hart Benton (fig. 9-12), Hosmer wrote, "Your kindness will now afford me an ample opportunity of proving to what rank I am really entitled as an artist unsheltered by the broad wings of compassion for the sex." Hosmer's statue of Senator Benton exemplifies the Neoclassical ideal of joining the values of antiquity—here demonstrated by the pose, drapery, and scroll—to subjects of the contemporary world.

Hosmer welcomed another American sculptor, Edmonia Lewis (1845–90), to Italy in the 1860s. Lewis's mother was a Native American from the Chippewa nation, and her father was an African American who worked, in Lewis's words, as a "gentleman's servant." Nicknamed "Wildfire," Lewis spent much of her youth with the Chippewas, but at the insistence of her brother she became a student at Oberlin College. Following an incident of racial violence directed toward her, Lewis traveled to Boston in 1863. There she developed her talents as a sculptor and her views as an abolitionist. *Forever Free* (fig. 9-13) was created shortly after Lewis arrived in Italy; it depicts the moment of the triumph of freedom for African American slaves, whose chains of bondage have just been broken. As a sculptor, Lewis was engaged not only by the theme of her works, which later would be expanded to reflect her Native American heritage, but also by the compositional challenge of creating multifigured groups.

CE	1800	1820	1840
EUROPE ART	**1806** CANOVA'S *NAPOLEON* **1806** ARC DE TRIOMPHE, PARIS, BEGUN **1811** INGRES'S *JUPITER AND THETIS* **1814–15** GOYA'S *THE THIRD OF MAY, 1808* **1818–19** GÉRICAULT'S *THE RAFT OF THE MEDUSA*	**1821** CONSTABLE'S *THE HAY WAIN* **1834** DAUMIER'S *RUE TRANSNONAIN, APRIL 15, 1834*	**1849** COURBET'S *THE STONE BREAKERS* **1850–51** PAXTON'S CRYSTAL PALACE **1852** BARRY AND PUGIN'S HOUSES OF PARLIAMENT OPEN, LONDON **1853** BONHEUR'S *THE HORSE FAIR*
HISTORY	**1815** Napoleon defeated at Waterloo	**1837** Victoria crowned, Great Britain	**1848** Revolutions in many European cities **1848** Marx and Engels's *Communist Manifesto*
ASIA ART	**19TH CENTURY** RAJPUT MINIATURE PAINTINGS, INDIA	**c. 1823–29** HOKUSAI'S *THIRTY-SIX VIEWS OF MOUNT FUJI*	**1849–53** KUNISADA'S *WOMAN FRIGHTENED BY THUNDER* **1858** HIROSHIGE'S *ONE HUNDRED FAMOUS VIEWS OF EDO*
HISTORY	**1644–1912** Qing dynasty, China		**MID-19TH CENTURY** British East India Co. becomes power in India
THE AMERICAS ART	**EARLY 19TH CENTURY** MANDAN HIDE PAINTINGS	**1832–41** GREENOUGH'S *GEORGE WASHINGTON* **1838** COLE'S *SCHROON MOUNTAIN*	**1845** BINGHAM'S *FUR TRADERS DESCENDING THE MISSOURI* **1851** LEUTZE'S *WASHINGTON CROSSING THE DELAWARE*
HISTORY	**1803** Louisiana Purchase	**1823** Monroe Doctrine	**1849** California gold rush begins
AFRICA ART	**19TH CENTURY** ASHANTI BRASS WEIGHT FIGURES	**1830–48** "ALABASTER MOSQUE," CAIRO	**19TH CENTURY** FRIDAY MOSQUE, BOBO-DIOULASSO (UPPER VOLTA)
HISTORY	**1805** Establishment of modern Egypt	**1832** Egypt defeats the Turks in Syria	
THE MIDDLE EAST ART	**1809** MASJID-I SHAH MOSQUE, TEHRAN, FOR FATH ALI SHAH QAJAR	**1826** NUSRETIYE MOSQUE, ISTANBUL **1839** TOMB OF SULTAN MAHMUD II, ISTANBUL	**1840s** DOLMABAHÇE PALACE, ISTANBUL
HISTORY	**1794–1925** Qajar dynasty, Persia, with capital at Tehran	**1820** Britain gains control of Persian Gulf states	**1853–56** Crimean War between Russia and Turkey

1861–75
GARNIER'S OPÉRA, PARIS

1863
MANET'S *LE DÉJEUNER SUR L'HERBE*

1863
SALON DES REFUSÉS, PARIS

1864
NADAR'S *GEORGE SAND*

1867–68
CARPEAUX'S *THE DANCE*

1872
MONET'S *IMPRESSION-SUNRISE*

c. 1873–74
DEGAS'S *THE REHEARSAL*

1884–86
RODIN'S *THE BURGHERS OF CALAIS*

1884–86
SEURAT'S *A SUNDAY AFTERNOON ON THE ISLAND OF LA GRANDE JATTE*

1887–89
EIFFEL TOWER, PARIS

1888
VAN GOGH'S *THE NIGHT CAFE*

1888
GAUGUIN'S *THE VISION AFTER THE SERMON*

1890–94
CÉZANNE'S *STILL LIFE WITH BASKET OF APPLES*

1893
MUNCH'S *THE SCREAM*

1868
Meiji Restoration moves Japanese capital to Tokyo

1877
Queen Victoria becomes Empress of India

1894–95
Sino-Japanese War

1898–1900
Boxer Rebellion, China

c. 1862
HOSMER'S *SENATOR THOMAS HART BENTON*

1867
LEWIS'S *FOREVER FREE*

1875
EAKINS'S *PORTRAIT OF DR. SAMUEL GROSS*

1883
ROEBLINGS' BROOKLYN BRIDGE COMPLETED

1884–88
RICHARDSON'S ALLEGHENY COUNTY COURTHOUSE

1885
HOMER'S *THE FOG WARNING*

1886
BARTHOLDI'S *STATUE OF LIBERTY* DEDICATED

1887–95
MCKIM, MEAD & WHITE'S BOSTON PUBLIC LIBRARY

1890–91
SULLIVAN, WAINWRIGHT BUILDING

1893–94
CASSATT'S *THE BOATING PARTY*

c. 1893
TANNER'S *THE BANJO LESSON*

1861–65
U.S. Civil War

1867
Dominion of Canada formed

1898
Spanish-American War

19TH CENTURY
BUSHONGO ROYAL FIGURES

1869
Suez Canal opens

1899
Boer War begins

1870s
DERVISH LODGE REBUILT AT SAHKULU SULTAN, NEAR ISTANBUL

1878–90
SIPAHSALAR MOSQUE, MADRASEH, TEHRAN

1876
New Ottoman constitution proclaimed

THE CONTINUATION OF NEOCLASSICISM

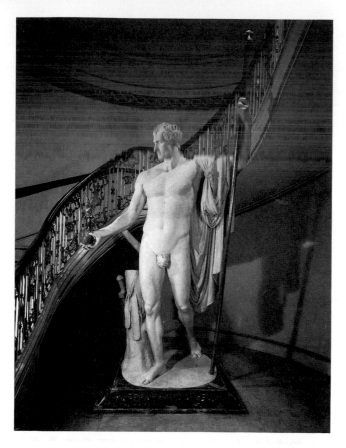

9-14. Antonio Canova. *Napoleon.* Designed by 1806. Marble with gilded bronze staff and figure of victory, height 11'. Wellington Museum, London. This work was commissioned by Napoleon, who wanted to be immortalized by Canova, then considered by many to be Europe's greatest artist. The sculpture was bought by the British government and presented to the victorious duke of Wellington, who had defeated Napoleon at Waterloo.

9-15. Jean-François-Thérèse Chalgrin and others. Arc de Triomphe, Paris. 1806–36. Height 164'. Inspired by ancient Roman triumphal arches, Napoleon decided to commemorate his military victories with this commission, the largest arch ever built. It was not completed until long after his downfall. For one of the sculptures on the arch, see figure 9-21.

How well sculpture conveys political concepts and how quickly the political situation changes are revealed in the monumental representation of Napoleon by Antonio Canova (1757–1822), commissioned by the emperor himself in 1802 (fig. 9-14). Napoleon is represented nude in the guise of Mars, ancient Roman god of war. By the time the sculpture was delivered, in 1811, Napoleon's position had become less secure. The heroic concept no longer seemed completely relevant, and Napoleon decided not to put the work on public display. After Wellington defeated Napoleon, he was given the statue as a trophy of victory, as well as a reminder of how quickly the powerful can fall. It is still displayed in Wellington's home in London.

Throughout the nineteenth century, Neoclassical architecture was popular, especially for public buildings and monuments. The Arc de Triomphe (fig. 9-15) is Napoleon's inflated and grandiose version of the ancient Roman triumphal arches, which honored victorious emperors, and its original function was exactly the same. Unfinished at his death, the sculptures added after it was completed honor instead the heroic people of the French Revolution.

The style of Jean-Auguste-Dominique Ingres (1780–1867) in *Jupiter and Thetis* demonstrates the continuing impact of the Neoclassical mode in painting (fig. 9-16). The sculpturesque modeling of the heroically posed Jupiter and the crisp drapery folds of Thetis's garment

1800	Volta invents the electric battery
1800	World population reaches 870 million
1800	U.S. population is 5.3 million; China's population is 295 million
1800	Beijing is world's largest city (1,100,000)
1804	Beethoven, Third Symphony (Eroica)
1806	**Canova, *Napoleon***

9-16. Jean-Auguste-Dominique Ingres. *Jupiter and Thetis*. 1811. Oil on canvas, 11'4 5/8" x 8'5 1/4". Musée Granet, Aix-en-Provence, France. This painting, based on an episode from the Trojan War delineated in the *Iliad* (I, 493–542), depicts Thetis, a sea nymph and mother of Achilles, pleading with Jupiter to look favorably upon a request she has delivered from Achilles.

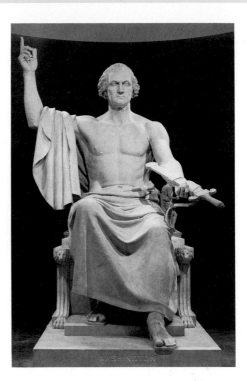

9-17. Horatio Greenough. *George Washington*. 1832–41. Marble, height 12'. National Museum of American History, Smithsonian Institution, Washington, D.C. Commissioned by Congress in 1832, this colossal work was intended for the Capitol Rotunda. Greenough, America's first famous sculptor, was an expatriate who worked in Italy, where his designs were carved by local stone carvers. The *George Washington* was completed and delivered in 1841, by which time the enthusiasm for Neoclassical sculpture in the United States had passed, and the sculpture was poorly received.

reveal Ingres's academic training. Painted while Ingres was working at the French Academy in Rome, *Jupiter and Thetis* was sent back to the Academy in Paris. The references to antiquity go beyond the theme, for the pose of Jupiter, the Roman equivalent of the Greek Zeus, king of the gods, was derived from the lost ancient cult statue of Zeus from his temple at Olympia. Created by Phidias, this magnificent sculpture of ivory and gold was considered one of the finest artistic accomplishments of classical civilization.

This lost statue of Zeus was also the inspiration for the monumental sculpture of George Washington (fig. 9-17) by Horatio Greenough (1805–52). In a typical Neoclassical effort to aggrandize and immortalize Washington—to clarify his significance for later generations—Greenough posed the great founder as the most powerful Olympian god. With rhetorical gestures, Washington offers us a sword and points upward in a declaratory manner, much like David's determined Socrates (see fig. 8-22). Most nineteenth-century Americans would not have known Greenough's source, and without this reference, the statue seemed at best ridiculous. The abrupt juxtaposition of Washington's face set on an idealized semi-nude body led to a disappointed reaction from the statue's patrons and the public. Blaming the harsh interior light of the Rotunda of the U.S. Capitol, Greenough had the sculpture moved outdoors, where it proved to be even less appreciated. The history of Greenough's *George Washington* reveals the increasingly rapid manner in which style and attitude can change—an important feature of the modern world. This impressive sculpture, with its monumental scale and commanding composition, continues to convey the heroic and even godlike characteristics often ascribed to Washington during the period of the early republic.

FRANCISCO GOYA

9-18. Francisco Goya. *The Execution of Madrileños on the Third of May, 1808*. 1814–15. Oil on canvas, 8'9" x 13'4"; the figures are life-size. Prado, Madrid. *Madrileños* is the name given to the residents of Madrid. Napoleonic troops occupied Spain from 1808 to 1814, and this painting is one of a pair by Goya that represents an uprising against the French in Madrid on May 2, 1808, and the execution of rebels and a number of innocent victims during the night of May 2–3. This was a decisive act in the consolidation of French power in Spain, and the French commander, Napoleon's brother-in-law Murat, announced that "yesterday's events have given Spain to the emperor." But the riots of May 2 also marked the beginning of Spanish resistance to the French occupation throughout the country (underground warfare is still called guerrilla warfare, from the Spanish term for "little war"). In 1814, after Napoleon was defeated, Goya petitioned the new Spanish government for support to "perpetuate with his brush the most notable and heroic actions or events of our glorious insurrection against the tyrant of Europe." The two paintings were commissioned by the government that same year.

Despite Goya's commission to perpetuate the "most . . . heroic actions of our glorious insurrection," *The Execution of Madrileños on the Third of May, 1808*, is a brutal and unsettling painting (fig. 9-18). It emphasizes a confrontation between helpless individuals and the inhuman power of an anonymous authority. The universality of Goya's interpretation overwhelms the specific event of the title. These Spaniards are not heroes but victims—perhaps even innocent victims—rounded up to be murdered by French troops. Goya represents the terror and helplessness they feel as they confront death from a faceless firing squad. More victims are marched slowly up the hill, testifying to the extent of the French brutality. Goya commemorates history while simultaneously condemning war and its effect on the individual.

The simple composition and focused light concentrate our attention on the terror and desperate helplessness of the central figure. The night setting, dramatic chiar-

1812	Byron, *Childe Harold*	
1812	Hegel, *Logic*	
1814–15	**Goya, *The Third of May, 1808***	
1817	Cullen Bryant, *Thanatopsis*	

1814–15

9-19. Francisco Goya. *Great Courage! Against Corpses!* c. 1810–15. Etching, 4 x 6" (No. 39 from *The Disasters of War* series). Goya's title for this series was *The Fatal Consequences of Spain's Bloody War with Bonaparte and Other Striking Caprichos.* The titles of the etchings in this series evoke Goya's intent: *With Reason or without It; One Cannot Bear to See This; No One Can Know Why; They Cry in Vain; And There Is No Remedy; This Is Worse, Even Worse, Barbarians!; Cartloads to the Cemetery; Bury and Shut Up; I Saw This; Why?*

oscuro contrast, and right-to-left composition heighten the drama, and Goya's loose brushstroke emphasizes the writhing movement of the victims. The color scheme is dull, with the exception of the red for blood splashed on the left foreground.

Goya published several series of prints, including a large group now known as *The Disasters of War.* Begun during the Napoleonic occupation and continued in the repres-

sive political period after the French withdrawal, they were not published until 1863, after Goya's death. In some of these prints, the nationalities of the French and Spanish soldiers are clear, but which are the torturers and which the tortured alternates. Other scenes, like the one reproduced here (fig. 9-19), are less specific; they provide Goya's comments on the terrible inhumanity created by war. Even the title condemns the futility and cru-

elty of this act. Many of the prints represent atrocities Goya witnessed during the occupation, and his cry of "Enough!" resonates across the centuries. The creation of these prints may have helped the artist deal with his emotions of helplessness, frustration, and sorrow, but the demons he expelled remain to haunt us. The **etching** medium, with its rough, scratchy lines, here serves as an appropriate vehicle for Goya's expression.

ROMANTICISM

9-20. Théodore Géricault. *The Raft of the Medusa*. 1818–19. Oil on canvas, 16'1" x 23'6". The Louvre, Paris. In preparing for this enormous painting, Géricault read published accounts of the event, interviewed survivors, and visited hospitals and morgues to study dying and dead people.

The momentous *Raft of the Medusa*, by Théodore Géricault (1791–1824), signals a departure in the development of history painting, for its subject is not a heroic event but a needless modern tragedy (fig. 9-20). When the French frigate *Medusa* sank off the African coast, the captain and senior officers commandeered the lifeboats, abandoning 150 other survivors to a makeshift raft. After floating for thirteen days, the fifteen who were still alive were rescued. Géricault represents the moment when they first sight the ship that will rescue them on the horizon. The inexperienced captain of the *Medusa* owed his position to his noble birth and his connections with the French government. Géricault's painting is intended both as a dramatic record of the event and as a condemnation of a government that would allow such a thing to happen. Whereas in the past most works of art that made a political statement were designed to sustain the government in power, Géricault's social and political consciousness demanded that he create a work that was critical.

The precise modeling of the figures and their dramatic gestures and varied poses reflect Géricault's study of the art of Michelangelo and Rubens, while the strong chiaroscuro, diagonal composition, and agitated figurative poses remind us of Baroque painting. But here these visual devices have been adapted to a theme of continuing and uncertain conflict. As the survivors excitedly catch sight of a ship on the horizon, they are in constant danger of being engulfed by the turbulent sea. Géricault's painting re-creates a frightful, emotional drama.

The Raft of the Medusa introduces us to Romanticism, a new style that challenged the dominance of Neoclassicism in the early nineteenth century. Later in the century, Émile Zola, the French novelist and critic (see page 455), would help

9-21. François Rude. *The Departure of the Volunteers of 1792* (popularly known as *"La Marseillaise"*). 1833–36. Limestone, height about 42'. Arc de Triomphe, Paris (see fig. 9-15). So stirring was Rude's sculpture that it soon received the nickname *"La Marseillaise,"* after the French national anthem, which was written in 1792 and first gained popularity when it was sung in the streets of Paris by troops from Marseilles. Commissioned by the French Government of King Louis Philippe

define Romanticism when he wrote, "A work of art is part of the universe as seen through a temperament." Romanticism stressed the subjective view of the artist, which meant that it was not dominated by a single, unified style. Romantic artists freely looked to a variety of past art styles, as well as to nature around them, to express their temperament. Opposing the rational and restrained aesthetic of Neoclassicism, Romanticism championed the unbridled spirit of the human imagination. The expression of the artist's feelings and convictions became paramount.

The powerful and contagious emotional surge of Romanticism is evident in the enormous high-relief sculpture, by François Rude (1784–1855), that decorates one of the piers of the Arc de Triomphe (fig. 9-21). An angry and determined figure representing the Genius of Liberty urges the people forward with a vigorous right-to-left movement. Despite the specific title, Rude depicts the soldiers in classical nudity or wearing ancient armor to express a universal theme—humanity's fight for liberty.

ROMANTIC LANDSCAPE PAINTING

9-22. John Constable. *The Hay Wain*. 1821. Oil on canvas, 51¼ x 73". The National Gallery, London

This interpretation of English scenery by John Constable (1776–1837) is affectionate, with its simple cart, humble cottage, and a dog standing at the river's edge (fig. 9-22). The composition is unaffected and natural, as if we have accidentally come upon this quintessential English scene. But Constable's painting is unified by the cloudy English atmosphere and by flecks of light and color—surprisingly loosely applied—that re-create the sparkling luminosity of the English countryside after the rain. Despite its naturalistic basis, the work can also be termed Romantic. Constable said that "painting is for me but another word for feeling."

Here the rush of feeling lies in Constable's love for and exaltation of his native countryside.

In the nineteenth century, landscape painting became a vehicle by which Romantic artists expressed their personal thoughts and emotions. One of the earliest was the German painter Caspar David Friedrich (1774–1840), who wrote:

The painter should depict not only what he sees before him, but also what he sees inside himself. . . . Close your physical eyes so that you see your picture first with your spiritual eye. Then bring forth what you saw inside

you so that it works on others from the exterior to their spirit.

Friedrich often encourages a quiet meditation before nature, as in his *Abbey in an Oak Forest* (fig. 9-23), in which a funeral procession of monks is moving slowly past the ruins of a Gothic structure. The barren, skeletal branches of the towering oak trees, their linear patterns echoing the window tracery of the Gothic ruins, are set against the somber, leaden sky, suggesting the void of death. Friedrich has captured one of the moods of nature, filling it with melancholy by the addition of the procession. Winter and time have

1821 **Constable,** *The Hay Wain*
1821 Egyptian hieroglyphics on Rosetta stone are deciphered
1823 Monroe Doctrine ends European colonialism on American continent
1823 Antislavery Society is founded in England

9-23. Caspar David Friedrich. *Abbey in an Oak Forest.* 1809–10. Oil on canvas, 3'8" x 5'8¹/₂". Schloss Charlottenburg, Berlin

9-24. Joseph Mallord William Turner. *The Slave Ship.* 1840. Oil on canvas, 35³/₄ x 48¹/₄". Courtesy, Museum of Fine Arts, Boston
Henry Lillie Pierce Fund

blanketed nature and the product of human endeavors. Friedrich and other nineteenth-century landscape artists (see fig. 9-33) sought to communicate the grandeur of nature and to thus inspire an almost religious reverence.

The concept of struggle was also an important theme of Romanticism. The human struggle against the seemingly overwhelming forces of nature is expressed in *The Slave Ship* (fig. 9-24), by Joseph M.W. Turner (1775–1851). This painting, ablaze with a fiery red sunset that almost consumes the activity of the theme, depicts a slave ship heading into a typhoon. Turner's evocative use of color and broad brushstrokes create an urgent, anxious feeling. To lighten the ship's load, the captain inhumanly has thrown overboard his cargo—the slaves. Although we witness their death struggle in the water, the final outcome of the brutal slavers and their ship will be determined by nature, as the ship itself faces the fury of the impending storm.

JAPANESE PRINTS

9-25. Katsushika Hokusai. *The Great Wave*, from *Thirty-six Views of Mount Fuji*. c. 1823–29. Woodblock print, 9$^{1/2}$ x 14^{3}/4". Courtesy, Museum of Fine Arts, Boston. The initial impetus behind a *ukiyo-e* woodblock print was from the publisher, who often dictated the subject matter and style. Its creation was the result of close and complex collaboration among a number of individuals. The design, created by the artist-designer, was carved into blocks of wood by a carver, who had to modify the artist's line from the original brush drawing; then it was printed by other specialists. Cooperation was essential, and compromise for aesthetic reasons or to enhance marketing must have been common. The earliest prints were black and white, with color applied by hand. With the development of color printing about 1741, each color was printed from a separately carved block; the coordination of printing so that each color was properly placed was a difficult technical procedure. Commissioned by the publisher William S. and John T. Spaulding Collection.

The particular combination of subject matter and style seen in these two prints is called *ukiyo-e* ("pictures of the floating world"). The term *floating* is here used in the Buddhist sense of something that is transient or evanescent, as experienced in everyday life and especially in the world of pleasure: theater, dancing, love, festivals, and the like. In both examples, we see the fleeting nature of *ukiyo-e*: in one, the rising of a huge wave that enframes a view of Mount Fuji; in the other, the humble but distinctive aspect of the cotton merchants' lane in Tokyo at one moment in time.

The term *ukiyo-e* is especially associated with Japanese woodblock prints. In Japan it is also used more broadly to describe a style that originated in painting and incorporated influences from a number of sources. These sources include the narrative picture scrolls (*emaki*, see pages 216–17) of the twelfth century, the decorative style brought to its peak by such painters as Sotatsu (see his *byobu*, fig. 7-48), bold Chinese compositions and brushwork incorpo-rated into the tradition of Japanese Kano painting, and aspects of naturalism drawn from both Japanese traditions and the West (the Western influence lies in the use of mathematical rules of Western scientific perspective). These elements came together in *ukiyo-e*, a new art that satisfied the demands and interests of the merchant and plebeian classes of urban Japan. *Ukiyo-e* prints, which were relatively inexpensive, were readily available for purchase by these new classes of collectors, and their bold colors and familiar subject matter gave them wide appeal.

The printing of single sheets and books had been known in East Asia since the eighth century, but this woodblock technique, traditionally used to produce cheap Buddhist icons, painting manuals, and textbooks, did not fully exploit the medium either technically or aesthetically. During the eighteenth century, however, the new interest in the urban, everyday world and the new market among the moderately well-to-do motivated the swift development of woodblock prints. The prints were mass-produced and responded quickly to changing urban fads and fashions.

During the eighteenth century, most *ukiyo-e* prints were dedicated to the representation of the figure, but as the popular taste for figure prints became more garish in the nineteenth century, some innovative artists-designers turned to urban and landscape subjects. Some of these were produced in series of prints around a central subject, such as *Thirty-six Views of Mount Fuji* by Hokusai (1760–1849) or *Fifty-three Stages of the Tokaido* (a travel guide) and *One Hundred Famous Views of Edo* (Tokyo) by Hiroshige (1797–1858).

Hokusai's *Thirty-six Views of Mount Fuji* holds the viewer's interest by the inventiveness in which Fuji, the sacred Japanese mountain, is in each print incorporated into the Japanese landscape or scenes of everyday life. Often, there are unusual and dramatic juxtapositions, as in *The Great Wave* (fig. 9-25), where the men in the skiff are dwarfed by the huge, clawing wave.

9-26. Ando Hiroshige. *Cotton Goods Lane, Odenma-cho Momen Dana*, from *One Hundred Views of Edo*. 1858. *Edo* is an earlier name for Tokyo. Woodblock print, 14 3/4 x 10". Art Institute of Chicago. The pristinely uniform architecture seen here was a particular feature of the *Odenma-cho* ("the cotton-goods merchants' quarter") and was unusual for wealthy Edo merchants. The enclosure of a row of several shops under a single roof is a house form usually reserved for backstreet tenements. The alternating crests and names identify three separate establishments, which are further defined by the low projecting ridges running down the roof face. According to the authorities, the cotton merchants were entitled to use the boxlike structure running along the entire roof as a distinguishing mark. The enclosures on top of the ridge held buckets that trapped rain water to be used in case of fire. Commissioned by the publisher Clarence Buckingham Collection 1928.301

The sense of imminent danger contrasts with the calm and majestic shape of the ever-present mountain in the background.

Cotton Goods Lane (fig. 9-26) by Hiroshige represents a street in the heart of Tokyo. The care taken with architectural details in the scene is matched in the handling of human activity. Hiroshige has shortened one of the cloth *noren* so that we can peer inside a shop, where the merchants sit among piles of cloth, presumably tallying the day's profits. The subtle disarray of the dress of the two geisha suggests that they are returning from providing entertainment and perhaps sharing drinks with the patrons. Hiroshige's technical virtuosity is evi-

dent, and his interest in rich, velvety color helps explain why his contemporaries referred to his renderings of the Japanese city and landscape as "lovely."

Although these artists were contemporaries and were both interested in depicting the transitory, Hokusai's subjects were less varied and particular than Hiroshige's. Hokusai's style is characterized by willful inventiveness and daring organization, while Hiroshige's focus is on the subtleties of a particular place and mood. Most of these print designers were also painters, but interest in their paintings has been eclipsed in the West by the popularity and availability of their prints.

HONORÉ DAUMIER AND THE POLITICAL PRINT

9-27. Honoré Daumier. *Rue Transnonain, April 15, 1834.* 1834. Lithograph, 11¹/₂ x 17⁵/₈". This print was published in *L'Association mensuelle*, July 1834. Probably commissioned by the publisher of the periodical

The dying baby lying under its dead father (fig. 9-27) is the most moving detail provided by Honoré Daumier (1808–79) in his condemnation of the brutality of French governmental policy in dealing with the working classes. The specificity of the title was chosen so that there could be no doubt about the subject. In April 1834, workers in Lyon and Paris, led by the secret Society of the Rights of Man, rioted to demonstrate against harsh working conditions and the passage of a new law forbidding unionization. On the night of April 14–15, a sniper in Paris killed an officer. In retaliation, a number of innocent residents of the sniper's building were killed by the police, including a woman and a child. Daumier's printer, Charles Philipon, wrote of this print:

> This is not caricature . . . it is a blood-stained page in the history of our days, traced by a vigorous hand and inspired by noble indignation . . . he has created a picture which will never lose its worth or duration, even if it consists of only black lines on a sheet of paper.

Daumier's print was publicly displayed and was sold in mass quantities in a journal in which Daumier's other political and humorous prints often appeared. Already in 1832, at the age of twenty-four, Daumier had served five months in prison because he had caricatured King Louis Philippe as Gargantua, but this experience did not weaken his determination to make statements through his prints about the moral and political problems and issues of his day.

Daumier made thousands of prints in a long career, and no one was safe from his attacks: radical artists, bored and quarrelsome married couples, naughty children, amateur artists, arrogant connoisseurs, corrupt politicians, and even figures from classical antiquity and mythology were lampooned. One of the popular political periodicals that published Daumier's work was called *La Caricature*. Its name helped popularize the term we use today for exaggerated and humorous representations.

Daumier's heroes most often came from the working classes. In *Freedom of the Press* (fig. 9-28), a youthful typographer, fists clenched, stands ready to defend free speech and the liberty of writers, artists, and publishers to comment on contemporary affairs. The vignette in the right background shows the defeated French king Charles X, who had been driven from power in 1830 in part as a result of criticism leveled by the press. Other European monarchs come to his aid as he is exiled. The sturdy hero looks toward the arrival of the current king, Louis, and his stance indicates that he is again ready to do battle to protect his rights.

The opinions and criticism revealed in popular prints by Daumier and others, however, eventually became too much for the government to bear. In 1835, laws were passed that proclaimed that "Frenchmen have the right to circulate their opinions in published form," but that "drawings" were such an "incitement to action" that complete liberty in this realm was no longer permitted. After this point, Daumier's prints became more humorous and less political.

9-28. Honoré Daumier. *Freedom of the Press: Don't Meddle with It*. 1834. Lithograph, 11¹/₂ x 17⁵/₈". This print appeared in *La Caricature*, March 1834. Probably commissioned by the publisher of the periodical

TECHNIQUE   LITHOGRAPHY

Lithography ("stone drawing"), invented in Germany in 1798, became the most popular print medium of the nineteenth century, as lithographs came into use to illustrate newspapers and books (fig. 9-29). Lithography is based on the affinity of grease for grease and the antipathy of water to grease. The **print form** is usually a very smooth slab of limestone on which the artist creates a composition using either a greasy crayon or lithographic ink applied with a pen or a brush. The resulting design adheres chemically to the surface of the stone. When the stone is moistened, the water stays only in the nongreasy areas and the greasy ink that is subsequently applied with a roller adheres only to the composition. A dampened paper is applied, stone and paper are put through a press, and a lithograph is created. The technique, spontaneous and relatively cheap, was especially appropriate for the mass media of the nineteenth and early twentieth century because the design can be mechanically transferred from the original print form to additional stones, allowing a large and rapid print edition.

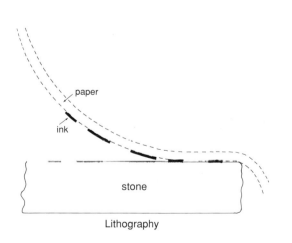

9-29. Diagram of the lithography technique

ROMANTIC REVIVAL ARCHITECTURE

9-30. Charles Barry and Augustus W. N. Pugin. Houses of Parliament, London. Begun 1836; opened 1852; completed 1870. Barry, who won the 1835–36 competition to design the new Houses of Parliament, hired Pugin to help with the detailing. The resulting Gothic Revival complex even has Gothic Revival inkwells and coatracks. Commissioned by Parliament and King William IV

The decision to rebuild the Houses of Parliament in the Gothic Revival style (fig. 9-30) was not based solely on aesthetic grounds. A more profound cultural and moral basis declared that the Gothic style was historically appropriate, for it had flourished in England during the late medieval period. And, more important for the nineteenth century, the Gothic was perceived as a style that expressed spiritual goodness, truth, and the properly reverent relationship between humanity and God, and it thus became the quintessential Christian style. One critic in 1836 described it as

> a style of architecture which belongs peculiarly to Christianity . . . whose very ornaments remind one of the joys

of life beyond the grave; whose lofty vaults and arches are crowded with the forms of prophets and martyrs and beatified spirits, and seem to resound with the choral hymns of angels and archangels . . . the architecture of Christianity, the sublime, the glorious Gothic.

The Romantic architects of the nineteenth century revived a multitude of historical styles, but each was understood within a specific cultural, moral, and historical context that encompassed both the nineteenth century and the period when the style originated. The Greek Revival in the United States, for example, as witnessed in a house in Demopolis ("City of the People"), Alabama (fig. 9-31), and in hundreds of banks, courthouses, churches, and homes throughout the country, was a response to a movement to find an architectural style appropriate for the political ideals of the young nation. Thomas Jefferson had championed the Neoclassical style (see pages 408–09), but the early nineteenth century turned more directly to the monuments of ancient Athens, history's first documented democracy, for inspiration. American architects and publishers produced how-to books with plans and elevations for Greek-style houses and churches, and all across the United States, buildings with handsome Doric porticoes—some in stone but many in wood, like this one—were erected.

In the United States, the Greek style was gradually supplanted in popularity by the Gothic Revival style. The house by A. J. Davis in New Bedford, Massachusetts (fig. 9-32), is decorated with the architectural vocabulary invented in the later Middle Ages for the great French Gothic cathedrals. The scalloped decoration (cusping) along the eaves and the lacy patterns of the porch posts—cut from wood—are

1836	**Barry and Pugin, Houses of Parliament begun**
1836	R. W. Emerson, *Nature*
1837–1901	Reign of Queen Victoria

9-31. Gaineswood, Demopolis, Alabama. 1842–c. 1860. The heritage of the early-nineteenth-century American enthusiasm for things Greek survives in structures, often by unknown or purely local architects, in the Greek Revival style in stone, wood, and stucco, in coordinating furniture and decorative arts, and in such place names as Demopolis; Troy, New York; Olympia, Washington; and Sparta and Athens, Michigan.

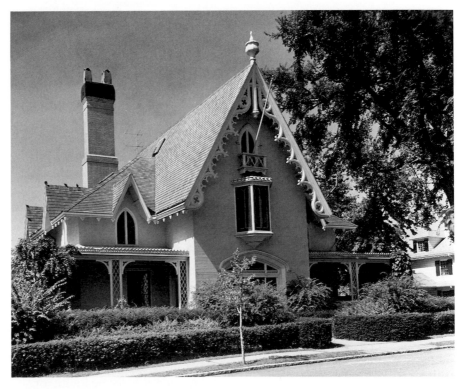

9-32. Alexander Jackson Davis. House for William Rotch, New Bedford, Massachusetts. 1845. Commissioned by William J. Rotch

an American version of the gilded ornamentation on a medieval Gothic reliquary. The widespread popularity of this "carpenter" Gothic movement and other revival styles can be explained in part by the cheap pattern books produced by architects and publishers that brought such fantasy within the range of every pioneer with a saw.

AMERICAN ROMANTIC PAINTING

9-33. Thomas Cole. *Schroon Mountain, Adirondacks.* 1838. Oil on canvas, 39³/8 x 63". Cleveland Museum of Art. Philip Hone, who had served as mayor of New York City, in 1838 wrote, "I think every American is proud to prove his love of country by admiring Cole."
Hinman B. Hurlbut Collection

A landscape is great in its proportion as it declares the glory of God, not the works of man. (Asher B. Durand, *Letters on Landscape Painting*, 1855)

Enthusiasm for the God-given beauty and richness of the American landscape is the subject of this painting (fig. 9-33) by Thomas Cole (1801–48). A dramatic natural confrontation is emphasized as the sweeping peak seems to soar victorious above the clouds. The season is autumn, when the American landscape offers a special coloristic splendor not found in the landscapes of Europe. Schroon Mountain is located near the source of the Hudson

River in the Adirondack Mountains, in New York State, and after visiting there in 1837, Cole wrote:

> The scenery . . . has a wild sort of beauty . . . quietness—solitude—the world untamed . . . an aspect which the scene has worn thousands of years. . . . I do not remember to have seen in Italy a composition of mountains so beautiful or pictorial as this.

Cole's emphasis on the uniqueness of American scenery is significant, for in his paintings, nationalistic spirit was joined to the ideal of the American landscape as a new Garden of Eden—a God-given paradise that

would guarantee the nation's future greatness. Cole himself was to write:

> Those scenes of solitude from which the hand of nature has never been lifted affect the mind with more deep-toned emotion than aught which the hand of man has touched. Amid them the consequent associations are of God, the Creator. They are his undefiled works, and the mind is cast into the contemplation of eternal things.

Later, the landscape painter Asher B. Durand wrote that every American family should own a painting of the American landscape, counseling

9-34. George Caleb Bingham. _Fur Traders Descending the Missouri._ 1845. Oil on canvas, 29 x 36". The Metropolitan Museum of Art, New York. Bingham's original title for this work was _French Trader and Half-Breed Son._ There is still debate about the identification of the tethered animal. In a later version of this same theme, however, it is clearly a bear cub.
Morris K. Jessup Fund, 1933 (33.61)

that it should hang in the parlor, over the table where the family Bible was kept.

Earlier American painters had concentrated on portrait painting (see page 406), an art that flourishes in democratic, mercantile societies. In the late-eighteenth and early-nineteenth centuries, however, a number of painters went to Europe to study, returning home full of enthusiasm for Neoclassical history painting (see page 410). They soon discovered that the intellectual subjects of history painting held little appeal for the American public or patrons. Beginning in the 1820s, American scenery was identified as the ideal subject for American artists, and it was Thomas Cole who

was recognized by his contemporaries as the first great painter of the American landscape. Landscape seemed an especially democratic art, for its meaning was immediately accessible to the public, without scholarly reference.

In the painting by George Caleb Bingham (1811–79), our romantic, atmospheric view of the wide American river is momentarily disrupted as a dugout canoe moves downstream, close to us and in sharp focus (fig. 9-34). The trailing smoke from the trader's pipe reveals the speed of the current. The old trader and his son look at us with contrasting expressions—the boy seems bemused, the father serious.

Bingham's composition places

the canoe parallel to the **picture plane** to emphasize both the horizontal vastness of the mighty river and its right-to-left movement. A surprising percentage of the painting is given over to the sky, where the sudden luminosity of dawn highlights the wispy clouds. The subdued colors and blurred forms of the atmospheric setting give emphasis to the foreground forms, which are richer in color and pattern and more precisely executed. These forms are in turn blurred in the splendidly painted reflection. Bingham's painting of life on the frontier, an evocation and exaltation of the American West, was intended for an audience in the urbanized cities of the East.

FRENCH REALISM: GUSTAVE COURBET

9-35. Gustave Courbet. *The Stone Breakers*. 1849. Oil on canvas, 5'3" x 8'6". Formerly Gemäldegalerie, Dresden (destroyed in 1945)

The art of painting can consist only in the representation of objects visible and tangible to the painter. An epoch can be reproduced only by its own artists. I mean by the artists who have lived in it. I hold that the artists of one century are fundamentally incompetent to represent the things of a past or future century. . . . It is in this sense that I deny the existence of an historical art applied to the past. (Gustave Courbet, 1861)

To our eyes, there is nothing offensive about *The Stone Breakers* (fig. 9-35), by Gustave Courbet (1819–77), for the scene of a youth assisting an older man in breaking stones for a roadbed is a **genre** subject, an objective view of life in the mid-nineteenth century. When it was first exhibited, however, *The Stone Breakers* shocked and angered critics and public alike. During the Neoclassical and Romantic eras, the significance of a painting was judged by the didactic virtue of its theme and by the painter's adherence to academic rules of composition and execution. Courbet broke these rules, insisting that the only goal of the artist was to reproduce "objects visible and tangible to the painter." To those schooled in the traditional attitudes about art, however, truly commonplace figures and subjects seemed trite, even vulgar.

Courbet's words were given an even fuller expression in *A Burial at Ornans* (fig. 9-36). We stand at the side of a grave during a funeral in Courbet's hometown, outside Paris. Virtually without comment, Courbet records the visual facts: a priest and attendants reciting prayers, the mourners and a gravedigger, a dog, and a hole in the ground in the immediate foreground. No spiritual promises of an "eternal reward" are apparent here. The emotional pulse of Romantic painting has given way to simple, direct observation.

When Courbet's *Burial at Ornans* and another large painting were rejected by the jury of the Universal Exposition of 1855, an infuriated Courbet withdrew the eleven pictures they had accepted and had his own exhibition building constructed,

9-36. Gustave Courbet. *A Burial at Ornans.* 1849. Oil on canvas, 10'3¹/₂" x 21'9". Musée d'Orsay, Paris

where, with customary bravado, he held a solo show in competition with the official exhibition. The so-called *Realist Manifesto*, which may have been written in part by the Realist writer and critic Champfleury, was actually the introduction to the catalog of Courbet's private exhibition:

The title of "realist" has been imposed upon me, as the men of 1830 had imposed upon them the title of "romantics." Titles have never given a just idea of things; were it otherwise, the work would be superfluous. Without trying to clear up the degree of correctness of a qualification which no one, one must hope, will be asked to understand exactly, I will limit myself to a few words of explanation to cut short any misunderstanding.

I have studied the art of the masters and the art of the moderns, avoiding any preconceived system and without prejudice. I have no more wanted to imitate the former than to copy the latter; nor have I thought of achieving the idle aim of art for art's sake. No! I have simply wanted to draw from a thorough knowledge of tradition the reasoned and free sense of my own individuality.

To know in order to do: such has been my thought. To be able to translate the customs, ideas, and appearance of my time as I see them—in a word, to create a living art—this has been my aim.

In a letter, Courbet wrote to a patron that Realism was "a holy and sacred cause, which is the cause of Liberty and Independence." Throughout the 1850s, Courbet's paintings gained greater public acceptance, although critics also became more vociferous, accusing him of being a propagandist for leftist or socialist causes. Courbet's redirection of subject matter toward the realism of the commonplace was an important influence on younger French artists, especially Édouard Manet and the Impressionists (see pages 454 and 460).

ACADEMIC ART

9-37. Emanuel Leutze. *Washington Crossing the Delaware.* 1851. Oil on canvas, 12'5" x 21'3". The Metropolitan Museum of Art, New York. When this painting was exhibited in New York in 1852, some 50,000 people paid to see it, and the wide sale of a reproductive engraving made it one of the most famous images in the United States. Leutze worked hard to make his painting authentic, but history buffs will note a number of errors.

Gift of John S. Kennedy, 1897

Washington Crossing the Delaware (fig. 9-37) exemplifies the Academic approach to history painting, with its blend of a serious subject, historical fact (or what passes for historical fact), artistic manipulation, precise detail, and a carefully digested blend of elements from the High Renaissance and Baroque. Although he had grown up in the United States, Emanuel Leutze (1816–68) returned to his native Germany to spend many years teaching and studying at the influ-

ential Academy at Düsseldorf. Many American painters studied there, returning to the United States to advocate the strict and precisely painted realistic style for which the Düsseldorf Academy and Leutze were famous.

The highest goal of Academic painters was to create history paintings of significant moral import, paintings that would document the past and provide inspiration and guidance for the future. In his painting, Leutze set out to express the sig-

nificance of Washington's crossing of the Delaware. His success can be judged by the manner in which his treatment continues to capture the public's enthusiasm. It is through this painting that generations of schoolchildren have come to understand a famous national event; rather than representing history, Leutze's painting has played a role in forming it.

The success of the picture is based on its precise and studied realism, a style that makes its his-

1850   London becomes the world's largest city (2,320,000)
1850–59   U.S. receives 2.5 million immigrants
1851   Leutze, *Washington Crossing the Delaware*
1851   First submarine cable, under the English Channel

9-38. Rosa Bonheur. *The Horse Fair.* 1853; retouched 1855. Oil on canvas, 8' x 16'7¹/2". The Metropolitan Museum of Art, New York. Like many European women artists in the period before 1900, Rosa Bonheur was the daughter of an artist. She and her sister and two brothers all began receiving art lessons while young; Rosa, the eldest and most successful, began to study at the Louvre at the age of fourteen and by nineteen was exhibiting in the Paris Salons. Her works enjoyed great critical and popular success. In 1865, the empress of France awarded her the Cross of the French Legion of Honor, declaring "genius has no sex." The youthful horse trainer in the center, wearing a black cap, may be a self-portrait.

Gift of Cornelius Vanderbilt, 1887 (87.25)

torical theme convincing, and on its striking composition, with a valiant Washington shown standing heroically against the wind.

The Horse Fair (fig. 9-38), by Rosa Bonheur (1822–99), was one of the most famous paintings of the nineteenth century. After creating a sensation at the Salon of 1853, it toured to crowds in the United States for three years. The painting's success can be attributed to its academic realism, which extends from an expert understanding of animal anatomy (Bonheur went often to horse fairs, disguised as a boy, to draw from the living animals) to the precise rendition of the pebbles in the foreground. The effective composition is the result of numerous studies of details and of the whole design. Most impressive is the powerful movement of the horses and men that surges, almost uncontrolled, across the breadth of this huge painting. Bonheur here modified her usually fine brushstroke for a bolder stroke to enhance the effect of rippling energy, and the natural colors of the horses are heightened by contrast with the brilliant colors worn by the grooms.

Paintings and sculptures of animals were popular during the nineteenth century, in part because they functioned as metaphors for the more human content that painters were reluctant to represent. The combination of grace and power in Bonheur's handsome horses communicates an ideal of energy and vitality.

NINETEENTH-CENTURY ART   **447**

NEW MATERIALS AND ENGINEERING IN ARCHITECTURE

The Crystal Palace (fig. 9-39) demonstrates two developments that transformed architecture during the second half of the nineteenth century: the importance of new, artificial materials and the advantages of prefabrication. This huge structure of prefabricated cast-iron membering and glass was made and erected in nine months, proving the speed and economy of such a procedure. The basic module used in the design of the building was not based on aesthetic principles but on a practical fact: the maximum size of the glass that could be manufactured was approximately 4 feet. The cast-iron components were based on the larger module of 24 feet, and no single prefabricated

9-39. Joseph Paxton. Interior, the Crystal Palace, London. 1850–51 (destroyed). Cast iron, wrought iron, and glass, length 1,848'; width 408'. Engraving by R. P. Cuff after W. B. Brounger. Drawings Collection, Royal Institute of British Architects, London. The Crystal Palace was an enormous structure erected to house the Great Exhibition of the Works of Industry of All Nations—the first in a series of nineteenth-century international exhibitions that presaged the world's fairs of our own day. The largest single enclosed volume erected up to that date, it covered almost one million square feet of floor space. It was later disassembled and rebuilt on another site. Commissioned by the Building Committee of the Commissioners of the Great Exhibition of the Works of Industry of All Nations

9-40. John A. and Washington A. Roebling. Brooklyn Bridge, New York. 1869–83. Stone piers with steel cables, maximum span 1,595′. John Roebling died in 1869, just as construction on the bridge was beginning, and his son brought his plans for the bridge to completion. Commissioned by the New York Bridge Company, under an act passed by the New York State Legislature

part was allowed to weigh more than a ton. Because it was intended to be a temporary, utilitarian structure (the exhibits of machinery and other works of art and industry were the focus), the references to earlier architectural styles demanded in nineteenth-century building were not required. One perceptive critic pointed out that "here the standards by which architecture had hitherto been judged no longer held good," but the fact remains that the Crystal Palace was not considered to be architecture with a capital *A*. There was no reevaluation here, as there was with virtually all other nineteenth-century structures of significance, which were endowed with references to traditional architec-

tural styles (see page 440).

The new technological investigations and accomplishments of the nineteenth century were widely published in books and technical journals, and thus their impact could be immediate and universal. Metal and glass were at first held to be fireproof, but iron proved to be susceptible to melting and collapse in a conflagration. Ironically, the Crystal Palace itself was ultimately destroyed by fire, but only in 1936.

New York City's Brooklyn Bridge, by John A. Roebling (1806–69) and his son Washington A. Roebling (1837–1926), pioneered another new material—steel (fig. 9-40). The advantages of using metal for bridges were first realized in a cast-

iron bridge erected in England in 1779. In bridge building, cast iron (an iron alloy that is easily cast but of low tensile strength) was subsequently replaced by wrought iron (a much purer, malleable iron), and then wrought iron was replaced by steel (a malleable iron alloy with very high tensile strength). The Brooklyn Bridge is more than half again as long as any earlier bridge, and its four huge cables are formed from parallel galvanized drawn-steel wires that were spun in place to create an ultimate strength of 71.5 tons per square inch. But despite the modern technology that made this huge span possible, the dramatic masonry supporting piers were given Gothic arches.

NINETEENTH-CENTURY ART **449**

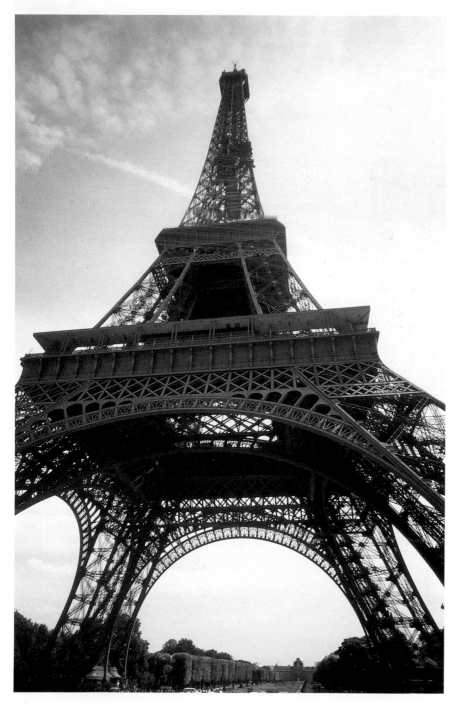

9-41. Gustave Eiffel. Eiffel Tower, Paris. 1887–89. Wrought-iron superstructure on a reinforced concrete base, original height 984'; current height 1,052'. Eiffel's design was the winning entry from 700 submissions in a competition to design a temporary structure for the Paris Universal Exposition of 1889, which celebrated the 100th anniversary of the French Revolution. Until the erection of the Empire State Building in 1930–32, the Eiffel Tower was the tallest structure in the world. Commissioned by Monsieur Lockroy, Minister for Trade and the General Commissioner for the Exhibition of 1889

possible for fairgoers to have fabulous views of Paris. But Eiffel also set out to design a pleasing structure, and he disguised the underlying modern grid frame on which the work is engineered with sweeping curves and dramatic proportions. Even so, the design was criticized as a monstrosity, and the architect Charles Garnier (see page 452) circulated a petition demanding that it be demolished.

But the most significant development in the later nineteenth century was the invention of the skyscraper (see page 480). As business and population were concentrated in rapidly growing cities, the need for expansion upward became evident. Louis Sullivan, in his *Autobiography of an Idea*, wrote: "The tall commercial building arose from the pressure of land prices, the land prices from pressure of population, the pressure of population from external pressure." In 1852, Elisha G. Otis invented the Otis safety elevator, which he demonstrated at a New York industrial fair in 1854. By 1857, the first commercial passenger elevator had been installed in a New York building, and in 1861 Otis made a significant improvement by patenting a steam-powered elevator. Before Otis's invention, the height of a building had been limited by how many flights of steps the owner was willing to make his clients climb. With an elevator, the height was limited only by the potentials of the material available and the economics of tall construction.

Most urban structures were of heavy masonry (that is, stone or brick) construction, and the taller the building, the heavier the lower stories had to be to support the tremendous weight of the increased height. All this changed with the development of the load-bearing steel cage, based on the new lower price of steel due to the invention of the Bessemer process (1855), and of reinforced concrete.

Before he won the competition to build a temporary structure for the Universal Exposition of 1889, Gustave Eiffel (1832–1923) had established an international reputation as an engineer and designer of bridges, locks, and the skeleton for the *Statue of Liberty* (see fig. 9-7). The purpose of his tower (fig. 9-41) was to provide a dramatic and unforgettable symbol for the exposition and, by elevators, to make it

9-42. William Le Baron Jenney. Detail of steel-frame construction, as used in the Fair Store, Chicago. 1890–91

9-43. François Hennebique. Diagram of monolithic reinforced-concrete joint; patented 1892

Load-bearing **steel-frame construction** (fig. 9-42) is based on an earlier development in wood, the **balloon frame**, in which wood joists are joined horizontally and vertically to create grids that become a skeletal structure for the building. Both outer "skin" and inner walls are attached to and hang from this skeleton.

Load-bearing steel-frame construction employs the same method, but the load-bearing members are prefabricated steel I beams. In tall buildings, the steel frame offers several significant advantages. The high tensile strength of steel, for example, makes possible a substantial reduction in both the amount of material needed and the thickness of the walls. In a brick- or stone-walled structure, each story that is added to the height means a significant increase in the thickness of the walls at the base:

> It was inherent in the nature of masonry construction to fix a new limit of height; as its ever-thickening walls ate up ground and floor space of

ever-increasing price, as the pressure of population rapidly increased. (Louis Sullivan, *The Autobiography of an Idea*, 1926)

Steel is much stronger than masonry, and its tensile strength means that the finished building will have the elasticity necessary to allow it to move and respond to the pressure from high winds, a problem in a masonry building, which will topple because it cannot sway.

Reinforced concrete (fig. 9-43), in which concrete is strengthened by embedded wire rods or mesh, was developed in France in the second half of the nineteenth century. The steel gives the concrete an impressive tensile strength. It is a remarkably flexible material and can be formed at the site, during construction, or prefabricated. As is typical of the nineteenth century, this economical new construction method was first used only for utilitarian structures such as mills.

LATE-NINETEENTH-CENTURY REVIVAL ARCHITECTURE

9-44. Charles Garnier. The Opéra, Paris. 1861–75. Commissioned by Emperor Napoleon II as one of the focal points for his rebuilding of the center of Paris

Many mid- to late-nineteenth-century buildings impress us by their scale, richness of materials, and inventive abundance of historical references. The style of the design for the Paris Opéra (fig. 9-44), by Charles Garnier (1825–98), has been called Second Empire Italianate Neo-Renaissance/Baroque, revealing the eclecticism of this building. More sumptuous than any Baroque structure, it established a standard of extravagant decoration for cultural institutions that would have a wide impact, affecting even the development of the motion picture "palace" in twentieth-century America. The opulence of the exterior, with its sculptures (see fig. 9-53), mosaics, and gilded details, is continued in the interior with a magnificent grand staircase, foyer, and auditorium. Garnier stated his philosophy in pointing out that a "staircase crowded with people was a spectacle of pomp and elegance"

and that "by arranging fabrics and wall hangings, candelabra . . . and chandeliers, as well as marble and flowers, color everywhere, one makes of this ensemble a brilliant and sumptuous composition." This is the kind of architecture that is popularly termed Victorian, whether it was built within the empire of Queen Victoria or not.

The courthouse and jail (fig. 9-45) erected in Pittsburgh by Henry Hobson Richardson (1838–86) for one of the world's great industrial centers use a modern version of the Romanesque style (see page 208) that avoids decoration to emphasize mass, weight, and solidity. The heavily **rusticated** walls, corner pavilions, and tall, centralized tower of the courthouse express the enduring authority of law and government. In contrast, the jail offers irregular masses, a lively silhouette, and unexpected placement of openings, effects that may refer to law-

lessness and a lack of order. This "iconography" is not accidental, for the building specifications from the Allegheny County commissioners indicated that "the buildings should suggest the purpose for which they were intended." A low bridge, inspired by examples in Venice, allows a secure transfer of the accused to trial in the courthouse. Richardson's particular, personal use of the Romanesque style had a widespread popularity in the 1880s. Perhaps its sheer weight and architectural presence were reassuring after the disruptive trauma of the Civil War. Richardson's first biographer wrote of the courthouse: "It is as new as the needs it meets, as American as the community for which it was built. Yet it might stand without loss of prestige in any city in the world." Richardson himself was most pleased with its massive scale: "If they honor me for the pigmy things I have already done, what will they

9-45. Henry Hobson Richardson. Allegheny County Courthouse and Jail, Pittsburgh, Pennsylvania. 1884–88. Richardson died without seeing these buildings completed; when he realized that he was seriously ill, he wrote: "Let me have time to finish Pittsburgh and I shall be content without another day." This illustration reproduces a print of the design Richardson submitted to win the competition for the project. It preserves the original appearance of the entrance portals and the steps, which are today modified. Commissioned by the Allegheny County Commissioners

say when they see Pittsburgh finished?"

In the closing decades of the nineteenth century, a monumental classical style was re-created in the works of America's most popular architectural firm, McKim, Mead, & White. Their white granite Boston Public Library (fig. 9-46) seems like a grandiose Renaissance palace. A row of impressive rounded arched windows emphasizes the second floor. The inspiration from Renaissance palaces is perhaps not purely aesthetic, for the trustees' commission was for a "palace for the people." A dignified inscription across the facade states the building's public purpose and patrons: "The Public Library of the City of Boston Built by the People and Dedicated to the Advancement of Learning." This is the most important building of a movement sometimes known as the American Renaissance.

9-46. McKim, Mead, & White. Public Library, Boston. 1887–95. Commissioned by the Trustees of the Library

ÉDOUARD MANET

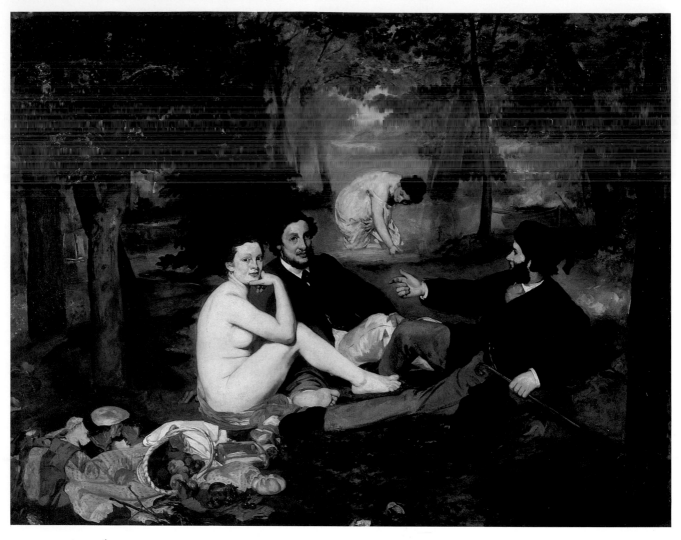

9-47. Édouard Manet. *Le Déjeuner sur l'herbe* (*The Picnic*). 1863. Oil on canvas, 7' x 8'10". Musée d'Orsay, Paris

A commonplace woman of the demimonde, as naked as can be, shamelessly lolls between two dandies dressed to the teeth. These latter look like schoolboys on a holiday, perpetrating an outrage to play the man, and I search in vain for the meaning of this unbecoming rebus. . . . This is a young man's practical joke, a shameful open sore not worth exhibiting this way . . . . The landscape is well handled . . . but the figures are slipshod. (A critique of *Le Déjeuner sur l'herbe*, 1863)

In *Le Déjeuner sur l'herbe* of 1863 (fig. 9-47), Édouard Manet (1832–83) created a scandal, even at the Salon des Refusés (see page 422). Its iconography is perplexing. We are unashamedly confronted by a female nude, her dress and undergarments thrown down near a basket of luscious fruit in the foreground. She is accompanied by two fully clothed men, while in the middle ground a second woman bathes in a small lake. The visual impact of Manet's style is equally powerful and unexpected, for the startling lack of modeling in the female nude and the large strokes of thick, rich paint had not been seen

in earlier French painting. The bold, luscious passages of paint that create the fruit are especially beautiful. In iconography, Manet based his *Le Déjeuner sur l'herbe* on the combination of dressed men and nude women seen in a well-known Renaissance painting in the Louvre, the *Concert Champêtre (Pastoral Concert)*, which at the time was thought to be by Giorgione (scholars today attribute it to Titian), while he took the figural composition intentionally from a print after the much-revered Raphael. Manet's updating of earlier artistic sources may have a deeper social meaning, representing the polarity of French

9-48. Édouard Manet. *Olympia*. 1863. Oil on canvas, 4'3" x 6'2³/4". Musée d'Orsay, Paris. Of Manet's *Olympia*, the later painter Cézanne would say, "Our Renaissance dates from it."

society, with the natural world confronting the artificial, or the painting may simply represent artists picnicking with their models. We shall probably never know the exact meaning or meanings, but we do know that from Manet onward, a new course was set for avant-garde painting of the late nineteenth century, as artists would begin to turn further and further away from prescribed academic rules in painting.

Two years after the French critics and public were shocked by *Le Déjeuner*, they were sent reeling by Manet's entry in the 1865 Salon (fig. 9-48). The scandal revolved around both Manet's methods of painting, with loose brushstrokes and flat areas of color, and his disrespect for proper subject matter. One of Manet's sources was Titian's *Venus of Urbino* (see fig. 6-35), a painting that had helped establish the theme of the reclining nude female figure as a subject for art. But now, in the pose usually reserved for an idealized female nude, Manet has realistically painted Victorine, a model. In addition, Manet has changed Titian's sleeping dog, a symbol of fidelity, into a lively black cat, a traditional symbol of lust in European art. Titian's servants attend to their work, but Olympia's maid brings flowers—a gift, it would seem, from a grateful or prospective client.

Even the title (*Olympia* was a generic term for a lower-class prostitute at the time) suggests the shocking subject of Manet's painting.

Manet did have his champions, however, and one was the noted author and critic Émile Zola. In writing a defense of Manet, Zola pointed out that Manet's paintings are responsive to life, rather than to academic traditions of art:

M. Manet's temperament is dry, trenchant. He catches his figures vividly, is not afraid of the brusqueness of nature and renders in all their vigour the different objects which stand out against each other. His whole being causes him to see things in splotches, in simple and forceful pieces. . . . Don't bother looking at the neighboring pictures. Look at the living persons in the room. Study the way their bodies look against the floors and walls. Then look at M. Manet's paintings: you will see that there lies truth and strength.

Manet's devotion to painting form as he saw it, irrespective of its meaning, is summarized in Zola's comments as one of Manet's subjects:

I remember posing for hours on end. . . . Now and again, half dozing as I sat there, I looked at the artist standing at his easel, his features taut, his eyes bright, absorbed in his work. He had forgotten me; he no longer realized that I was there.

When Manet died in 1883, Zola, Degas, and Monet all served as pallbearers. Renoir and Pissarro paid their respects, and even the reclusive Cézanne came to Paris from Provence.

EARLY PHOTOGRAPHY AND PHOTOGRAPHIC TECHNIQUE

9-49. Nadar (Gaspard-Félix Tournachon). *George Sand*. 1864. Albumen print, 7⁷/₈ x 6¹/₄". George Eastman House, Rochester, New York. "George Sand" was the pen name of Aurore Dupin, a French novelist and feminist.

Nadar's portrait of George Sand (fig. 9-49), with its controlled lighting and careful attention to pose and detail, was part of a series that included the major French literary and artistic figures of the mid-nineteenth century. That such a series should be produced is not novel, but that it was produced using the relatively new photographic medium greatly assisted the legitimization of photography. Nadar (1820–1910) pioneered the use of interior studio

lighting in portraits that communicated the dignity of his sitters.

One of the components of photography (from the Greek *photo*, "light," and *graphis*, "to write" or "to describe") dates back centuries. The **camera obscura** (from the Latin, meaning "dark room") was an enclosed box with an opening at one end. Rays of light passing through the opening projected an inverted image on the opposite wall. The camera obscura had been in use

since the Renaissance, primarily as an aid in understanding perspective. Artists traced the projected image inside the "camera." What was lacking, however, was a method to "fix" that image, a process whereby it could be made permanent. In the early eighteenth century, it was discovered that silver salts were light sensitive, and, building on this and other, more recent advances, Joseph-Nicéphore Niépce in 1826 created the first photograph using a camera obscura and a pewter plate coated with bitumen, a light-sensitive substance. Niépce's first photograph required an eight-hour exposure time.

In 1829, the elderly Niépce formed a partnership with Louis Daguerre, who, in 1837, successfully produced the first **daguerreotype**, which used a chemically treated silver-plated sheet of copper to retain the image. The result was a far clearer image than Niépce's, with a greatly reduced exposure time. Improvements in the next decade made the daguerreotype practical, with an exposure time of

1864	**Nadar,** *George Sand*
1866	First transatlantic cable
1867	Russia sells Alaska to the U.S.

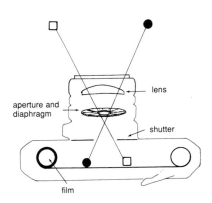

9-50. Diagram of a camera

lens

aperture and diaphragm

shutter

film

9-51. Oscar Rejlander. *The Two Paths of Life*. 1857. Combination albumen print, 16 x 31". George Eastman House, Rochester, New York. To achieve this tableaulike effect, Rejlander photographed the background and each of the figures separately. These thirty negatives were then printed on one photographic paper.

30–60 seconds. Daguerre's excited claim, "I have seized the light, I have arrested its flight," announced the beginning of modern photography.

Developments in photography quickened. In 1839, William Henry Fox Talbot, a British scientist, invented the photographic negative, allowing multiple prints to be made from the same exposed plate, and by midcentury glass-plate negatives were being used to produce remarkably sharp images. Our illustration (fig. 9-50) shows a modern version of a camera.

The early relationship between photography and art was, at best, a difficult one. Some photographers, such as Oscar Rejlander (1813–75), sought to make photography an art by copying the traditional themes found in contemporary Academic Art. *The Two Paths of Life* (fig. 9-51) represents an allegorical subject. As a photograph, it is impressive for its size and technical achievement, for it is a combination of thirty negatives individually printed on a single sheet of paper. The young men on

each side of the elderly father must choose between a life of virtue or of vice. Such an overtly theatrical subject was related to the publicly accepted values of Academic Art (see page 446). Here photography was trying to "copy" painting to win public acceptance.

It was, however, in portraiture that photography found its most immediate and popular use. The reduced exposure time and affordable price made photographic portraits available to almost everyone. Julia Margaret Cameron (1815–79) developed a distinctive style that emphasized the face of the sitter (fig. 9-52). Cameron was fully aware that photography is not just a medium that reproduces reality. Speaking of her portraits, she wrote:

> When I have such men before my camera, my whole soul has endeavoured to do its duty toward them in recording faithfully the greatness of the inner man as well as the features of the outer

9-52. Julia Margaret Cameron. *Alfred Lord Tennyson*. 1865. Silver print, 10 x 8". Royal Photographic Society, London. Cameron, who began photography only in her late forties, after she received a camera as a gift, was primarily self-taught. The poet Tennyson was a friend and neighbor.

man. The photograph thus taken has been almost the embodiment of a prayer.

LATE-NINETEENTH-CENTURY SCULPTURE

9-53. Jean-Baptiste Carpeaux. *The Dance*. 1867–68. Plaster model, height 15'. Musée de l'Opéra, Paris. Commissioned by Charles Garnier, the architect of the Opéra

9-54. Marcello (Adèle d'Affry, Duchess Castiglione-Colonna). *Pythia*. 1870. Bronze, height 9'6". The Opéra, Paris. "Marcello" was the pseudonym used by a talented and highly successful female sculptor who exhibited at the Paris Salons beginning in 1863. This work was shown at the 1870 Salon, where it was purchased by Charles Garnier to decorate the Grand Foyer of the Paris Opéra (see fig. 9-44).

As architectural sculpture, *The Dance* (fig. 9-53), by Jean-Baptiste Carpeaux (1827–75), is part of a tradition that includes the Parthenon and Gothic cathedrals (see figs. 3-72, 4-89). Charles Garnier designed the Opéra (see fig. 9-44) with large reliefs by the main entrances representing the various arts. Carpeaux, however, went beyond Garnier's intention, making his figures virtually freestanding, an effect further enhanced by their energetic movement. The exuberant, winged male allegory of Dance leaps upward and outward, while the smiling female nudes encircle him, moving outward into our space in a dance. Carpeaux's allegory communicates the joy of dancing, but originally its nudity shocked contemporary Parisians, who demanded its removal.

Movement conveys a different emotional state in Marcello's *Pythia*, who was the oracle at the sanctuary of Apollo at Delphi and, therefore, the most important prophetess of the ancient Greek world (fig. 9-54). After breathing fumes emanating

1867–68	**Carpeaux, *The Dance***
1867	Karl Marx, *Das Kapital*
1867	New York establishes a free public school system
1867	Strauss, "The Blue Danube Waltz"
1867	Baseball's curve ball pitch is invented

9-55. Edgar Degas. *Little Fourteen-Year-Old Dancer.* c. 1881. Wax, silk, satin ribbon, and hair, height 39". Collection Mr. and Mrs. Paul Mellon, Upperville, Virginia. Degas's model was a Belgian girl studying at the Opéra in Paris.

from the earth, the Pythia, who was believed to be possessed by Apollo, would answer queries and predict future events, employing dramatic gestures and language that were often incomprehensible. Marcello (1836–79) gives the beautiful young woman a pose that conveys her convulsed state. As she jerks forward, her breasts swing out to either side. The smoothness of the flesh is sharply contrasted with the multiple drapery folds and with the unruly,

flying hair. The snakes hidden in her hair, attributes of Apollo, startle the viewer. *Pythia* is a convincing representation of Greek religious ecstasy as it was understood during the nineteenth century.

Little Fourteen-Year-Old Dancer (fig. 9-55), the only sculpture Edgar Degas (1834–1917) ever exhibited, is now one of his most popular works, and a number of bronze casts, with real cloth tutus and satin ribbons, were produced after his death and are visible in museums. Degas's original, now in a private collection, is of wax, a material used for popular sculptures that were meant to be intensely realistic, combined with real fabric and hair (this is the same technique still in use for the naturalistic figures seen in wax museums around the world). Degas followed the popular tradition by coloring the wax to resemble flesh, and he heightened the illusionistic reality of the figure by using a silk faille bodice, a tutu of tulle and gauze, fabric ballet slippers, and a satin ribbon to tie back a wig of real hair partially covered with wax. Degas's appropriation of a multimedia technique that mimics the world of reality is consistent with the attitudes of the French Realist and Impressionist painters. By creating a sculpture that had the colors and textures of reality, he, like the Impressionists, was questioning the relationship between vision and art.

When Degas's sculpture was shown at the Sixth Independent Exhibition in 1881, the critics recognized its novelty but received it with hostility because the model

was not attractive:

He chooses her from among the most odiously ugly; . . . she is sturdy and carefully studied, but what is the use of these things in the art of sculpture? Put them in a museum of zoology, anthropology, or physiology, fine; but, in a museum of art, forget it! (Nina de Villars, 1881)

I do not always ask that art be graceful, but I do not believe that its role is to represent only ugliness. (Elie de Mont, 1881)

. . . a dancer in wax of a strangely attractive, disturbing, and unique Naturalism . . . The vicious muzzle of this young, scarcely adolescent girl, this little flower of the gutter, is unforgettable. (Jules Claretie, 1881)

The modernity of Degas's work did not go unnoticed, however, as Joris-Karl Huysmans wrote in 1883:

The terrible realism of this statuette makes the public distinctly uneasy, all its ideas about sculpture, about cold, lifeless whiteness [compare fig. 9-17], about those memorable formulas copied again and again for centuries, are demolished. The fact is that on the first blow, M. Degas has knocked over the traditions of sculpture, just as he has for a long time been shaking up the conventions of painting.

I, IPRE. IIONIJ A

9-56. Claude Monet. *Impression-Sunrise.* 1872. Oil on canvas, 19$^{1/2}$ x 25$^{1/2}$". Musée Marmottan, Paris. When their paintings were rejected for the Salon exhibitions, a group of painters, some of whom we today classify as Impressionists, decided to hold independent exhibitions. The first of a series of eight such exhibitions was held in Paris in 1874; it included this painting. The exhibition was sponsored by a group that called itself the Anonymous Society of Painters, Sculptors, Engravers, Etc., a title that indicates the diverse nature of the group's members, who had banded together to create independent exhibitions and not because of any notion of stylistic unity. Monet's painting *Rue St.-Denis Festivities on June 30, 1878* (see fig. 9-2) was included in the Fourth Independent Exhibition, in 1879.

Impressionist paintings such as Monet's *Impression-Sunrise* engage us immediately by their subtle depictions of nature (fig. 9-56). Here Monet's representation of the interaction of light, atmosphere, and color heightens our awareness of the beauty in the seascape at dawn. But it is important to realize that Monet did not set out to paint a beautiful picture. His goal was to create a painting that recorded reality as he saw it. As an Impressionist, he wanted to capture in paint the visual effect of reality as it appeared to him at that mo-

ment. Monet was especially sensitive to transitory effects of color—how color changes in response to shifting light and varying atmospheric conditions. In *Impression-Sunrise*, the combination of the moving surface of the water and the red/orange rays of the sun provides a perfect vehicle for his demonstration.

Impressionism had a strong scientific basis, although this is not immediately obvious in looking at Impressionist paintings. A critic of the First Independent Exhibition said that Monet, Renoir, Degas, and

Morisot should be called by the "new term *impressionists*. They are impressionists in the sense that they render not the landscape, but the sensation produced by the landscape." The use of the term *Impression* by Monet in his title and the painters' subsequent adoption of the term *Impressionism* suggest the influence of new theories about the physiology of perception. The new color theory emphasized the presence of color within shadows and, in asserting that there was no black in nature, inspired the Impression-

1869	Suez Canal opens
1870	Rome becomes the capital of Italy
1871	Trade unions legalized in Britain
1872	**Monet, _Impression-Sunrise_**
1873–75	Daniel Chester French, _Minuteman_

9-57. Claude Monet. _Gare St.-Lazare, Paris_. 1877. Oil on canvas, 32¹/₂ x 39³/₄". Fogg Art Museum, Harvard University, Cambridge, Massachusetts. This painting was exhibited at the Third Independent Exhibition, in 1877.
Maurice Wertheim Collection

ists to ban black from their palette. In addition, Impressionism is based on an understanding of the interrelated mechanisms of the camera and the eye: just as a photograph is created by light as it passes through a lens to make an impression on light-sensitive paper, so is our vision the result of the light and color that create an "impression" on the back surface of the eyeball. By embracing the principle that subject matter is less

important than depicting what is perceived and by determining that painting should represent as closely as possible what the eye sees, the Impressionist painters are clearly related to the earlier Realism of Courbet and the innovations of Manet (see pages 444 and 452). Their works look so different from Courbet's and Manet's because of their scientific interest in how the eye sees and because of their deter-

mination to capture quickly the richness of color that exists in nature, whether in light or in shadow.

Monet's emphasis on painting visual reality means that his subjects are scenes or views of the world around him, but it is not accidental that he was one of the first painters of the modern urban cityscape. By painting the city streets and the railroad station, as in the _Gare St.-Lazare_ (fig. 9-57), Monet

9-58. Auguste Renoir. *A Luncheon at Bougival* (now known as *The Luncheon of the Boating Party*). 1881. Oil on canvas, 4'3" x 5'8". The Phillips Collection, Washington, D.C. This work was included in the Seventh Independent Exhibition, in 1882.

emphasized the actuality of modern life. In the railroad station, the open air in the background interacts with the light that filters down through the glass roof and the billowing smoke of the engines to provide another appropriate vehicle for Monet's investigation of the ever-changing patterns of light, color, and atmosphere. An Academic painter would never have chosen such a subject but, if required to paint it, would have rendered the clouds of smoke in tonalities of gray. Monet sees not merely gray but shades of blue and lavender as well.

Although Auguste Renoir (1841–1919) embraced the ideas and employed the techniques of the Impressionists, he was interested in human life and relationships, which led him to favor compositions with human figures rather than land-scapes. One of his most popular works is certainly *A Luncheon at Bougival*, with its everyday subject, casual composition, strong strokes of arbitrary color, and bold **impasto**—the latter is especially evident in the beautiful shimmering glasses and bottles of wine on the table (figs. 9-58, 9-59).

A Luncheon at Bougival was singled out for praise by critics when it was exhibited in the Seventh Independent Exhibition in 1882, and one critic captured the contemporary, momentary quality of Renoir's subject in writing that the painting is:

a charming work, full of gaiety and spirit, its wild youth caught in the act, radiant and lively, frolicking at high noon in the sun, laughing at everything, see-ing only today and mocking tomorrow. For them eter-nity is in their glass, in their boat, and in their songs.

It was this emphasis on the momentary and the everyday that made paintings such as this one unacceptable to the Salon juries, who favored history paintings of literary subjects that had been exe-cuted with controlled academic technique.

9-59. Auguste Renoir. *A Luncheon at Bougival*, detail

TECHNIQUE **IMPRESSIONISM**

To capture the subtle effects of ever-changing light, Monet and the other Impressionists painted outside, on the spot, working quickly with loose, bold strokes of color to catch the impression of color in nature before the light changed. The increased brightness of Impressionist paintings (one critic even complained that they made his eyes hurt) was in part made possible by the use of a canvas covered with white underpainting rather than the beige, tan-reddish, or even darker ground that had been traditional since the Renaissance. In addition, an invention of the Industrial Revolution—the collapsible, sealable tube—made it prac-

tical for the Impressionists to paint outside, while the development of synthetic pigments meant that the intense colors they needed were no longer prohibitively expensive. Monet applied paint in rich, thick strokes of virtually pure color, without black. The bold physical presence of these strokes and the heightened color emphasize the surface of the painting. Monet also used a painting stroke that maximized accidental effects of color. By dipping a relatively wide brush into two or more pigments, he allowed the colors to blur and blend as the brush stroked the canvas.

EDGAR DEGAS, BERTHE MORISOT, AND MARY CASSATT

9-60. Edgar Degas. *The Rehearsal.* c. 1873–74. Oil on canvas, 18 x 24". Fogg Art Museum, Harvard University, Cambridge, Massachusetts

Bequest of Maurice Wertheim, 1951

Edgar Degas disliked being referred to as an Impressionist and preferred to call himself a realist or an independent. His work nevertheless demonstrates many similarities to Impressionist works, and he exhibited in several of the Independent Exhibitions. Degas's realism is in part revealed by his subject matter, for, no matter how romantic we may find his representations of ballerinas today, they were considered neither an appropriate nor a beautiful theme for art in his own day. He was often criticized for picking unattractive dancers by critics who did not realize that, like the other Impressionists, he was emphasizing the realities of modern life (see page 461). He also shared with the Impressionists a taste for strong and even arbitrary color, despite the fact that most of his work represents figures in rather subdued interiors. The subtlety of natural light in an interior space provided him with a distinct challenge.

In addition to his concern with light and color, Degas had a special interest in the interaction between movement and composition. One contemporary critic wrote that "Degas continues to be passionately devoted to movement, pursuing it even in violent and awkwardly contorted forms." He found that movement, especially the repeated, choreographed movement of dancers onstage or in rehearsal, had a greater intensity when seen from an unexpected viewpoint. In *The Rehearsal* (fig. 9-60), the strong diagonal recession of the dancers' parallel arms and legs and of the windows in the room creates a thrusting perspective; this in turn is balanced by the empty space in the right foreground. The broad brushstrokes reemphasize the pictorial surface. The influence of Japanese proto-types (see fig. 9-3) for Degas's work is evident in the diagonal recession and in the cutting off of the forms by the edges. Degas's peculiarly realistic viewpoint was discussed by one of his friends, Edmond Duranty, who published a pamphlet, *The New Painting*, in 1876, in which Duranty pointed out how our visual field is limited by "the frame that endlessly accompanies us . . . cutting off the external view in the most unexpected ways, achieving that endless variety and surprise that is one of reality's greatest pleasures."

We can see the same unusual viewpoint and the compositional motif of the strong diagonal thrust cut off by the edges in *Marine* (fig. 9-61), by Berthe Morisot (1841–95). When this work was shown in the First Independent Exhibition, a critic remarked, "What a lovely vagueness [there is] in the distance at sea where the tiny points of masts tilt!"

c. 1873–74	**Degas,** ***The Rehearsal***
1873	Jules Verne, *Around the World in Eighty Days*
1874	Women's Christian Temperance Union is founded

Morisot, who once wrote, "My ambition is limited to the desire to capture something transient," remains true to Impressionist principles in striving to capture the strong visual qualities of an actual view. The parasol shields the face of the woman—Morisot's sister Edma, also a painter—and as a result her features are left a blur; her identity is less important than her function as a colored form within the composition. Light reflects from the warm brown of the stone railing to create a pink shadow on her white dress.

Mary Cassatt (1845–1926), an American who trained in France and spent most of her life working there, exhibited in several of the Independent Exhibitions. In writing about works by Cassatt at the Sixth Independent Exhibition in 1881, a critic defined Impressionist practice:

> Like her brothers in independence, Manet and Degas, Cassatt works relentlessly to bring her eyes to a state of sensitivity, nervous excitement, even irritation, so she can seize the smallest flicker of light, the smallest atom of color, and the slightest tint of shadow.

Another critic, however, voiced the frequent complaint that Impressionist paintings were unfinished, lamenting that Cassatt had changed her style and was now "aspiring to the partially completed image."

Cassatt's *The Boating Party* (fig. 9-62) reveals the inspiration both of Degas and of Japanese prints in the realistic but unexpected viewpoint it enforces. We are behind the rower, and his dark, bold silhouetted form sets off the pastels of the rest of the composition. Cassatt maximizes re-

9-61. Berthe Morisot. *Marine (The Harbor at Lorient)*. 1869. Oil on canvas, 17^{1}/$_{8}$ x 28^{3}/$_{4}$". National Gallery of Art, Washington, D.C. Berthe Morisot, one of the founders of the Impressionist movement, exhibited in seven of the eight Independent Exhibitions, and her works were also accepted at many of the Salon exhibitions. The artist presented this work to Manet after he admired it. After her death in 1895, a large exhibition of her work was arranged by Monet, Renoir, Degas, and the poet Stéphane Mallarmé.

Ailsa Mellon Bruce Collection

9-62. Mary Cassatt. *The Boating Party*. 1893–94. Oil on canvas, 35^{1}/$_{2}$ x 46^{1}/$_{8}$". National Gallery of Art, Washington, D.C.

Chester Dale Collection

alism in the partial profile of the rower and the foreshortening of the child's head. Neither is an attractive view, but both are realistic and skillfully executed. Large areas of unmodeled color and the potent compositional shapes of the green interior of the boat and the partial view of the sail emphasize the two-dimensional quality of her composition. In the greater solidity with which she endows her figures, Cassatt reveals her independence within the Impressionist movement.

AMERICAN REALISM: THOMAS EAKINS AND HENRY TANNER

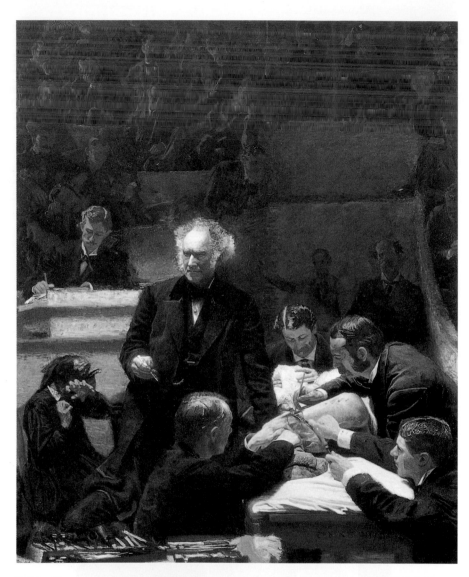

9-63. Thomas Eakins. *Portrait of Dr. Samuel Gross.* 1875. Oil on canvas, 8' x 6'6". Jefferson Medical College of Thomas Jefferson University, Philadelphia. Eakins's realistic portrayal of surgery at Jefferson Medical College reveals how medical practice has changed. In Eakins's day, surgeons operated in their street clothes, and operations were scheduled between 11:00 A.M. and 3:00 P.M. to take advantage of the daylight in the college's amphitheater.

To Thomas Eakins (1844–1916), the Philadelphia physician Samuel Gross was a heroic figure. Gross was a respected surgeon and professor at Jefferson Medical College and a physician with an international reputation. A pioneer in using new techniques in surgery, he was an inspiring educator, teaching medical students both surgical procedures and the human purpose that stood behind the medical profession. Gross specifically emphasized the significance of clinical instruction, and Eakins represented him in the operating amphitheater at work (fig. 9-63). He is performing an operation in which he specialized, a new, lifesaving treatment for osteomyelitis (infection of the bone), when the diseased bone is cut away. At the same time, he is also teaching, and Gross looks up from the incision in the thigh of the patient, an expression of intense concentration on his face as he searches for words to convey to aspiring doctors the significance of his life's work. He holds a bloody scalpel, the sudden sight of which makes the elderly woman to the left, most likely the patient's mother, cringe.

Eakins's light is focused and concentrated, and the powerful chiaroscuro contrast makes Gross, teacher and surgeon, a dramatic figure. The sharp overhead light directs our attention to Gross's head, silhouetting it against the dark background. The craggy features of the face are emphatically three-dimensional, stressing the serious line of the mouth and throwing the eyes into meditative shadow. Eakins emphasizes the light as it catches Gross's bushy hair and vigorous sideburns. This visually electrifying effect suggests that Eakins is searching for a concrete metaphor for the intensity of Gross's thoughts. The original painting has an overall warm harmony, the result of red underpainting, which unifies and heightens the limited palette, with its strong blacks, flesh tones, and areas of white. Punctuation marks of red draw our attention to the pen of the clinical recorder, the incision, and the bloody hand and scalpel of the surgeon. In contrast to the abstract treatment of Gross's head, his hand and scalpel jump out because they seem to be exactly in focus. Eakins, himself a photographer, seems to have thrown the other parts of his composition out of focus (note especially the loose painting of the instruments in the immediate foreground) to draw attention to the skilled hand and its tool, making them the focal point in his composition. The contrast in treatment between the head and hand is not accidental: while the physical aspect of Gross's accomplishment is completely comprehensible, the workings of his intellect cannot be discerned.

Eakins painted *Portrait of Dr. Samuel Gross* specifically to submit to the arts section at the Centennial Exposition, to be held in Philadelphia in 1876. It was rejected, apparently because the subject was not considered appropriate; other, less significant works by Eakins were accepted. Through the influence of Gross, the painting was exhibited in the medical department of the exposition.

The African American painter Henry O. Tanner (1859–1937) studied with Eakins at the Pennsylvania Academy from 1880 to 1884, but his mature style merged Eakins's realism with stylistic

9-64. Henry O. Tanner. *The Banjo Lesson.* c. 1893. Oil on canvas, 48 x 35". Hampton University Museum, Hampton, Virginia. Tanner was the first African American artist to achieve an international reputation.

effects learned from the French Impressionists. Tanner moved permanently to Paris in 1891; in 1896, he received an honorable mention at the Salon; and in 1897, his work was awarded a gold medal. In *The Banjo Lesson* (fig. 9-64), the choice and interpretation of the theme grow from Eakins's example, but the lighter palette, softer light, and more delicate brushstroke reveal the influence of the new French style of Impressionism.

AUGUSTE RODIN

9-65. Auguste Rodin. *The Burghers of Calais*. 1884–86. Bronze, height 6'10$^{1/2}$". Hirshhorn Museum and Sculpture Garden, Smithsonian Institution, Washington, D.C. In 1884, the city of Calais in northern France commissioned Rodin to fashion a public monument that would honor six leading citizens (burghers) who, in 1347, had offered themselves as hostages to the English king Edward III, who had laid siege to the city. The burghers were ready to sacrifice their lives if their city would be spared. Edward III was so impressed with their courage that he spared both the burghers and Calais.

Auguste Rodin (1840–1917) was commissioned to create *The Burghers of Calais* (fig. 9-65) as a public monument that would display the courage and civic virtue of the Calais burghers. But the work disappointed many at first because it lacked the overtly heroic antique references that then dominated public sculpture. Rodin's re-creation of the six hostages, with its realism and psychological honesty, however, played an important role in bringing a fresh vision of the human figure to late-nineteenth-century sculpture. From his study of the works of such sculptors as Donatello

and Michelangelo, Rodin understood how gesture and expression could reveal an inner psychological state. Here the individual burghers betray philosophical questioning, acceptance, defiance, and sorrow. Through Rodin's sculpture, the burghers are revealed to us as human beings like ourselves, not idealized superheroes.

To understand better the impact of Rodin's work, we must keep in mind that Neoclassical and Romantic attitudes still dominated public sculpture. Rodin's physical and psychological naturalism seemed to run counter to critical and public

taste, and the psychological depth of Rodin's work was missed by many critics.

Rodin's *Monument to Balzac* (fig. 9-66) is an audacious sculpture in both theme and execution. The great novelist is shown wrapped in the heavy robe in which he worked late at night. His dramatic posture and penetrating facial features vividly communicate the fury of creative inspiration. Balzac's face and massive robe seem to be emerging from the plaster, from the raw material from which the sculpture was first formed. This unfinished quality contributes to our perception of a

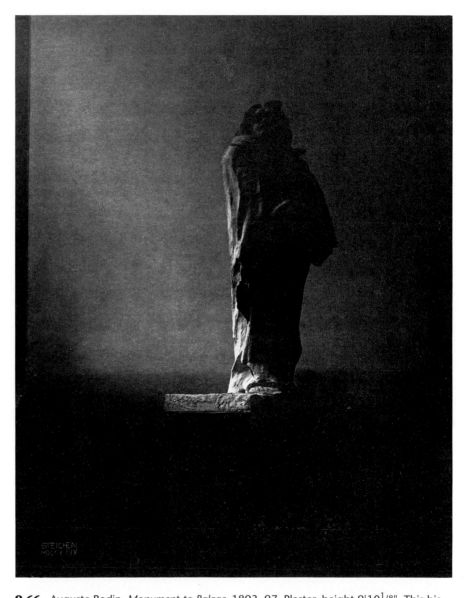

9-66. Auguste Rodin. *Monument to Balzac.* 1893–97. Plaster, height 9'10¹/₈". This historic 1908 photograph of the plaster model is by Edward Steichen, one of America's foremost photographers. Steichen so successfully captured the creative ambiance of Balzac that, on seeing Steichen's photographs, Rodin remarked, "You will make the world understand my Balzac through these pictures. They are like Christ walking in the desert." The sculpture was commissioned by the Société des Gens de Lettres in honor of Balzac, who had been the group's second president. Unhappy with Rodin's interpretation, they rejected the monument.

transformation; Rodin, in displaying the process of bringing form from the raw material, has visually expressed the creative energy that has seized Balzac.

Stating his philosophy on the relationship of art and the artist to nature, Rodin wrote:

I grant you that the artist does not see Nature as she appears to the vulgar, because his emotion reveals to him the hidden truths beneath appearances. But, after all, the only principle in art is to copy what you see. . . . There is no recipe for improving nature. The only thing is to see. Oh, doubtless a mediocre man copying nature will never produce a work of art, because he really looks without seeing, and though he may have noted each detail minutely, the result will be flat and without character. . . . The artist, on the contrary, sees; that is to say, his eye, grafted on his heart, reads deeply into the bosom of nature.

WINSLOW HOMER

9-67. Winslow Homer. *The Fog Warning*. 1885. Oil on canvas, 30 x 48". Courtesy, Museum of Fine Arts, Boston
Otis Norcross Fund

The unusual cloud bank rolling in from the background of *The Fog Warning,* by Winslow Homer (1836–1910), warns the fisherman that he is suddenly in mortal danger, for it signals the arrival of a particularly fast-moving and dangerous fog (fig. 9-67). The hunter, preying on nature, suddenly becomes the hunted. Homer's composition heightens the mood of instability and uncertainty by representing the small rowboat being heaved upward by a large swell. The right-to-left thrust of the rowboat is counter to the movement of the fisherman's home vessel in the background, which seems about to sail out of the range of vision. The realistic colors—yellowish-white for the sky, green for the sea, and shades of brown for the boat and the fisherman—are somber and appropriate for this theme.

The bold composition, the diagonal thrust of the boat, and the truncated oar reveal the influence of Japanese woodcuts. Homer's brushstrokes are broad and simple; note especially the rough strokes in the foreground that represent the foamy waves.

The power of natural forces and their challenge to humanity are themes that recur in Homer's most significant works. A New England individualist, Homer spent many winters living in isolation along a particularly dramatic and treacherous stretch of the Maine coastline, where he had many opportunities to observe the power of a turbulent sea.

TECHNIQUE   **WATERCOLOR AND GOUACHE**

9-68. Winslow Homer. *The Blue Boat*. 1892. Watercolor over graphite, 15¹/₈ x 21¹/₂". Courtesy, Museum of Fine Arts, Boston
Bequest of William Sturgis Bigelow

Watercolor is aptly named, for it is a medium in which ground pigments are mixed with water and, as an adhesive binder, a little gum arabic. It is usually applied to white paper. The brilliant light effects possible in watercolor are evident in *The Blue Boat*, by Homer (fig. 9-68). The liquidity of the medium is apparent in the broad strokes that convincingly render sky and water. Watercolor is transparent, and in some areas Homer has laid one color over another, creating veils of color. The strong white of the paper shows through in the clouds and water in *The Blue Boat*. Homer commonly added a few touches of **gouache** (an opaque watercolor) to strengthen certain areas.

As early as the 1780s, English artists had begun to work seriously with watercolor. Homer was one of the founders of the American Watercolor Society, an organization that helped popularize the medium among professional artists in the United States. Previously, watercolor had been used for the most part by amateurs.

POST-IMPRESSIONISM: GAUGUIN AND SEURAT

9-69. Paul Gauguin. *The Vision after the Sermon.* 1888. Oil on canvas, 28³/₄ x 36¹/₂". National Gallery of Scotland, Edinburgh

9-70. Paul Gauguin. *Where Do We Come From? What Are We? Where Are We Going?* 1897. Oil on burlap, 4'6³/₄" x 12'3¹/₂". Courtesy, Museum of Fine Arts, Boston
Tompkins Collection

Parisian Paul Gauguin (1848–1903) painted *The Vision after the Sermon* in the rural area of Brittany, in northern France, which he visited in 1888 to divert his mind and art from what he felt were the restrictive artistic and social pressures of Paris (fig. 9-69). The painting depicts Breton women, deep in prayer, experiencing a vision. We seem to be standing behind the group of women in native dress and a priest in the right foreground. A tree limb creates a strong diagonal across the composition, separating the left middle ground from the "vision" to the right, which represents the Old Testament figure

Jacob wrestling with an angel, a story in which God tested Jacob's enduring love. Visual tension results from the conflict between the flat red ground, which creates a strong planarity, and the perspective suggested by the diminution of size. The heavy outlines of the figures combine with the patternlike configuration of the Breton headdresses to create a simple yet forceful composition. Although the red ground may have been inspired by a religious festival that included the blessing of horned animals and bonfires that cast a red glow over the fields at night, Gauguin's choice of color also carries a symbolic content. The red ground symbolizes the theme of struggle, and in choosing it, Gauguin has freed himself from the traditional use of color to describe nature. Here it is used in an abstract, expressive way.

Gauguin left his wife and family, as well as a successful brokerage career in Paris, to seek a more natural, unindustrialized environment, first in Martinique, then in Brittany and later Arles in southern France, and

9-71. Georges Seurat. *A Sunday Afternoon on the Island of La Grande Jatte*. 1884–86. Oil on canvas, 6'9$^{1}/_{2}$" x 10'1$^{1}/_{4}$". The Art Institute of Chicago

Helen Birch Bartlett Memorial Collection

finally in Tahiti, in the South Seas. In attempting to remove himself from Western centers of civilization, Gauguin sought an unbridled artistic and psychological response to nature.

During his second Tahitian period, Gauguin, in poor health, nearly broke, severely depressed, and planning suicide, painted what he envisioned as a summation of his art and life (fig. 9-70). His suicide attempt failed, and he later detailed the meaning of the painting in a letter. The woman, child, and dog in the right foreground symbolize birth and the innocence of life. The figure near the center tries to pick a fruit from the tree of knowledge in an attempt to understand the meaning of life, while in the left foreground "an old woman approaching death . . . reconciled and resigned to her thoughts" is joined by "a strange white bird [that] represents the futility of life." In the right middle ground, two standing clothed figures betray the sorrow that life's knowledge can bring; the idol to our left expresses the forces that rule our primitive passions. The abstraction of Gauguin's colors and forms

plays an important role in communicating his content and demonstrates how far he has moved away from Impressionism.

By the time of the last Independent Exhibition in 1886, Impressionism, which a decade earlier had been considered revolutionary, was gaining increasing critical and public acceptance. New avant-garde styles were now being explored by artists such as Gauguin, who had moved from Impressionism to more individualized styles. *Post-Impressionism* is the generic term now used to embrace the diversity of these individual styles—styles that laid the foundation for modern art.

Georges Seurat (1859–91) was the youngest of the Post-Impressionist painters. His monumental painting *A Sunday Afternoon on the Island of La Grande Jatte* (fig. 9-71), which was two years in preparation and execution, exemplifies his theo-

ries of Divisionism, which was also called Neo-Impressionism. The still, transfixed quality of the scene reminds us of works of the Renaissance painter Piero della Francesca (see fig. 5-1), whose work Seurat admired. But the classicism of Renaissance art has been updated, joined with the modern perception of light and color begun by the Impressionists. Seurat systematized contemporary scientific advances in color theory to create what he termed optical painting. Colored paint is methodically applied in a series of small dots (now popularly known as Pointillism, a term not used by Seurat), usually in complementary colors. The resulting surface, covered with thousands of controlled spots of color, is both vibrant and luminous, at once relating to the surface of the picture plane and to forms in an illusory depth bathed in natural light.

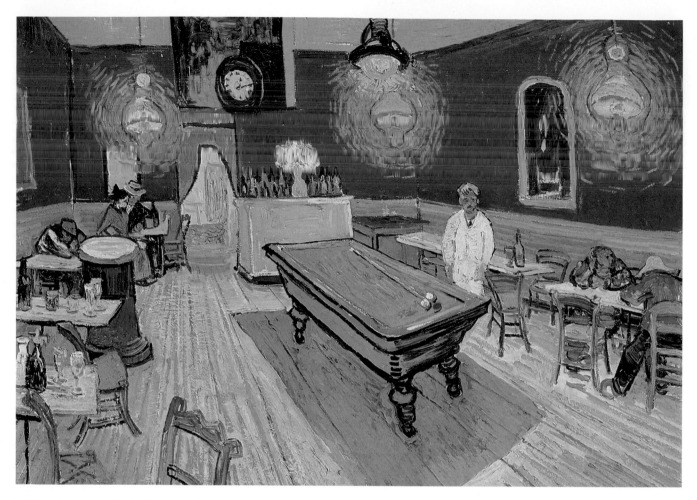

9-72. Vincent van Gogh. *The Night Cafe*. September 1888. Oil on canvas, 27^{1}/2 x 35". Yale University Art Gallery, New Haven, Connecticut. Van Gogh painted *The Night Cafe* in Arles, in the south of France, where he lived in 1888–89. Vincent wrote that when he painted this picture he stayed up three consecutive nights, sleeping only during the day. On September 17, 1888, he wrote to his brother Theo that "the problem of painting night scenes and effects on the spot and actually by night, interests me enormously."
Bequest of Stephen C. Clark

Today I am probably going to begin the interior of the Cafe where I eat, by gas light, in the evening.

It is what they call here a Cafe de Nuit (they are fairly frequent here), staying open all night. "Night prowlers" can take refuge there when they have no money to pay for a lodging, or are too tight to be taken in. All those things—family, native land—are perhaps more attractive in the imaginations of such people as us . . . than they are in reality. I always feel I am a traveller, going somewhere and to some destination.

If I tell myself that the somewhere and the destination do not exist, that seems to me very reasonable and likely enough. . . .

The room is blood red and dark yellow with a green billiard table in the middle; there are four citron-yellow lamps with a glow of orange and green. Everywhere there is a clash and contrast of the most disparate reds and greens in the figures of little sleeping hooligans, in the empty, dreary room, in violet and blue. The blood-red and the yellow-green of the billiard table, for instance, contrast with the soft tender . . . green of the counter, on which there is a pink nosegay. The white coat of the landlord, awake in a corner of that furnace, turns citron-yellow, or pale luminous green. (Vincent van Gogh, letter to his brother Theo from Arles, September 8, 1888)

The Night Cafe is one of the powerfully emotional paintings in a series of works created during Van Gogh's stay in Arles (fig. 9-72). Van Gogh later referred to Arles as the place where "I attain[ed] the high yellow note," suggesting that this was a particularly strong point in his career. Here he adopted the Japanese belief that the color yellow is symbolic of hope. However, Arles was also a place of despair for Van

Gogh, which may help explain the intensity of the Arles works. He said that this painting, given to his landlord in exchange for rent, was "one of the ugliest pictures I have done."

The ugliness of which he writes is intentional, for in this painting color is used arbitrarily, allowing him to express personal meanings and emotions through the "clash and contrast" of glaring yellow, bright green, and "blood" red. In a letter to his brother Theo, who was living in Paris, he explained the psychological impact that he wanted the painting to have:

> I have tried to express the terrible passions of humanity by means of red and green . . . the cafe is a place where one can ruin oneself, run mad, or commit a crime.

Van Gogh's goal is in part conveyed to us by the claustrophobia of the tense and threatening atmosphere. Drunks slump over tables within a tilted and close perspective space that is unnerving for the viewer. Van Gogh was here experimenting with the relationship between color, space, theme, and emotions. His

efforts make him one of the forerunners of the expressionist trends that become important in the twentieth century (see page 526). He wanted to express the mood he senses at the cafe, and in doing so, he reveals some of his feelings about his own alienation.

In the early 1880s, Van Gogh was involved briefly in the rapidly changing styles of French painting. Like many other artists, he began to collect Japanese prints (see fig. 9-3), and in *The Night Cafe* we sense their influence in the bold delineation of the forms, the intricate patterning of horizontal and vertical lines, the unusual viewpoint, and the vivid, arbitrary colors. The oddly exaggerated perspective of the painting may also be attributed to other influences, for evidence suggests that Van Gogh may have suffered from temporal-lobe epilepsy; some aspects of his art may have been influenced by the visions he experienced during the beginning of a seizure. We also know that Van Gogh often spent his limited money on alcohol, rather than food, and absinthe, one of the artist's common indulgences, is known to affect the occipital lobe, which controls vision.

9-73. Vincent van Gogh. *The Starry Night.* June 1889. Oil on canvas, 29 x 36$^{1}/4$". Collection, The Museum of Modern Art, New York. Van Gogh can be classified as a Post- or Counter-Impressionist because after painting in the Impressionist style (he saw the Eighth, last Independent Exhibition in 1886 in Paris), he developed his own personal style. Van Gogh eloquently revealed his understanding of his own intense personality and his loneliness by writing, "One may have a blazing hearth in one's soul and yet no one ever comes to sit by it. Passersby see only a wisp of smoke rising from the chimney and continue on their way."

Acquired through the Lillie P. Bliss Bequest

In *The Starry Night* (fig. 9-73), painted in 1889, Van Gogh displays his fascination with the earth and sky, and his philosophies of life and death and their connection to nature:

> For my own part, I declare I know nothing whatever about it, but to look at the stars always makes me dream, as simply as I dream over the black dots of a map representing towns and villages. Why, I ask myself, should the shining dots of the sky not be as accessible as the black dots on the map of France? If we take the train to get to Tarascon or Rouen, we take death to reach a star. One thing undoubtedly true in this reasoning is this, that while we are alive we cannot get to a star, any more than when we are dead we can take the train. (Vincent van Gogh, letter to his brother Theo, mid-July 1888)

This depiction of night "in situ," as Van Gogh described it, reveals his continuing interest in a favorite subject, the flamelike cypress tree used in France and Italy to mark graves. Almost black, the tree dominates the foreground. The night sky overwhelms the little town of St.-Rémy, but the expansiveness of space and the solidity of the earth are formally linked: the tip of the cypress tree crosses the nebula, and the steeple of the church enters the area of the sky.

In a letter to his brother, Van Gogh wrote that he felt that nighttime was more colorful than the day—as is suggested here by the vividness and luminosity of the celestial bodies. Deeply saturated colors—purple and violent green—clash, and a thickly painted "glow" surrounds each star, planet, and the moon. These qualities seem to express Van Gogh's testament that there are lives and colors on other planets, and perhaps even better conditions. Here the artist projects his own destiny: death represents not an ending but a metamorphosis.

The significance of nature for Van Gogh is apparent in the following quotation, from a letter he wrote to Theo in September 1889, right after Theo was married:

> Well, do you know what I hope for, once I let myself begin to hope? It is that a family will be for you what nature, the clods of earth, the grass, the yellow corn, the peasant, are for me, that is to say, that you may find in your love for people something not only to work for, but to comfort and restore you, when there is need for it.

The *Self-Portrait* of 1889 (see fig. 9-11) was probably painted shortly after Van Gogh left the hospital in St.-Rémy in early January 1889. His ear is still bandaged from the self-mutilation he had inflicted in December, when he cut off part of his ear, probably to punish himself because of a quarrel he had had with Paul Gauguin. Van Gogh sent this painting to his family in the Netherlands, probably to reassure them of his health. The very fact that he could paint again revealed his ability to control his feelings, and although he does not deny that he damaged his ear, he shows himself as somber and meditative, smoking his pipe. The placement of the green coat against the red background and the blue cap against orange demonstrates his understanding of how to use complementary colors to achieve rich coloristic and dramatic effects. The violent juxtaposition of the red and orange draws attention to Van Gogh's solemn eyes. As he wrote, "[I find myself filled with] a certain undercurrent of vague sadness, difficult to define. . . . My God, those anxieties—who can live in the modern world without catching his share of them?"

POST-IMPRESSIONISM: CÉZANNE

9-74. Paul Cézanne. *Still Life with Basket of Apples.* 1890–94. Oil on canvas, 24 3/8 x 31".
The Art Institute of Chicago
Helen Birch Bartlett Memorial Collection

"I want to make of Impressionism something solid and durable, like the art of the museums," wrote Paul Cézanne (1839–1906). In his paintings, Cézanne set himself an impossible task: he wanted to establish an equilibrium between the vivacious color and solid form of three-dimensional objects and the two-dimensional surface of the picture plane. He sought to achieve both illusionistic solidity and a strong compositional structure in two dimensions. His frustration with Impressionism was twofold: Impressionist painters did not create paintings that were compositionally strong, and they were not interested in endowing painted objects with three-dimensional solidity. Cézanne wrote: "In art, everything is theory, developed and applied in contact with nature." It is the union of na-

ture with the philosophical truth of the flatness of a painting's surface that absorbed Cézanne's attention.

Cézanne's *Still Life with Basket of Apples* (fig. 9-74) demonstrates his ability to render objects with solidity—note the white napkin, with its deep angular folds and pockets of shadow. The pieces of fruit have a physical presence that is in part the result of an unexpected richness of color, exemplifying Cézanne's dictum that "when color is richest, form is fullest." He modeled the fruit with pure, unmixed colors, juxtaposing, for example, yellow with green and red. He thereby created a richer effect than that produced by the typical academic practice of rendering modeling by reducing coloristic intensity by adding white or black. Cézanne does not outline his forms to distinguish

them from each other. They have rather loosely painted edges, and it is the internal color that creates their solidity. Cézanne once said, "The secret of drawing and modeling resides in the contrasts and relationships of tone."

If we analyze Cézanne's *Still Life with Basket of Apples* as an illusion or as an exercise in accurate drawing, it is a failure: neither the front nor the back edges of the table, for example, are continuous; the wine bottle, itself tilted, offers a distinctive contour on each side; and the pastries stacked on the plate are tilted upward. But our observations are based on the wrong questions. In Cézanne's work, these visual "inaccuracies" reveal the moving viewpoint of the artist relative to the objects being painted. Renaissance scientific perspective insisted that

1890–94   **Cézanne, *Still Life with Basket of Apples***
1890   Emily Dickinson poems are published
1890   Oscar Wilde, *The Picture of Dorian Gray*

9-75. Paul Cézanne. *Mont Ste.-Victoire.* 1904–6. Oil on canvas, 25⁵/8 x 31⁷/8". Private collection. Mont Ste.-Victoire in Provence, a symbol of Cézanne's local area, is one of his favorite subjects. In 1901–02, he built a study in the countryside with a large window facing the mountain.

the artist's (and therefore the viewer's) eye be at a fixed point. Cézanne, on the other hand, expresses a basic fact of vision: our understanding of an object or space is based on our movement relative to that object or space. The difference in the edges of the table, for example, results because the table edge is seen from lower or higher, closer or farther viewpoints. The issues Cézanne has selected to investigate are difficult ones to resolve. Later, Picasso would praise Cézanne for his "restless striving."

The structured pictorial surface Cézanne accomplished is best expressed in his later works (fig. 9-75).

Although the most significant monument in the landscape is the powerful, thrusting mountain, Cézanne has constructed his painting out of blocks of color and no one area or object is less strong than another. Cézanne urged painters to "see in nature the cylinder, the sphere, the cone," and this painting demonstrates his approach. Surface strength is also accomplished by intermingling blocks of limited color—in this case violet, green, ocher, and blue; the violet of the atmospheric perspective reappears in the foreground, and the green of the middle ground is also found in the sky. When this work is compared to an

Impressionist painting, such as *Impression-Sunrise* (see fig. 9-56), two completely different effects can be noted. Cézanne has sacrificed the ravishing, momentary subtlety of color that forms the foundation of Monet's accomplishment in his attempt to create a landscape that has an enduring strength and power. In ancient times, Mont Ste.-Victoire was believed to be a holy mountain, a home of the gods, and in Cézanne's painting it is once again endowed with a mysterious presence. Cézanne's paintings had an important impact on developments in the twentieth century: Matisse called him the "father of us all."

THE BEGINNINGS OF THE SKYSCRAPER

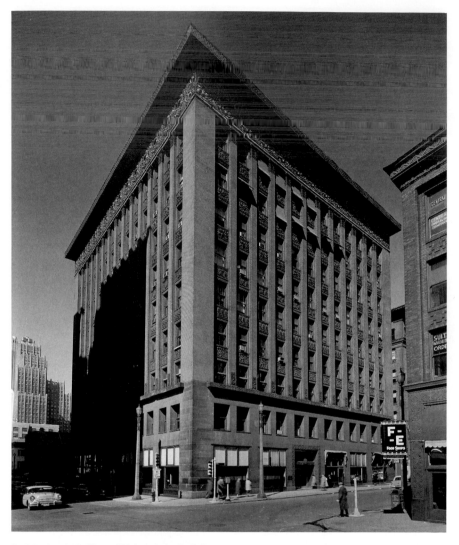

9-76. Louis Sullivan. Wainwright Building, St. Louis, Missouri. 1890–91. Commissioned by Catherine Wainwright and her son, Ellis Wainwright, a brewing magnate and commercial leader

What is the chief characteristic of the tall office building? And at once we answer, it is lofty. . . . The force and power of altitude must be in it. . . . It must be every inch a proud and soaring thing, rising in sheer exultation that from bottom to top it is a unit without a single dissenting line. (Louis Sullivan, *The Tall Office Building Artistically Considered*, 1896)

To accomplish his lofty exaltation, Louis Sullivan (1856–1924) based his Wainwright Building on a design concept analogous to that of a column (fig. 9-76). The first two stories act as a base that supports the unimpeded vertical members, which rise like flutes on a column to support a cornice, decorated with foliage ornament, that crowns the structure like a capital. This intelligible design hides the load-bearing steel-frame construction, which other early skyscraper architects had emphasized by creating a grid of balanced horizontals and verticals (see page 451). Sullivan chose instead to stress the vertical articulation. Only every second vertical element corresponds to the interior steel cage. In addition, the vertical elements dominate because the windows are recessed between them, and the horizontal membering, obscured behind recessed panels of decorated terra-cotta, is reduced in importance.

The integrity of the design depends on the proportional relationships between the parts and the whole, which Sullivan has carefully calibrated. The wide corners balance and set off the elegant, narrow verticals between the windows, while the effulgent decorative terra-cotta at the cornice level, a full story high, unites with the narrow uppermost cornice to provide an elegant final closure that defines the mass of the structure. The decorated panels below each window provide a typically Sullivanesque touch,

1890–91	
1890–91	**Sullivan, Wainwright Building**
1890	One-third of U.S. population now resides in cities and towns
1890	Los Angeles population is 50,000
1893	Dvorák, New World Symphony
1893	Henry Ford builds his first car
1893	Tchaikovsky, Symphonie pathétique

9-77. Louis Sullivan. Carson-Pirie-Scott Store (formerly Schlesinger and Meyer Department Store), Chicago. 1899; enlarged 1903–4 and 1906. Commissioned by Leopold S. and Daniel Meyer

offering a pleasant decoration for office workers in adjacent buildings. The total effect is of a finely articulated mass, elegant and substantial at the same time.

The most impressive developments in skyscraper architecture occurred in Chicago, where a devastating fire in 1871 leveled much of the city. During the closing decades of the century, the city's rapidly increasing population spurred a building boom. Sullivan's last major commission was the design for the Schlesinger and Meyer Department Store (fig. 9-77). The idea of a huge urban store carrying luxury items for middle- and upper-class patrons was novel, and Sullivan emphasized elegant public entrances and huge plate-glass windows on the lower floor by fantastic cast-iron ornamentation of his own design. The upper floors, with their huge "Chicago" windows and very plain terra-cotta decoration, refer in a streamlined fashion to the concealed steel cage, but note that the horizontal members are emphatically wider and therefore dominant. Sullivan's sensitivity to the shape and placement of the building as a whole is evident in the cylindrical tower at the corner, an unexpected element adding a vertical punctuation mark that makes the horizontal sides even more forceful. Here Sullivan completely avoids any historical references, creating a building that is one of the first works of modern architecture.

EDVARD MUNCH

9-78. Edvard Munch. *The Scream.* 1893. Oil, pastel, and casein on cardboard, 35-1/4 x 29". National Gallery, Oslo. Munch originally titled this work *Despair*.
© 1996 The Munch Museum/The Munch-Ellingsen Group/Artists Rights Society (ARS), New York

I was walking along the road with two friends. The sun set. I felt a tinge of melancholy. Suddenly the sky became a bloody red.

I stopped, leaned against the railing, dead tired, and I looked at the flaming clouds that hung like blood and a sword over the blue-black fjord of the city.

My friends walked on. I stood there, trembling with fright. And I felt a loud, unending scream piercing nature. (Edvard Munch, *Diary*, 1892)

The composition of *The Scream* (fig. 9-78) expresses the personal anxiety of Edvard Munch (1863–1944) by creating a formal tension that reinforces the psychological tension that is the theme. As in Munch's description, the sky is a blood red. Its undulating rhythms melt into the blue-black waters of the fjord. The perspective of the bridge is unnatural. Its sharp angle creates a visual tension, for it is caught between the flatness of the picture plane, which is emphasized by the shapes of clouds and water, and the illusory space established by the diminution of Munch's com-

panions and the ships on the fjord. The curving rhythm of Munch's body, transformed into an existential symbol, incorporates itself into the rhythms of the environment. He is becoming one with nature, realizing his worst agoraphobic nightmare. As the figure screams, its face is distorted to resemble a skull, with the iconographic association of death. These visual manipulations communicate an emotional impact not as a representational image, but as a symbol of a schizophrenic psychological state.

The terrifying tension Munch felt that evening was in part the result of his alcoholism and a dread of open spaces. In this condition, Munch experienced himself being pulled into his environment, losing his identity. He heard a scream within him, the scream of nature "dying"

1893	**Munch, *The Scream***
1895	Oscar Wilde, *The Importance of Being Earnest*
1895	First professional football game
1895	H. G. Wells, *The Time Machine*
1896	First modern Olympic Games held, in Athens
1896	Chekhov, *The Sea Gull*
1898	Pierre and Marie Curie discover radium
1900	Half of all U.S. working women are farmhands or domestic servants
1900	World population reaches about 1.65 billion

9-79. Edvard Munch. *The Frieze of Life* exhibition. Photograph of the installation at Leipzig, Germany, 1903. Munch divided the exhibition into four sections: Seeds of Love, Flowering and Passing of Love, Life Anxiety, and Death. *The Scream* was exhibited in the Life Anxiety section. The paintings along the wall seen here are, from left to right, *The Red Vine, The Scream, Angst, Evening on Karl Johan Street, Death in the Sickroom, By the Deathbed,* and *Death and the Child.*

© 1996 The Munch Museum/The Munch-Ellingsen Group/Artists Rights Society (ARS), New York

in flaming bursts at sunset. The inner scream became so intense that Munch, looking at us, screams to relieve the pain within.

The Scream was one of a series of twenty-two paintings and prints that Munch exhibited as a coordinated group in the opening years of the twentieth century. The exhibition was titled *Motifs from the Life of a Modern Soul,* yet it more often carried the simpler title *The Frieze of Life* (fig. 9-79), which better suggests Munch's intent to represent the flowering and passing of love, life's anxieties, and death. As a young person growing up in Norway, Munch had led a bohemian life, and the ideas for the paintings began with his personal, subjective experiences, which were then transformed into broader symbolic themes.

For Munch, the emotionally expressive abstraction of forms was a way of creating art that possessed what he termed a "deeper meaning," one that conveyed the content of the human soul. The impact of his art had a profound effect on the development of early modern painting.

10-1. Giacomo Balla. *Speeding Automobile—Study of Velocity.* 1913. Oil on cardboard, 26 x 37⁷/₈".
Municipal Gallery of Modern Art, Milan, Italy

© 1997 Estate of Giacomo Balla/VAGA, New York, NY

INTRODUCTION TO TWENTIETH-CENTURY ART

"A roaring motorcar which seems to run on machine-gun fire is more beautiful than the *Victory of Samothrace*" (see fig. 3-78), wrote Filippo Marinetti, an Italian poet of the Futurist movement, in 1908–09. The works chosen to introduce the twentieth century relate the dynamism of modern art to the vigor of modern life reflected in Marinetti's words. *Speeding Automobile—Study of Velocity* (fig. 10-1), by the Futurist artist Giacomo Balla (1871–1958), is an abstract representation that can be related to a 1910 *Futurist Manifesto*, which declared:

> [T]he gesture . . . we would reproduce on canvas shall no longer be a fixed moment in universal dynamism. It shall simply be the dynamic sensation itself.

Balla's painting represents the propulsive energy of a speeding car; the sequential placement of diagonal lines communicates dynamic force. Balla, an associate of Marinetti's, has visualized the poet's remarks on the new aesthetic of beauty as exemplified by a "roaring motorcar."

The sleek, aerodynamic design of Pininfarina's Cisitalia "202" GT car (fig. 10-2) is both superbly functional—it cuts the wind resistance—and aesthetically elegant. Even standing still, the car gives the impression of movement. In function and appearance, both Balla's painting and Farina's automobile are works characteristic of the twentieth century.

HISTORY

The decades that opened the twentieth century were characterized by a population boom, unprecedented improvements in living conditions in the Western world, and technological revolution that had the kind of impact on the arts that the poet Marinetti and the painter Balla glorified. By the 1890s, electric lighting and motors were common, and the radio, invented by Guglielmo Marconi in 1895, greatly facilitated communication over vast geographic areas. Television was introduced in the 1920s, computers in the 1940s. One dramatic example of the astounding pace of modern technology was air and

10-2. Pininfarina (designer). "Cisitalia 202 GT" Car. 1946. Aluminum body, 49" x 57^5/8" x 12'5". Manufacturer: S.p.A. Carrozzeria Pininfarina, Turin, Italy. The Museum of Modern Art, New York

Gift of the manufacturer

space flight. In the United States, the 1903 flight of the Wright brothers at Kitty Hawk, North Carolina, was followed by rapid advances; Charles Lindbergh soloed across the Atlantic in 1927, and in 1969 Neil Armstrong became the first human to set foot on the moon. As this book is being revised, Russian and American astronauts are orbiting the globe together.

Advances in technology were often set against a backdrop of political conflict, war, and violent revolution. By the end of the first decade of the twentieth century, the European nations and Great Britain had built up enormous armed forces. Germany, Austria-Hungary, and Italy were allied against Great Britain, France, and Russia. War became inevitable after Archduke Ferdinand, heir to the throne of Austria-Hungary, was assassinated in 1914. The "Great War," now known as World War I, erupted within months. Although all parties hoped it would be of short duration, it lasted, stagnated in trench warfare, until 1918. The United States committed its armies in 1917. The 1919 Treaty of Versailles ended World War I, but the harsh restrictions imposed on Germany set the foundation for yet another conflict. Before World War I ended, events in Russia had brought a new political force to the world scene. A populist revolution of 1917 overthrew Czar Nicholas II, and a "dictatorship of the proletariat" was established by a well-organized party of Bolshevik Communists headed by Vladimir Lenin. Lenin withdrew Russia from World War I in 1918, but internal civil war ended only in 1921. In 1923, the Union of Soviet Socialist Republics (USSR) was formed. Communist parties outside of the USSR were federated with

10-3. Vladimir Tatlin. Historic photograph of the model of the Monument to the Third International Communist Conference. 1919–20. The model, 16 feet tall, was of wood and netting; the final building, which was to be built of iron painted red and glass, would have been more than 1,300 feet tall.

© 1997 Estate Vladimir Tatlin/VAGA. New York, NY

Soviet communism in 1919 to form the Third International. In proposing a structure that would provide a center for world communism, Vladimir Tatlin (1885–1953), a Russian artist who had visited the **avant-garde** art centers of Berlin and Paris in 1913, offered an ambitious spiraling architectural form (fig. 10-3). The dynamic energy

10-4. Max Beckmann. *Departure.* 1932–33. Oil on canvas, 7'3/4" x 3'9³/8" (center); 7'3/4" x 3'3¹/4" (each wing). The Museum of Modern Art, New York

Given anonymously, by exchange. © 1996 Artist Rights Society (ARS), New York/VG Bild-Kunst, Bonn

of the Communist party was to be expressed by glass-enclosed meeting rooms that would revolve around the building's axis. The lowest level—a cube—would turn once per year, the pyramid in the center once per month, and the upper, cylindrical chamber once per day. This ambitious structure, designed to convey the modernity of communism to the world, was never built, and later Soviet structures abandoned the modern style for a severe version of classicism.

Following World War I, economic instability arose as nations returned to peacetime industrial production. Prosperity seemed assured by the late 1920s, but an economic collapse in 1929 plunged the world into a great depression, which in the United States would leave about one in four workers without a job. Compounding the American economic ruin, a drought in the Southwest devastated farming.

During the 1930s, as the West struggled to regain economic stability, the Nazi government of Adolf Hitler took control in Germany, and the Fascist dictators Benito Mussolini in Italy and Francisco Franco in Spain seized power. In 1939, another world war broke out in Europe. World War II reached global involvement following Japan's attack on the American naval base at Pearl Harbor, Hawaii, in 1941. This war ended with the defeat of Germany and Japan, but the explosion of the atomic bomb over Hiroshima, Japan, on August 6, 1945, ushered in the nuclear era, with its constant threat of atomic and nuclear weapons.

Departure (fig. 10-4), by Max Beckmann (1884–1950), is a potent image of frustration and inhumanity born of the scars left on Europe from World War I and the growing totalitarian regime of Nazi Germany. The two wings represent scenes of torture and mutilation, while in the center panel the precious realization of freedom is symbolically rendered with the departing queen holding a child. The figurative exaggerations, harsh brushstrokes, and severe colors contribute to the expression of brutality. Beckmann wrote of the painting:

> On the right wing you can see yourself trying to find your way in the darkness, lighting the hall and staircase with a miserable lamp dragging along tied to you as part of yourself, the corpse of your memories, of your wrongs, of your failures, the murder everyone commits at some time of his life—you can never free yourself of your past, you have to carry the corpse while Life plays the drum. The Queen carries the greatest treasure—Freedom—as a child in her lap. Freedom is the one thing that matters—it is the departure, the new start.

The economic depression of the 1930s and World War II had a profound impact on the world. Increasing industrialization in the United States and the prosperity and development that this industrialization made possible in America, Europe, and Japan led gradually, after the war, to an even greater distance between the developed nations and other countries. The struggle to be free from foreign domination led to the dissolution of the British Empire and independence for many countries, but in many cases independence did not lead to broad well-being for the citizens or to the establishment of democratic governments. Tension between the industrialized

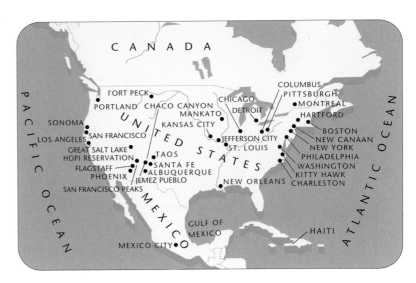

10-5. Maya Lin. *Vietnam Veterans Memorial.* 1982. Black granite, length 500'. The Mall, Washington, D.C. The jury that selected this winning entry in the competition affirmed that two criteria, stated in the program for the competition, were uppermost in their minds—that the monument should "make no political statement regarding the war or its conduct" and that it should be "reflective and contemplative in nature." Commenting on her conception for the memorial, Lin wrote, "I didn't want a static object that people would just look at, but something they could relate to as on a journey, or passage, that would bring each to his own conclusion." Lin's monument is designed so that the walls point toward the Washington Monument and the Lincoln Memorial. Chosen by the competition jury appointed by the Vietnam Veterans Memorial Fund

nations and third-world countries and the struggle for decreasing resources have grown almost continuously during the second half of the twentieth century, and they promise to be increasingly disruptive factors in the twenty-first century.

In the United States, both foreign and domestic conflicts have marked the years since 1945. Between 1950 and 1953, the United States sent a large contingent of troops to the United Nations force that fought in Korea to stop the aggression of Communist North Korea. The 1950s also witnessed an intensification of the civil rights movement. Led by Martin Luther King, Jr., a Baptist minister who would receive the Nobel Peace Prize in 1964, African Americans were in the forefront of the struggle to achieve equality and dignity in human and legal rights. By the early 1960s, American combat troops were becoming deeply involved in a war between North and South Vietnam. In America, efforts to sustain this military involvement were met with bitter domestic divisiveness. By 1973, U.S. forces were withdrawn. In Washington, the *Vietnam Veterans Memorial* (fig. 10-5), designed by Maya Lin (b. 1960), lists the more than 58,000 names of Americans who lost their lives in that conflict. It is an unprecedented public monument. Simple and direct in design, it creates a solemn environment. The polished surface of the granite on which the names are etched reflects the transient life before it,

while the names impose themselves, constantly reminding us of the human suffering and loss that are the ultimate costs of conflict.

Politically, the pulse of change has quickened even more as we approach the end of the twentieth century. Throughout the world, there have been challenges to autocratic and tyrannical rule. After a military coup in Burma (Myanmar) in 1988, opposition demonstrators were shot down in Rangoon. Daw Aung San Suu Kyi, an opposition leader who later, in 1991, was awarded the Nobel Peace Prize, reacted by asserting that "you can't solve political problems by massacring people." In 1989, Chinese troops killed antigovernment demonstrators—mostly workers and students—in Beijing. Yet during that same year, the Berlin Wall, one of the most poignant realities of the Cold War, was torn down, and Germany was reunited after forty-five years. On January 1, 1992, the Soviet Union, a center for world communism for more than seventy years, was formally disbanded. In 1990, Nelson Mandela was released from a South African prison to confront apartheid ever more forcefully; in 1994 he was elected president of South Africa.

At the same time, nationalism became an increasingly serious problem. The 1990s have seen regional ethnic violence in Bosnia-Herzegovina in the former Yugoslavia, in Chechnya in the former Soviet Union, and in Rwanda in Africa. In these and other conflicts, hundreds of thousands of individuals died, were murdered, or were forced to become homeless refugees. Attempts to broker peace have failed in most cases. Nationalism has probably been a factor in art since prehistoric times, but beginning in the Renaissance in Italy, it became an increasingly important factor; art was a means by which the singularity of a culture, a location, a population could be defined and promoted. In the twentieth century, art has continued to be a force of national identity on many levels.

In 1991, a coalition of forces defeated Iraq in the Persian Gulf war after Kuwait was invaded. In subsequent

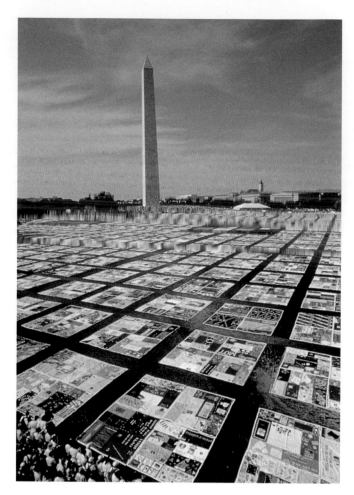

10-6. The Names Project, San Francisco. *AIDS Memorial Quilt*, as displayed on the Ellipse facing the White House in October 1996

years, terrorist bombs killed six people at the World Trade Center in New York City in 1993 and 160 people at the Federal Building in Oklahoma City in 1995. The words of Daw Aung San Suu Kyi, cited above, have yet to be heeded.

Another struggle arose on the medical front—AIDS. As a memorial to those who had lost their lives to this pandemic, the American-based Names Project began the creation of an enormous quilt. Each 3-by-6-foot panel contains the name, the image, and sometimes even some of the clothing or possessions of a person who has died from AIDS. Although there is no particular limitation, most of the people commemorated were Americans. The panels were created not by a particular artist or group of artists but by friends or relatives of the deceased; artistic training has here been judged less important than personal knowledge and commitment. During the fall of 1996, when the *AIDS Memorial Quilt* had expanded to more than 37,000 panels, it was displayed in its entirety in Washington, D.C. for a few days (fig. 10-6). Like the *Vietnam Veterans Memorial*, the quilt commemorates individuals. In its vast size and communal

spirit, the *AIDS Quilt* acknowledges the scope of this modern disease and becomes both a memorial and cogent social commentary. The concern about AIDS is evident worldwide; for a Japanese example, see Masami Teraoka's *AIDS Series: Makiki Heights Disaster* (see fig. 10-146).

INTELLECTUAL AND SCIENTIFIC ACTIVITY

Scientific advancements during the twentieth century have been revolutionary in many areas. In physics, Albert Einstein's general theory of relativity demonstrated the relationship of geometry to gravity and radically modified our concept of space and time. Our understanding of the very essence of matter itself has been altered, as the atom has been reduced to its subatomic components.

Throughout the twentieth century, major philosophical movements have influenced visual expression. The Existentialist writings of Jean-Paul Sartre and Simone de Beauvoir, for example, emphasized the singularity and isolation of the individual in modern society. Meaning, they argued, is not conferred on us by external forces; it is actualized by individual choices, the consequences of which are solely our responsibility. Existentialism also emphasized the importance of the moment and the fact that we really live only in the present. Their philosophical arguments can be related to the distinctive elongated figures in the sculptures of Alberto Giacometti (1901–66). His standing or walking figures, as in *City Square* (fig. 10-7), are recognizably human, upright, and dignified but lack the particular features that would give them individuality. Their rough contours make them seem nervous or agitated, and they are placed so that there seems to be no physical or psychological interaction. Even the spaces that separate them become poignant barriers to communication. Although the title of the work suggests a space that would normally be bustling with abundant human activity, here the figures seem to exist in solitude and only within themselves. In *City Square*, Giacometti has given visual form to the Existential concepts that were so strongly felt in post–World War II Europe.

Twentieth-century developments in psychology have greatly influenced the course of art, especially in the movements of Surrealism and Abstract Expressionism (see pages 544 and 554). Using therapeutic approaches that included free association and the interpretation of dreams in treating his patients, Sigmund Freud established the active and even dynamic role of the human unconscious in guiding behavior. To Freud, unmasking the subconscious was the key to understanding the human mind. Carl Jung extended, modified, and at times countered Freud's theories to develop additional psychological insight into human behavior. Jung advanced

10-7. Alberto Giacometti. *City Square.* 1948. Bronze, 8^1/2 x 25^1/8 x 17^1/4". The Museum of Modern Art, New York

Purchase. © 1996 Artists Rights Society (ARS), New York/ADAGP. Paris

the notion of a "collective unconscious," a layer of unconscious that underlies the personal unconscious and that carries the inherited disposition of our species. The collective unconscious was revealed by the common use of archetypal images, such as the circle, across diverse cultural traditions.

Radical changes were introduced in twentieth-century music. Igor Stravinsky's ballet music for *The Rite of Spring* (1913), with its driving, primal rhythms and fragmented melodies, nearly caused the audience to riot at its first performance. In Germany, the composer Arnold Schönberg devised a new system of musical tonality; Schönberg's pantonality (which is commonly referred to as being atonal) is a free but not unstructured use of musical tones without traditional chord progressions or resolutions. At mid-century, the American composer John Cage began to incorporate elements of chance into his work. One composition from 1952, titled *4'–33*, has a performer come on stage and sit at a piano for 4 minutes and 33 seconds. During this time, the unpredictable sounds from the audience and other accidental noises "create" the musical experience. Cage's avant-garde concept of music has been influential for contemporary poets, painters, and performance artists (see page 570).

ART OF THE TWENTIETH CENTURY

Twentieth-century art is often referred to as modern art, although the terms are not exactly synonymous. The concept of modernism is relative within the context of history and until recently was virtually limited to Western art. It expresses an attitude that distinguishes a current time from the immediate past. Renaissance artists, for example, felt themselves to be working in a "modern style." In the history of art, developments in the nineteenth century countered well-established traditions in art, laying the foundation for the radical and rapid changes that have occurred in this century. These changes in twentieth-century art have been so distinctive that the term *modern* is applied in both a chronological and a descriptive sense to the works of avant-garde art that challenged earlier traditions. Modernism was a Western construct that only became common elsewhere when artists wanted to challenge the status quo or when they wanted to promote Western values and ideas.

The present century has brought a variety of artistic experiences unparalleled in the history of art. Throughout the century, the avant-garde has rapidly expanded the traditional limits of art by developing new styles, by working in new materials, and by questioning accepted artistic practice. One area in which avant-garde artists made an important contribution was in the theater, designing stage sets and costumes. Picasso, Matisse, Malevich, De Chirico, and Bakst, for example, all designed sets and/or costumes for the ballets presented in Paris and elsewhere by the Ballets Russes under the direction of the group's founder, Sergey Diaghilev. Their decor accompanied modern music commissioned by Diaghilev from Stravinsky, Prokofiev, Ravel, Poulenc, Satie, and others. Diaghilev's original choreographer, Michel Fokine, transformed the very nature of ballet by insisting on dramatic expression in gesture and movement and demanding that dancers use their whole body to convey the emotional message of the music and the subject; other choreographers who worked with Diaghilev included the dancers Vaslav Nijinsky and George Balanchine. Nijinsky choreographed and danced the lead in the Ballets Russes's *L'Aprés-midi d'un Faune* (*The Afternoon of a Faun*), set to music written in 1894 by Claude Debussy. The theme, from antiquity, inspired

10-8. Leon Bakst. *Faun*, ballet costume design for Nijinsky for *L'Aprés-midi d'un Faune*. 1912. Gouache, watercolor, and gold on paper mounted on cardboard, 11³/4 x 10¹/2". Wadsworth Atheneum, Hartford, Connecticut. For this costume, Bakst has been inspired by the Art Nouveau style, which flourished in Europe and the United States between about 1880 and 1920. Art Nouveau's emphasis on sinuous line and the natural forms of leaves and flowers and on the hand-crafted object, often made of the finest materials, is in part a reaction to the Industrial Revolution. Art Nouveau subject matter is often sensuous, a development related to the freer morality that was beginning to become common during these years. Commissioned by Sergey Diaghilev for the Ballets Russes production of the ballet

The Ella Gallup Sumner and Mary Catlin Sumner Collection Fund

10-9. Edward Hopper. *Nighthawks*. 1942. Oil on canvas, 30 x 60". The Art Institute of Chicago
Friends of American Art Collection

Leon Bakst (1866–1924) to base the women's costumes on the attire seen in ancient Greek art, but his design for Nijinsky in his role of the Faun (fig. 10-8) responded both to the popular Art Nouveau style and to the need for a costume that would heighten the erotic and sinuous movements that Nijinsky choreographed for the Faun, a creature of nature, half animal and half man, who in the ballet experienced his first sexual awakening. Although it was said that the ballet shocked *"le tout Paris"* ("all Paris"), its revolutionary qualities were championed by the sculptor Rodin, among others. In the context of the ballet, Bakst's costume became kinetic art within a collaboration among artists at a moment when freedom of expression was being explored in all the arts.

More traditional currents in art, including realism and illusionism, have also been sustained throughout the century, although critics at the time often ignored the work of artists who worked outside the more "modern"

10-10. Andy Warhol. *Green Coca-Cola Bottles*. 1962. Oil on canvas, 6'10¹/₄" x 4'9". Whitney Museum of American Art, New York

Purchase, with funds from the Friends of the Whitney Museum of American Art. © 1996 The Andy Warhol Foundation for the Visual Arts/Artists Rights Society (ARS), New York

10-11. Georgia O'Keeffe. *Evening Star III*. 1917. Watercolor on paper, 9 x 11⁷/₈". The Museum of Modern Art, New York

Mr. and Mrs. Donald B. Straus Fund. © 1996 The Georgia O'Keeffe Foundation/Artists Rights Society (ARS), New York

mainstream. Edward Hopper (1882–1967) developed a personal style and iconography devoted to the theme of the loneliness and isolation of the individual. Hopper's settings could be anywhere in America, and his people are ordinary, nameless figures from the middle class. We have to be careful not to infuse these images with the nostalgia that their settings and costumes now evoke, for Hopper intended his paintings to represent the here and now. In *Nighthawks* (fig. 10-9), painted in 1942, we are cut off from the quiet individuals inside the diner, and the harsh interior light exposes the lack of communication that Hopper so often emphasizes in his images of modern urban life. At times, representational art achieved avant-garde status, as in Andy Warhol's *Green Coca-Cola Bottles* (fig. 10-10), which focused visual attention on consumer commercialism.

It is, however, abstraction and nonobjectivity that have become the hallmarks of twentieth-century art. Continuing formal developments advanced by the Post-Impressionist artists, twentieth-century artists expanded the vocabulary of visual expression. Georgia O'Keeffe's *Evening Star III* (fig. 10-11) is from a series of watercolors inspired by viewing the evening star at sunset, but representational associations have here been abstracted to express the rhythmic pulsations of the star over the landscape. O'Keeffe's painting communicates a sensation rather than the appearance of a scene. *The Kiss* (fig. 10-12), by Constantin Brancusi (1876–1957), with its compact, rectangular masses joining two abstract figures, conveys the essence of unity. For Brancusi, the expression

10-12. Constantin Brancusi. *The Kiss*. 1909. Limestone, height 35¹/₄". Tomb of T. Rachevskaia. Montparnasse Cemetery, Paris

© 1996 Artists Rights Society (ARS), New York/ADAGP, Paris

10-13. Helen Frankenthaler. *Tobacco Landscape.* 1964. Acrylic on canvas, 5'9¹/₂" x 7'5¹/₄". Private collection

of a concept, which in this sculpture is the wholeness of two individuals as symbolized by the kiss, overrode concerns of naturalism.

Some artists totally denied any representational aspects in their work. *Tobacco Landscape* (fig. 10-13), by Helen Frankenthaler (b. 1928), for example, is a nonobjective painting belonging to a style from the 1960s called Post-Painterly Abstraction. Using a water-soluble, plastic-based paint known as **acrylic**, which is flexible and quick-drying, Frankenthaler poured thin **washes** onto the raw canvas, creating an expressively fluid composition.

In viewing twentieth-century art, we witness a tremendous expansion of the materials used by artists. Traditional mediums, such as marble, bronze, and wood for sculpture, will be joined by commonplace, found objects, and even discarded junk in creating **assemblage** works. Even the raw earth has become a significant medium of artistic expression (see fig. 10-112). In composing *Sky Cathedral* (fig. 10-14), Louise Nevelson (1900–88) assembled cut and scrap pieces of wood—parts of furniture, architectural decoration, and the like—in each box. The individual boxes were then arranged to form a wall-like construction. The overall black paint unites the piece, integrating the multiple, diverse forms. Shadows within and among the boxes increase a sense of mystery. In Nevelson's assemblage sculptures, the commonplace has been transfigured.

After mid-century, the fashioning of an art object became less important to some artists. In the **happenings** of the 1950s and 1960s, artists, usually without a preconceived script, performed and directed the activity of the audience during a quasi-theatrical event, often outside the confines of a museum or gallery. *Household* (fig. 10-15), by Allan Kaprow (b. 1927), for example, was commissioned by Yale University. Happenings and performance art (see pages 570–71) have countered traditional definitions of the work of art as a tangible object. Another thrust of artists late in this century has been to break down the distinctions between "high" and "low" art. In the early 1980s, Keith Haring (1958–90) was inspired by the vigor and simplicity of street graffiti, and he began to draw bold chalk compositions onto the black paper that was pasted over ads whose rental time had expired in New York City subway stations. This series of more than 5,000 drawings became known as *Art in Transit* (fig. 10-16); the title refers not only to the location of these chalk drawings but also to their continual removal by the authorities and to the manner in which they boldly challenged the traditional notion of art. Haring's linear, energetic figures are, in the artist's words, "open to everyone," and in a typical democratic, twentieth-century manner, he often kept the meaning of each composition somewhat vague in order to allow for personal interpretation.

10-14. Louise Nevelson. *Sky Cathedral*. 1958. Wood painted black, 9'7" x 11'3". Albright-Knox Art Gallery, Buffalo, New York

George B. and Jenny R. Matthews Fund, 1970

10-15. Allan Kaprow. From *Household*, a Happening commissioned by Yale University, 1964

10-16. Keith Haring. *Art in Transit*. 1982. Graffiti in New York City subway station

Courtesy Estate of Keith Haring

10-17. Bill Viola. *The Sleep of Reason.* 1988. Video and sound installation: 3 videotape projectors, 1 monitor, ¹/₄" videotape, 2 channels, sound, color and black and white, 14'1" x 19'3" x 22 (3.5 x 4.8 x 8.6 m). Carnegie Museum of Art, Pittsburgh

Gift of Milton Fine and Gift Fund for Specific Acquisitions 88.33

Installation art, which also denies the tradition of a work of art as a unique, singular object, fashions a temporary environment within a gallery space (see figs. 10-134, 10-138, 10-139, 10-140) or, as in the case of Judy Pfaff's *cirque, Cirque,* a permanent object within a large, usually public space (see fig. 1-14). *The Sleep of Reason* (fig. 10-17) by Bill Viola (b. 1951) is a video and sound installation; upon entering a room, we are confronted by a simple arrangement of commonplace objects, including a rather everyday chest with a lamp, a vase of flowers, a clock, and a television set on top. The video shown on the television represents a man sleeping. Suddenly, however, the room goes dark, and huge images of attacking birds, lunging Dobermans, crashing waves, and other disturbing images are projected on the walls, accompanied by thunderous, even terrifying noises. We are jolted from a comfortable perception of reality and, it seems, trapped in a small space surrounded by nightmarish visions. The title of Viola's installation makes reference to a late-eighteenth-century print by the Spanish artist Francisco Goya titled *The Sleep of Reason Produces Monsters.* In Goya's print, a sleeping artist, his head resting on a desk, is beset by winged monsters; Goya clarified the meaning of the image in the accompanying text: "Imagination abandoned by reason produces impossible monsters; united with her, she is the mother of the arts and the source of all their wonders." For both Goya and Viola, creativity is examined within the interrelationship between reason and imagination. Viola's installation, however, removes us from being observers and forces us to enter a dialogue within this interrelationship.

Western artists have often identified modernism with a search for newness. This search also has led architects to the creation of a more purely formal aesthetic that countered the eclecticism and abundant decoration

10-18. Indian village women creating a *mandana,* Rajasthan, India. 1994. Rice paste on floor resurfaced with red ocher and cow dung wash

of the late nineteenth century. At times, this aesthetic was imbued with philosophical meaning, as with the Bauhaus, although in this case an inspiration was found at the Japanese Katsura Villa, outside the Western tradition (see figs. 7-46, 7-47). In recent decades, however, the formalist approach has been challenged by architects who have sought to rehumanize our architectural environments and to question those concepts that have defined Western architectural tradition.

In many rural areas of today's world, however, the quest for newness is not a dominant feature in either art

10-19. Sergey Eisenstein. *Potemkin*, detail of film stills. 1925. Eisenstein's film dealt with the 1905 mutiny aboard the Russian ship *Potemkin* and the failed anti-czarist uprising.

10-20. Sergey Eisenstein. *Potemkin*, detail of film stills

or architecture. Often, the creation of intentionally repetitive art is part of an effort to link generations of individuals. For important occasions, such as a marriage, the birth of a child, or a festival, for example, women in the villages in Rajasthan in India paint *mandanas*, or floor designs, at the threshold, on the walls, or in the inner rooms of their houses (fig. 10-18). Each design is produced by following hereditary prescription; women learn from their mothers the precise drawings and techniques required for each *mandana*. Most often the purpose of the *mandana* is spiritual; it acts as a visual prayer to secure blessings on the household. *Mandanas* are but one example of a host of temporary art forms that are regularly created around the globe to reinforce the continuity of ethnic or regional cultural values. In the cultures in which these works are created, they are probably not thought of as "art" in the traditional Western sense, and the women who create them are not thought of as "artists." But the works they create, albeit ephemeral, have a serious purpose that is similar to many of the works that are considered to be art in the West. As communication makes our global community smaller and more accessible, we can more easily understand the integrity to be found in these distinct and meaningful traditions.

One modern international medium of artistic expression is cinema. In the late nineteenth century, experimental photographers succeeded in presenting a "moving picture" by projecting a sequential series of photographs taken at exposures as quick as 1/2000 of a second. The forerunner of our motion-picture projector, however, was the Vitascope, invented by Thomas Armat and manufactured by Thomas Edison in 1895. The projector achieved the illusion of movement by rapidly projecting a series of still photographic images in sequence. The persistence of our vision, from the image retained on the retina of the eye, lets our minds interpret the rapidly shown still frames as continuous movement. By 1895, the Lumière brothers had opened the first public movie theater in France, and soon their *cinématographie* was being shown throughout Europe.

Like other art forms, cinema is primarily a visual experience. Techniques of shooting can effectively manipulate our perspective as we remain stationary. But special to film is the depiction of movement over a course of time. The expression of a continued time has been an important element in many works of art, but with cinema, not only is time actual but our perception of it may be altered by various methods of editing—the "cutting and pasting" of sequences of film together. Sergey Eisenstein's editing in *Potemkin* (figs. 10-19, 10-20), rapidly shifting us from scenes of Cossacks firing into a crowd to scenes expressing the anguish of the people, conveys the tragedy of the event. The efficacy of the modern medium of cinema was vividly expressed by the Swedish director Ingmar Bergman when he stated:

I can transport my audience from a given feeling to the feeling that is diametrically opposed to it, as if each spectator were on a pendulum. I can make an audience laugh, scream with terror, smile, believe in legends, become indignant, take offense, become enthusiastic, lower itself, or yawn with boredom. . . . I am able to mystify, and I have at my disposal the most astounding device [the motion-picture camera] that has ever, since history began, been put into the hands of the juggler.

The twentieth century has transformed art to such an extent that the artist may become the work of art, in performance art, and the work of art as an object may be

10-21. Jacob Lawrence. *Self-Portrait*. 1977. Gouache on paper, 23 x 31". National Academy of Design, New York

deemed less important than the concept or idea to create it. Joseph Kosuth's *One and Three Chairs* (see fig. 10-107), for example, seems to refer to the potential of an art object rather than being one in itself.

THE TWENTIETH-CENTURY ARTIST

The thing that interests me today is that painters do not have to go to a subject matter outside themselves. Modern painters work in a different way. They work from within. (Jackson Pollock, 1951)

Pollock's statement, made at mid-century, summarizes the experience of the artist in this century. The rapidity of social change, the impact of technology, and new artistic freedoms have altered many traditional notions of the role and identity of the artist. The twentieth-century artist has forged a new independence with diverse materials, and often works of art are imbued with a highly introspective content. This aspect of self-gratification in art leads us to experience many works as a revelation of the artist's inner self (see Pollock's work, figure 10-87). It is almost as if this disclosure of the inner self, which in the past was usually restricted to self-portraits, is the main content of many twentieth-century works of art. But the diversity and subjectivity of this new freedom have also posed problems in the critical evaluation of art and even in the identity of the artist. Having broadened the definition of art, customary notions con-

cerning the education of artists and the parameters of a work of art have been opened to a flood of conjectural questions concerning quality, value, and meaning.

The three self-portraits shown here demonstrate how several twentieth-century artists have used the self-portrait as a means of self-examination. Jacob Lawrence, a contemporary African American artist (b. 1917; see also page 541), painted his *Self-Portrait* when he was elected to membership in the National Academy of Design (fig. 10-21); it joined hundreds of portraits and self-portraits of other members in the Academy's collection. Lawrence's direct and compelling painting alludes to both the physical and the intellectual processes of creativity. He is surrounded by the tools and products of his profession, including, in the upper left background, a work from his *Harriet Tubman* series, which narrated the life of the former slave who, before the Civil War, was responsible for freeing more than 300 slaves. The laborer below the Harriet Tubman painting and the tools and paintings on the shelf refer to Lawrence's *Builders* theme, which had its roots in the artist's youth in Harlem, where he associated with cabinetmakers and carpenters. For Lawrence, this theme symbolized human aspiration, which, in the artist's words, "came from my own observation of the human condition."

The Two Fridas, a double self-portrait by the Mexican artist Frida Kahlo (1910–54), is a complex image filled with symbolism (fig. 10-22). Although the two figures hold hands and are joined by a common blood system, the duality Kahlo felt is revealed by the contrasting costumes, Mexican and European. Her dual heritage is like-

10-22. Frida Kahlo. *The Two Fridas*. 1939. Oil on canvas, 5'9" x 5'9". Museo de Arte Moderno, Mexico City

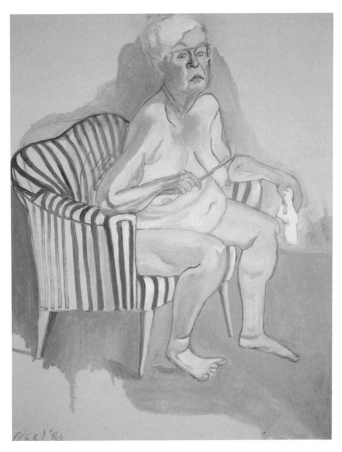

10-23. Alice Neel. *Nude Self-Portrait*. 1980. Oil on canvas, 54 x 40". National Portrait Gallery, Washington, D.C.

wise expressed in the two hearts, for the figure in the European dress has her chest ripped open in a reference to Aztec sacrificial practices, while the other figure's heart resembles Catholic representations of the Sacred Heart of Jesus. This revealing, if enigmatic, work was painted as Kahlo was being divorced, and the open artery on her lap may refer to her suffering at this time. Such personal self-revelation is not unusual in twentieth-century art.

From later in the century, the *Nude Self-Portrait* of Alice Neel (1900–84) is a bold statement of the new honesty of the artist (fig. 10-23). The stern modeling and rather austere pose portray a psychological presence that coexists with the probing, unashamed honesty of the nude figure. Such introspective and deliberate honesty, revealed within a wide variety of visual means, can be one of the keys to understanding the modern artist.

The role of the patron, so important in most art before the nineteenth century, was reduced even further in the course of the twentieth century. As Jackson Pollock's quote reveals, the attitude held by artists and the public alike is that artists work "from within." Although most twentieth-century works are created by the artist independently, without a patron or any con-trolling dictates from outside, there are still exceptions. Most architects, for example, cannot afford to build a building just to see if someone will buy it. Architects are the most likely of all twentieth-century artists to work on commission, although the mindset of the period is such that some architects, once they understand the function of the building and the particular needs of the client, refuse advice about anything that might concern design. Other examples of patronage might be large public monuments, where clients request a work, informing the artist of the price they are willing to pay, the particular location, and the needs (for example, commemoration or decoration) that the work is intended to fulfill, but here again the artist usually remains free to create a personal solution to these problems.

Artists of the twentieth century have had to respond to a different world from that of their predecessors. Technology and the immediacy of communication have brought us into an era in which isolation is increasingly rare and where the developments in ecology, economics, political change, and even local conflict can have a strong impact on a large part of the world. Artists, like the rest of us, are caught up in global tension, uncertainty, and promise.

GLOBAL TIMESCOPE: TWENTIETH-CENTURY ART

	1900		1920

EUROPE ART

1905–06
MATISSE, *THE JOY OF LIFE*

1907
PICASSO, *LES DEMOISELLES D'AVIGNON*

1909–10
BRAQUE, *VIOLIN AND PALETTE*

1911–12
PICASSO, *STILL LIFE WITH CHAIR CANING*

1912
DUCHAMP, *NUDE DESCENDING A STAIRCASE, NO. 2*

1912
ARCHIPENKO, *WALKING WOMAN*

1913
GONCHAROVA, *ELECTRIC LIGHT*

1913
KIRCHNER, *STREET, BERLIN*

c. 1913
KANDINSKY, *FIRST ABSTRACT WATERCOLOR*

1914
DE CHIRICO, *THE MELANCHOLY AND MYSTERY OF A STREET*

1914–19
DUCHAMP, *BOTTLE RACK, FOUNTAIN, AND OTHERS*

1919
BAUHAUS FOUNDED

1923–24
RIETVELD, SCHRÖDER HOUSE

1931
DALÍ, *THE PERSISTENCE OF MEMORY*

1937
PICASSO, *GUERNICA*

1938
MOORE, *RECUMBENT FIGURE*

HISTORY

1914–18
World War I in Europe

1917
Russian Revolution

1919
Treaty of Versailles redraws map of Europe

1936–39
Spanish civil war

1939–45
World War II

ASIA ART

HISTORY

1904–05
Japan defeats Russia

1911
Chinese revolution overthrows Manchu dynasty

1921
Chinese Communist party founded

THE AMERICAS ART

20TH CENTURY
HOPI KACHINA FIGURINES

1909
WRIGHT, ROBIE HOUSE

1923–28
RIVERA *NIGHT OF THE RICH*

1928
DEMUTH, *I SAW THE FIGURE 5 IN GOLD*

1930
STIEGLITZ, *EQUIVALENT*

HISTORY

1911
Revolution in Mexico

1929
Stock market crash in U.S. begins Great Depression

AFRICA ART

20TH CENTURY
BWA RITUAL DANCERS

20TH CENTURY
GUINEAN WOODEN ANCESTRAL FIGURES

20TH CENTURY
SUDANESE GRAVE FIGURES

HISTORY

MIDDLE EAST HISTORY

1912
Ottomans lose European lands

1919–25
Wahabi dynasty conquests (modern Saudi Arabia)

1950–54
LE CORBUSIER, NÔTRE-DAME-
DU-HAUT

1945
U.N. Charter signed

1947
British give India independence

1953
OZU, *TOKYO STORY*

1957
First earth satellite (U.S.S.R.)

1958
E.E.C. is formed

1961
Berlin Wall is built

1972
Strategic Arms pact

1990
Reunification of Germany

1992
Commonwealth replaces U.S.S.R.

1989
HASEGAWA, SHONANDAI
CULTURAL CENTER

1993
YU, *WITH LOVE, WHITNEY*

1994
KAWAGUCHI, *COACERVATER*

1941
Japan attacks U.S. base at Pearl
Harbor, Hawaii

1949
JOHNSON, GLASS HOUSE

1952
POLLOCK, *CONVERGENCE*

1954
ALBERS, *HOMAGE TO THE SQUARE:
AFFECTIONATE*

1949
People's Republic of China
established

1954
JOHNS, *FLAG*

1956
HAMILTON, *JUST WHAT IS IT . . .*

1958
FRANK, *TROLLEY, NEW ORLEANS*

1973
U.S. role in Vietnam War ends

1965
KOSUTH, *ONE AND THREE CHAIRS*

1968
JUDD, *UNTITLED*

1969–70
SMITHSON, *SPIRAL JETTY*

1970
HANSON, *TOURISTS*

1980–82
GRAVES, PORTLAND PUBLIC
SERVICE BUILDING

1980–85
KIEFER, *MIDGARD*

1983
SCHAPIRO, *WONDERLAND*

1983–88
EISENMAN, WEXNER CENTER

1990
GRAVES, *CANOPTIC LEGERDEMAIN*

1954
Brown v. Board of Education, U.S.
Supreme Court rules against
school segregation

1959
Fidel Castro becomes premier of
Cuba

1962
Cuban missile crisis

1995
Oklahoma City bombing kills 169

1957
Ghana gains independence

1960
Benin, Burkina Faso, Zaire, and
Nigeria gain independence

1994
Nelson Mandela elected
president of S. Africa

1948
Israel established

1967
Third Arab-Israeli War

1991
War in the Persian Gulf

FAUVISM

10-24. Henri Matisse. *The Joy of Life*. 1905–06. Oil on canvas, 5'8¹/2" x 7'9³/4". The Barnes Foundation, Merion, Pennsylvania. When it was exhibited in 1906, *The Joy of Life* was singled out for criticism. The painter Paul Signac complained that Matisse had "gone to the dogs."

© 1996 Succession H. Matisse/Artists Rights Society (ARS), New York

I cannot copy nature in a servile way, I must interpret nature and submit it to the spirit of the picture—when I have found the relationship of all the tones the result must be a living harmony of tones, a harmony not unlike that of a musical composition. . . .

The chief aim of color should be to serve expression as well as possible. . . . What I dream of is an art of balance, of purity and serenity devoid of troubling or depressing subject-matter, an art . . . like an appeasing influence, like a mental soother, something like a good armchair in which to rest from physical fatigue. (Henri Matisse, *Notes of a Painter*, 1908)

In Matisse's representation of the mythical land of Arcadia (fig. 10-24), lovers embrace and dance to the strains of music. The sinuous nudes who inhabit this verdant pasture are defined by the same curving, rhythmic lines that describe trees and foliage, suggesting a harmony between humanity and the natural order. The colors are intense and vibrant. Matisse's monumental painting descends from a tradition of pastoral images that began in antiquity and was revived during the Renaissance and Baroque periods. In this twentieth-century interpretation, the diminution of the figures indicates spatial recession, but the broad areas of unmodulated bold color and the powerful flowing linear rhythms create a patterned, flat composition that adheres to the picture plane.

In the opening years of the present century, Matisse, who during the 1890s had painted with an Impressionist palette, assimilated artistic influences from the Post-Impressionists and began to make paintings in which color, independent of descrip-

1900	London is the largest city in the world, with population of 6.5 million
1902	Leon Trotsky escapes from Siberian prison to live in London
1904	Henry James, *The Golden Bowl*
1904	Puccini, *Madama Butterfly* premieres, Milan
1904	Rolls-Royce Company founded
1905–06	**Matisse, *The Joy of Life***
1905	Russian sailors mutiny aboard the ship *Potemkin*

10-25. Henri Matisse. *The Dance*. 1909–10. Oil on canvas, 8'5" x 12'8". Hermitage, St. Petersburg. Commissioned by Sergey Shchukin, a wealthy Russian businessperson and important patron of both Matisse and Picasso. Matisse had shown Shchukin a preliminary design in Paris, and Shchukin wrote back to Matisse from Moscow: "I find 'The Dance' of such nobility that I have decided to defy Russian bourgeois attitudes and to place on my staircase a subject with NUDES. It will be necessary to have a second painting, of which the subject might well be music. . . . In my house we have a great deal of music. Each winter there are some ten classical concerts (Bach, Beethoven, Mozart). The panel 'Music' should indicate in some way the character of the house." Shchukin brought Matisse to Moscow for a visit in 1911.

© 1996 Succession H. Matisse/Artists Rights Society (ARS), New York

tive reality, was exalted for its expressive and sensuous self. Matisse worked in Paris with a group of painters who were exploring this liberation of color, and at a Parisian exhibition in 1905, their works were displayed in a room with a classicizing sculpture, causing the critic Louis Vauxcelles to remark: "*Donatello au milieu des fauves!*" ("Donatello among the wild beasts!"). This witty denunciation gave the name *Fauvism* to this new style.

Within a few years, Matisse was experimenting with further simplifying his style. His boldest experiments were undertaken in a pair of paintings dedicated to Dance and Music, created for the stairwell of the Moscow home of Sergey Shchukin, a sophisticated Russian patron. Shchukin, whose interest in the shockingly modern art of Matisse and Picasso paralleled the Russian interest in revolutionary statements in music, ballet, literature, and politics, purchased many of Picasso's and Matisse's most modern works when he visited their studios in Paris. In *The Dance* (fig. 10-25), Matisse took the dancing figures from the center of *The Joy of Life* and expanded them so that they seem ready to burst out of the boundaries of the huge canvas. The figures are almost lifesize, and the powerful curves of their shapes and of the composition as a whole make their movement seem impulsive and unstoppable. The figures are organic and full of life, and yet Matisse avoided using traditional modeling to suggest three-dimensionality. Another aspect of Matisse's boldness is the manner in which he limited the colors to four. He set the warm orangish hue of the figures and their outlines against two hues from the opposite side of the color wheel: blue and green. The drama and the impulsive movement of the dance are conveyed here with limited means and careful control on the part of the artist.

AFRICAN ART AND RITUAL

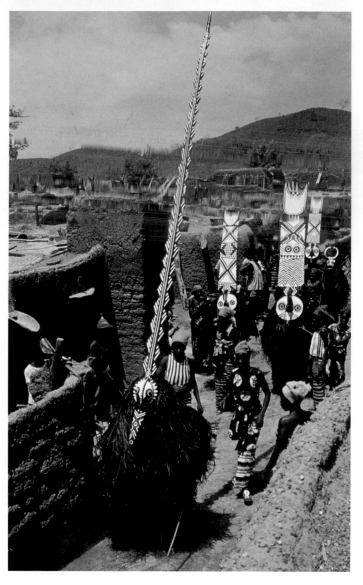

10-26. Bwa culture. Ritual dancers wearing painted wooden plank masks and related raffia body suits at annual purification rites. 20th century. Plank masks of wood, paint, and raffia. Burkina Faso, Upper Volta River region

These people wearing painted wooden masks and fiber body suits (fig. 10-26) are participants in rites that the Bwa perform to sustain social balance in their communities and to mark the cycle of seasonal renewal and rebirth. Masks relate to animals and are used to influence and to ensure social harmony. These wooden masks are constructed of planks that extend laterally or above a face with ringed eyes. Decoration is geometric (lozenges, checks, triangles, and chevrons) and has been interpreted both in terms of animals that are represented and in terms of the forces or principles with which those animals are associated. The fiber suits and masks use and portray the fruits of the seasonal cycle that is essential to their agricultural economy. The masks and costumes appear according to that cycle: with the coming of rain and the drying of the terrain after the harvest, as well as when social conditions merit attention and community action.

The Bwa, like other traditional societies across Africa, have a highly articulated spiritual/ritual life that blends the concerns and conduct of daily life with the rhythms of the natural environment. For the Bwa, that environment is the savannah just below the desert, which stretches across the continent. They live in small kin-based communities surrounded by the land that they farm. Life is con-

nected to the land, and people are closely connected to each other.

The visual arts of sub-Saharan Africa are sets of objects, acts, and performance that express and affirm beliefs. The human expression that we call African art is found in masks and costumes, figurative sculpture, body decoration, clothing, decorative arts, instrumental and vocal musical composition and performance, dance, oral performance, and the ways in which all or some of these are brought together in ritual life. Each detail carries or expresses meaning, sometimes multiple meanings depending on the audience and the performer. For example, a chevron in contrasting colors may represent the feathers of a particular bird and the opposition of dark and light. While the artist is recognized for the fullness and effectiveness of her expression, art is seen as the presentation of recurring themes, unchanging elements in daily life. Repetition, affirmation, and continuity are the messages of the arts in Africa.

Outside the major political centers, the village is the dominant political unit. The Upper Volta River region can be divided into as many autonomous political units as there are villages. Although the villages are not isolated from each other, distinct and localized patterns of culture, including language and arts, have been maintained. All these groups, however, share a concept about the relationship of human life to nature and perform a series of ritual activities that are outfitted with ritual dress, dance, and music.

In this region agriculture is the predominant source of wealth. The fear of drought or of a delay in the arrival of the rainy season is a source of mental stress that the farmers of the dry savannah ease through a highly developed and elaborate scheme of institutions and rites intended to preserve the relationship between nature, the source of all life, and survival. The Bwa see nature as essentially benevolent, but the needs, mistakes, and offenses of people upset it. The function of the ritual performances is to chase away the evil that is bound to occur in human communities. This purification role of the dances is indispensable to the cycle of renewal and is directly linked to the creation myth. Such rites are necessary at times of transition—birth, entering adult life, death, planting, and harvest.

The Bwa hold that Wuro, the Supreme Being, installed harmonious order among the sun, rain, and earth at creation. Human beings, given their lifeways and weaknesses, threaten that equilibrium. The techniques of agriculture involve violation of the soil and that outrages Soxo, the divinity of the bush, and through him, Wuro the Creator. Moreover, if one transgresses the taboos (laws) of society, a sequence of calamities will occur: drought leads to starvation, sickness, sterility, and sometimes even death. Wuro gave some of his bounty to Dwo, who acts as mediator between God and human life to restore balance. Dwo is incarnated in the leaf masks of the Bwa.

Leaf masks and body suits cover the entire body of the dancer (fig. 10-27) and are made in the bush after the millet crop is safely stored. The leaves are from a local tree, the karité (a type of mahogany), and are tied together with vegetable fiber. Feathers or a straw crest indicate that the mask is male. The leaf masks enter the village at dusk and roam the alleys, lightly brushing against storehouses, huts, and the people of the village. The rustling leaves collect all the dust particles, which represent the offenses of human beings. They cleanse what they touch of all their impurities and thus absorb the evil that has accu-

20th century	Bwa ritual dancers
1906	All-India Muslim League founded by Aga Khan
1908	Congo Free State becomes the Belgian Congo
1909	First women admitted to German universities

10-27. Bwa culture. Ritual dancer wearing leaf mask and related body suit. 20th century. Leaves of the karité tree ("bastard mahogany"), fiber, straw, and colored string. Burkina Faso, Upper Volta River region

mulated throughout the year. They purify the village. The masks and body suits are perishable and their potency is spent in this activity. They, too, are part of the life cycle and must be regenerated at the end of the next agricultural season.

The human community also is regenerated by participation in renewal rites of nature that take place at the end of the dry season, before the first rain falls and planting begins. These rites signify the end of the period of mourning, are a rite of purification, and appeal to the spirits of the underworld. They require the presence of leaf, fiber, and sculpted masks.

Fiber masks are plaited and dyed by blacksmiths, and their natural materials are associated with substances of the bush. They are decorated with clan emblems linked to veneration of human lineage. The wooden, sculpted masks are usually rendered in animal form and represent the protective spirits of the village. They include the male flat-

horned buffalo, the female buffalo with circularly sectioned horns, the warthog, the cock with its crest, the toucan, the fish, the antelope, and the serpent, which can be as much as 10 feet long. The *Bird of the Night*, or butterfly mask and body suit (see fig. 1-13), appears after the first rains of the season. As the fluttering movements of the butterfly are imitated by the dancer, the essence of the animal is invoked.

As with many African arts, the masks were collected by Western artists, anthropologists, and collectors in the late nineteenth century because they were moved by the masks' direct and powerful formal expression; usually, however, only the carved and painted wooden masks were preserved and exhibited, while the related body suits, constructed of more perishable materials, and the leaf mask and body suit were not included. Only recently have these masks begun to be understood in their own context by outsiders.

NATIVE AMERICAN ART

10-28. Hopi culture, Arizona. Kachina figurines. 20th century. Cottonwood roots adorned with mineral paints and other natural materials. The Heard Museum, Phoenix, Arizona

Fred Harvey and Barry Goldwater Collections

20th century	**Hopi kachina figurines**
1906	San Francisco earthquake
1907	Oklahoma is admitted as forty-sixth state

10-29. Hopi culture, New Mexico. Hemis Kachina. 20th century. Feathers, yarn, buckskin, and grass. The design of the headdress, with stepped designs called *tablitas*, refers to clouds. The figure holds cattails.

These wooden figurines (fig. 10-28), called *kachin-tihus* (or ka-china "dolls"), were carved by Hopi, a people living in northeastern Arizona. The elaborate headdresses, some of them fitted with birds' feathers, are thought to assist in transmitting messages to and from the spirits. Another kind of ka-china—a supernatural being who acts as an intermediary between the gods and human beings—is a human figure (fig. 10-29) wearing a ritual outfit and headdress that are not unlike those on the small wooden figurines. As with most Native American art, these examples must be seen as functional—that is, they were not produced solely for their own sake as decorative objects but were meant to serve social and religious purposes. Each example is invested with sacred symbolism.

10-30. Hopi culture. First Mesa, Walpi Village in the foreground, Hopi Reservation, Arizona. 20th century. Seaver Center for Western History Research, Los Angeles County Museum of Natural History

The spirits with whom these kachinas are intended to communicate are thought to live in the San Francisco Peaks and are believed to visit the Hopi at their current home in Arizona during the first half of the year, when the planting of new crops is being prepared. Among their many powers, these important spirits are thought to exercise control over weather. The Hopi were and still are farmers who grow corn, beans, and squash. Because of their dependence on agriculture in this arid region, they have developed a complex religious life centered around rainmaking and crop fertility.

In the Hopi religion, there are three manifestations of kachinas: the spirit, a human acting as a spirit,

and a carved figurine. The spirit, which cannot be seen, is impersonated in rituals by members of the Hopi community. By placing masks over their heads and wearing elaborate ritual dress and headdresses, these men and women are regarded as having taken on the supernatural character of the kachina spirit. Through special masks, costumes, paint, and actions of the impersonators, the otherworldly spirits are given power, substance, and personality. Kachina figurines are miniature representations (8–10 inches tall) of the masked impersonators.

There are about 250 kachina personalities, though a limited number are favored. They personify a variety of natural elements, includ-

ing clouds, rain, crops, animals, and even such abstract concepts as growth. Archaeological evidence shows that kachina dolls have been in use since the Hopi first inhabited the southwestern United States, between 1350 and 1400.

The Hopi culture was not much disturbed by European influence until the late nineteenth century, and the Hopi claim that they, more than any other North American people, live "in the old way." Since 1882, the Hopi have been officially confined to government reservations in northeastern Arizona (see map, page 489). This is the traditional homeland of the Navajo and the Zuni as well and is typified by steep-walled canyons and isolated mesas formed by the steady down-cutting of rivers. Hopi communities are based on cooperation, as their survival in such a difficult environment depends on shared responsibility. They count on ceremonies to give them unity and cohesiveness. Group rituals depend on cooperation and are important models for the whole community to witness.

Hopi villages seem to grow directly out of the mesa top, and their building materials and shapes give them continuity with the living rock on which they are built (fig. 10-30). This is often called an organic mode of building, for there is little conscious separation between what is made by human hands and what is natural environment.

Hopi village life is organized around the plaza, a central space left open for the performance of ritual dances. Preparation for such rituals takes place in an underground chamber called a *kiva*, which represents the underworld from which the Hopi believe their people emerged in primordial times. Among other beliefs, the *kiva* is where the ritual of growing new food plants for the coming season takes place. This ritual is performed by men, whose upward movement from the dark *kiva* to the open daylight symbolically reenacts the Hopi "origin myth," in which the Hopi emerged from the chaos of the underworld to begin settled agricultural life on the mesas.

Ceremonies in the *kivas* and plaza take place over a seven-month period beginning in December. In the winter, when the earth's vegetation is dormant and covered with snow, the kachina rituals are held at night in the *kivas*. These dances, which include figures dressed as warriors and hunters, emphasize combat and death. Spring and summer rituals take place in the outdoor plaza in daylight and are associated with fertility, themes of growth, and regeneration. They are happy, boisterous occasions involving both men and women in ritual dress who sing and dance in an ordered and stately fashion. Some kachina dancers, however, represent ogres, whose role is to admonish everyone, especially children, to obey the rules of Hopi society. In a society based on cooperation rather than authoritarian control, such kachinas are important for assuring social stability. The kachina figurines serve a didactic purpose: to remind Hopi children of religious and social mores. They are not toys; these art forms are clearly an integral part of life and are thought to ensure Hopi survival.

THE ORIGINS OF CUBISM

10-31. Pablo Picasso. *Les Demoiselles d'Avignon.* 1907. Oil on canvas, 8' x 7'8". The Museum of Modern Art, New York. The Avignon to which the title refers is a street in Barcelona's red-light district.

Acquired through the Lillie P. Bliss Bequest. © 1996 Estate of Pablo Picasso/Artists Rights Society (ARS), New York

Les Demoiselles d'Avignon, by Pablo Picasso (1881–1973), is a harsh and aggressive painting (fig. 10-31). Inside a brothel, we confront five naked prostitutes with abstracted anatomies. Three figures conceal their faces behind vividly painted African masks that both hide their identity and communicate a frightening ferocity. Picasso considered these masks "magic things" that added a mysterious potency to the work. Compounding the psychological anxiety communicated by these masked figures is a composition that sets formal elements in violent visual combat: warm flesh tones and shades of pink and rust are set against icy blues, while spatial illusionism seems denied by the flat, abstract shapes, despite the manner in which the nude entering from behind parted drapes and the ***repoussoir*** table and still life suggest perspectival recession. The nude figures are discordantly composed of geometric, angular facets and organic, curving passages. *Les Demoiselles d'Avignon*, a paradox of formal and psychological tensions, threatened the tradition of illusionism that had characterized painting since the Renaissance.

The painting began, however, in a less-anguished, more-traditional

10-32. Georges Braque. *Houses at L'Estaque*. 1908. Oil on canvas, 28 3/4 x 23 5/8".
Hermann and Margit Rupf Foundation, Kunstmuseum, Bern, Switzerland
© 1996 Artists Rights Society (ARS), New York/ADAGP, Paris

spirit. In the spring of 1907, Picasso, a young Spanish artist working in Paris, took up the challenge of painting a monumental modern composition of female nudes. After seeing a 1906 Paris retrospective of Cézanne's paintings, Picasso began to apply the planar, geometric simplifications of Cézanne's forms to the study of the human figure. In a preliminary study for the painting, two clothed male figures were surrounded by five female prostitutes. This confrontation, as well as the still-life arrangement on the table, suggests a traditional *memento mori* theme to express the idea that all physical pleasure is passing.

Les Demoiselles d'Avignon seemed a brutal and ugly painting to many of Picasso's friends, including the French painter Georges Braque (1882–1963), but Braque was inspired by the manner in which Picasso was wrestling with the question of pictorial structure and the issues raised by Cézanne. In the summer of 1908, Braque was in southern France, the landscape that had earlier been transformed by Cézanne (see fig. 9-75). Braque's *Houses at L'Estaque* (fig. 10-32) develops the planar simplification and faceted surface structure of Cézanne's paintings, but in contrast to Cézanne's intention, now the houses seem to lack solidity and weight. Braque's eccentric use of modeling highlights different areas of the landscape simultaneously and reinforces the planarity of the pictorial surface.

Reviewing a 1908 exhibition of Braque's paintings in Paris, which included *Houses at L'Estaque*, the French art critic Louis Vauxcelles (who had earlier given us the name *Fauvism*) wrote that Braque "despises form, reduces everything . . . to cubes. Let us not make fun of him, since he is honest. And let us wait." Cubism, the style that would result from these experiments by Picasso and Braque, would become one of the most influential movements of early-twentieth-century art.

FRANK LLOYD WRIGHT, ROBIE HOUSE

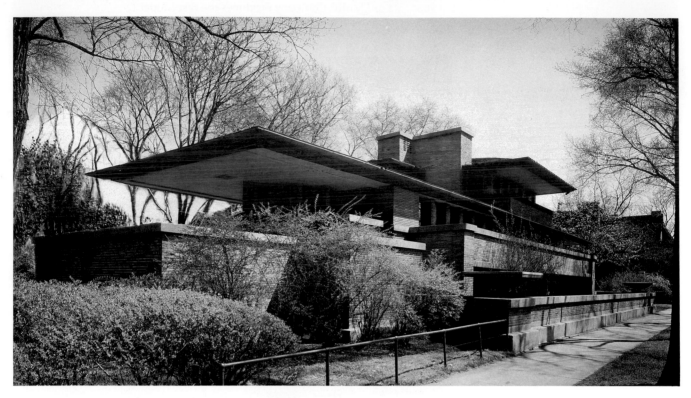

10-33. Frank Lloyd Wright. Exterior, Robie House, Chicago. 1909. Wright's Prairie-style designs, including this house, were published in Europe in 1910. They influenced later developments in modern European architecture, including de Stijl and the Bauhaus. Commissioned by Frederick C. Robie, a relatively young and successful manufacturer of bicycles

Wright's Robie House (fig. 10-33) is distinguished by an emphatic horizontal design, with rooms and porches extending out from a central core defined by the chimney mass. The structure is so severe and modern in appearance that it is a surprise to realize that the Robie House, with its contemporary appearance, was designed and constructed in the first decade of the twentieth century. Frank Lloyd Wright (1867–1959) had worked as an assistant to Louis Sullivan from 1888 to 1893, but by 1900, Wright had developed a new and personal style. In the opening years of this century, he designed a series of private homes in the Chicago area that shared similar compositional qualities, including an emphasis on the horizontal features of the design. Wright's style at this time, which was inspired by the flatness of the

10-34. Dining room, Robie House, with original furniture designed by Wright. The patron wrote later that he selected Wright as his architect in part because he did not want his house to have "a lot of junk—a lot of fabrics, draperies, and what not, or old-fashioned roller shades with the brass fittings on the ends—in my line of vision, gathering dust and interfering with window washing. No sir . . . ." Wright's sleekly modern furniture and his windows, with their integral, stained-glass decoration, fit the client's expectations.

10-35. Frank Lloyd Wright. Plan of Robie House

terrain where the homes were built, is known as the Prairie style.

In the Prairie style, Wright developed what he termed his organic theory of architecture. The organic concept governs both the design of the structure and its relationship to the site. The cantilevered projections (see below) from the core of the house help to blur the distinction between inside and outside, while the abstract, geometric massing of the architectural forms creates a distinctly modern effect.

The interior design of the rooms continues the geometric emphasis apparent from the outside. Wright's use of furniture, much of which he created specifically for each house, is distinctive for its severely geometric design and its hand-crafted elegance (fig. 10-34). It reiterates and complements the architectural forms and, in its rich use of wood and modern decorative elements, enhances the intimate scale of the rooms.

Viewing the plan, one becomes aware of another feature of Wright's organic theory (fig. 10-35). The spatial flow from room to room, around the central core of the fireplace and stairway, is free and unobstructed; rooms are not boxed off. Interior spaces merge with each other. A new continuity of interior spatial design is established.

The decorative features of the house's exterior are minimal. Instead of applied ornamentation, Wright utilized the color and texture of the materials themselves. On the exterior, red brick contrasts with powerful horizontal accents in stone. The unadorned planarity of the exterior walls would become one of the distinguishing features of modern architecture.

Certain features of Wright's organic theory are antithetical. For example, the desire to merge the house with the environment is countered by the severely geometric and planar design, but it was precisely the balancing of contrasting design features that distinguishes Wright's achievements.

TECHNIQUE   THE CANTILEVER

The **cantilever,** an architectural support system utilized by Wright in both the Robie House and Fallingwater (see fig. 1-6), projects a horizontal architectural member out into space without external support. It is counterbalanced by a weight on the interior end. The materials used in the construction of a large cantilever must possess a high tensile strength; usually steel beams and reinforced concrete are used. For this reason, the cantilever as a method of construction has reached its fullest expression in modern architecture.

ANALYTICAL CUBISM

The theme of Georges Braque's *Violin and Palette* (fig. 10-36) is traditional: a still-life arrangement of a violin, a music stand with sheet music, a painter's palette hung on a **trompe l'oeil** nail at the top, and green folds of drapery as a backdrop. Each of these common elements, however, is broken up into disengaged fragments. The violin, for example, is composed of a series of planes or facets that represent parts of the violin as seen from different points of view. They have been reassembled to form a highly abstract composition on the picture plane of the painting.

Braque's fragmented violin is in part the result of influences stemming from Cézanne, who introduced planar modeling and multiple viewpoints in his paintings from the late nineteenth century (see fig. 9-74). From 1907 onward, Picasso and Braque, working together in Paris, experimented with this analytical abstraction, applying it to figural and landscape representations. By the fall and winter of 1909–10, they had developed Cubism.

Since the Renaissance, naturalistic illusionism had been a primary concern of painting. Cubism confronted that tradition by asserting a new independence for the painted image. Given the visual clues that Braque offers us in *Violin and Palette*, we conceptually understand, for example, that one of the images refers to a violin. The image does not represent a particular violin as seen from a specific viewpoint. Rather, the simultaneous viewpoints suggest the essence of a violin—those shapes, forms, and colors that define a violin as a distinct object, different from the music stand,

10-36. Georges Braque. *Violin and Palette.* 1909–10. Oil on canvas, 36¹/₈ x 16⁷/₈".
Solomon R. Guggenheim Museum, New York

© 1996 Artists Rights Society (ARS), New York/ADAGP, Paris

1909–10	**Braque, *Violin and Palette***
1910	Igor Stravinsky's *Firebird* is performed in Paris
1910	Halley's comet returns
1910	U.S. population reaches 92 million; 13.5 million are foreign-born
1910	Race-car driver Barney Oldfield drives 133 mph

sheet music, palette, or drapery. In this process of analysis, seeing becomes both visual and conceptual; we perceive time and space as a total experience, unlike the illusionistic tradition of painting, which fixes a viewpoint at a moment in time.

The initial phase of Cubism, which analyzes objects from different viewpoints to re-create them as planar facets lying near or on the picture plane, is known as Analytical Cubism. The process of abstraction inherent in this visual and conceptual analysis led to ambiguities of interpretation, but Cubism never became nonobjective.

In 1911, a new element was introduced into Analytical Cubist paintings that further emphasized the surface: letters and musical symbols. Picasso's *"Ma Jolie"* (fig. 10-37) contains words, a treble clef sign, and a hint of the five lines of the musical staff. While the shapes of the letters reinforce the planarity of the painting's surface, they also act as a clue, for they were taken from a current popular song. The words also become a reference for the viewer, for above them we can glimpse shapes that suggest a figure holding a stringed instrument. The color has been reduced because Picasso's primary interest is in examining form; color, which depends on light, is deemed extraneous to form. However abstract, the painting offers the persistent observer a representation of a posed model. The network of planar shapes has given a new aesthetic to painting, one that asserts the surface as a two-dimensional field for assembling references to the world.

10-37. Pablo Picasso. *"Ma Jolie"* (*Woman with a Zither or a Guitar*). 1911–12. Oil on canvas, 39³/₈ x 25³/₄". The Museum of Modern Art, New York. *Ma Jolie* (French for "My Pretty One") has a double meaning here. It refers both to the words in a popular song and to the name Picasso used for his new lover, Eva, who probably posed for this painting.

Acquired through the Lillie P. Bliss Bequest. ©1996 Estate of Pablo Picasso/Artists Rights Society (ARS), New York

SYNTHETIC CUBISM

10-38. Pablo Picasso. *Still Life with Chair Caning*. 1911–12. Collage of oil and pasted oilcloth, simulating chair caning, on canvas, oval 10⁵/8 x 13³/4". Musée Picasso, Paris

© 1996 Estate of Pablo Picasso/Artists Rights Society (ARS), New York

The upper portion of Picasso's *Still Life with Chair Caning* (fig. 10-38) bears the familiar fragmentation of Analytical Cubism. This arrangement of objects includes an oyster shell, lemon slices, a knife, a pipe, and a wineglass, while the *JOU*—the beginning of the French word *journal* ("newspaper")—indicates the presence of a newspaper. These objects have been painted over chair caning. But this chair caning, which seems to be the most realistic aspect of the work, is itself an illusion, for it is in actuality cheap printed oilcloth pasted onto the canvas. Even the frame dares us to consider new expectations of painting, for it is common, ordinary rope instead of a traditional frame.

Picasso's use of the collage medium (see below) is an extension of the questions first posed by Analytical Cubism. Now the issues are compounded, for the reality of the painted, conceptualized Cubist still life is joined to printed oilcloth that looks like yet another reality: chair caning. With Picasso's Cubist collage, we are exposed to the paradoxical realities of life and art; although we can recognize the artificial and artful composition of still-life objects, the oilcloth disguises its reality behind the illusion of chair caning.

Still Life with Chair Caning ushers in a new phase of Cubism in which painted elements are combined with commonplace materials. The resulting works join traditional artistic mediums with materials previously considered outside the realm

1911–12   **Picasso, *Still Life with Chair Caning***
1911   Marie Curie wins Nobel Prize for chemistry
1911   Italy occupies Tripoli
1911   Revolution in Mexico
1911   Arnold Schönberg, *Manual of Harmony*

10-39. Pablo Picasso. *Three Musicians*. 1921. Oil on canvas, 6'7" x 7'3³/4". The Museum of Modern Art, New York

Mrs. Simon Guggenheim Fund. © 1996 Estate of Pablo Picasso/Artists Rights Society (ARS), New York

of art. This second phase of Cubism is known as Synthetic Cubism.

Soon the effects of the Synthetic Cubist collage were translated wholly into painting, as seen in Picasso's *Three Musicians* (fig. 10-39). Although some of the patterned areas of this work appear to be collage materials, all in actuality are painted. The abstracted figures retain an objectivity that is clearly recognizable, while the reality of the picture plane is simultaneously emphasized. The tradition of the picture plane as an element through which we view an illusion of space has been overturned. Painting now asserts itself as a completely flat surface.

TECHNIQUE   **COLLAGE AND ASSEMBLAGE**

The term *collage*, from the French word *coller* ("to glue"), is used to designate works of art that incorporate such materials as pieces of newspaper, cloth, colored paper, and the like. With their Synthetic Cubist collages and **assemblage** sculptures, Picasso and Braque extended the range of materials accepted in art and influenced later avant-garde movements, including Futurism, Dada, and Surrealism.

The term *assemblage* has broader connotations than *collage*, although historically the word has been used to include collage. Assemblage usually involves a combination of actual three-dimensional objects, some of which are "found" objects from the household or the junkyard, into a coherent composition. Examples of assemblage include Duchamp's "ready-mades" (see fig. 10-56) and the works of Louise Nevelson (see fig. 10-14).

THE INFLUENCE OF CUBISM

NU DESCENDANT UN ESCALIER

10-40. Marcel Duchamp. *Nude Descending a Staircase, No. 2.* 1912. Oil on canvas, 58 x 35". Philadelphia Museum of Art. When Duchamp's *Nude* was shown in the Armory Show in the United States, it became the butt of many jokes and cartoons, including one entitled *The Rude Descending a Staircase (Rush Hour at the Subway)*, published in the *New York Evening Sun* on March 20, 1913.

Louise and Walter Arensberg Collection. Artists Rights Society (ARS), New York/ADAGP, Paris

1911	The Qing dynasty in China dissolved
1911	Chinese Republic proclaimed
1912	**Duchamp, *Nude Descending a Staircase, No. 2***
1912	Carl Jung, *The Theory of Psychoanalysis*
1912	*S.S. Titanic* sinks

Cubism was tremendously influential on developments in early-twentieth-century art, from Paris to New York, Tokyo, and Moscow. The techniques of planar fragmentation, used in Cubism to portray a conceptual vision, were adapted to express different artistic philosophies. Marcel Duchamp (1887–1968), for example, used a complex sequence of fragmented planes to describe the dynamic movement of a figure descending a staircase (fig. 10-40).

In Italy, the portrayal of the dynamism of modern life was the aim of a group of avant-garde artists who called themselves Futurists. Their task, as expressed in the 1910 *Futurist Manifesto*, was to free Italy from its past artistic traditions and thrust it forward into the twentieth century. The Futurist artists also embraced political anarchy. Among other defiant statements, the manifesto declared:

> that all subjects previously used must be swept aside in order to express our whirling life of steel, of pride, of fever and of speed.
> that the name of "madman" with which it is attempted to gag all innovators should be looked upon as a title of honor.
> that universal dynamism must be rendered in painting as a dynamic sensation.

Futurist works in painting and sculpture were a response to the challenge established in their manifesto. The intensity of speed suggested in Balla's *Speeding Automobile* (see fig. 10-1) meets the demand for "dynamic sensation," as does the implied stride by Umberto Boccioni

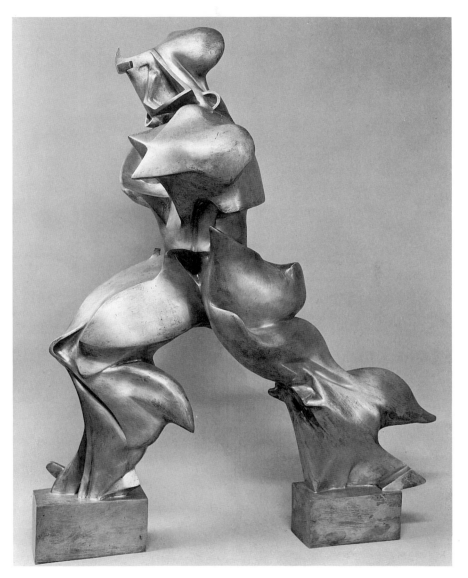

10-41. Umberto Boccioni. *Unique Forms of Continuity in Space.* 1913 (cast 1931). Bronze, height 43⁷⁄₈". The Museum of Modern Art, New York
Acquired through the Lillie P. Bliss Bequest

(1882–1916) in his *Unique Forms of Continuity in Space* (fig. 10-41). Forms that suggest both working, moving muscles and sweeping drapery folds are thrust outward into space in order to convey the energy of a quickly striding figure. The sculpture is dramatically different when seen from varied viewpoints. Boccioni wrote:

No one can any longer believe that an object ends where another begins. . . . We therefore . . . proclaim . . . the complete abolition of definite lines and closed sculpture. We break open the figure and enclose it in the environment.

ABSTRACTION IN SCULPTURE

10-42. Alexander Archipenko. *Walking Woman.* 1912. Bronze, height 26³/8". Collection Frances Archipenko-Gray

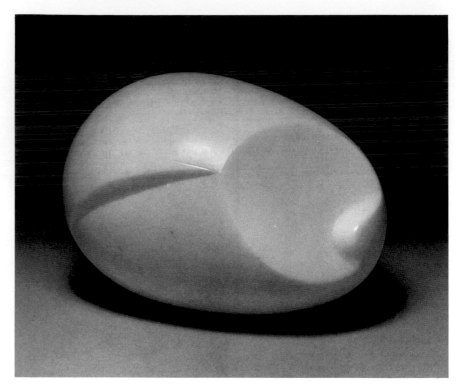

10-43. Constantin Brancusi. *The Newborn.* 1915. Marble, height 5⁵/8". Philadelphia Museum of Art

Louise and Walter Arensberg Collection. Artists Rights Society (ARS), New York/ADAGP, Paris

The influence of Cubism led to further experimentations in sculpture as well as in painting. In *Walking Woman* (fig. 10-42), Alexander Archipenko (1887–1964) displays the impact of the simplified planar abstraction that we associate with Cubism. Note how the dissected lower left leg resembles the forms of Duchamp's *Nude Descending a Staircase* (see fig. 10-40). What is novel, however, is Archipenko's transformation of the interpretation of mass in space. He has opened voids in the head and torso areas, where previous figural sculptures had always asserted the strongest concentrations of mass.

Parallel to these Cubist-inspired developments in abstract sculpture, another evolution in sculpture was occurring. In 1904, Brancusi, a Romanian artist, took up residence in Paris. Working in a variety of traditional sculptural mediums and often guided by a subjective synthesis of diverse traditions—including the simplified, abstract features of African and Romanian folk sculpture—Brancusi reduced representational images to elemental forms. Evolving a style based on organic abstraction, Brancusi noted:

> They are imbeciles who call my work abstract; that which they call abstract is the most realist, because what is real is not the exterior form but the idea, the essence of things.

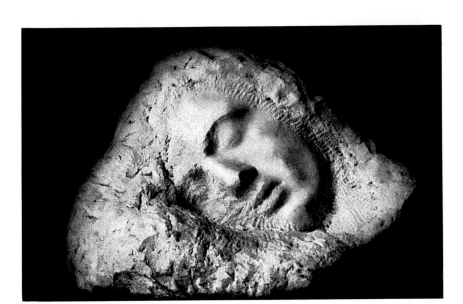

10-44. Constantin Brancusi. *Sleep.* 1908. Marble, height 10". National Gallery, Bucharest
© 1996 Artists Rights Society (ARS), New York/ADAGP, Paris

10-45. Constantin Brancusi. *Bird in Space.* c. 1924. Polished bronze, height 49 3/4". Philadelphia Museum of Art

Louise and Walter Arensberg Collection. © 1996 Artists Rights Society (ARS), New York/ADAGP, Paris

Brancusi's concern with portraying the "essence of things," an artistic philosophy that he shared with other members of the European avant-garde, led to the abstraction evident in *The Newborn* (fig. 10-43). The particulars of a baby's head and facial features have been reduced to a primordial egg form with sweeping arcs uniting the forehead with the nose and gaping mouth; the abstracted forms communicate the essence of the cry of a new life. Brancusi had started in a more traditional mode.

Sleep, from 1908 (fig. 10-44), displays representational facial features, and Rodin's influence is felt in the consciously unfinished forms of the work and in the manner in which the form of the head seems to evolve from the enveloping marble. Seven years later, in *The Newborn,* Brancusi's transformation of form was complete.

One of Brancusi's aphorisms was "simplicity is not an end in art, but one arrives at simplicity in spite of oneself in drawing near to the reality of things." With *Bird in Space* (fig. 10-45), Brancusi draws us close not to the essence of a natural form, as we have seen above and met earlier with *The Kiss* (see fig. 10-12), but to the essence of a dynamic sensation. The soaring verticality of the gently swelling bronze form and its mirrorlike surface, which further denies its minimal mass, communicate a propulsive yet graceful energy. Here Brancusi proclaims the essence of flight.

MALEVICH AND THE RUSSIAN AVANT-GARDE

10-46. Natalya Goncharova. *Electric Light.* 1913. Oil on canvas, 41$^{1}/_2$ x 32". Musée National d'Art Moderne, Centre National d'Art et de Culture Georges Pompidou, Paris

© 1996 Artists Rights Society (ARS), New York/ADAGP, Paris

10-47. Kasimir Malevich. *Suprematist Composition: White on White.* 1918. Oil on canvas, 31$^{1}/_4$ x 31$^{1}/_4$". The Museum of Modern Art, New York

Early in this century, the electric light bulb became one of the symbols of modern technological advancement. *Electric Light* (fig. 10-46), by Natalya Goncharova (1883–1962), renders an electric lamp not as a static form but as pure radiant energy. The painting pulsates with light; widening, concentric circles of intense colors emit piercing diagonal rays. And just as intense light can seem to dematerialize its immediate surroundings, in the painting the brilliance of the light seems to float in an indeterminate space. In both concept and presentation, Goncharova's painting clearly states its modernity.

The planar fragmentation of forms seen here is derived from Analytical Cubism, while the iconographic interpretation and dynamic linearity owe a debt to Italian Futurism. In the opening decades of the twentieth century, the works of avant-garde artists were known to Russian artists through periodicals, exhibitions, and private collections in Moscow and St. Petersburg. Goncharova's earlier paintings celebrated traditional Russian themes, but under the influence of Cubism and Futurism, she became one of the leaders of the avant-garde in Russia. Beginning in 1911, Goncharova and her husband, Mikhail Larionov (1881–1964), created a new artistic movement that they called Rayonism. This abstract movement, which sought to give visual expression to dynamic forces, was short-lived, but its impact was felt by other artists, including Kasimir Malevich (1878–1935).

Malevich knew and exhibited with Goncharova and Larionov. By about 1913, however, his Cubist-inspired paintings gave way to geometric abstraction in an attempt, as he would later write, "to free art from the burden of the object." The resulting series of paintings consisted of nonrepresentational compositions dominated by simple geometric shapes. One painting,

Suprematist Composition: White on White (fig. 10-47), reduces the formal elements of the painting to two squares of white that are separated only by the slightest value contrast. Using geometric and coloristic purity, Malevich intended to communicate pure uncorrupted emotion. He titled this new style Suprematism, writing:

> The Suprematists have deliberately given up the objective representation of their surroundings in order to reach the summit of the true "unmasked" art and from this vantage point to view life through the prism of pure artistic feeling. (Malevich, *The Non-Objective World,* 1927)

Within the innovative spirit of early-twentieth-century art, traditional interpretations of mass and space in sculpture were constantly and vigorously questioned. The Russian sculptor Naum Gabo (1890–1977) was among the artists who challenged that tradition. Through Cubism, Picasso had introduced construction as a method of sculpture. It was the Russian avant-garde artists of Constructivism, however, who legitimized the approach to modern sculpture. Gabo was a medical and science student in Munich from 1909 to 1914. While there, he was inspired by an interest in the history of art and in the artists' group Der Blaue Reiter (see page 526). Working in Norway during World War I, Gabo, through his brother Anton Pevsner, became aware of the revolutionary spatial implications and geometric shapes of Cubism. Late in 1915, Gabo began to create a series of heads constructed from cardboard, plywood, or thin metal sheets (fig. 10-48). In these works, the geometric configuration of the constructed planes, whose edges define surface boundaries, also creates internal voids, or pockets, of space. These voids now

1913   Goncharova, *Electric Light*
1913   Suffragists march in Washington, D.C.
1913   First multimotored aircraft

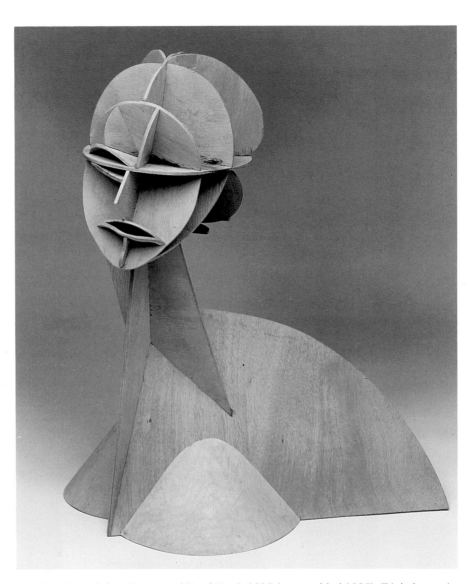

10-48. Naum Gabo. *Constructed Head No. 1.* 1915 (reassembled 1985). Triple-layered plywood, height 21¹/4". Collection Städelsches Kunstinstitut und Städlische Gallerie, Frankfurt. To retain an identity distinct from his brother, Anton Pevsner, who was equally influential in the spread of Constructivism, Naum Pevsner changed his surname to Gabo.

become a positive element in our perception of the head.

Understanding the impact of this approach, as it defied the traditional mass/space relationship of sculpture, Gabo wrote:

> We consider space from an entirely different point of view. We consider it as an absolute sculptural element, released from any closed volume, and we represent it from inside with its own specific properties. . . . In our sculpture space has ceased to be for us a logical abstraction or a transcendental idea and has become a malleable material element.

GERMAN EXPRESSIONISM: DIE BRÜCKE

10-49. Ernst Ludwig Kirchner. *Street, Berlin.* 1913. Oil on canvas, 47$^{1}/_{2}$ x 35$^{7}/_{8}$". The Museum of Modern Art, New York. This painting was later included in a 1937 exhibition of "degenerate art" organized by Germany's Nazi government. The exhibition was meant to demonstrate to the public that many works of modern German art were created by artists who were insane and deviant. The show toured Germany until 1941, and Nazi propaganda records state that it was viewed by 3,200,000 persons.
Purchase

"The modern light of the cities, the movement in the streets—there are my stimuli. . . . Observing movement excites my pulse of life, the source of creation." For Ernst Ludwig Kirchner (1880–1938), who wrote these words, the dynamic interaction of color and movement on a city street was the paragon of modernity. In *Street, Berlin* (fig. 10-49), arbitrary, intense colors are joined with sharply stylized figures and a distorted perspective to communicate not only the animation of twentieth-century urban life but also the decadence of wealthy Germans on the brink of World War I.

The seeds of the modern movement known as German Expressionism were planted in the late nineteenth and early twentieth centuries by Van Gogh, Munch, Matisse, and the Fauves. Expressionist tendencies, such as distortion of form and intensification of color, had surfaced earlier in the history of German art in the work of artists such as Dürer and Grünewald (see figs. 6-20, 6-39). In the opening years of the twentieth century, artists looked to these artistic precedents to find forms that would express the intensity of feeling that they believed was part of the Northern cultural tradition.

In 1905, a group of young architectural students in Dresden formed an association that they called Künstler-Gruppe Brücke ("Artists Group of the Bridge"). As an associ-

ation, Die Brücke was based on the medieval guilds, and the artists lived and worked together as a community. The symbol of the bridge, adopted from Nietzsche's writings, indicated that they conceived their role as a transitory force by which "all the revolutionary and surging elements" of modernism could bring German art to a new and fulfilling future. The artists of Die Brücke turned away from academicism, looking instead for inspiration to the stylizations and spirituality that they perceived in medieval, African, and Oceanic art. Die Brücke held its first exhibition in 1906.

Although not directly related to Die Brücke, the graphic art of Käthe Kollwitz (see fig. 1-19) may be considered within this expressionist context.

Die Brücke's cultural kinship with earlier German traditions led to an interest in the prints of Dürer, and one aspect of the movement was a revival of the woodcut medium. Emil Nolde's *Prophet* (fig. 10-50) is a traditional religious subject, but unlike earlier heroic treatments of this theme, such as the prophets on the Sistine Chapel ceiling (see fig. 6-30), the intentionally rough features and stark black-and-white contrasts communicate an immediate and intensely personal religious experience. In his autobiography, Nolde wrote, "A work becomes a work of art when one re-evaluates the values of nature and adds one's own spirituality."

10-50. Emil Nolde. *Prophet*. 1912. Woodcut, 13 x 9"

GERMAN EXPRESSIONISM: DER BLAUE REITER

10-51. Wassily Kandinsky. *First Abstract Watercolor.* c. 1913. Watercolor and ink, 19¹/₄ x 25". Musée National d'Art Moderne, Centre National d'Art et de Culture Georges Pompidou, Paris. Kandinsky identified this as his first nonobjective watercolor, dating this experiment to 1910, but later scholars have suggested that the work more probably dates to about 1913.
© 1996 Artists Rights Society (ARS), New York/ADAGP, Paris

Vibrant passages of color and line burst on the surface of this abstract watercolor (fig. 10-51) by Wassily Kandinsky (1866–1944). This ebullient composition of colored shapes and lines does not correspond to any reality in nature; the painting can therefore be termed nonobjective. This important breakthrough, which led to many later developments in twentieth-century art, was accomplished by a number of artists during the second decade of the century.

Kandinsky had begun a career as a law professor when, in 1896, he left Russia to study painting in Germany. His education had included studies in art and music, but the decision to become a professional artist was made in 1895, when he viewed a Moscow exhibition of Impressionist paintings. Particularly impressed by the intense color of one of Monet's *Haystack* paintings, Kandinsky wrote: "I had the impression that here painting itself comes into the foreground; I wondered if it would not be possible to go further in this direction." As Kandinsky traveled throughout Europe, he studied German Expressionism and Fauvism, and, returning to Munich in 1908, he painted a series of landscapes that pulsate with color.

A chance occurrence assisted in clarifying Kandinsky's thoughts about nonobjective painting:

It was the hour of approaching dusk. I was coming home with my box of paints after sketching, still dreaming and caught up in my thoughts about the work I had done, when suddenly I found myself face to face with an indescribably beautiful picture drenched with an inner glow. At first I

c. 1913   Kandinsky, *First Abstract Watercolor*
1913   Thomas Mann, *Death in Venice*
1913   Prentice-Hall, Inc., founded

10-52. Franz Marc. *The Large Blue Horses*. 1911. Oil on canvas, 3'5 5/16" x 5'11 1/4". Walker Art Center, Minneapolis
Gift of the T.B. Walker Foundation, Gilbert M. Walker Fund, 1942

hesitated, then I rushed toward this mysterious picture in which I could discern no visible subject, but which appeared to be completely made up of bright patches of color. Only then did I discover the key to the puzzle. It was one of my own paintings, standing on its side against the wall. . . . I knew for certain now that the depiction of objects in my paintings was not only unnecessary but indeed harmful.

The realization that painting could communicate an emotional content without recognizable subject matter was a catalyst in Kandinsky's thoughts about art and the expressive values of color. These issues occupied not just his paintings but also his writings. In late 1911, Kandinsky published *Concerning the Spiritual in Art*, in which he asserted that the function of art was to release us from a "nightmare of materialism" by revealing an "internal truth" that awakens the human spirit. The key to this awakening was the "psychic effect" that colors could evoke:

> Color is a power which directly influences the soul. Color is the keyboard, the eyes are the hammers, the soul is the piano with many strings. The artist is the hand which plays, touching one key or another, to cause vibrations in the soul.

In writing *Concerning the Spiritual in Art*, Kandinsky drew from many varied and rich sources, including Expressionism, Fauvism, and African and Oceanic art. Expressing a kinship with non-Western artists, Kandinsky wrote, "Like ourselves, these artists sought to express in their work only internal truths, renouncing in consequence all consideration of external form." The musical innovations of Arnold Schönberg added further inspiration. "[Schönberg's] music leads us into a realm where musical experience is a matter not of the ear but of the soul alone—and from this point begins the music of the future."

Kandinsky believed that the emotional power of music could be paralleled by abstraction in painting.

In 1911, Kandinsky, Marc, and other Expressionist artists working in Munich formed an artists' group, which they called Der Blaue Reiter ("The Blue Rider"); the title was derived from a work by Kandinsky that depicted an abstract rider and horse unified by a single value of blue. Der Blaue Reiter was an association of artists who sought to communicate the spiritual values that lie behind the facade of appearances.

In *The Large Blue Horses* (fig. 10-52), by Franz Marc (1880–1916), the curving, swelling contours of the landscape intentionally echo the forms of the horses' backs, expressing the artist's belief in the harmony of animal life within nature. For Marc, the blue of the horses communicated a spiritual principle and the ideal of hope, while the red of the landscape symbolized what the artist called "brutal and heavy" matter. Marc's paintings wed line, form, and color in an attempt to express the essential concord in the environment.

TWENTIETH-CENTURY ART   **527**

FANTASY

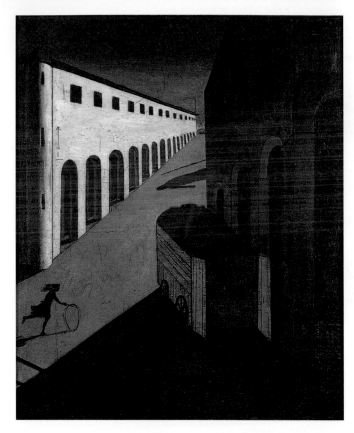

10-53. Giorgio de Chirico. *The Melancholy and Mystery of a Street.* 1914. Oil on canvas, 34¼ x 28½". Private collection

© 1997 Foundation Giorgio de Chirico/VAGA, New York, NY

10-54. Marc Chagall. *Birthday.* 1915. Oil on cardboard, 31¾ x 39¼". The Museum of Modern Art, New York

Acquired through the Lillie P. Bliss Bequest. © 1996 Artists Rights Society (ARS), New York/ADAGP, Paris

Formerly we used to represent things visible on earth, things we either liked to look at or would have liked to see. Today we reveal the reality that is behind visible things, thus expressing the belief that the visible world is merely an isolated case in relation to the universe and that there are many more other, latent realities. (Paul Klee, 1920)

The attempt to express visually a reality that supersedes that of the objective, physical world distinguishes the early-twentieth-century avant-garde movements of Fauvism, German Expressionism, and Cubism. Another approach to this challenge is found in the works of the artists of fantasy, painters who, questioning rationalist views, explored the expression of their personal, inner visions.

As its title hints, *The Melancholy and Mystery of a Street,* by Giorgio de Chirico (1888–1978), opens to us a world that is disturbing and possibly even forbidding (fig. 10-53). The forms are representational. The arcaded buildings, the wagon, and even the intense light are features that can be found in many Italian piazzas. In De Chirico's painting, however, stark **chiaroscuro** is joined with an exaggerated perspective to create an unexpectedly dramatic spatial illusion. The anxiety created by the convergence of diagonals is heightened by the iconography. The setting is void of life except for a young girl, who innocently plays with a hoop. Her path will take her into the menacing emptiness of the piazza, where the shadow of a large statue falls, almost threateningly, across her path. De Chirico's manipulation of representational forms opens the world of the subconscious and the frightening exaggeration we often sense in dreams. De Chirico considered his paintings to be metaphysical—that is, they offered encounters with mysterious truths beyond our understanding.

In 1912, De Chirico expressed in words the process of his creative invention. He wrote:

I believe that as from a certain point of view the sight of someone in a dream is a proof of his metaphysical reality, so, from the same point of view, the revelation of a work of art is the proof of the metaphysical reality of certain chance occurrences that we sometimes experience in the way and manner that *something* appears to us and provokes in us the image of a work of art, an image, which in our souls awakens surprise—sometimes, meditation—often, and always, the joy of creation.

The juxtaposition of dissociated objects in De Chirico is intended to beckon the unconscious within us.

Marc Chagall (1887–1985) journeyed to Paris from his native Russia in 1910. In *Birthday* of 1915 (fig. 10-54), he shares with us his celebration of love with his new wife, the ecstasy of which elevates the artist off the ground to surprise his bride with a kiss. Although he never forgot his Jewish heritage and the decorative, colorful qualities of Russian folk-art traditions, Chagall was deeply inspired by the avant-garde styles that were invigorating the Parisian art scene. *Birthday* weds the joyful colors of Fauvism and Russian folk art with the multiple viewpoints and simplified planar structure of Cubism. The emphasis on emotion seen here is typical of Chagall's commitment to representing familial and societal relationships. Here, all these elements are combined into a liberated and highly personal aesthetic. Later, Chagall disdained the literary associations of "anecdote" and "fairy tales" that critics saw in his paintings, stating that his works "are only pictorial arrangements of images that obsess me." This emphasis on

1914	**De Chirico, *The Melancholy and Mystery of a Street***
1914	World War I begins
1915	Albert Einstein develops the general theory of relativity

10-55. Paul Klee. *Ad Parnassum*. 1932. Oil on canvas, 39 x 42". Kunstmuseum, Bern, Switzerland. Klee's wife was a piano teacher, and the title of this work may derive from *Gradus ad Parnassum* (*Steps to Parnassus*), a series of piano exercises based on scales for the beginning piano pupil.

© 1996 Artists Rights Society (ARS), New York/VG Bild-Kunst, Bonn

the "art" evident in his paintings is an attempt to stress their modernity, but the importance of subject and emotion in his works is evident.

The Swiss artist Paul Klee (1879–1940) usually worked on a small scale, but *Ad Parnassum* is one of his larger and most ambitious works (fig. 10-55). Klee set out to discover elemental symbols: here the pyramid suggests not only the mysteries of ancient Egypt but also, because of the title, Mount Parnassus near Delphi, which was sacred to the ancient Greeks as the home of the Muses, who inspired creative activities. The red circle that suggests the sun may refer to the role of the sun in world religions, as well as to the concept of gradual enlightenment. The division of the surface into tiny squares of pure color creates a precious and beautiful effect that evokes the shimmering nature of light as it illuminates a form. From a multitude of smaller forms, monumental constructions can be created: from stone blocks come pyramids; from scales,

symphonies. But ultimately the full expressive content of Klee's work becomes a matter of individual perception and understanding. Klee believed that there were visual equivalents for spiritual states, and as so often in his work, the few simple forms of *Ad Parnassum* suggest deep and elemental mysteries.

Like Henri Rousseau, whose naïvely direct yet purposeful paintings were championed by young avant-garde artists in Paris (see fig. 9-8), these painters of fantasy often did not view themselves as depicting the bizarre or fanciful. They equated reality with an inner vision. Questioned about this, Chagall responded, "I am against the terms 'fantasy' and 'symbolism' in themselves. All our interior world is a reality—and that perhaps more so than our apparent world." In the visual communication of this "interior world," these artists opened a path of artistic exploration that would lead to Dada (see pages 530–31) and Surrealism (see pages 544–45).

DADA

10-56. Marcel Duchamp. *Bottle Rack, Fountain,* and other works; reproductions of works originally created between 1914 and 1919. Installation, Moderna Museet, Stockholm

© 1996 Artists Rights Society (ARS), New York/ADAGP, Paris

Marcel Duchamp was an artist of unprecedented and unsettling works that still seem shocking to us today, although some were done more than eighty years ago (fig. 10-56). On the pedestals in the gallery, where we expect to find sculpture, Duchamp has placed a manufactured *Bottle Rack*, a common object used at the time for drying bottles. In 1914, Duchamp felt that he could confer an artistic dignity on a bottle rack by designating it a work of art. Another pedestal supports an upended porcelain urinal, officially titled *Fountain*. Duchamp signed the urinal "R. Mutt," a pun on the name of the company that manufactured it, the Mott Works Company. On the wall behind is a reproduction of Leonardo's "*Mona Lisa*" (see fig. 6-16), which Duchamp defaced by adding a mustache, goatee, and, at the bottom, the letters *L.H.O.O.Q.,*

which suggest the French phrase for "She has a hot ass." If all of this appears absurd to you—and it certainly did to critics and the public in the early twentieth century—then you are beginning to understand the function of these objects as works of art. Duchamp, a Parisian avant-garde artist who came to New York in 1915, asserted that "found objects" or "ready-mades" could be works of art. Although they were mass-produced objects intended for a functional use, Duchamp felt that by his saying they were art and by exhibiting them within a gallery, they had entered into the realm of art.

Duchamp never officially declared himself a Dadaist (see below), but his works from 1913 onward, especially the ready-mades, are formally and spiritually akin to those produced by Dada artists. As an artistic, musical, and literary movement, Dada was officially con-

secrated in 1916 at the Cabaret Voltaire in Zurich. Dada intentionally bred confusion, and even the origin of the title remains, appropriately, a matter of uncertainty: two of Dada's founders—writers Richard Huelsenbeck and Hugo Ball—state that the word, which is French for "hobbyhorse," was discovered by chance in a German-French dictionary, but another founder—the German painter Hans Richter—holds that it was simply the Slavonic word for "yes," and that *da, da* meant only "yes, yes."

Other theories as to the origin of the term have been advanced, but what defined Dada was a nihilistic mocking of traditional values in the arts and, by extension, Western society as a whole. This artistic anarchy grew from a profound psychological disgust. Dada glorified the irrational. The Swiss artist Jean Arp (1887–1966), for example, cre-

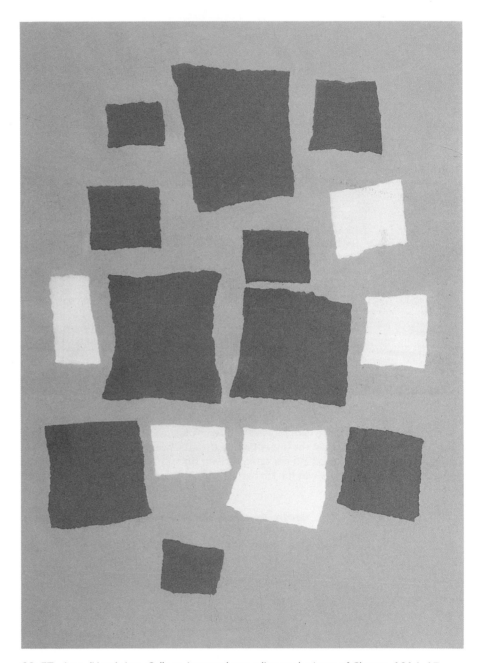

10-57. Jean (Hans) Arp. *Collage Arranged according to the Laws of Chance.* 1916–17. Torn and pasted paper, 19^{1}/$_{8}$ x 13^{5}/$_{8}$". The Museum of Modern Art, New York Purchase. © 1996 Artists Rights Society (ARS), New York/VG Bild-Kunst, Bonn

ated collages by dropping torn pieces of paper randomly onto a paper surface and then gluing them into place (fig. 10-57). These works were composed according to chance. In the words of Arp:

> Dada aimed to destroy the reasonable deceptions of man and recover the natural and unreasonable order. Dada wanted to replace the logical nonsense of men of today by the illogically senseless. That is why we pounded with all our might on the big drum of Dada and trumpeted the praises of unreason. . . . Dada is senseless like nature.

The senselessness and nihilism of Dada, however absurd, were born from an even greater absurdity, World War I. Dada was an art of social protest, a protest against the senseless slaughter and destruction of life and meaning that, at the time, was continuing without an end in sight. "We searched for an elementary art that would, we thought, save mankind from the furious madness of these times" (Jean Arp).

DE STIJL AND THE BAUHAUS

10-58. Gerrit Rietveld. Schröder House, Utrecht, The Netherlands. 1923–24. One of the radical aspects of this house is the placement of a large, flexible living space with moving and removable partitions on the upper floor; Rietveld, sensitive to the conservative attitudes of the local authorities, labeled the upper floor as the attic when he submitted his plans for their permission. The patron was Truus Schröder-Schräder, a widowed interior designer with three children who wanted a functional, easy-to-maintain house. Her studio was located on the lower floor, as was the kitchen. She took an active part in the planning of the house.

10-59. Gerrit Rietveld. Plan of Schröder House

1922   Oswald Spengler, *The Decline of the West*
1922   James Joyce, *Ulysses*
1923–24   **Rietveld, Schröder House**

10-60. Gerrit Rietveld. Interior, Schröder House. Visible in this interior view are the movable sliding walls and some of the built-in furniture that Rietveld designed for the Schröder House. The goal was a completely unified formal and aesthetic expression—what the *De Stijl Manifesto* called a "structural affinity between object and environment." Also visible here is his famous "red and blue" chair, designed about 1918. The forms of the chair are completely geometric: only the need to make some concession to the requirements of the human body explains the two diagonal forms. A durable formal solution, the chair was designed to be mass-produced at a reasonable price for mass consumption. The colors are carefully controlled, with the structure composed of black bars with yellow ends, and the seat and back given over to one blue and one red plane. The restriction to complementary colors is typical of the de Stijl philosophy.

Schröder House, designed by Gerrit Rietveld (1888–1964), is without historical reference. Its simplicity and severity of form make it seem new even today: it offers a timeless modernity (figs. 10-58–10-60). At the same time, it is neither simple nor simplistic. The contrasts between wall and opening, solid and void, horizontal and vertical, aggressive and recessive forms establish complex interrelationships, and the composition, which is determinedly asymmetric in both two and three dimensions, is enhanced by the precision with which the forms are defined. On both exterior and interior, openness integrates the forms of the house with the surrounding space. The Schröder House is a powerful and convincing example of the "equilibrium of equivalent relationships" that was one of the aesthetic goals of the de Stijl movement.

De Stijl ("*The* Style") was founded in 1917 in Amsterdam by several Dutch artists who felt a mission to carry abstraction to what they termed "its ultimate goal." The group was motivated in part by the tragic events of World War I and was inspired by such modern philosophical movements as Theosophical Mysticism and Neopositivism. Their utopian aspirations are revealed in the name, which suggests that this is the ultimate style, the perfect style that, mass-produced, could satisfy all humanity for the rest of the world's history. This search to find a visual equivalent for spiritual and philosophical purity led to the development of a completely new and abstract style in architecture, painting, sculpture, and the decorative arts. Their motivation was ethical, for they felt that a perfectly balanced and serene art could carry the qualities of harmony and purity into the very soul and being of the viewer. Their ultimate goal was to bring about world understanding, unity, and peace. They avoided individualism and subjectivity, arguing that these concepts had led the world into war:

> The old tends to the individual. The new tends to the universal. The struggle between the individual and the universal is revealed in both the world war and contemporary art.

They wanted to create an art that was universal and comprehensible to all humanity, regardless of nationality or creed. "Man adheres only to what is universal," wrote Piet Mondrian, one of the movement's founders, in 1919.

These profound goals reached fulfillment in a series of works produced by Mondrian between the

10-61. Walter Gropius. Workshop wing, Bauhaus, Dessau, Germany. 1925–26. The Bauhaus was an influential modern school of architecture and design.

classrooms
laboratories

classrooms
offices
library
workshops
studios

workshops
exhibition room
stage
dining room
kitchen

GROUND FLOOR

SECOND FLOOR

N

10-62. Walter Gropius. Plan of Bauhaus

two world wars (see fig. 1-16). In these abstractions, which are characterized by a studied balance between forms and colors, Mondrian hoped to accomplish, in his words, an "equilibrium of opposites." The universality of this goal, with its search for worldwide peace, is related to the philosophical statements made by other modern thinkers and artists, as well as to the contemporary founding of the

World Court and the League of Nations, which led eventually to the establishment of the first worldwide governmental body, the United Nations, after World War II.

Walter Gropius's philosophy on the unity of the arts guided his design for the new home for the Bauhaus at Dessau (figs. 10-61, 10-62). The structure at Dessau exemplified the modernist aesthetic. A complex of classrooms, library, and offices is

externally unified by planes of reinforced concrete walls and vast expanses of windows. A rectilinear design, with verticals and horizontals meeting at right angles, governs the plan and determines the exterior articulation. The plain, unornamented surfaces used throughout the building contribute to its modern, clean appearance. The interior design of the classrooms and even the desks and chairs respond to the

10-63. Walter Gropius. Student dormitory room, Bauhaus

design aesthetic that governs the entire structure. Gropius's own office had furniture of his design and a rug, wall hanging, and lighting created in the Bauhaus workshops. The student dormitory room illustrated here reveals how strictly the Bauhaus aesthetic could govern an environment (fig. 10-63). This is what Gropius meant by the "complete building" when, in 1919, he wrote:

> The ultimate aim of all visual arts is the complete building! . . . Today the arts exist in isolation, from which they can be rescued only through the conscious, co-operative effort of all craftsmen. . . . Architects, sculptors, painters, we must all return to the crafts! For art is not a "profession." There is no essential difference between the artist and the craftsman.

Gropius, a German architect and industrial designer, had played a leading role in founding the Bauhaus in 1919 at Weimar. The name *Bauhaus*, chosen by Gropius, is derived from the *bauhütte*, the medieval German builders' lodge, which housed the masters and craftspeople who built the great cathedrals of the late Middle Ages. The recent Arts and Crafts Movement and Art Nouveau's unity of design had reinforced Gropius's belief in the total integration of the arts. Unlike those late-nineteenth-century movements, however, the Bauhaus philosophy of design was guided by the technology and materials of industrial production.

The design of the building at Dessau, where the Bauhaus relocated in 1924, was itself inspired by the rectilinear massing of Frank Lloyd Wright's Prairie-style designs (see page 512) and by the geometric planarity of de Stijl architecture. The resulting building, with its clean, precise, and almost mechanistically tuned appearance, does not display a regional or national identity. The Bauhaus style has reduced the essence of design to a visual common denominator. It promised, with the assistance of modern technology, a future in which a total design aesthetic would not be restricted by cultural or national boundaries. Reacting to the horror of World War I, the Bauhaus offered a utopian vision where art and architecture would assist in the realization of our common human heritage.

In 1933, Adolf Hitler, then chancellor of Germany, manifesting the intolerance that totalitarian regimes commonly share toward the avant-garde, ordered the Bauhaus closed. Like apostles to foreign lands, those who had worked at the Bauhaus carried its philosophy throughout Europe and to the United States.

DIEGO RIVERA AND MEXICAN MURAL PAINTING

10-64. Diego Rivera. *Night of the Rich*. 1923–28. Fresco, Ministry of Education, Mexico City. Commissioned by José Vasconcelos and Puig Casauranc, ministers of public education

Only the work of art itself can raise the standard of taste. Art has always been employed by the different social classes who hold the balance of power as one instrument of domination—hence, as a political instrument. One can analyze epoch after epoch—from the stone age to our own day—and see that there is no form of art which does not also play an essential political role. . . . What is it then that we really need? An art extremely pure, precise, profoundly human, and clarified as to its purpose. (Diego Rivera, 1929)

These mural paintings by Diego Rivera (1886–1957) are on the third floor of an open courtyard in the Ministry of Education building in Mexico City (figs. 10-64, 10-65). They are but 2 of 124 murals that the artist painted during the decade of the 1920s. The scenes present a direct and didactic contrast between the debauchery of the rich, which includes excessive drinking and hoarding money, and the quiet, peaceful sleep of the poor peasants after an honest day's work. A few of the peasants remain awake into the night, educating themselves by lamplight. In the left background of *Night of the Poor*, the Marxist content of the mural is reinforced as bourgeois onlookers disdainfully watch; in *Night of the Rich*, revolutionary soldiers observe the decadent behavior of the wealthy ruling class.

These scenes, and indeed the entire cycle of paintings, are unyielding expressions of class struggle.

They communicate the purposes and promises of the Mexican Revolution, which began in 1911 with a dramatic demand for economic and social reform. A decade of internal civil strife and bloodshed followed, and only during the 1920s and 1930s would some of the aims of the 1911 revolution be realized. Rivera's paintings propagandize the causes and goals of the continuing revolution.

The impact of Rivera's murals is direct and immediately comprehensible, for here the artist has eschewed modernist abstraction in favor of an easily understood representational form and content. Rivera, who had traveled in Europe, returned home in 1921 to join with other Mexican artists in creating a unique and forceful style that, while borrowing elements from Expressionism and Cubism, was also rooted in the bold, severe forms of much Central and South American native art. In the hands of the Mexican muralists, art became a vehicle to promote social awareness; in Rivera's words:

> Mural painting must help in man's struggle to become a human being, and for that purpose it must live wherever it can; no place is bad for it, so long as it is permitted to fulfill its primary functions of nutrition and enlightenment.

10-65. Diego Rivera. *Night of the Poor.* 1923–28. Fresco, Ministry of Education, Mexico City. These frescoes are from the final cycle of paintings, begun by Rivera in 1927, for the Ministry of Education. The images in this cycle are loosely related to the words of two revolutionary songs (*corridos*), which appear on the painted festoons. In part, one of the *corridos* reads: "The clock strikes one, two, and the rich keep awake thinking what to do with their money so that it keeps multiplying. It's only seven o'clock at night and the poor have gone to rest. They sleep very peacefully because they are tired. Blessed the tree that yields fruit, but very ripe fruit. Yes, gentlemen, it is worth more than all the hard dollars."

1923–28	**Rivera, *Night of the Rich***
1924	Mahatma Gandhi fasts to protest Hindu-Muslim violence
1925	New York, population 7.8 million, is the largest city in the world
1925	Alan Locke, *The New Negro*
1925	F. Scott Fitzgerald, *The Great Gatsby*
1926	A. A. Milne, *Winnie the Pooh*
1927	Charles Lindbergh becomes the first person to fly across the Atlantic alone

MODERNISM IN AMERICAN PAINTING

Among the rain
and lights
I saw the figure 5
in gold
on a red
fire truck
moving
tense
unheeded
to gong clangs
siren howls
and wheels rumbling
through the dark city.
(William Carlos Williams,
"The Great Figure," 1921)

Charles Demuth (1883–1935), inspired by this poem by the distinguished American poet William Carlos Williams, intended this painting as a modern portrait of the poet; *W.C.W.*, *Carlos*, and the nickname *Bill* appear in the painting (fig. 10-66). This is one of Demuth's "poster portraits," a series inspired by the stark forms and lettering of advertising billboards. The vibrant 5 is repeated, just as the accompanying "gong clangs" and "siren howls" would have echoed off the hard surfaces of the city streets. The blocky red forms refer to the fire truck, the white circles suggest the streetlights, and the quickly pulsating forms of the composition as a whole visually suggest the jerky rhythm of the poem. The style, with its sharp edges and flat, unmodeled forms, developed in the 1920s in the United States and is known as Precisionism.

In the first four decades of the twentieth century, the influence of modern European art played a significant role in the development of modernism in the United States, aided by exhibitions organized by

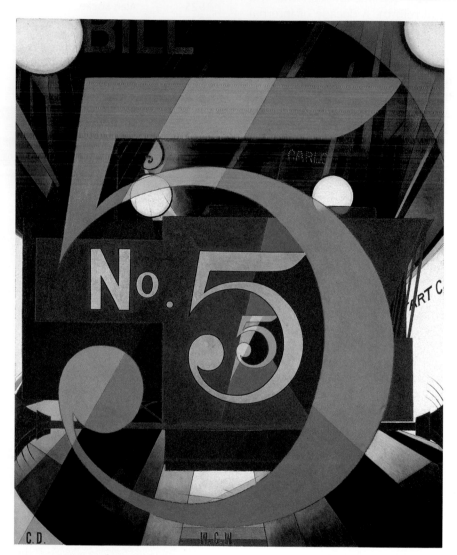

10-66. Charles Demuth. *I Saw the Figure 5 in Gold*. 1928. Oil on composition board, 36 x 29^{3}/$_{4}$". The Metropolitan Museum of Art, New York
The Alfred Stieglitz Collection, 1949

Alfred Steiglitz at Gallery "291" (see page 542). At the same time, however, the Americans maintained an independent stance and were less willing to give up subject matter than were their European counterparts. Instead, they searched for contemporary American subjects and evolved styles adapted from one or more twentieth-century European styles. Until 1940, American modernism was conservative by European standards.

Precisionist style is evident in

American Landscape (fig. 10-67), by Charles Sheeler (1883–1965), but here the tradition of illusionism continues to dominate. The precise linear rendering of the machinery and the industrial buildings is more than a stylistic device, for it also suggests the role of efficiency in successful industry. Only smoke, sky, and water—now channeled to serve an industrial function—show transient movement. In the nineteenth century, the quintessential American landscape had been a wilderness scene that res-

1928 **Demuth, *I Saw the Figure 5 in Gold***
1928   Penicillin is discovered to have antibacterial properties
1928   Joseph Stalin's first five-year plan
1928   D. H. Lawrence's *Lady Chatterley's Lover* denied publication in England
1929   Kodak introduces 16mm color movie film

10-67. Charles Sheeler. *American Landscape.* 1930. Oil on canvas, 24 x 31". The Museum of Modern Art, New York. While he was a young art student, Sheeler also worked as an architectural photographer, and this industrial landscape was painted after he was commissioned to document in photographs the Ford Company's River Rouge plant. Sheeler wrote: "Photography is nature seen from the eyes outward, painting from the eyes inward. . . . Photography records inalterably the single image, while painting records a plurality of images willfully directed by the artist."
Gift of Abby Aldrich Rockefeller

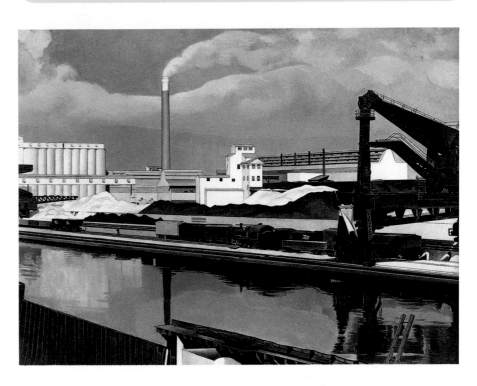

onated with the painter's wonder before sublime nature (see fig. 9-33). Following World War I, the machine and industry emerged as heroes. The satisfying nature of Sheeler's composition lies in his carefully calibrated composition, which reveals his idea "that pictures realistically conceived might have an underlying abstract structure."

A similarly precise treatment of forms is evident in the well-known and much-caricatured *American Gothic* (fig. 10-68) by Grant Wood (1892–1942). Wood grew up in the American Midwest, and his intent in the painting was to capture the qualities of hard work and determination that he saw in his family and in many of the citizens of the small towns of Iowa. Wood intended that

10-68. Grant Wood. *American Gothic.* 1930. Oil on composition board, 29^7/$_8$ x 24^7/$_8$". The Art Institute of Chicago. The *Gothic* in the title refers to the Gothic revival window in the modest Iowa farmhouse behind the figures. When *American Gothic* was shown at an exhibition in Chicago in 1930, it won a prize and was purchased for the museum by the Friends of American Art for $300. It was Grant Wood's first prize and his first purchase by a museum.

10-69. Georgia O'Keeffe. *The Lawrence Tree.* 1929. Oil on canvas, 31¹/₁₆ x 39³/₁₆". Wadsworth Atheneum, Hartford, Connecticut. The novelist D. H. Lawrence and his wife, Frieda, were friends of O'Keeffe when she spent the summer of 1929 in New Mexico. O'Keeffe wrote: "I spent several weeks up at the Lawrence ranch that summer. There was a long weathered carpenter's bench under the tall tree in front of the little old house that Lawrence had lived in there. I often lay on the bench looking up into the tree—past the trunk and up into the branches. It was particularly fine at night with the stars above the tree." Lawrence described this tree as "a great pillar of pale, flaky-ribbed copper" and wrote about the wind "hissing in the needles like a nest of serpents."
Ella Gallup and Mary Catlin Sumner Collection. © 1996 The George O'Keeffe Foundation/Artists Rights Society (ARS), New York

his figures, whom he identified as a man and his daughter (note the family resemblance and the difference in ages), suggest how the values of the pioneers were being perpetuated into the modern period by later generations. When the painting was exhibited in 1930, it became clear that it could mean different things to different people; while one critic suggested that the painting "has a touch of humor and a heart of gold," another said that it revealed "what is Right and what is Wrong with America." An art historian has recently pointed out that a sympathetic and supportive interpretation of the characters was more often found in the Midwest, while harsher interpretations came from critics outside the Midwest. In discussing the characters as he represented them, Wood himself said that he had "no intention of holding them up to ridicule" and that although "these people had bad

points . . . to me they were basically good and solid people."

O'Keeffe's *The Lawrence Tree* (fig. 10-69) forces us to take an unusual viewpoint—looking directly up—on a starry evening in the American Southwest. O'Keeffe abstracts from nature, using limited colors and forms that are rendered with almost no modeling. But in the subtle organic shape of the tree, she suggests not only its growth patterns but its arching expansiveness. The poetic, evocative position we assume emphasizes the scope and scale of nature in an almost pantheistic fashion. The appreciation for the majesty of nature that so moved American nineteenth-century artists found a worthy modern successor in O'Keeffe.

The art of Thomas Hart Benton (1889–1975) is a product of Regionalism, an antimodern movement that flourished in the American Midwest in the late 1920s and early

1930s. Regionalist American artists painted local subject matter in a simple, realistic, and comprehensible style. Such an art is determinedly chauvinistic and can perhaps be related to a need during the Great Depression for a reassurance that finds comfort in nostalgia. Benton's large, didactic murals exalted the history and folklore of a specific region: among his ambitious programs is a wall dedicated to *Pioneer Days and Early Settlers* (fig. 10-70) in the Missouri State Capitol. The wall is divided by painted geometric bands that establish an active compositional pattern. The figures, drawn in Benton's unique and energetic style, reenact local history and legend. The heroism of work, conveyed by the figures to the right— these were inspired by the nudes of Michelangelo (see fig. 6-29)—is a common theme in Benton's art. Such paintings were more than imaginative re-creations of America's past; they were intended to offer criticism, as well as models and inspiration for the future. Benton himself denied the significance of modern art for his work, stating: "I wallowed in every cockeyed 'ism' that came along, and it took me ten years to get all that modernist dirt out of my system." In summarizing his work, he wrote: "I have a sort of inner conviction that . . . I have come to something that is in the image of America and the American people of my time."

The *Toussaint L'Ouverture Series*, by Jacob Lawrence, joined historical research with intensely personal memories of history lectures the artist had heard during his youth in Harlem (fig. 10-71). Lawrence's work communicates his brutal theme with immediacy: harshly abstract figures, sharp contrast of colors, and even the movement of the tall grass, which is waving like flames, add to the violence of the scene. Like other Social Realist artists in the United States during the 1930s and 1940s, Lawrence uses his work as a vehicle for protest, demonstrating a brutal historical reality. Discussing the purpose of his art in relation to social justice, Lawrence wrote:

Having no Negro history makes the Negro people feel inferior to the rest of the world. I don't see how a history of the United States can be written honestly without including the Negro. . . . We don't have a physical slavery, but an economic slavery. If these people, who were so much worse off than the people today, could conquer their slavery, we certainly can do the same thing.

10-70. Thomas Hart Benton. *Pioneer Days and Early Settlers.* 1935–36. Oil and egg tempera on linen mounted on panel, size of wall 25' x 14'2". State Capitol, Jefferson City, Missouri. Before receiving this important commission in his home state, Benton had received commissions for mural cycles at the New School for Social Research in New York City, in the library of the Whitney Museum of American Art, and for the State of Indiana's exhibit at the 1933 Chicago World's Fair. The Missouri cycle, which Benton called *A Social History of Missouri*, encompasses three walls; on this wall, Benton depicted early settlers, including a trader giving whiskey to a Native American in exchange for furs, the legend of Huck Finn and Jim with a paddleboat named *Sam Clemens,* and early construction that leads back to a view of later governmental structures. Benton's portrayal is not completely positive, as is seen in the smaller scenes below, with a cruel slave driver and the violent expulsion of the Mormons. The public and the Missouri legislature criticized these works for not being more idealistic, and Benton was accused of degrading his state's history and image. Commissioned by the Missouri legislature

© 1997 T. H. Benton and R. P. Benton Testamentary Trusts/VAGA, New York, NY

10-71. Jacob Lawrence. *Toussaint L'Ouverture Series, No. 10: The Cruelty of the Planters Led the Slaves to Revolt, 1776. These Revolts Kept Springing Up from Time to Time—Finally Came to a Head in the Rebellion.* 1937–38. Gouache on paper, 11 x 17". Amistad Research Center, Aaron Douglas Collection, Tulane University, New Orleans. The forty-one panels of Lawrence's *Toussaint L'Ouverture Series* tell how the hero, a Haitian slave named Toussaint L'Ouverture, freed his country from French rule during the late-eighteenth and early-nineteenth centuries. The republic of Haiti, founded by L'Ouverture, was the first black republic established in the Western Hemisphere.

PHOTOGRAPHY

10-72. Alfred Stieglitz. *Equivalent*. 1930. Chloride print. The Art Institute of Chicago
The Alfred Stieglitz Collection

Equivalent, by Alfred Stieglitz (1864–1946), is an evocative image; the moon and its light are diffused through clouds in the upper right, while below, separated by the diagonal thrust of a cloud, an impenetrable darkness enters the composition (fig. 10-72). The photograph was produced without staging or significant darkroom manipulation, but the emphasis is less on the representational quality of the image than on abstract patterns of light and dark to create a somber, pensive mood.

When Stieglitz began his *Equivalent* series in 1922, he was already an established artist. In 1902, he had broken away from the conservative posture of traditional photography to form the Photo-Secession Group. One year later, he founded *Camera Work*, a quarterly publication that stressed, with numerous illustrations, an ever-widening range of photographic innovation.

In 1905, Stieglitz founded an art gallery at 291 Fifth Avenue in New York City. "291," as the gallery was known, brought the art of the European avant-garde to the United States. Exhibitions included works by Cézanne, Brancusi, Picasso, and such American artists as Charles Demuth and Georgia O'Keeffe. In 1917, Stieglitz began to decrease his gallery and publication involvements to devote fuller attention to photog-

10-73. André Kertész. *Distortion No. 4.* 1933. Gelatin silver print. Estate of Kertész. Kertész's *Distortion* photographs, commissioned by a French magazine in 1933, were not published until 1976.

1930	**Stieglitz, *Equivalent***
1930	Sinclair Lewis wins Nobel Prize for literature for *Babbitt*
1930	First analog computer is placed in operation
1930	World population nears 2 billion

10-74. Margaret Bourke-White. *Fort Peck Dam*, photograph for the cover of the first issue of *Life* magazine, November 23, 1936. Bourke-White was one of the original staff photographers for *Life* magazine. During World War II, she became the first woman photographer to work with the U.S. armed forces. Commissioned by the editors of *Life* magazine

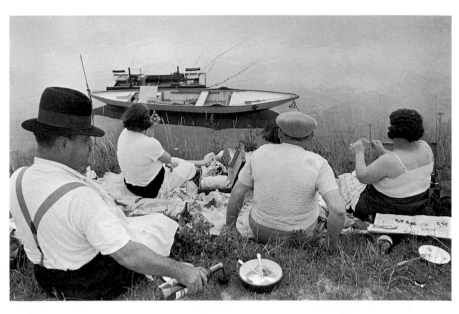

10-75. Henri Cartier-Bresson. *Sunday on the Banks of the Marne*. 1938. Gelatin silver print

raphy. Stieglitz's work and vision helped establish photography as an independent artistic medium.

An important advance in photography in the 1920s was the development of the hand-held, lightweight, 35 mm roll-film camera. No longer burdened by bulky equipment, the photographer now had a new freedom of mobility. One artist who took full advantage of this freedom was André Kertész (1894–1985). In 1933, Kertész, a leading Hungarian photojournalist working in France, created a series of photographs with figurative distortion reminiscent of expressionist tendencies (fig. 10-73) and Surrealism. Kertész achieved these effects by photographing models reflected in "fun house" mirrors with varied surfaces.

The cover story for the first issue of *Life* magazine was a photo essay by Margaret Bourke-White (1904–71) about a dam being constructed at Fort Peck, Montana (fig. 10-74). Her photographs revealed both the strength and the promise of industrial development, as is evident in her powerfully abstract compositions of the steel-and-concrete structure and in the dynamics of the lives of the men and women who were bringing the dam into existence.

The French photographer Henri Cartier-Bresson (b. 1908) has sought to communicate in his work what he termed "the decisive moment" in an image where overt activity uncovered a deeper psychological understanding. In *Sunday on the Banks of the Marne* (fig. 10-75), Cartier-Bresson has captured, in a summary manner, the activity of a picnic—wine is being poured and food eaten. From our viewpoint, we have joined the picnickers for lunch, but we can also observe, with some wit, how their corpulent bodies contrast with the sleek design of the boat. Cartier-Bresson believed that a photograph should seize both the scene in front of the eye and what the eye sees when it looks inward, into the self of the photographer.

SURREALISM

10-76. Salvador Dalí. *The Persistence of Memory*. 1931. Oil on canvas, 9^1/$_2$ x 13". The Museum of Modern Art, New York
Given anonymously. © 1996 Demart Pro Arte/Artists Rights Society (ARS), New York

In the hallucinatory world before our eyes (fig. 10-76), watches—sturdy, metallic timekeepers—grow limp and decay like organic refuse; one attracts a fly; ants converge on another. One watch has melted over a biomorphic form that bears a fantastically conceived profile portrait of the artist. A smooth, satiny beach gives onto a limitless expanse of mirror-smooth water abutted by cliffs. Within this landscape of stillness, the limp watches suggest the inevitable decay of the passing of time.

This painting, by Salvador Dalí (1904–89), succeeds in conveying its subconscious, dreamlike vision by the uncanny juxtaposition and fantastic manipulation of representational objects. This emphasis on the subconscious realm introduces us to Surrealism, a literary and artistic avant-garde movement that began in Europe in the early 1920s. The roots of Surrealism were the metaphysical paintings of De Chirico and the found-object constructions and collages of Dada (see pages 528 and 530). Dalí's fantasy conveys a frightening psychological oppression in part because its combination of unexpected elements eludes any obvious interpretation.

Surrealism was inexorably bound with the psychoanalytic theories of Sigmund Freud; we know, for example, that Dalí read Freud's writ-

10-77. André Masson. *Battle of Fishes*. 1927. Chalk, charcoal, conté crayon, and oil on canvas, 14¹/₄ x 28³/₄". The Museum of Modern Art, New York

James Thrall Soby Collection Bequest. © 1996 Artists Rights Society (ARS), New York/ADAGP, Paris

ings while he was a still a student in Madrid. André Breton, the French writer who authored the first *Surrealist Manifesto* in 1924, acknowledged Freud's revolutionary discoveries when, in defining *Surrealism*, he wrote:

> SURREALISM, n. Pure psychic automatism, by which it is intended to express verbally, in writing, or by any other means the real process of thought. Thought's dictation, in the absence of all control exercised by the reason and outside all aesthetic or moral preoccupations.

The Surrealist translation of the unconscious into visual form was realized in the figurative works of Dalí and René Magritte, where representational or fantastically conceived forms are juxtaposed within a spatial illusion.

The abstraction of *Battle of Fishes* (fig. 10-77), by André Masson (1896–1987), is the result of automatism, a concept related to Freud's use of "free association" to divulge the subconscious. Breton used the word *automatism* in his definition of Surrealism, and in describing the process for writing an automatist Surrealist composition, Breton suggested that you should "write quickly without any previously chosen subject, quickly enough not to dwell on, and not to be tempted to read over, what you have written." This process of "automatic" writing was viewed as a revelation of the subconscious. In art, lines or colors were quickly set down on a surface, without reference to a preconceived theme. The conscious mind would then associate these nonobjective marks with objective forms. In Masson's work, the ferocious battle among fishes that has evolved exhibits his intense anxieties about the brutality of nature, feelings that were born of the physical and mental wounds he received in World War I.

PABLO PICASSO, *GUERNICA*

10-78. Pablo Picasso. *Guernica.* May 1–June 4, 1937. Oil on canvas, 11'5$\frac{1}{2}$" x 25'5$\frac{3}{4}$". Museo Nacional Centro de Arte Reina Sofía, Madrid. Picasso placed the painting on extended loan to the Museum of Modern Art in New York for many years, stipulating that it be given to Spain and her people only when democracy was restored. The painting was returned to Spain in 1981. Commissioned by the Republican Government of Spain

© 1996 Estate of Pablo Picasso/ Artists Rights Society (ARS), New York

Despite the perplexity of highly abstract shapes, which owe a formal debt to Synthetic Cubism, the *Guernica* mural, inspired by the bombing of an innocent Spanish town during the civil war of 1936–39, achieves an immediate impact (fig. 10-78). An architectonically stable composition underlies the surface tumult, for the verticality of the two side figures, the woman with upraised arms to the right and the woman cradling the dead child on the left, acts to secure the central group, which is resolved in the shape of a triangle. This simplified geometric order imparts an underlying strength to the composition.

The restriction of the color palette to black, white, and values of gray and the newspaperlike lines across the body of the horse remind us of the reporting of disastrous events in newspapers. It was by reading such reports that Picasso learned of the disaster at Guernica (see map, page 486). Writing later,

the American painter Ad Reinhardt considered the *Guernica* a "design that diagrams our whole present dark age," and of the limited color range Picasso used, Reinhardt stated, "The dead have no color."

Picasso refused to elaborate on the particular intentions he invested in each figure, preferring to encourage the viewer to understand the work on an emotional, intuitive level. On the right and left sides of the composition, two women, shrieking in anguish with eyes transformed to the shape of tears, look toward the heavens, source of their pain and death. The figure on the left holding a dead child adapts the Pietà theme (see fig. 5-62) to this nightmare, while the woman to the right cries from the flames that have engulfed her house. Below her, another woman drags her mangled leg and, with arms outstretched, seems to be pleading for help. Above, an oil lamp, reminiscent of the light held by allegorical figures

of Truth and Liberty, is thrust into the chaos. This light, however, is overwhelmed by the harsh radiance from the bare electric bulb, added to the composition only in the final stages of painting (fig. 10-79). Previously, this area had represented the sun or an eye. The change to the electric light is most likely an allusion to technology, which, during the bombing of Guernica, was unleashed as a malevolent and destructive force.

In the central group, a horse has been lanced; its head is twisted back, and the pointed tongue becomes a silent scream of pain and accusation. Although the horse may symbolize the suffering of Spain, it also expresses the totality of a conflict that involves all of nature. The bull suggests brute power, perhaps in reference to Franco and fascism (see below). Below the horse are the dismembered remains of a fallen soldier. His hand, while still clutching a broken sword, also clings to a

1933   Books by Jewish and non-Nazi authors are burned in Germany
1933   Approximately 60,000 artists, writers, and musicians leave Germany
1937   Picasso, *Guernica*

10-79. Pablo Picasso. *Guernica.* Photograph of the painting on May 11, 1937, by Dora Maar. This is the first of seven photographs made of the work in progress. Many of the main themes are already established, but virtually all will be dramatically reworked. Note that at this early point defiance on the part of the dead warrior is expressed by his upraised arm and fist.

© 1996 Estate of Pablo Picasso/Artists Rights Society (ARS), New York

delicate flower, the only promise of hope in this image of suffering and death.

The brutal Spanish civil war was the result of conflicting political ideologies and of internal tensions that were centuries old. In 1931, the Bourbon monarchy, which had ruled Spain since 1700, was replaced by a republican government that promised social and economic reform, including the redistribution of land and the secularization of certain governmental functions controlled by the Church. Such reforms, which were aimed at countering the political power of wealthy landowners and the clergy, provoked the formation of conservative alliances. During the increasing civil disorder after the elections of 1936 (won by the republicans), General Francisco Franco, claiming allegiance to his nation rather than to any political group, led an insurrection that immersed Spain in civil war. Nazi Germany and Fascist Italy aided Franco, while the USSR assisted the leftist coalition, which included the Communists. The major Western democracies maintained an official position of neutrality, but many individuals supported the republican cause when the cruel reality of Franco's oppression became apparent. After three years and the loss of hundreds of thousands of lives, Franco established an authoritarian rule that continued until his death in 1975.

In January 1937, in the midst of the civil war, the republican government commissioned Picasso, who was living and working in France, to paint a mural for the Spanish Pavilion at the World's Fair scheduled to open in Paris that year. Picasso had yet to settle upon an exact theme when news of the events of April 26 reached him. On that day, Franco had used his Nazi allies to conduct the first "total" air raid. In what seems to have been an experiment in saturation bombing, the historic city of Guernica, a town of no strategic military significance, was bombarded for more than three hours. When Picasso learned of the bombing, he started to paint a work that would be an invective against both the particular event and the senseless brutality of conflict.

Picasso, whose republican sympathies had already been manifested in satirical etchings that were called the *Dream and Lie of Franco,* wrote:

> In the panel on which I am working which I shall call Guernica, and in all my recent works of art, I clearly express my abhorrence of the military caste which has sunk Spain into an ocean of pain and death.

The story is told that while viewing a photograph of *Guernica,* a Nazi official queried Picasso, "So it was you who did this?" The reply came sharply, "No, you did!"

SCULPTURE IN THE 1930S AND 1940S

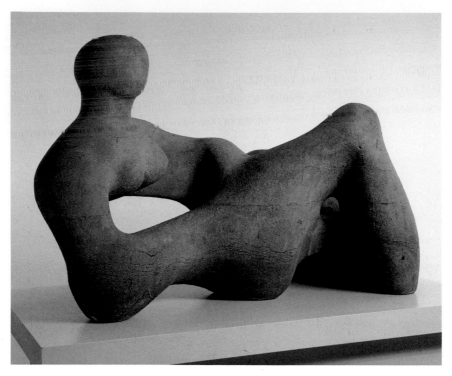

10-80. Henry Moore. *Recumbent Figure*. 1938. Gray-green Hornton stone, length about 54". Tate Gallery, London. Moore's sources for this style encompass not only modern European sculpture but also the powerfully abstract forms of African and pre-Hispanic art.

Reproduced by permission of the Henry Moore Foundation

*R*ecumbent Figure (fig. 10-80), by Henry Moore (1898–1986), is immediately recognizable as a reclining female figure—one of the traditional themes of Western art. Like many of its antecedents (see figs. 6-34, 6-35), it suggests a voluptuous figure. Although the positions of the head and breasts are evident and the figure is clearly propped up on one elbow, the torso below the breasts is an open cavity, and other forms suggest hips, a knee, and legs, without informing us of the exact pose. Moore's massive, simple forms also suggest the hills and gullies of a landscape. The sculpture interrelates with its environment through the powerful masses and unexpected openings that surround and mold space. Moore has written that

"sculpture in air is possible, where the stone contains only the hole, which is the intended and considered form." The interrelationships of the abstract forms, however, suggest the organic qualities of a living, breathing figure with a potential for movement. Moore never denies the dignity and beauty of the human body, and many of his figures are heroic in scale and in content.

During the 1930s and 1940s, sculptors' interest in abstraction took a number of forms. Henry Moore and Barbara Hepworth (1903–75) guided the development of British abstract art in the 1930s, but Hepworth's sculpture moved further into abstraction. In *Sculpture with Color (Oval Form)*, mass and space become integral elements in a com-

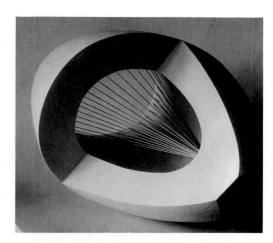

10-81. Barbara Hepworth. *Sculpture with Color (Oval Form), Pale Blue and Red.* 1943. Painted wood with strings, length 18". Private collection

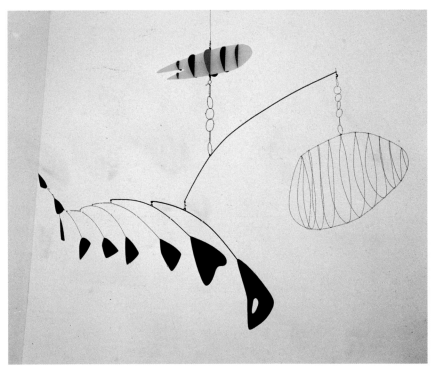

10-82. Alexander Calder. *Lobster Trap and Fish Tail.* 1939. Hanging mobile: painted steel wire and sheet aluminum, 8'6" x 9'6". The Museum of Modern Art, New York. Commissioned by the Advisory Committee for the stairwell of the museum

© 1996 Artists Rights Society (ARS), New York/ADAGP, Paris

position that simultaneously reveals itself as exterior form and interior structure (fig. 10-81). The contrast between exterior and interior is reinforced by color, while the taut strings relate the interior cavity to the exterior surface. Hepworth wrote that this structural relationship of color and string was associated with her perception of nature:

> The colour in the concavities plunged me into the depth of water, caves, or shadows deeper than the carved concavities themselves. The strings were the tension I felt between myself and the sea, the wind or the hills.

In a later comment, she elaborated on the significance of nature:

> In the contemplation of Nature we are perpetually renewed, our sense of mystery and our imagination is kept alive, and rightly understood, it gives us the power to project into a plastic medium some universal or abstract vision of beauty.

A new type of sculpture, named **mobiles** by the artist Marcel Duchamp, was shown at an exhibition in 1932 by the American artist Alexander Calder (1898–1976), who had first been trained as an engineer. Calder's earliest mobiles were moved by hand cranks or motors, but by 1932 they evolved into the lightweight, delicately balanced, suspended sculptures, moved by air currents, that have spawned so many popular variations. Although most of Calder's mobiles are completely abstract, the title of the present example suggests that the graceful movements of the curvilinear forms are a reference to swimming fish (fig. 10-82). In Calder's mobiles, the intimate relationship between form and space attains a new complexity as air currents move the forms slowly through space to create ever-new compositions.

The title that Isamu Noguchi (1904–88) gave his over-lifesize *Kouros* reveals that these abstract forms refer to a standing male figure (fig. 10-83), and we are encouraged to compare the sculpture with idealized

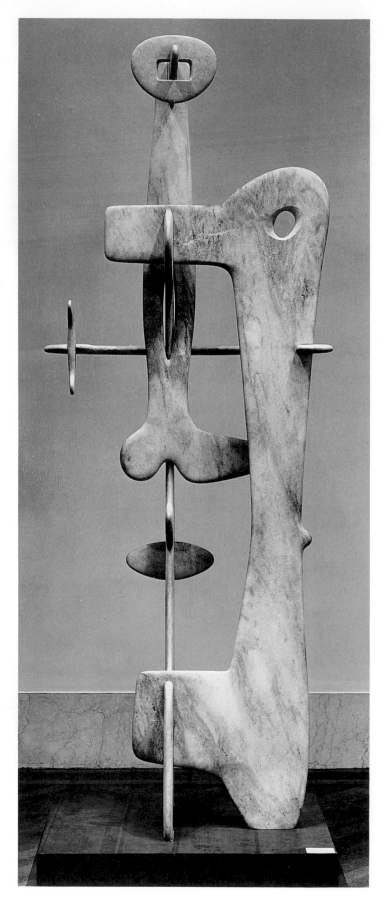

10-83. Isamu Noguchi. *Kouros.* 1944–45. Pink Georgia marble, height 9'9". The Metropolitan Museum of Art, New York. The slabs of stone are not fastened together, and the sculpture can be disassembled. Noguchi's involvement with Greek themes came in part from his collaboration as a set designer with Martha Graham, the innovative American dancer whose modern ballets were often based on mythic themes.

Fletcher Fund, 1953

10-84. Joseph Cornell. *Medici Slot Machine.* 1942. Construction, 13^{1}/$_{2}$ x 12 x 4^{1}/$_{4}$". Private collection. Cornell intended that his boxes be held in the hands and moved so that the loose elements could rattle and be rearranged.

ancient Greek statues of the sixth and fifth centuries BCE (see figs. 3-57, 3-59). As a modern artist, Noguchi reinvents the human form, substituting thin slabs of stone that interlock at right angles as support for the solid, rounded mass that is central to the body. The individual slabs, however, offer organic shapes and subtly rounded edges that are related to the flowing interpenetration of forms that characterizes a living human form. The frailty of forms and the instability of structure may be intended to convey the emotional anxiety Noguchi sensed in 1944–45, near the end of World War II, when he felt a need for "constant transfusions of human meaning into the encroaching void."

In his boxes, Joseph Cornell (1903–73) combines three-dimen-sional objects and two-dimensional charts, photographs, maps, and/or reproductions of works of art, all joined within shallow, glass-fronted enclosures. His unexpected juxtapositions of the concrete with the illusory can be poignant, enigmatic, and nostalgic. Each becomes a secluded and private universe intended to stimulate a viewer's imagination and memories. In speaking of a box that made a reference to soap bubbles, Cornell said, "Shadow boxes become poetic theaters or settings wherein are metamorphosed the elements of a childhood pastime."

In *Medici Slot Machine*, a reproduction of a sixteenth-century painting of a young nobleman is viewed through a glass with crossed lines, like a gunsight, perhaps to suggest the way that we target the past from a distance (fig. 10-84). A compass and a watch spring in the circular opening below suggest both space and time. The frame around the boy is covered with old maps of ancient Rome, perhaps a reference to the Renaissance interest in antiquity, while the ball, jacks, and game pieces below refer to the entertainments enjoyed by youth in all periods. These are at best suggestions of Cornell's meanings—the true modernity of Cornell's boxes lies in how they encourage individual, unconscious interpretations. Even the name enhances this quality of personal meaning. Like many modern artists, Cornell avoids reference to specific meaning by selecting names that increase a viewer's sense of wonderment and expectation.

INTERNATIONAL STYLE ARCHITECTURE

10-85. Philip Johnson. Glass House, New Canaan, Connecticut. 1949. The Glass House, the architect's own home, is secluded on a large estate, and privacy is not a problem. A brick cylinder placed asymmetrically provides a fireplace and the enclosure necessary for the bathroom and mechanical equipment. A counter forms the kitchen area, and a freestanding block of closets, not visible in this view, provides storage space.

Glass House, by Philip Johnson (b. 1906), is a satisfying combination of pure geometric form, subtle proportional relationships, and elegant materials (fig. 10-85)—an outstanding example of the modern architectural movement known as the International Style. This style, named by Johnson in 1932 in the context of an architectural exhibition held at the Museum of Modern Art in New York, is based on the refined glass box. It was expressed as early as the 1920s in works by the German architect Ludwig Mies van der Rohe (1886–1969), who later became the director of the Bauhaus (see page 535). Mies emigrated to the United States in 1937 and became a citizen in 1944. The International Style only came to full fruition after World War II, when Mies was commissioned to create a number of works, including skyscrapers in Chicago and New York and an entire campus for the Illinois Institute of Technology in Chicago. These popularized the style and led to its adaptation throughout the Western world. By the 1960s, virtually every Western capital had many metal and glass skyscrapers.

Even while it was under construction, the Seagram Building was recognized as an especially elegant and impressive modern structure (fig. 10-86). Mies's choice of materials reveals his goals of harmony and elegance, for the exposed structural I beams are composed of bronze that exactly matches the amber-tinted glass. The building is tall and wide when seen from the front, but its relative thinness gives it a soaring refinement. The proportions of the design are based on a simple modular system much like the satisfying Early Renaissance architecture of Brunelleschi (see fig. 5-35). The open lower stories, where there are a bank of elevators and a small glassed lobby, lighten the structure and help establish the proportional integrity of the whole. The building in every way reflects Mies's personal motto, "Less is more." Because it occupies less than one-half of the site, the building does not have to conform to the restrictions of New York City's

1949	**Johnson, Glass House**
1949	U.S. minimum wage raised from 40 to 75 cents an hour
1949	George Orwell, *1984*
1949	People's Republic of China is established
1950	World population exceeds 2.5 billion

set-back law, which explains the staggered rooflines of so many Manhattan buildings. The structure is placed on a large plaza that sets it off as a gigantic sculptural form.

The glass box represents a pure ideological statement without historical precedent or references, but in its materials it is a product of the machine culture. Its origins lie in mass production, prefabrication, and the glorification of the precision of the machine. Even more importantly, it shares in the utopian ideals that had inspired de Stijl (see page 532), one of its sources; as pure architecture, expressing the Platonic ideal with thoroughly modern materials, it shares in the idealism of much twentieth-century thought.

Despite the purist, reductive beauty of Johnson's Glass House and Mies's Seagram Building, the International Style quickly reached a dead end. The glass box is an impersonal object, and as cities all over the world became crowded with such buildings, many people felt that their environment had become a cold and sterile place in which to live and work. Because the emphasis is on purity of design at the expense of function, such buildings—all of which look similar—demonstrate little interest in the needs of the client or of the people who work in them. In their modern purity, they ignore the subtle relationships to site, climate, or local architectural tradition that were crucial for so many earlier works of architecture.

10-86. Mies van der Rohe. Seagram Building, New York. 1956–58. The International Style glass-box skyscraper became popular with corporate America because it projected a modern, up-to-date image for the business it housed. Few buildings in this style, however, have the sophisticated elegance of the Seagram Building. Philip Johnson, who assisted Mies in the design of the building, was largely responsible for the creation of the interior spaces. Commissioned by Joseph E. Seagram and Sons Corporation, under the advisement of Phyllis Bronfman Lambert

ABSTRACT EXPRESSIONISM AND POST-PAINTERLY ABSTRACTION

10-87. Jackson Pollock. *Convergence.* 1952. Oil on canvas, 8 x 13'. Albright-Knox Art Gallery, Buffalo, New York
Gift of Seymour H. Knox, 1956. © 1996 Pollock-Krasner Foundation/Artists Rights Society (ARS), New York

My painting does not come from the easel. I hardly ever stretch my canvas before painting. I prefer to tack the unstretched canvas to the hard wall or the floor. I need the resistance of a hard surface. On the floor I am more at ease. I feel nearer, more a part of the painting, since this way I can walk around it, work from the four sides and literally be in the painting. . . .

I continue to get further away from the usual painter's tools . . . I prefer sticks, trowels, knives and dripping fluid paint or a heavy impasto with sand, broken glass, and other foreign matter added.

When I am in my painting, I'm not aware of what I'm doing. It is only after a sort of "get acquainted" period that I see what I have been about. I have no fears about making changes, destroying the image, etc., because the painting has a life of its own. I try to let it come through. It is only when I lose contact with the painting that the result is a mess. Otherwise there is pure harmony, an easy give and take, and the painting comes out well. (Jackson Pollock, 1947)

Convergence bursts forth with the dynamism of exuberant colors and interpenetrating layers of undulating paint (fig. 10-87). This weblike mass of colors and rhythms offers a new and provocative approach to painting; it records the process by which the artist's unconscious has been laid bare. Pollock's method of painting is derived from Surrealist automatism, and while creating these innovative works, Pollock, often described as being in a trance-like state and moving with the grace of a dancer, aggressively flung paint onto the canvas, the action of his arm being guided by his unconscious (fig. 10-88). But unlike Surrealist automatism, Pollock did not consciously complete the image to bring it within the realm of objectivity. The painting communicates a raw, expressive energy.

But what are we to make of all this? What does it mean for us to confront this painterly record of an artist's unconscious? Surrealism, one of the roots of Abstract Expressionism (defined below), was bound to the psychoanalytical investigations of Freud, but Carl Jung's concept of a "collective unconscious" is equally significant here. As Pollock has exposed his human unconscious, we should be able to draw meaning intuitively from the painting, as its large scale, abstract rhythms, and intense colors meet an unconscious response in us.

Pollock's drip paintings exemplify one style within Abstract Expressionism, a movement that, beginning in New York after World War II, thrust the United States into the avant-garde of Western art. As we have seen, the roots of Abstract Expressionism were grounded in the psychoanalytical theories of Freud and Jung and in Surrealism. During the 1930s, with the rise of Nazi Germany casting an increasingly foreboding shadow over Europe, many leading European artists came to the United States. The impact of their work and their presence was felt in a major 1936 exhibition of Dada and Surrealism at New York's Museum of Modern Art. European artists, some of whom opened their studios as teachers, found a particularly responsive audience among a younger generation of American artists who, bound with a collective American identity resulting from the common hard-

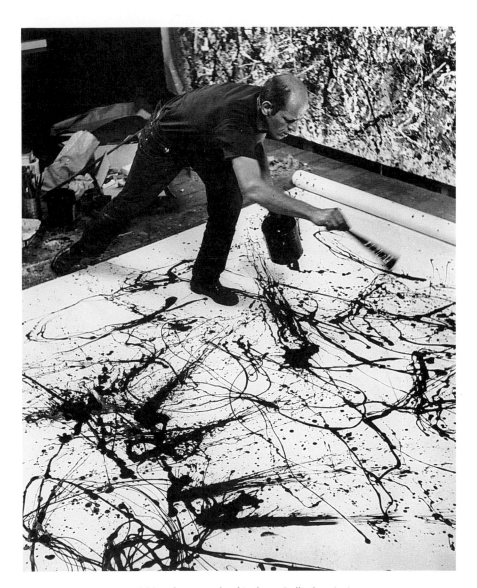

10-88. Photograph of Jackson Pollock painting

ships of the Depression, were searching for new avenues of expression. With Surrealism illuminating one of the avenues, these American artists assumed control of the avant-garde in the late 1940s.

The term *Abstract Expressionism* had been used earlier in the century to designate the nonobjective paintings of Kandinsky, but it was resurrected in 1946 to describe the works of a group of American painters centered in New York (these artists are also sometimes referred to as the New York School). What joined these artists was not a unified style but a common attitude that stressed the unique individuality of each creative act. These artists were also familiar with the

10-89. Mark Rothko. *White and Greens in Blue.* 1957. Oil on canvas, 8'6" x 7'. Private collection, New York
© 1996 Kate Rothko-Prizel & Christopher Rothko/Artists Rights Society (ARS), New York

philosophy of Existentialism, with its emphasis on the importance of the experience of the present moment (see pages 490–91); their interest in the actual techniques of creation are an important aspect of the movement.

Within the stylistic differences of the Abstract Expressionist painters, we can discern two fundamental ap-

proaches; one, termed Action Painting by the critic Harold Rosenberg in 1952, was a free, gestural expression of paint on the canvas, as demonstrated by the paintings of Jackson Pollock. Another mode, exemplified by the work of Mark Rothko (1903–70), is referred to as Color Field painting. It displayed limited areas of color within simple and controlled,

nonobjective compositions, leaving the shapes and colors to communicate an aesthetic and/or emotional experience.

Rothko, who arrived at this mode of expression after experimenting with the human form and with Surrealist biomorphic compositions, always insisted that paintings must be about something,

10-90. Morris Louis. *Saraband.* 1959. Acrylic resin on canvas, 8'5¹/8" x 12'5". Solomon R. Guggenheim Museum, New York. The title of the painting is derived from a stately European court dance of the seventeenth and eighteenth centuries. This abstract work would have been titled after it was completed. Perhaps the repeated rhythmic patterns and flowing shapes of the composition suggested this title to the artist.

that they must have a strong content:

> It is a widely accepted notion among painters that it does not matter what one paints as long as it is well painted. This is the essence of academicism. There is no such thing as a good painting about nothing. We assert that subject matter is crucial and only that subject matter is valid which is tragic and timeless.

In Rothko's *White and Greens in Blue* (fig. 10-89), horizontal planes stacked vertically carry associations of nature, such as landscape and sky, while also establishing a hierarchical order. The interplay of these elements is joined to an emotive use of color. We draw a melancholic sensation from the sobriety of the colors. The densely darkened green rectangles that weigh down the bottom rectangle of white seem to convey unconsciously the suppression of hope.

Rothko, believing in the evocative nature of his paintings, became increasingly sensitive to charges that his work lacked content, that it was only an exercise in color relationships. An interviewer once posed the question of content to Rothko, who replied:

> I'm interested in expressing only basic human emotions—tragedy, ecstasy, doom, and so on—and the fact that lots of people break down and cry when confronted with my pictures shows that I communicate these basic human emotions. . . . The people who weep before my pictures are having the same religious experience I had when I painted them, and if you, as you say, are moved only by their color relationships, then you miss the point.

The development of Abstract Expressionism provoked the exploration of new techniques. Both Pollock and Rothko experimented by staining raw or unprepared artists' canvas with highly liquid acrylic paint, a technique that produced different effects from the traditional application of brushed paint. Among the artists who adopted the resulting style, which was named Post-Painterly Abstraction by the art critic Clement Greenberg, were Helen Frankenthaler (see fig. 10-13) and Morris Louis (1912–62). In creating *Saraband*, Louis poured acrylic resin onto the canvas and then inclined it at different angles as the paint flowed over and soaked into the canvas (fig. 10-90). The result is a luminous painting composed of rhythmic color veils whose transparency and overlapping forms deny traditional figure/ground distinctions. The staining technique negates the autographic movements of the artist that had been so important in Abstract Expressionism. In *Saraband*, color and canvas are wed in a planarity whose only texture is that of the canvas itself. Even the white color of the canvas becomes an important element of the composition. By questioning the roles of picture plane and illusory space, the artists of this group achieved a reductive purity in abstract painting.

LE CORBUSIER

10-91. Le Corbusier. Exterior, Nôtre-Dame-du-Haut, Ronchamp, near Belfort, France. 1950–54. Le Corbusier, "the crowlike one," is the nickname of the French architect Charles-Édouard Jeanneret. Nôtre-Dame-du-Haut is built in the foothills of the Alps, on the edge of a high promontory overlooking the town of Ronchamp. It marks the site of an earlier chapel, destroyed in World War II, that had displayed a miracle-working statue of the Madonna now incorporated into the new structure. In ancient times, this area had been sanctified by a pagan shrine. An outside altar and pulpit are used when pilgrimage crowds become too large to be accommodated within the chapel. The building is constructed of reinforced concrete. Commissioned by Canon Lucien Ledeur of Besançon, who hoped the building would help initiate a renaissance in church art and architecture

In its highly personal, nonrepeating forms, the chapel at Ronchamp by Le Corbusier (1887–1965) offers a dramatic, individualized alternative to the geometric purity of the contemporary International Style in architecture. Like the great French Gothic cathedrals, this structure sets out to astonish and move us by its unexpected and mysterious form and structure (figs. 10-91, 10-92). The sweeping roof seems thin and billowing, like an air-filled sail. Although the roof is made of natural brown-gray cement, its detachment from the thick, curving walls below gives it a particular lightness. The sail-like roof of Nôtre-Dame-du-Haut creates a relationship with nature, for it seems to respond to the winds that sweep the promontory site. The structural system is based on nature, for Le Corbusier was inspired by a crab

10-92. Le Corbusier. Axonometric projection of Nôtre-Dame-du-Haut

1950–54	**Le Corbusier, Nôtre-Dame-du-Haut**
1951	U.S. population reaches 153 million
1952	First hydrogen device is exploded
1952	First pocket-sized transistor radios

10-93. Le Corbusier. Interior, Nôtre-Dame-du-Haut. The interior, approximately 43 x 82', has pews for only about fifty worshipers.

shell he picked up on a beach.

On the interior (fig. 10-93), the darkness and the thick, roughly textured walls suggest a mysterious cave, while a slit of light between wall and ceiling and the sagging shape of the ceiling itself reinforce the billowing sail effect of the exterior. The thick wall is pierced by irregularly sized and spaced windows filled with stained glass on which traditional religious symbols (a dove, the sun) and phrases ("Marie," "Blessed among Women") have been painted. Like sculpture in the round, the building forces us to move to understand it, and as we explore the structure, three chapels—mysteriously lit by hidden windows in towers—are discovered. The building becomes an adventure and, for some, a journey of personal religious discovery. In discussing the building, Le Corbusier called it "totally free architecture," describing it as "sculpture 'of an acoustical nature,' that is to say projecting afar the effect of its forms and, in return, receiving the pressure of the surrounding spaces. The key is light and light illuminates shapes and shapes have emotional power."

FILM IN JAPAN

10-94. Yasujiro Ozu (director). *Tokyo Story.* 1953. Shukichi (the father) and Tomi (the mother). Script by Kogo Noda and Yasujiro Ozu; photographed by Yuharu Atsuta. The running time of the film is 135 minutes.

Tokyo Story, by the filmmaker Yasujiro Ozu (1903–63), was released on November 3, 1953. Popular in Japan, it was also one of very few Japanese films of this period to be shown abroad. The film focuses on a modern, middle-class Japanese family, the relationships among its members, and how they are affected by events in their everyday lives. Ozu's message concerns how events gradually lead to the dissolution of the traditional family structure that is so important in Japanese life and society. Rather than stressing the cause of domestic turbulence, he emphasized its effect on individual family members. Incidents in everyday life gradually reveal the nature of the characters. These confrontations of family members within the context of daily life are subtle, familiar, and easy for Japanese as well as Western audiences to appreciate. The subject crossed cultural boundaries and allowed viewers in the West a glimpse of Japan not common in the postwar period.

Produced in the context of war weariness and disillusion, this film appeared only one year after the end of the Allied occupation of Japan. The reforms carried out during the postwar period were drastic. Land-reform programs had made owner-farmers out of tenants, the new "peace constitution" had defined the emperor as a "symbol of state" instead of a source of sovereignty, and a long bill of rights gave certain privileges to individuals. The abandonment of war as an "instrument of national policy" meant the renouncement of any buildup of weapons and armies. The civil code was revised in accordance with the sentiments of the new democratic constitution, and as a result the traditional powers of the family head, which were built into the old code, were supposed to disappear. Such reforms had a profound effect on both national policy and everyday life. Made in the midst of these sweeping reforms, *Tokyo Story* reveals the inevitable and unresolved conflict between the demands of life in the modern industrial era and traditional Japanese cultural mores and values, especially those centered around family life. The film examines that conflict thematically and cinematically.

Tokyo Story is integrated around three elements: story, theme, and cinematography. The story is a complex three-part tale that focuses on the parents' relationships with their children. The first section is set in the town of Onomichi, where the old couple lives. The middle section sees the parents at a reunion with their children in Tokyo. Both their son and daughter are busy with their own lives and send the parents off to a hot-springs resort, ostensibly as a treat but actually to get rid of them. The only kindness they

10-95. Yasujiro Ozu (director). *Tokyo Story.* The family at the funeral of the mother

experience in Tokyo is found with the widow of their third son, who had been killed in the war. The third section, back in Onomichi, depicts the death and funeral of the mother. The children are called to her deathbed, but she is so ill that she cannot recognize them. The children hurry away after the funeral, but the daughter-in-law stays behind to see the old father settled in. Then she, too, must return to Tokyo, leaving the father in the empty house to contemplate the lonely years that lie ahead.

Ozu's central theme is how one comes to terms with the dissolution of the family and, ultimately, with death. Three alternative solutions are examined, each described in the reactions of the children. Several of the characters are resigned and accept these conditions with sensitivity. Others lack compassion, are indifferent, and regard separation of the family as inevitable. The youngest refuses to accept the dissolution and tries to shore up the family once again. These choices are presented as complementary to one another, and dynamic conflict never arises. Resolution is never reached, and the theme of transience triumphs. The psychological tension created by this thematic and visual structure keeps the viewer aware of the conflicts inherent in modern life.

Given his attachment to daily family scenes and events, Ozu sets a slow pace that echoes the unfolding of life in the everyday world. The camera is literally fixed at the eye level of someone seated on the floor on a straw tatami mat in a traditional Japanese house. He uses only three standard shots—long, medium, and close-up—repeating them again and again. The medium shot is the basic unit, and the scenery in each frame is presented with austere formal symmetry (fig. 10-94). Although these standard shots are repeated, they frame the subtle psychological and emotional relationships of the moment (fig. 10-95).

Both the framing and the pacing of the film confirm the aesthetic standards that had been held for centuries among Japanese artists and support Ozu's reputation as the most traditional of Japan's filmmakers. His visual and thematic sensibilities—an emphasis on simplicity and directness and an interest in the notion of the transience or impermanence in life—closely resemble those of Zen artists. His black-and-white films have been compared to Zen temple gardens, where simple, unadorned arrangements of dry rocks and raked sand are meant to elicit complex responses (see fig. 6-73). Ozu's tale, told in the modern medium of film and focused on a problem common to the modern world, expresses unmistakably traditional Japanese values.

THE RETURN TO THE OBJECT: JASPER JOHNS AND ROBERT RAUSCHENBERG

10-96. Jasper Johns. *Flag.* 1954–55 (dated on reverse 1954). Encaustic, oil, and collage on fabric mounted on plywood, 42^1/$_4$ x 60^5/$_8$".
The Museum of Modern Art, New York

Gift of Philip Johnson in honor of Alfred H. Barr, Jr. © 1997 Jasper Johns/VAGA, New York, NY

Flag (fig. 10-96), by Jasper Johns (b. 1930), strikes us as a blatantly representational image, even more so when we consider that it was created in the mid-1950s, when various modes of nonobjectivity ruled the avant-garde in painting. The composition is clearly and intentionally recognizable, but in place of the solid colored shapes of red, white, and blue that we expect in a flag, Johns has substituted a painterly texture whose thinness in places reveals collage elements underneath. Johns's painting is not a flag of the United States. The artist has carefully manipulated the surface to emphasize the reality of the painting as a mixed-medium work of paint and collage. This artistic transformation is intended to drain the image of its immediate symbolic content. Johns thus forces us to realize that the painting itself is first and foremost a composition of shapes and colors—an object.

During the early 1950s, a group of artists reacted to the nonobjective aesthetic that had dominated the American avant-garde with Abstract Expressionism and Hard-Edge painting. Artists such as Johns and Robert Rauschenberg (b. 1925) began to incorporate, in the most literal of ways at times, representational imagery and recognizable objects in their work. This served at least two purposes: It avoided the sometimes uncomfortable defensiveness viewers felt with nonobjective art while simultaneously offering the image, or its combination with actual "found objects," as a given fact of our experience, without reference to symbolic comment. There

1954

1953	Eisenhower is inaugurated as president of the U.S.
1954–55	**Johns, *Flag***
1955	Tennessee Williams, *Cat on a Hot Tin Roof*

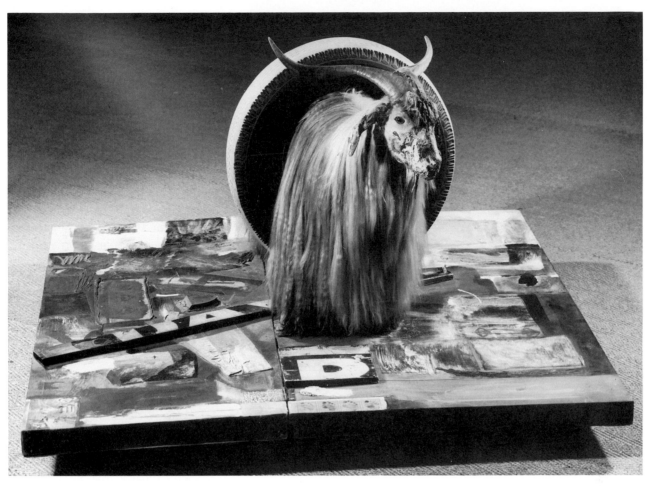

10-97. Robert Rauschenberg. *Monogram*. 1959. Construction, 3'6" x 6' x 6'. Moderna Museet, Stockholm

© 1997 Robert Raushenberg/VAGA, New York, NY

is no precise name for this artistic activity of Johns and Rauschenberg in the mid-1950s. It is sometimes referred to as Neo-Dada, but although there is a similarity to Dada in the use of found objects, the artistic transformation of common images and objects and the different philosophical context of the 1950s make these works distinct from earlier Dada.

In *Monogram* (fig. 10-97), Robert Rauschenberg attached a stuffed Angora goat that had a used tire around its midsection to a base that joined collage elements with broad, gestural strokes of paint. Rauschenberg referred to these works as "com-bines," for they associated elements of life with those of art in a "matter of fact" manner that was inspired by the avant-garde musical compositions of John Cage (see page 491). In the words of Rauschenberg:

Any incentive to paint is as good as any other. There is no poor subject.

Painting is always strongest when in spite of composition, color, etc., it appears as a fact, or an inevitability, as opposed to a souvenir or arrangement.

Painting relates to both art and life. Neither can be made. (I try to act in the gap between the two.)

A pair of socks is no less suitable to make a painting with than wood, nails, turpentine, oil, and fabric.

A canvas is never empty.

Amid the abstraction of the American avant-garde, these works of Johns and Rauschenberg emphasized the literal role of the object in the work of art.

HARD-EDGE AND OP ART

10-98. Josef Albers. *Homage to the Square: Affectionate.* 1954. Oil on canvas, 31⁷/₈ x 31⁷/₈". Musée National d'Art Moderne, Centre National d'Art et de Culture Georges Pompidou, Paris

© 1996 The Josef and Anni Albers Foundation/Artists Rights Society (ARS), New York

The colors in my paintings are juxtaposed for various and changing effects. They are to challenge or to echo each other, to support or oppose one another. The contrasts, respectively boundaries, between them may vary from soft to hard touches, may mean pull and push besides clashes, but also embracing, intersecting, penetrating.

Despite an even and mostly opaque application, the colors will appear above or below each other, in front or behind, or side by side on the same level. (Josef Albers, c. 1964)

Affectionate (fig. 10-98) is one of a series of paintings of virtually identical composition by Josef Albers (1888–1976). In all these works, square planes of color are set within larger square planes. Differences of color lead to varying perceptions of spatial illusion created without reference to representational forms. In this painting, the red square of the center appears suspended in advance of the darker, burgundy-colored square behind. This spatial configuration, however, is confounded by the lighter colors of the outer two squares, creating a complicated spatial illusion.

Albers, who studied and then taught at the Bauhaus, moved to the United States in 1933. His preference for controlled, geometric compositions derives from the Bauhaus design aesthetic. Early in his career, Albers studied the process of how we perceive and understand illusionism in painting through a series of works that created spatial illusions with nonrepresentational, geometric elements. Albers's studies continued throughout his career, culminating in a series of paintings in the 1950s titled *Homage to the Square*. In the United States, generations of artists were influenced by his teaching and his works.

The term *Hard-Edge Abstraction* was coined in 1958 to indicate a type of abstract painting whose shapes met in clearly defined edges. In the 1960s, Frank Stella (b. 1936) began to work with a series of shaped canvases that broke the rectangular format traditional for paintings. In *Empress of India* (fig. 10-99), the angular outward movement of the lines seems to have determined the boundaries, or shape, of the canvas. To Stella, the destruction of the traditional pictorial format opened to the viewer a greater understanding of the painting as a physical object—a support with colors attached. As Stella said in 1966:

> I always get into arguments with people who want to retain the old values in painting—the humanistic values they always find on the canvas. My painting is based on the fact that only what can be seen is there. It is really an object. . . . All I want anyone to get out of

10-99. Frank Stella. *Empress of India.* 1965. Metallic powder in polymer emulsion paint on canvas, 6'5" x 18'8". The Museum of Modern Art, New York

Gift of S.I. Newhouse, Jr. © 1996 Frank Stella/Artists Rights Society (ARS), New York

my paintings, and all I ever get out of them is the fact that you can see the whole idea without any confusion. What you see is what you see.

Drift 2 (fig. 10-100), by Bridget Riley (b. 1931), exemplifies another movement from the 1960s known as Op art, short for Optical art. It was a descendant of Albers's nonobjective illusory compositions and Hard-Edge Abstraction. Its medium is **emulsion**, a liquid mixture in which one of the elements does not mix with the others but remains suspended in minute droplets. Although *Drift 2* is a flat canvas, its pattern is composed so that it seems to surge and undulate before our eyes. This illusion of movement, however, is dependent on our perception of the optical effects of pattern. Op art questions the very process by which we see and understand.

10-100. Bridget Riley. *Drift 2.* 1966. Emulsion on canvas, 7'7^1/$_2$" x 7'5^1/$_2$". Albright-Knox Art Gallery, Buffalo, New York

POP ART

10-101. Richard Hamilton. *Just What Is It That Makes Today's Homes So Different, So Appealing?* 1956. Collage, 10¼ x 9¾". Kunsthalle, Tübingen, Germany. Hamilton's collage was part of a 1956 London exhibition titled "This Is Tomorrow."

"Popular (designed for mass audience); Transient (short-term solution); Expendable (easily forgotten); Low Cost; Mass Produced; Young (aimed at Youth); Witty; Sexy; Gimmicky; Glamorous; Big Business." These words were used by the British artist Richard Hamilton (b. 1922) to describe Pop art. Hamilton's collage *Just What Is It That Makes Today's Homes So Different, So Appealing?* was both a visual manifesto and a prophetic statement of Pop art (fig. 10-101). The inspiration for Pop art was found in the commercialism that developed, particularly in the United States, after World War II. Hamilton's work engages us on different levels; the almost-nude figures

"update" the tradition of the nude in Western art, yet here they also represent a modern couple and they remind us of one of the rules of advertising—sex sells. They are surrounded by the conveniences and products of modern life, while the "fine arts" include a comic book as a framed picture and a canned ham as a table sculpture. The collage is laced with witticisms, including the use of the word *pop* on the Tootsie Roll wrapper and a portrait of John Ruskin, a conservative nineteenth-century British art critic. Yet within this environment of commercially produced images and intellectual puns, we are greeted with more profound considerations. The ceiling design is actually a photo of the

earth taken from space, and the "pattern" of the rug is really a photograph of densely packed humanity on a beach.

In the United States, the literal objectivity of artists like Johns and Rauschenberg (see pages 562–63) assisted in the development of Pop art. *As I Opened Fire*, by Roy Lichtenstein (b. 1923), is fashioned after a drawing in an out-of-date adventure comic book that the artist has blown up to an enormous size (fig. 10-102). The expression of the thoughts of the pilot across the top and the emblazoned *BRAT!* are a natural adjunct to the bold and simple style of the planes and blazing guns. The strong areas of flat color, contained by heavy black outlines, are in places created by enlarged patterns of dots inspired by the process used to print color illustrations in comic books and newspapers. Lichtenstein thus draws our attention not only to the overtly melodramatic imagery of the comic book, itself a representative subject of post–World War II culture, but also to the processes by which images are created for mass consumption.

Pop art celebrated objects and ideas that were not only familiar but also banal in their content. Nowhere was the habitual repetition of commercialization felt more fully than in the works of Andy Warhol (see fig. 10-10), who wrote, "The reason I'm painting this way is that I want to be a machine, and I feel that whatever I do and do machine-like is what I want to do." Many of Warhol's images were silk-screened by assistants at his workshop, The Factory, suggesting an equation between the processes of art and consumer production. But if Warhol's rows upon rows of Coke bottles, Campbell soup cans, images of Marilyn Monroe, or

1956   Hamilton, *Just What Is It . . . ?*
1956   Fidel Castro begins campaign to oust Cuban dictator Batista
1957   Leonard Bernstein's musical *West Side Story* opens in New York

10-102. Roy Lichtenstein. *As I Opened Fire.* 1964. Magna on canvas, each panel 5'8" x 4'8". Stedelijk Museum, Amsterdam

© Roy Lichtenstein

accident scenes are born from an aesthetic numbness produced by the commercial environment, they also communicate how we are in danger of becoming unfeeling "products" within an industrialized environment. American Pop art had an international impact, and even influenced young artists working in China (see pages 592–93).

In the realm of public sculpture, Pop art overturned the traditional values that had been associated with monumental sculpture in public spaces. Claes Oldenburg (b. 1929) altered the scale or texture of commonplace, manufactured objects (fig. 10-103). The recent installation of groups of scattered shuttlecocks on the lawns on both sides of a museum in Kansas City adds a playful yet thought-provoking contrast to the classically inspired design of the building and its ostensibly serious purpose as a repository for great art. Oldenburg once remarked that "The important thing about humor is that it opens people. They relax their guard and you can get your serious intention across."

10-103. Claes Oldenburg and Coosje van Bruggen. Shuttlecocks (detail, one of four). 1994. Aluminum and fiberglass-reinforced plastic, painted with polyurethane enamel; each 17'10¼" high. Each shuttlecock weighs approximately 5,500 pounds. The Nelson-Atkins Museum of Art, Kansas City, Missouri. The artists found many associations between the shuttlecock form and the Western location of this commission, including the visual analogy to Native American feathered headdresses. Commissioned by the Nelson-Atkins Museum of Art and the Morton I. Sosland Family

Purchase: acquired through the generosity of the Sosland Family. © Claes Oldenburg/Coosje van Bruggen

10-104. Robert Frank. *Trolley, New Orleans,* published in *The Americans*. 1958. Gelatin silver print, 7^1/2 x 8^1/2". The Art Institute of Chicago

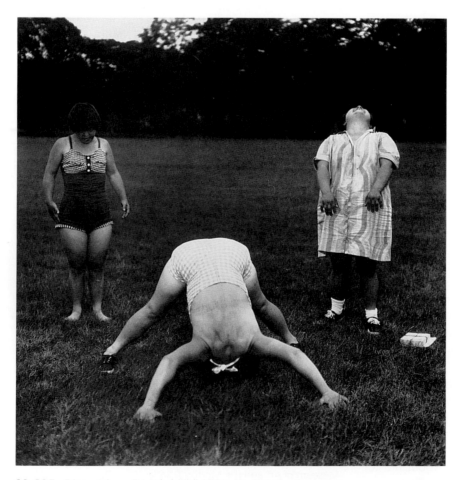

10-105. Diane Arbus. *"Untitled (6)."* 1970–71. Gelatin silver print
Copyright © The Estate of Diane Arbus, 1972. Courtesy, Robert Miller Gallery, New York

10-106. Jerry N. Uelsmann. *Untitled.* 1984.
Photograph
Courtesy of the artist

This photograph of a trolley in New Orleans by Robert Frank (b. 1924) has the appearance of a common snapshot (fig. 10-104). The image is at an angle to the picture plane, yet the effect is precisely calculated. The windows create a grid pattern that formally separates the people, who engage our attention. The formal divisions caused by the windows reinforce the apparent psychological separateness of the people; they do not communicate with each other. Frank's photograph is a poignant statement both of human alienation and of segregation in the American South during the 1950s.

Frank, who was born in Switzerland and came to the United States in 1946, traveled thousands of miles throughout the United States, armed with his 35mm camera, in 1955 and 1956. His photographic essay *The Americans*, which demonstrated the vigor of a new photographic aesthetic that revealed the reality often hidden behind the facade of commercial glamour in the postwar United States, had an enormous impact on American photographers. His new "snapshot aesthetic" is one of a number of developments that have distinguished photography since World War II.

We see a similar approach in the work of Diane Arbus (1923–71). Like Frank, she worked in fashion photography. In the late 1950s, she turned toward a more introspective use of the medium. Arbus's photograph, taken at a home for developmentally disabled women, is both disturbing and compelling (fig. 10-105). Arbus takes us into a realm that is too often ignored. She once commented, "I really believe there are things which nobody would see unless I photographed them."

The works of Frank and Arbus are "straight" photographs; the image has not been altered by extensive darkroom manipulation. Artistic and technical creativity in the darkroom, however, has led other artists to unexpected and even surreal results. Jerry Uelsmann (b. 1934), for example, has written that "for me the darkroom functions as a research laboratory." Uelsmann's photograph (fig. 10-106) was created through the use of multiple enlargers and exposures to a sheet of photographic paper. By masking parts of images on the easels of different enlargers and exposing the same piece of photographic paper on one easel and then another, Uelsmann constructs photographs of composite images. Uelsmann's photographs often reach to our subconscious in a surrealist manner; here, for example, three stoic faces from an ancient Roman grave sculpture and three footprints on a beach remind us of the transitory nature of life. The aesthetic and technical achievements of recent photographers have helped us appreciate a new and far-reaching potential in photography. Much of their work creatively denies the popular axiom that "photographs don't lie."

CONCEPTUAL, PERFORMANCE, INSTALLATION, AND VIDEO ART

10-107. Joseph Kosuth. *One and Three Chairs.* 1965. Wooden folding chair, photographic copy of a chair, and photographic enlargement of a dictionary definition of a chair; chair 32³/₈ x 14⁷/₈ x 20⁷/₈" (82 x 37.8 x 53 cm); photo panel, 36 x 24¹/₈" (91.5 x 61.1 cm); text panel, 24 x 24¹/₈" (61 x 61.3 cm). The Museum of Modern Art, New York
Larry Aldrich Foundation Fund. © 1996 Joseph Kosuth/Artists Rights Society (ARS), New York

One and Three Chairs (fig. 10-107), by Joseph Kosuth (b. 1945), informs us of three different realities. First, there is the reality of the folding chair placed between a full-scale photograph of the same chair and a printed definition of chair taken from a dictionary. The photograph is a second reality, but it bears an illusory image of the chair. Finally, the definition communicates a verbal description of a chair. The idea that we form from the definition exists in our minds and might therefore be termed a conceptual reality. *One and Three Chairs* presents the actuality, the image, and the idea of a chair, thus demonstrating the relationship between an object and communicative methods of signifying that object.

Kosuth's emphasis on the creative idea and the process of expressing that idea are characteristic of conceptual art. The term *conceptual art* was first used in the early 1960s to designate an artistic philosophy that held the supremacy of the artist's concept and the process intended to achieve it over the actual execution of the work. This modern tradition of stressing the intellectual creative act began with Dada, and especially the "readymades" of Marcel Duchamp.

Conceptual art requires that the concept for a work of art be documented, but that documentation need not take the form of a finished, crafted work. It might, for example, be expressed verbally or in another visual medium. In 1967,

another conceptual artist, Sol Lewitt, wrote:

> In Conceptual Art the Idea or concept is the most important aspect of the work . . . all planning and decision are made beforehand and the execution is a perfunctory affair. The idea becomes the machine that makes the art.

Another contribution from the 1960s that continues to expand the definitions of art is performance art. Historically, such art is related to the happenings of the 1950s. Performance art, which celebrates a temporal experience for an audience, is not geared toward making an object; rather, the artist becomes the work of art, freely acting within a theatrical environment. Performance artists often use a multimedia approach. Joseph Beuys (1921–86), a German artist who was a major practitioner of performance art, incorporated a wide variety of props in his "actions" (as he termed his performances), from found objects to live animals. Beuys, a pilot shot down in a barren frozen area of the Crimea during World War II, used performance art as a means to communicate autobiographical experiences in a symbolic manner, causing us to question the

10-108. Joseph Beuys. Photographic negatives with brown-cross between glass plates in iron frame, 28 x 21 x 2" (71.1 x 53.3 x 5 cm) with frame. Photos by Ute Klophaus from Beuys's *Iphigenia/Titus Andronicus*. May 1969. This work premiered during an avant-garde theater festival in Frankfurt, Germany. The performance consisted of selected simultaneous readings of Goethe's *Iphigenie* and Shakespeare's *Titus Andronicus* while Beuys, who designed the "set," acted on stage. Beuys's actions included spreading margarine on the stage floor and occasionally clashing cymbals.

© 1996 Artists Rights Society (ARS), New York/VG Bild-Kunst, Bonn

deeper values in our lives. Beuys believed that performance art could reawaken the mind and soul (fig. 10-108).

On the contemporary scene, performance-concerts by Laurie Anderson (b. 1947) synthesize sight and sound. High-tech light displays and projections are synchronized with a pulsating musical background while Anderson's "talking songs" reflect on the issues and realities we face in life. In her 1992 tour (fig. 10-109), her subjects included "War Is the Highest Form of Modern Art," "My Grandmother's Hats," and "The Cardinal Points."

With video art, television becomes a medium of artistic enterprise. Nam June Paik once remarked, "As collage technique replaced oil paint the cathode ray tube will replace the canvas." Viewing *Electronic Highway* (see fig. 1-1), we focus simultaneously on multiple association of reality and time. The video montage reminds us of the fast-paced gloss of MTV, offering a plethora of information that is only possible through the advances in electronic communication.

Conceptual, performance, and video art have broadened the boundaries of art beyond any traditional definitions, raising intriguing questions about the nature of art as we approach a new millennium.

10-109. Laurie Anderson. Performance-concert of *Stories from the Nerve Bible*. 1992

THE DEVELOPMENT OF MINIMAL ART

10-110. Donald Judd. *Untitled*. 1968. Eight stainless-steel boxes, each 48" square and placed 12" apart. Private collection

© 1997 Donald Judd Estate/VAGA, New York, NY

A series of eight stainless-steel boxes is set directly on the floor, without the pedestals common to the display of sculpture (fig. 10-110). Identical in size and finish, they have been fabricated by metalworkers to the artist's specifications, and the placement of each box and its position in the series have been precisely calibrated. Each box displaces an identical amount of space. Although it might be said that each box retains an individual and objective integrity, the set of eight boxes becomes an indivisible sculptural unit. The highly finished surfaces, the precise manner in which they are related, and the purity of the geometric compositions deny the autographic quality of the hand of the artist in their creation. Such art dissociates itself from those qualities that we usually ascribe to sculpture. These boxes are, simply, visual facts, and they remind us of our own existence in space and the visual nature of our own being.

Donald Judd (1928–94) is the artist of this series of boxes, which exemplifies a style that developed in the 1960s known as Minimalism. The roots of Minimal art extend back

1968

1965	World population reaches 3.3 billion
1965	*Help*, a Beatles film, is released
1967	First human heart transplant
1967	U.S. population exceeds 200 million
1968	**Judd, *Untitled***

10-111. Agnes Martin. *Night Sea*. 1963. Oil on canvas with gold leaf, 6 x 6'. Private Collection, London. Agnes Martin's work is fundamental for the development of Minimalism, but she does not refer to herself as a Minimal artist.

in the twentieth century to the structural and spatial considerations of Russian Constructivism, the manufactured ready-mades of Duchamp (see fig. 10-56), and the Hard-Edge Abstraction of such artists as Frank Stella (see fig. 10-99). As an alternative to the emphatic personal emotionalism of Abstract Expressionism, Minimalism presented the work of art as an object of elemental form with the least amount of visual components and divorced from either symbolic or personal expression. Judd, who holds academic degrees in philosophy and art history and was well known as an art critic before the advent of Minimalism, wrote in 1965:

> It isn't necessary for a work to have a lot of things to look at, to compare, to analyze one by one, to contemplate. The thing as a whole, its quality as a whole, is what is interesting. The main things are alone and are more intense, clear, and powerful.

In the late 1950s, Agnes Martin (b. 1912) began a series of paintings based on simple grid patterns. Although her work was influential for later Minimalists, her position within Minimal art is unique. *Night Sea* (fig. 10-111) is composed of a grid of shimmering gold leaf over a soft, almost atmospheric, veil of shaded blue. Her composition is formally related to the structured approach of Minimalism; however, the interaction of the radiant geometric lines against the subtle changes of the ground color creates a surface and an effect that are atypical of the objective, planar surfaces of most Minimal painting. Agnes Martin's paintings encourage an intuitive, almost meditative, response.

EARTH AND LAND ART

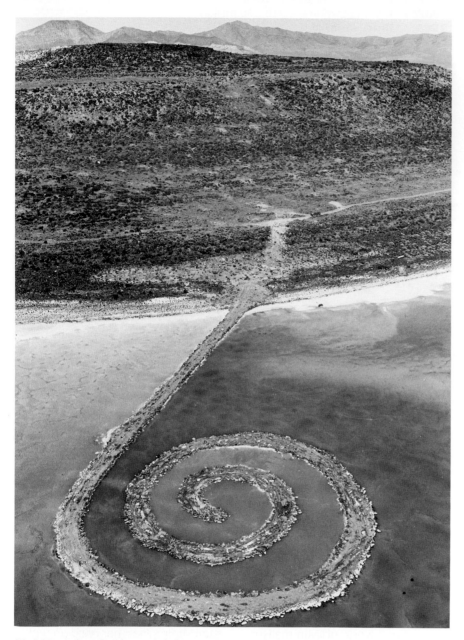

10-112. Robert Smithson. *Spiral Jetty*. 1969–70. Black rock, salt crystals, earth, and red water (algae), diameter 160'; coil length 1,500'; width 15'. Great Salt Lake, Utah. This photograph shows the jetty soon after it was first completed. Smithson died in 1973 in an airplane crash while working on a later project.

Spiral Jetty in the Great Salt Lake (see map, page 489) is an aggressive and dramatic gesture in the natural landscape (fig. 10-112). Robert Smithson (1938–73) used assistants and huge earth-moving equipment to create the work. The top of the jetty functioned as the roadbed as the rock was moved into place in the lake. The jetty was meant to be walked on and to be seen from the shore and the sky. The resulting form, which is both regular and open, transformed the quality and color of the water within the jetty, for the encircled areas of water heated to a higher temperature, changing the amount and color of the local algae. But Smithson's mark on the landscape was not meant to be permanent. He knew it was a temporary structure that would eventually be transformed, if not obliterated, by the forces of nature. Recently it has been hidden by an unexpected rise in the water level of the lake. Although the geometric purity of the spiral form can be related to formalism and Minimalist art, it also has a historical and iconographic content. Smithson learned that early Mormon settlers believed that the Great Salt Lake was bottomless and connected to the Pacific Ocean by an underground canal and that from time to time Pacific currents would cause huge whirlpools to form on the lake's surface. His choice of design was based on this legend.

Beginning in the 1960s, a number of American artists became interested in producing large-scale works of art in the natural environment. This type of art became known as earth art, land art, or environmental art. Some artists moved large amounts of earth, creating a personal statement and transforming the land in a manner offensive to environmentally minded citizens. Others were determined to reassert and even re-create the natural quality of nature. Some projects took advantage of the natural forces in nature: ice, flowing water, wind, even animals and birds. All redirected attention to nature, making us see it with new eyes and a new awareness, and raising the issue of the importance of nature in modern, industrialized society.

Running Fence, by Christo (b.

1969–70   **Smithson,** *Spiral Jetty*
1969   *Sesame Street* program is introduced on PBS
1969   Woodstock music festival

10-113. Christo and Jeanne-Claude. *Running Fence, Sonoma and Marin Counties, California.* 1972–76 (now removed). 2,050 steel poles set 62' apart; 65,000 yards of white woven synthetic fabric, height 18'; total length 24¹/₂ miles. © Christo 1976. The planning stages of this work began in 1972. The project was completed in four days and remained standing for fourteen. Christo and Jeanne-Claude's determination to create works on such a large scale that they must be executed with the assistance of a large number of workers is related to their interest in involving the broader community; this cooperative and inclusive approach is in direct opposition to the exclusive, individualistic tradition of most modern Western art.

1935) and Jeanne-Claude (b. 1935), crossed the hills of California north of San Francisco to run into the sea, highlighting by its existence not only the forms of the landscape but also, as it caught the changing effects of light and the shifting winds, the constant movement inherent in nature (fig. 10-113). Perhaps its best vantage point was from an airplane, for only thus could the enormous scope of the project be encompassed in a single view. Part of the creative act for Christo and Jeanne-Claude is not just conceiving and executing a project but raising the funds (through the sale of preparatory drawings and prints), acquiring the legal permissions required, finding workers who will help with the intensive, large-scale labor of the project, and creating a reasonable timetable so that the project can be completed on schedule. Their early works included projects in which objects were stacked (a project to create a great **mastaba** form by stacking 2 million oil barrels has not yet been completed) or the wrapping of objects or buildings in fabric that was then bound with ropes, including the wrapping of more than 1 million square feet of the cliffs of the coast of Australia in 1969. In 1971–72, Christo and Jeanne-Claude closed off a valley in Colorado with an orange nylon curtain 365 feet high and 1,368 feet long (documented in a film, *Valley Curtain*), and in 1983 they surrounded eleven small islands in Biscayne Bay in Miami with 6 million square feet of bright pink polypropylene fabric, exaggerating their natural shapes and turning them into a sequence of enormous pink flowers. Two recent projects involved series of umbrellas on either side of the Pacific, in Japan and California, and wrapping the historic and symbolic Reichstag building in Berlin in silver-colored fabric. This last project, conceived in 1971, was only carried out in 1995.

THE NEW REALISM

10-114. Duane Hanson. *Tourists*. 1970. Fiberglass and polyester, polychromed, 5'4" x 5'5" x 4'3". Scottish National Gallery of Modern Art, Edinburgh. As time passes and clothing styles change, Hanson's figures seem more historic and less naturalistic, but when first created they were meticulous re-creations of individuals whom one might meet on the street. Other figures by Hanson include *Traveler with Sunburn*, *Couple with Shopping Bag*, and *Football Player*.

The interaction between art and life, and our perception of both, take on new meaning with the sculptures of Duane Hanson (b. 1923). The figures seem as real as the actual clothing, camera, and other props. At exhibitions of Hanson's works, viewers commonly speak to the works of art, having mistaken them for living individuals. Hanson casts these fiberglass-reinforced polyester resin figures from molds made from the models and paints the "skin" with meticulous attention to pores, surface blemishes, and other individualistic details. Although the resulting figures share in the visual world of reality, their mute presence and arrested poses create an uncanny gulf between the sculpture and ourselves. Hanson's figures approach, but cannot participate in, life.

Tourists (fig. 10-114) is an example of Hyper-Realist sculpture, itself part of a broader movement known as New Realism that emerged in the late 1960s and early 1970s. Actually, realism in art had never left the twentieth century; Pop art, for example, was first greeted with the label *New Realism*. To many artists, critics, and connoisseurs, realism seemed outmoded when compared to avant-garde abstract and nonobjective art, but given the visual and psychological dearth left by Minimalism, the public and many art dealers embraced this resurgent realism. The meticulous crafting of a work of art again became an element to be enjoyed, even if, on a more profound level, it forced viewers to confront the banality of modern life.

The call to realism was met by painters, many of whom developed techniques that utilized photographs. In viewing *Double Self-Portrait* (fig. 10-115), we seem to be standing on an urban sidewalk, facing the large glass windows and doors of a diner. In these panes of glass, myriad forms—cars, buildings, and street signs—are reflected. It is as if we can "see" in two directions at the same time. Reflected in the lower right area of the central pane of glass is the artist, Richard Estes (b. 1936), with his camera on a tripod. To the left, you can see the second, smaller reflection of the artist that explains the work's title. Estes's camera alerts us that the vivid **trompe l'oeil** realism of the painting is in part based on Estes's photographs of the different ele-

1970   Hanson, *Tourists*
1970   Vietnam War protests lead to deaths of four youths at Kent State University
1970   Alexander Solzhenitsyn wins Nobel Prize for literature
1970   Tokyo is the largest city in the world, with population of 21.5 million

ments of the scene. In the final composition, he combined these images with a sharp-focus painted realism, leaving us to explore the conflict between visual reality, photographic information, and the painted surface.

Audrey Flack (b. 1931), who invests her Photo-Realist paintings with psychological and emotional content, begins by arranging a still-life composition that combines objects suggesting both personal and universal meaning. The series of paintings from the mid-1970s that included *Queen* (fig. 10-116) can be related to traditional Vanitas iconography (see fig. 7-41). The watch and the transient beauty of the flower and fruit stress the passage of time, while more personal objects—make-up, photographs, a key chain, a card, and a chess piece—suggest additional layers of meaning. When she is pleased with her arrangement, Flack photographs it with color-slide film. She then projects slides onto a canvas and paints following the guidelines offered by the projected image. Her use of an **airbrush** (a small, high-quality paint sprayer) softens the contours of the objects, giving the finished painting a suggestive and even sensual effect. This soft focus combines with the iconography of the objects to appeal to our emotions in a way that is quite different from the sharp focus and detached objectivity of Estes's urban scene. The fact that Flack's huge, dazzling objects leap out toward us by overlapping the gray border gives them a compelling presence. These modern trompe l'oeil artists delight and intrigue us, just as their ancient Roman counterparts entertained Philostratus the Younger (see page 129).

10-115. Richard Estes. *Double Self-Portrait*. 1976. Oil on canvas, 24 x 36". The Museum of Modern Art, New York

Mr. and Mrs. Stuart M. Speiser Fund. © 1997 Richard Estes/VAGA, New York, NY/Marlborough Gallery, NY

10-116. Audrey Flack. *Queen*. 1975–76. Oil and acrylic on canvas, 6'8" x 6'8". Private collection

Courtesy Louis K. Meisel Gallery

POSTMODERNISM

10-117. Michael Graves. Portland Public Service Building, Oregon. 1980–82. This model shows one of the architect's designs for the building. When built, the extravagant bows on the side of the structure were flattened and the "acropolis" of structures on the roof, which was originally intended to house the building's mechanical functions, was omitted. The huge figure of Portlandia over the main entrance was designed by the American sculptor Raymond Kaskey. Commissioned by the City Government of Portland

10-118. Mark Tansey. *Purity Test*. 1982. Oil on canvas, 6 x 8'. Collection of the Chase Manhattan Bank, N.A.
Courtesy Curt Marcus Gallery, New York © Mark Tansey

Portland Public Service Building (fig. 10-117), by Michael Graves (b. 1934), represents the Postmodern style of architecture; by abandoning the "modern" glass box and reintroducing traditional architectural elements and ideas, Postmodernism defines itself as a new style that has moved beyond the modern. Although the Portland Building contains a reference to modernism in its rectangular form, its Postmodern elements include references to historic architectural traditions in its giant **pilasters**, blocklike **Doric capitals**, and enormous **keystone** and the adherence to the concept of the building as an anthropomorphic emblem. Graves's building also returns to the use of traditional symbols: the distinct areas of green, terra-cotta, and blue into which the structure is divided, for example, refer to water, earth, and sky. The huge figure of Portlandia over the main entrance, which is taken from the city's seal, represents a break from the abstract sculpture usually associated with modern public buildings. Here, the symbolism of ornament is wedded to a frolicsome attitude of visual delight.

According to the architectural critic Charles Jencks, the death of "modern" architecture occurred at 3:32 PM on July 15, 1972, in St. Louis, Missouri, when the failed Pruitt-Igoe housing project, which had won a national design award in 1951, was dynamited. With its geometric design, flat roofs, and complete avoidance of ornament, the project had exemplified the purist aesthetic of the International Style (see pages 552–53), but the impersonal nature of its design did not endear it to its residents, and the project eventually fell victim to vandalism and became a site for drug dealing. The destruction of the project by the St. Louis housing authority made it clear that the modern style of architecture was meeting neither individual needs nor social realities in a pluralistic world.

The term *Postmodernism*, first applied to architecture, is also used to refer to developments in other art forms that are characterized by a pluralistic approach to style, medium, and interpretation, as well as a disavowal of the belief in the value of modernism. Postmodernism's emphasis on plurality makes it difficult to offer a succinct definition of the movement, but it is possible to discuss its primary features. Postmodernism, for example, welcomes the artistic past into the present.

1971	Swiss women granted the right to vote
1972	Richard Nixon visits China and U.S.S.R.
1973	Pablo Picasso dies
1979	Shah of Iran forced into exile
1980–82	**Graves, Portland Public Service Building**

The process of appropriating, or adapting, traditional art forms into contemporary works allows us to question and examine the role of tradition and context. Postmodernist art celebrates diversity and is unafraid to examine social, political, and historical issues. It is a vehicle that can help us locate and define ourselves within our culture. As the contemporary architect Robert Stern has written:

> The fundamental shift to post-modernism has to do with the reawakening of artists in every field to the public responsibilities of art. Once again art is being regarded as an act of communication.

The development of the Postmodernist aesthetic in art can be related to contemporary developments in French intellectual thought during the 1970s. Critical methods of inquiry based on the writings of Jacques Derrida, Jean Baudrillard, Julia Kristeva, and others offered a new philosophical basis for artistic exploration. The paintings of Mark Tansey (b. 1949) are particularly responsive to this intellectual current. Tansey's compositions are based on his personal response to older images and his thoughtful meditation on history and tradition. In one image, for example, he shows a painter (a self-portrait?) on a ladder with a paint roller, painting out Michelangelo's *Last Judgment*; in another painting, based on a historic photograph of a military surrender, he represented *The Triumph of the New York School*, with the French artists Matisse and Picasso surrendering their preeminence in

art to the American Jackson Pollock and the influential modernist art critic Clement Greenberg. Tansey's paintings are often sepia toned or monochromatic in a reference to old photographs. Although this photographylike quality sets up an expectation of veracity with the viewer, it is challenged by the implausible nature of the image.

In Tansey's *Purity Test* (fig. 10-118), a group of Native Americans on horseback views Robert Smithson's *Spiral Jetty* (see fig. 10-112) from atop a bluff. The juxtaposition poses intriguing questions. The manner in which the Native Americans are represented is a caricature that has a greater resemblance to nineteenth-century paintings of the American West than to historical accuracy. Nevertheless, the work raises the question of how Native Americans might have responded to *Spiral Jetty*, a modern, abstract work in the Great Salt Lake that is based on prehistoric earthworks created by Native Americans and on a legend common among early Mormon settlers. Tansey's naturalistic representation also forces us to wonder what myths Native Americans may have had about the source and meaning of the Great Salt Lake. In the final analysis, we are reminded of the vast differences that can separate cultures and of the difficulties that can be experienced when cultures clash.

Such communication may, at times, include facing the reality of one's cultural past. Sigmar Polke (b. 1941) is one of a group of German Neo-Expressionist artists who have confronted the legacy of their country's past. The dark, looming image of the watchtower in Polke's *Hochstand* (fig. 10-119) calls to mind

10-119. Sigmar Polke. *Hochstand*. 1984. Acrylic, lacquer, and cotton, 10'8" x 7'4". Private collection, New York

the concentration camps of World War II and the guarded borders of the divided Germany. In addition, *Hochstand*, like much Postmodernist work, involves a complex layering of imagery. The watchtower seems to be both emerging from and sinking into a ground of patterned fabric. Besides their historical references, Polke's paintings can also refer formally to stages in modern art. Here the printed fabric pattern alludes to both Pop art and to the P + D (Pattern and Decoration) movement (see pages 584–85), while the overall darkness and dribbling of the paint may refer to the gestural technique used by the Abstract Expressionist painters (see pages 554–57). Polke's complex image can remind us of past political realities at the same time it warns us not to let memory fade behind the numbing onslaught of media culture.

ARCHITECTURE SINCE 1970

10-120. Peter Eisenman. Wexner Center for the Visual Arts, Columbus, Ohio. 1983–88. Commissioned by the Ohio State University and Leslie H. Wexner, Chairman of the Board, The Limited

Eisenman's architecture speaks to us with words for which there are no substitutes, about the disorder of the modern world, about the weakness of all human action, about the fallibility of our knowledge, about our alienation from our own places. It is a text which speaks. But its speech does not consist in telling any definite tale . . .

These remarks by the contemporary Spanish architect Ignasi de Sola-Morales help to prepare us for a new architectural experience that seemingly is full of contradictions.

In winning the commission to design the Wexner Center for the Visual Arts at the Ohio State University, Columbus, Ohio, in 1983 (fig. 10-120), Peter Eisenman (b. 1932) accepted the challenge to create a building intended to exhibit not only traditional art forms but also whatever new art forms may be created in the future. The result is a building that proclaims its modernity and challenges traditional architectural form. The design of the Wexner Center, set between two existing buildings, is based on a grid that relates it not to the immediate university environment but to the grid patterns of the city of Columbus. Eisenman in this way makes reference to the historical survey grid first established in the early 1800s, when this area was part of the Northwest Territory. Tradition and history are thus affirmed, but through the use of forms that simultaneously assert the modernity of the structure.

The fortresslike towers that make up part of one of the entrances are based on the forms of a towered armory that once stood on this site, but a close look reveals that the towers are not complete. Other architectural elements exhibit a similar subversion of architectural

1983–88 **Eisenman, Wexner Center**
1983 Drought causes widespread famine in Africa
1983 Sally Ride is first U.S. shuttle astronaut in space

10-121. Renzo Piano and Richard Rogers. Georges Pompidou National Arts and Cultural Center, Paris. 1971–78. The center incorporates not only museum spaces for permanent and temporary exhibitions, but a public library and an audiovisual center. Commissioned by Georges Pompidou, president of France, and later named for him

form: arches are not complete, the supporting function of some columns is denied, and both form and space assume shapes that defy our visual expectations. At one and the same time, the Wexner Center is related to and discordant with Western architectural traditions.

Critics are still debating whether the Wexner Center is an example of Deconstructivist architecture or not, but some of the concepts that we encounter here introduce us to Deconstructivism, an art theory that is rooted in the literary philosophy of Jacques Derrida and others (see

also page 579). In literary deconstruction, where the concept originated, texts are dismantled and freely reassembled without regard to original intent or underlying content. Meaning becomes changeable, it is argued, and depends on the context and the relationship to the reader.

In architecture, Deconstructivism demands that we have a profound understanding of historic architectural forms so that we can understand the manner in which traditions are countered or violated. New possibilities arise as we ques-

tion the validity of traditions and ponder their role in current developments; the seeming instability of design and form at the Wexner Center embodies complex ideas and suggests that an inherent conceptual instability has pervaded the practice of designing and building structures.

Since about 1970, architecture throughout the world has undergone sweeping transformations (see also pages 578–79). At the forefront of many of the newer developments was the Pompidou Center in Paris (fig. 10-121), by Renzo Piano (b.

10-122. Charles Moore (in collaboration with U.I.G. and Perez Associates Inc.). Piazza d'Italia, New Orleans, 1975–80. The piazza was designed to provide the Italo-American population of New Orleans with a piazza where the annual festival of Saint Joseph could be celebrated. The central fountain is in the shape of the map of Italy, with the water from the fountain flowing down courses that follow the routes of major Italian rivers.

1937) and Richard Rogers (b. 1933). At first glance, the architecture of the Pompidou Center seems to be completely honest. Not only are the structural elements exposed—without and within—but air-circulation ducting, escalators, and other mechanical equipment are brought into public view and even emphasized. Bright colors are used to designate each different mechanical function, so that we are constantly aware of the operating systems needed to keep the building functioning; in such a program, the mechanical systems also function as decoration. Inside, all the walls are movable, and each space can be redesigned as needed. It is not only an adventure in architecture but also a demonstration in understanding the complex workings of the advanced technology of a huge contemporary building. Leaving the mechanicals on the exterior allows for their easy replacement when they wear out or when new technology becomes available. Rogers has written:

> I believe in the rich potential of a modern industrial society. Aesthetically one can do what one likes with technology for it is a tool, not an end in itself, but we ignore it at our peril. To our practice its natural functionalism has an intrinsic beauty.

Architects have been inspired by the direct bluntness of industrial "architecture," such as oil refineries and grain elevators, where function forms the design.

In Postmodern architecture (see pages 578–79), some architects have revived historical architectural vocabulary and references in a creative and even playful nontraditional manner since 1970. In Piazza d'Italia (fig. 10-122), columns and capitals representing numerous orders (see page 95), arches, including a triumphal arch, and inscriptions from the classical tradition are transformed by Charles Moore (1925–1993) through the use of bright and unexpected colors, neon outlining,

10-123. Zaha Hadid. Vitra Fire Station, Weil-am-Rhein, Germany. 1993. Commissioned by the Vitra Furniture Manufacturing Company

stainless steel, and varied scale. Some of the "columns" are composed of flowing water, with the streams of water wittily suggesting fluting, and two human masks that spout water into the fountain from a Roman arch are self-portraits of the architect. When viewed from above, the center of the composition is the island of Sicily, the area from which most New Orleans Italians came. At night, dramatic lighting gives the piazza a dazzling, commercial quality.

If the Piazza d'Italia embraces historical references, the Fire Station (fig. 10-123) by Zaha Hadid (b. 1950), an Iraqi-born architect, appears to deny them completely.

The stark concrete walls of her building are joined at unexpected angles, while strong diagonal accents impart a dynamism to the building that may be related to its function as a fire station. The architectural forms are both simple and boldly conceived; the manner in which the masses of the building jut into space encourages us to conceive the building as sculptural and to be aware of how it relates to and energizes the space around it.

Both Hadid and Eisenman were featured in the 1988 Deconstructivist architecture exhibition at the Museum of Modern Art in New York City, and they share some of the design aspects and theories of this style. Both, for example, construct buildings in which the most basic elements of the design avoid right angles. While Eisenman's Wexner Center makes a connection with history through a relationship with a previous building on this site and with the history and design of the Ohio city where it is built, Hadid's building can be related to the early modern movement of Russian Suprematism (see pages 522–23). By reinterpreting these forms in a huge scale in architecture, Hadid's building engages us in the current dialogue between architectural structures and shifting meaning.

PATTERN AND DECORATION

10-124. Miriam Schapiro. *Wonderland.* 1983. National Museum of American Art, Smithsonian Institution, Washington, D.C. Acrylic and fabric on canvas, 7'6" x 12'

The painting is me, torn in two. I present myself as the painter who can organize and master a huge canvas and then there's the other side of me which belongs to all women who were not liberated—all my ancestors who were trapped in a world where they were punished for being women, where nothing they did was good enough. That's what the painting is about.

In these words, Miriam Schapiro (b. 1923) shares with us the meaning of *Wonderland* (fig. 10-124). This large, multimedia work resembles a giant quilt; pieces of needlework, collected during the artist's visit to Australia, are assembled across the surface of the canvas and combined with painted areas. The embroidered detail of a woman and kitchen in the center offers a stereotypical view of women's work, a view that is challenged by Schapiro's artistic creation in the rest of the work.

Schapiro's multimedia *Wonderland* exemplifies what she has termed a "femmage." The term *femmage*, a contraction of *female* and *image*, is also related to the French words *femme* ("woman") and *hommage* ("homage" or "respect"). The iconography of *Wonderland* is specifically feminine; Schapiro writes that her femmages

explore and express a part of my life which I had always dismissed—my homemaking, my nesting. . . . The collagists who came before me were men who lived in cities and often roamed the streets at night scavenging, collecting material, their junk, from urban spaces. My world, my mother's and grandmother's world, was a different one. My "junk," my fabrics allude to a particular universe, which I wish to make real, to represent.

Wonderland complements Schapiro's feminist sensibility in the large scale of the work, its incorporation of

10-125. Joyce Kozloff. *Los Angeles Becoming Mexico City Becoming Los Angeles*. 1992–93. Watercolor, lithographs, and collage on paper, 22 x 87". Private collection

Courtesy DC Moore Gallery, New York

fabric, its decorative composition, and the traditional association of the fiber arts with women artists.

Schapiro's vibrant painting belongs to a style often referred to as P + D, an abbreviation for *Pattern and Decoration*. P + D utilizes repeated nonobjective shapes inherent in decorative motifs, some of which, as here, have been derived from traditional sources. Unlike the severe, impersonal abstraction of Hard-Edge or Minimal art (see pages 564–65, 572–73), P + D revels in bold colors and less-constrained compositions.

For Schapiro and other artists in this movement, P + D joined a Postmodern concern for content with artistic traditions drawn from all over the world. Over the past centuries, as Western art academies developed a qualitative hierarchy of themes in painting, pattern and decorative work was relegated to an inferior position, outside the realm of fine art. Yet decorative and patterned compositions, with their implied planarity, have been at the core of many artistic traditions, including Anglo- and Hiberno-Saxon art, Islamic art, and Native American art. In addition, P + D has drawn strength from popular and domestic art forms, such as textiles, that historically have been associated with women.

The rise of P + D in the 1970s coincided with the impact of feminism on art history, contemporary art, and art criticism. One goal of feminist art and criticism is to recover the significant, yet too often neglected, contributions of women in art. Another goal is to explore the issue of a female aesthetic. The principles of feminism influenced the works of Schapiro and many other artists, including Joyce Kozloff (b. 1942).

Kozloff has received a number of commissions for public spaces in which she has demonstrated her personal response to the historical and social traditions of the particular location. *Los Angeles Becoming Mexico City Becoming Los Angeles* (fig. 10-125) is one of a series of map projects that culminated in a large installation for Mankato State University in Mankato, Minnesota, in which Kozloff created tile panels that refer to twelve cities around the world, including Ravenna and Florence, Italy, and Vladivostok, Russia, which lie on the same latitude as Mankato. In the Los Angeles/Mexico City piece, however, the title and the manner in which the maps and cultural references (including an Aztec map) are combined suggests not a similarity in location, as in the Mankato piece, but an interweaving of cultures that is creating a new and modern synthesis in both cities. These cities, which rank among the largest in the world, are becoming more and more alike. Kozloff writes that she thinks "of cities as rich, interlocking patterns related to my own earlier decorative work, in which I had always juxtaposed cultural references. I'm struck by the extraordinary geometrics . . ."

NEO-EXPRESSIONISM

10-126. Anselm Kiefer. *Midgard*. 1980–85. Oil and emulsion on canvas, 11'10" x 19'9¾". Carnegie Museum of Art, Pittsburgh. The broken shape in the center that resembles an artist's palette relates to Kiefer's performance art; in one of his performances, he dropped a clay palette and it shattered. As a symbol, this may refer to the Nazi suppression of German artists during the 1930s and also to the difficulty of being an artist in an age dominated by science.

Anselm Kiefer (b. 1945) drew inspiration from Nordic mythology for his panoramic painting (fig. 10-126). Its title, *Midgard*, which is written several times on the surface of the painting, means "Middle Garden," a name traditionally given to the earth by the ancient Norse gods. In Norse mythology, the destruction of the earth comes after three years of winter, when the Midgard serpent and other demons destroy the old gods and all life in a purification that can lead, then, to regeneration. Using enormous scale, a comfortless composition, and barren colors (the artist employed a blowtorch to achieve a scorched effect), Kiefer explores and expands

one of the initial and invigorating currents of twentieth-century art, expressionism. *Midgard* is a dramatic painting of a traditional mythological subject that, in Kiefer's reinterpretation, has the power to grip the contemporary imagination.

Countering the impersonal traits of recent abstraction, Neo-Expressionism reinvests an emotional and empathetic content in painting. *Midgard* seems to express dread and desolation in the vast scorched earth that stretches before us; it is as if our nightmares of nuclear holocaust have become manifest. The only sign of life is the snake in the central foreground, which is moving slowly but inexorably toward a

labyrinthine circular area of land that also represents a broken artist's palette. Kiefer's painting is ultimately ambiguous in its meaning, but the snake and the seashore setting have been seen by some critics as indications of renewal, and the painting may not be as pessimistic as it first seems to be.

Within the pluralistic world of Postmodernism, Neo-Expressionism arose in the early 1980s as a reaction to what some artists perceived to be the emotional aridness of Minimalism and Conceptualism. Neo-Expressionism is an international movement. Nourished in Germany and Italy, it then found adherents in the United States.

10-127. Robert Colescott. *Les Demoiselles d'Alabama: Vestidas.* 1985. Acrylic on canvas, 8' x 7'8". New York, Collection of Hanford Yang

Courtesey Phyllis Kind Gallery, New York

These artists revived the emotionally laden gestural brushwork and intense colors of Europe's earlier Expressionist painters. Appropriation of imagery, as we have already seen in the work of Sigmar Polke (see fig. 10-119), became a means of defining contemporary conflict on many levels, from personal through global.

In the United States, the paintings of Robert Colescott (b. 1925) have questioned concepts of identity within a multicultural society. In *Les Demoiselles d'Alabama: Vestidas* (fig. 10-127), the African American artist parodies Picasso's 1907 painting *Les Demoiselles d'Avignon* (see fig. 10-31), which is regarded as a formative work in the history of modern art. Picasso's abstracted prostitutes are now dressed in garish and revealing clothing, and their racial identities have been expanded to include both black and white women.

Such a direct incorporation of art-historical references opens us to various levels of meaning, as questions of cultural traditions and their transmission are posed. Specifically, the racial transformation of three of Picasso's figures leads us to realize the glaring omissions of minority artists from Western art surveys, as well as the uninformed appropriation of African art by early modern artists. The issues dealt with by Colescott, from individual identity through the broader context of societal inclusion and noninclusion, are effectively communicated through powerful compositions and an expressive use of content, color, and brushwork.

JAPANESE ARCHITECTURE

10-128. Itsuko Hasegawa. Shonandai Cultural Center, Fujisawa City, Japan. 1989

At first sight, the Shonandai Cultural Center (fig. 10-128), designed by Itsuko Hasegawa (b. 1941), seems both futuristic in its vision and overwhelming in its size. The center was built to house a variety of spaces for different purposes, including a theater, community center, and children's pavilion. Fully two-thirds of the enormous Cultural Center is built underground, where rooms and passageways are arranged around a sunken garden. Above ground level, the futuristic-looking structures are set within a garden complex, providing green spaces, a stream, and a pond for quiet contemplation. The gable-roofed buildings are meant to suggest Japanese village architecture, but Hasegawa also views them as reminiscent of mountains when they are seen from the garden. The large spheres symbolically refer to

the world, the moon, and the cosmos. The union of nature, village, and universe here is based in the purpose of the center, which is to help the people of Fujisawa City understand their position as citizens of both local and world communities. Writing about the concept for the Shonandai Cultural Center, Hasegawa noted:

A basic theme of this project was to accept those things that had been rejected by the spirit of rationalism—the translucent world of emotions and the supple and comfortable space woven by nature—and to create a landscape filled with a new form of nature where devices enable one to hear the strange music of the Universe.

As in the West, architects in Asia are consistently challenging traditions with innovative designs and the use of new techniques and materials. But whereas the Western theory of Deconstructivism seeks to subvert tradition, avant-garde Asian architects have been concerned with redefining our relationship to architecture and to the natural environment. This relationship is the starting point for many progressive Japanese architects, including Hasegawa and Tadao Ando.

The Water Temple (fig. 10-129), by Tadao Ando (b. 1941), was designed as an addition to an older, traditional Buddhist temple that follows the conventions first laid out for Japanese Buddhist architecture at Horyuji (see fig. 4-36). Ando's new temple at the same site, however, breaks decisively with this tradition; the new structure has been described by one critic as "less a building than a series of shaped sensual experiences."

Ando controls our entrance to the temple through a series of concrete walls that guide us and then focus our field of vision on a large, serene pool. This controlled spatial passage suggests that we should undertake a psychological transition as Ando prepares us to enter the spiritual environment of the temple. In the large elliptical pool grow a number of lotus plants, whose blossoms float on and help define the flat and serene surface of the water (in Buddhism, the lotus is a symbol of enlightenment). As paths direct our passage along the edge of the pool, we unexpectedly discover a stairway that descends into the surface of the water. This staircase

10-129. Tadao Ando. Water Temple, Island of Awaji, Japan. 1992. Honpukuji is affiliated with Old Shingon, a Tantric Buddhist sect that emphasizes meditation based on two mandalas. Commissioned by Honpukuji

leads down to the circular shrine that lies underneath; the convex ceiling of the central area of the shrine is the bottom of the pool. The rather narrow form of this staircase as it moves into the water leads us to expect a dark, underwater space, but the red-painted shrine itself is, when reached, unexpectedly lit from windows in a "light room" set where the enveloping hillside drops away. The central circular area, with a statue of the Buddha flanked by the two mandalas of the Shingon

sect, is surrounded by square rooms to be used for the tea ceremony (see pages 344–45). The progression of spaces, materials, and colors Ando has created for the viewer is intended, obviously, as a metaphor for the sponsoring religion.

Ando himself wrote that his architecture is intended to create a place "for the spirit to rest." Untraditional in its design, Ando's Lotus Pond Hall uses contemporary innovation to fulfill its centuries-old religious and cultural function.

APPROPRIATION

10-130. Nancy Graves. *Canoptic Legerdemain*. 1990. Stainless steel, aluminum mesh, resin, and paper, 7'1" x 7'11" x 3'1". National Gallery of Art, Washington, D.C. The title refers to the representation of Egyptian canopic burial jars in the relief and to the artful trickery with which the artist has hidden references to several past cultures in a single work.
Gift of Graphic Studio/University of South Florida and the artist, in honor of the fiftieth anniversary of the National Gallery. © 1997 Nancy Graves Foundation/VAGA, New York, NY

Canoptic Legerdemain by Nancy Graves (1940–95) is a complex three-dimensional interweaving of formal and iconographic elements (fig. 10-130). In many ways, it is an adroit and erudite summation of recent developments in art. Based on the appropriation of art-historical, archaeological, and mythological imagery from the ancient Egyptian, Early Christian, and Byzantine civilizations, some imagery in the work, such as the head of the Empress Theodora (see fig. 4-27) and the Egyptian hunting scene (see fig. 3-28), is already familiar to us. The uncoiling snake near the center

of the composition has associations with many ancient beliefs, particularly the biblical account of the temptation of Adam and Eve.

Although *Canoptic Legerdemain* is a visual and psychological feast, it is also exemplary of the use of modern technology in art. Laser-cut steel, which was produced from a computer program of Graves's drawings, is joined by a host of materials, from cast and molded resins to more traditional lithographs. Here the mix of painting and sculpture demonstrates the breakdown of barriers between mediums that is typical of Post-

modernism. The composition relates art to technology, connects two-dimensional to three-dimensional forms, and unites the past to the present in art. In its expansive vitality, *Canoptic Legerdemain* exemplifies many of the issues that we shall meet in contemporary art, especially appropriation.

The term *appropriation* designates both a process and an aspect of Postmodernism (see pages 578–79). Although Nancy Graves drew upon art-historical images in the creation of *Canoptic Legerdemain*, other artists have opened themselves to influences from a seemingly endless

10-131. Cindy Sherman. *Sèvres Porcelain Soup Tureen: Madame de Pompadour (née Poisson).* 1990. Silk-screened and hand-painted on Limoges porcelain. Frick Art Museum, Pittsburgh. The inside bottom of the tureen features a silk-screened version of a photograph of dead fish entwined with ropes of pearls. This is surely a play both on the original use for the tureen and on Madame de Pompadour's maiden name, which is the French word for *fish*.

Gift of Mr. and Mrs. Richard M. Scaife

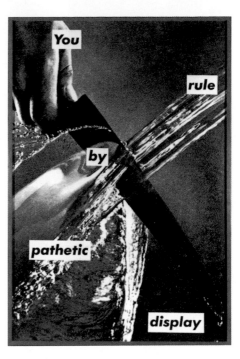

10-132. Barbara Kruger. *Untitled (You Rule by Pathetic Display).* 1982. Photograph, 6'1" x 4'1". Krannert Art Museum and Kinkead Pavilion, University of Illinois at Urbana-Champaign

Purchased by the Art Acquisition Fund

repertoire of commercial and contemporary cultural images. These images, often including printed texts, are divorced from their original context and are transformed to create new meanings. This recontextualization is a vehicle for some artists to examine social values and to address the inequalities people face in their daily lives. In appropriation art, not only has iconography been recast, but also the formats for works have assumed commercial modes, including electronic billboards, posters, T-shirts, and even soup tureens. This commercialization of mediums has assisted the deconstruction of our understanding of art forms, opening us to new possibilities in art.

The earliest photographs of Cindy Sherman (b. 1954) featured the artist herself posed in costumes and settings that re-created the dramatic, posed "stills" that were used to advertise movies in the 1940s and 1950s. The tureen illustrated here (fig. 10-131) is related to a later development, when she photographed herself costumed and in the poses of historical figures or figures in well-known paintings. The shapes, colors, and decorative motifs of the tureen and its platter are appropriated directly from the French eighteenth-century rococo style, but Sherman's modern addition is her silk-screened self-portrait as Madame de Pompadour in a setting that resembles the French royal residence at Versailles (see figs. 7-43–7-45). Sherman's low-cut dress and her seductive pose, with her eyes half-closed, refer to the rococo interest in seduction and sexuality. Her contemporary use of images from the past poses many questions concerning the multiple levels of artifice in our society and the multiple personae we may assume to meet this artifice.

Works by Barbara Kruger (b. 1945) are found in a variety of formats, from T-shirts to photomontages (fig. 10-132). Her compositions, inspired by the aesthetics of advertising, are direct. But whereas advertising most often promotes a stereotypical viewpoint, Kruger's works question and even de-mythologize such attitudes. *Untitled (You Rule by Pathetic Display)* is a feminist critique of male-dominated power structures, in which sexism, cutting like a knife, interrupts and destroys the natural flow of human relations and the advancement sought by women. The prominent knife suggests a further reference to domestic violence, yet the theme of the work, the inanity of power that rules by brute force, may also be interpreted on a more universal level.

AVANT-GARDE CHINESE ART

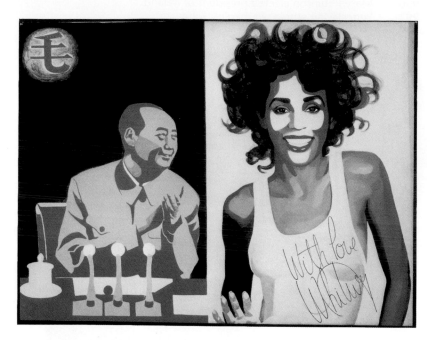

10-133. Yu Youhan. *With Love, Whitney.* 1992. Acrylic on canvas, 41 x 57". Courtesy, Hanart T Z Gallery, Hong Kong

Yu Youhan (b. 1943) painted *With Love, Whitney* (fig. 10-133) using familiar images: the revolutionary leader Mao Zedong and the American popular singer Whitney Houston. Mao is shown applauding one of his own principles; Whitney applauds her own music. The two images were copied in acrylic on canvas from official photographs and were meant to draw attention to the similarity between the manner in which a public image has been created for each well-known personality. Yu has created many paintings with similarly politically charged themes using the impersonal style of presentation made famous by such American Pop artists as Andy Warhol (see fig. 10-10). The Chinese call this style Political Pop, and Yu considers himself to be part of the "Avant-Garde Movement" created by a few young artists who were influenced by ideas about their responsibility to society. Their ideas have had a strong effect on the Chinese art world of the most recent period.

The Avant-Garde Movement, which was possible only after the Cultural Revolution (1977–87), is based on the commitment of certain artists to declare their individuality, which they thought of in a new way in China in the 1970s. These artists used their notion of "humanism" to refer to concepts of human freedom or individualism. The Stars Group, for example, who advocated criticism of society and called for an awakening of human nature, was the most controversial in the early years of the Chinese Avant-Garde Movement. When they were excluded from the National Art Gallery Exhibition in Beijing in 1979, they exhibited their works on a fence outside. The authorities immediately shut down their exhibit, and the response of the Stars Group was to demonstrate for individual human rights in the streets of Beijing. From this time on, Chinese artists played a revolutionary role in Chinese society and politics.

The Chinese Avant-Garde Movement includes artists who have an independent vision of their own work, even though the Group's direction has changed over time. These artists are at the edge of society and are part of the intellectual culture, not the official or popular culture. Their goal is to make way for freedom of spirit and expression in a society that, through its official strictures and internal social mechanisms, has not allowed for original thought. From 1979 to 1989, these artists acted on the principle that art could change society and make it free. Their art was politically motivated and critical. By attacking and destroying the traditional order in the art world, they thought that they could lead the way to freedom.

The artists in this movement who take a long view of culture do not limit their thoughts to immediate social concerns or problems, and most of their work is conceptual and philosophical. Some emphasize that life is instinct, others that life is accommodation. All oppose a society that suppresses human nature, and at the same time they praise a pure and simple life. Some have turned to depictions of rural life, of life among the many ethnic minorities in China, or of erotic and sexual encounters.

In *Mirror for Analyzing the World*, Xu Bing (b. 1955) emphasized other concepts. (fig. 10-134). Under the influence of Chan Buddhism (Zen Buddhism in Japan), he fabricated 4,000 characters that no one could read, even though they look like traditional Chinese characters. He then used traditional printing techniques to produce long scrolls and books. According to his interpretation of Chan thought, what is important is the laborious artistic process. The work of art is useless in itself. Xu compared his process of creation to the mindless diligence of Chan Buddhist labor, which was thought to empty the mind of useless knowledge and lead to enlightenment. His installations were thought of as extravagant, and critics argued that they expressed nihilist, absurdist, and tragic feelings.

After the Tiananmen Square Massacre on June 4, 1989, and the crushing of the "Democracy Movement" by the Chinese government, avant-garde art in the People's Republic of China changed. At that time, Zhang Peili, an artist working in Hangzhou, said:

> Before the Massacre, there was so much noise, a deafening roar of protest. Then the tanks came and everyone immediately fell silent. That silence was more terrifying than the tanks.

After the massacre, the socially critical aspect of the Avant-Garde Movement could no longer be expressed directly; displays of avant-garde art were banned, and artists could no longer use the visual and performing arts to express criticism of the government and the social order. Artists lost faith in the idea that an individual work could change society, but they began to write that art could function to make the *artist* free—and that to be free was no small matter.

Since 1989 and the government attacks on intellectual culture, the Avant-Garde Movement in China has weakened. With the increasing emphasis on the immediate economic benefits of any activity, both official and popular culture have common priorities that are significantly different from those of the intellectuals. Artists today confront the twin challenges of a commodi-

10-134. Xu Bing. *Celestial Book: Mirror for Analyzing the World.* 1988. Installation with printed paper. Installed February 5, 1989, National Academy of Art, Beijing, People's Republic of China

fied society and an entrenched art world. With the suppression of Chinese critics, critical recognition, and intellectual culture, the artists lost their most important audiences. Many of the most prolific avant-garde artists are now living and working outside of the People's Republic of China, while those working inside have to exhibit and sell their work abroad.

The idealism of the previous period has given way to ironic playfulness of the sort found in Yu's *With Love, Whitney*. This sort of Political Pop is not shown in China but has become very popular outside of the People's Republic in Chinese communities in Hong Kong, Taiwan, and Singapore, for example, and has many buyers in the West. This particular painting, for instance, is part of the collection of the China Club, a private club in Hong Kong.

Many recent avant-garde paintings and installations transcend the level of psychological and personal feelings of the earlier period to make more universal statements. They have the potential to be dangerous to the traditional artistic culture in China because they seek to create a viable alternative to the older art. Whether they will replace the traditional styles (see pages 198–201) is yet to be seen. Chinese art styles in the twentieth century rest on three legs: traditional brush painting, realism imported in the beginning of the twentieth century from Europe and the former Soviet Union, and the many streams of international (and largely Western) modern twentieth-century art. The work of the two artists discussed here appropriate from all of these traditions and are part of the global context of the 1980s and 1990s.

RECENT DEVELOPMENTS

10-135. Yoichiro Kawaguchi. *Coacervater.* 1994. CD-ROM, Video

From the late 1980s and into the 1990s, the tempo of artistic innovation has continued to accelerate while the diversity of forms and purposes of art have, at the same time, widened. The goal of this concluding section is to illuminate, rather than exhaust, the internationalization and multifaceted communication of "art present." This internationalization is expressed, for example, in several works by Japanese artists that are related to global interests while at the same time maintaining certain distinct Japanese qualities.

One increasingly important manner of creating art is through the use of computers, and it also seems clear that the exhibition and distribution of art on CD-ROMs will continue to grow in the years ahead. Although some dealers and museums have been hesitant to exhibit such work, an international exhibition in Helsinki in 1995 devoted to the theme of "Public/Private" included a number of CD-ROM presentations on computer terminals by artists from Australia, England, Finland, Japan, and the United States. The space in which these works were exhibited was often the most crowded area of the museum, and it was clear that children and teenagers were especially interested in this new type of art. Some of the CD-ROMs were interactive, allowing the museum audience to participate in the colorful developments being presented on the screen. One of the Japanese artists, Yoichiro Kawaguchi (b. 1952), offered *Coacervater* (fig. 10-135), in which there was a continuous, flowing change from one abstract form to another in a sequence of mesmerizing effects. This reproduction shows only one brief view of the continuously developing patterns invented by the artist with the aid of the computer.

At the same time, however, another Japanese artist, Nobuo Sekine (b. 1942), has continued to work in a more traditional manner. Sekine utilizes space on an environmental scale; it is handled in a way that draws both from traditional Japanese conceptions of landscape gardening and from contemporary concerns for preparing an environment that shares pleasure with the public. In *Plaza of Mother Earth* (fig. 10-136), monumental basalt sculptures, resembling megalithic formations from Japanese prehistory, are set within a gardenlike space. The juxtaposition of the rough "natural" state of the rock and the regularly designed spiral floor with its meticulously "finished" setstone base creates an aesthetic tension (or vitality) that was often thought to approximate *ki* (*qi*, in Chinese, see page 201), or the universal life force. The essential features (potential) of

10-136. Nobuo Sekine. *Plaza of Mother Earth*, Navel Park, Showa-machi, Japan. 1989. Basalt and environmental sound

the rock itself are emphasized—they are both roughhewn and polished and were left showing the process of being worked and changed. Application of this concept is well known in many Japanese arts, especially those of Zen Buddhist inspiration, such as the garden and the tea ceremony (see pages 344–45). But unlike traditional Zen gardens, which were exclusive, private places, Nobuo Sekine's spaces are constructed for the public. In this sense, he shares a concern of present-day environmental artists worldwide.

The shaped canvas paintings of Elizabeth Murray (b. 1940), which traverse the boundaries between painting and sculpture, have their roots in the formalism of the 1960s, particularly the shaped canvases of Frank Stella (see fig. 10-99). Unlike the Hard-Edge, intellectual abstraction of Stella, however, Murray's irregularly shaped canvases and use of strong color create a dramatic and even an emotional impact. In their complex, vital spatiality and surging, often-aggressive forms, they suggest the tensions that are part of everyday life. *Cracked Question* engages us both visually and intellectually (fig. 10-137). The intense colors and three-dimensional seething of the canvas create a tension that is reinforced by the fragmenta-

tion of a common and easily recognized symbol; the question mark itself becomes the source of questions. We are led away from old bonds or ideas to search for new relationships and meaning. Murray has asserted a deeper and more personal content of her work, for when she was asked if her paintings are political, she replied, "I want my work to reflect my feelings about the society we live in; [they're] political in that sense."

Lothar Baumgarten (b. 1944) is a contemporary German artist whose site-specific installation celebrates the achievements of an early-nineteenth-century Native American

10-137. Elizabeth Murray. *Cracked Question.* 1987. Oil on six canvases, 13'5¼" x 16'2" x 1'11½". Cordiant Group, Ltd., London

10-138. Lothar Baumgarten. *The Tongue of the Cherokee*, detail. 1985–88. Installation with painted, laminated, and sandblasted glass, 100 x 43'. Permanently installed at the Carnegie Museum of Art, Pittsburgh. Commissioned by the 1988 Carnegie International

named Sequoya. Baumgarten's installation (fig. 10-138) is viewed by looking up to a glass ceiling where letter shapes appear on many of the glass panels. These are the eighty-four letters of the Cherokee alphabet as it was invented by Sequoya, who seems to have been the only person in history to develop his own alphabet; he did not understand English, but he used English letters, without a knowledge of their relationship to sound, as a basis, and he added additional letters of his design. In the nineteenth century, Sequoya's alphabet was widely used by the Cherokees, and between 1828 and 1834, the *Cherokee Phoenix* was published in two languages and alphabets—Cherokee and English. The Cherokee language largely died out with the suppression of the Native American population, and Baumgarten's monumental work, which scatters the letters and their accents like random decoration, comments on its demise. This installation informs us both of personal achievements and of the consumption of one culture by another.

We Are Leaving Here Forever (fig. 10-139) is an installation by the Ukrainian artist Ilya Kabakov (b. 1933). Entering the darkened rooms with flashlights in hand, the museum visitors became something of archaeological intruders witnessing the remnants of a former collective human presence. In a two-story structure constructed inside the museum, large rectangular openings in the upper-level corridors looked down on a central space. This temporary installation represented an orphanage in the moments just after the children have left, never to return. All that remained were furniture, trash, and pieces of paper, some of which were scattered in corners or posted on the walls. In the large central space, pieces of trash and scraps of paper with phrases in Ukrainian and English were suspended from clotheslines. The words and phrases refer to the anxious voices of the departed occupants or to the faceted network of bureaucratic and personal existence.

Kabakov's installations are haunting and evocative. The suspended bits of paper and trash recall the Stalinist decrees of forced communalization that denied privacy to self and family. But the installation also spoke on a symbolic level of an interval between the immediacy of the remembered past and anxiety about the imminence and uncertainty of the future. Of this anxious time, Kabakov wrote:

> Nothing remains but a sea of useless papers, in which merciless orders, precise timetables, touching letters and notes are all mixed together. Some recall the past and mourn for it. Almost all are full of terror before the imminent uncertainty that awaits them.

On another level, Kabakov's installation reminds us of the insecurity that former Soviets face now that the USSR no longer exists.

The installations of Jenny Holzer (b. 1950) employ the high-tech mediums of electronic advertising to present continuous series of short statements that she calls truisms. Prompted by graffiti art in the 1970s, Holzer clandestinely placed posters in public areas near where she lived in New York City; each poster contained a philosophical or popular maxim. Clichés such as "Absolute Submission Can Be a Form of Freedom," "Money Creates Taste," and "Dying for Love Is Beautiful but Stupid" seemed to offer a trenchant commentary on contemporary social issues. Gradually, Holzer developed a conceptual art using computer-controlled light-emitting diode (LED) machines (fig. 10-140). Here, the medium of pop-

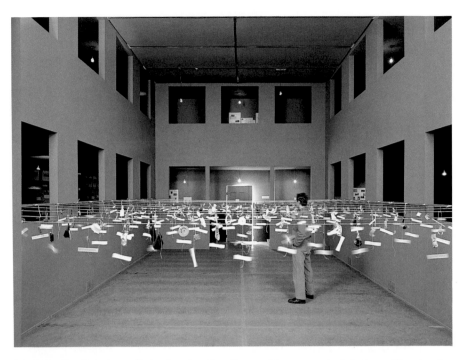

10-139. Ilya Kabakov. *We Are Leaving Here Forever*. Temporary installation with mixed media. Installed at the Carnegie International Exhibition at the Carnegie Museum of Art, Pittsburgh, 1991–92. Commissioned by the 1992 Carnegie International

10-140. Jenny Holzer. *Untitled (Selections from Truisms, Inflammatory Essays, The Living Series, The Survival Series, Under a Rock, Laments, and Mother and Child Text)*. Temporary installation with extended helical tricolor LED electronic display signboard, 11" x 162' x 4". Installed at the Solomon R. Guggenheim Museum, New York, 1989–90. Solomon R. Guggenheim Museum, New York. Commissioned by the Guggenheim Museum
Partial gift of the artist, 1989

10-141. Faith Ringgold. *Tar Beach*. 1988. Acrylic on canvas, and tie-dyed and pieced fabric, 6'2" x 5'9". Solomon R. Guggenheim Museum, New York

10-142. Louise Bourgeois. *Cell II*, detail. 1991. Mixed media, 6'11" x 5' x 5'. Carnegie Museum of Art, Pittsburgh
© 1997 Louise Bourgeois/VAGA, New York, NY

ular advertising is turned upon itself, revealing how we are manipulated by language, especially the media world's use of it. Holzer gets inside the system, using light bars and short, snappy, visual "sound bites," to critique it and to deconstruct or reveal the mode of manipulation.

I will always remember when the stars fell down around me and lifted me up above the George Washington Bridge. . . . Sleeping on Tar Beach was magical. Laying on the roof in the night with stars and skyscraper buildings all around me made me feel rich, like I owned all that I could see.

These words form part of the narrative text that Faith Ringgold (b. 1930) used to enframe her multimedia work *Tar Beach* (fig. 10-141). ("Tar Beach" is the colloquial name

given to a rooftop in the inner city at night.) Ringgold's work shares with us the realities and dreams of the African American experience in Harlem. Rich in the complexity of its visual, thematic, and psychological association, *Tar Beach* is composed of acrylic paint on canvas, with tie-dyed and pieced fabric attached to the surface. The quilt reminiscences recall the work of feminist artists in P + D painting (see pages 584–85), while the abrupt but purposeful transitions of perspective communicate the naïveté of children as they stare at buildings and stars from the roof. Ringgold's work visually is simple and direct, yet its human message is multilayered.

Unlike the contemporary artists discussed previously, Louise Bourgeois (b. 1911) belongs to a generation of earlier modern artists. An accomplished painter and sculptor who was thoroughly schooled in Surrealism, she first achieved prominence in the 1940s and 1950s. In

the early 1990s, she created a series of *Cells*; each *Cell* or unit was the size of a very small room, and each was defined by a grouping of old, hinged doors of various sizes, all painted in various shades of blue. Inside the *Cells*, combinations of found objects and precisely sculpted forms created an almost surrealistic atmosphere. Viewers are not permitted to enter the *Cells*; our vision of the objects in the interiors was confined to peering through windows and narrow openings between the doors.

In *Cell II* (fig. 10-142), old perfume bottles and Bourgeois's white marble sculpture of hands, with fingers tightly intertwined, are arranged on a circular mirror. Bourgeois has revealed that for her the clenched hands symbolize the indestructibility of pain, while the perfume bottles represent the fleeting scents of pleasure. This juxtaposition of opposite, intense sensations gives, in Bourgeois's words, "meaning and shape to frustration and suffering." By making us voyeurs, Bourgeois reveals not only this private drama of pain but also our inability to mediate or help. Finally, the *Cells* remind us of our ultimate isolation from one another. Drawn from personal experiences and remembrances, Bourgeois's *Cells* communicate the inescapable fact of human pain: "What happens to my body has to be given a formal abstract shape. So you might say, pain is the ransom of formalism."

Visitors to the 1991 Spoleto Festival USA in Charleston, South Carolina, were greeted by numerous site-specific works of art on the theme of "Places with a Past." A temporary installation by the American artist Ann Hamilton (b. 1956) was dominated by an enormous pile of approximately 48,000 carefully folded indigo-blue work clothes (fig. 10-143). Hamilton's intent in creating this "monument" was to celebrate the common person; the shirts and pants were meant to praise the achievements of "blue collar" workers and, especially, to emphasize the labor of the women who cared for these clothes. But there was yet another level to the experience of Hamilton's work. Throughout the course of the installation, a woman sat at a table and quietly erased the texts from old history books. To the artist, the act of erasing the text from a dated, conventional history book suggested that we need to create a new space in history to record the accomplishments of everyday people.

In *Indigo Blue*, the commonplace is made monumental in order to draw attention to the importance of ordinary events and people in American history. The revisualized photograph (fig. 10-144) by Morimura Yasumasa (b. 1951), on the other hand, might at first glance seem to be a simple re-creation of Manet's *Olympia* (see fig. 9-48). But Morimura has not merely reconstructed Manet's setting and pho-

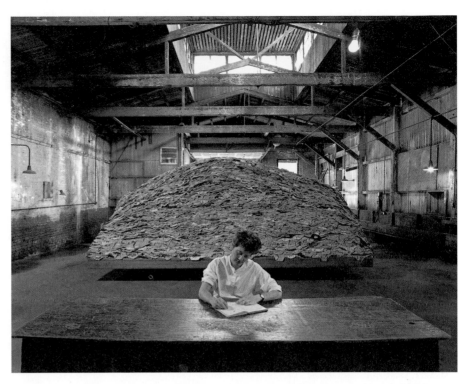

10-143. Ann Hamilton. *Indigo Blue*. Temporary installation with a woman participant and mixed media for "Places with a Past," Spoleto Festival USA, Charleston, South Carolina, 1991. The site that Ann Hamilton used for a site-specific installation in Charleston was on Pinkney Street, which, the artist discovered, had been named for Eliza Lucas Pinkney, the woman who in 1744 first grew indigo in the American colonies. This was the initial impetus for the installation *Indigo Blue*. Commissioned by the Spoleto Festival USA

10-144. Morimura Yasumasa. *Portrait (Futago)* (after Édouard Manet, *Olympia*, 1863). 1988. Color photographs, four panels, 6'10^{11}/16" x 9'10^{1}/2". Carnegie Museum of Art, Pittsburgh. In Japanese, *futago* means "twin."

10-145. Yukinori Yanagi. *Hinomaru Illumination (Amaterasu and Haniwa).* 1993. Neon and painted steel, with reproductions of ceramic *haniwa* figures; each *haniwa* approx. 39³/8" high. Installation at The Museum of Art, Kochi, Japan, 1993

tographed models in the positions made famous by Manet; that this is a complex photographic reconstruction becomes obvious when we recognize that the two figures are the same person in different costumes and makeup. This helps explain the term *futago* ("twin") used in the title. The fact that this is a man is apparent from the reclining figure; it is Morimura himself who has assumed the two female roles in the composition. Most of Morimura's work consists of photographs in which the artist takes the roles of figures in famous paintings or of contemporary popular heroes from the entertainment world. At first, we are astonished and amused, but gradually the serious message of Morimura's work asserts itself. It

becomes apparent that his use of computer-generated and photographic imagery is a commentary on the techniques through which cultural information is transmitted today and on how easily falsehood is possible. The photographs may represent Morimura's attempt to make a work that will be as shocking in his day as Manet's was in nineteenth-century Paris. Further, the superimposition of a Japanese artist into a Western work may allude to Japan's twentieth-century appropriation of Western culture and, at the same time, retention of an inherently Japanese integrity. On a more personal level, Morimura's work raises the issue of what it would be like to change sexes, or what it would be like to be a white

prostitute or a black maid in nineteenth-century France, or what it would be like to be Manet's model and to have to pose naked before an artist for many hours. The image should perhaps be understood within the political, economic, and social upheavals that Japan has experienced, especially since the death of Emperor Hirohito in 1989. Morimura's art is more than Postmodern appropriation. It questions Japan's identity at the close of this century, it raises problems about the role of the artist in society, and it asks us to understand ourselves and our relationship to others and to history in a new light.

Morimura's revisualized photographs are a multilevel social commentary. The *Hinomaru* series,

10-146. Masami Teraoka. *AIDS Series: Makiki Heights Disaster*. 1988. Watercolor on paper, mounted as four-panel screen, 6'5½" x 12'11". Private collection
Courtesy Pamela Auchincloss Gallery, New York

begun in 1990 by the Japanese artist Yukinori Yanagi (b. circa 1959), aims at deconstructing the myth that the Japanese people are a single "family" ruled by their emperor. Yanagi writes:

> The ruling powers of Japan have always resorted to political myths in order to reinforce the country's unity. . . . As a modern nation state, Japan fabricated a myth of "one people" . . . [arguing] that all Japanese, no matter how diverse, are children of the Emperor.

Yanagi's art champions diversity by satirizing fanatical nationalism. In *Hinomaru Illumination* (fig. 10-145),

row after row of repetitive figures based on the prehistoric Japanese *haniwa* type (see fig. 4-3) are grouped in an orderly manner, facing a neon "Rising Sun" flag. Although banned since the end of World War II, this flag has survived as a symbol for ultranationalist groups. *Haniwa* figures were created to surround and protect the tombs of early Japanese emperors; here, they symbolically take on the character of modern company workers, whose individual identity is suppressed in the name of corporate profit. By exposing the myth of "racial purity" perpetuated by ultranationalists, Yanagi attempts to open Japanese culture to the nondiscriminatory acceptance of minorities; his is an art of social meaning.

The work of Masami Teraoka (b. 1936) also speaks to the confrontation between East and West. Working within a bold style derived from that of Japanese *ukiyo-e* prints (see fig. 9-25), Teraoka makes huge paintings (fig. 10-146) that are mounted on folding panels, like traditional Japanese screens (see fig. 7-48). Teraoka's subjects—a couple shown in bed, enormous animals, and fighting figures, all combined with panels of calligraphic text—are clearly inspired by traditional Japanese themes. But the modern subject of *Makiki Heights Disaster* is a couple living with the fear of AIDS. To the right, a woman informs her lover that he must use a condom; the immense snake that menaces them is symbolic of the disease. The

10-147. James Turrell. Roden Crater project. 1974–present. San Francisco Volcanic Field, near Flagstaff, Arizona. Turrell plans to complete the Roden Crater project sometime between 2000 and 2010.

rest of the painting is filled with menacing references to suffering and death. Using both narrative and symbol, Teraoka's art becomes a weapon of social consciousness.

The Roden Crater project (fig. 10-147), by American artist James Turrell (b. 1943), is a decades-long work near Flagstaff, Arizona (see map, page 489), that remains to be completed. The goal is to create a natural observatory that is, in many ways, similar to those created by prehistoric peoples at Stonehenge (see fig. 2-9), by the Anasazi at Chaco Canyon, New Mexico, and by other early societies elsewhere. Using the movements of celestial bodies—the sun, moon, stars, and planets—the crater will track the passage of time. Without damaging the shape and beauty of the crater, Turrell has planned to construct four spaces that will be oriented to the four cardinal directions; each will be

designed to catch, reflect, or enclose natural light in a particular, often mysterious manner. Some of the rooms will function like a larger version of the **camera obscura** that was used by the Dutch seventeenth-century painter Vermeer and others; at Roden Crater, the image of the surface of the moon, for example, will be projected onto the wall of one of the chambers every 19.81 years. On a huge scale, Turrell has set out to re-create for modern observers at least a hint of the sensitivity to the rhythms of the sky and the changing seasons that was common among our prehistoric ancestors. That these cycles are still important to us is clarified by Turrell when he says that

there is a cycle of fertility that comes from the lunar cycle and it's the cycle almost all plants and animals

relate to. Humans have the same twenty-nine day cycle with fertility.

The Roden Crater project will be accomplished by creating spaces that are intended to be permanent—there is no high technology, and nothing will ever wear out. Like Stonehenge, it will continue its relationship to the heavens even if there is no one there to watch.

In many ways, the twin Petronas Towers in Kuala Lumpur, Malaysia (see map, page 588), designed by the American architect Cesar Pelli (b. 1926), express the artistic, economic, and social transitions that mark our era. When completed, the Petronas Towers (fig. 10-148) will become the world's tallest buildings—a statistic that is made more impressive by the fact that there are two towers, not just one. They will probably soon be eclipsed,

10-148. Cesar Pelli. Petronas Towers, Kuala Lumpur, Malaysia. Construction of towers completed in 1997. Height of each tower 1,483'. Previously the world's tallest building had been the Sears Tower in Chicago, Illinois, at 1,454 feet. Already in the planning stages at the Manhattan offices of Kohn Peterson Fox Associates is the Mori Shanghai, 95 stories and 1,509 feet tall, to be built in Shanghai, China. Petronas Towers was commissioned by the Malaysia National Petroleum Company.

however, by taller structures now being planned. By the year 2000, six of the ten tallest buildings are expected to be in Asia—illustrating dramatically the changing patterns of world economic development. At the same time, however, it should be recognized that new developments in electronics and computers mean that there is a decreased need for the huge amounts of office space demanded in American cities in the past.

The towers, which will house the offices of the national petroleum company, are part of a complex that includes other corporate offices, a hotel, a mosque, and a park. Although the structure was designed by an American, Malaysian engineers are playing key roles in the construction, and the enormity of the project is bringing an infusion of new technology and new industries to Kuala Lumpur.

In designing the towers, Pelli broke away from the International Style (see pages 552–53), which had dominated skyscraper architecture for decades. In fact, the design alludes to Islam, the official state religion of Malaysia: the plan of each tower is based on the traditional Islamic emblem of the eight-pointed star. Sunshades of stainless steel are intended to help control the tropical sun and heat, while the design emphasizes an openness to the environment. The towers are joined by a "skybridge." In a statement that is applicable to much of the art and architecture we have examined in this book, Pelli believes that the combination of towers and bridge is meant to suggest a gateway that "symbolizes the threshold between the tangible and spiritual worlds."

GLOSSARY

Definitions in the glossary are intentionally short; for further information and illustrations, consult the references listed. Words in CAPITAL LETTERS within an entry are defined in the glossary. An abbreviation used here is e.g., meaning for "example."

A BACUS: on a DORIC capital, the flat slab between the rounded ECHINUS and the ENTABLATURE; see fig. 3–60 and p. 93.

ACID BATH: a shallow tray of acid used in the ETCHING technique; see pp. 378–79.

ACROPOLIS: in ancient Greek cities, a fortified citadel and the site of the most important civic and religious buildings. The most famous is in Athens and is now called simply the Acropolis.

ACRYLIC PAINT: a fast-drying synthetic paint MEDIUM developed about 1960; see fig. 10–13.

AERIAL PERSPECTIVE: see ATMOSPHERIC PERSPECTIVE.

AIRBRUSH: a device for spraying paint or other liquid media. The medium is mixed with compressed air and sprayed through a nozzle; see fig. 10–116.

AISLES: corridors flanking a large central area; Old St. Peter's Basilica has two aisles on either side of its central NAVE (figs. 4–12, 4–13). Also known as side aisles.

ALTAR: a raised structure, usually tablelike, on which offerings are sacrificed, incense burned, or sacred objects kept. Christian altars usually consist of a consecrated slab—traditionally of stone and called a mensa—on a base.

ALTARPIECE: a painted and/or sculpted work of art that stands as a religious image upon and at the back of an ALTAR; see the Van Eycks' *Altarpiece of the Lamb* (figs. 5–25, 5–26).

AMBULATORY: a circular or semicircular vaulted passage, as at Chartres (fig. 4–82).

AMPHITHEATER: a circular or oval building with tiered seats for sports and entertainment, developed by the ancient Romans; e.g., the Colosseum or Flavian Amphitheater (figs. 3–108, 3–109, 3–110).

AMPHORA: an ancient Greek vase used to store olive oil, honey, or wine; see fig. 3–55.

ANICONIC: the representation of a deity by symbols rather than by figural form, as at Sanchi (fig. 3–86).

ANNULAR VAULT: a structural system composed of a series of vaults arranged in a curving or circular configuration; for examples see the ancient Roman Colosseum (figs. 3–108—3–110) and the AMBULATORY at Chartres (fig. 4–82).

APSE: in architecture, an area composed of a half cylinder or semipolygonal form surmounted by a half dome or VAULTING, as at Old St. Peter's (fig. 4–13) and Chartres (fig. 4–82).

AQUEDUCT: a structure used to transport water in ancient Roman times; e.g., the Pont du Gard (fig. 3–114).

ARCADE: a series of ARCHES with their supporting COLUMNS or PIERS, as in the nave arcades at Chartres (fig. 4–80) and Santo Spirito (fig. 5–35).

ARCH: a means of construction in which an opening, often semicircular, is spanned by a series of wedge-shaped elements (VOUSSOIRS and a KEYSTONE); see fig. 3–113 and p. 132.

ARCHITECTURE: a structure, usually functional, that encloses and defines space.

ARCHITRAVE: in architecture, the lowest part of an ENTABLATURE; see fig. 3–60 and p. 93.

ARCHIVOLTS: the moldings that enframe the TYMPANUM in a Romanesque or Gothic church; often decorated with sculptures, as at Vézelay (fig. 4–63).

ART: traditionally, defined as an object made by a person or persons that communicated a message, concept, or belief. Today art includes so many different kinds of products (including ephemeral performances, for example) that an all-encompassing definition is no longer possible.

ART THEORY: the discussion and establishment of philosophical ideals concerning the goals of art.

ASSEMBLAGE: a work of art that combines actual three-dimensional objects, some of that may be "found" objects from the household or the junkyard; see fig. 10–97.

ATMOSPHERIC PERSPECTIVE: a device, used in painting to suggest PERSPECTIVE, in which forms nearer the horizon are blurred and their color is less intense and higher in VALUE, while the sky gradually shades from blue toward white above the horizon, as in Perugino's *Christ Giving the Keys* (figs. 1–15, 5–22). Also known as aerial perspective.

ATRIUM: an open courtyard, sometimes surrounded by a COLONNADE, found at the entrance to a Roman house (fig. 3–89) or a Christian church (fig. 4–13).

AVANT-GARDE: a French term meaning advanced guard, which, in the nineteenth century, was applied to artists or movements considered to be new, radical, and often revolutionary. For example, the ideas and work of Gustave Courbet were regarded as avant-garde within the context of mid-nineteenth-century French painting; see pp. 444–45.

AVATAR: the descent of a deity into our time and space; an incarnation of a Hindu god; see the *Descent of the Ganges* (fig. 4–2).

AXIAL COMPOSITION or ORGANIZATION: a compositional pattern with a central AXIS and BILATERAL SYMMETRY, giving an impression of balance; see Botticelli's *Birth of Venus* (fig. 5–56).

AXIS: the imaginary straight line that passes through the center of figures or forms, or through an architectural composition. An analysis of the axes of a work helps establish its COMPOSITION.

AXONOMETRIC PROJECTION: a geometrical drawing that depicts a building in three dimensions.

BALDACCHINO: a canopy over an altar or throne; e.g., Bernini's at St. Peter's (fig. 7–19).

BALLOON FRAME: an architectural structure in which wooden beams are joined horizontally and vertically to create a gridlike structural system; e.g., Davis's wooden house (fig. 9–32).

BALUSTRADE: a low parapet or barrier formed of uprights, called balusters, topped by a rail.

BARREL VAULT: a deep ARCH that normally requires continuous BUTTRESSING; see fig. 3–113 and pp. 132–35. Also known as a tunnel vault.

BASILICA: to the ancient Romans, a large building used for public administration, as in the Basilica Ulpia in Rome (fig. 3–120). In Christian times, a specific type of structure, with a central NAVE, CLERESTORY, flanking AISLES, and APSE, as at Old St. Peter's (figs. 4–12, 4–13).

BAS-RELIEF: relief sculpture in which flattened figures or forms project only very slightly from the background; e.g., the *Palette of Narmer* (figs. 3–15, 3–16). Also known as low relief.

BATTERED WALL: a wall that slopes or slants inward toward the top, as in ancient Egyptian MASTABAS (fig. 3–20) and PYLONS (fig. 3–24).

BAYS: individual units of space defined by the PIERS and VAULTS in a vaulted structural system; the plan of the Gothic cathedral of Chartres (fig. 4–82), for example, reveals that the NAVE is seven bays long. Bays also refer to the vertical divisions of the exterior or interior surfaces of a building, as marked by such elements as windows, BUTTRESSES, COLUMNS, etc.

BILATERAL SYMMETRY: representations of people and objects in which both halves look essentially identical.

BOOK OF HOURS: a book of private devotions with prayers for the seven canonical hours of the Roman Catholic church. Sometimes contains a calendar and is illustrated with illuminations (figs. 5–11, 5–12).

BUON FRESCO: see FRESCO.

BURIN: a tool with a sharp metal point used in the decoration of Greek vases (fig. 3–54) and in making ETCHINGS (see pp. 378–79).

BURR: the tiny raised filings of copper on either side of the groove created in the DRYPOINT technique; the burr catches the ink and creates rich areas of deep, soft shadow; see pp. 378–79.

BUTTRESS, BUTTRESSING: the projecting support that counteracts the outward thrust of an ARCH or wall; see figs. 3–113, 4–84, and pp. 226–27.

CALLIGRAPHY: fine penmanship or beautiful writing (figs. 4–31, 4–79).

CALYX KRATER: an ancient Greek bowl with handles used for mixing wine with water; see fig. 3–55.

CAMERA OBSCURA: an enclosed box with an opening that allows an image to be projected inside the box; sometimes used by artists, including Vermeer (fig. 7–16), as a tool for understanding PERSPECTIVE recession.

CANTILEVER: a support system in which an architectural member projects horizontally into space, beyond its supports, as in Wright's Fallingwater (fig. 1–6).

CAPITAL: the decorated top of a COLUMN, PIER, OR PILASTER; often helps effect an aesthetic transition from the vertical COLUMN to the horizontal ENTABLATURE; for examples from the Greek and Roman ORDERS, see fig. 3–60.

CARITYA: a sacred Buddhist site, complete with a shrine, MONASTERY, lecture hall, and other structures, as at Nara (figs. 4–36, 4–37, 4–37b).

CARPET PAGE: a manuscript page with complex, abstract, decorative patterns, usually Hiberno-Saxon, as in the page from the Lindisfarne Gospels (fig. 4–30).

CARTOON: a full-size drawing for a painting.

CARVING: in sculpture, a subtractive process in which form is created by cutting into a medium, usually stone or wood, thereby releasing, or subtracting, excess parts of the medium (see fig. 5–29). The term also may refer to works of art fashioned by this technique. See also MODELING.

CASEIN: a technique of painting in which PIGMENTS are mixed with a milk protein; see fig. 9–78.

CASTING: a method of producing a copy of a three-dimensional object by pouring a hardening material into a mold; see fig. 3–66 and p. 97.

CAST SHADOWS: the shadows cast by an object onto surrounding surfaces and objects. In a painting, these shadows help increase the ILLUSIONISM, as in the ancient Roman still life (fig. 3–107).

CATACOMB: an underground complex of tunnels and rooms, used in ancient Roman times by Romans, Jews, and Christians for burial purposes; for a painting from a catacomb, see fig. 4–8.

CATHEDRAL: in western Christianity, a church that marks the residence of a bishop; for example, Chartres (figs. 4–80, 4–81, 4–82, 4–83).

CENTERING: the temporary wooden support upon which an ARCH or VAULT is constructed; see fig. 3–113 and p. 132.

CENTRALLY PLANNED: denotes an architectural design in which regularized units radiate, usually at 90° angles, from a central area, often surmounted by a dome, as in the original High Renaissance design for St. Peter's in Rome (fig. 6–25).

CHAITYA HALL: an Indian Buddhist architectural form with a pillared, central nave, two side aisles, an ambulatory, and a high barrel vault; many are carved out of living rock with a STUPA in the apse; see the Great Stupa at Sanchi, pp. 110–13, and the Kailasantha Temple (fig. 4–39).

CHA NO YA: the Japanese tea ceremony; see the art of Zen, pp. 344–45.

CHIAROSCURO: in painting and printmaking, the use of a contrast of VALUES to create effects of MODELING; see the Roman still life (figs. 3–107, 6–45).

CHOIR: in a Christian church, an enclosed area near the altar where the monks or nuns chant the services, as at Chartres (fig. 4–82).

CHUMON: the entrance gate to a Japanese Buddhist temple area, as at Horyu-ji (figs. 4–36, 4–37).

CLERESTORY: in architecture, an area elevated above adjacent rooftops, usually along a central AXIS. Its purpose is to allow light into the interior, and it has windows on the sides, as in the Egyptian HYPOSTYLE hall (fig. 3–25), Old St. Peter's (fig. 4–12), Chartres (figs. 4–80, 4–81), Santo Spirito (fig. 5–35), and elsewhere.

CLOISTER: an open court within a monastery, usually with an open ARCADE or COLONNADE; see figs. 4–46, 4–47.

CLUSTER PIER: in the Gothic structural system (fig. 4–84), a pier with groups of COLONNETTES, as at Chartres (fig. 4–81). Also known as a compound pier.

COFFERING, COFFERS: in architecture, recessed geometrical panels—often square—that decorate the interior surface of a VAULT; see the coffers of the DOME of the ancient Roman Pantheon (fig. 3–117) and elsewhere (fig. 7–23).

COLLAGE: a composition in which pieces of materials such as newspaper, cloth, or colored paper are glued to a canvas, paper, or other surface, as in Picasso's *Still Life with Chair Caning* (fig. 10–38).

COLLOCATION: the idea that an artist created a specific work for a specific location and that it is adjusted for that location and the spectator's viewpoint, as in Caravaggio's *Conversion of St. Paul* (fig. 7–11) and Rembrandt's *Militia Company of Captain Cocq* (fig. 7–22).

COLONNADE: a continuous row of columns supporting an ENTABLATURE or ARCHES; see the Parthenon (figs. 3–68, 3–70).

COLONNETTE: a slender, columnar decorative motif, common in Gothic architecture, as at Chartres (fig. 4–81), where groups of colonnettes create COMPOUND PIERS that support the NAVE ARCADE.

COLOR PALETTE: the selection of colors used by an artist; for an example of a restricted color palette, see Mondrian's *Diamond Painting* (fig. 1–16).

COLOSSAL ORDER: see GIANT ORDER.

COLUMN: a freestanding cylindrical support, often FLUTED and with a CAPITAL, used in POST-AND-LINTEL construction, as at the Parthenon (fig. 3–68).

COMPLEMENTARY COLORS: colors found opposite each other on the color wheel (see fig. 1–17), which form a neutral gray when mixed but create a vibrant contrast when placed side by side. The complementary color of each of the primary colors (red, yellow, and blue) is obtained by mixing the remaining two primaries; the complementary of red is green (yellow and blue); the complementary of yellow is violet (red and blue); and the complementary of blue is orange (red and yellow).

COMPOSITION: the arrangement or organization of the various elements of a work of art; e.g., the balanced symmetry of Perugino's *Christ Giving the Keys to St. Peter* (fig. 1–15).

COMPOUND PIER: see CLUSTER PIER.

CONCRETE: as developed by the ancient Romans, fast-drying hardening volcanic sand used in architectural construction; see pp. 132–35.

CONTRAPPOSTO: a term describing the position assumed by the human body when the weight is borne on one leg while the other is relaxed; e.g., the *Doryphorus* (fig. 3–67). Contrapposto creates a figure that seems to be relaxed and yet suggests the potential for movement.

CORBEL: an architectural member created as each successive vertical layer of building material, e.g., stone, brick, or wood, projects from the previous layer. It often supports a CORNICE; see pp. 132–35.

CORINTHIAN ORDER: one of the ancient Greek ORDERS; see fig. 3–60 and p. 93.

CORNICE: a projecting MOLDING surmounting and emphasizing a WALL or ARCH. Note the prominent interior cornices of the Pantheon (fig. 3–117) and the heavy cornice capping the Medici Palace (fig. 5–39).

CROSS-HATCHING: in drawings and PRINTS, superimposed layers of parallel lines (HATCHING) at an angle to one another, used to create shadows and MODELING, as in fig. 6–21.

CROSSING: in a Christian church, the area where the NAVE intersects the TRANSEPTS; for diagrams, see figs. 4–12, 4–84.

CROSS SECTION: an architectural diagram that shows how a building would look from the inside if it were cut by a vertical plane from side to side; for a cross section of the Parthenon, see fig. 3–71. See also LONGITUDINAL SECTION.

CROSS VAULT: a structural system formed by two TUNNEL VAULTS intersecting at right angles; see fig. 3–113 and pp. 132–35.

CRUCIFORM BASILICA: a BASILICA with TRANSEPTS, forming a Latin cross plan, as at Old St. Peter's (fig. 4–13).

CUN: in Chinese painting, small brushstrokes dabbed on quickly to create the sense of a particular texture, as in Li Cheng's painting (fig. 4–51).

DAGUERREOTYPE: the earliest practical photographic process; see pp. 456–57.

DEVARAJA: cult of the god-king in the Khmer kingdoms in Cambodia; an amalgam of a state cult and religion. See Angkor Wat, pp. 214–15.

DIMINUTION: a device used in drawing and painting to help suggest PERSPECTIVE. Forms are represented as progressively smaller to suggest their distance from the viewer; see Perugino's *Christ Giving the Keys to St. Peter* (fig. 1–15).

DIPTYCH: two equal-size panels hinged to fold shut or simply hang side-by-side. Most are painted; some are carved in RELIEF.

DOME: an architectural structural system that can be understood as an ARCH rotated 180° around a central axis; see fig. 3–113 and p. 133.

DORIC ORDER: the most vigorous and austere of the ancient Greek architectural ORDERS; see fig. 3–60 and p. 93.

DRESSED STONE: blocks of stone used for construction, each of which is carefully cut and trimmed for its specific place and purpose, as at the ancient Roman Pont du Gard (fig. 3–114).

DRUM: a cylindrical or polygonal wall set atop a building and used to support a DOME; see fig. 5–37.

DRUMS: the individual cylindrical units that are combined to create the SHAFT of a COLUMN; due to the ravages of time, the drums of the columns of the Parthenon are clearly visible today (fig. 3–68).

DRYPOINT: an INTAGLIO printmaking process; see fig. 7–34 and pp. 378–79.

ECHINUS: on a DORIC CAPITAL, the rounded, cushion-shaped MOLDING below the ABACUS; see fig. 3–60 and p. 93.

EDITION: a group of prints made from a single PRINT FORM in one of the print-making processes; see figs. 6–23, 7–34, 9–29. In current practice, artists sign and number each print in an edition.

ELEVATION: an architectural diagram that shows the exterior or interior surfaces of a building and their decoration diagramatically, without the recession and distortion that would result from a single viewpoint; see figs. 6–27, 6–28. Elevation can also refer to one exterior side of a building.

EMULSION TECHNIQUE: a painting technique using a liquid mixture in which one of the elements is suspended as minute droplets, as in fig. 10–100.

ENCAUSTIC: a technique of painting using PIGMENTS dissolved in hot wax; see fig. 4–21.

ENGAGED COLUMN: see HALF COLUMN.

ENGRAVING: an INTAGLIO printmaking process; see fig. 6–23 and pp. 310–11.

ENTABLATURE: the upper part of an architectural ORDER, which usually includes ARCHITRAVE, FRIEZE, and CORNICE; see fig. 3–60.

ENTASIS: the bulging of a DORIC column about one-third of the way up from the base, creating an effect of muscular elasticity; for a subtle example of entasis see the columns of the Parthenon (fig. 3–68).

ETCHING: an INTAGLIO printmaking process; see fig. 7–34 and pp. 378–79.

ETCHING GROUND: the acid-resistant, resinous mixture used to coat the PRINT FORM (a metal plate) in the ETCHING process; see pp. 378–79.

ETCHING NEEDLE: the sharp steel instrument used in the ETCHING technique; see pp. 378–79.

EXPRESSIVE CONTENT: the emotions and feelings communicated by a work of art.

FACADE: the front or principal face of a building, as in Palladio's San Giorgio Maggiore (fig. 6–63).

FAIENCE: colorfully glazed earthenware or pottery, whether in the form of sculpture, decorative tiles, or functional vessels; see the Minoan *Snake Goddess* (fig. 3–32).

FERROCONCRETE: see REINFORCED CONCRETE.

FIGURE-GROUND RELATIONSHIP: the contrast between form (or positive elements) and background (or negative ground) in a work of art; see Piero's *Duke of Urbino* (fig. 5–6).

FLUTES, FLUTING: shallow vertical grooves on the SHAFT of a COLUMN that

accentuate the column's cylindrical quality; see fig. 3–60.

FLYING BUTTRESS: a structural element in the form of an open half arch that counteracts the outward thrust of an ARCH or VAULT; see fig. 4–84.

FORESHORTENING: the technique used in a painting or RELIEF SCULPTURE to suggest that figures, parts of the body, or other forms are shown in sharp recession, as in Mantegna's *Foreshortened Christ* (fig. 5–50).

FORMAL ANALYSIS: a visual examination and analysis of a work of art that studies how the integral parts of a work of art are united to produce its historical and/or individual style. Introductory formal analyses of works of art are offered for figs. 1–4, 1–6—1–12, 1–15, 1–16.

FORUM: the official center of an ancient Roman town, with temple, marketplace, and governmental buildings; see the forum in Rome (fig. 3–95).

FREESTANDING: see SCULPTURE IN THE ROUND.

FRESCO: a technique of painting directly on a plaster wall or ceiling, usually when the plaster is still wet, as in Giotto's Arena Chapel (fig. 4–98) and Michelangelo's Sistine Chapel ceiling (fig. 6–30); see figs. 3–106, 4–101. Also known as buon fresco. See also FRESCO SECCO.

FRESCO SECCO: a technique of FRESCO painting in which the paint is applied to dry plaster.

FRIEZE: the middle section of the horizontal ENTABLATURE in the ancient Greek and Roman ORDERS; see fig. 3–60 and p. 93.

FUNCTION: the purpose for which a work of art was created; e.g., the function of the Egyptian sculpture of *Menkaure and His Wife, Queen Khamerer-nebty* (fig. 1–2) was to provide a home for the souls of the pharaoh and his queen throughout eternity.

GABLE ROOF: the most common type of roof, formed by two planes that slope downward from a central beam, as on the Parthenon (fig. 3–70). Also known as a pitched roof.

GENRE PAINTING or SCULPTURE: a representation of everyday life, as in Leyster's *Gay Cavaliers* (fig. 7–13).

GESSO: a mixture of glue (size) and gypsum or chalk used to coat a surface that will be gilded or painted, usually with TEMPERA PAINT. Also used to build up BAS-RELIEF sculpture and to mold elaborate picture frames before GILDING.

GIANT ORDER: PILASTERS or COLUMNS that

span more than one story of a structure; e.g., the pilasters on the exterior and interior of Michelangelo's design for New St. Peter's in Rome (figs. 6–27, 6–28). Also known as colossal order.

GILDING: the covering of a work of art or part of a work of art with gold leaf or some other gold-colored substance; the background of Giotto's *Madonna* is gilded (fig. 4–95).

GIORNATA: from the Italian word meaning "day." Giornata lines are produced when areas of plaster (*intonaco*) overlap one another in a FRESCO. In the true fresco technique, these areas of *intonaco* would be painted in one day, before the plaster dried, hence the term *giornata;* see figs. 3–106 and 5–17.

GLAZES: in the art of oil painting, thin layers of superimposed translucent varnish, often with a small amount of pigment added, to modify color and to build up a rich, sonorous color effect; used by Jan van Eyck (figs. 5–32, 5–33), Titian (figs. 6–41, 6–43), and others. In pottery, the glaze is a thin layer of a colored material that fuses with the surface when heated; the glaze provides the hard and colorful surface of a pottery vessel.

GOUACHE: opaque WATERCOLOR paint.

GREEK CROSS PLAN: a central plan with four arms of equal dimension placed at 90° angles, usually surrounding a DOME, as in Bramante's and Michelangelo's design for New St. Peter's (figs. 6–25, 6–26).

GRISAILLE: the monochromatic painting of objects, often to simulate stone sculpture; see fig. 5–26.

GROIN VAULT: see CROSS VAULT.

GROUND PLAN: an architectural diagram that shows how a building would look from above if it were truncated by a horizontal plane approximately one meter above floor level; see figs. 4–82, 7–24.

GUILDS: legal organizations of merchants, craftspeople, and artists, rather like trade unions, that flourished in the later Middle Ages and the Renaissance. Guilds established standards for training and production and commissioned works of art; see the niches at Orsanmichele in Florence (figs. 5–9, 5–10).

HALF COLUMN: a half-round decorative COLUMN attached to a supporting wall. Also known as an engaged column.

HALF-HIPPED ROOF: a type of roof construction in which the ends are vertical and partly HIPPED, or they are hipped using two different angles, as at Nara (fig. 4–36).

HALO: a radiance of light, visually represented as a golden circle or disc, surrounding the head of a holy figure, as in the Byzantine mosaic at Mount Sinai (fig. 4–19).

HAPPENING: a quasi-theatrical event, common in the 1950s and 1960s, in which artists, usually without a preconceived script, performed and encouraged the spontaneous participation of the audience; see fig. 10–15.

HATCHING: in drawings and prints, closely spaced series of parallel lines that create effects of MODELING, as in fig. 6–21. See also CROSS-HATCHING.

HIERARCHICAL SCALE: the representation of figures who are more important politically (or socially) as larger than less important figures, as in *Ti Watching a Hippopotamus Hunt* (fig. 3–28).

HIGHLIGHTS: in painting, areas of HIGH VALUE color which suggest light hitting the form to create MODELING; see the highlights on the metal pitcher in the Roman still life (fig. 3–107).

HIGH RELIEF: RELIEF SCULPTURE in which the forms project substantially from the background; e.g., the altar at Pergamon (fig. 3–82).

HIGH VALUE: a relatively light color, as in the high value of the yellow trousers in Goya's *Execution of Madrilenos on the Third of May* (fig. 9–18).

HIPPED ROOF: a type of roof construction in which the ends are sloped instead of being vertical.

HISTORICAL CONTEXT: the ideas, beliefs, or attitudes current in the period when a work of art was created. Historical context also encompasses how the work of art was perceived by its audience.

HISTORICAL SIGNIFICANCE: an understanding of how a work of art reveals the ideas, beliefs, or attitudes current in the period when that work of art was created.

HISTORICAL STYLE: a clearly recognizable artistic tradition (see FORMAL ANALYSIS) characteristic of a particular historical or artistic period.

HUE: the property of a color that distinguishes it from others; also the name of a color; see fig. 1–17.

HYPOSTYLE: a type of architectural construction in which the interior space is crowded with continuous rows of COLUMNS or posts, as in the Egyptian hypostyle hall (fig. 3–25) and the Mosque at Córdoba (fig. 4–41).

ICON: a special term used in Orthodox Christianity to refer to a painting of a religious subject, as in fig. 4–21.

ICONOGRAPHY: the art-historical study of the subject matter of a work of art, including the investigation of the symbolism and the meaning of the subject in the culture that produced it.

ICONOLOGY: the investigation of how the iconography of a work is related to the HISTORICAL CONTEXT.

IDEALIZATION, IDEALIZED: the improvement and abstraction of forms to conform to contemporary cultural standards of perfection and beauty; e.g., *Menkaure and His Wife, Queen KhamererNebty* (fig. 1–2).

ILLUMINATED MANUSCRIPT: a handwritten book with painted decoration, common in medieval and Renaissance Europe; see figs. 4–20, 4–30, 4–31, 4–44, 4–58, 4–79, 5–11, 5–12.

ILLUSIONISM, ILLUSIONISTIC: when the objects represented in a work of art (usually a painting) seem to be tangible and weighty, existing within actual space; e.g., Perugino's *Christ Giving the Keys* (fig. 1–15); see pp. 126–29.

IMPASTO: raised brushstrokes of thick paint, usually oil, as in Titian's *Rape of Europa* (fig. 6–46).

INCISED RELIEF: see SUNKEN RELIEF.

INDIVIDUAL STYLE: the particular formal qualities (see FORMAL ANALYSIS) used by an individual artist; e.g., the bold colors, thick paint, and heavy brushstrokes characteristic of the works of Van Gogh (figs. 9–11, 9–72, 9–73).

INFILLING: see WEB.

INSTALLATION: a work of art that consists of an ensemble of objects, often three-dimensional, that are especially arranged by the artist for a particular location or site (see fig. 10–140).

INTAGLIO PROCESS: a printmaking process in which the lines to be printed are incised into the surface of the PRINT FORM, such as in the engraving, etching, and drypoint processes; see figs. 6–23, 7–34.

INTENSITY: the level of richness or saturation of a color; note the very intense red used in Van Gogh's *Night Cafe* (fig. 9–72).

INTERLACE: common in medieval art and architecture, ornament composed of intertwined line-form elements, such as stylized vines and/or animal forms.

IONIC ORDER: one of the ancient Greek architectural ORDERS; see fig. 3–60 and p. 93.

ISOCEPHALY: a COMPOSITION, usually relatively unnaturalistic, in which the heads of the figures form a horizontal line; see the mosaic of *Theodora and Attendants* at Ravenna (fig. 4–27).

ISOMETRIC PROJECTION: an architectural diagram that includes both a ground plan and a view of the exterior and/or interior from a specific point of view below or above the structure; for an isometric projection of a temple at Karnak, see fig. 3–27.

JAMBS: the areas flanking an ARCH, doorway, or window; in Romanesque and Gothic churches, the jambs are often decorated with sculpted figures, as at Amiens (fig. 4–90).

KACHIN-TIHU: a small wooden figure or doll (also known as a kachina doll) made by members of the Hopi people (fig. 10–28).

KAMI: in the Shinto religion, Japanese nature spirits thought to endow all things; see the Shinto Shrine at Ise, pp. 162–63.

KEYSTONE: the central VOUSSOIR of an arch, rib, or vault; see fig. 3–113.

KONDO: the main hall at a Japanese Buddhist temple-MONASTERY complex, as at Horyu-ji (figs. 4–36, 4–37, 4–37b).

KUFIC: a style of Arabic CALLIGRAPHY, sometimes used as virtually pure ornament.

KYLIX: an ancient Greek drinking cup; see fig. 3–55.

LACQUER: a hard, opaque varnish with a high-polish surface. Originally derived from the sap of a tree native to China, lacquer was used to fashion objects of functional art and religious utensils in East Asia.

LAY ARTIST: during periods when much artistic production was controlled by monks and nuns, a lay artist was one who lived and worked in the city, outside of the MONASTERY, and was often a member of a GUILD.

LEKYTHOS: an ancient Greek container to hold olive oil; see fig. 3–55.

LINEAR: the technique in painting, drawing, or printmaking of creating sharply defined forms or precisely delineated contours, as in Leonardo da Vinci's *Vitruvian Man* (fig. 5–58).

LINEAR PERSPECTIVE: developed in fifteenth-century Europe, a method of representing three-dimensional objects on a two-dimensional plane. Linear perspective has all parallel edges and lines converging as ORTHOGONALS toward one or more VANISHING POINTS on a two-dimensional surface. Also called scientific perspective.

LINGAM: a phallic symbol in the Hindu religion associated with the God Siva; see the Kailasantha Temple, Ellora, India (fig. 4–39).

LINTEL: the horizontal beam spanning an

opening, as in the POST-AND-LINTEL SYSTEM (fig. 3–22).

LITHOGRAPHY: a printmaking process; see fig. 9–29 and p. 439.

LONGITUDINAL SECTION: an architectural diagram that shows how a building would look from the inside if it were sliced by a vertical plane from front to back; see the Pantheon (fig. 3–116) and New St. Peter's (fig. 6–27).

LOST-WAX BRONZE CASTING: a technique of CASTING bronze and other metals; see fig. 3–66 and p. 97.

LOW RELIEF: relief sculpture in which flattened figures or forms project only very slightly from the background, as in the *Palette of Narmer* (figs. 3–15, 3–16). Also known as BAS-RELIEF.

LOW VALUE: a relatively dark color, as in the low value of the background in Goya's *Execution of Madrilenos on the Third of May* (fig. 9–18).

LUNETTE: a semicircular area enclosed by an ARCH, as at the Byzantine church of San Vitale (fig. 4–25).

MADKSOURAH: a special enclosure in a MOSQUE reserved for the calif (ruler), as at Córdoba (fig. 4–41).

MANDALA: a diagram of the Buddhist cosmos, used as a basic design motif in Buddhist art, as at Sanchi (fig. 3–84).

MANDORLA: an oval or almond-shaped HALO that surrounds the body of a holy figure, as in the Byzantine mosaic at Mount Sinai (fig. 4–19).

MANUSCRIPT: a handwritten book produced in medieval and Renaissance Europe. If it has painted decoration, it is known as an ILLUMINATED MANUSCRIPT; see figs. 4–30, 4–31 and 5–11, 5–12.

MASTABA: a rectangular Egyptian burial monument, with BATTERED WALLS and a flat roof; see fig. 3–20.

MEDIUM/MEDIA: the material or materials of which a work of art is composed, or the technique used to create it; e.g., oil paint on canvas (fig. 9–73), bronze (fig. 5–41), and etching (fig. 7–33).

MEGALITH: a very large stone of irregular shape (not DRESSED) used in prehistoric monuments; see Stonehenge (fig. 2–9).

METALPOINT: a graphic arts technique of drawing with a fine-pointed metal rod, often silver, on paper prepared with a special coating, called a ground. The faint metal line oxidizes to a light brown.

METOPES: the square areas between the TRIGLYPHS in the FRIEZE area of the ENTABLA-TURE of the DORIC ORDER; sometimes deco-

rated with sculpture, as at the Parthenon (fig. 3–70); see fig. 3–60 and p. 93.

MIHRAB: in a MOSQUE, the ARCH or niche on the QIBLA wall that indicates the direction of Mecca, to which Muslims turn in prayer, as that at Córdoba (figs. 4–41, 4–42, 4–43).

MINARET: the tower in a MOSQUE complex, usually tall and slender, from which the Muslim faithful are called to prayer five times a day; see Hagia Sophia (fig. 4–23).

MIXED-MEDIA: a term used to describe a work composed of a variety of different materials, usually encompassing elements of painting, sculpture, and even architecture (see fig. 10–97).

MOBILE: a sculpture that moves, usually a lightweight, delicately balanced suspended work; see the example by Calder (fig. 10–82).

MODELING/TO MODEL: in painting, drawing, or printmaking, the creation of an effect of weight and mass in an object by the manipulation of VALUE to create HIGHLIGHTS and SHADING, as in fig. 5–57; in sculpture, an additive process in which form is created with a malleable medium such as clay; see CARVING as a subtractive process.

MOLDING: an ornamental band, depressed or projecting, that gives definition to an architectural surface.

MONASTERY: a religious establishment that houses a community of persons who have withdrawn from the world to pursue the religious life; see examples from St. Gall and Cluny (figs. 4–46, 4–47).

MONOCHROMATIC: term used to describe a painting or drawing created by shades of black and white or values of a single color, as in Picasso's *Guernica* (fig. 10–78).

MOSAIC: a pattern made of small pieces (TESSERAE) of stone, tile, or glass, used on floors, walls, or ceilings; see Roman floor mosaics (figs. 3–53, 3–80) and the wall and ceiling mosaics at San Vitale (figs. 4–25—4–28).

MOSQUE: a place of worship in the Islamic religion, as at Córdoba (figs. 4–41, 4–42, 4–43).

MOUND ARCHITECTURE: an early type of architectural construction characterized by the creation of a solid mass, as in the Sumerian ZIGGURAT (fig. 3–7) and the Egyptian pyramids (fig. 3–17).

MUDRA: a hand gesture of Buddha, as in fig. 4–38. Each traditional gesture conveys its own meaning.

MURAL PAINTING: large wall decorations;

e.g., those at the Villa of the Mysteries (fig. 3–103) and Giotto's Arena Chapel (fig. 4–98).

NAOS: the walled inner sanctuary of a Greek temple, where the cult statue is housed (fig. 3–71).

NARTHEX: an entrance hall or vestibule, often found in Christian churches, as at Old St. Peter's Basilica (fig. 4–13).

NATURALISM, NATURALISTIC: when the elements or forms within a work of art closely resemble the appearance of those forms in nature; e.g., Bernini's *Apollo and Daphne* (fig. 1–4).

NAVE: the large central hall, usually AXIAL and often with a CLERESTORY, that characterizes the BASILICA plan (see Old St. Peter's, fig. 4–13, and many Christian churches).

NAVE ARCADE: the series of ARCHES that divide the NAVE from the AISLES; see fig. 4–84.

NONOBJECTIVE: when the forms in a work of art do not resemble forms in the visual world; e.g., Mondrian's *Diamond Painting* (fig. 1–16). Also known as nonrepresentational.

NONREPRESENTATIONAL: see NONOBJECTIVE.

NUNNERY: a religious establishment that houses a community of women who have withdrawn from the world to pursue the religious life.

OBA: the name of the monarch in Benin society when the Portuguese arrived there in 1485; see the royal ancestral shrine at Benin (fig. 4–104) and pp. 238–39.

OCULUS: a circular opening in a wall or at the apex of a DOME, as in the ancient Roman Pantheon (fig. 3–117).

OIL PAINT TECHNIQUE: a technique developed in the fifteenth century in which the pigments are mixed with the slow-drying and flexible MEDIUM of oil; see figs. 5–33, 5–34 and pp. 272–73.

ORDERS: a series of Greek and Roman architectural systems that give aesthetic definition and decoration to the POST-AND-LINTEL SYSTEM; see fig. 3–60.

ORTHOGONALS: the converging diagonal lines that meet at the vanishing point in the SCIENTIFIC PERSPECTIVE system, as in Donatello's *Feast of Herod* (fig. 5–23). In reality these lines would be parallel; see fig. 5–24 and p. 263.

OVERLAPPING: a device used in painting and relief sculpture to help suggest perspective. Forms are placed in front of other forms to suggest their relative placement within the illusion of space.

PAGODA: the European name for a tall tower, often with a series of roofs over successive storeys, that marks sacred Buddhist sites in China and Japan, as at the Horyu-ji complex (figs. 4–36, 4–37).

PAINTERLY: in painting, the technique of using large brushstrokes and flecks of paint to define form; see figs. 6–44, 7–21.

PANATHENAIC AMPHORA: an ancient Greek vase awarded as a prize at the Olympic Games; see fig. 3–55.

PARCHMENT: the skin on a calf, sheep, or other animal which is scraped, stretched, and dried to be used as a surface for writing. Used in the medieval period for MANUSCRIPTS.

PASTEL: a drawing medium made of ground pigments mixed with gum water.

PATRON: the person, persons, or organization that asks an artist or artists to create a work of art. Usually they pay for the work.

PATTERN BOOK: a book of images, prepared as an artist's tool, that preserves a tradition of images that can be copied; see fig. 4–6.

PEDIMENT: the triangular end of a GABLE ROOF; in a Greek temple this area is often decorated with sculpture; see figs. 3–49, 3–72, 3–73, 3–74.

PENDENTIVES: in a domed structure, the curved triangular segments that provide a transition from the four supporting piers to the circular base of the dome, as at the Byzantine church of Hagia Sophia (fig. 4–22). For a diagram see fig. 3–113.

PERIPTERAL: a term that describes a building with an exterior PERISTYLE; e.g., the Parthenon (fig. 3–70).

PERISTYLE: a continuous row of COLUMNS that completely surrounds the exterior of a structure, e.g., the ancient Greek Parthenon (fig. 3–70), or an inner courtyard, as in fig. 3–89.

PERSPECTIVE: depth. An illusion of perspective is suggested in many paintings; e.g., Perugino's *Christ Giving the Keys to St. Peter* (fig. 1–15). Devices that help suggest the illusion of perspective include LINEAR PERSPECTIVE, ATMOSPHERIC PERSPECTIVE, DIMINUTION, and OVERLAPPING.

PICTORIAL RELIEF: relief sculpture that conveys an illusion of depth by using a subtle transition from high to progressively lower relief. See Donatello's *Feast of Herod* (fig. 5–23) and Ghiberti's *Story of Jacob and Esau* (fig. 5–27).

PICTURE PLANE: the flat surface of a pic-ture. The picture plane, denied in such illusionistic works as Perugino's *Christ Giving the Keys to St. Peter* (fig. 1–15), is emphasized as a positive element in many nineteenth- and twentieth-century paintings, such as Mondrian's *Diamond Painting* (fig. 1–16).

PIECE-MOLD CASTING: a method of CASTING metal objects developed in ancient China in which the mold for receiving molten metal is made of a number of sections fitted together and then packed in sand before casting. See p. 79.

PIER: the vertical supports used in an ARCHED or VAULTED structural system; see the supports of the ancient Roman Pont du Gard (fig. 3–114) and the nave piers of the Gothic cathedral at Chartres (figs. 4–80—4–84).

PIETÀ: an iconographic theme in which the dead Christ is shown being held by his mother, as in Michelangelo's *Pietà* (fig. 5–62).

PIGMENT: the substance, usually ground, that is used to give color in the TEMPERA, FRESCO, and early OIL painting techniques.

PILASTER: a shallow, virtually flat version of the columns of the Greek and Roman ORDERS; pilasters are usually decorative, not structural. See fig. 8–3.

PITCHED ROOF: see GABLE ROOF.

PLAN: see GROUND PLAN.

PLATE: the thin metallic plate used as a PRINT FORM in ENGRAVING and ETCHING; see figs. 6–23, 7–34.

POLYCHROME: painted in many colors and often used to describe sculpture.

POLYPTYCH: a work of art composed of four or more leaves or panels.

POESIE: the Venetian name for a theme from mythology treated in a nostalgic and romantic manner; see Titian's *Rape of Europa* (fig. 6–46).

POINTED ARCH: an ARCH in which the sides rise to a point at the apex, as in Gothic architecture (figs. 4–80, 4–84, 4–85).

PORTICO: a sheltered space for walking; usually refers to a COLUMN-lined projection in front of the main entrance to a classical structure.

POST-AND-LINTEL SYSTEM: a simple system of architectural construction in which horizontal architectural members (LINTELS) are supported by vertical supports (posts); see fig. 3–22 and p. 66.

POTTER'S WHEEL: a revolving platform on which clay vessels of regular and often graceful shape are formed. Examples of wheel-produced vessels include the ancient Greek pots shown in fig. 3–55.

PRESENTATION DRAWING: a finely fin-ished drawing made to be given to a collector or friend.

PRIMARY COLORS: red, yellow, and blue. These are HUES that in theory are pure and not the combination of any other hues. On the color wheel (fig. 1–17), all other colors are understood as mixtures of these three hues.

PRINT: a work of art produced by one of the printmaking processes, including WOODCUT, ENGRAVING, ETCHING, DRYPOINT, LITHOGRAPHY, and silkscreen.

PRINT FORM: the surface—wood, copper, steel, glass, stone, etc.—to which ink is applied in any of the PRINTMAKING processes; see figs. 6–23, 7–34, 9–29.

PRINTMAKING: a series of techniques (WOODCUT, ENGRAVING, ETCHING, DRYPOINT, LITHOGRAPHY, silkscreen, and others) by which prints are produced.

PSALTER: a manuscript of the Psalms of David, as in the *Paris Psalter* (fig. 4–20).

PSEUDO-PERIPTERAL: a building that seems to have a PERISTYLE, but many of the COLUMNS are HALF COLUMNS or PILASTERS; e.g., the Roman Temple of Portunus (fig. 3–88).

PURE COLOR: a color at maximum or full intensity; a HUE without the addition of white, black, or other colors that would reduce the INTENSITY of the color; e.g., the colors used by Mondrian in his *Diamond Painting* (fig. 1–16).

PUTTI: figures of male babies, sometimes male baby angels, popular in Renaissance art, as in Mantegna's frescoes in the Camera Picta (figs. 5–48, 5–49).

PYLON: the entrance gate to an Egyptian temple complex, with broad BATTERED towers and flagpoles; see fig. 3–24.

QI: Chinese cosmic spirit; used in aesthetics to describe the "life" or spirit of a painting; see Chinese landscape painting, pp. 198–99.

QIBLA: in a MOSQUE, the wall that indicates the direction of Mecca, toward which Muslims turn in prayer; see Córdoba (figs. 4–42, 4–43).

QUADRIGA: a sculptural monument that consists of a figure in a chariot with four horses; the *Charioteer* (fig. 3–65) was part of a quadriga.

REALISM, REALISTIC: the use of subject matter drawn from actual life and experience; e.g., fig. 7–16. Not to be confused with the nineteenth-century movement known as Realism (figs. 9–35, 9–36, 9–63).

RED-FIGURE STYLE: style of Greek vase painting from c. 530 BCE to the third century BCE in which the background of a scene is painted with a clay SLIP that turns black in firing, leaving the designs in the natural reddish tones of the clay. Details are also painted with slip and so appear as black lines.

REFECTORY: the dining hall in a MONASTERY or NUNNERY; the location for Leonardo da Vinci's painting of the *Last Supper* (fig. 5–60).

REINFORCED CONCRETE: concrete strengthened with embedded wire rods or mesh; see fig. 9–43. Also known as ferroconcrete.

RELIEF: sculpture in which the design extends from a background surface.

RELIEF PROCESS: a PRINTMAKING process in which the lines and surfaces to which the ink adheres are higher than the parts that are not to be printed; e.g., the WOODCUT process; see fig. 6–23 and pp. 310–11.

RELIEF SCULPTURE: sculpture in which the figures or forms are united with a background; examples of relief sculpture types include LOW or BAS-RELIEF (figs. 3–15, 3–16), HIGH RELIEF (fig. 3–82), SUNKEN RELIEF (fig. 3–10), and PICTORIAL RELIEF (fig. 5–23).

RELIQUARY: a container for a sacred relic, as in fig. 4–1.

REPOUSSOIR: an object in the immediate foreground of a painting that establishes the frontal plane of the illusionistic space; e.g., the low fence in the FRESCOED room known as *Livia's Garden* (fig. 3–105).

REPRESENTATIONAL: when a work of art reproduces the appearance of forms in nature; see Bernini's *Apollo and Daphne* (fig. 1–4).

RIBS: raised structural elements that outline and help support a ribbed VAULT, as at the Gothic cathedral of Chartres (figs. 4–80, 4–81); see fig. 4–85 and p. 226.

ROUND ARCH: also sometimes called a true arch, it is a half-round opening that rises at the SPRINGING from upright supports.

RUSTICATION: the practice of covering building surfaces with massive, rough-cut stones, often with deep-cut grooves at the joints.

SARCOPHAGUS: a stone coffin, sometimes decorated with sculpture; see fig. 4–10.

SCIENTIFIC PERSPECTIVE: see LINEAR PERSPECTIVE.

SCREEN WALL: a non-supporting wall, usually with broad expanses of windows, that fills the opening under an ARCH or VAULT, as at the Byzantine church of Hagia Sophia (fig. 4–22). It is screen walls that sheathe the exterior of a modern steel-frame skyscraper.

SCRIPTORIUM: the room or rooms in a MONASTERY where MANUSCRIPTS are copied and illustrated, as in the St. Gall plan (fig. 4–46).

SCULPTURE IN THE ROUND: sculpture that is fully three-dimensional and finished on all sides; e.g., French's *Minuteman* (fig. 1–11). Also known as freestanding.

SECONDARY COLORS: colors created by mixing two of the PRIMARY COLORS; the secondary colors are orange (red and yellow), green (yellow and blue), and violet (red and blue).

SHADING: in painting, drawing, and printmaking, progressive decreases in the VALUE and INTENSITY of colors to suggest the changes that result when light hits a form; note the progressive darkening on the face of the *Mona Lisa* (fig. 6–16). See also MODELING.

SHAFT: in architecture, the vertical cylindrical form that supports the ENTABLATURE; for example, Doric columns are shafts (fig. 3–69).

SHAMANIC: describing a practice in which individuals, called shamans, claim to make contact with and influence gods, spirits, and forces in unseen realms while in ritualized trance states.

SHIFTING PERSPECTIVE: the use of multiple viewpoints in a painting or drawing, as in Li Cheng's and Cézanne's paintings (figs. 4–50, 9–74) or in Cubism (figs. 10–36, 10–37).

SHIN NO MIHASHIRA: a heart pillar buried deep in the ground below the Inner Shinto Shrine at Ise; thought to be the place where the KAMI reside; see pp. 162–63.

SHINTO: indigenous Japanese nature religion with a central focus on reverence for KAMI; see pp. 162–63.

SHODEN: the main shrine building at Ise dedicated to the National Shinto Cult at the Naiku (Inner) Shrine; see pp. 162–63 and fig. 4–18.

SIDE AISLE: see AISLE.

SILVERPOINT: a drawing technique using a sharpened point of silver on specially prepared paper or parchment; e.g., Rembrandt's drawing of his fiancée Saskia (fig. 7–29).

SITE: the specific setting or location for which a work of art or architecture was designed; e.g., the location of Wright's Fallingwater over a waterfall (fig. 1–6).

SIVA: one of the three main Hindu gods, known as the Preserver; see Hindu art at Ellora, pp. 186–87.

SLIP: clay particles and water, sometimes used to decorate a pottery vessel, as in figs. 3–54, 3–56.

SPANDRELS: in architecture, the triangular surfaces to the sides of an ARCH, between the top of the arch and the SPRINGINGS on either side.

SPOLIA: materials taken from an earlier structure and reused, as in the columns and capitals at Old St. Peter's (fig. 4–12) and the Mosque in Córdoba (fig. 4–41).

SPRINGING: the level at which an ARCH or VAULT begins to curve inward and upward; see fig. 3–113 and pp. 132–35.

SQUINCH: ARCHES, LINTELS, and/or CORBELS that jut across the corners of a square space to support a dome and to make the transition from the square space to a polygonal or round one; see the squinches that support the dome at Córdoba (fig. 4–43). See also fig. 3–113.

STAINED-GLASS WINDOWS: windows composed of pieces of colored glass joined by lead strips; see fig. 4–94 and p. 231.

STATES: the successive printed stages of a print, especially common in Rembrandt's ETCHINGS and DRYPOINTS (figs. 7–33, 7–35).

STEEL-FRAME CONSTRUCTION: an architectural structure in which steel beams are joined horizontally and vertically to create a gridlike structural system; see fig. 9–42.

STEREOBATE: the stepped platform that forms the base for a Greek temple; the top step is known as the stylobate; see fig. 3–60.

STILL LIFE: a painting of fruit, flowers, game, or ordinary domestic objects. The still life developed as a popular genre in Northern European painting in the seventeenth century.

STUPA: a large hemispherical Buddhist shrine, erected to hold a relic or mark a holy site, as in the Great Stupa at Sanchi (fig. 3–83); the form evolved from earlier burial mounds.

STYLE: a complex concept with several meanings, including HISTORICAL STYLE and INDIVIDUAL STYLE.

SUBJECT MATTER: see ICONOGRAPHY.

SUNKEN RELIEF: an Egyptian style of RELIEF SCULPTURE in which the figures are recessed into the surface (fig. 3–10). Also known as incised relief.

TABLERO: in Mesoamerican architecture, a heavy, projecting, rectangular MOLDING outlined by a thick frame, as in the Pyramid of Quetzalcóatl at Teotihuacán (fig. 3–122).

TAOTIE: the stylized monster mask that decorates early Chinese bronzes (figs. 3–1, 3–2).

TECHNIQUE: how an artist or artists uses materials (the MEDIUM or MEDIA) to create a work of art; e.g., the vigorous, heavy OIL brushstrokes of Van Gogh (figs. 9–72, 9–73) or the highly polished finish of Michelangelo's *Pietà* (fig. 5–62).

TEMPERA PAINT TECHNIQUE: a painting technique in which the pigments are combined with egg. The support is usually plaster-coated wood and the background is often decorated with gold leaf, as in Giotto's *Madonna* (fig. 4–95). See also fig. 4–100.

TENEBRISM: a dramatic contrast of light and dark used by Caravaggio and his followers; see pp. 358–61.

TENSILE STRENGTH: the internal longitudinal strength in a stone, steel, or wood beam which enables it to support itself without breaking.

TERRA-COTTA: a hard earthenware, glazed or unglazed.

TESSERAE: the individual cut pieces of stone, glass or other materials used in the MOSAIC technique (see fig. 4–28). One piece is a tessera.

THRUST: the outward force created by an ARCH or VAULT; this must be counterbalanced by BUTTRESSING; see fig. 3–114 and pp. 132–35.

TORII ARCH: two posts capped by two beams—the topmost beam flaring upward—found at the gateway to the sacred precinct of a SHINTO shrine.

TOU-KUNG BRACKET: in Chinese and Japanese architecture, CANTILEVERED brackets, often multiple and complex, that support the beams and roof of a structure, as at Horyu-ji (fig. 4–36).

TRANSEPT: in a cross-shaped Christian church, cross arms placed perpendicular to the NAVE; see fig. 4–13 and p. 160.

TRANSVERSALS: lines that are parallel to each other in reality that recede parallel to the picture frame in the LINEAR PERSPECTIVE system; see fig. 5–24 and pp. 262–63.

TRANSVERSE ARCH: an ARCH that separates one BAY from the next in a series of arched VAULTS.

TRAVERTINE: a limestone, found especially along the Tiber River in Italy, pocked with small spongy holes.

TRIFORIUM: in Gothic construction, an arcaded passageway above the NAVE ARCADE (fig. 4–84) and below the CLERESTORY, as in the cathedral at Chartres (figs. 4–80, 4–81).

TRIGLYPH: in the Doric FRIEZE, the area between the METOPES, decorated with vertical grooves; see fig. 3–60 and p. 93.

TRIPTYCH: a three-part altarpiece or work of art.

TRIUMPHAL ARCH: a kind of free-standing monumental ARCH. They were first erected along routes of victorious returning Roman armies in the second century BCE and later created as nonfunctional commemorative public monuments.

TROMPE L'OEIL: illusionistic painting that emphasizes realistic effects to convince the viewer that the painted scene or object is actually real and not painted, as in Mantegna's Camera Picta frescoes (figs. 5–48, 5–49).

TRUMEAU: the central supporting post between the two sides of a double door, which in Renaissance and Gothic churches is often decorated with sculpture, as at Amiens (figs. 4–89, 4–92).

TUFA: a soft, porous rock that hardens with exposure to air; used in construction.

TUNNEL VAULT: see BARREL VAULT.

TYMPANUM: the LUNETTE over the doorway of a church, which is often decorated with sculpture, as in Romanesque (figs. 4–63, 4–64, 4–65) and Gothic (fig. 4–90) structures.

UNDERDRAWING: a preparatory drawing done directly on the plaster or canvas and over which the artist paints the finished work.

VALUE: the relative darkness (LOW VALUE) or lightness (HIGH VALUE) of a HUE.

VANISHING POINT: in a work created using the LINEAR PERSPECTIVE system, the vanishing point is the place where the converging ORTHOGONALS would converge if continued, as in Donatello's *Feast of Herod* (fig. 5–24).

VANITAS: a type of STILL LIFE showing objects that symbolize the impermanence of life, such as skulls, withered flowers, and clocks, and intended as reminders of the futility of amassing knowledge, wealth, and earthly possessions represented by stacks of books, coins, and jewels and fancy garments.

VAULT, VAULTING: a structural system based on the ARCH, including the TUNNEL (or BARREL) VAULT, the CROSS (or GROIN) VAULT, and the DOME; see fig. 3–113 and pp. 132–35.

VEHICLE: the drying liquid in which painting pigments are suspended; as it dries, it adheres the color to the surface.

VELLUM: fine PARCHMENT prepared from calfskin used for the pages in MANUSCRIPTS.

VILLA: a country house, as in the Villa Rotonda by Palladio (fig. 1–7).

VISHNU: one of the three main Hindu gods, known as the Creator; see Hindu art at Ellora, pp. 186–87.

VOLUTE: the spiral scroll motif that characterizes the capital of the IONIC ORDER; see fig. 3–60.

VOLUTE KRATER: an ancient Greek vase used for the mixing of wine with water; see fig. 3–55.

VOUSSOIRS: the individual blocks of stone (or bricks) that compose an ARCH; see fig. 3–113 and pp. 132–35.

WASH: ink thinned with water, applied with a brush to add effects of shadow, as in Rembrandt's *A Man Rowing* (fig. 7–28).

WATERCOLOR: pigments mixed with water (and gum arabic as a drying agent); used in Homer's watercolor *The Blue Boat* (fig. 9–68).

WEB: the surfaces of a Gothic RIB VAULT; see fig. 4–85. Also known as infilling.

WESTWORK: a church entrance with a centralized APSE enclosing a chapel on the second story and two flanking towers, typical of Carolingian churches, as in the St. Gall monastery plan (fig. 4–46).

WOODCUT: a relief printmaking process; for a diagram, see fig. 6–23 and pp. 310–11.

YAKSHA, YAKSHI: ancient Indian nature spirits that became gods and goddesses of fertility, as at Sanchi (fig. 3–85).

ZEN: a form of Buddhism (known in China as Chan) that teaches that there is no Buddha except that in one's own nature; only through meditation can one reach one's own Buddha nature; see Zen art, pp. 344–45.

ZIGGURAT: a stepped pyramid of mud brick, used by the Sumerians and the Assyrians as a sacred site; see fig. 3–7.

BIBLIOGRAPHY

This is a general, broad bibliography intended to lead the reader to more specific books on individual sites, monuments, artists, and movements. As a rule, it includes only the most important sources, and only those in English.

GENERAL

Broude, Norma, and Mary D. Garrard. *Feminism and Art History: Questioning the Litany.* New York: Harper & Row, 1982.

Elsen, Albert E. *Purposes of Art.* New York: Holt, Rinehart and Winston, 1981.

Encyclopedia of World Art. 15 vols. New York: McGraw-Hill, 1959–68.

Fernie, Eric (selection and commentary by). *Art History and Its Methods: A Critical Anthology.* San Francisco: Chronicle Books, 1995.

Fleming, John, Hugh Honour, and Nikolaus Pevsner. *The Penguin Dictionary of Architecture.* New York: Viking, 1991.

Goldwater, Robert J., and Marco Treves. *Artists on Art.* New York: Pantheon, 1974.

Gombrich, E. H. *Art and Illusion.* New York: Pantheon, 1972.

————. *The Story of Art.* Oxford: Phaidon, 1995.

Hartt, Frederick. *Art: A History of Painting, Sculpture, Architecture.* New York: Abrams, 1992.

Holt, Elizabeth G. *A Documentary History of Art.* 2 vols. Garden City, N.Y.: Doubleday, 1981.

Honour, Hugh, and John Fleming. *The Visual Arts: A History.* Upper Saddle River, N.J.: Prentice Hall, 1995.

Janson. H. W., and Anthony F. Janson. *History of Art.* New York: Abrams, 1997.

Kemal, Salim, and Ivan Gaskell. *The Language of Art History.* Cambridge, Eng.: Cambridge University Press, 1992.

Kemp, Martin. *The Science of Art: Optical Themes in Western Art from Brunelleschi to Seurat.* New Haven, Conn.: Yale University Press, 1989.

Kostof, Spiro. *The Architect: Chapters in the History of the Profession.* New York: Oxford University Press, 1986.

————. *A History of Architecture: Settings and Rituals.* New York: Oxford University Press, 1995.

Lee, Sherman E. *A History of Far Eastern Art.* New York: Abrams, 1994.

Nochlin, Linda. *Women, Art, and Power and Other Essays.* New York: Harper & Row, 1988.

————. and Ann S. Harris. *Women Artists: 1550–1950.* Los Angeles: Los Angeles County Museum of Art; New York: distributed by Random House, 1976.

Sayre, Henry M. *Writing About Art.* Upper Saddle River, N. J.: Prentice Hall, 1995.

Stokstad, Marilyn. *Art History.* New York: Abrams, 1995.

Sullivan, Michael. *The Arts of China.* Berkeley, Calif.: University of California Press, 1984.

Tansey, Richard G. and Fred S. Kleiner. *Gardner's Art Through the Ages.* Fort Worth, Tex.: Harcourt Brace & Company, 1995.

Trachtenberg, Marvin, and Isabelle Hyman. *Architecture, from Prehistory to Post-Modernism,* New York: Abrams, 1986.

Turner, Jane, ed. *The Dictionary of Art.* 34 vols. New York: Grove's Dictionaries, 1996.

Wittkower, Rudolf and Margot. *Born Under Saturn.* New York: Norton, 1969.

PREHISTORIC AND ANCIENT

Adam, Robert. *Classical Architecture: A Comprehensive Handbook to the Tradition of Classical Style.* New York: Abrams, 1991.

Adams, Richard E. W. *Prehistoric Mesoamerica.* Norman, O.K.: University of Oklahoma Press, 1996.

Addiss, Stephen. *How to Look at Japanese Art.* New York: Abrams, 1996.

Aldred, Cyril. *Egyptian Art in the Days of the Pharaohs 3100–320 B.C.* New York: Thames and Hudson, 1985.

Amiet, Pierra. *The Ancient Art of the Near East.* New York: Abrams, 1980.

Berrin, Kathleen, and Esther Pasztory, eds. *Teotihuacan: Art from the City of the Gods.* New York: Thames and Hudson, 1993.

Boardman, John. *Greek Art.* London: Thames and Hudson, 1996.

————. *The Oxford History of Classical Art.* Oxford/New York: Oxford University Press, 1993.

————. *The Parthenon and Its Sculptures.* Austin, Tex.: University of Texas Press, 1985.

Boëthius, Alexander. *Etruscan and Early Roman Architecture.* New Haven, Conn.: Yale University Press, 1987.

Brendel, Otto. *Etruscan Art.* New Haven, Conn.: Yale University Press, 1995.

Brilliant, Richard. *Arts of the Ancient Greeks.* New York: McGraw-Hill, 1973.

Collon, Dominique. *Ancient Near Eastern Art.* Berkeley, Calif.: University of California Press, 1995.

Craven, Roy. *Indian Art: A Concise History.* New York: Thames and Hudson, 1986.

Henig, Martin. *A Handbook of Roman Art.* Ithaca, N.Y.: Cornell University Press, 1983.

Grand, Paule M. *Prehistoric Art: Paleolithic Painting and Sculpture.* Greenwich, Conn.: New York Graphic Society, 1967.

Groenewegen-Frankfort, H. A., and Bernard Ashmole. *Art of the Ancient World.* Englewood Cliffs, N.J.: Prentice Hall, 1972.

Kubler, George. *Art and Architecture of Ancient America.* Harmondsworth, Eng.: Penguin, 1990.

MacDonald, William L. *The Architecture of the Roman Empire.* 2 vols. New Haven, Conn.: Yale University Press, 1982.

Mason, Penelope. *History of Japanese Art.* New York: Abrams, 1993.

Miller, Mary Ellen. *The Art of Mesoamerica: From Olmec to Aztec.* New York: Thames and Hudson, 1996.

Pollitt, J. J. *The Art of Greece 1400–31 B.C.* (Sources and Documents). Cambridge, Eng.: Cambridge University Press, 1990.

————. *Art and Experience in Classical Greece.* Cambridge, Eng.: Cambridge

University Press, 1972.

————. *The Ancient View of Greek Art.* New Haven, Conn.: Yale University Press, 1974.

————. *The Art of Rome c. 753 B.C.–A.D. 337* (Sources and Documents). New York: Cambridge University Press, 1983.

————. *Art in the Hellenistic Age.* Cambridge, Eng.: Cambridge University Press, 1986.

Ramage, Nancy. *Roman Art: Romulus to Constantine.* Englewood Cliffs, N.J.: Prentice Hall, 1996.

Smith, William Stevenson. *The Art and Architecture of Ancient Egypt.* New Haven, Conn.: Yale University Press, 1988.

Strong, Donald. *Roman Art.* Harmondsworth, Eng.: Penguin, 1988.

Ward-Perkins. J. B. *Roman Architecture.* New York: Rizzoli, 1988.

————. *Roman Imperial Architecture.* Harmondsworth, Eng.: Penguin, 1981.

ART FROM 200 TO 1400

Conant, Kenneth J. *Carolingian and Romanesque Architecture.* Harmondsworth, Eng.: Penguin, 1978.

Davis-Weyer, C. *Early Medieval Art 300–1150* (Sources and Documents). Englewood Cliffs, N.J.: Prentice Hall, 1986.

Dodwell, C. R. *The Pictorial Arts of the West, 800–1200.* New Haven, Conn.: Yale University Press, 1993.

Ettinghausen, Richard, and Oleg Grabar. *The Art and Architecture of Islam, 650–1250.* New Haven, Conn.: Yale University Press, 1992.

Frisch, T. G. *Gothic Art 1140–ca. 1450* (Sources and Documents). Toronto: University of Toronto Press, 1987.

Grodecki, Louis. *Gothic Architecture.* New York: Rizzoli, 1991.

Hearn, M. F. *Romanesque Sculpture.* Ithaca, N.Y.: Cornell University Press, 1981.

Huntington, Susan. *Art of Ancient India: Buddhist, Hindu, Jain.* New York: Weatherhill, 1985.

Krautheimer, Richard. *Early Christian and Byzantine Architecture.* Harmondsworth, Eng.: Penguin, 1986.

Mango, Cyril. *The Art of the Byzantine Empire 312–1453* (Sources and Documents). Cheektowga, Ont.: University of Toronto Press, 1986.

————. *Byzantium.* London: Weidenfeld and Nicolson, 1980.

————. *Byzantine Architecture.* New York: Rizzoli, 1991.

Os, H. W. van. *The Art of Devotion in the Late Middle Ages in Europe, 1300–1500.* Princeton, N.J.: Princeton University Press, 1994.

Petzold, Andreas. *Romanesque Art.* New York: Abrams, 1995.

Rodley, Lyn. *Byzantine Art and Architecture.* Cambridge, Eng./New York: Cambridge University Press, 1994.

Snyder, James. *Medieval Art: Painting, Sculpture, Architecture 4th–14th Century.* New York: Abrams, 1989.

Swaan, Wim. *The Gothic Cathedral.* New York: Park Lane, 1981.

White, John. *Art and Architecture in Italy, 1250–1400.* New Haven, Conn.: Yale University Press, 1993.

Wilson, David M. *Anglo-Saxon Art from the Seventh Century to the Norman Conquest.* Woodstock, N.Y.: Overlook Press, 1984.

FIFTEENTH AND SIXTEENTH CENTURIES

Blair, Sheila. *The Art and Architecture of Islam 1250–1800.* New Haven, Conn.: Yale University Press, 1994.

Cole, Alison. *Virtue and Magnificence: Art of the Italian Renaissance Courts.* New York: Abrams, 1995.

Cole, Bruce. *The Renaissance Artist at Work.* New York: Harper & Row, 1983.

Gilbert, Creighton. *Italian Art 1400–1500* (Sources and Documents). Evanston, Ill.: Northwestern University Press, 1991.

Harbison, Craig. *The Mirror of the Artist: Northern Renaissance Art in Its Historical Context.* New York: Abrams, 1995.

Hartt, Frederick. *History of Italian Renaissance Art.* New York: Abrams, 1994.

Heydenreich, Ludwig, and W. Lotz. *Architecture in Italy 1400–1600.* New Haven, Conn.: Yale University Press, 1996.

Klein, Robert, and Henri Zerner. *Italian Art, 1500–1600* (Sources and Documents). Evanston, Ill.: Northwestern University Press, 1989.

Kristeller, Paul O. *Renaissance Thought and the Arts: Collected Essays.* Princeton, N.J.: Princeton University Press, 1990.

Paoletti, John T., and Gary M. Radke. *Art in Renaissance Italy.* New York: Abrams, 1997.

Rosand, David. *Painting in Cinquecento Venice: Titian, Veronese, Tintoretto.* New Haven, Conn.: Yale University Press, 1986.

Snyder, James. *Northern Renaissance Art.* New York: Abrams, 1985.

Stechow, Wolfgang. *Northern Renaissance Art 1400–1600* (Sources and Documents). Evanston, Ill.: Northwestern University Press, 1989.

Wittkower, Rudolf. *Architectural Principles in the Age of Humanism.* New York: St. Martin's Press, 1988.

SEVENTEENTH AND EIGHTEENTH CENTURIES

Blunt, Anthony. *Art and Architecture in France 1500–1700.* New Haven, Conn.: Yale University Press, 1988.

Crow, Thomas E. *Painters and Public Life in Eighteenth-Century Paris.* New Haven, Conn.: Yale University Press, 1985.

Enggass, Robert, and Jonathan Brown. *Italy and Spain 1600–1750* (Sources and Documents). Evanston, Ill.: Northwestern University Press, 1993.

Gerson, H., and E. H. ter Kuile. *Art and Architecture in Belgium 1600–1800.* Baltimore, Md.: Penguin, 1978.

Guth, Christine. *Art of Edo Japan: The Artist and the City 1615–1868.* New York: Abrams, 1996.

Haskell, Francis. *Patrons and Painters: A Study in the Relations Between Italian Art and Society in the Age of the Baroque.* New Haven, Conn.: Yale University Press, 1980.

Held, Julius, and Donald Posner, *Seventeenth and Eighteenth Century Art: Baroque Painting, Sculpture, Architecture.* New York: Abrams, 1971.

Levey, Michael. *Painting and Sculpture in France, 1700–1789.* New Haven, Conn.: Yale University Press, 1993.

Rosenberg, Jakob, Seymour Slive, and E. H. ter Kuile. *Dutch Art and Architecture 1600–1800.* New Haven, Conn.: Yale University Press, 1987.

Schama, Simon. *The Embarrassment of Riches: An Interpretation of Dutch Culture in the Golden Age.* Berkeley, Calif.: University of California Press, 1988.

Varriano, John. *Italian Baroque and Rococo Architecture.* New York: Oxford University Press, 1986.

Wittkower, Rudolf. *Art and Architecture in Italy 1600 to 1750.* Harmondsworth, Eng.: Penguin, 1973.

NINETEENTH AND TWENTIETH CENTURIES

Arnason, H. H., and Marla F. Prather. *History of Modern Art.* 4th ed. New York: Abrams, 1998.

Atkins, Robert. *ArtSpeak: A Guide to Contemporary Ideas, Movements, and Buzzwords.* New York: Abbeville Press, 1990.

————. *ArtSpoke: A Guide to Modern Ideas, Movements, and Buzzwords 1848–1944.* New York: Abbeville Press, 1993.

Baigell, Matthew. *A Concise History of American Painting and Sculpture.* New York: Harper & Row, 1984.

Boimé, Albert. *A Social History of Modern Art.* Chicago: University of Chicago Press, 1990–93.

Broude, Norma. *Impressionism: A Feminist Reading: The Gendering of Art, Science, and Nature in the Nineteenth Century.* New York: Rizzoli, 1991.

Clark, T. J. *Image of the People: Gustave Courbet and the 1848 Revolution.* Princeton, N.J.: Princeton University Press, 1982.

————. *The Painting of Modern Life: Paris in the Art of Manet and His Followers.* Princeton, N.J.: Princeton University Press, 1989.

Curtis, William J. R. *Modern Architecture Since 1900.* San Francisco: Chronicle Books, 1996.

Daval, Jean-Luc. *Photography: History of an Art.* New York: Rizzoli, 1982.

Eitner, Lorenz. *Neoclassicism and Romanticism 1750–1850 (Sources and Documents).* New York: Harper & Row, 1989.

————. *An Outline of 19th Century European Painting: From David through Cézanne.* New York: HarperCollins, 1989.

Fry, Edward. *Cubism.* London: Thames and Hudson, 1985.

Gaggi, Silvio. *Modern-Postmodern: A Study in Twentieth-Century Arts and Ideas.* Philadelphia; University of Pennsylvania Press, 1989.

Gates, Henry Louis. *Africa: The Art of a Continent: 100 Works of Power and Beauty.* New York: Abrams, 1996.

Hamilton, George H. *Nineteenth and Twentieth Century Art.* New York: Abrams, 1971.

————. *Painting and Sculpture in Europe 1880–1940.* New Haven, Conn.: Yale University Press, 1993.

Herbert, Robert L. *Modern Artists on Art.* Englewood Cliffs, N. J.: Prentice Hall, 1986.

————. *Impressionism.* New Haven, Conn.: Yale University Press, 1991.

Holt, Elizabeth G. *From the Classicists to the Impressionists.* New Haven, Conn.: Yale University Press, 1986.

Hopi, Kachina, Spirit of Life. The California Academy of Sciences. Seattle: distributed by University of Washington Press, 1980.

Hughes, Robert. *The Shock of the New.* New York: Knopf, 1992.

Hunter, Sam, and John Jacobus. *Modern Art: Painting, Sculpture, Architecture.* New York: Abrams, 1992.

Janson, H. W. *19th-Century Sculpture.* New York: Abrams, 1985.

Levin, Kim. *Beyond Modernism: Essays on Art from the '70s to '80s.* New York: HarperCollins, 1989.

Lucie-Smith, Edward. *American Art Now.* New York: Morrow, 1985.

————. *Art Today.* London: Phaidon, 1995.

————. *Movements in Art Since 1945.* New York: Thames and Hudson, 1995.

McCoubrey, John. *American Art 1700–*

1960 (Sources and Documents). Englewood Cliffs, N.J.: Prentice Hall, 1965.

Munroe, Alexandra. *Japanese Art After 1945: Scream Against the Sky.* New York: Abrams, 1994.

Newhall, Beaumont. *The History of Photography, from 1839 to the Present Day.* New York: Museum of Modern Art, 1982.

Nochlin, Linda. *Impressionism and Post-Impressionism (Sources and Documents).* Englewood Cliffs, N.J.: Prentice Hall, 1966.

————. *Realism and Tradition in Art 1848–1900 (Sources and Documents).* Englewood Cliffs, N.J.: Prentice Hall, 1966.

Noever, Peter, and Regina Haslinger, eds. *Architecture in Transition: Between Deconstruction and New Modernism.* New York: te Neues, 1995.

Phillips, Tom. *Africa: The Art of a Continent.* New York: te Neues, 1995.

Rewald, John: *Post-Impressionism: From Van Gogh to Gauguin.* New York: Abrams, 1990.

————. *The History of Impressionism.* New York: Abrams, 1990.

————. *Studies in Impressionism.* New York: Abrams, 1986.

————. *Studies in Post-Impressionism.* New York: Abrams, 1986.

Rosenblum, Robert, and H. W. Janson. *Nineteenth-Century Art.* New York: Abrams, 1984.

Selz, Peter. *Art in Our Times.* New York: Abrams, 1981.

Smagula, Howard. *Currents, Contemporary Directions in the Visual Arts.* Englewood Cliffs, N.J.: Prentice Hall, 1989.

Thompson, Robert Farris. *African Art in Motion: Icon and Act.* Los Angeles: University of California Press, 1979.

Varnedoe, Kirk. *A Fine Disregard: What Makes Modern Art Modern.* New York: Abrams, 1990.

Wheeler, Daniel. *Art Since Mid-Century.* Englewood Cliffs, N.J.: Prentice Hall, 1991.

Wilmerding, John. *American Art.* New York: Viking, 1982.

INDEX

Note: Page numbers in *italics* refer to illustrations. Names of architects and artists whose work appears in this book are in CAPITALS.

Aachen, Germany: Palace Chapel, 192–93; *193*

Abbey Church of La Madeleine, Vézelay, France, 210–11, 228; *210*

Abbey Church of Ste.-Foy, Conques, France, 208–9, 211; *208, 209, 211*

Abbey in an Oak Forest (FRIEDRICH), 434–35; *435*

Abraham Feeding the Three Angels (Byzantine mosaic), *170*

abstract art: de Stijl, 533; *532*; geometric, 522–23; Hard-Edge, 564–65, 573; Post-Painterly, 554, 557; sculpture, 520–21, 548–49; *520, 521, 548*

Abstract Expressionism, 490–91, 524–27, 554–57, 562, 573, 579

Abu Simbel, Egypt: Temple of Ramesses II, 59–60; *60*

Academic Art, 422, 446–47, 457; *446, 447*

Achilles and Ajax Playing Draughts (EXEKIAS), 88; *88*

Acropolis, Athens, 86; *86*

Action Painting, 556

ADAM, ROBERT (English): 340; Osterley Park House, 394; *395*

Adam and Eve (DÜRER), 308, 310; *308, 310*

Ad Parnassum (KLEE), 529; *529*

Aegean art: Minoan and Mycenaean, 74–77

Affectionate (ALBERS), 564; *564*

Africa, 34–35; Benin shrine, 239; *238*; Bwa masks and body suits, 26, 28, 504–5; *28, 504, 505*; Edo head, 239; *238*; Ife head, 238; *238*; Nok head, 42–43; *42*; ritual practices, 420–21, 504–5; royal art, 238–39; Wodaabe calabashes, 35; *35*

AIDS Memorial Quilt (NAMES PROJECT), 490; *490*

AIDS Series (TERAOKA), 490, 601–2; *601*

Akhenaten with Nefertiti and Their Children (Egyptian relief), 59; *59*

ALBERS, JOSEF (American): *Homage to the Square*, 564; *564*

Alberti, Leon Battista: *On Architecture*, 287; *On Painting*, 247, 263, 267, 285; *On Sculpture*, 40

Alexander the Great, 60, 86, 87, 106–7; battle with Darius, 107–8, 334–35; *108, 335*; portrait busts of, 107; *107*

Alfred Lord Tennyson (CAMERON), 457; *457*

Allegheny County Courthouse and Jail, Pittsburgh (RICHARDSON), 452–53; *453*

Allegorical Portrait of Sarah Siddons as the Tragic Muse (REYNOLDS), 398, 406; *407*

Allegory of the Outbreak of War (RUBENS), 365; *365*

Allegory of Time and Lust (BRONZINO), 332; *332*

Altar of Peace (Roman), 119; *119*

Altar of Zeus and Athena, Pergamon, 108; *109*

Altarpiece of the Lamb (VAN EYCK), 261, 264, 265; *261, 264, 265*

ALTDORFER, ALBRECHT (German), *Battle of Alexander and Darius*, 334–35; *335*

American art, *see* United States

American Gothic (WOOD), 539–40; *539*

American Landscape (SHEELER), 538–39; *539*

Amiens: Nôtre-Dame, 228; *228, 229*

Analytical Cubism, 514–15, 516, 522

Ancestors of Christ (Gothic), 228; *229*

ANDERSON, LAURIE (American): *Stories from the Nerve Bible*, 571; *571*

Andokidas Painter (Greek), 88

ANDO, TADAO (Japanese): Lotus Pond Hall, Honpukuji, 588–89; *589*

Angkor Wat, Kampuchea Cambodia, 214–15; *214, 215*

Anglo-Saxon metalwork, 174, 176; *175*

ANGUISSOLA, SOPHONISBA (Italian), *Portrait of the Artist's Three Sisters*, 301

Ankhuf (Egyptian sculpture), 61; *61*

Annunciation (Gothic), 220; *221*

Annunciation with Patrons (CAMPIN), 256–57; *256, 257*

ANTHEMIUS OF TRALLES (Byzantine): Hagia Sophia interior, 168–69; *168*

Aphrodite of Knidos (PRAXITELES), 104–5; *105*

Apollo and Daphne (BERNINI), 21, 354; *20*

Apollo and the Battle of the Lapiths and the Centaurs (Greek), 84; *84*

appropriation, 590–91

ARBUS, DIANE (American): *Untitled 6*, 569; *568*

Arcadian Shepherds (POUSSIN), 382–83; *382*

Arc de Triomphe, Paris (CHALGRIN), 428, 433; *428*

Archaic period, 85, 87, 88, 90–91

ARCHIPENKO, ALEXANDER (Russian), *Walking Woman*, 520; *520*

architectural forms: arches, 114, 116, 120, 122, 132–35, 209, 226, 275; *133, 134, 135, 226, 428, 449*; atria, 117, 276; *116*; cantilevers, 513; *23*; centrally planned churches (LEONARDO), 287, 312; *287*; classical orders, 93; *92*; domes, 134–35, 161, 169, 191, 213, 275, 296–97, 313, 370; *134, 161, 168, 191, 213, 275, 296, 370*; flying buttresses, 226; *226*; fountains, 353; *352*; how to read diagrams, 69; monasteries, 164, 167, 194–95; pagodas, 182, 397–98; *182*; skyscrapers, 450, 480–81, 552–53, 603; stupas, 110–13, 197, 243; *tou-kung* bracketing, 183; *183*; vaults, 114, 116, 120, 122, 132–35, 161, 226, 318; *132, 133, 134, 226*

architectural materials: concrete, 114, 116, 120, 122, 131, 132–35, 451; *132, 133; 451*; post-and-lintel construction, 68, 132; *66, 68, 132, 183*; steel-frame construction, 451; *451*

architecture: American, 22, 24–25, 489–99, 512–13; analyzing, 22–25; Assyrian, 80–81; Baroque, 351, 353–54, 367, 370–71; Bauhaus, 534–35; *534, 535*; Buddhist, 110–13; Byzantine, 168–72, 339; *168, 170*; Carolingian, 192–93; Chinese, 179–81, 244–45; Deconstructivist, 581, 583, 588; de Stijl, 533; Doric, 93, 94–95, 99, 100–101, 131; early Christian, 160–61, 194–95; Egyptian, 59, 61, 64–69; eighteenth-century, 394, 399; *395*; Etruscan, 116; Federal style, 408–9; Gothic, 218–27, 326, 405; *222–27*; Gothic Revival, 441; Greek, 87, 93, 94–95, 100–101, 116; Greek Revival, 441; Hindu, 186–87; International Style, 552–53, 578, 603; Islamic, 339; *338*, Italian, 24–25, 274–77, 353–54;

Japanese, 22, 24, 388–89, 588–89; Khmer, 214–15; Neoclassical, 408–9, 422, 428, 441; Neolithic, 43–45; nineteenth-century, 420, 422, 423, 428, 440–41, 448–53, 452–53; Ottoman empire, 339; *338*, Persian, 80–81; Postmodern, 578–79, 582; Prairie style, 513, 535; Renaissance, 258, 274–77, 312–13, 330, 367; Rococo, 404–5; Roman, 116, 120–22, 130–39, 408; Romanesque, 195, 208–9, 452; Romantic, 422, 440–41; seventeenth-century, 351–52, 367, 386–89; sixteenth-century, 340–41; twentieth-century, 22, 24–25, 499, 512–13, 532–35, 558–59, 578–83, 602–3; Victorian, 423, 452–53

Arch of Titus, Rome, 121–22; *121*

Arena Chapel, Padua, frescoes (GIOTTO), 234–35; *234, 235*

ARP, JEAN (Swiss): 530–31; *Collage Arranged According to the Laws of Chance*, 531; *531*

Arrival and Reception of Marie de' Medici at Marseilles (RUBENS), 364; *364*

art academies, 34, 200, 301, 398, 446–47

Art in Transit (HARING), 494; *495*

Artist Drawing a Lute with the Help of a Mechanical Device (DÜRER), 281; *281*

Art Nouveau style, 418, 423, 492; *492*

Arts and Crafts Movement, 418, 423

ASAM, EGID QUIRIN (German), *Assumption of the Virgin*, 405; *405*

Ascension (Byzantine mosaic), 213; *213*

As I Opened Fire (LICHTENSTEIN), 566; *567*

assemblage work, 494, 517

Assisi: San Francesco, 227; *227*

Assumption and Coronation of the Virgin (TITIAN), 326–27; *327*

Assumption of the Virgin (ASAM), 405; *405*

Assyrian art, 80–81

Athens, 398; Acropolis, 86; *86*; Parthenon, 100–103, 119, 458; *100, 101, 102, 103*

At the Moulin Rouge (TOULOUSE-LAUTREC), 419; *419*

Augustus, Roman emperor: 99, 115–16, 118–19, 121; *118*; *Res Gestae*, 119

Augustus Prima Porta (Roman), *118*

automatism, 545, 554

Autun, France: Cathedral of St.-Lazare, 148, 211; *211*

avant-garde art, 34, 420, 423, 455, 491, 528, 529, 535, 542, 555, 562, 576; Chinese, 592–93; Russian, 522–23

Bacchic Mysteries (Roman fresco), *126*

Bactrian Camel with Pack Saddle (Chinese earthenware), 178, 181; *179*

BAKST, LEON (Russian): 491–92; *L'Aprés-midi d'un Faune* costume, 418, 423, 492; *492*

Baldacchino (BERNINI), 366; *366*

BALDOVINETTI, ALESSO (Italian): *Portrait of a Young Woman*, 279; *278*

BALLA, GIACOMO (Italian), *Speeding Automobile—Study of Velocity*, 486, 519; *486*

Banjo Lesson, The (TANNER), 467; *467*

Banquet of the Officers of the Civic Guard of St. George (HALS), 368; *368*

Bar at the Folies-Bergère (MANET), 418; *418*

BARMA (Russian): Cathedral of St. Basil the Blessed, Moscow, 296–97; *296*

LIST OF CREDITS

The authors and publishers wish to thank the museums, galleries, libraries, and churches for permitting the reproduction of works of art in their collections. Photographs have been supplied by the owners or custodians of the works of art, except for the following, whose courtesy is gratefully acknowledged. Numbers refer to illustrations.

ACL, Brussels: 5–19, 5–25, 5–26; Archivi Alinari, Florence: 1–4, 3–49, 3–53, 3–67, 3–81, 3–92, 3–98, 4–10, 4–68, 5–5, 5–8, 5–9, 5–10, 5–27, 5–35, 5–37, 5–38, 5–49, 5–50, 6–1, 6–14, 6–15, 6–48, 6–52, 7–4, 7–19, 7–23; courtesy Tadao Ando: 10–129; Ferdinand Anton, Munich: 3–122; © 1997 The Art Institute of Chicago, All Rights Reserved: 9–5, 9–26, 9–71, 9–74, 10–9, 10–68, 10–72, 10–104; Erich Lessing/Art Resource, New York: 8–12; Bildarchiv Foto Marburg, Germany: 3–11, 8–13, 8–14; Scala/Art Resource, New York: 3–80, 4–26, 4–27, 5–1, 5–20, 5–55, 6–13, 6–32, 6–36, 7–3; B. Arthaud, Grenoble: 4–71; © 1991 Asian Art Museum of San Francisco. All rights reserved: 4–3; James Austin: 4–65; The Avery Library, Columbia University, New York: 3–111; © J.H. Morris/Axiom Photographic Agency, London: 3–18; © Jim Holmes/Axiom Photographic Agency, London: 6–4; Dirk Baaker: 10–13; Bardazzi Fotografia, Florence: 3–46; © The Barnes Foundation, Merion, PA: 10–24; Bauhaus Archiv, Berlin © 1969: 10–63; courtesy the Municipality of Bayeaux: 4–59; © Carol Beckwith/Estall Photograph: 1–23; Raffaello Bencini, Florence: 4–43; Bibliothèque Nationale, Paris: 9–27, 9–28; courtesy Xu Bing: 10–134; A. Boethius and J. B. Ward-Perkins, *Etruscan and Early Roman Architecture*, 1970: 3–112; Boston Public Library: 9–46; Photographie Bulloz, Paris: 9–21; Caisse Nationale des Monuments Historiques et des Sites, Paris © Arch.Photo. Paris: 4–60, 4–62, 4–63, 4–64, 4–83, 4–92, 7–45, 8–1, 9–53; Piero Codato, Cameraphoto, Venice: 4–98, 6–41, 6–42, 6–43, 6–44, 6–68; Canali Photobank, Capriolo, Italy: 1–15, 1–20, 3–87, 3–95, 3–96, 3–103, 3–104, 3–105, 3–107, 3–109, 4–28, 4–95, 4–96, 4–97, 4–99, 5–4, 5–15, 6–33, 6–35, 6–69, 7–9, 7–11, 7–25, 7–26; Soprintendenza Archeologica all'Etruria Meridionale courtesy Canali Photobank, Capriolo, Italy: 3–48; Canali/Bertoni courtesy Canali Photobank, Capriolo: 5–29; Eugenio Cassin, Florence: 5–28; Leo Castelli Gallery, New York: 10–110; Chicago Architectural Photo Co.: 10–34; Chicago Historical Society: 9–42; Editions Citadelles & Mazenod, Paris: 3–28, 3–44; Jean Vertut courtesy Editions Citadelles & Mazenod, Paris: 3–12;

Geoffrey Clements: 10–10; © The Cleveland Museum of Art, 1997: 2–7; Comstock, London: 4–48; Comstock, New York: pp. 144–45, 4–41; © George Gerster/Comstock, New York: 4–49; Kenneth J. Conant, *Cluny*, 1968: 4–47; Paula Cooper Gallery, New York: 10–137; A. C. Cooper, Ltd., London: 7–7; Corbis-Bettman, New York: 8–19; courtesy The Council for the International Biennale in Nagoya: 10–1450; Jeffrey Crespi: 10–28; Crown Copyright, Ministry of Public Buildings and Works: 2–9; Prudence Cuming and Associates, Ltd, London: 10–81; Deutsche Fotothek, Dresden: 9–35; Deutscher Kunstverlag, Munich: 4–45; Deutsches Archäologisches Institut, Rome: 3–90, 3–93, 4–14; Deutsches Archäologisches Institut, Athens: 3–36; Byzantine Visual Resources © 1987, Dumbarton Oaks, Washington, D.C.: 4–67; courtesy Eisenman Architects: 10–120; Nikos Kontos courtesy Ekdotike Athenon, Athens: 4–19; Eliot Elisofon: 4–39, 4–70, 4–104; © Peter Aaron/ESTO. All rights reserved: 10–5; © Wayne Andrews/ESTO. All rights reserved: 8–3, 9–32; © Richard Byrant/ESTO/Arcaid. All rights reserved: 10–123; Ezra Stoller © ESTO. All rights reserved: 10–91; Edmund B. Feldman, *Thinking About Art*, 1985: 3–72, 4–84; Bruce Fleischer: 4–103; Fotocielo, Rome: 7–20; Fotostudio C.N.B., Bologna: 6–8; Fototeca Unione, Rome: 3–88, 3–94, 3–101, 3–108; Alfred Frazer and Henry A. Millon, *Key Monuments of Architecture*, 1965: 3–62, 3–100; French Government Tourist Board, New York: 9–44; Gabinetto Fotografico Nazionale, Rome: 5–62, 6–66, 7–1; Gabinetto Fotografico Piazzale degli Uffizi: 5–21; Gabinetto Fotografico, Florence: 6–31; © Andrew Garn, New York: 10–86; Mark Garvin: 10–109; GEMS, New York: 4–23; Alexandre Georges: 10–85; German Research Project Mohenjodaro/RWTH Aachen: 3–30; Photographie Giraudon, Vanves: 4–90, 4–91, pp. 240–41, 5–11, 5–12, 5–57, 7–15, 8–4; Erwin R. Goodenough, *Jewish Symbols in the Greco–Roman Period*, Bollingen Series 37, Vol.II: *Symbolism in the Dura Synagogue*, © 1964, Princeton University Press (photographs by Fred Anderegg), reprinted by permission of Princeton University Press: 4–6, 4–7; Gianfranco Gorgoni, New York: 10–112; Foto Grassi, Siena: 5–24; Paschall and Taylor courtesy Michael Graves: 10–117; *Guernica/ Pablo Picasso*, 1947: 10–79; David Heald © The Solomon R. Guggenheim Foundation, New York: 10–36, 10–90, 10–140, 10–141; Mr. T. Hara, Yokohama: 6–70; Susan Harder Gallery, New York: 10–73; Cyril M. Harris, *History of Architecture Sourcebook*, 1977: 3–110; Hassia: 3–33; Hedrich Blessing, Chicago: 1–10, 9–76; Bill Engdahl,

Hedrich-Blessing, Chicago: 10–33; *Yksityinen/ Julkinen (Private/Public)*, exhibition catalogue, Helsinki, Museum of Contemporary Art/ARS Fennica, 1995: 10–135; Lucien Hervé, Paris: 10–93; Hickey-Robertson, Houston: 10–84; © Colorphoto Hinz, Allschwil-Basel: 2–1, 2–3; Hirmer Fotoarchiv, Munich: 3–4, 3–6, 3–7, 3–8, 3–15, 3–17, 3–23, 3–32, 3–38, 3–47, 3–51, 3–57, 3–59, 3–64, 3–65, 3–76, 3–79, 4–8, 4–25, 4–55; Hirschl and Adler Modern, New York: 10–108; Hispanic Society of America, New York: 9–19; John D. Hoag, *Islamic Architecture*, Electa Editrice, Milan and Harry N. Abrams, Inc., New York, © 1975/1977: 6–62; HOA-QUI, Paris: 1–13, 10–26, 10–27; Peter Horner: 9–8; Stephen P. Huyler, Camden, ME: 10–18; © Department of Archaeology/ Government of India: 3–31; *Irish Historical Series*, © 1977: 4–94; Isabella Stewart Gardner Museum, Boston: 6–47; Italian State Tourist Office, New York: 3–108; Jeanne-Claude: 10–113; Thomas Jefferson Memorial Foundation, Inc.: 8–21; Phyllis Kind Gallery, New York: pp. 484–85; Kostas Kontos, Athens: 3–35, 3–58, 3–68; Kurt Lange: 3–16; © 1997 Gary Layda, Metropolitan Government of Nashville: 3–71; E. Levy, Paris: 9–15; Library of Congress, Washington, DC: 9–31, 9–40; Tony Linck, Fort Lee, NJ: pp. 36–37, 2–8; Jannes Linders, Rotterdam: 10–58, 10–60; MAGNUM Photos, New York: 10–75; Gene Markowski: 3–83; Foto MAS, Barcelona: 4–56, 5–2, 6–37, 6–38; Mauritshuis, The Hague: pp. 346–47; Lawrence Wodehouse and Marian Moffet, *A History of Western Architecture*, © 1989, reproduced by courtesy of Mayfield Publishing Company, Mountainview, CA: 7–24; Norman McGrath, New York: 10–122; Louis K. Meisel Gallery, New York: 10–116; James Mellart, *Catal Hüyük*, 1967: 2–6; The Metropolitan Museum of Art, New York: 6–18, 6–20, 6–21, 6–22, 6–28; All Rights Reserved, The Metropolitan Museum of Art: 3–9, 3–13, 3–25, 3–50, 3–70, 8–7, 9–37, 10–83; copyright © by The Metropolitan Museum of Art: 3–56 (1986), 5–3 (1987), 5–13 (1996), 5–14 (1996), 6–55 (1980), 6–58 (1990), 7–38 (1981), 8–22 (1980), 9–34 (1988), 9–38 (1979), 10–66 (1986); courtesy Asian Art Department, The Metropolitan Museum of Art: 3–39, 3–40; courtesy of the Michigan-Princeton-Alexandria Expedition to Mt. Sinai: 4–21; Ferdinando Leopoldo del Migliore, *Firenze, Citta Nobilissima Illustrata*, Arnaldo Forni Editore: 5–39; Ministry of Education, Mexico City: 10–64; Missouri Department of Natural Resources, Missouri State Museum: 10–70; Allan Mitchell: 10–53; Archivio Fotografico, Monumenti Musei e Galerie Pontificie, The Vatican: pp.

48–49, 3-1, 3-54, 3-77, 3-102, 4-9; Munch Museet, Oslo: 9–79; courtesy Musée d'Art et d'Histoire, Fribourg: 9– 54; Archivo fotográfico Museo Nacional Centro de Arte Reina Sofía: 10–78; Museum of Modern Art, New York: 9–66, 10–61; Museum of Modern Art/Film Stills Archive: 10–19, 10–20, 10–94, 10–95; photo © copyright 1997 The Museum of Modern Art: 9–9, 9–73, 10–2, 10–4, 10–7, 10–11, 10–31, 10–37, 10–39, 10–41, 10–47, 10–49, 10–54, 10–57, 10–67, 10–76, 10–77, 10–82, 10–96, 10–99, 10–107, 10–115; © Hans Namuth, New York: 10–88; © 1996 Board of Trustees, National Gallery of Art, Washington, D.C.: 6–3; Archives, National Gallery of Art: 4–69; Victor Boswell © National Geographic Society: 5–60; Prints Division/New York Public Library, Astor, Lenox and Tilden Foundations: 6–19; Nippon Television Corporation, Tokyo: pp. 292–93, 6–29; 6–30; 6–49; © Stiftung Nolde, Seebüll, Germany: 10–50; Sara Krulwich/New York Times Pictures: 1–14; Shigeo Okamoto: 1–5, 7–47; Robert Paine and Alexander Soper, *The Art and Architecture of Japan*, 1955 © Yale University Press/Pelican History of Art: p. 183; J. Apicella copyright © Cesar Pelli and Associates: 10–148;

Philadelphia Museum of Art: 1–19; The Pierpont Morgan Library, New York: 7–33; Port Authority of New York and New Jersey: 9–6; Studio Fotografico Quattrone, Florence: 5–6, 5–16, 5–18, 5–56, 6–7, 6–12, 7–18; Schlesinger Library, Radcliffe College, Cambridge, MA: 9–12; Lois Fichner Rathus, *Understanding Art*, © 1989: 4–12, 4–13, 4–85; Agence Photographique de la Réunion des Musées Nationaux, Paris: 3–42, 3–45, 3–78, 4–78, 5–44, 6–6, 6–16, 7–17, 7–31, 7–39, 8–9, 9–1, 9–20, 9–36, 9–47, 9–48; Rijksmuseum, Amsterdam: 7–35; Roger-Viollet, Paris: 9–2; Jean Roubier, Paris: 3–114; Studio Lourmel, Paris: 9–56; Bob Schalkwijk, Mexico City: 10–65; E. G. Schempf: 10–103; © 1997 Valerie M. Shepherd: 3–85, 3–86; Shinkenchiku-sha, Tokyo: 10–128; Edwin Smith: 4–86; Archives, Smithsonian Institution, Washington, D.C.: 10–29; Society for the Preservation of New England Antiquities, Boston: 1–11; Holly Solomon Gallery, New York: pp. 14, 15; Soprintendenza al beni Artistici e Storici di Venezia: 5–58; courtesy Steinbaum Krauss Gallery, New York: 10–124; Richard Stoner: 10–17, 10–139; William Struhs, Charleston, SC: 10–143; Wim

Swaan: 4–88, 4–93, 6–60; C.Z. Swiechowski: 4–61; Mark Theissen courtesy the Names Project Foundation, San Francisco: 10–6; Time Picture Syndication, New York: 10–74; Michel Desjardins, Agence TOP, Paris: 5–48; Marvin Trachtenberg, New York: 1–7, 3–61, 3–97, 3–99, 4–22, 4–75, 4–81, 4–87, 9–41; courtesy James Turrell: 10–147; Ed Roseberry, University of Virginia: 8–20; © The Board of Trustees of the Victoria & Albert Museum, London: 8–6; Vincent van Gogh Foundation/National Museum Vincent van Gogh, Amsterdam: 9–3; John C. Vincent: 6–67; Ann Hutchison © Virginia Museum of Fine Arts: pp. 392–93; Vizzavona, Paris: 7–43; 7–44; Gemeinnützige Stiftung Leonard von Matt, Buochs, Switzerland: 3–91, 4–57; Yasatuda Wantanabe, Shinto Art: *Ise and Izumo Shrines*, 1974: 4–16; Ron Warren: 10–119; H. Wehmeyer, Hildesheim, Germany: 4–54; Etienne Weill, Paris: 10–12, 10–121; courtesy David C. Wilkins: 1–18, 7–22, 7–116, 4–3, 5–30, 5–41, 5–42, 5–46, 6–61, 6–63, 6 64, 6–73; © Nina Williams: 10–48; ZEFA, Dusseldorf: 3–121.

Artists' Copyrights: © 1997 The Josef and Anni Albers Foundation/Artists Rights Society (ARS), New York: 10– 98; © The Estate of Diane Arbus, 1972: 10–105; © 1997 Artists Rights Society (ARS), New York/ADAGP, Paris: 10–7, 10–12, 10–32, 10–36, 10–40, 10–43, 10–44, 10–45, 10–46, 10–51, 10–54, 10–56, 10–77, 10–82; © 1997 Artists Rights Society (ARS), New York/VG Bild-Kunst, Bonn: 10–4, 10–55, 10–57, 10–108; © 1997 Estate of Giacomo Balla/ Licensed by VAGA, New York, NY: 10–1; © 1997 T. H. Benton and R. P. Benton Testamentary Trusts/Licensed by VAGA, New York, NY: 10–70; © 1997 Louise Bourgeois/ Licensed by VAGA, New York, NY: 10–142; © 1997 Foundation Georgio de Chirico/Licensed by VAGA, New York, NY: 10–53; © Christo 1976: 10–113; © 1997 Demart Pro Arte/Artists Rights Society (ARS), New York: 10–76; © 1997 Richard Estes/Licensed by VAGA, New York, NY: 10–115; © Audrey Flack/Louis Meisel: 10–116; © Helen Frankenthaler: 10–13; © 1997 Nancy Graves Foundation/Licensed by VAGA, New York, NY: 10–130; Reproduced by permission of the Henry Moore Foundation: 10–80; © 1997 Jasper Johns/ Licensed by VAGA, New York, NY: 10–96; © 1997 Donald Judd Estate/Licensed by VAGA, New York, NY: 10–110; © André Kertész Estate: 10–73; © 1997 Joseph Kosuth/Artists Rights Society (ARS), New York: 10–107; © Joyce Kozloff: 10–125; © Roy Lichtenstein: 10–102; Henri Cartier-Bresson © MAGNUM Photos, New York: 10–75; © Agnes Martin: 10–111; © 1997 Succession H. Matisse/Artists Rights Society (ARS), New York: 10–24, 10–25; Courtesy of Mondrian Estate/ Holtzman Trust: 1–16; © Yasumasa Morimura: 10–144; ©

1997 The Munch Museum/The Munch-Ellingsen Group/Artists Rights Society (ARS), New York: 9–78; © Stiftung Nolde Seebüll, Germany: 10–50; © 1997 The Georgia O'Keeffe Foundation/Artists Rights Society (ARS), New York: 10–11, 10–69; © Claes Oldenburg/Coosje van Bruggen: 10–103; © 1997 Estate of Pablo Picasso/Artists Rights Society (ARS), New York: 10–31, 10–37, 10–38, 10–39, 10–78, 10–79; © 1997 Pollock Krasner Foundation/Artists Rights Society (ARS), New York: 10–87; © 1997 Robert Rauschenberg/Licensed by VAGA, New York, NY: 10–97; © Faith Ringgold: 10–141; © 1997 Kate Rothko-Prizel & Christopher Rothko/Artists Rights Society (ARS), New York: 10–89; © Miriam Schapiro: 10–124; courtesy of Cindy Sherman and Metro Pictures: 10–131; © 1997 Frank Stella/Artists Rights Society (ARS), New York: 10–99; © 1997 Estate of Vladimir Tatlin/Licensed by VAGA, New York, NY: 10–3; Margaret Bourke-White, LIFE Magazine, © Time, Inc: 10–74; © Bill Viola: 10–17; © 1997 The Andy Warhol Foundation for the Visual Arts/Artists Rights Society (ARS), New York: 10–10; © Nina Williams: 10–48; © 1997 Estate of Grant Wood/Licensed by VAGA, New York, NY: 10–68.

Diagrams: 1–9, 3–13, 3–55, 3–63, 3–66, 3–73 above, 3–106, 3–113, 4–100, 4–101, 5–17, 5–22, 5–34, 6–23, 7–34, 9–29, 9–50 by Marlene Boyle. 2–10, 3–24, 3–26, 3–41, 3–73 below, 3–116, 4–11, 4–15, 4–85 above, 6–25, 6–26, 9–43 by John McKenna.

Maps by Paul J. Pugliese.

The authors and publishers wish to acknowledge the following publications, from which quotations were taken: p. 21: Ovid, *Metamorphoses*, trans. by R. Humphries, Bloomington: Indiana University Press, 1969; p. 86: Susan Woodford, *The Parthenon*, Cambridge, Eng.: Cambridge University Press, 1981; p. 179: Arthur F. Wright, "Symbolism and Function: Reflections on Changan and Other Great Cities," *Journal of Asian Studies*, Vol. 24, No. 4, August 1965, p. 669. Reprinted with permission of the Association for Asian Studies, Inc.; p. 291: Giorgio Vasari, *Lives of the Most Eminent Painters, Sculptors and Architects*, trans. by Gaston Du C. de Vere, New York: Harry N. Abrams, Inc., 1979. All rights reserved; p. 305: Giorgio Vasari, *The Lives of the Artists*, vol. 1., trans. by George Bull, Harmondsworth: Penguin Classics, 1987. © George Bull, 1965; p. 305: *The Complete Poems of Michelangelo*, trans. by J. Tusiani, New York: The Noonday Press, 1960; p. 314: Translation by Creighton Gilbert, from *Complete Poems and Selected Letters of Michelangelo*, Princeton: Princeton University Press, 1980; p. 398: Sir Joshua Reynolds, *Fifteen Discourses Delivered in the Royal Academy*, New York: E.P. Dutton, 1911; pp. 410, 444, 445, 469, 502, 536: Robert Goldwater and Marco Treves, *Artists on Art: From the XIV–XX Century*, New York: Pantheon Books. © 1945 by Pantheon Books, Inc. Renewed 1973 by Goldwater and Treves. By permission of Pantheon books, a division of Random House, Inc.; pp. 459, 462, 464, 465: Translation from Charles S. Moffett et al., *The New Painting: Impressionism 1874–1886*. © 1986 by The Fine Arts Museum of San Francisco. Reprinted with permission.

N 5300 .W64 1997
Wilkins, David G.
Art past, art present

HOLYOKE COMMUNITY COLLEGE
ELAINE NICPON MARIEB LIBRARY